2107 CURIOUS WORD ORIGINS, SAYINGS & EXPRESSIONS

FROM

WHITE ELEPHANTS

TO

A SONG & DANCE

CHARLES EARLE FUNK

DRAWINGS BY TOM FUNK

2107
CURIOUS WORD ORIGINS, SAYINGS & EXPRESSIONS
FROM
WHITE ELEPHANTS
TO
A SONG & DANCE

CHARLES EARLE FUNK

DRAWINGS BY TOM FUNK

GALAHAD BOOKS
NEW YORK

First Galahad Books edition published in 1993.

Galahad Books
A division of BBS Publishing Corporation
386 Park Avenue South
New York, NY 10016

Galahad Books is a registered trademark of BBS Publishing Corporation.

Published by arrangement with Harper Collins Publishers, Inc.

Library of Congress Catalog Card Number: 93-78584

ISBN: 0-88365-845-3

Printed in the United States of America.

CONTENTS

A HOG ON ICE

And Other
Curious Expressions

*To the memory
of my mother,
Cynthia Ellen Funk*

FOREWORD

CURIOSITY about the origin of an expression that my mother frequently used started the investigation which has led to the contents of this book. Whenever she saw a pompous person strutting down the street, a girl leading the way to a restaurant table without heeding the head waiter's guidance, a young man with hat atilt jauntily striding along without a care in the world, a baby who had just learned to walk ignoring the outstretched hand of its mother, such a person, she always said with a toss of her own head, was "as independent as a hog on ice." She meant cockily independent, supremely confident, beholden to no one.

Now my mother was born and brought up on a farm in southern Ohio, in a region wholly given over to farms. She knew full well that a hapless hog that found itself upon the ice would be utterly helpless, unable to rise, its feet sprawled out in all directions. So why did she use this expression with such a contrary meaning? Of course, I never thought to ask her while she was living; I doubt now, in fact, that she could have told me. It was a saying that she had picked up from her own elders, and they in turn from the generation that preceded.

The homely expression, though not extinct, is rarely heard nowadays; so it was not until a few years ago that I found that my wife, whose forebears dwelt in eastern Massachusetts from Puritan days, was just as cognizant of the simile as I—and knew no more of its origin. Then, of course, I turned to the collection of phrase books on my shelves—to Holt's *Phrase Origins*, FitzGerald's *Words and*

7

Phrases, Brewer's *Dictionary of Phrase and Fable*, Walsh's *Handy-Book of Literary Curiosities*, Hyamson's *Dictionary of English Phrases*, Apperson's *English Proverbs and Proverbial Phrases*, and others old and new—but none even listed the saying. The dictionaries were next to be consulted. Of all of them, not one listed and defined the expression as a whole, though the Supplement, published in 1933, to the huge *Oxford English Dictionary* came within an ace of so doing. There, under "hog" it listed the phrase, "like, or as, a hog on ice," giving it the definition, "denoting awkwardness or insecurity." It credited the saying to the United States and gave two quotations showing its use. The first, from a Vermont paper of 1894, really illustrated the definition, for it pertained to a certain horse which, upon a racetrack, would be as awkward as a hog upon the ice. The second, taken from Carl Sandburg's "The Windy City," from *Slabs of the Sunburnt West*, read: "Chicago fished from its depths a text: Independent as a hog on ice." The editors slipped, however, in the inclusion of this quotation under the definition, for it does not fit. A reading of the entire poem shows that Sandburg used the full phrase, "independent as a hog on ice," in the sense that my mother knew it—to indicate that "the Windy City" was quite able to stand upon its own feet, had supreme confidence and self-assurance.

My next step, then, was to refer to the vast resources of the New York Public Library, to enlist the aid of some of its researchers, and especially to consult the complete file of *Notes & Queries*, the British monthly publication that since 1850 has been the recognized medium for the exchange of antiquarian information among its readers. I found nothing. Subsequently, I may say here, direct appeal to the readers of *Notes & Queries* was equally non-productive, nor did the larger resources of the Chicago Public Library, extended through the courtesy of its librarian, Mr. Carl B. Roden, yield anything that I did not already know.

In the meantime I had been questioning my friends and acquaintances. Some, especially of a younger generation, had never heard the expression, but almost all those within my own generation or older were familiar with it, or had heard it in childhood. Upon further inquiry I found that the localities in which these people had known the phrase included all the northern states from Maine to Illinois; later, through correspondence, I was able to add many of the southern states, though in Georgia "pig" was more familiar than "hog." Perhaps by chance, none to whom I wrote west of the Mississippi had ever heard the expression. Parenthetically, one friend recalled from his youth an old codger who, when asked how he was, would respond, "Oh, just as independent as a hog on ice; if I can't stand up I can lay down." No one else knew this additional line.

The search was momentarily halted in its early stages because, having no farm experience myself, I could not positively state from my own knowledge, in answer to a question, that a hog was actually helpless upon the ice. The questioner had heard, he said, that by virtue of its sharp hoofs a hog had no trouble whatever in maneuvering itself upon ice. So I sent an inquiry to the Bureau of Animal Industry, U. S. Department of Agriculture, to make certain. The reply, from Mr. John H. Zeller, Senior Animal Husbandman, In Charge Swine Investigations, reads, in part:

The facts are that a hog on a smooth icy surface cannot move about in a normal manner. The pads on the feet are smooth and offer no resistance to slippery or smooth icy surfaces. His feet slide out from under him, the legs will either spread as the animal sprawls out on the ice, or they will be drawn under him. In either case, after several attempts to arise, he refuses to try to get on his feet. The hog usually has to be skidded or dragged off the ice to a firm footing before he attempts to move about in the usual manner.

So, reassured on this point, my search proceeded.

The fact that the gelid independent hog was known, apparently, throughout all the eastern states some eighty or more years ago, made me wonder whether it may have been connected in some way with a historical episode. Digging back, I recalled that after the Revolutionary War our newly created republic had its independence, all right, but that, through internal squabbles and lack of credit abroad, for many years this independence had very nearly the grace and security of a hog on ice. Perhaps some satirist of that period had coined the phrase, and perhaps it had been disseminated through a political song. Again the resources of the library were called upon, and more letters were sent—this time to historians and to writers of historical fiction. Again the library was non-productive—no satire and no song or ballad could be found in which the phrase appeared. The historians, without exception, had heard the saying. Professor Charles Beard found my theory of a Tory satirical origin interesting and plausible, but could offer no clue; Arthur Schlesinger, Jr., did not recall its occurrence in any of his readings upon the Jacksonian period. Two other eminent scholars, one born in Illinois, the other in Indiana—had always vaguely supposed, from childhood, that the saying had somehow arisen from the meat-packing industry in Chicago or in Cincinnati, without recalling that, prior to about 1880 when refrigeration was introduced, meat was preserved by salting, drying, corning, smoking, pickling, or the like, but not by freezing. Furthermore, if the saying were associated with packing, a sheep or a cow when frozen would be just as independent as a hog.

But the historical novelist, Kenneth Roberts, drew my attention away from the probability of American coinage, for he replied to my request by saying that he had always known the expression, that it was commonly used by his grandmother in her home in New Hampshire when he was young. Then he added: "A lot of expressions which I later found to be old English were in common use in our family—which came from Godalming near Stratford-on-Avon in the early 1630s. So I suspect that 'independent as a hog on ice' is older than you think." He gave his own explanation of the simile: "I strongly suspect the phrase was applied to people who were idiotically independent: that a man who was *that* independent was getting himself exactly nowhere, like a spread-eagled hog."

Because two acquaintances who were born in Ireland had told me that they had heard the expression in the "Ould counthry," I had already briefly considered Ireland as the possible source of the saying—its transmission throughout all of the eastern United States could readily be accounted for by the great Irish immigration of 1820-1840 into all of the eastern states. But I had discarded the likelihood, for, as Padraic Colum reminded me, there is no ice in Ireland and hogs are called pigs. I had concluded that my earlier informants, who had been brought to this country when very young, had heard it here and assumed that it was Irish. But now, along with Roberts' opinion, came a letter from Peter Tamany of San Francisco, notable collector of unusual words, in which he said that his mother, a woman of seventy-five, born near Macroom, County Cork, had often heard the saying as a young girl. Then a chance acquaintance in New York City, a man of sixty-five, hailing from Belfast and still owning land near that city, told me that, though one hears the expression rarely now in Northern Ireland, it is still well known among the older folks. Then, too, H. L. Mencken, who wrote that he had known it in Baltimore from boyhood, said that he had always had the impression that it was of Irish origin. Professor Harold W. Thompson, folklorist and writer, also thought it likely to have been an Irish importation, and then added—"but what would the Irish immigrant know about ice? Would the Irish peasant ever have hogs on ice? Also, why is a hog on ice independent? Is it because he has attained the dignity of death?"

The net result of these latter opinions was that I abandoned my earlier thought of an American origin. Despite the evidence of use in Ireland, however, I agreed with Colum, Thompson, and others that probability of an Irish origin was not likely. Hence, in Ireland as in America, it must have been an importation. But from where? Sir William Craigie, co-editor of the Oxford English Dictionary, thought it most improbable that England could have been the source, both because of the rarity of ice and because "pig" is also British use, rather than "hog." Sir St. Vincent Troubridge advanced similar arguments and, like all previous English acquaintances whom I had consulted, had never heard the expression in England. But, at about that stage of my search, I began to get returns from another direction.

A fellow worker, an Englishwoman, interested in my search had been in correspondence with her brother, Leslie Campbell Stark, living in the north of England. Though he was not himself acquainted with the expression, he began to make inquiries and learned, surprisingly, that the usage was known in northern England, especially among the old-timers and more especially among his Scottish acquaintances. This news altered the entire trend of my thought and caused me to take up again a line of reasoning that, early in the search, had been abandoned as wholly untenable. Possibly, though no one now could give the reason, the expression was of Scottish origin. If so, this would explain its occurrence in Northern Ireland and its spread in the United States. My mother was of Scottish descent, and perhaps—though I have not attempted to pursue this theory—the saying has persisted particularly among other such families. And if the expression was Scottish, then perhaps the allusion to a swine was indirect. I might say here also that it is by no means unknown for a word or saying to survive in America that has long been obsolete in England; the incongruity of this saying would especially appeal to American or Irish ears, lending strength to its survival.

If one looks in the dictionary—an unabridged dictionary—he will see that, in the game of curling, a Scottish game played upon ice, the word "hog" is used to describe a curling stone under certain conditions. That is, when a player does not give his stone sufficient impetus to cause it to slide beyond a certain distance, that stone, when it comes to rest, is called a "hog." No explanation of the name has been given, but the Century Dictionary, published originally in 1889, says of the entry, "Origin obscure; by some identified with hog (i. e., swine), as 'laggard stones that manifest a pig-like indolence,' or, it might be thought, in allusion to the helplessness of a hog on ice, there being in the United States an ironical simile, 'as independent as a hog on ice!'" Incidentally, this appearance of the phrase in the Century Dictionary is its earliest occurrence in print; at least, no earlier appearance has been found. The Century did not list the phrase separately nor offer any further explanation of it.

Back toward the beginning of my search, I had thought for awhile that this curling stone afforded an ideal explanation of the phrase, that the "hog," lying indolently upon the course, was free and independent, by its immobile state blocking the way of subsequent stones to be played, forming a hazard. But the thought was short-lived, for when I read over the rules of the game I saw that the stone does not constitute a hazard, for the "hog" is removed from the course as soon as it comes to rest. It blocks nothing and attains no

12

independence! Reluctantly, therefore, I had dismissed this explanation of the phrase from further consideration.

But now, after tracing the simile back to a probable Scottish origin, it seemed feasible to look again into this game. Its antiquity is not known, but it dates at least to the early sixteenth century, for of a number of early crude stones that have been found in the beds and along the shores of Scottish rivers and ponds, one has the date 1509 cut in its side. No earlier reference in literature has been found, however, than 1620, and no prescribed set of rules is known to have been drawn up or followed until another century had passed. So, because no writer mentioned the sport, it is apparent that curling, like many other games started very humbly, perhaps among a group of boys who, at first, had improvised a game of bowls on the ice, using small stones as the pins and larger ones in place of balls. Perhaps, because round stones to roll over the ice could not be found, they used flattened stones that could be slid. Older lads or men taking over the game would then undoubtedly have introduced refinements and hazards unthought of by boys—ultimately leading through the centuries to the exacting rules and highly polished, heavy stones, rounded, as of today. But in its early days I think the method of play had local differences wherever the game was played—such, at least, has been the history of most games. When, later, teams of players were organized and competition was introduced, then some agreement had to be reached as to method of play. But, again, if other sports are any criterion—and we need only to look back over the few brief years in the history of baseball or basketball for an example—curling undoubtedly underwent many changes before the rules of the eighteenth century were put down on paper.

Hence, though my conclusion cannot be proved, I think that sometime during the early centuries of the game, perhaps by accident one of the awkward, heavy stones did not have enough momentum to carry it to its destination and it stopped halfway along the course. I think that someone made the suggestion that it be allowed to stay there as an extra hazard, and I think that, because of its unwieldiness and its inertness, becoming partly frozen into the ice, some player with a sense of humor likened it to a hog—and the name stuck. If this hypothesis be correct, then the very fact that the stone occupied a central position, showing no regard to its interference with subsequent players, like an automobile driver who "hogs" the center of a road, made it appear self-assured, cocky, and independent, and thus gave rise to the humorous simile that came down through the centuries. Perhaps—to explain the later development leading to the present removal of the "hog"—there may have been a tendency among some players to encumber the course with their curling stones deliberately, thus blocking the game. So, perhaps, the rule was made that a stone must traverse five sixths of the course, as at present—passing a line upon the ice still known as the "hog score"—before it would be permitted to remain on the ice and exert its independence. This theory, as the Century Dictionary suggests, would give us "laggard stones that manifest a pig-like indolence."

No one has tried to make an individual collection of all the common sayings in the English language; there are thousands of them. They have come from all the trades and professions; they have come from the courts of kings and from beggars' hovels; they have come from churches and cathedrals and they have come from gambling hells and bawdy houses. A large number have come from the sea, because England existed through maritime trade for many centuries and the speech of her sailors has become commonplace in every British port. Many have come from the battlefield or the arts of warfare; others from the hunt or the fisherman's boat. Many have come down to us from the loom and the spindle, because weaving, once introduced into England from the Continent, became a staple industry, practiced throughout the kingdom. The farmer's field and his livestock and the housewife and her domestic chores have supplied many more. But aside from these serious occupational sources, a lesser number have been derived from games and sports. These latter include the pastimes of children, the rough outdoor and indoor sports and games of boys and men, and games of skill and chance.

These sayings, whatever the source, have become folk sayings, adopted into the common speech of English-speaking peoples generally, for they became part of the language. Thus, we in America, though we have added and are still adding many more expressions peculiar to this country which will pass on to our children's children, are using phrases and sayings in our common speech that hark back to the days of the Wars of the Roses and the House of Tudor. Along with them are sayings from other languages which also have become English folk sayings. A few of these have come, apparently, from Scandinavian sources—such as, "to run the gantlet," "to cook one's goose," and, perhaps, "to pay through the nose"; a number have come from France, both from the common speech and from French literature, which is not surprising when one considers that for two centuries after the Norman Conquest it was a toss-up between French or English as the common language and that French was the court language for three centuries more. Some of the sayings that we use every day are nothing more than English translations of Latin, Greek, or Hebrew—and this, too, is not surprising, for Latin, until recent centuries was the literary language of all learned, scholarly people throughout Europe, and even to the days of our own grandparents every schoolboy had to be proficient in both Latin and Greek; and, of course, the Old Testament, from which we have many familiar sayings, was a Hebrew document.

Many of these sayings are nothing more than figurative applications of commonplace utterances. They require no explanation, because almost no one's imagination is so weak that the allusion is not immediately evident. In my study I have discarded the obvious and have considered only those that, for one reason or another, I regard as curious or especially picturesque or out of the ordinary. Some, of modern vintage, have been included for perhaps no better reason than that they have struck my fancy, or because I thought it worth while to record what I know or surmise to be the explanations back of their use. An amusing expression, either one that is incongruous or that involves a play upon words, is quick to seize the popular fancy and seems to live until there is scarcely more than a ghost left of the original circumstance that caused its popularity. The clue leading to its source many depend upon some former dialectal word or expression, or upon some ancient practice among certain tradesmen, or upon some obscure local event or custom, or upon some long-forgotten diversion. Such sayings I have tried to trace. These threads provide the reasons for such old phrases as "higher then Gilderoy's kite," "to leave in the lurch," "to kick the bucket," "from pillar to post," and scores of others. But in some expressions no trace remains by which we can step with any confidence to the source. No one knows, with certainty, what was originally meant by the admonition, "to mind one's *p*'s and *q*'s," nor why, when things were neatly arranged, they were said to be "in apple-pie order," nor why a person with a broad smile was said to "grin like a Cheshire cat." These and others in this category must have been readily understood at one time, and the allusions must have been so clear and definite that no one thought it necessary to describe them. Each must have been based upon a common practice, an incident, a spectacle, or the like that was familiar to all among whom the saying was first introduced; but, even as today, no one then made a written record because no one had any reason to believe that the saying would persist and become commonplace.

Does any family, for example, make a record of the words or sayings peculiar to it? I doubt it, though sometimes they are apt and worthy of perpetuation. One such, still used among the third generation of a family that I was once privileged to know, might have been written, from the sound, "peebidess." It was used, variously, to designate an ambitious but impoverished family or community, or something vainly pretentious, or even something that had once been fine but had become bedraggled or faded—anything, that is, deserving of commiseration. Eventually I learned that the first generation of users—five clever sisters—had coined it for secret conversation, using initials: "*P*. but *S*.," poor but struggling.

One does not expect to be able to discover who the one individual was, in any given instance, who first took an innocent remark or incident and gave it a metaphorical twist. We say that some came from Shakespeare or Spenser or Chaucer, but it is really not very likely that these or other writers would take the chance that their readers or audience would grasp the point of some wholly new witticism. All that we can do, then, is to trace the written record back and thus, in most instances, find out approximately when the saying came into use. (We do not often find that, as with the independent hog, two or three centuries have passed before some writer has made use of the saying.)

So what I have done herein is to take those curious sayings that I have selected, give to each the figurative meaning that it has acquired, show, whenever possible, how that meaning has come about, and make an approximate estimate of the time it came into use in English speech. Occasionally, to lend vividness to the account, I have taken the reader back into ancient ways and practices, or I have quoted from old texts. The intent has been, with due regard to accuracy, to use such means as were available to enable the reader to retain the sources of these sayings in his memory. To this end, also, the aid of my nephew, Tom Funk, was enlisted to scatter some of his black-and-white "spots" throughout the text.

The collection ranges over some two thousand years of time, for along with curious sayings of former centuries are included some coined within recent decades—"hitting on all six," "on the nose," "behind the eight ball," "Bronx cheer" are examples. Here again, with a few exceptions, the actual origins are elusive. Someone must have devised the gesture of touching his nose as an indication that the timing was exact; someone must have been the first to designate a peculiarly raucous, derisive sound as a "Bronx cheer"; it may be a natural way among automobile mechanics to say that a smoothly running engine is "hitting on all four," or "hitting on all six," depending upon the number of its cylinders, but someone must have been the first to take this and use it figuratively. I have been unable to learn who were the authors of these and like phrases, though it is likely that they are living. Positive information from any reader will be appreciated.

The material for many of these sketches has been collected over a number of years in connection with other work, collected through correspondence, through newspaper clippings, through the files of *Notes & Queries*, through encyclopedias and dictionaries, and through scores of other reference works which have been checked one with another. I am especially indebted to the Oxford English

17

Dictionary and to the Dictionary of American English for references to early literary use of many of the expressions discussed and for various quotations of such use, and to the former, in many instances, for valuable etymological clues. In a few instances, Apperson's *English Proverbs and Proverbial Phrases* has supplied references to earlier usage than had been found by the editors of either of those dictionaries.

A HOG ON ICE

*And Other
Curious Expressions*

in a blue funk

It would be interesting if, through family records, I could bring an unsuspected source into view which would explain why this expression means "in a state of dire panic," or from another record determine why a stooge for an auctioneer, one who makes fictitious bids to stimulate higher bids, is called a "Peter Funk"; but, alas, no such records are known. An actual Peter Funk who thus served an auctioneer may have lived, in some part of the United States, but the unusually full record of the American family from 1710 to 1900 has no mention of such an individual. The English phrase, "in a funk," was Oxford slang back in the middle of the eighteenth century, and seems to have been borrowed from a Flemish phrase, "in de fonck siin," which also meant "in a state of panic"; but no one has been  able to figure out why the Flemish *fonck* meant "panic." Perhaps some ancestor, for the early American branch spelled the name "Funck" and came from lands bordering the Flemings, may have lived in such panic that his name, slightly misspelled, became a synonym for great fear. No one can say.

"Blue" was inserted into the phrase about a hundred years after the Oxford adoption. The adjective had long been used to mean "extreme," and its addition merely intensified the state of panic ascribed to the phrase.

Incidentally, the first literary mention of the mythical "Peter Funk" is in the book by Asa Green, *The Perils of Pearl Street*, published in 1834. The book is a humorous narrative of mercantile life in New York City and, obviously, the author invented the names of most of the characters he describes. Possibly this name was also invented, though the author says that Peter Funk was a name familiar to generations of merchants.

21

to put the kibosh on

To put an end to; to stop; to dispose of. One thinks of this as being modern slang, in use only a few years, but readers of Dickens, if they remember *Sketches by Boz*, may recall the sketch, "Seven Dials." This is a description of a squalid locality in London, so benighted that even the "ladies" were usually engaged in fisticuffs. One such battle was egged on by a young potboy, who, as Dickens wrote it, roared to one of the "ladies," "Hooroar, put the kye-bosk on her, Mary!" That sketch was published back in 1836, so our "modern slang" is somewhat more than a hundred years old.

There has been considerable speculation about the origin of the word "kibosh." A correspondent to *Notes & Queries* some years ago advanced the theory that it was of Yiddish origin meaning eighteen pence, and began as a term used in auctions, as an increase in a bid. Recently, another correspondent to the same publication suggested that it may be a corruption of the Italian *capuce*, a tin lid, and that it may have been employed by street vendors of ice-cream—"Put the kibosh on," meant to put the lid back on the container.

But I am indebted to Padraic Colum, well-known Irish author, for what I take to be the true explanation. In a letter to me he says: " 'Kibosh,' I believe, means 'the cap of death' and it is always used in that sense—'He put the kibosh on it.' In Irish it could be written 'cie bais'—the last word pronounced 'bosh,' the genitive of 'bas,' death."

to knock (or *beat*) the tar out of

We use this with the meaning, to beat, whip, or belabor without mercy. Though credited to the United States and with no earlier record of use than the twentieth century, I think it likely that the expression may have been carried to this country by some Scottish or north-of-England sheepherder who may have used it in a literal sense. Many centuries ago it was learned that a sore on a sheep, as from an accidental cut in shearing, could be protected against the festering bites of flies if smeared with tar. In fact, back in 1670, the proverb is recorded by John Ray, "Ne're lose a hog (later, a sheep) for a half-penny-worth of tarre." But when tar once gets embedded into a sheep's wool, its removal is difficult. So I surmise that our present saying was first used in its literal sense, to beat a sheep's side for the removal of tar.

hell-bent for election

"Hell-bent," an American term, means so determined as to be regardless of the consequences, even hell itself. An article in *Knickerbocker Magazine* in an issue of 1835 describes a band of Indians as "hell-bent on carnage." The present "all out" is a mild substitute for the same thing. But "hell-bent for election" means speed, speed so great as to be heedlessly reckless. The meaning seems to be derived from the political race made by Edward Kent, in 1840, for election to the governorship of Maine. He was a Whig, and, though Maine was then normally Democratic, he had served as governor for one term, had been defeated for re-election by John Fairfield, and was again running against Fairfield in 1840. The Whigs were determined to win; they were "hell-bent for the election" of Kent and probably used that slogan in the campaign, for their victory was celebrated by a song that ran, in part:

> *Oh have you heard how old Maine went?*
> *She went hell-bent for Governor Kent,*
> *And Tippecanoe and Tyler, too!*

spick and span

For the past two hundred years we have been using this to mean very trim and smart, thoroughly neat and orderly, having the appearance of newness, but for the two hundred years preceding that, or from the middle of the sixteenth century to the middle of the eighteenth century, the phrase was always "spick and span new," and had no other meaning than absolutely and wholly new.

The phrase has had an interesting history. It started, so far as the records show, about 1300 as just "span-new," meaning perfectly new, or as new as a freshly cut chip, for "span," in olden days, meant a chip. At that time, chips were used for spoons, so "span-new" really meant a newly cut spoon, one that had not yet been soiled by use.

"Spick" was not added until late in the sixteenth century, presumably for no better reason than alliteration. A "spick" really meant a splinter, or, also, a spike. Actually, it had no particular meaning when added to "span-new," but it would be interesting if I could say that the original purpose of the "spick," or splinter, was to impale meat, as we use a fork today, when the "span" was laid aside.

cock-and-bull story

The French have a phrase, *coq-à-l'âne*—literally, cock to the donkey—which they use in exactly the same sense as we use cock-and-bull; concocted and incredible; fantastic. A cock-and-bull story is one that stretches the imaginations somewhat beyond the limits of credulity. Many learned attempts have been made, both in

French and English lore, to discover the precise origin of the phrase, which has appeared in English literature since about 1600, but nothing has yet been determined. Probably it came from a folk tale, one concerning a cock and a donkey, in France, and a cock and a bull, in England. A writer back in 1660, Samuel Fisher, speaks of a cock and a bull being metamorphosed into one animal, but more likely in the original fable the two barnyard animals engaged in conversation. As no farmer would believe that such conversation was possible, he would be apt to label any incredible tale as a "cock-and-bull story."

not dry behind the ears

As innocent and unsophisticated as a babe. A saying that came directly from the farm, where many others have also arisen, for it alludes to a newly born animal, as a colt or a calf, on which the last spot to become dry after birth is the little depression behind either ear. The figurative use seems to be wholly American, too homely to have attained literary pretensions, but undoubtedly in familiar use through the past hundred years or longer.

24

in the bag

With success assured; all over but the shouting. The saying is new; that is, it has become generally known throughout America, where it originated, since about 1920. In card games or the like, the person doing the playing may use it when he wishes to free his partner's mind from anxiety. An earlier expression with the same inference was "all wrapped up"; that is, in allusion to merchandise, success was assured and merely awaited delivery. When paper bags succeeded wrapping paper for the holding of groceries or the like, the later saying succeeded the older.

to be (or go) woolgathering

To be engaged in trivial employment; to indulge in aimless reverie. Though this expression has long had such figurative meanings, its origin was literal; people did actually wander in a seemingly aimless manner over the countryside gathering the fragments of wool left by passing sheep on bushes or fences against which they brushed. Such people were "woolgatherers," and it is likely that in some countries children are so employed today. The figurative sense was in use as long ago as the middle of the sixteenth century, as in Thomas Wilson's *The arte of rhetorique*, "Hackyng & hemmyng as though our wittes and our senses were a woll gatheryng."

to cool one's heels

To be kept waiting, as when you have a train to catch, but must see a prospective customer who keeps you nervously fuming in his outer office. The figurative meaning dates back to the early seventeenth century, and the phrase, though the evidence is scant, was apparently preceded by the more literal, "to cool one's hoofs." Here, the allusion is to a draft horse or saddle horse which takes advantage of a period of rest by lying down. "To kick one's heels" is a later variant, from about the middle of the eighteenth century, with the same meaning, except that impatience is always implied. Here the allusion is to a restless horse which, when kept standing, kicks its stall. "To kick up one's heels" has two meanings, each different, and having no similarity with the foregoing. In one sense

25

the phrase means playfulness, especially that of an elderly person who momentarily affects the careless spirits of a child. Here the allusion is to a horse which, turned out to pasture, frisks about briefly with the careless abandon of a colt. In the other sense it means to trip a person; that is, to cause the person to kick up his own heels by falling flat.

to ride the high horse; on one's high horse

Away back in the fourteenth century John Wyclif records that in a royal pageant persons of high rank were mounted on "high"  horses, meaning that they rode the so-called "great horses," or heavy chargers used in battle or tournament. Hence, the use of such a horse was presumptive evidence that its rider was, or considered himself to be, a person of superiority or arrogance. The custom died, but the expression remains. "To ride the high horse" means to affect arrogance or superiority, to act pretentiously. From it we have the derived phrase, "on one's high horse," which we use descriptively of a person who affects to scorn those who or that which he feigns to believe beneath his notice.

to have two strings to one's bow

Anciently, the bowman who went forth to battle was ill prepared unless he carried two or more bowstrings. Otherwise he would be utterly useless if the one on his bow were to snap. Thus, probably long before Cardinal Wolsey recorded it in 1524, the expression had acquired the figurative meaning still in use, to have two (or more) resources, or to be prepared with alternate plans for carrying out one's intent.

dyed in the wool

Probably back beyond the days of Jacob—who gave his favorite son, Joseph, " a coat of many colors"—it was known that if the wool were dyed before it was made up into yarn, or while it was still raw wool, the color would be more firmly fixed. The figurative sense—to have one's habits or traits so deeply ingrained as to be inflexible—seems not to have been used in England before the late sixteenth century, for a writer of that period thought he had to explain his meaning when he used it. This was odd, for England was largely dependent upon her textile industry then and earlier for her existence, and any allusion to that industry should have been immediately evident to any Englishman.

all over but the shouting

Success is so certain that applause only is lacking. Though the earliest appearance of the saying in print appears to be in the works of the Welsh writer on sports, Charles James Apperley, in 1842, to my notion the expression has the earmarks of American origin. I would infer that the real origin might have pertained to a hotly contested early American election. The results would not be positively known until the ballots were all counted, but one of the parties might be so sure of success—through the sentiments of the voters at the polls, for instance—as to have little doubt of the outcome. With him, the election was over and nothing was lacking but the plaudits of the multitude.

to fall between two stools

The French is, *être assis entre deux chaises*, literally, to be seated between two seats, and the meaning, as in English, is to fail through lack of decision. It cannot be determined, but the French is probably the older saying, the English no more than a translation. The earliest English record is in John Gower's *Confessio amantis*, of 1390, "Betwen tuo Stoles lyth the fal, Whan that men wenen best to sitte (Between two stools lieth the fall when one thinks one is sitting best)." The allusion is, of course, to the concrete fact: a man seeing a seat at his left rear and one at his right rear, is likely to miss each of them.

to take the bull by the horns

If you have inadvertently insulted your employer's best customer, you must eventually "take the bull by the horns"—screw your courage to the sticking point, and tell the boss what happened; for we use the expression to mean, to face an unpleasant, difficult, or dangerous situation with such courage as one can muster and with the hope that such decisive action may avert disastrous consequences.

In all probability this saying is derived from the Spanish bullfighting, from that division of the contest in which, after planting their darts into the neck of the maddened bull, the *banderilleros* endeavor to tire him out by urging him to rush at their cloaks, by leaping upon his back, and by seizing him by the horns to hold his nose down. But possibly the saying came down from the brutal old English sport of bull-running, as it was called. This sport originated, it is said, in the reign of King John, or about the year 1200, and in the little market town of Stamford, Lincolnshire. Annually upon the thirteenth of November and promptly at eleven o'clock a bull was turned loose in the market place. Men and boys, then, with clubs and dogs pursued the animal, trying to drive it upon the bridge over the Welland River. There, those with courage tried to seize the furious beast and tumble it into the river, grasping it by the horns to do so. When the bull swam ashore to adjacent meadows, miry at that season, the run was continued until both the mob and the bull, spattered with mud, were utterly fatigued. The bull was then slaughtered and its meat sold, at a low price, to those who had participated in the run. The sport was finally abolished in 1840.

to feather one's nest

To provide for one's comfort; especially, for comfort in later life by amassing wealth. The import is to the practice of many birds which, after building their nests, pluck down from their breasts to provide a soft lining that will be comfortable during the long hours of setting upon the eggs. The oldest English literary occurrence is in 1553, but a more typical example is that used in 1590 by the young poet, Robert Greene, "She sees thou hast fethred thy nest, and hast crowns in thy purse."

to ring the changes

To state something over and over again in different ways. It comes from the art of bell ringing, which first came into popularity in the seventeenth century. A "change" means the order in which a series of bells are rung. Thus, with a series of 4 bells, as in the Westminster chimes, it is possible to ring 24 changes without once repeating the order in which the bells are struck. With 5 bells, 120 changes can be rung, for the variety increases enormously with the increase in the number of bells. With 12 bells, the greatest number used in change ringing, the huge figure of 479,001,600 changes is possible—possible, but not probable. The greatest number ever actually rung upon church bells is reported to have been 16,000 changes, and this took somewhat more than nine hours—and the physical exhaustion of the ringers. All the possible changes with any series of bells constitutes a "peal," but when we use the expression in the figurative sense, we convey the idea of repetition *ad nauseum* by saying, "She rang *all* the changes."

to wear one's heart on one's sleeve

Though Shakespeare was the first to use this saying, thus indicating an ostentatious display of one's limitless devotion, he was merely adapting another phrase current in his day and which he himself used in an earlier play. It was Iago, in *Othello*, who wore his heart on his sleeve, professing a devotion to his master, Othello, which, with him, was altogether feigned. The usual phrase of that period was to pin (a thing) upon one's sleeve. Shakespeare uses this in *Love's Labor's Lost*, where Biron, speaking of Boyet, says, "This gallant pins the wenches on his sleeve," meaning that Boyet is openly devoted to all wenches.

to know beans

This is usually in the negative; one who doesn't know beans is appallingly ignorant or is wholly unacquainted with the subject under discussion. It is likely that the expression arose from some story that went the rounds in America early in the nineteenth century, but, if so, the story has been lost. It is possible, however, that it arose from some dispute over the cowpea, which, despite the name, is more nearly related to the bean than to the pea and which is often called either the black-eyed bean or the black-eyed pea. But, as Walsh suggests, it is more likely that the reference was to the famous city of Boston, "the home of the bean and the cod," the city of culture, the hub of the universe, where it would be a mark of the sheerest ignorance not to know that Boston baked beans, to be fit to eat, must be made of that variety of small white bean known as "pea bean."

It might be, of course, that this American expression was contracted from the British phrase, "to know how many beans make five"—a silly saying that probably got started several centuries ago by having children learn to count by using beans. When little Cecil got far enough advanced to know how many beans made five, he was very intelligent and well informed, which is what the phrase means.

to put (or set) the cart before the horse

To get the order of things reversed, as to give the answer to a riddle while attempting to give the riddle. This common occurrence must also have been common among the ancient Greeks and Romans, for they also had sayings that agree with ours. The Greeks said, "Hysteron proteron," which meant, literally, the latter the former.

 The Romans said, "Currus bovem trahit præpostere," or, literally, the plow is drawn by the oxen in reversed position, and this, as a matter of record, is the way the saying first appeared in English. It is found in Dan Michel's *Ayenbite of Inwyt* (*Remorse of Conscience*), a translation by Dan Michel of a French treatise, written by Laurentius Gallus, in 1279, into the dialect of Kent. Michel renders it "Moche uolk of religion zetteth the zouly be-uore the oksen, (Many religious folk set the plow before the oxen)." In the course of the next two hundred years the English version became the present usage.

It must be recalled, of course, as the artist has shown, that some coal mines, cut as tunnels, are so laid out that a coal cart, when filled, could go by gravity out to the open, the horse or mule being needed chiefly to get the empty cart back to the face of the mine. But actually, on the outward trip, the horse is reversed in its shafts to act as a holdback, keeping the full cart from going too rapidly.

small fry

We use this humorously when speaking of young children. Our ancestors for the past four hundred years have done the same, so the humor is somewhat antique. But the joke is on us, because even in the remote day when we borrowed "fry" from the Norse, it meant the children of a man's family. That meaning died out, however, and the present humorous usage is rather a reference to the numerous progeny (or "fry") of salmon. And even now it implies a considerable number of small children.

of the first water

Water, in the sense of luster or brilliancy as applied to diamonds or pearls, is presumably a meaning that was borrowed, in translation, from Arabic gem traders, for the same expression is found in other European languages. Three centuries ago, diamonds were graded as first water, second water, or third water, those of the first water being white stones of the highest quality. The old method of grading died out before 1850, but "of the first water" remains in the language to indicate that the person or thing to which it is applied exemplifies the perfection of a flawless diamond. Even "a liar of the first water," would surpass all other liars in the perfection of his falsehoods.

Hobson's choice

The choice of taking what is offered or having nothing at all. Thomas Hobson, who died in 1630 at the ripe age of eighty-five or eighty-six, was a carrier, with his stables in Cambridge and his route running to London, sixty miles away. He was popular among the students of the university, for he drove his own stage over the long route, becoming well known to his passengers, and also because he was entrusted with the privilege of carrying the university mail. Not all the students kept riding horses, and Hobson had extra horses

31

in his stables which could be hired by them, thus becoming, it is said, the first in England to have conducted such a business. But Hobson, according to an article by Steele in the *Spectator* a hundred years later, had observed that the young men rode too hard, so, rather than risk the ruin of his best horses, which were most in demand, he made an unvarying rule that no horse be taken except in its proper turn—that, or none at all. "Every customer," said Steele, "was alike well served according to his chance, and every horse ridden with the same justice."

Hobson's death was said to have been the result of idleness forced upon him while the black plague was raging in London. He had the distinction, however, of being the only person to have been honored by an epitaph written by John Milton, or, in fact, by two such epitaphs. Either is too long to be quoted in full, but the second, filled with puns upon his occupation and the cause of his death may be quoted in part:

> *Merely to drive the time away he sickened,*
> *Fainted, and died, nor would with ale be quickened.*
> *"Nay," quoth he, on his swooning bed outstretched,*
> *"If I mayn't carry, sure I'll ne'er be fetched,*
> *But vow, though the cross doctors all stood bearers,*
> *For one carrier put down to make six bearers."*
>
> *Ease was his chief disease; and to judge right,*
> *He died for heaviness that his cart went light;*
> *His leisure told him that his time was come,*
> *And lack of load made his life burdensome,*
> *That even to his last breath (there be some that say't),*
> *As he were pressed to death, he cried, "More weight."*

Maundy Thursday

The day before Good Friday, the Thursday next before Easter. To most persons not of the Roman Catholic or Episcopalian faiths the designation of this day is incomprehensible, for the term "maundy" now appears in no other connection. It originated from the thirteenth chapter of John, in which the Last Supper and the ceremony and doctrine of humility are described. The thirty-fourth verse, it will be recalled, reads, "A new commandment I give unto you, That ye love one another." The Latin for "a new commandment" is *mandatum novum*, and these are the words that begin the first antiphon sung after the commemorative observance of the Lord's Supper and the ceremony, in England, of the washing of the feet of a number of poor persons by some member of the royal family or other important person. *Mandatum novum* became early abridged to *mandatum*, and in the common speech of the thirteenth and fourteenth centuries this became further abridged to mandee, monde, maunde, and so on, ultimately becoming maundy. The original commandment itself lost its significance and became applied to the ceremonial washing of feet, except in the observances of some religious denominations.

to get (or have) cold feet

An American doesn't need to be told that the meaning is to lose one's nerve, to become craven. The slang expression originated during my youth, probably in the early 1890's, but, as has been the case from the earliest times, no one took the trouble to give it a date or to record the exact source. I think it likely that its origin was a literal statement. Some wife, hearing a noise during the night, may have aroused her worthy but timorous husband to investigate the source. He, poor wight, may have said that his feet were too cold—meaning, literally that his feet were so cold and the floor so icy that he couldn't even chase a mouse. "Ya-a-ah," she may have retorted, "you and your cold feet!" And, if she were like some wives, she lost no time in passing the word around among all his friends that "Ed had such cold feet last night he couldn't even get out of bed for fear a mouse would bite him."

to cotton to (a thing or person)

We are apt to look upon this as recent, forgetting that it was used by Dickens (*Old Curiosity Shop*) more than a hundred years ago with just the present meaning, to get along with or to like a thing or person. And it was not original with Dickens, for it was used more than thirty years earlier. In fact, the usage appears to be little more than an extension of a meaning that was popular back in the middle of the sixteenth century, in a phrase, now obsolete, "This gear cottons," meaning this matter goes well or prospers. The origin is lost, but probably referred in some manner to the readiness with which cotton adheres to a napped surface.

one-horse town

The "one-horse town" is American; we use the expression disparagingly to designate a town of such limited resources, so sleepy and doless, that one horse might be able to do all its necessary transportation. The usage first reported (1855) credits the expression to New Orleans, but as it was reported a few years later as far north as Boston, a place notably reluctant to accept new terms, it is more than likely that it had come into wide popular use quite a long while before it appeared in print.

kangaroo court

Nowadays, a kangaroo court is rarely heard of except in jails or similar institutions where a mock court, independent of regular legal procedure, is set up by the inmates to try a fellow prisoner for some alleged offense. Sometimes such courts are set up merely for amusement, as diversions against the tedium of imprisonment, and are then nothing but travesties of legal processes. Originally, however, these irregular courts were resorted to in frontier communities, usually for the trial and condemnation of persons committing offenses against the community. The source of the name is mysterious, for it is American rather than Australian; I have not found evidence of its use in Australia at any time. But as the date of origin appears to coincide closely with the gold rush to California in 1849, the guess may be hazarded that the name was in humorous allusion to the early purpose of such courts, to try "jumpers" who, resorting to desperate measures, seized the mining claims of others. As the long arm of government had not yet reached the "diggings," the improvised courts were as irregular as those in today's jails, and perhaps they were sometimes equally unfair.

34

red-letter day

Such a day may be traced back to the fifteenth century, though in that period the allusion was to a holy day of some sort, such as one memorializing a saint or a church festival. The name came from the custom of using red or purple colors for marking those days upon the calendar, a custom that is still followed generally in showing the dates of Sundays and holy days by red figures on our present calendars. From this ancient custom arose the practice of designating any memorable date as a red-letter day.

not to know (one) from Adam

Wherever this is used the speaker means that he would be wholly unable to recognize the person of whom he speaks, probably a person once known but now forgotten. The source and antiquity are wholly unknown, but it may be that we owe it to the ancient argument over Adam's possession of a navel. Artists, such as Michelangelo, Van Eyck, and Titian, in their paintings of the Creation, always showed both Adam and Eve with navels, but many critics insisted that they could not have possessed them. "Otherwise," we may surmise that they said, "one could not tell ordinary people from Adam!" The argument was used as the basis of the contribution by Dr. Logan Glendenning, in  1944, "The Case of the Missing Patriarchs, to a symposium, *Profile by Gaslight*, which purported to be "the private life of Sherlock Holmes," and which contained fancied episodes about the great detective written by a number of his admirers. Dr. Glendenning recounted an adventure of Holmes after he had died: Consternation reigned in Heaven because Adam and Eve had been missing for several eons. Holmes, whose astuteness was known in Heaven, was assigned to the search. He alone knew all others from Adam and could speedily pick out the missing pair, for he alone of all the myriads who preceded him through the pearly gates knew that they would be the only two without navels.

root hog or die

This means to get down to hard work or suffer the consequences, to shift for oneself. The earliest literary use so far reported goes back only to 1834, to Davy Crockett's autobiography, *A Narrative of the Life of David Crockett*, written just two years before his death at the Alamo. It is likely, however, that this typical Americanism goes back to much earlier pioneering days. It arose, undoubtedly, from the everyday observance of the fact that a hog, if left to forage for himself, is not in much danger of starving. He will root with his snout, or, to use another American term, he will "hog," or appropriate greedily, whatever he can find in the nature of food. It is possible, of course, that the original sense was a command, as it were, to a hog to start rooting or suffer death. But in the use that I have always heard "hog" had merely the force of a verb, one of a triplet, "to root, hog, or die"—just as the phrase, "eat, drink, and be merry."

black Monday

Nowadays, in schoolboy lingo, this is the day after Easter, the day when school is resumed after the Easter holidays. But, although school children may not know it, the day after Easter has been called "black Monday" in England for many centuries as the anniversary of several different tragedies or ominous events. The first was a tragedy, but historical authenticity is uncertain. According to an account written several centuries after the event, on the day after Easter in the year 1209 a large number of English people who had taken residence in Dublin were massacred by the Irish. Five hundred were said to have been slain. Then in 1357, according to an account written in Latin, "the Black Prince," Edward, Prince of Wales, sustained terrific losses in France on the day after Easter because of a great storm. Also, in the year 1360, according to another ancient chronicle, on the fourteenth day of April, or the day after Easter, during the siege of Paris by Edward III, the day was "a ffoule derke day, so bytter colde, that syttyng on horse bak men dyed." Each of these two latter events were said by the respective chroniclers to have been the occasion which gave rise to the term "black Monday"; but be that as it may, the day was actually so called as long ago as the latter part of the fourteenth century.

to rain cats and dogs

When we use this we don't refer to a gentle shower, but to a terrific downpour. Perhaps, because such rain is usually accompanied by heavy thunder and lightning, the allusion was to a cat and dog fight. As far as the records show, this form of the slight exaggeration originated with Jonathan Swift in his *Complete collection of genteel and ingenious conversation*, usually referred to as *Polite Conversation*, written in 1738; but it might have occurred to him to use a politer phrase than was used by a wit eighty-five years earlier who, describing a downpour, said it rained "dogs and polecats."

to show the white feather

To behave in a cowardly manner; to act pusillanimously. The expression comes from the cockpit, the arena or ring where game-cocks are pitted against one another to see which can vanquish the other. Cockfighting is one of the oldest of sports; it is recorded among early Chinese accounts and was practiced in ancient India, Persia, and Egypt. Throughout all this period birds have been selected for fighting abilities and high wagers have been staked between owners, and between friends of each, on the relative prowess of their cocks. But about two centuries ago—at least, no earlier mention has been found—someone made the discovery that if a cock had so  much as one white feather in its tail, that bird was certain to be a poor fighter, that he would run from the other bird and put up no fight at all. Whether this is true or not—and, if true, it seems strange that it was not known hundreds of years earlier—it became fully believed and passed into a byword that, when applied to a person, became a stigma of cowardice.

on the anxious seat (bench)

We use this nowadays to mean in a state of worry or anxiety, but the literal meaning alludes to the "mourners' bench," or seat especially assigned to those of a congregation who, affected by the exhortations of a preacher, have become anxious over their future state and seek repentance. The literal phrase was in use early in the nineteenth century, but the oldest record of the figurative use is in Harriet Beecher Stowe's *The Pearl of Orr's Island*, published in 1862.

to hold water

The literal sense, such as applied to a sound pitcher or bowl, gradually acquired in the early seventeenth century a figurative meaning, as if testing a pitcher for soundness by filling it with water —if unsound, the water would leak out. Thus, figuratively, an unsound argument or fallacious reasoning would not "hold water" if it failed to stand a test.

to acknowledge the corn

This purely American expression means to admit the losing of an argument, especially in regard to a detail; to retract; to admit defeat. It is somewhat over a hundred years old, one account of its origin giving it the date of 1828. In this account, plausible, though unverified, a member of Congress, Andrew Stewart, is said to have stated in a speech that haystacks and cornfields were sent by Indiana, Ohio, and Kentucky to Philadelphia and New York. Charles A. Wickliffe, member from Kentucky, questioned the statement, allowing that haystacks and cornfields could not walk. Stewart then pointed out that he did not mean literal haystacks and cornfields, but the horses, mules, and hogs for which the hay and corn were raised. Wickliffe then rose to his feet, it is said, and drawled, "Mr. Speaker, I acknowledge the corn."

The other account carries no date, but takes us to New Orleans where an upriver countryman is alleged to have fallen among card-sharps. Before the evening was over the farmer had lost not only his purse, but the two barges of produce, one of corn and one of potatoes, which he had brought to market. But in the morning when he went to the river, possibly intending to deny his losses, he found that the barge loaded with corn had sunk during the night and, of course, was now worthless. So when his creditor arrived, demanding that he turn over both potatoes and corn, he said, "I acknowledge the corn, but, by golly, you shan't get the potatoes."

to break the ice

Our present figurative use came, of course, from the maritime necessity of breaking up the ice upon rivers and channels for the navigation of ships and boats in winter. The early extended sense, indicating preparation of a pathway for others, did not arise until late in the sixteenth century—the earliest instance is from the epilog of a curious work written in 1590 by Henry Swinburne, *A briefe Treatise of Testaments and last Willes*: "The author therefore in aduenturing to breake the yse to make the passage easie for his countrymen, failing sometimes of the fourd, and falling into the pit, may seeme worthie to be pitied." From this metaphorical usage the present sense—to break down a stiff reserve between persons—was slow in developing, or at least was not recorded for another hundred and fifty years.

to walk Spanish

When Jeffie grabs the smaller Johnny by the collar and the seat of the pants, raises him until he must walk on tiptoe and hustles him out of the room, Johnny is "walking Spanish." (Later in life, Johnny may "walk Spanish" by himself by just tip-toeing cautiously out of a place where he may decide he doesn't want to be.) Neither of the youngsters has any notion that their great-great-grandfathers a hundred and twenty-five years ago were saying and doing the same thing. Possibly one could go back another generation or two, but recorded use dates only to 1825. The source is American, and there is little doubt that it alluded originally to the practices attributed to pirates of the Spanish Main in the treatment  of prisoners. Obviously, a captive would be reluctant to "walk the plank" except under compulsion. He might resist even the prod of a knife; but if lifted and partly choked by a powerful buccaneer, the propulsion would be resistless, and, willy-nilly, he would find himself in the sea.

to go scot free

To be exempt from payment, punishment, or penalty. Except in this expression, and in the somewhat rare "to pay one's scot," this meaning of "scot" is almost unknown in America. But it comes straight from Old English; it then meant, as now, a payment, or, especially, one's share in the cost of some entertainment; later it came to mean also a tax. Hence, "to go scot free" is, literally, to be free of payment or tax.

a bolt from the blue

It is a bolt of lightning from the clear, blue sky that is meant. Such a phenomenon is, at least, unexpected and is also startling. Thus the news of the Japanese attack on Pearl Harbor was a bolt from the blue, in the figurative sense. Literary record of the use of the saying dates only to 1888, but it is likely that it existed in common speech many years earlier.

an Achilles' heel

A vulnerable spot. In the *Iliad,* Homer's marvelous legend, Achilles, the hero of the story, was the son of a king, Peleus, and of the sea-goddess, Thetis, and a great-grandson of no less than Zeus himself. The account that Homer gives of the boyhood of so remarkable a being is reasonably prosaic; that is, he was at least brought up on land, even though his tutors did include a centaur. But later writers than Homer felt compelled to provide greater details. Thus, according to one account, the real reason why Achilles was fearless in battle was because he knew that everyone was powerless to hurt him. That was because his mother had dipped him in the river Styx—the river that encircles Hades—and had thus made him invulnerable. He would have been living yet, perhaps, but the god Apollo, who was no friend, knew that Thetis had slipped—she had held Achilles by the heel when she dipped him and had neglected to get that heel wet. Apollo whispered that secret to Paris, mortal enemy of Achilles, who deliberately aimed an arrow at this unprotected heel, the one spot that was vulnerable, and thus caused the death of the hero. (Incidentally, the tendon leading upward from the rear of the heel is even today called "Achilles' tendon.")

to paddle one's own canoe

This was probably used in nothing but its literal sense until the appearance in *Harper's Monthly*, in 1854, of a song by Dr. Edward P. Philpots. Since then, however, it has been more frequently used to mean, to show one's independence. The refrain of the song ran:

> *Voyager upon life's sea:—*
> *To yourself be true,*
> *And whate'er your lot may be,*
> *Paddle your own canoe.*

a dog in the manger

Aesop, back about 600 B.C., is said to have told his master about a dog which went to sleep in a manger full of hay. According to the fable, the ox, for whom the manger had been filled, came up to it for his rations, whereupon the dog, roused from his slumbers, snapped at the ox and drove him away. The ox, annoyed by this behavior, accused the dog of being churlish, because, he said, "You are unable to eat the hay yourself but will not leave it for those who can." Or, in the quaint words of John Gower, in *Confessio Amantis*, written about 1390, "Thogh it be noght the houndes kinde To ete chaf, yit wol he werne (prevent) An oxe which comth to the berne (barn), Therof to taken eny fode."

to set the Thames on fire

It is the English river that is referred to, not Connecticut's. But the saying has been used of other rivers and with the same thought—in Ireland of the Liffey, in the United States of the Hudson, and in Germany of the Rhine. The German saying—*Er hat den Rhein und das Meer angezündet* (He has set the Rhine and the ocean afire)—dating back to about 1580, is of earlier vintage than the English by about two hundred years. In all instances, the figurative meaning is to build up a reputation for oneself, as if by such a miraculous stunt as to set a river afire; to do something wonderful.

A writer in *Notes & Queries*, about eighty years ago, advanced the theory that, perhaps through similarity of pronunciation, the English saying might originally have been, "to set the temse on fire"

41

—"temse" being an old-fashioned name for the sieve used in bolting meal. Thus, "He will never set the temse on fire," he argued, might have had reference to some extremely slow workman. There is no historical basis for this theory, however.

till the cows come home

Although cows are always milked twice a day, mornings and evenings, this very old homely saying refers to the time that cows, with udders painfully full, come to the home gates for the morning  milking. The saying, used as long ago as 1600, seems at first to have always indicated disgracefully late hours, mostly hours spent riotously; but Swift, in 1738, applied it to time spent by a slugabed who did not arise before the evening milking: "I warrant you lay abed till the cows came home," he wrote in *Polite Conversation*. The amplified expression, "Till hell freezes over and the cows come skating home over the ice," is very modern.

to raise Cain

In the United States, one raises Cain when he causes a disturbance, or, perhaps, when one gets so angry that he loses his temper. The saying is generally believed to refer to the first child of Adam and Eve, Cain, who killed his brother, Abel, through jealousy and whose name has always been synonymous with fratricide. It is not surprising that the first literary use of the expression should have this reference, a witticism in the *St. Louis Pennant* of 1840: "Why have we every reason to believe that Adam and Eve were both rowdies? Because . . . they both raised Cain."

It seems more likely to me, however, that the expression was originally a play upon words. Cain was, it is true, a son of Adam and Eve; but for many centuries and to the present time in Scotland and Ireland, the Gaelic word "cain" or "kain" or "cane" has meant the rent of land, payable in produce. One who "raises cain" is actually raising the produce to pay for his land. Some Scottish or Irish

42

settler in the United States may have used the term literally in all seriousness to a jocular neighbor. There is no evidence supporting the hypothesis, however.

to draw the longbow

The longbow was the type of bow said to have been used by Robin Hood; that is, a bow about the length of a man, as distinguished from the old short bow used at the Battle of Hastings, or from the crossbow. The longbow, as compared with either of the others, was greatly superior in range and in accuracy. Famous archers vied with one another in using the longbow, and great tales were told of their prowess. One archer, according to an old ballad, was so skilled that, in an exhibition before the king, he split a slender wand at a distance of 400 yards (almost a quarter of a mile), then to impress the king still more, he tied his own seven-year-old son to a stake, balanced an apple upon the lad's head, and, from a distance of 120 yards, split the apple.

Great tales were told of the remarkable shots these English bowmen made—and the tales lost nothing in the telling. They became as discredited as the modern fish story. Hence, anyone believed to be telling a fantastic story was said to draw the longbow. Probably the saying came into use long before the seventeenth century, though the first literary record appeared late in that century.

on the horns of a dilemma

A dilemma, in logic, is a form of argument in which a participant finds himself in the embarrassing predicament of having to make a choice of either of two premises, both of which are obnoxious; it is a trap set by an astute person to catch an unwary one, like answering yes or no to the question, "Have you stopped beating your wife?" Because one may be caught and impaled upon either of the alternatives, each of them has been called a "horn." Medieval scholars, writing in Latin, used the expression, *argumentum cornutum*, horned argument. Nicolas Udall, in his translations of the adages collected (in Latin) by Erasmus explains the saying in the language of 1548: "Thys forked questyon; which the sophisters call

43

an horned question, because that to whether of both partyes a bodye shall make a direct aunswere, he shall renne on the sharpe poyncte of the horne."

by hook or by crook

This phrase is so old that it has become a recognized part of the language. It appears in the writings of John Wyclif and of John Gower, both of whom were contemporaries of Chaucer. It meant then, as it does today, "in one way or another; by fair means or foul"; but no one knows why it has that meaning. Attempts to solve the riddle have been numerous; various theories have been advanced and stoutly defended, but none yet has been definitely proved. The most plausible relates to the old forest laws of England, laws by which all forest lands of the country were the private property of the king. The sole right of the common people to enter these forests without permission was, it is said, for the removal of dead wood from the ground or dead branches from the trees; of the latter, only such branches as could be brought down "by hook or by crook," that is, by the use of no stouter instrument than a reaper's hook or a shepherd's crook. But in order to satisfy the meaning, "by fair means or foul," we must assume that some of the ancient shepherds found an excuse to tend their sheep with crooks that were exceedingly long or unusually heavy.

to turn the tables

Metaphorically speaking, we turn the tables upon another fellow when we put him in the predicament that we have been occupying, or into a similar one. There is no connection with "turning the other cheek." The saying arose during the early 1600s, some three centuries ago, and seems to have been applied to some popular card game in which a player, when at a disadvantage, might reverse the position of the board and thus shift the disadvantage to his adversary. Or possibly the original sense of the expression was the same as we now indicate by "duplicate," as in duplicate bridge, that after a series of hands of cards had been played, the table was turned and the same series of hands was replayed, each player holding the hand previously held by an opponent.

Brewer has an interesting theory that the expression is derived from an ancient Roman masculine fad of purchasing costly tables. After such a purchase, the matron of the house, chided for a purchase of her own, was alleged to "turn the tables" by reminding her spouse of his extravagance. Marital customs of Roman days were not unlike the present, so it is not unlikely that the matrons did thus defend themselves, but evidence is lacking that our metaphor had such an origin.

to keep the pot boiling

Even among the ancients the container often signified the thing contained; the Romans used *olla*, pot, many times instead of the meat within the pot, and so did our own forbears. Hence, when they said that they must keep the pot boiling, they meant that they must have something within the pot, which, when removed, would be edible; that is, that they must supply meat or other material for a stew, provide a livelihood. This was the only figurative meaning from the sixteenth to the nineteenth century; it gave rise to such allied sayings as "to go to pot" (to cut up and prepare for the pot; hence, in present usage, to become disintegrated), "potboiling," (doing something, usually something of no great merit, that will provide for one's immediate needs).

at (or on) first blush

Anciently, a blush was a glimpse, a momentary view. This was the sense that we find in the late fourteenth-century poem, "Joseph of Arithmathie": "Aftur the furste blusch we ne michte him biholden (After the first glimpse we could not behold him)." This sense dropped out of use during the sixteenth century, however, except in the present phrase.

to carry coals to Newcastle

The current American equivalent is "to sell refrigerators to the Eskimos." The idea is of doing something that is the height of superfluity. In explanation, Newcastle—or Newcastle upon Tyne, to use the official name of this ancient English city—lies in the center of the great coal-mining region of England. Vast quantities of coal are shipped out of it by rail and by sea every day. Hence, he would be a fool indeed who brought coal from another region into the place where it was naturally so plentiful. The saying was recorded by Heywood in 1606; as he labeled it common even then, it may well go back a century or two earlier. Similar sayings occur in all languages.

to talk turkey

A century ago, it would seem, the turkey was considered a pleasant bird, for when such expressions as "to talk turkey" or "to say turkey" were used, the allusion was to a pleasant conversation. A young man "talked turkey" to a good-looking girl, if he had the chance. Perhaps that was because a young man in the presence of a

pretty girl gets so tongue-tied that his remarks sound as meaningless as the gobble of a turkey. But sometime within the past fifty or sixty years the gobble of the turkey acquired a sterner note; it began to have the qualities of the voice of a father berating his son for the dent in the fender of the family car, or that of the employer who, in no uncertain tones, jumps down the throat of a clerk for a heedless error.

There is a legend, variously reported, that is often used in explanation of the way this expression arose: Two men, one an Indian, went for a day's hunting. They shot several birds, among them one or more turkeys; but when it came time to divide the bag, the smart white man, thinking to take advantage of an ignorant savage, always arranged the counting in such way that the turkeys fell to his share. The Indian, however, was not so gullible as he seemed. Finally he faced his companion. "Ugh," he said, "All time you talk turkey. Now I talk turkey to you."

46

in hot water

Perhaps because hot water is so easily obtainable these days, we think of the figurative hot water, meaning a trouble, a scrape, or a difficulty, as being a modern expression. No, indeed! People first got into trouble thousands of years ago, though English-speaking people didn't refer to it as "hot water" until about the beginning of the sixteenth century. Possibly the allusion was to the ancient way that unwelcome guests were sometimes warded off—by heaving a kettleful of boiling water, when available, upon troublesome intruders. But, oddly enough, more than two centuries after the figurative use was a matter of record, James Harris, before starting on the great diplomatic career that eventually caused him to be created Earl of Malmesbury, supposed that "in hot water" was a modern phrase of his period, and called it such, in 1765, in one of his letters.

to eat humble pie

This, meaning to humble oneself, to apologize or abase oneself profoundly, was originally a play upon words, a jocular substitution of humble for umble wherein the meaning of humble was retained. Umble pie was, and maybe still is in some parts of England, a pasty made of the edible inward parts of an animal, usually a deer. The umbles were considered a delicacy by most persons, although some thought them to be fit only for menials. And the pie made of those parts was also variously appreciated; it graced some tables, but James Russell Lowell, in 1864, said, "Disguise it as you will, flavor it as you will, call it what you will, umble-pie is umble-pie, and nothing else."

Etymologically the phrase is interesting; though in present use it is humble pie, jocularly derived from umble pie, umble is one of a number of English words which originally had an initial "n." Thus, just as apron was originally napron, adder (the snake) originally nadder, so umble was originally numble. But there would have been no point to the joke then, without an initial vowel to which cockney "h" might be prefixed.

to haul (rake, bring, or fetch) over the coals

Until comparatively recent times the sin of heresy was, in many countries, punishable by death. In England, during the fifteenth and sixteenth centuries, one found guilty of departing from the creed and tenets of the church might be condemned to death by burning. Thus, the earliest uses of this expression, back in the sixteenth century, referred to the literal punishment of heretics— one would be fetched over the coals literally unless he speedily reformed his actions and beliefs. From the use of the expression as a threat, almost at once it became a synonym for the sense in which we use it today—to reprimand severely, to censure caustically.

wet blanket

This, one might have supposed, is certainly an example of recent American slang, but it was used in Scotland more than a hundred years ago, and with exactly the meaning in which we use it today— one who puts a damper on anything, especially upon any jollity; one who emits gloom. The expression was used in 1830 by the Scottish novelist, John Galt, in *Lawrie Todd, or the Settlers in the Woods*: "I have never felt such a wet blanket before or syne." But as this novel contains sketches of American frontier life, the author creates an illusion of American slang.

to sweat blood

To perform such arduous toil or to be in such physical agony that the sweat in which one is bathed seems to be one's blood draining away. The allusion is to the agony of Jesus on the Mount of Olives: "And being in an agony he prayed more earnestly: and his sweat was as it were great drops of blood falling down to the ground." The expression had only a religious use until about the seventeenth century.

a big shot

A person of importance. This slang use is quite recent, developed within the current century, but it is a lineal descendant of "a big gun," dating from the middle of the last century, and which in turn sprang from the union of "a great gun" and "a big bug" of the early nineteenth century.

the lion's share

Why this always means the greater part in any allotment, especially the part that one gives to the "boss" or that, in serving the dessert, mother apportions to father, takes us back to one of Aesop's fables. Two versions have come down to us, which is not surprising, for old Aesop is supposed merely to have told his fables, leaving it to others to write them out in later centuries.

In one of these, a lion, an ass, and a fox went hunting, with the understanding that the prey should be divided among them. A large fat stag was caught, and the ass was appointed to divide it. This he did with scrupulous exactitude, apportioning an equal amount, as best he could, to each of them. But this enraged the lion, who felt that his size, prowess, and dignity had been insulted. He was so infuriated that he flew at the ass and killed him. Then the fox undertook to divide the stag into proper portions; and, being crafty and not wishing to follow the fate of the ass, he nibbled off a small piece for himself and left all the rest to the lion.

In the other version, there were four hunters, a lion, a heifer, a goat, and a sheep. Again the prey was a large fat stag, but in this story the lion did the dividing. He divided it neatly enough into four equal portions, taking the tastiest part for himself. But, having done so, he took another portion, saying that it was his by right of being the strongest. A third portion followed, because, he said, it was his by right of being the most valiant. The fourth portion belonged, he said, to the others—and then he added, "But touch it if you dare!"

to get the bird

Actors get the bird when the performance is so bad that the audience rebels, by hissing or booing, or, in more recent years, by executing the Bronx cheer. The expression was the forerunner of getting the raspberry. It dates from about the middle of the nine-teenth century, being first recorded in Hotten's *Dictionary of Modern Slang* in 1859. But, in turn, this expression was preceded by its logical forerunner, "to get the goose," in allusion to the hissing of the goose, a theatrical phrase that goes back at least to the beginning of the nineteenth century.

between the devil and the deep sea

On the horns of a dilemma; between Scylla and Charybdis; facing equally perilous dangers. William Walker, in 1670, when com-piling his *Phraseologia Anglo-Latina; or Phrases of the English and Latin Tongue*, included this expression in his list, probably finding it used by some earlier writer of Latin; but if so, his source is no longer known. The phrase is listed, however, by James Kelly, in 1721, in his *Complete Collection of Scotish Proverbs*. The view that it is of Scottish origin is supported by the fact that it is to be found in the account written by Colonel Robert Monro, a doughty Scot, *His Expedition with the worthy Scots Regiment called Mac-Keyes Regiment*, relating to his service under Gustavus Adolphus of Sweden between 1621 and 1632. Monro described one engagement, in which he found himself exposed not only to the fire of the enemy, but also to Swedish guns that were not sufficiently elevated, and said, "I, with my partie, did lie on our poste, as betwixt the devill and the deep sea." This is the earliest English use of the phrase that has yet been found.

to blow hot and cold

To be inconsistent; to vacillate. We are indebted to one of Aesop's fables for this meaning. A satyr, he tells us, came upon a traveler in the winter who was blowing upon his fingers. "Why do you do that?" asked the satyr. "To warm my fingers," replied the traveler, "they are nearly frozen." The satyr led the man to his cave where he poured out a mess of hot pottage and laid it before his guest. Thereupon the traveler began to blow the smoking dish with all his might. "What! Is it not hot enough?" cried the satyr. "Indeed, yes," answered the man, "I am trying to cool it." "Away

50

with you," said the alarmed satyr, thrusting the man out of the cave, "I will have no dealings with one who can blow hot and cold from the same mouth."

to know the ropes

To be familiar with all the details. There have been differences of opinion about the origin of this saying, for it so happens that the earliest records make it appear that the phrase was first used by the gentry of the racetracks, and, because of that, some hold that by "ropes" the allusion is to the reins of a horse's harness; that one "knows the ropes" who best knows the handling of the reins. But, as with many other phrases, this one, I think, undoubtedly originated among sailors. An experienced sailor, in the days  of sailing vessels, was one who was familiar with the bewildering array of ropes leading to all parts of the many sheets of canvas under which the vessel sailed. Such a man literally "knew the ropes."

to split hairs

In these days, one engaged in the occupation of splitting hairs might very likely be engaged in some profound scientific work—trying, perhaps, to find some microscopic cause for the dividing of long hair at the ends. But three hundred years ago when the phrase was coined there was no thought of scientific research; it meant to divide into exactly even amounts, so precisely as to afford no slightest advantage. A hundred years later, however, it became an ironic figure of speech; one who would split hairs was one who would argue endlessly over fine distinctions, over differences of trivial importance, and this is the sense still in use.

all beer and skittles

The phrase occurs more generally in British literature than in American. Dickens used it (with "porter" instead of "beer") in *Pickwick Papers*, in the scene in which Mr. Pickwick, convicted of breach of promise, is introduced to Fleet Prison as a debtor. His conductor has shown him that other debtors manage to have a pretty good time. "It strikes me, Sam," said Mr. Pickwick to his faithful Achates, Sam Weller, "that imprisonment for debt is scarcely any punishment at all." "Ah, that's just the wery thing, sir," rejoined Sam, "they don't mind it; it's a regular holiday to them—all porter and skittles."

Skittles was a game quite similar to ninepins; so "porter and skittles" or "beer and skittles" was equivalent to a very pleasant occasion, a time of feasting and playing. The expression occurs generally in the negative, as, "life is not all beer and skittles"; i.e., life is not an unmixed pleasure.

best bib and tucker

One's best clothes. The expression as a whole dates from the late eighteenth century. The bib was an article of attire similar to that worn by children then and now, but also formerly worn by girls and women, and extending from the throat to the waist. The tucker, to quote a historian of 1688, was "a narrow piece of Cloth which compasseth the top of a Womans Gown about the Neck part"; it was often a frill of lace over the shoulders. Men whose calling required an apron, such as mechanics or drovers, sometimes wore a bib; no man ever wore a tucker. The expression, therefore, was originally never applied to a man, but when the literal meaning of the words became dimmed, either a man or a woman was said to don his best bib and tucker when he dressed up for some momentous occasion.

to steer (or sail) between Scylla and Charybdis

To steer a mid-course between perils. Scylla, according to Homer's *Odyssey*, was a fearful monster that dwelt in a cavern on the face of a high cliff that overlooked a narrow channel of the sea. She had six heads, each on a long neck, and from every ship that passed each mouth seized a sailor. On the opposite rock grew a wild fig tree, beneath which Charybdis, three times a day, sucked in and regorged the sea. It was the fate of Odysseus (or, in Latin, Ulysses) to sail between these two perils, to try to avoid the loss of his crew from the monster and the loss of his ship in the whirlpool at the base of the opposite rock. Odysseus lost both his crew and his ship, saving his own life by clinging to the fig tree.

to curry favor

"Fauvel" was the name of a fallow-colored horse, in the four-teenth-century allegory, *Roman de Fauvel*, a horse used to symbolize fraud and cunning. The allegory achieved great popularity in France as well as in England. Perhaps in ironic jest, a person who indulged in fulsome flattery was said "to curry Fauvel," meaning that he sought by fraud and cunning to gain the good will of the person he flattered. This, in the English spelling of that day became corrupted into "to curry Favel," and a toady or sycophant became known as a "curry-favel." Popular speech took up the phrase, but the popular ear did not hear it quite correctly; so *favel*  became *favor* several hundred years ago, and gave us an expression, "to curry favor," that had no literal meaning, but which was used then, as now, to mean to flatter subtly in order to gain some end. In French, many years ago, they made a verb of "Fauvel"—*faufiler* —which has the meaning of our entire phrase.

to lead apes in hell

This expression was common in the times of Shakespeare and is found in *The Taming of the Shrew* in the lines where Katharina says to her father, "Nay, now I see she is your treasure, she must have a husband; I must dance bare-foot on her wedding day and for your love to her lead apes in hell." Beatrice uses the same expression in *Much Ado about Nothing*. Another writer of the same period gives us the meaning in the lines, " 'Tis an old proverb, and you know it well, that women dying maids lead apes in hell." But why spinsters were ever consigned to such an ignoble fate after death, and what was the source or the age of the proverb, were probably unknown even in Shakespeare's days.

53

to spill the beans

To upset the plans; to relate something fully or prematurely; to let the cat out of the bag; to upset the apple cart. This American saying came into general use early in the present century, and, of course, the incident that gave rise to it, whatever it may have been, was not recorded. Very likely it was an actual occurrence, possibly an important occasion at which, say, baked beans were to have been the main dish. Just before serving, or perhaps at the table, the bean pot may have broken, not only causing a mess generally, but also upsetting the plans. The extended sense, telling something that should not be told, or telling something in detail, seems to have been added from the older, "to know beans," to know what is what.

to walk the chalk

In present-day American use, one who is made "to walk the chalk" must walk a line of rectitude and sobriety, not deviating a hair's breadth, or he must obey the rules closely. The significance is alleged to have been of nautical origin, a straight chalk line drawn along the deck, or a narrow lane between two lines, to test the  sobriety of a sailor; if he could not walk the length of the line placing each foot directly on it, or if he was unable to keep within the two lines of the lane, he was adjudged to be too drunk for duty and was clapped into the brig. By the time the expression had become a matter of literary record, back in 1823, however, the test was military and altogether a friendly competition among soldiers to discover who was the most sober. The British say that the original test was a custom in the American navy, but the Dictionary of American English has no record of it.

Both in England and America, however, there was another meaning of "to walk the chalk (or chalks)." It is now obsolete in America, but its meaning was to take one's speedy departure. Mark Twain used it in *Sketches, New and Old*, "If anybody come meddlin' wid you, you jist make 'em walk chalk." This usage is recorded in England as early as 1842, though the original allusion cannot be ascertained.

to turn turtle

One must remember that "turtle" applies, scientifically speaking, to the marine member of the family, and that "tortoise" should properly be used to describe the land or fresh-water member. The sea beastie is the one most highly prized for food, nowadays chiefly appearing on the menu as "turtle soup." Our English-speaking ancestors, however, called both the land and sea species "tortoises" until the middle of the seventeenth century, for it was not until then that they began to realize that the huge marine creature, unknown to them before the travels of Columbus, Cabot, and other explorers, was not just an overgrown land specimen. Sailors started to speak of this animal as a "turtle," probably thinking that they were giving it the French name, *tortue*, though in reality they were giving to this quadruped a name that had previously been applied only to the bird which we now call "turtle dove."

Also some time in the seventeenth century, sailors found that these sea monsters were edible, if one could first capture them. Caribbean natives, they observed, waited until one of the reptiles came ashore to lay her eggs, then, seizing her by one of her flippers, turned her over on her back. Thus careened, she was absolutely helpless. This the sailors called "turning the turtle." Later, because a ship that had been capsized bore a fancied resemblance to an overturned turtle, sailors called such capsizing, "turning the turtle." Ashore, that saying was adopted for anything that was upside down.

to bark up the wrong tree

To mistake one's course of action; to be on the wrong course; to have one's attention diverted from the intended object. Literally, this American phrase referred to a hunting dog used in the pursuit of raccoons. When this nocturnal animal takes to a tree, the dog is supposed to stay at the foot of the tree and bay until its master arrives. But, in the dark, if the dog mistakes the tree in which the 'coon has taken refuge, the hunter may lose it entirely. The expression must have been very popular in the early nineteenth century, especially by writers of western life and tales, for in rapid succession it appeared in the works of James Hall, David Crockett, and Albert Pike.

to hold the bag

When one is left holding the bag he is being made the scapegoat, he has been left in an awkward predicament not of his own devising, or blamed for or punished for all the faults committed jointly by himself and others. George Washington may have been familiar with the saying during the Revolutionary War, for it was used by an  American army officer, Major Royall Tyler, in literature for the first time, when, in 1787, he wrote the first comedy to be written and produced in America. This young officer had participated in the suppression of Shays's Rebellion in the previous year and, in his play, has one of his characters say, "General Shays has sneaked off and given us the bag to hold."

There was a much earlier expression, dating back to the sixteenth century, "to give the bag," which meant to give one the slip, to elude someone, and also, to abandon. It is likely that the bag that was given was the same bag as that which one was left holding. Neither the bag of the sixteenth century nor its contents, if any, is identified, but as the saying was used in speaking of a servant or apprentice who left without notification, it is highly probable that the original bag was empty, that the servant had absconded with his master's cash, leaving him only an empty purse.

to jump out of the frying pan into the fire

The same expression or one closely allied to it is common to many languages; in the second century the Greek equivalent was "out of the smoke into the flame"; the Italian and Portuguese, "to fall from the frying pan into the coals"; the Gaelic, "out of the cauldron into the fire," and the French, from which the English may be a translation, "to leap from the frying pan into the fire (*tomber de la poêle dans le feu*)." The sense of the expression has always been to escape one evil predicament by leaping into another just as bad or worse.

English usage is traceable to a religious argument that arose between William Tyndale, translator of the Bible into English, and Sir Thomas More, best remembered now as the author of Utopia. The argument started in 1528 upon the publication of a paper by More, *A Dialoge concerning Heresyes*. This elicited a treatise from Tyndale in 1530, *An Answere unto Sir Thomas Mores Dialoge*, and this in turn brought forth from More, two years later, *The Confutacyon of Tyndales Answere*, wherein More brings in our expression, saying that his adversary "featly conuayed himself out of the frying panne fayre into the fyre." It is a little grim to recall that Tyndale was publicly strangled and burned as a heretic in 1536, but that More was not alive to rejoice, for he, a year earlier, had been hung, through perjured testimony, as a traitor because he would not approve the bigamous marriage of Henry VIII to Anne Boleyn.

the apple of one's eye

Literally this is the pupil of the eye. In ancient times it was called an apple because it was thought to be a solid globular body. But even by the time of King Alfred—that is, in the ninth century—because injury to the pupil would render one blind, the expression had come to mean that which one holds dearest.

to be caught flat-footed

Unlike "flat-footed" in the phrase, "to come out flat-footed," one is caught flat-footed when undecided or unprepared. It is likely that the term came from the American game of football, for it applies most pertinently to the player who, having received the ball on a pass, is caught by an opposing player before he has moved from his tracks.

within an ace of

About as close as possible; on the very edge of. At dice, an ace is the lowest number, and ambsace—literally, both aces, from the Old French, *ambes as*—is the lowest possible throw, hence the epitome of bad luck, almost nothing. Thus, "ambsace" very naturally came to mean an extremely small point; less of a point than would be represented by the pip of a single ace. And, in the same figurative manner, "within ambsace of" measured a degree of closeness that was no more than half a pip or jot. This latter wording appears to have been the original form of the expression; but, through careless use or faulty hearing, this became corrupted into the only form heard today, "within an ace of," though both wordings were in use in the seventeenth century.

to fly the coop

This is American slang, apparently twentieth century, though it is likely that it was criminal cant originally and may date back to  the nineteenth century. "Coop" is slang for prison, jail; the original meaning was, therefore, to escape from prison. By later extension the phrase has come to mean to depart unceremoniously from any place, especially from a place that has begun to feel confining or restrictive. Thus a boy at school tells his fellows that he is going "to fly the coop," when he intends to "play hooky"; that is, to leave the school grounds without permission. Or, humorously, one at a party that he does not enjoy, is said "to have flown the coop" if he has left without formal leave-taking.

Attic salt

This has nothing to do with anything that may be found in one's attic, but refers rather to Attica, the ancient kingdom and republic of Greece. The people of this country, especially of its capital, Athens, were noted for the delicacy and refinement of their wit. It was so nobally piquant or salty that even in Rome it was described as *sal Atticum*, of which our phrase, "Attic salt," is merely the translation.

through thick and thin

Through evil times and good; through foul weather and fair; steadfastly. The expression may be traced back to Chauncer's *The Reeves Tale* where, in the escapade of the clerk's horse, we read:

58

And whan the hors was loos, he gan to goon
Toward the fen ther wilde mares renne,
Forth with "wi-he!" thurgh thikke and eek thurgh thenne.

But Spenser, in *The Faerie Queene*, supplies the best clue to the probable original meaning in the lines:

His tyreling Jade he fiersely forth did push
Through thicke and thin, both over banck and bush.

That is, if the rider was pushing his steed over a straight course and over "banck and bush," he was also likely to be going through both thickets and thin woods; and this, it is thought, was the original expression, so old that it had been contracted even before the time of Chaucer.

a fidus Achates

A faithful Achates; a steadfast friend. The saying comes from Virgil's *Aeneid* where Achates is described as the friend who accompanied Aeneas on all his wanderings.

Jim Crow

You can read about Thomas D. Rice in the encyclopedia. He was a comedian of a hundred years ago, turning to Negro minstrelsy almost at the outset of his theatrical career and rapidly attaining especial eminence in this field. He introduced a number of popular songs of that period—one especially, about 1835, with the title "Jim Crow," that became extremely popular.  The first verse and chorus of this song, which was accompanied with an appropriate dance step, ran:

Come, listen all you gals and boys,
I'se just from Tucky hoe;
I'm goin' to sing a little song,
My name's Jim Crow.

Chorus   *Wheel about and turn about and do jis' so;*
Ebery time I wheel about I jump Jim Crow.

It cannot be stated positively that "Jim Crow," as an appellation of a Negro, arose from this song or that the appellation was of earlier date. No earlier record exists, yet across the ocean, in London, a book against slavery, with the title *The History of Jim Crow*, came out just a few years after the song was first heard. And, not long ago, The Negro Year Book for 1925 recorded the career of a Negro slave of the early nineteenth century, one Jim Crow, born in Richmond, who, eventually freed by his master, went to London and amassed a considerable fortune.

to have one's heart in one's shoes

This is no more than the current version of a very old saying that describes extreme fear. An ancient humorist, wishing to imply that his heart sank lower with fear than another's could, wrote, in the early fifteenth century, that his heart fell down into his toe. Successively through the centuries, and depending somewhat upon the costume of the period, the heart has metaphorically sunk to one's heel, to one's hose, to one's boots.

to play second fiddle (or *violin*)

In order to produce the harmony desired by the composer of an orchestral piece, someone must be willing to play the violin of lower tone, or second violin, while another plays the first violin and the leading part. Hence, metaphorically, we speak of anyone who occupies a subordinate position, especially of a person who steps from a leading position into the lesser status, as one who plays second fiddle. And we use the expression also to describe a suitor who, though still smiled upon by the girl of his heart, is not her favorite but is her second choice should the first fail her. Both the academic "violin" and the colloquial "fiddle" have been used in the expression for some two centuries or more, but the latter is more common in America.

amen corner

Who started it and just when is not on the record, but there is little doubt that the "amen corner" was familiar in some American churches, probably Methodist, early in colonial history. Some little church, very likely, began it by placing a bench for the deacons in a corner up toward the front of the congregation, perhaps so that they might the better see who was not paying attention to the sermon. These deacons or other saints, perhaps to keep awake themselves or perhaps merely to show how closely they were following the preacher's discourse, began to express approval audibly, instead of just nodding the head, whenever he said something particularly fitting. This was done by saying "amen," perhaps quietly or perhaps with great enthusiasm and unction when aroused by the dramatic fervor of some portion of the sermon. The original experiment was undoubtedly a success because the practice spread to other churches. This special seat was originally called the "deacons' bench"—a term later applied to a settee in front of a fireplace—but, though not in print before 1868, the disrespectful and popular name given to it was the "amen corner."

Many years later, toward the end of the nineteenth century, the newspapers of New York City began to call a room of the Fifth Avenue Hotel, reserved especially for the group of politicians currently in power, the "amen corner," possibly because the last word in regard to city politics was said there.

Of independent formation, a street corner in London, no longer in existence, was anciently known as the Amen Corner. It was so called because, on Corpus Christi Day, the monks proceeding to St. Paul's Cathedral, singing the *Pater Noster* (thus giving the name "Paternoster Row" to the street they traversed), reached the turn of the road as they sang the *Amen*.

once in a blue moon

It means extremely infrequently, so rarely as to be almost tantamount to never. From literary evidence the unusual tinge to the face of the moon which led someone to call it a "blue moon" was not observed until after the middle of the last century; nevertheless it is highly probable that this phenomenon had been observed by mariners some centuries earlier, but, like many other notions and expressions long familiar to seafaring men, it did not come to the notice of writers for many, many years. But, with another thought in mind, as long ago as 1528 a rimester published these lines:

61

Yf they saye the mone is belewe,
We must beleve that it is true.

Then the next year "green cheese" entered the picture in the lines of another writer: "They woulde make men beleue . . . that ye Moone is made of grene cheese."

Apparently, then, there were two schools of thought back in the early sixteenth century—one maintaining that "ye Moone" was made of "grene" cheese, and the other stoutly affirming that it was "belewe." Actually these ancient humorists were just punsters with a taste for metaphor; for by "green cheese," it was not the color but the freshness that was referred to—the moon, when full and just rising, resembling both in color and shape a newly pressed cheese. By "blue cheese" the ancient reference was to a cheese that had become blue with mold, metaphorically transferred, probably, to the comparatively rare appearance of the moon on unusually clear nights when the entire surface of the moon is visible although no more than a thin edge is illuminated. Thus, our phrase, "once in a blue moon" may actually date back to the sixteenth-century saying that "the mone is belewe."

none of one's funeral

The explanation of this American saying appears in the first printed account of its use. This was in the Oregon *Weekly Times* in 1854: "A boy said to an outsider who was making a great ado during  some impressive mortuary ceremonies, 'What are you crying about? It's none of your funeral.'" The boy meant, of course, that the funeral was of no concern to the bystander. I have no doubt, however, that the boy quoted by the Oregon paper was merely using an expression that was already long current, at least in the West. It traveled widely and may have been taken east by returning forty-niners or others, for within the next two decades it appeared in many eastern sections of the country and was heard even on the floor of Congress.

to pull wires (or *strings*)

A wirepuller these days is one who uses political influence or the like to gain some end or to win an advantage. We in the United States have known such people for the past hundred years. But the original wirepuller was the artist in a marionette show who manipulated the strings or wires that moved the limbs of the puppets.

to cast sheep's eyes at

"To kesten kang eien upon yunge wummen," was the Old English way of expressing the same thought. In modern words, that would read, "to cast wanton eyes upon young women," to gaze upon them amorously. John Skelton, who was decidedly a humorous versifier of the early sixteen century, softened those amorous looks of the young swains of his day by endowing upon them the soft, tender eyes of the sheep, for to him is credited the first use of "casting sheep's eyes" at the fair women of his day. His namesake and fellow humorist of our day, "Red" Skelton, might say, "Oh yeah! Sheep's eyes in wolves' clothing!"

swan song

In ancient times, back when it was thought that a crocodile wept after eating a man, it was also the belief that a swan, unable all its life to sing like other birds, would burst forth into glorious song when it felt the approach of death. According to Plato, Socrates explained the song as one of gladness because the swan, sacred to Apollo, was shortly to be able to join the god it served. As Apollo was the god of poetry and song, it was also the belief that the souls of a poet passed after death into the body of a swan. These ancient beliefs may .be traced through all European literature; in England, we find them in Chaucer, Shakespeare, Byron, and many other writers. From this picturesque source we owe the allusion to the last work of any poet, writer, or orator as his "swan song," supposedly the culmination of all his artistry, his finest work.

to go off half-cocked

This is what we say in America; the British equivalent is "to go off half-cock" or "at half-cock." Either way the meaning is to speak or do something hastily, without adequate preparation, prematurely. The original reference, back in the middle of the eighteenth century, was to the musket which, if the hammer was cocked halfway, was

 supposed to be locked, safe against accidental discharge. But sometimes the mechanism was faulty, the hammer would be released, and the gun would be prematurely discharged, with the musketeer wholly unprepared. The thought has been expressed that the allusion is to what happens when a hunter, excited upon seeing his quarry, attempts to shoot his gun without releasing the trigger from the safety position while it is still half-cocked; hence, that he was unprepared. But such reasoning seems faulty, for, as nothing would happen, the gun could not be said to "go off."

to come out flat-footed

There are no ans, ifs, nor buts in the statement of one who "comes out flat-footed"; you know exactly what he means and where he stands. We picture him as planted firmly on both feet, with an air of defiance, daring one to try to shake him from his opinion. The expression originated in the United States; the earliest record of its use yet found is 1846, though "flat-footed" alone, in the sense of determined, positive, is found some twenty years earlier.

not a Chinaman's chance

Having no chance at all; afforded no opportunity whatever. In the early days of the California gold rush something over forty thousand Chinese came into the United States, most of them staying in California. They were not popular in the gold camps, for they were willing to work for almost nothing and, unable to speak the language, were despised by the Americans. Human life was held none too highly in the lawless camps, and a Chinese, friendless and alone, ignorant of American ways, was fair sport for anyone. He had no rights that were respected; even self-defense was not accepted, in a miner's court, against any injury he might commit against another. His chance of survival against any charge was negligible.

proud as (or pleased as) Punch

"Punch" is the chief character, the hump-backed clown, in the comic puppet show, Punch and Judy. The dialog differs, probably, with every showman, but invariably "Punch" is a pompous vainglorious character who in the end lords it magnificently over his shrewish wife, "Judy," and is conspicuously pleased or proud over his ultimate victory, thus giving rise to our present expression.

Probably there are now few children in America or in England who have ever seen a "Punch and Judy Show," but before the days of the "movies" these puppet shows were very popular, exhibited at every old-time county fair. The show originated in Naples about 1600, and is attributed to a comedian, Silvio Fiorillo. In the Italian play, the name of the chief character was Pulcinello; when the show came to England, that name became Punchinello, later contracted to Punch. The British humorous weekly, *Punch*, founded in 1841, owes its name to this old comic show and still carries a figure of the old clown on its masthead.

upside down

Strangely enough, we have had this expression only since the time of Queen Elizabeth. Before that, when one wanted to say that a thing was overturned or in a state of disorder, he said it was "upsedown," or, with the same meaning, "topsy-turvy." From a variety of evidence, the early form of *upsedown* was *up so down*, but nothing has yet been found that would explain this Old English usage, nor, indeed, explain the source of "topsy-turvy."

to keep the ball rolling

The host or hostess, if properly conforming with the precepts of Emily Post, "keeps the ball rolling" at a dinner-party or other occasion by maintaining conversation or relating some anecdote or by providing other entertainment that will keep the interest of the guests from flagging. The saying is of British origin, dating back to the eighteenth century, and alludes either to the game of Rugby or to the game of bandy, probably the latter. Bandy, which is called hockey in America, dates back at least to the sixteenth century, but the puck is a small ball, even when the game is played on the ice. Needless to say, either in this game or in Rugby, if the ball is not in motion interest in the game has certainly flagged.

greasy luck

To a Nantucketer, this is just a way of saying "good luck!" It is a hang-over from the days of whaling, and meant that the well-wisher hoped that the whaleman would quickly fill his ship with oil.

to knuckle under (or down)

Nowadays we usually think of the knuckles as the joints of the fingers, but there was a time when the knuckle meant the knee or the elbow, especially the rounded part of the bone when the joint is bent. This sense survives chiefly in allusion to a joint of meat and in certain phrases. Thus, "to knuckle under," meaning to submit to—

or acknowledge oneself defeated by —another, carries back to the time when one knelt before one's conqueror in token of submission, put the knuckles of one's knees to the ground. Some writers use "to knuckle down," with the same implication.

"To knuckle down to" carries a different significance. It arises from the early inclusion of the bones of the spinal column as "knuckles" also. Hence, one knuckles down to work when he puts his back into it, when he applies himself diligently to it.

Of course, as any small boy knows, one "knuckles down" in the game of marbles; he gets the knuckles of his fingers on the ground, if an adversary insists, so that when he is ready to shoot, his marble will be directly above the spot where it had come to rest, not "fudged" a few inches closer to an opposing marble.

to play ducks and drakes

To squander foolishly or carelessly. The allusion is to the ancient pastime of skipping stones over the water, in some places called "playing ducks and drakes" because the stones, skimming over the surface, are supposed to resemble water fowl rising from a pond. Many stones, thrown even by an expert, fail to skip, and all eventually lose momentum and are lost beneath the water. So, a person who takes his patrimony and spends it carelessly, getting only a brief enjoyment from it, has been said to play ducks and drakes with his money. The figurative allusion dates from the beginning of the seventeenth century; the game was described, in 1585, by John Higgins in *The Nomenclator, or Remembrancer of Adrianus Junius:* "A kind of sport or play with an oister shell or stone throwne into the water, and making circles yer it sinke. . . . It is called a ducke and a drake, and a halfe-penie cake."

to see which way the cat jumps

We use this in a figurative sense as meaning to notice how events are shaping (so as to be able to act accordingly). It is the general assumption that the saying came from the game of tipcat, which boys have been playing since the sixteenth century at least. In this game the "cat" is a short stick of wood, about an inch and a half or so in diameter and five or six inches long, each end tapered from the center like the frustum of a cone. In playing the game the "cat" is struck on one of its tapered ends with sufficient force to cause it to spring into the air and is then knocked away by the player. To strike the "cat" while in the air the player must observe closely the direction of its spring.

But figurative expressions do not often arise from boys' games; they are more likely to achieve permanence from the sports of men. For this reason it seems to me that the source of the expression is more likely to have been the same ancient sport which produced the expressions, "room to swing a cat," and "to let the old cat die." That is, the "cat" in this instance was probably tied within a leather sack which in turn, hung from a tree, was used as a target in archery. The sportsman had literally to watch how the cat jumped in order to be able to hit the target.

to pour oil on troubled waters

It was known to both Pliny and Plutarch, in the first century A.D., that oil poured upon a stormy sea would quiet the waves. Five centuries later, according to the Venerable Bede, Bishop Aidan, an

Irish monk of Iona, also knew this "miracle," for after foretelling that a storm would arise, he gave the seamen of a certain vessel some holy oil and advised them to pour it upon the water to calm the sea and permit the vessel to ride through the storm. But, perhaps because oil was not plentiful, this knowledge seems either to have been lost or to have remained a scientific fact, for we do not find it again referred to until Benjamin Franklin, in 1774, refers to Pliny's statement in some correspondence. But when whale fishing became a great industry, beginning toward the end of the eighteenth century, and oil in large quantities was available, especially on whaling vessels, it is likely that the scientific phenomenon was often made use of. By the middle of the nineteenth century, at least, the fact was so well known that the expression began to be used metaphorically. Oil poured on troubled waters, as we use it today, means something offered for easing a troubled condition.

blood, toil, tears, and sweat

Winston Churchill had just been appointed prime minister. The war against Germany had been going badly; an attempt to overcome the German invasion of Norway had met with severe losses, and British morale was at low ebb in the spring of 1940. The populace and Parliament hoped for miracles, but Churchill wanted them to know that grim reality faced them and that they must throw off their lethargy. "I have nothing to offer," he told the House of Commons on May 13, "but blood, toil, tears, and sweat."

But, as a writer in *Notes & Queries* (1944) points out, it is likely that Churchill drew, consciously or unconsciously, from the following passage in John Donne's *An Anatomie of the World* (1611):

> *Shee, shee is dead; shee's dead; when thou knowst this,*
> *Thou knowst how drie a Cinder this world is,*
> *And learn'st thus much by our Anatomy,*

That 'tis in vaine to dew, or mollifie
It with thy teares, or sweat, or blood: nothing
Is worth our travaile, griefe, or perishing,
But those rich joyes, which did possesse her heart,
Of which she's now partner, and a part.

Or, perchance, from these satirical lines from Byron's "The Age of Bronze":

Safe in their barns, these Sabine tillers sent
Their brethren out to battle—Why? For rent!
Year after year they voted cent. by cent.,
Blood, sweat, and tear-wrung millions—why? for rent!
They roared, they dined, they drank, they swore they
*   meant*
To die for England—why then live?—for rent!

stripped to the buff

Buff, as we use it most frequently today, is a color, a light yellow. But it is also the name given to a soft, undyed and unglazed leather, especially a leather made from a buffalo hide, for it was from this leather that the color got its name. Someone, about three hundred years ago, facetiously referred to his own bare skin as his "buff," perhaps because it was tanned by the sun and had the characteristic fuzzy surface of buffalo leather. The name stuck, but is now rarely used except in the phrase above, which, of course, means divested of one's clothing.

to sleep like a top

To sleep so soundly as to be utterly quiescent. Efforts have been made to derive the "top" in this saying from the French *taupe*, mole, and thus imply that one sleeps as quietly as a mole; but this solution does not hold, for the French idiom is not *dormir comme une taupe*, but *dormir comme un sabot*, in which *sabot* means a top. The saying has been in English literature since the late seventeenth century, and from its first appearance the evidence is that the analogy refers to the state of apparent immobility of a rapidly spinning top.

69

hue and cry

Nowadays this just means a great to-do over some matter, especially one accompanied by clamor. But originally, and at least until the early part of the nineteenth century, it was the outcry raised by one who had been robbed, or by the constable or other officer of the law, calling upon all honest men to join in the chase and capture of the thief. One who failed to join the chase was liable to punishment. The expression is very old, dating back at least to the time of Edward I, or the late thirteenth century. In Norman-English spelling it was *hu e cri*, and it seems probable that the ancient meaning of "hue," in this saying, was a whistling or the sound of a horn, or a yell or hoot of some recognized nature, which was followed by a cry such as, "Stop thief! Stop thief!"

a wild-goose chase

Back in Shakespeare's time this was a game played on horseback, with two or more players. It began, apparently, with a race to see which player could take the lead; then, willy-nilly, the losers followed him at set intervals wherever he might choose to lead. The name came from the resemblance to wild geese in flight, each following the leader and at an even distance from one another. It is this game that is referred to in the dialog between Mercutio and Romeo, in Act II, scene 4, of *Romeo and Juliet.* Mercutio says, "Nay, if thy wits run the wild-goose chase, I have done; for thou hast more of the wild-goose in one of thy wits than, I am sure, I have in my whole five: was I with you there for the goose?" Romeo answers, "Thou wast never with me for anything when thou wast not there for the goose." And this style of repartee continues for another thirty lines or so.

But that sport went out of fashion within a few years and was remembered only as representing a wilful and erratic course taken by those who indulged in the chase. By the middle of the eighteenth century, even that much of the origin of the name was forgotten, and, in 1755, Dr. Samuel Johnson defined wild-goose chase as, "A pursuit of something as unlikely to be caught as a wild goose." This has come to be the accepted meaning—a vain pursuit of something, which, even if attained, would be worthless.

to have an ax to grind

To flatter a person or to be obsequious when seeking a favor from him. It is from a story entitled, "Who'll turn the grindstone?" first published in the Wilkesbarre *Gleaner* in 1811, often credited to Benjamin Franklin, but actually written by Charles Miner. It purports to relate an incident in the boyhood of the author: One morning a man with an ax over his shoulder greeted the boy most pleasantly and asked if his father had a grindstone. When the boy said, "Yes," the man complimented him upon his good looks and intelligence and asked if he might borrow the use of the stone. The boy, flattered by the attention, was sure that he could. The man then remarked that the boy appeared to be unusually strong for his age. Of course, the  lad fell for all this flattery, and before he knew it he had been inveigled into turning the stone until the very dull ax was as sharp as a razor. Just then the school bell was heard to ring; the man's manner changed abruptly, and without a word of thanks or a coin, he berated the boy for being a sluggard and ordered him to be off instantly so as not to be late for school. The author closed his tale with the comment, "When I see a merchant over-polite to his customers, begging them to taste a little brandy and throwing half his goods on the counter—thinks I, that man has an ax to grind." The story was reprinted later in a collection, *Essays from the Desk of Poor Robert the Scribe*, confused by many persons with *Poor Richard's Almanac* and for that reason associated with Franklin.

hand over fist (or *hand*)

At first, this was a nautical expression with a very literal meaning —advancing the hands alternately, as in climbing a rope, hoisting a sail, or the like. Then, still nautical, it acquired a figurative sense— advancing continuously, as if by pulling something toward one by a rope. Thus, in overtaking another vessel rapidly, one spoke of coming up with it "hand over hand." In America, early in the nineteenth century, this second meaning acquired a further extension—hauling in rapidly, as if by reeling in a fish; and, Americans being flippant, the second "hand" became "fist," so that now we say of a friend that he is making money "hand over fist" when his fortunes are in the ascendency.

to get (set, or *put*) one's back up

Cats have been doing this, when angry, as long as there has been a feline family; but, from the written evidence, it has been only some two centuries that human beings have figuratively been arching their backs when aroused into anger.

to keep the wolf from the door

Because the wolf, from remote antiquity, has been noted for its ravenous appetite, seemingly never able to get enough to eat, it has

always stood as a symbol for hunger, for want and necessity, in English as well as in other languages. The figurative intent was so well understood as far back as 1457 that John Hardyng saw no cause to explain his meaning when, in his *Chronicle*, he wrote, "Endowe hym now, with noble sapience By whiche he maye the wolf werre (ward off) frome the gate."

room to swing a cat

Space in which to move around freely. This is generally used in the negative, "no room to swing a cat," meaning cramped quarters. It was a common saying, according to the records, as long ago as the middle of the seventeenth century, and the origin is not certain. The popular notion is that "cat," in the phrase, was originally a contraction of "cat-o-nine-tails," but this could not be so, for this instrument of punishment was not in use until about a hundred years after the phrase was first recorded.

Of course, the original phrase may have been literal—room in which to hold a cat by the tail and swing it around one's head—but I find it difficult to think of a reason for indulging oneself in this form of exercise. I think instead that it originated in the ancient archery sport to which Shakespeare refers in *Much Ado about Nothing*, where Benedick says, "Hang me in a bottle like a cat, and shoot at me," the "bottle" here being a leather sack in which a live cat was placed to make a swinging target when the sack was hung from a tree. Thus, I think, "room to swing a cat" meant space enough to use for such archery practice.

to fish in troubled waters

"Troubled waters" is itself an idiomatic phrase, used since the sixteenth century to mean mental perturbation or disquiet. And at about the same period our ancestors fished in the same kind of water; that is, they took advantage of another's mental perturbation to gain something desirable for themselves. The earliest instance of use thus far located is in Richard Grafton's *Chronicle of England*, "Their perswasions whiche alwayes desyre your unquietnesse, whereby they may the better fishe in the water when it is troubled." The allusion is to the fact that, as fishermen know, fish bite best when the water is rough.

to paint the town red

Nowadays this has no greater significance than to go on a spree, usually in company with others of like mind. As far as the records go, the term is less than a hundred years old, but as is so often the case, usage probably antedates the printed record by several generations. I think it likely that the first town that was painted red was one actually fired by American Indians on the warpath, one outlined by the pigment of red flame. Figurative paint was probably applied, in later years, by young cowboys from outlying ranches who, bent on riotous revelry, rode into the main streets of a town whooping at the top of their lungs and firing their guns into the air as if actually a band of Comanches.

But Professor T. F. Crane, of Cornell, formerly president of the American Folklore Society, offered the opinion some twenty years ago that the peoples of the earth since the dawn of time have used "red" as a symbol of violence; hence that the expression is a natural figure of speech, signifying "to do violence in town."

too big for one's breeches

A youngster, or an adult for that matter, who struts around trying to impress others with his importance, is said to be "too big for his breeches." Just as with the independent hog on his chunk of ice, this expression gives us another instance of an absurdly recent first appearance in print of an obviously old expression. The first  appearance is credited to H. G. Wells, and as recently as 1905. But the expression was in use in America before 1850, at least in the Ohio farming region in which my mother was raised, and is undoubtedly much earlier, probably going back to the eighteenth or even the seventeenth century. "Too big for one's boots," very probably a euphemism of the vulgar "breeches," was respectable enough to appear in print by 1879. Today we have moved to the other extreme: he of the swelled buttocks of 1850, of the swelled foot of 1880, is now called a swellhead, or is said to have a head too big for his hat.

a horse of another color

Something of a different nature from that under consideration. Just how long it has been that this phrase has had such a meaning is anyone's guess. It was known by Shakespeare, though he used it as "a horse of the same color" when describing the plot hatched up by Sir Andrew Aguecheek and Sir Toby Belch, in *Twelfth Night*, to get Malvolio in Dutch with his mistress, Olivia. Shakespeare didn't explain the meaning, so it must have been well known to his audiences, but there is no earlier record of its use.

The probabilities are that the expression was a natural statement, possibly made by some favorite princess at a tournament or a race. She may have thought that her favored knight or horse was losing, when, seeing otherwise by better view, she exclaimed, "Oh, but that is a horse of another color!" Delighted courtiers would have repeated the saying on all occasions. Or, perhaps, the saying may have been derived from the archeological mystery, the celebrated White Horse of Berkshire. This is a crudely delineated figure, on an enormous scale, of a galloping horse, excavated in the chalk of a hill in western Berkshire. It is 374 feet long, covering about two acres of ground. Legend attributes the figure to a commemoration of the victory of King Ethelred and his brother Alfred (later, Alfred the Great) over the Danes in 871, but the figure is unmistakably of much greater antiquity. It would have become undistinguishable from the surrounding terrain many centuries ago, however, were it not for the custom of the people of the neighborhood to make it "a horse of another color" periodically by cleaning out the grass and debris from the trenches by which the figure is outlined.

to go against the grain

In wood, the fibers are arranged in parallel lines which run lengthwise along the line of growth of the original tree, and this we call the grain of the wood. The wood may be easily split, sawed, or planed along those parallel lines, or, as we say, "with the grain." We use "against the grain" to describe a cut that runs transversely across those lines, whether at right angles or obliquely. It is the long oblique cut that tends to produce slivers; one's fingers or a plane run smoothly in one direction over such a cut, but snags upon splinters if run in the other direction. This latter direction is more explicitly described as "against the grain," and from it we derive our figurative saying, "to go against the grain," by which we mean to be opposite to one's inclination or preference, or, especially, to be repugnant to one's feelings.

to catch a Tartar

To have a bull by the tail; to stir up a hornet's nest, or, in plain English, to take something that one expects to be advantageous and find it to be an unpleasant attachment that one cannot be rid of— like marrying a woman for her money and finding her to be not only miserly, but also a nagging scold. The saying seems not to be older than about the middle of the seventeenth century; Dryden was the first to record it. But for its source we can do no better than, with tongue in cheek, to repeat the story given by Francis Grose in his *Classical Dictionary of the Vulgar Tongue*, published in 1785. He says, "This saying originated from a story of an Irish soldier in the Imperial service, who, in a battle against the Turks, called out to his comrade that he had caught a Tartar. 'Bring him along, then,' said he. 'He won't come,' answered Paddy. 'Then come along yourself,' replied his comrade. 'Arrah,' cried he, 'but he won't let me.' "

to beat about the bush

So far as I know, batfowling was never an American sport. Perhaps game has always been too plentiful. But we have to go way back to this ancient practice in the fifteenth century for the origin of this expression. Batfowling was nothing more than the hunting of birds at night, the hunter armed with a light with which to  dazzle the sleepy birds, and a bat with which to kill them. (The next day they formed his repast, ba-ked in a pye!) Or, in some instances, the hunter would use a net for trapping the birds, hiring a boy or someone else, armed with a bat, to stir up the birds asleep in a bush. The birds, attracted by the light, would fly toward it and become entangled in the net. When there were more birds in a flock than could roost on a single bush, the batfowlers usually beat the bushes adjacent to the one on which the main flock was asleep, thus literally beating about the bush to reach their main objective. So when today Junior says, "Daddy, are you going to use the car tonight?" we recognize that, like the batfowlers of old, he is "beating about the bush," approaching indirectly the subject he has in mind.

to lick into shape

This we do when we take something formless or not fully in readiness to meet the critical eyes of the world and put it into form or make it ready. The saying comes from the ancient belief that, to quote from the unknown translator (about 1400) of de Guilleville's *The pylgremage of the sowle*, "Beres (bears) ben brought forthe al fowle and transformyd (are born all foul and shapeless) and after that by lyckynge of the fader and moder (by licking of the father and mother) they ben brought in to theyr kyndely shap."

The belief, probably arising from the fact that, at birth, the cubs are hairless and very small, as well as the fact that the mother usually keeps them concealed in her remote den for four or five weeks, is of great antiquity. The saying was used by the Roman writer, Donatus, in discussing the great care taken by Virgil when writing his *Georgics*. He said: "Cum Georgica scriberet, traditur cotidie meditatos mane plurimos versus dictare solitus ac per totum diem retractando ad paucissimos redigere, non absurde carmen se more ursae parere dicens et lambendo demun effingere."

to rule the roost

This is the American expression, and, according to the record, we and our grandsires before us and their sires or grandsires also used it when expressing mastership or authority. The original analogy was, undoubtedly, the rooster, who is cock of the walk in the hen-yard. It is very likely, however, that the American saying was

strongly influenced by the far older British saying which conveys the same meaning, "to rule the roast." And this usage goes back at least to the fifteenth century—"What so euer ye brage or boste, My mayster yet shall reule the roste." The origin of the British expression has caused a great deal of speculation. The usual assumption is that it alluded to the lord of the manor who presided over the roast of meat at the table; but I find myself in agreement with the minority in the belief that the actual ancient word was that which we pronounce "roost" today. Formerly, along with door, floor, brooch, other words now spelled with a double "o" were also pronounced with a long "o," and there is excellent reason to suppose that "roost" was one of them. This, together with the fact that modern "roast" was formerly sometimes spelled "roost," makes it fairly convincing to me that the ancient intent was in full accord with the modern American expression, or that the old-time master who exercised full authority, along with the cock of the barnyard, actually "ruled the roost."

a hair of the dog that bit you

Customarily, this applies to a drink taken as a pick-me-up on the morning after a spree, to a drink taken for relief from an excess of drinks. Heywood, in 1546, thus recorded it in his *Dialogue conteynyng prouerbes and epigrammes:* "I pray the leat me and my felow haue A heare of the dog that bote vs last night—And bitten  were we both to the braine aright." The curious name for the practice comes from a widely accepted medical doctrine that goes back at least to the sixteenth century and was probably the common folk belief many centuries before that. That is, it was generally and seriously believed that if one were bitten by a dog suffering from rabies (by a "mad dog"), one's chance of recovery was greatly improved if a hair from that dog could be secured and bound upon the wound. It may be pertinent to remark that, though this treatment was still recommended up to the middle of the eighteenth century, its efficacy is now doubted; possibly the same could be said of the morning pick-me-up.

gone to Jericho

According to the Bible (II Samuel x), Hanun, to whom David had sent his servants as a mark of respect for Hanun's father, who had just died, was persuaded that they were actually spies; he had them seized, half their beards shaved off, and then sent them back to their master in derision. The servants, ashamed of their disgraced condition, were unwilling to return to Jerusalem and sent word of their plight to David. He sent word back, "Tarry at Jericho until your beards be grown."

78

But it was a much later king who inspired our present expression. Henry VIII, it is said, had a place of retirement on a small stream called "Jordan," near Chelmsford, which he called "Jericho." Like the servants of David, he may first have gone there to be in seclusion while his beard grew, but his later visits at least, were supposedly in company with a paramour of the moment. At any rate, his courtiers and ministers recognized that, officially, no one knew where the king might be whenever his servants announced that he had "gone to Jericho." It is for that reason that the expression has come to mean any indefinite or nameless place.

to give a wide berth to

The word "berth" came into the language early in the seventeenth century from sources unknown. It was a nautical term employed to mean roomway for a ship in which to operate. The early phrase was "to give a good (or, a clear) berth to," which meant, literally, to avoid, or to keep well away from, and we give it the same meaning today, though rarely with reference to a ship.

to put the screws on

Among the instruments of torture used, especially in Scotland, in the late seventeenth century was the screw or thumbscrew. It was a clamp or vise applied to one or both thumbs of the victim which could be tightened under the slow and inexorable pressure of a screw. The device was used for extorting confession from an accused, or for exacting money from a victim. Another name for the device was the thumbikins, and an earlier machine, probably intended for compressing the fingers, was known as the pilliwinks.

One who has suffered the accident of having his (or, more likely, her) fingers caught in an electrically operated clothes wringer can faintly imagine the continued and excruciating agony of relentlessly applied compression of the thumbs. To one who had once suffered the agony, no more than a threat to "put the screws on" was probably necessary to compel acquiescence. Memory of the torture survives only in the phrase which we use to indicate moral, rather than physical pressure.

like a Trojan

According to legend, the people of Troy, especially those who accompanied Paris in his abduction of Helen, were endowed with prodigious strength, endurance, energy, and capacity. English acceptance of the legend dates back to the Benedictine chronicler of the fourteenth century, Ranulf Higden; but it was not until the nineteenth century that English and American writers began to compare the powers of their fictional heroes—for lying, for working, for drinking, and even for swearing—with these Trojan heroes.

an itching foot

Though it is only within the past fifty years, apparently, that we in America have used this to mean a craving to travel, we have  ancient precedent for such a figurative expression. Away back in the thirteenth century a writer used "an itching ear" to mean a craving to hear gossip, and, later, one with "an itching tongue" was one with an inordinate desire to repeat gossip. Even today one with "an itching palm" craves money. There seems no end to the itching that one may have.

in apple-pie order

That which is said to be "in apple-pie order" has a perfection of orderliness, but no one has been able to figure out the reason for this with certainty. The expression is of British origin, and has been used since early in the nineteenth century at least. Some have tried to figure that it may have been derived from "cap-a-pie," which, in English usage, means "from head to foot," but there is no known instance of such an expression as "cap-a-pie order," and the expression itself seems meaningless. A very recent philologist, Bruce Chapman, asserts confidently: "The phrase comes from the French *nappes pliées*, meaning 'folded linen,'" but he does not cite any instance of the use of this French phrase in English literature, and, unable to find any instance myself, I cannot support his derivation, plausible though it may appear. If only some cookbook of, say, 1800 could be found, possibly we might learn that some unusually finicky cook had prescribed a most precise manner or arrangement in which an apple pie should properly be concocted, so precise as to earn the derision of all proficient cooks who thereupon made "apple-pie order" notorious.

full as a tick

Some suppose that the tick to which this simile alludes is the bed-tick, the old-fashioned flat, rectangular bag of cloth which was stuffed with feathers, straw, or the like to form a bed. It had to be full, of course, or one might find one's poor bones resting on the floor. But the tick that is really meant is the disgusting, bloodsucking insect that attacks the skin of man or other animal, burying its head into the flesh and becoming fat and bloated.

to grease (a person's) palm

When you enrich someone with money in the hope or expectation of having a favor from him in return, you "grease his palm." The present expression has been in vogue since the beginning of the eighteenth century, changed since the early sixteenth century only in the substitution of "palm" for "hand." Our present form, however, is a direct translation of a French phrase of the Middle Ages, "oindre la paume à quelqu'un." Littré, the French philologist, tells of an ancient story about an old woman whose two cows had been seized by the provost and who then received the advice that she would have saved herself from trouble had she first "greased his palm."

to bring down the house

To call forth such wild applause, as at a theater, that the very walls seem to tremble and be about to fall. Possibly this could be done actually, for, we are told, a regiment marching in cadence across a bridge could cause its destruction. I have not heard, however, that applause has ever been so continuous and tumultuous as that. Perhaps the expression was used by those who described the effect of a play by Will Shakespeare upon his audience, but, if so, no one thought to record it. Its first use in print did not come until more than a century after Shakespeare died.

to cut the coat according to the cloth

A tailor, making such a coat, would pay no attention to the pattern in the cloth nor to warp or woof; he would make it out of  whatever material there was at hand, taking advantage of every scrap, regardless of the appearance of the ultimate garment. It is likely that tailors—and mothers—have been thus adapting themselves to circumstances—which is the meaning of the phrase—since Jacob made Joseph a patchwork coat of many colors, for the saying has great age. It had become proverbial in England by the time Heywood compiled his *Dialogue conteynyng Prouerbes and Epigrammes* in 1546, but no one can tell how much earlier it had been in common English speech.

blind tiger

This name for a place where liquor is illegally sold is scarcely more than sixty years old, though the reason for the appellation can now only be surmised. I think it likely that the "blind tiger" began its career in the back room of a faro establishment, for this game was known more than a hundred years ago, in America, as "tiger." As the game itself was often conducted illegally, it would be perfectly in keeping that a second license for selling booze in a "blind tiger" would not be secured.

We have the game of faro to thank also for "to buck the tiger." In less picturesque words this means to play against the bank; hence, to gamble. This, too, was known a century ago. According to Walsh, *Appleton's Journal* traced "tiger" to a figure of a tiger appearing with one of the Chinese gods of chance; the figure, it is said, is used in China as a sign before the entrance to a gambling house.

to hold one's horses

Originally, this had nothing but its literal meaning—to keep one's team of horses from getting excited. In the United States somewhat more than a hundred years ago, however, the expression began to be applied to people, always as a mild adjuration. And because of an assumed rustic source, the suggestion that one control one's temper or patience is generally phrased, placatingly, "Now, just hold your hosses."

to run (something) into the ground

Bartlett, back in 1859, thought that this American phrase probably came from hunting, "to express the earthing of a fox or other game." But because the sense has always been to overdo (a matter), to carry (something) to extremes, Bartlett's explanation fails to satisfy. In my opinion, the phrase was probably of nautical origin. It may have been said of an eager youngster learning to sail, or even of an experienced helmsman who, upon reaching his home port after a long voyage, had so strong a desire to see his family as to overshoot the landing. Thus, in an excess of zeal, one might literally run (a vessel) into the ground.

ghost writer

Ghosts, as everyone knows, are invisible, unseen. So it is with the ghost writer; he is the unseen anonymous person who actually writes for hire or love the articles or the speeches that a prominent person gets the credit for having written. Until a decade or so ago such persons, from about 1850, were just called ghosts—somebody thought it a bit more dignified to add "writer." In fact, ghostwriting is an honorable profession these days. Recent presidents, engrossed upon important affairs of state, have had no time to prepare public speeches that are, say, primarily political in nature. Someone who is familiar with the views of the important person is called upon  to write the speech that will be used, but the public is led to believe that the important personage has himself written the speech. Ghostwriting has become such a profession these days that ghosts may be found who, for a price, will write a speech, an essay, or an article upon any given subject. Even an occasional book, ascribed to some "big shot," is actually the work of a ghost.

manna from heaven

A windfall; something providential. That is the current figurative use of the expression; but, as any biblical student knows, the real manna from heaven was that spoken of in the sixteenth chapter of Exodus, "a small round thing, as small as the hoar frost on the ground," which provided the needed food for the children of Israel on their journey out of Egypt.

in the dog house

Aside from the literal sense, this modern expression is used to mean that a person is undergoing punishment of some sort. It is usually used to denote the treatment, mental or physical, meted out to a man by his spouse for some misdemeanor. Probably the original allusion was to a "gay dog," a man who, in his wife's opinion, had been somewhat too gay and jovial, or perhaps had been roving too far from his own fireside. And, just as the punishment for a roving dog is to be confined to his kennel, so the two-legged gay dog deserved similar treatment.

a month of Sundays

This has become just a glib expression for a long time. But when coined, a hundred years ago—first as "a week of Sundays," then, in amplification, as "a month of Sundays"—it meant an interminable length of time, especially to a young person—and possibly, if the truth were known, to many an older person. In those days a well brought-up person was obliged to observe Sunday with the utmost decorum; not only no games, but no levity was permitted. To a child or young person of any spirit, the day seemed never ending. The utmost of dreariness, a veritable eternity to such a person would be seven or thirty Sundays in succession.

to play fast and loose

When something has been promised and the promise is accepted in good faith, but never fulfilled, he who made the promise has "played fast and loose" with the person to whom it was made; that is, he was not trustworthy. The expression was the name of a game known and played as far back as the first half of the sixteenth century. It was a cheating game played at village fairs by sharpers, usually gipsies. A belt or strap was doubled and coiled in such a manner that, when laid edgewise, it appeared to have a loop in its center. That was the trick; for the loop seemed to be so definitely a loop that it was not difficult to persuade a rustic that he could easily fasten the belt to the table by running a skewer through the loop. After bets were placed the sharper skilfully unrolled the belt, which had had no loop in it at all. The game must have been quite popular, for it was mentioned by many writers of the period. Shakespeare spoke of it in *King John*, in *Love's Labor's Lost*, and in *Antony and Cleopatra*. In more recent years the same trick has been known as "Prick the Loop," or "Prick the Garter."

hell for leather

In America we'd say, "in a hell of a hurry," with the same meaning; but this is a British expression, apparently originating in the British army in India. Possibly Kipling coined it, for he was the first to record it, though he may have been actually quoting army speech. His first usage is in *The Story of the Gadsbys*, in that portion of the story ("The Valley of the Shadow") where Mrs. Gadsby is just emerging from "the Valley." His second use of the expression is in Mulvaney's episode with "My Lord the  Elephant," in *Many Inventions*. Though the term must originally have referred to the terrific beating inflicted upon leather saddles by heavy troopers at full speed, even by Kipling's time it had acquired a figurative sense indicating great speed, on foot, by vehicle, or by horse.

to hold a candle to (someone)

This is usually in the negative—so-and-so can't, or isn't fit to, or isn't able to hold a candle to such and such—and we mean that the party of the first part fares poorly by comparison with the party of the second part. The development of the present-day simile came somewhat gradually from an ordinary custom of the sixteenth century and later. Because of poorly lighted streets it was customary for a servitor with a lighted candle to accompany his master when on foot. It was a menial service, one that required no training nor skill, nothing more than familiarity with the way. One who did not know the road was, literally, not fit to or not worthy to hold a candle to a superior. But by the eighteenth century, the sense of worthiness or of comparative ability had become the intent of the phrase, as illustrated by John Byrom's "Epigram on the Feuds between Handel and Bononcini," printed in a 1725 issue of the *London Journal*:

> *Some say, that Seignior Bononchini*
> *Compar'd to Handel's a mere Ninny;*
> *Others aver, to him, that Handel*
> *Is scarcely fit to hold a candle.*
> *Strange! that such high Disputes shou'd be*
> *'Twixt Tweedledum and Tweedledee.*

The positive expression, "to hold a candle to (someone)," was, literally, to act as an assistant to one by holding a light for him. In our present electric-lighted age we do not appreciate the inadequacy of candles for illumination until some emergency obliges us to return to them. On such occasion, if we try to play cards we find that candles not only interfere with our arms, but that the light falls in the eyes of the players rather than on the cards. Our ancestors, who had no better light than candles, had the same difficulty. Hence, when playing cards or dicing, they employed a servitor to hold the light where needed, paying him for both his services and the light. So when the game was going poorly or indifferently, one might find that one's winnings were too light to defray these expenses. This literal fact gave birth to the proverb, "the game is not worth the candle," which we use conveniently to mean that the returns from a given enterprise are not worth the effort expended upon it.

to cut didos

This is something that a Britisher doesn't do. He cuts a caper or otherwise cavorts around. There is nothing to show that George Washington cut any didos, though it is likely that others were doing so during the latter part of his life, for probably the expression was coined about that time. It was widely enough known to be used in *A Narrative of the Life & Travels of John Robert Shaw, the Well-Digger*, an autobiography published in 1807. Whoever coined the dido left us no certain clue of its origin; he may have alluded in some manner to the trick performed by the mythological queen, Dido, who founded Carthage. When she landed in Africa, according to the story, she bought from the trusting natives only the land that could be enclosed with a bull's hide. Having agreed upon the price, the crafty queen then proceeded to cut the bull's hide into a continuous cord slightly thicker than a hair, and thus encircled enough land upon which to build the walled city of Carthage. Some dido!

to pull the wool over one's eyes

A very roundabout way of saying to hoodwink, to delude. The expression is said to have originated in the United States, probably because the earliest use of the expression in print that has yet been found is American. But this was in a newspaper, so it must have been widely known at that time, 1839, because the meaning was not explained. The actual source was likely to have been much earlier, and perhaps in England. Quite probably, "wool" was jocularly used for hair, and perhaps for the hair that composed a wig. Hence, the expression may have originated in a practice, either sportive or malicious, of pulling the wig of some nabob over his eyes to blind him temporarily, perhaps for the purpose of snatching his purse, or perhaps just teasingly.

to be caught with one's pants down

When such a respectable family publication as *The Saturday Evening Post* gives its sanction to this homely American expression, notice of its origin may properly be taken. Despite the fact that the appearance of the phrase in the *Post* is its first in print (1946), so far as is known, in all likelihood its popular usage goes back a hundred years. Maybe longer. Maybe it was anciently "to be caught with one's breeches down"; but the expression was never considered to be decorous enough to appear in print, so we cannot be certain of its age.

The figurative meaning is, of course, to be taken completely by surprise; to be wholly unprepared. But the literal meaning, I think, takes us back to the days when white frontiersmen were exposed to peril if their muskets were not actually at hand. Even at the risk of death, the wants of nature must be met, and in such circumstances a lurking Indian would indeed catch one in a state of embarrassing unpreparedness.

cock of the walk

This is he who "rules the roost," who permits no doubt of his supremacy. The figurative use is so common, especially as applied to a young dandy strutting along the sidewalk, that we are not likely to wonder why a rooster would be upon a promenade nor how long its cockiness would last if it were. But, especially in England, "walk" has a particular application. It means a place set aside for the feeding and exercise of domestic animals; or, in this instance, a chicken yard. The literal cock of the walk, therefore, is the rooster in a given chicken yard. The figurative expression seems to have been in use little more than a century.

to keep one's fingers crossed

This we do, either actually or mentally, when wishing the success of something or hoping that nothing unpleasant will happen or anything will interfere with one's plans. The expression appears to be wholly American and, probably, of Negro origin. Probably it arose from the superstition that making the sign of the cross would avert evil; hence, that it would bring good luck.

In all likelihood the firm belief among American children that a lie doesn't count as a lie if one's fingers are crossed while it is being spoken, comes from the same superstition. That is, as every child knows, some dire punishment is likely to be meted out if one tells a lie; but, since evil may be averted if a cross be made of one's fingers, therefore, by specious reasoning, if one is not punished for the telling, no lie has been told.

brass hat

The modern extension of this slang appellation means any person in authority, especially one who has an overbearing manner. Originally it was British army slang; one of the earliest instances of its literary use was by Kipling, in *Many Inventions*, in 1893, in the story, "In the Rukh." Soldiers used it to designate a general, because the quantity of gold braid about that officer's dress cap made it shimmer in the sun as if the entire cap were of shiny brass. Kipling puts it into the speech of the head ranger of all India, a gigantic German in the British service, and the manner of use indicates that the appellation was already in wide use. The German, Muller, explaining his theory that best efficiency among subordinates is obtained by visiting them unexpectedly, says:  "If I only talk to my boys like a Dutch uncle, dey say, 'It was only dot damned old Muller,' and dey do better next dime. But if my fat-head clerk he write and say dot Muller der Inspecdor-General fail to onderstand and is much annoyed, first dot does no goot because I am not dere, and, second, der fool dot comes after me he may say to my best boys: 'Look here, you haf been wigged by my bredecessor.' I tell you der big brass-hat pizness does not make der trees grow."

to put a spoke in one's wheel

Whenever you are not in accord with another person's plans or projects, you "put a spoke in his wheel" by taking some action that will interfere with or impede his progress. The expression goes back to the sixteenth century and alluded to the use, by carters, of an extra spoke or bar which could be thrust between the spokes of a wheel so that that wheel would drag and serve as a brake in descending a hill.

to keep under one's hat

One would suppose that this warning would be as old as the first hat, but its actual history appears to have been no earlier than the closing years of the nineteenth century. What is kept under the hat, of course, is retained within the head; that is, it remains a secret.

up the spout

When we say that something is or has gone "up the spout," we mean, usually, that plans have gone awry, that affairs are hopeless. This is literal as well as figurative, for "spout" is slang for a pawnbroker's shop, to which we turn when things are desperate and we need cash. Mr. Pickwick, as readers of Dickens' works will know, discovered that meaning when he visited Fleet Prison to see his friend, Mr. Alfred Jingle, who, imprisoned for debt, had pawned his coat, boots, and other raiment for food; he had sent them, Jingle said, to "Spout—dear relation—uncle Tom."

The real spout was, in former days, the hoist or elevator within a pawnbroker's shop by which articles pawned were carried to an upper floor for storage. Such articles literally went "up the spout." The literal meaning is old enough to have been recorded in *A new and comprehensive vocabulary of the flash language* by James H. Vaux in 1812.

to rob Peter to pay Paul

Speculation has been rife for centuries over the origin of this common saying; every avenue has apparently been explored, but the original allusion is still a mystery. In English it dates back at least to the fourteenth century; the French have a similar saying at least as old, and there is, in Latin, a twelfth-century phrase, "Tanquam si quis crucifigeret Paulum ut redimeret Petrum, (As it were that one would crucify Paul in order to redeem Peter)." The verbs have varied from time to time, depending upon the desired application. Thus we find that one has borrowed from or unclothed Peter to pay or to clothe Paul, but "rob" is the oldest English usage, so recorded in Wyclif's *Select English Works*, written about 1380. The thought has always been, to take something (usually money) that is needed for one purpose and use it for another.

to drag a red herring over the track (or trail)

Red herring is nothing more than herring that has been cured by smoke, a process that changes the color of the flesh to a reddish hue. The herring is intended to be eaten after such curing, but dog trainers learned long ago that red herring had a peculiarly persistent odor and was very useful, if trailed over the ground, for training a dog to follow a scent. The author of *The Gentlemen's Recreation*, in 1686, advised that if a dog could not be trained by dragging a dead cat or dead fox, a red herring, having a more powerful odor,  could be employed, and it could not fail to serve the desired purpose.

But that which leaves so strong a scent can be used for bad purposes as well as good. A dog that gets a good whiff of red herring will lose any other scent that it has been following. Criminals who have been chased by bloodhounds have used that knowledge to advantage. So when our small son, trying to divert our attention from the pink stickiness on his cheek, shows us the daub of jam on the cat's back, we accuse him of dragging a red herring over the track, figuratively, by trying to turn our suspicions aside.

to get (or give one) the sack

Cotgrave, in his *Dictionaire of the French and English Tongues*, published in 1611, shows us that we are still using, by translation, an expression known to the French more than three centuries ago. The same saying in Dutch is used in the Netherlands and can be traced there back to the Middle Dutch. It meant, in all cases, to be dismissed (or to dismiss one) from employment.

Because the expression goes back to the Middle Ages, the theory has been advanced that the "sack" was one in which an itinerant worker carried his tools and, if his work were unsatisfactory, he would receive notification thereof by the return of his sack by his employer. That explanation would carry the implication that it was the custom for all workmen to leave their tools lying around unprotected, which is highly improbable. It would also imply that the craft guilds had sent forth an unprepared master workman.

Evidence is lacking, but I think it probable that the "sack" of the Middle Ages was always figurative, that it alluded to the ancient Roman punishment of putting a condemned person into a sack and drowning him in the Tiber. That form of punishment was common throughout Europe in the Middle Ages and persisted in Turkey until the nineteenth century. The figurative usage may have begun as a threat of fatal punishment, just as today we "fire" an employee when he is discharged, likening him to the bullet sent away, or fired, or discharged from a gun.

a gone coon

Legend has it that this expression, which is applied to a person or thing in a hopeless situation, originated in the Revolutionary War. An American spy, it is said, seeking information on the number of British forces that were to be attacked, dressed himself in raccoon furs and, by night, stealthily climbed a tree overlooking the British

camp. He hoped that the protective coloration of the fur would shield him from discovery. To his dismay, however, he had scarcely taken his position when a British soldier, on a nocturnal raccoon hunt, approached the tree and spotted what he supposed to be an unusually large specimen of this tasty animal. The Briton took careful aim and was just about to fire, when the American called out, "Don't shoot! I'll come down. I know I'm a gone coon." It so terrified the Briton to hear a raccoon talk, the legend goes, that he dropped his gun and ran away in panic.

But Captain Frederick Marryat, British author, who wrote a notably fair *Diary in America*, in 1839, had not heard this alleged earlier version. When he asked what the origin of the expression was, he was told that it was attributed to a certain Captain Martin Scott of Vermont, an army officer with a prodigious reputation as a sharpshooter. According to the story that was told:

His fame was so considerable that even the animals were aware of it. He went out one morning with his rifle, and spying a raccoon upon the upper branches of a high tree, brought his gun up to his shoulder; when the raccoon perceiving it, raised his paw for a parley. "I beg your pardon, mister," said the raccoon, very politely; "but may I ask if your name is Scott?"—"Yes," replied the captain— "Martin Scott?" continued the raccoon—"Yes," replied the captain —"Captain Martin Scott?" still continued the animal—"Yes," replied the captain, "Captain Martin Scott"—"Oh! then," says the animal, "I may just as well come down, for I'm a gone coon."

to be neither fish nor flesh

No evidence has been found, either in proof or denial, yet the fact that the earliest record of this phrase coincided almost exactly with the break between Henry VIII and the Pope, a break that could not have occurred unless preceded by a long period of disaffection, makes me suspect that the original significance of the expression was theological. One who abstained from neither fish nor flesh when days of fasting were prescribed were neither Roman Catholics nor Dissenters, neither one thing nor the other—just plain irreligious.

Merely to intensify a lack of distinction indicated by the phrase, someone appended, "nor good red herring." This is not a recent appendage, for it was recorded as long ago as 1546 by John Heywood, in his *Dialogue conteynyng Prouerbes and Epigrammes.* Probably because herring is not as popular in the United States as in England, we have substituted "fowl" for "red herring" and, unaware of early significance, when anything cannot be definitely classified or its nature fixed, we say that it is "neither fish, flesh, nor fowl."

to let the old cat die

Both in England and America when one permits a swing to come to rest one "lets the old cat die," yet no one knows positively why this saying is used. It seems to be so old that the original allusion is lost. In my opinion, however, it comes from the same source as the other common saying, "room to swing a cat." We may find it hard to realize now, but the time was not very remote when no one was at all concerned over the sufferings of dumb animals. Thus, as Shakespeare reports in *Much Ado about Nothing*, there was an ancient archery sport in which a cat was put into a sack (a leather bottle, according to Shakespeare) which, in turn, was suspended from a tree; the efforts of the cat to escape provided a swinging target. Probably it was no part of the sport to kill the cat, but it is more than likely that the poor beast was at least injured before the marksmen wearied of the sport. So, I think, rather than to open the bag and run the risk of getting severely scratched by the injured animal, both bag and cat were left swinging from the tree until "the old cat died."

straight from the horse's mouth

When we hear someone say he had such and such a piece of information "straight from the horse's mouth," we know that he means that he received it from the highest authority, from the one person whose testimony is beyond question. The expression comes from horse-racing and has to do with the age of the racers. Scientists  tell us that the most certain evidence of the age of a horse is by examination of its teeth, especially those of the lower jaw. The first of its permanent teeth, those in the center of the jaw, do not begin to appear until the animal is two and a half years old. A year later the second pair, those alongside the first, begin to come through, and when the animal is between its fourth and fifth year, the third pair appears. Thus, no matter what an owner may say of the horse's age, by an examination of its lower jaw an experienced person can get his information at first hand, straight from the horse's mouth.

to put one through a course of sprouts

To give one a thorough and disciplined course of training, or, by extension, to give one a grueling examination. What the source may have been cannot now be determined, though the Americanism is not much more than a hundred years old. The "sprouts" could have been children, and the "course of sprouts" could have indicated a severe course of instruction.

caviar to the general

Something that is an acquired taste; something too racy or too unfamiliar to be acceptable to the general public. The expression is from Shakespeare's *Hamlet*, Act II, scene 2, in which Hamlet, speaking of a play, says, ". . . it was never acted . . . the Play I remember pleased not the Million, 'twas Cauiarie to the Generall."

between cup and lip

Four centuries ago the saying was "between cup and mouth," at least it is so recorded in *Prouerbes or Adagies*, by Richard Taverner, published in 1539: "Manye thynges fall betweene ye cuppe and the mouth." The saying itself, however, is much older than that, for Taverner was merely translating into English the Latin collection of adages, *Chiliades adagiorum*, published by Erasmus in 1508. In one form or another, it is found in many languages.

Usually, in English, the saying occurs in the form of a proverb, "There's many a slip between cup and lip," signifying that there is nothing certain in life, that though one may have a cup at his mouth ready to swallow its contents, something may even then prevent the drinking. Erasmus wrote it, "Multa cadunt inter calicem supremaque labra," and is believed to have taken it from Greek. The origin is said to have come from the following legendary incident: Ancæus, a son of Neptune, was especially skilful in the cultivation of his vineyard, and drove his slaves exceedingly hard at this work. One year, a slave, worn out by toil, prophesied that the master would never taste the wine from that harvest; but when the fruit was gathered and the first wine was being pressed from it, Ancæus sent for the slave to show how poor a prophet he was. "There's many a slip between cup and lip," replied the slave as Ancæus raised the goblet to his mouth, and just at that moment another slave rushed up, crying that a wild boar was destroying the vineyard. Ancæus dropped the cup, ran to the fields to drive off the marauder, but the ferocious beast turned upon his pursuer and gored him to death before anyone could come to his aid.

the fat is in the fire

Back in the early sixteenth century when this saying first came into use the meaning of it was that the project, whatever it might have been, had become wholly ruined. The thought was, I suppose, that meat being broiled upon a spit is ruined by the resulting flame if a chunk of the fat drops into the fire. In this original sense the proverb is found in John Heywood's *A Dialogue conteynyng Prouerbes and Epigrammes*, published in 1562. But in the course of the next hundred years the meaning became altered to the present sense, and now we use the phrase to mean that an action of some sort has occurred which will lead to further action or from which great excitement, as of anger or indignation, will result.

Adam's off ox

The form commonly used is "not to know one from Adam's off ox," meaning to have not the slightest information about the person indicated. The saying in any form, however, is another of the numerous ones commonly heard but of which no printed record has been found. But in 1848 the author of a book on *Nantucketisms* recorded a saying then in use on that island, "Poor as God's off ox," which, he said, meant very poor. It is possible that on the mainland "Adam" was used as a euphemistic substitute.

The off ox, in a yoke of oxen, is the one on the right of the team. Because it is the farthest from the driver it cannot be so well seen and may therefore get the worst of the footing. It is for that reason that "off ox" has been used figuratively to designate a clumsy or awkward person.

faster than greased lightning

Denoting the acme of speed, than which nothing could be faster. This appears to be one of the instances of American hyperbole about

96

which British visitors to our shores, a century ago, were always complaining—or secretly envying. Our ancestors, in the days of Washington, Adams, and Jefferson, were not content to indicate great speed in such a trite manner as "faster than lightning"; instead, knowing that a cart with greased wheels will go faster than if the wheels were dry, they merely greased the lightning.

the jumping-off place

Originally, this imaginary place was the edge of the earth, the ultima Thule. From there, one could proceed no farther, other than to leap straight into hell. At least, such appears to have been the thought of our American pioneering forebears in the late eighteenth or early nineteenth century when this description was first applied. Perhaps it was an adaptation from some Indian belief, but, of course, by the early nineteenth century it was applied figuratively to any place, as a God-forsaken town, a desolate waste, any hopeless out-of-the-way spot, which one might deem to be literally next door to hell.

a bad egg; a good egg

A bag egg figuratively is like a bad egg literally—a person, or an egg, that externally appears to be wholesome and sound but, upon closer acquaintance, is found to be thoroughly rotten. By some strange chance this slang usage did not develop until about the middle of the past century, though even Shakespeare called a young person an "egg," as when, in *Macbeth*, the murderers, seeking Macduff, encounter and slay his young son, with the words, "What you egg! Young fry of treachery!"

A good egg, the converse of a bad egg, did not come into popular use until the early part of the present century, and it seems to have first been British university slang, probably first used at Oxford.

to heap coals of fire on one's head

To return good for evil, and thus make the recipient uncomfortable. The passage most often quoted is from the Old Testament,

Proverbs xxv, 21, 22: "If thine enemy be hungry, give him bread to eat; and if he be thirsty, give him water to drink: For thou shalt heap coals of fire upon his head, and the Lord shall reward thee." It is possible that the ancient Hebrew writer had some old metaphor in mind, but the usual explanation of the biblical passage is that the coals of fire upon one's head might melt him into kindliness. It reminds us that our word "remorse," which has a somewhat similar meaning, comes from the Latin *re* plus *morsus*, which has the literal meaning, a biting or gnawing again.

tit for tat

A blow for a blow; an ill deed for an ill deed. This phrase, which expresses a moderate retaliation, goes back only about four centuries in its present form, but before that it was "a tip for a tap," which goes back certainly a hundred years earlier and probably much more than that. A "tip," in Middle English, was a light blow; a "tap," then as now, was also a light blow. So the expression is far weaker than the old Hebrew adage, "an eye for an eye, and a tooth for a tooth." We use it chiefly in reference to speech: an insult for an insult; an unkind remark in return for an unkind remark. Probably the original expression was influenced by the French phrase, *tant pour tant*, literally, so much for so much.

chip of the old block

One who has the characteristics of a parent, usually a son with those of his father. The expression goes back to the early seventeenth  century and, if some of the early sermons of Bishop Robert Sanderson quote it correctly, the original form showed less disrespect to dad. It ran, "chip of the *same* block." The allusion is not difficult to follow: if one takes a block of stone and knocks a chip from it, the chip will carry all the characteristics of the larger portion.

eager beaver

Though its reputation has been questioned in recent years, the beaver has been long noted for persistent industry. This reputation gave us the simile, "to work like a beaver," some two hundred years ago. And, of course, industrious persons have long been likened to the beaver—"So-and-so is a veritable beaver." We English-speaking peoples are gluttons for rimes—as, witness, such compounds as pell-mell, hodge-podge, helter-skelter—so, within the past few years, some bright spirit did the best he could and began referring to some individual who was particularly, and somewhat offensively, avid in his industry as an "eager beaver."

neither hide nor hair

This sounds like such a typically western American expression that it is surprising to find that, though American, it is merely the reverse of one so old that it might have been known to Chaucer. The ancient saying was "in hide and hair," and the meaning was "wholly, entirely." The American phrase means "nothing whatsoever." Our first record of it occurs in one of the early works of Josiah G. Holland, *The Bay Path*, published in 1857: "I havn't seen hide nor hair of the piece ever since." Holland, it may be recalled, wrote under the pen name of Timothy Titcomb and, in 1870, founded *Scribner's Magazine*.

the Brain Trust

Despite the contention that this term was used as a title to a newspaper article in 1903, the name attained no popularity until 1933. In the previous summer, after his nomination for the presidency by the Democratic party, Franklin Delano Roosevelt surrounded himself with a group of advisers to aid in mapping out his election campaign. James M. Kieran of The New York *Times*, assigned to "cover" Mr. Roosevelt at the time, groped for a descriptive name for this group. He tried, it is said, "brains department" but found it too unwieldy, and then hit upon "brains trust." Other reporters ignored his coinage for a time, but after Roosevelt's election and inauguration, when the college professors who had assisted in the campaign were found to have become also a kitchen cabinet of advisers in the administration, Roosevelt himself began to speak of the group as his "brain trust," using the singular form that has since outmoded the original

99

designation. The term is no longer limited in application to a presidential group of advisers, but is applied, sometimes ironically, to any group that establishes the policies of an organization, whether intelligently or not.

to take a message to Garcia

The incident, in time of war, was not unusual; it was not particularly hazardous; but as dramatized by Elbert Hubbard in the March, 1900, issue of his famous magazine, *The Philistine*, it fired the imagination as keenly as if it had been an adventure of a knight of King Arthur's court. The United States, in defense of Cuba, had declared war against Spain. In April, 1898, the American chief of staff wished certain information from the leader of the Cuban forces, General Calixto Garcia, but was unable to establish any communication with him through the Spanish blockade. Accordingly, a young lieutenant, Andrew Rowan, was dispatched from Washington to make his way into Cuba and to find General Garcia, though no one in Washington knew just where the insurgent general might be. Rowan landed secretly on the coast of Cuba in a small boat, learned through local patriots where to look for Garcia, made his way to the general, got the information that he sought, and, with the same privacy, retraced his route to the coast and back to Washington.

The resourcefulness of the young lieutenant was, of course, praiseworthy in the extreme. It was that aspect of the incident which called forth the best of Hubbard's skill. He made it into an impressive sermon to young people, a lesson in success. "To take a message to Garcia" became a byword; it meant, "Show that you are resourceful and inventive, that you can accept responsibilities and can carry them through to success."

sold down the river

Though this is now used with wryful humor, as of a baseball player whose contract is sold to a team of lower rating or of an employee who is transferred to a more humble position than he formerly held, there was a time when it was literal and tragic—when it was used in connection with the domestic slave trade of the southern states. The importation of slaves into the United States was illegal after 1808 (though undoubtedly many thousands were smuggled into the country during the following years) and it then became profitable to build up a domestic trade. Hence, because cotton and sugar plantations of the South and Southwest were expanding by leaps and bounds, slaves from the worn-out tobacco belt of the upper South were readily purchased from their masters by dealers and were then transported down the Mississippi River to the markets at Natchez or New Orleans. Regrettably, many dealers regarded slaves to be as insensitive as cattle, so "sold down the river" meant the loss of all ties, the breaking up of families, and, usually, transportation into the most exhausting of labor under notoriously severe and brutal masters.

cut out of whole cloth

Wholly false; without foundation of truth. Back in the fifteenth century, "whole cloth" was used synonymously with "broad cloth," that is, cloth that ran the full width of the loom. The term dropped into disuse along in the eighteenth century, except in the figurative sense. In early use, the phrase retained much of the literal meaning; a thing was fabricated out of the full amount or extent of that which composed it. Thus we find, in the sixteenth century, "I shalbe contente . . to lende you the choyce of as many gentle wordes and loovelye termes as we . . . use to deliver ower thankes in. Choose whether you will have them given or yeeldid . . . kutt owte of the whole cloathe, or otherwise powrid owte." But by the nineteenth century it would appear that tailors or others who made garments were pulling the wool over the eyes of their customers, for, especially in the United States, the expression came to have just the opposite meaning. Instead of using whole material, as they advertised, they were really using patched or pieced goods, or, it might be, cloth which had been falsely stretched to appear to be of full width.

to get (or give one) the mitten

When a lady fair—an American one—rejects her suitor, she gives him the mitten; he gets it. This has been in American usage for at least a hundred years. *The Knickerbocker*, a New York periodical, back in July of 1847 wondered how the expression had originated, but it seems clear that the intent of the phrase was that the suitor, requesting the hand of his lady, received instead only it empty, fingerless and insensate covering. The saying apparently has no relationship at all to the medieval custom popularized by Sir Walter Scott. Then, when a knight exhibited his courage and skill in combat upon the jousting field, he might wear or display the glove of the lady of his choice. The meaning then, however, was the reverse of our present phrase.

to get down to brass tacks

Like many other of our common sayings, this appears to have alluded originally to some specific operation, something that would call for the removal of successive layers until the brass tacks which held the structure together were exposed to view. For, as we in America use the expression, it means to get down to the fundamentals, to get to the bottom of a thing, to get to the business at hand. But the original allusion is lost; literary uses have reference only to the figurative sense, and are too recent to afford any clue to the purpose of the first brass tacks. Because tacks, other than ornamental, are made of copper rather than brass, I surmise that "brass" was a figurative use. I think, therefore, that the phrase was originally nautical, that the reference was to the cleaning of the hull of a ship, to scraping the barnacles off so thoroughly as to expose the bolts which held its bottom together. Those bolts were, of course, of copper, but "brass tacks" would be a typical American substitution for "copper bolts." The recently advanced supposition that the saying originated from the brass upholstery tacks placed upon counters in drapers' shops for use in measuring lengths of cloth, seems fanciful to me, for that practice is not old and tacks of that description are of comparatively modern manufacture.

lame duck

In the United States we know a "lame duck" as a congressman who, having run for re-election in November and having been defeated at the polls, still has several months of his term to serve before he bows out more or less gracefully to his successful rival.* But why "lame" and why "duck"? We must go to London for the answer, to a street known as Exchange Alley  which, prior to 1773, was the place where London stockbrokers conducted their business. It was the old-time Wall Street of London, and just as we now refer to "the Street," meaning Wall Street, so "the Alley" then meant Exchange Alley. This alley was the scene of the wildest stock speculation of all time, the noted South Sea Bubble of 1720—stock of the South Sea Company which, in that year, opened at 128½ a share in January, rose to 330 in March, to 550 in May, to 890 in June, and finally touched 1000 a share in July when the directors of the company sold out and the bubble exploded.

Exchange Alley was the place where stockbrokers were first divided into two classes, bears and bulls. And it was also the place which saw, all too frequently, a third class—those who were cleaned out; those who could not meet their financial obligations. These latter came to be known as "lame ducks." Why? Because, to the amused spectator, they "waddled out of the Alley!"

the ghost walks

Salaries are to be paid! The expression is now heard in any line of business: "Friday's the day the ghost walks." "The ghost walks on the fifteenth of each month." The "ghost" is the paymaster, nowadays, or the cashier or whoever may be the distributor of salary or wage. But the expression arose in the theater some ninety years ago, in a profession in which salaries were uncertain and at a time when the whims of the manager might lead to slow pay. The most probable origin of the expression credits it to the actor who, in *Hamlet*,

---

* Although since the passage of the Lame Duck Amendment, the twentieth, in March 1932, lame ducks no longer exist.

had the part of the ghost of Hamlet's father. According to the story, when Hamlet spoke the lines, "I will watch tonight; Perchance t'will walk again," the actor playing the ghost, off stage, shouted back, "I'll be damned if he will unless our salaries are paid."

to knock into a cocked hat

The cocked hat, especially that of the eighteenth and early nineteenth centuries, was permanently out of shape, with the brim turned up along three sides, giving the hat the outline of a triangle. The style was generally affected by officers of both the American and British armies during the Revolutionary War. Undoubtedly the hat was ridiculed by the soldiery, because, in its distorted shape, so much of the hatbrim was wholly useless. Hence, in camp lingo, to knock a fellow soldier into a cocked hat meant that he would be knocked out of shape and rendered useless, and that is still the meaning that we attach to the expression and the meaning in which it first appeared in print, in 1833, when, in depicting American life in his period, it was used by James Kirke Paulding in *Banks of the Ohio*. Some have credited the expression to a bowling game played in the United States about the middle of the nineteenth century. In this game, only the three corner pins were set up, and the player was allowed three balls to a frame. The name given to the game was "cocked hat," probably in allusion to the triangular arrangement of the pins. But the oldest record of the game is in 1858, so it is unlikely that our phrase was in any way the outcome of this short-lived game.

a man of my kidney

This saying is not now in frequent use; we are much more likely to say, "a man after my own heart," which carries the same meaning. But we find it used by Shakespeare and other writers of bygone years. The explanation takes us back to the philosophy of the Middle Ages, to the time when the temperament of men was supposed to be governed by their "humours." A person who was sullen or gloomy was supposed to have too much black bile, which gives us, from the Greek, the word "melancholy"; one who was irascible was supposed to be bilious, giving us "choler"; one of ruddy complexion was supposed to be cheerful, hopeful, and amorous, hence, full of blood, giving us "sanguine"; one of dull and sluggish nature, or cool and self-possessed, was supposed to have an excess of phlegm, giving us "phlegmatic." In the same philosophy, the kidney was supposed to be the seat of the affections; thus, in the original sense, "a man of my kidney" meant a person whose temperament and disposition were the same as those of the speaker.

to reckon without one's host

To neglect important facts in reaching a conclusion. This seems to have been a failing known also to our remote ancestors; at least, so long ago that the phrase had become proverbial when, in 1489, William Caxton printed (on his new wooden printing press) his own translation of the French *Blanchardyn and Eglantine*. In that early example of English printing may be found the passage, "It ys sayd in comyn that 'who soeuer rekeneth wythoute his hoste, he rekeneth twys for ones.'" But, as shown in this quotation and in others of the next hundred years—"Thei reckened before their host, and so paied more then their shotte came to"; and "He that countis without his oist, Oft tymes he countis twyse"—the tendency of our ancestors, unlike that of the present era, was to include more factors into the reckoning than should have been considered, even "twyse" as many.

to buy a pig in poke

Other languages have similar expressions, all dealing with the folly of buying something that one has not seen. In England, from time immemorial, it has been a pig, a young or suckling pig in a bag, for in ancient days the term "pig" was used only of very young swine, three or four months old, and still small enough to be carried to market slung over the shoulder in a stout "poke," the old-fashioned name for a bag smaller than a sack. The peasantry was apparently not above taking a runt to market and trying to sell it without opening the bag, because, as was undoubtedly the excuse, everyone knew how hard it would be to catch the piglet if it got loose. But the peasantry was also not above other tricks. Some investigators into bygone practices allege that, instead of a runt, it was a cat that was offered to the unwary customer. This view is supported by the French saying, "acheter chat en poche (to buy a cat in a sack)," a saying used, in translation, by John Wyclif in the fourteenth century. A canny purchaser, doubting the integrity of the dealer, however, might refuse to buy without an examination of the contents, thus giving rise to the related saying, "to let the cat out of the bag."

There was also an ancient saying, "When the pig is offered, hold open the poke." It's meaning was to be quick to seize an opportunity when it is offered. The allusion was again to the elusiveness of a pig; if not seized and put into the purchaser's bag, or if the bag were not fully open to receive it, the buyer's chance of recovering it was slim. Both sayings are recorded in Heywood's *A Dialogue conteyning Prouerbs and Epigrammes*, published in 1546.

to beard the lion

To be uncommonly and rashly brave; literally, to be so courageous as to dare to seize a lion by the beard. The saying is most familiar to us, perhaps, from the lines in Scott's *Marmion:*

> *. . . And dar'st thou then*
> *To beard the lion in his den,*
> *The Douglas in his hall?*
> *And hop'st thou thence unscathed*
> *to go?*
> *No, by St. Bryde of Bothwell, no!*

Scott was drawing upon a much older proverb, however, one cited by Shakespeare in *King John*, "You are the Hare of whom the Prouerb goes, Whose valour plucks dead Lyons by the Beard." Shakespeare quoted from Thomas Kyd's *The Spanish Tragedie*, perhaps—"Hares may pull dead lions by the beard." But the original source was undoubtedly the Latin saying, "Mortuo leoni et lepores insultant (And hares leaping at dead lions)."

by the skin of one's teeth

The use is always in respect to some calamity that has been avoided by so narrow a margin as to be measurable by the lining of a tooth. But originally, as found in Job xix, 20, the preposition "with" was used, not "by"—"And I am escaped with the skin of my teeth." But Job meant that he had escaped with nothing left but the skin of his teeth. The modern American expression and its meaning did not appear until approximately the beginning of the nineteenth century.

tarred with the same brush

The sense is always that of sharing, perhaps to a lesser degree, the faults or iniquities of another, of being defiled to some extent in the defilement of another. The record of usage goes back only to the late eighteenth century, though we may find its origin six centuries earlier. Early American usage, largely vanished now, alluded to a person of mixed blood; in Scotland the allusion was to sheep which had been smeared with tar as a protection against ticks. But it is likely that the real origin takes us back to the Crusades, to the introduction, in England at least, of the punishment, "tarring and feathering." This punishment could never have been humane, but when decreed by Richard the Lion-Hearted, in 1191, the chance of the survival of the victim must have been slight. A translation of that edict by Hakluyt, in 1589, reads, in part: "Concerning the lawes and ordinances appointed by King Richard for his navie the forme thereof was this . . . item, a thiefe or felon that hath stolen, being lawfully convicted, shal have his head shorne, and boyling pitch poured upon his head, and feathers or downe strawed upon the same whereby he may be knowen, and so at the first landing-place they shal come to, there to be cast up."

Through succeeding centuries tarring and feathering became a punishment for various misdemeanors inflicted, chiefly, by mobs. The nature of the punishment also varied. Rather than "boyling" pitch upon the shorn scalp, which must have horrible disfigured or killed the victim, the tar was heated enough to be viscid and was usually brushed, not poured, upon the scalp of the victim. Unless friendly hands and means were found to dissolve the tar, it would stay there a long time, for attempts to remove it otherwise would remove the skin with it. But when there was an accomplice of the chief victim, we may surmise that such a lesser rogue was punished less severely. Instead of hot tar and a pillowful of feathers, he may have received a swipe of the tarbrush and some of the feathers as a warning to mend his ways.

Tarring and feathering was not, of course, always applied only to the scalp. The culprits were often stripped, and both tar and feathers applied to the whole body. In frontier regions of the United States, as Mark Twain reminds us in *Huckleberry Finn*, villains thus treated by indignant townsmen might suffer the further indignity and torture of being set astride a rail, carried to the edge of the town, and warned against returning.

behind the eight ball

This modern expression has come to mean in a hazardous position; in a state or condition of embarrassment or peril from which it is difficult or impossible to extricate oneself; hence, out of luck; jinxed. The expression originated from the game of pocket billiards or, popularly, Kelly pool. But, though the origin seems to have been no longer ago than about 1919 or 1920, there are already at least two versions of the manner in which the phrase assumed its meaning.

The popular version says that it comes from a variant of the game of Kelly pool in which the players must pocket all fifteen balls, except that numbered "eight," in numerical order. But the eight ball, which is usually colored black, is considered unlucky, and if a player in the course of his shots has the misfortune to hit or touch the eight ball with the cue ball, he is penalized. Thus if, during the play, the cue ball comes to rest on such a spot that the eight ball lies between the next ball to be played, the player may be faced with an impossible shot or one that can be made only by skilful cushion shots.

Such a game as that just described is played, and it is easy to see that "behind the eight ball" would come to mean a hazardous position. But there is very good reason to believe that the phrase came first; that this variant of Kelly pool was a later development, making use of the phrase to introduce a new element of difficulty in the regular game.

The real story of the phrase, according to Charles C. Peterson, the noted billiardist, is that it originated in 1919 in a billiard room on John Street, New York, where a group of businessmen met each noon for a game of Kelly pool. In this game each player draws a number, and, if there are more than eight players, a player drawing a number higher than eight has no possible chance of winning. In this group of players, according to Peterson, "One player, time after time, day after day, would shake a number higher than eight. This became especially trying, because the group always placed side bets on lucky numbers under eight. One day when the 'pot' was extra interesting this player got an unusually high number. With a roar he threw it down and bellowed, 'I never have any luck! I'm always behind that doggoned ! ! * * ! ! eight ball!' "

Peterson says that the expression was first brought to his attention during a championship billiard tournament at the Hotel Astor, New York, in 1920, when Hoppe, Schaefer, and Cochran were contesting. He heard the full story in 1933 from Otto Reiselt, of Philadelphia, who gave the name of the unlucky originator of the expression as Allie Flint.

to stew in one's own juice

To suffer the consequences of one's own act. This, or its variant, "to fry in one's own grease," is very old. In the latter form it appears in a thirteenth-century tale of Richard the Lion-Hearted, and there is a French equivalent, *cuire dans son jus*. It is presumable that the older expression, at least, was originally literal; one fried in his own grease who, having committed some act punishable by such means, was burned at the stake.

to laugh in one's sleeve

To be secretly amused, whether in derision or just to avoid offense through open laughter, is to laugh in one's sleeve. The saying dates from the first half of the sixteenth century when, as one would suppose, the sleeves of a gentleman's costume were distinctly over-size, large enough to conceal one's whole head, let alone the mouth. The French, at the same period and earlier, laughed in their capes, which were large and flowing; and the Spaniard could conceal his amusement by laughing in his beard.

Bronx cheer

This somewhat disgusting sound expressing contemptuous dis-approval, the reverse of a cheer—a vibrating sound partly uttered through loosely closed lips and partly through the nose—seemingly owes its present name to the unusual skill displayed by the residents of the northern geographical section of New York City, or to spec-tators at athletic sports events held in that borough, in loudly producing this vocal effect. Before, roughly, a dozen years ago, the same sound was called "the raspberry," usually written "razz-berry"; to "get the raspberry," or "to give one the raspberry" was in slang use as early as the 1890s and is still regarded as a more refined expression than "Bronx cheer," if refinement may be considered in this con-nection. "Raspberry" was and is frequently shortened to "the berries." The British equivalent is "to get, or to give (one) the bird," a usage that traces back to theatrical slang of the middle nineteenth century.

It has been gravely suggested that the use of "raspberry" as the name of the sound arose from the resemblance to the noise pro-duced by a rasp grated over metal. I don't think so. I think that the word should be written "razzberry," that it was a humorous exten-sion developed from the slang, "to razz," to mock at or make fun of"; and that the latter term was originally a contraction of "to razzle-dazzle," meaning to bamboozle, banter, or deceive. And this latter verb, it may be recalled, came from the American invention in the 1880s of the razzle-dazzle, a kind of merry-go-round with an undulating platform, thus giving its passengers the combined pleasures of dizziness and seasickness.

to knock (something) galley-west

Aunt Sally, if you remember *Huckleberry Finn*, got so upset when trying to count the silver spoons—sometimes making a count of nine, sometimes ten, thanks to Huck's manipulations—that she seized the spoon basket, slammed it across the room, and knocked the cat "galley-west." It means that the cat was knocked upside down, topsy-turvy, into a state of confusion. Mark Twain's use happens to be the first on record, and one would almost expect to learn that he had coined the expression. Perhaps he did, but it is more likely that he heard it from someone else, either during the years that he was a pilot on the Mississippi or during the time he spent in western mining camps, for the term was already fairly common when, in 1882, he wrote *Huckleberry Finn*.

In fact, it is reasonably certain that the American "galley-west" is a corruption of the dialectal English "collyweston." This, used with much the same meaning—askew, awry, confused—has been traced by C. L. Apperson to 1587, and may be much earlier. The ultimate source is not known, but may have come from the name or nickname of an individual. In some English counties, there has long been a saying, "It's all along o' Colly Weston," used when anything has gone wrong. But whether "Colly Weston" was ever an actual person or just the name of a mischievous elf, like Robin Goodfellow, is not on the records.

another county heard from

Someone who has listened to—but has taken no part in—a debate or argument, finally breaks his silence. "Another county heard from," someone else is sure to remark brightly. The allusion is to the presidential election of 1876; Tilden and Hayes had had a neck-and-neck campaign; neither the Democrats nor the Republicans had been overscrupulous, and the results of the election were in grave doubt. Tilden, Democratic nominee, was believed to have carried all the southern states, but on the day after the election, word was sent out from the Republican headquarters that Hayes had carried Florida, Louisiana, and South Carolina. A recount of the ballots was ordered and, during the next several months, the suspense was high. Tallies from the various counties were so slow that as each came in a wearied public ironically remarked, "Another county heard from."

to skin the cat

In America, as any country boy knows, this means to hang by the hands from a branch or bar, draw the legs up through the arms and  over the branch, and pull oneself up into a sitting position. As we must abide by the record, we cannot say positively that the name for this violent small-boy exercise is more than a century old, but it is highly likely that Ben Franklin or earlier American lads had the same name for it. No one got around to putting it into print until about 1845. One can't be certain why the operation was called "skinning the cat," but maybe some mother, seeing it for the first time, saw in it some resemblance to the physical operation of removing the pelt from a cat, first from the forelegs and down over the body.

pieces of eight

This expression intrigued me as a youngster; it turned up in all the yarns about the Spanish Main, but was so obscure. Eight what? Actually, there was nothing mysterious about it, the term was merely the plural of the Spanish dollar which, having the value of eight reals, was stamped with a large figure 8. Until as late as our War Between the States the Spanish dollar was in general circulation in the United States, its value being almost the same as the United States dollar. It was from the Spanish dollar, or piece-of-eight, that we have our fictitious unit, the "bit," valued artificially at twelve and a half cents. The bit is, of course, the real, or one eighth of the dollar; "two bits" is twenty-five cents; "four bits" is fifty cents.

to draw (or pull) in one's horns

The use of this figure of speech with the meaning, "to retract, or to check oneself," has been traced back to the fourteenth century.

The allusion is to the snail which, when its hornlike tentacles touch something strange, possibly perilous, immediately retracts one or both of them.

iron curtain

Not often is a phrase, coined for a particular occasion, immediately seized upon, and widely used. This phrase, however, so aptly described a condition which was disturbing half the globe that it achieved immediate popularity. It was coined by Winston Churchill who, as prime minister of Great Britain during World War II, had an unequaled view of European politics during those critical years. The rise of Russian influence over eastern Europe disturbed him, accompanied as it was by rigid censorship and closed borders. When, no longer prime minister, he visited the United States in 1946, he felt free to express his misgivings. In a speech on March 5 at Fulton, Mo., where he was receiving an honorary degree from Westminster College, he expressed his concern in the following words:

From Stettin in the Baltic to Trieste in the Adriatic, an iron curtain has descended across the continent. Behind that line lie all the capitals of the ancient states of central and eastern Europe. Warsaw, Berlin, Prague, Vienna, Budapest, Belgrade, Bucharest, and Sofia, all these famous cities and the populations around them lie in what I might call the Soviet sphere, and all are subject, in one form or another, not only to Soviet influence but to a very high and in some cases increasing measure of control from Moscow.

to return to one's muttons

The English saying is a direct translation from the French, *revenon à nos moutons*. The literal meaning in the French phrase is the same as the English, and the figurative meanings are also the same— to return to the subject under discussion or consideration. For the origin we must go to a sixteenth-century play, *Pierre Pathelin*, written by the French poet, Pierre Blanchet. Pathelin (often spelled Patelin) is a lawyer who has, through flattery, hoodwinked Joceaume, the local draper, into giving him six ells of cloth. While this injury is still rankling, Joceaume also discovers that his shepherd has stolen some of his sheep. He has the shepherd haled before the magistrate and there finds to his amazement that the shepherd has the rascally Pathelin as his lawyer. The draper, sputtering in indignation, tries to tell the magistrate about his loss of the sheep, but each time that he sees Pathelin he begins to rave about the cloth of which he has been defrauded. The judge begins to get somewhat confused, but tries to keep Joceaume to his charges against the shepherd: "Revenon à nos moutons (Let us return to our sheep)," he repeats time and again.

to have bees in one's bonnet

To be slightly daft or crazed. The original saying, which dates at least to the sixteenth century was, "to have a head full of bees," or "to have bees in the head, or in the brain." That association of  craziness with bees humming in the head undoubtedly antedates that period, for the expression is recorded by John Heywood, in 1546, in his *Dialogue conteining the nomber in effect of all the prouerbes in the Englishe tongue*, though no earlier quotation has been found. According to Apperson, the poet, Robert Herrick was the person who introduced the bonnet into the expression. This was found in Herrick's "Mad Maid's Song," written in 1648: "Ah! woe is mee, woe, woe is mee, Alack and well-a-day! For pitty, sir, find out that bee, Which bore my love away. I'le seek him in your bonnet brave, I'le seek him in your eyes."

just under the wire

One who no more than barely catches a train, who has hardly settled himself in a theater seat before the curtain rises, who in a moment more would have been too late for whatever the event might be, is said to be "just under the wire." The expression comes from the racetracks. The winning horse is the first to go "under the wire"—the "wire" being a figment of the imagination, but denoting the exact line that marks the finish of a race. But in many races, though the winning horse receives the major part of the purse, the second, third, and often the fourth horses are also "in the money"—that is, receive a share of the prize. Thus a horse that just noses ahead of the fourth (or sometimes fifth) horse to cross the finish line is "just under the wire."

to sow one's wild oats

To indulge in dissipation, or to conduct oneself foolishly. The saying has been common in its present sense for at least four hundred years, for a writer of that period speaks of young men at "that wilfull and unruly age, which lacketh rypenes and discretion, and (as wee saye) hath not sowed all theyr wyeld Oates." The reference is to a genus of cereal grass, known as wild oat (*Avena fatua*), that flourishes throughout Europe. It is little more than  a weed and is very difficult to eradicate. The folly of sowing it is comparable to the folly shown by young men who, thoughtlessly, commit an act or begin a practice the evil of which will be difficult to eradicate.

I'm from Missouri

In America, extreme skepticism is indicated by one who says, "I'm from Missouri," though actually the residents of that state are no more incredulous than are other Americans. The expression is said to have originated during the course of some extemporaneous humorous remarks by Willard D. Vandiver who was, at the time, a representative to Congress from Missouri. The occasion, according to the Washington *Post*, May 31, 1932, was an impromptu address before the Five O'clock Club of Philadelphia in 1899. The previous speaker had made some extravagant assertions, it was said, for the productiveness of the prosperous state of Iowa. In casting doubt on some of those statements, Vandiver said, "I come from a country that raises corn, cotton, cockleburs, and Democrats. I'm from

Missouri, and you've got to show me." The implication of hard-headedness and shrewdness immediately appealed to the natives of Missouri, and especially the last part of their congressman's statement, and it was not long before they began to call themselves citizens of the "Show Me" state—and for all others, when some speaker drew the longbow, to smile and say, "I'm from Missouri."

the whole kit and caboodle

In its entirety, this phrase is American; it is a somewhat more refined expression than the earlier, "the whole kit and bilin'." Both forms mean lock, stock, and barrel; the whole lot, omitting nothing. But "the whole kit" is plain English—the entire outfit; the whole lot, either of things or persons. "Bilin'," of course, was corrupted from "boiling," which meant a seething mass, especially of persons; so "the whole kit and bilin'" originally meant the entire group of people and their equipment. Later it was limited to define just all the people in a group.

But along with the common expression, "the whole kit and bilin'," there was a more refined American phrase, "the whole kit and boodle," for "boodle" was apparently Americanized from the Dutch word *boedel*, property, estate, goods. And just because we like to have alliteration in our speech, someone tried to put a "*k*" before "boodle," giving us, "the whole kit and caboodle." By the way, it was this same Dutch word, corrupted to "boodle" also, that was later used in a sinister sense to mean money—money acquired by graft or bribery.

holding the bag (or sack)

We saw elsewhere how "to let the cat out of the bag" was connected with the other familiar saying, "to buy a pig in a poke." Proof is lacking, but it seems to me that the unfortunate wight who bought a pig in a poke and soon after let a cat out of the bag, could very well have served as the prototype of the person who was left holding the bag. This saying is also old, and from its first appearance in literature has meant "left in the lurch," holding responsibili-

116

ties that one has not contracted which have been evaded by the one who should bear them.

balled up

This has been used, in the sense of confused, embarrassed, entangled, only since about 1880, if we allow seven or eight years of that puristic period for a slang expression to break into print. Really, however, the slang use is little more than a natural extension of the normal use of the verb, "to ball," which is to form or to be formed into a ball—one balls a hank of yarn, for instance. But our phrase does not come so much from the state that grandma's knitting yarn sometimes got into, as from grandpa's horses. When driven during spring thaws or over soft winter snows, the snow often  became packed into rounded icy balls on the hoofs of the horses; it became "balled" or "balled up." Not only was progress difficult, but sometimes the horses were unable to keep their footing. When they fell, either singly or in pairs, the state of confusion and entanglement was exasperating, giving rise to the present use of the expression.

to pass the buck

There is no uncertainty about the source of this term. Poker. But, just as the origin of the American game of poker is shrouded in mystery, so is the origin of this phrase. Probably both the name of the game and the game itself come from an old German game, *pochspiel*, which was also a game of bluff, but this is little more than a guess. The game seems to have developed in the United States during the first quarter of the nineteenth century; first as straight poker, and later, about 1845, with draw poker its earliest modification. Until comparatively recent years, poker was not what would have been called a "gentlemen's game"; it was a game for the barroom or for the lumber or mining camp. Few of the men who played it were literate, and, therefore, the reasons or the occasions for some of the terms used in the game were not recorded. No one knows, for instance, how "stud poker" got its name. It may be, as someone has surmised, that a stud horse was the stake in an early exciting stage of its development. Our present phrase, "to pass the buck," came into use probably around the time of the Civil War, though Mark Twain, in 1872, gives us the earliest record of it. The "buck" was some sort of object passed from one player to another as a reminder that the next deal would fall to the second person. Because of the present-day practice of using a pocket knife for the purpose, and because early knives often had buckhorn handles, it has been suggested that "buck" came from that source. That is possible, but, in my opinion, unlikely. Knives carried by the poker players of that period were more likely to be hunting knives than pocket knives, and were too large for so slight a purpose. A buckshot would have served the need, or, possibly, a bucktail carried as a talisman.

bats in one's belfry

One wonders why such a typical Americanism was not coined until early in the present century. I suspect that it must have come  from the fertile imagination of Sime Silverman, the editorial genius and apt word-coiner who guided the theatrical journal, *Variety*, until his death in 1933, but if so, I find no proof. The earliest record is in 1911, in a novel by Henry Sydnor Harrison. Even the derivative, "batty," a slang equivalent for crazy, was a later development. The explanation is simple: as "belfry" is that part of a church tower in which the bells are hung, it suggests, therefore, the head. Bats are known to be frequenters of bell towers; they fly around crazily; ergo, they are crazy. Hence, to have bats in one's belfry is to be crazy in the head.

to put in one's best licks

Through some queer chance, the word "lick" in American speech acquired the meaning "a spurt of speed; also, a burst of energy."

This meaning found its way into print early in the nineteenth century. Our present phrase was derived from that sense and is graphically illustrated by the line from *Polly Peablossom's Wedding*, published in 1851 by T. A. Burke. The line reads, "I saw comin' my gray mule, puttin' in her best licks, and a few yards behind her was a grizzly." We also say, to put in "solid" licks, or "good" licks.

Annie Oakley

In theater or show parlance, an "Annie Oakley" is a free pass to the show. The real Annie Oakley, born in 1860, was an expert American markswoman. During the years when William F. Cody, perhaps better known as "Buffalo Bill," was touring the country with his Wild West Show, organized in 1883, one of his stellar attractions from 1885 to 1902 was this marvelous markswoman. Her full name was Phoebe Anne Oakley Mozes; she was not a "westerner" at all, but hailed from Ohio; her husband, whom she married at the age of fifteen, was Frank Butler, a vaudeville actor. Her marksmanship was exceptional; her most notable achievement, it is said, was by 1000 shots with a rifle to break 942 glass balls tossed in the air. In the Wild West Show a playing card, such as the ten of diamonds, was pinned to a target and, in successive shots, she would center a shot in each one of the pips. It was through this latter accomplishment that her name became synonymous with a complimentary pass to a show, because the card, when thus perforated, resembled a theater ticket which the manager has punched before issuing it as a pass.

to come to the end of one's rope (or tether)

"Tether" is the older word, but with either "rope" or "tether" the saying goes back many centuries. In original usage the expression alluded apparently to a cow or other domestic animal, perchance a dog, staked for grazing or for protection by a rope attached to its neck. The range of the animal was thus limited. If a cow, it could not graze beyond the limit of its rope; if a dog, it could not get at a stranger, no matter how fiercely it might run or lunge, who kept outside the circle of its tether. Thus, "to come to the end of one's rope" had the literal meaning, to reach the limit of one's resources.

But both rope and tether early became sinister synonyms for the hangman's rope. From this, the saying acquired a second and more devastating meaning by which we use it to signify that one has been effectually checked in the commission of crime, has reached, figuratively, if not literally, the noose of the hangman. It is probable that this extended meaning was effected, in part at least, by the old proverb, "Give him enough rope and he'll hang himself."

to lay an egg

This modern slang expression has no bearing whatsoever upon the output of a hen. It means, "to fail; to flop; to fail to produce an intended result." The "egg" in the expression is shortened from the older slang meaning of "goose-egg," which, in sporting circles, means a cipher, a nought, a zero, from the resemblance of the

outline of the egg to a cipher, o. In an inning of baseball, for example, the score of a team which has no runs is shown by the figure o, a cipher. That team "lays an egg."

"Goose-egg" in this sense had attained some degree of respectability by 1886, for in that year it is recorded that the New York *Times*, in reporting a baseball game, said, "The New York players presented the Boston men with nine unpalatable goose eggs in their contest on the Polo Grounds yesterday." The American usage, however, is merely a transference from the British "duck" as the layer of such eggs, for, as readers of Charles Reade's *Hard Cash* will discover, as long ago as 1863 and earlier, the British were describing one who failed to score at cricket as having "achieved a duck's egg." Sports writers of today leave the bird nameless.

the spit an' image

Though spelled and contracted in different ways—spit and image, spitting image, spittin' image, spitten image—the intent is always the same, an exact likeness, a counterpart. It usually refers to an infant or child whose features and mannerisms strongly reflect those of one of its parents. The origin of the expression has been variously ascribed; thus, for example, the late O. O. McIntyre, newspaper columnist, offered the ingenious suggestion that it may have been an American Negro corruption of "spirit and image," that the child possessed the spirit and was the image of its parent.

In my opinion, however, the expression is partly English and partly American. The records show that "spit," in such form as "the spit of his father," was used in England early in the nineteenth century. It seems certain that the origin of the noun in this sense was derived from an earlier use of the verb, going back over some two hundred years, for earlier records show such expressions as, "as like (a person or animal) as if spit out of his mouth."

"Image" seems to have been a redundancy added in America. It was not needed, and only serves to intensify the close resemblance which the speaker observes. Records do not show that the doubled term was in use much before the middle of the past century.

to turn the heat on

This seems originally to have been underworld slang, probably a rough interpretation of "to be grilled" in its figurative sense. It means, to be subjected to a severe cross-examination, as by police officers in grilling a suspected criminal; but of course in ordinary use a youngster will say that his dad turned the heat on when asking how the fender of the car got dented. The expression is quite recent.

to be hand in glove

To be on such terms of intimacy that the relationship is almost that of the glove to the hand. Literary usage dates back to 1678, but in those days and until late in the following century the phrase was "hand and glove," a form rarely heard nowadays.

white elephant

That large portrait of your wealthy Aunt Jane, given by her and which you loathe but do not dare to take down from your wall; that large bookcase, too costly to discard, but which you hope will be more in keeping with your future home; these, and a thousand other like items are "white elephants"—costly, but useless

possessions. The allusion takes us to Siam. In that country it was the traditional custom for many centuries that a rare albino elephant was, upon capture, the property of the emperor—who even today bears the title, Lord of the White Elephant—and was thereafter sacred to him. He alone might ride or use such an animal, and none might be destroyed without his consent. Because of that latter royal prerogative, it is said that whenever it pleased his gracious majesty to bring about the ruin of a courtier who had displeased him, he would present the poor fellow with an elephant from his stables. The cost of feeding and caring for the huge animal that he might not use nor destroy—a veritable white elephant—gave the term its present meaning.

Incidentally, as a matter of English history, Charles I of England had the sad experience of receiving such a gift, a figurative, if not literal, white elephant. In 1629, just at the time that the king, faced with a recalcitrant Parliament, was desperately trying to raise funds by any measures, even to the extent of bartering the crown jewels, the Emperor of Siam sent him an elephant and five camels. Though the account does not say that the elephant was white, the cost of keeping the beast, estimated at £275 a year, was so great that the queen was obliged to put off her "visit to 'the Bath' to a more convenient season, for want of money to bear her charges," for, as the record goes on to say, aside from that cost for feed and care, "his keepers afirme that from the month of September until April he must drink, not water, but wyne, and from April unto September he must have a gallon of wyne the daye."

to swallow (a tale) hook, line, and sinker

We use this saying of a person so exceedingly gullible as to accept a yarn or statement, no matter how fantastic, at its face value. The allusion is to a hungry fish, so voracious as to take into its maw not only the baited fish hook, but the leaden sinker and all the line between, thus falling an easy prey to the fisherman. It is an American expression and, though undoubtedly long and widely used earlier, was first recorded in the course of a congressional debate in 1865. There was a British antecedent, however, that had the same meaning and a similar piscatorial background—to swallow a gudgeon. This goes back to the sixteenth century at least, used by John Lyly in his romance, *Euphues*, in 1579. And a later writer, still in the sixteenth century, spoke of one who had swallowed the gudgeon and had been entangled in the hook. A gudgeon, incidentally, is a small fish often used as bait, a minnow.

to come out at the little end of the horn

To fail in an undertaking; especially, to fail after one has bragged about a result that promised large returns. Such has been the meaning of this expression for more than three hundred years. From the statement made by John Fletcher, in *A Wife for a Month* (1625)—"the prodigal fool the ballad speaks of, that was squeezed through a horn" —it appears that the saying arose from some old popular ballad, one that has not survived. But the allusion has come to us through other channels. George Chapman, in *Eastward Hoe!* written in collaboration with Jonson and Marston (1605), says, "I had the Horne of Suretiship ever before my eyes. You all know the deuise of the  Horne, where the young fellow slippes in at the Butte end, and comes squesd out at the Buckall." And a correspondent to *Notes & Queries* (Seventh Series) described an old painting ascribed to the sixteenth century that he had seen, on which was depicted a huge horn into which a man had been thrust, the head and arms emerging from the small end; underneath were the lines:

This horne emblem here doth show
Of svretishipp what harm doth grow.

From these we can surmise that the lost ballad probably related the sad experience of a young man who, coming into a fortune, accepted bad advice in the handling of it. It would appear that, under the promise of handsome dividends, he became surety for a false friend and, having to pay the obligation, lost all his heritage in the bitter experience. The moral probably pointed to the ease with which money can be lent, like entering the mouth of a horn, but the lender may find himself squeezed and stripped when promises are not fulfilled.

not amount to Hannah More

This saying, equivalent to "not amount to a hill of beans," is a common way of telling a young person around Gloucester, Massachusetts, that he doesn't show much promise. The saying was also current in some parts of England many years ago, but why the name of Miss Hannah More became bandied about in such manner is a mystery. Hannah More, born near Bristol, England, in 1745, the daughter of a boarding-school master, began to write while still in her teens, and to have those writings published. A friend of the actor, Garrick, she wrote two slightly successful tragedies. But before she was thirty her work turned to moral and religious topics and, in 1795, one of these, *Cheap Repository Tracts*, had such success that two million copies of it were circulated in its first year. In 1809 her most successful work, *Coelebs in Search of a Wife*, which despite its title was a religious novel, reached the remarkable sale, for that period, of ten editions in its first year. It was very popular, also, in the United States. She died at the ripe age of eighty-eight after a long bedridden period during which she produced a half-dozen or so other serious works. After such a notable career, it is odd that her name ever became a word of disparagement. The suggestion has been offered that, despite her assiduous work, nothing ever came of it; but if that be the interpretation, thousands of other names might be infinitely more appropriate.

124

to beat the Dutch

Though "Dutch courage" as a synonym for sham courage and "Dutch consolation" as a synomym for "Well, it might be worse," date back to the days of rivalry in arms and commerce between the countries of Holland and England, "to beat the Dutch" is traceable only to late American colonial days. Under English rule of New York descendants of the early Dutch settlers became successful merchants and traders, just as their forefathers as citizens of New Amsterdam had been. They dealt in good wares which they offered at fair prices, and he who would excel any of these merchants had good reason to boast that he had, literally, beat the Dutch. From that early literal meaning the phrase became a popular expression used to denote surprise or wonderment, and often interchangeable with "to beat the band." In the presidential campaign of Martin Van Buren his Dutch ancestry was used against him in a popular song that ran:

> *We'll beat the Dutch,*
> *Hurrah for Tyler!*
> *We'll beat the Dutch,*
> *Or bust our b'iler.*

a fig for your opinion, not worth a fig, not to care a fig

These sayings, which express contempt, may go back to ancient Greece, to a region where figs were so plentiful as to have almost no value. But more probably we got the worthlessness of a fig from Italy, where a gesture—the thumb thrust between the fingers—said to have an indecent significance, is called a "fig" and has been for many centuries expressive of the deepest contempt. It is interesting to note that English writers of the sixteenth century referred to this gesture as "a fig of Spain."

The Italian source is said to have originated in the twelfth century, as the result of an event in Milan. The citizens of that proud city, resenting its seizure by Frederick Barbarossa in 1158, overthrew its conqueror in 1159 and drove him from the city. His empress, in derision, was placed upon a mule, facing its tail, and escorted outside the city walls. But in 1162 Frederick recaptured Milan, razed its buildings, and humiliated its citizens. Those who were taken prisoners were compelled, on pain of death, to take a "fig"—in the slang of that day, the droppings of a mule—between his teeth and to repeat to his captors, "Ecco la fica, (Behold the fig)."

a wolf in sheep's clothing

Young people of today think they are very up to date when they refer to a carnally minded man, young or old, as a "wolf," but the fact is that they are, roughly speaking, some twenty-five hundred years behind the times. So anciently were such men known that Aesop, who lived in Greece about 600 B.C., told a fable about them.

He likened them to a wolf who got admission into a sheepfold by wrapping himself in the skin and fleece of a sheep. Thus, under the pretense that he was an innocent and harmless as a sheep, he was able to seize and devour unsuspecting young lambs that took his fancy.

The fables of Aesop were so familiar in Greece and the countries with which she enjoyed commerce that, possibly, this fable may have been the source of the passage in Matthew vii, 15: "Beware of false prophets, which come to you in sheep's clothing, but inwardly they are ravening wolves." Or, perhaps, to-day's ravening "wolf" got his name from the biblical passage, rather than directly from the fable, though no one can be certain.

to grin like a Cheshire cat

Lewis Carrol popularized the Cheshire cat in *Alice's Adventures in Wonderland*, in which the grinning cat disappeared gradually from Alice's view and the last to vanish was the grin, but the saying is much older than this account. It has been traced back to the writings of John Wolcot, better known under his pseudonym, Peter Pindar, whose numerous satires appeared between 1782 and 1819. But the saying must have originated some time before Wolcot's use, for by 1850, when people began to be interested in seeking its allusion, no grandsire or grandam could be found who had positive knowledge. One novel opinion was that, because Cheshire was a county palatine—that is, had regal privileges—the cats, when they thought of it, were so tickled that they couldn't help grinning. But the most likely opinion was that some influential family in Cheshire, with a lion rampant as its crest, employed some sign painter to paint the crest on the signboards of many of the inns. The painter was none too sure of the appearance of a lion and the final result looked, to the countryfolk, like an attempt to depict a grinning cat.

to stick one's neck out

When you vounteer for something that may have a bad ending, when you enter an argument in which you may turn out to be a poor second, or whenever you deliberately take the chance of being hurt, literally or figuratively, you are sticking your neck out. The saying is modern American slang, an outgrowth of the earlier, "to get it in the neck," both of them alluding to the neck of a chicken stretched for the ax. The other saying attained popularity during the last quarter of the nineteenth century.

to carry the torch for one

It is the torch of love that is understood in this modern American term, though sometimes no more than the torch of loyalty, for the "torchbearer" is one who is loud in his praise of a friend. But the torch has long been an emblem of enlightenment and of burning devotion, and, in 1775, Richard Sheridan used the expression, "The torch of love," in his epilog to *The Rivals*.

rope of sand

Nothing could be less cohesive or less stable. With just such meaning the expression has been used through the past three hundred and fifty years, ironically describing a treaty, contract, or the like which has no force, as a "rope of sand" binding the two parties. As used by Sir Francis Bacon and other sixteenth-century writers, one was supposed "to knit a rope of sand." Samuel Butler, the satirist, wrote in 1712, "I leave to my said children a great chest full of broken promises and cracked oaths; likewise a vast cargo of ropes made with sand."

127

to make one's mouth water

To anticipate something with great eagerness. Literally, and the original sense, one referred to the actual drooling that one experiences over the prospects of sinking one's teeth into a comestible that exudes a particularly delightful aroma, as a schoolboy from Boston might say. The experience must have been as early as mankind, but  it may be that early English cooking occasioned no such outpouring of saliva, for it was not until 1555 that the saying appeared in English print, and then in reference to some West Indian cannibals. The historian, Richard Eden, in *The Decades of the Newe Worlde or West India*, wrote, "These craftie foxes . . . espying their enemies afarre of, beganne to swalowe theyr spettle as their mouthes watered for greedines of theyr pray."

worth one's salt; to earn one's salt

We may as well take these together, for it is only the use of "salt" in these phrases that is interesting. Because of the origin of the word, one would expect to be able to find that either of the expressions could be traced to ancient Latin, but actually the first of them, the earliest, goes back only to the first quarter of the nineteenth century. "Salt," in these expressions, is no more than an etymological play upon the source of the word "salary," perhaps a source that was not understood before 1800. In the days of the Roman legions, a soldier received a part of his pay in the form of a salarium, a salary, which was actually an allowance for the purchase of salt (Latin, *sal*). Salt was not so easily obtainable in those times, but even then the Roman generals knew that this mineral was essential to health and vigor. A soldier who was not worth or did not earn this small allowance was worthless indeed.

to beat the band

This saying has become so trite as to be employed for almost any element of amazement or of any superior accomplishment or achieve-

128

ment; as, Well, if that doesn't beat the band! or, She cooks to beat the band; or, The baby yelled to beat the band. The expression isn't very old; at least, no literary record of it has been dug up earlier than fifty years ago, but, probably because of its enticing alliteration, it has acquired great general use in the United States. Its origin seems to have been literal, a desire to arrive at some spot before a band of musicians leading a parade had passed that spot, thereby enabling one to see the entire parade. Sometimes one had to whip up one's horses to get there, or, if a small boy, run on the wings of the wind, but the later pleasure made the haste worth while.

to jump the gun

This expression is of racing origin, especially foot racing. A contestant so keyed up as to spring from the starting mark a moment before the starter fires his pistol is said to jump the gun." The expression is also used in hunting game, as when a pheasant "jumps the gun" by being startled and taking flight before the sportsman's gun is in readiness. Hence, the phrase has acquired a general slang meaning of beginning a thing before preparations for  it are in readiness. In this figurative sense the usage is recent, probably not longer than within the past twenty-five or thirty years.

to stab in the back

We use this now always figuratively, to deliver a cowardly blow, physically or against one's character, and we usually use it with reference to such a delivery by one who was thought to be friendly, or at least not suspected to be inimical. The literal origin goes back to the times when footpads, with a dagger beneath the cape, would unconcernedly approach and pass an unsuspecting victim, quickly flash out the knife as the pedestrian was passing and thrust it into his back, grabbing his purse as he fell, and dashing away from the scene.

to take the cake

To receive or merit a prize or honor; hence, to excel at something. This expression did not arise from the "cakewalk," but the cakewalk got its name from the expression. Even two hundred years ago "cake" denoted an award or honor of some sort, and he who received it, "took the cake." American usage can be traced back a hundred years. The cakewalk, originally a Negro entertainment in which couples competed for a cake by the grace or style of walking, came into notice only in the last quarter of the nineteenth century.

to shoot the bull

This American slang, which originated in the gutter or, rather, the barnyard, now means to talk pretentiously, to talk wisely and freely upon subjects about which one knows little. It developed from the American institution known as a "bull session," a gathering of men, usually young men, in which each airs his knowledge or offers his opinions upon any subject toward which the conversation, often smutty, veers. "Bull" in each instance refers generically to a type of commodity, known euphemistically as "booshwah," found abundantly upon cattle farms, which forms a cheap fertilizer and reeks unpleasantly. Both "bull session" and "to shoot the bull" are developments of the twentieth century.

crocodile tears

It is proverbial that a crocodile moans and sobs like a person in great distress in order to lure a man into its reach, and then, after devouring him sheds bitter tears over the dire fate of its victim. Thus "crocodile tears" is synonymous with hypocritical grief, make-believe deep sorrow. Belief in the proverb is found in ancient Greek and Latin literature, so it was natural that un-traveled Englishmen, to whom a crocodile was unknown, accepted the belief as a statement of fact in early days. In the *Voiage and Travaile of Sir John Maundeville*, written about 1400, we read that "Cokadrilles. . . . Theise Serpentes slen men, and thei eten hem wepynge." Other English writers repeated the fable, and we find it even in Shakespeare's works.

going to town

Usually in our jocular use of this phrase we slur it to "goin' to town." It means alert and eager, full of life and vivacity, in the state or condition in which Fortune shines upon one. Although a very modern expression, we must seek its significance in the backwoods days of more than half a century ago when, for many persons, a visit to a town was a momentous event.

One prepared several days in advance for such a trip, getting one's clothes in order and making up a shopping list. The trip and the visit itself were filled with interest. The occasion, if the  weather were fine, was one of great good fortune. In modern usage the phrase retains much of that same spirit of high adventure.

out on a limb

At a disadvantage, as one would be if actually upon the limb of a tree, hanging on for dear life and being pelted or shot at by an enemy. The expression is of American origin and dates from the latter part of the ninteenth century. Its earliest literary appearance was, in 1897, by Alfred Henry Lewis who, under the pen name of Dan Quin, wrote *Wolfville*, one of a series of tales about life in a frontier town.

to get the brush-off

If your employer dismisses you, or if your boy friend ceases to call, or if the newcomer on the next street rejects your friendly advances, you are—in modern American slang—getting the brush-off; you are being put aside. The thought seems to be that one is likened to an undesirable piece of lint or streak of dirt that is brushed from a garment. But there is also the possibility that the allusion is to a Pullman porter who, sensing a poor tip from one of his charges, gives that person a few flicks with his brush and passes on to a more likely customer.

131

to give a lick and a promise

If small Johnny has taken the facecloth and lightly washed his mouth and cheeks, he has given himself a lick and a promise—about what the cat could do in one hasty swab of the tongue and a promise of a complete job in the dim future. We say that one who has worked half-heartedly or in a slovenly manner has given the work a lick and a promise. The homely saying is common in both England and America; it is undoubtedly several centuries old, but examples of literary use are not recorded.

to chew the rag

To talk, or to make a speech; especially, to talk at length, to grumble continuously, or to rant. As with any slang expression, the parentage and time of birth of this cannot be positively determined. Records of written use are simultaneous in England and the United States, in 1885—army slang in England, newspaper use in this country; so it is certain that the man in the street of either country had been using the expression a long time before that. But this noun, rag, I think, never had any connection with the ordinary rag, a strip of cloth. It seems to have been formed from the verb, to rag—which, in dialectal English back in the eighteenth century, meant, to scold; hence, to annoy, tease; also, to wrangle. No one knows the source of this "rag," but it is supposed to have been a contraction of "bully-rag."

As to chewing, in this figurative sense pertaining to words, we can find that use in Shakespeare. In *Measure for Measure*, he has Angelo chewing a name; that is, saying it over and over. And away back in the sixteenth century, the expression, "to chew the cud," meaning to ruminate upon a matter, was already proverbial.

to have a bone to pick

The bone, originally, was a bone of contention—some difference of opinion to argue about or to settle, thus resembling an actual bone tossed between two dogs to determine which should be the master. One has a bone to pick with one when one has an argument to settle or something disagreeable to discuss or have explained. Usage goes

132

back to the middle of the sixteenth century, but the expression may well have been derived from, or another form of, the earlier phrase, "to have a crow to pluck," which was used at least a hundred years earlier, but for which no satisfactory explanation has been discovered.

sword of Damocles

When Dionysius was ruler of Syracuse, back in the fourth century B.C., the courtier, Damocles, wishing to curry favor, began to praise the ruler one day. He exclaimed over the power that Dionysius wielded, extolled his great wealth, and admired, above all, the luxurious life that he led and the comfort with which he was surrounded. Dionysius, it is said, began to grow somewhat weary of this fulsome flattery, and asked the courtier if he would himself like to experience such a life. Naturally, Damocles would like nothing better. So the ruler ordered that a bath should be prepared for Damocles, that he be arrayed in fine raiment, that a feast be set before him, and that dancers and singers should entertain him while he ate. All this was done, and when Damocles had finished his sumptuous repast he lay back on the couch upon which he had been reclining, and was aghast to see over his head a heavy sword, hanging by a single hair. He jumped from the couch, asking the meaning of so ominous a threat. "That," said Dionysius, "is the threat of calamity that always imperils the life of anyone in high position, for others are always seeking his downfall." The story is told by various ancient writers, but the simile, expressing imminent danger, was not employed in English literature until a scant two hundred years ago.

to do (or pull) a brodie

This expression has a variety of meanings, depending largely upon where and by whom it is used, and whether "to do" or "to pull" is the accompanying verb. In sporting circles, "to do a brodie" is, generally, to take a chance, sometimes a daring chance. In theatrical circles and in some other instances, "to pull a brodie" is to produce a failure or a "flop," or to commit a blunder, or to fail or be defeated ignominiously.

Curiously, though the slang expressions are quite recent, scarcely more than ten years old, the source lies in an event, or series of events, of sixty years ago, especially one event that was recalled in the celebration of the sesquicentennial of the completion of the Brooklyn Bridge.

Steve Brodie, who was born about 1863 near the Brooklyn end of the great bridge that was begun when he was a lad, took great interest in its construction through the years of his boyhood. It is said that he was not too bright, intellectually, and that the imposing structure stimulated a zeal to acquire a personal fame or to do something that, to his notion, would celebrate the completion of the bridge. The height of the bridge from the lowest chord of the span is 135 feet at the center. Steve vowed that he would jump from it at that point.

Though completed in 1883, the bridge was not opened to traffic for several years. In the meantime, Steve Brodie's intention had become known among the frequenters of the saloon where he worked and eventually someone or some group made him a bet of $200 that he would not make the jump. According to the New York *Times* of July 24, 1886, young Brodie actually made the leap at two o'clock of the previous day, July 23, after eluding policemen on the bridge who had been instructed not to permit the hazardous undertaking. The account runs that he had been "well prepared" against injury by external applications of whisky and bandages. Friends were waiting in a rowboat beneath and picked him up as he returned to the surface; he complained of a "pain," which seems to have been alleviated by liberal applications of whisky, internally this time, and, though arrested for endangering his life, he suffered no further injury than a deflation of ego through a caustic upbraiding from the judge.

Two years later, according to the New York *Tribune* of November 10, 1888, Brodie jumped off the railroad bridge over the Hudson River at Poughkeepsie in the early hours of the previous day, a leap of 212 feet, as reported; this time to win a bet of $500. And the same authority stated that he had previously jumped from the Allegheny Bridge in 1881, a leap of 76 feet; from High Bridge, N. Y., in 1886, 111 feet; and from both the Covington, Ky., and the St. Louis bridges in 1887, as well as the Brooklyn Bridge.

But, fifty years later, when the semicentennial of the completion of the Brooklyn Bridge was being celebrated, no one could be found who could testify that any of these leaps had actually been made. Brodie had died when he was in his Forties; the newspaper reporter who related each picturesque elusion of the police for each jump and the subsequent "rescues," was a close friend of Steve's, and was always one of the "rescuers." Doubt was evinced that the "jumps" were anything but gags, hoaxes, for the sake of cheap notoriety; that each "jump," which might have been a daring chance, was actually a failure, a flop. Thus the lateness of the phrase and the present-day meanings are derived not from events that may or may not have occurred actually, but from subsequent suspicions and investigations that, fifty years later, threw doubt on the authenticity of those events and brought Brodie's name into contempt.

bull of Bashan

A person with a stentorian voice and powerful build is said to be a "bull of Bashan." The reference is to the Bible, to Psalms xxii, 12: "Many bulls have compassed me: strong bulls of Bashan have beset me round. They gaped upon me with their mouths, as a ravening and a roaring lion." The conquest of Bashan by Moses (Deuteronomy iii, 14), known as the land of giants, was a memorable feat to the Israelites; there are a number of references to it in the Old Testament. The size and power of the cattle were especially impressive.

from Dan to Beersheba

All over the world; from one side of the world (or the country) to the other. The expression comes from the Bible—Judges xx, 1— telling of the assembly of Israelites from one end of the country to the other to do battle against the Benjamites—from the city of Dan at the north end of the Land of Israel and from the city of Beersheba at the south end, and all points between. As far as the Israelites were concerned, that area embraced the world.

on (or *aboard*) *the bandwagon*

One who climbs or gets on or aboard the bandwagon, in the United States, is he who accepts or espouses a popular movement or cause that some leader has organized. It had a political origin—from the parades honoring a candidate for office and led by a loud band of musicians riding upon a large dray. For the effect upon his con-stituents, some local leader would, as the band approached, vauntingly mount the wagon and ride through his district, thus advertising his endorsement of the candidate. Though the band, the wagon, and the practice were long a feature in American pre-election politics, the phrase dates only from the second presidential campaign of William Jennings Bryan.

to whip (or *beat*) *the devil around the stump*

To evade a responsibility or duty in a roundabout manner; to get deviously around a difficulty. It may be that this old American expression is an offshoot of the familar "up a stump," which means in perplexity, in confusion, and which in turn came from the use of a tree stump as a platform for making a speech—one mounted upon a stump might well be confused and have stage fright. But if there was any connection, the explanation cannot be found now. In 1786, the date when the earliest record of the expression occurs, it was credited to Virginia. Possibly there was some allusion to the biblical admonition, "Get thee behind me, Satan," but it is more likely that it came from some folk tale once current in the South.

to teach one's grandmother to suck eggs

To offer needless assistance; to waste one's efforts upon futile matters; especially, to presume to offer advice to an expert. This particular expression is well over two hundred years old; it is just a variation of an older theme that was absurd enough to appeal to the popular fancy. One of the earliest of these is given in Udall's translation of *Apophthegmes* (1542) from the works of Erasmus. It reads: "A swyne to teache Minerua, was a prouerbe, for which we saie in Englyshe to teache our dame to spynne."

the goose hangs high

Things are propitious; all is well. This is sometimes regarded as a corruption of "the goose honks high," on the supposition that, in fair weather, the geese fly high and honk as they fly. The editors of the *Dictionary of American English*, however, report that they find "no convincing evidence" of such a corruption. Dr. Frank H. Vizetelly, in his *Deskbook of Idioms and Idiomatic Phrases* (1923), considers that the expression alludes to the one-time cruel American sport of gander pulling. As described in 1818 by Henry B. Fearon, in his *Sketches of America*, "This diversion consists in tying a live gander to a tree or pole, greasing its neck, riding past it at full gallop, and he who succeeds in pulling off the head of the victim, receives the laurel crown." Presumably Dr. Vizetelly thought that if the gander (or goose) was tied to the tree high enough, the contestants were assured of good sport.

to take for a ride

This may be jocular or serious; one is sometimes taken for a ride when he suffers nothing more severe than being kidded, made the butt of some joke. But in a sinister and the original sense the person taken for the ride rarely returns. The expression was of underworld origin, coined in the United States during the wave of criminality after World War I, when rival gangs of law-breakers waged warfare on each other. Anyone incurring the displeasure of a gang chieftain was likely to be invited by a henchman to go for a ride in the car of the latter, ostensibly to talk matters over and clear up the misunderstanding. The victim rarely returned from such a trip; his body might later be found by the police—or might not.

to let the cat out of the bag

If all the truth were known, our ancestors probably knew and practiced more sales tricks than the sliest and most unscrupulous merchants ever heard of today. Elsewhere is told one reason why a person was warned not "to buy a pig in poke," but, so it is said, there was another more potent reason—one might not get even a  stunted piglet; the wriggling contents of the bag, so like a lively pig, might be a cat. A luckless tradesman, who may not have examined each poke carefully that he had bought from a countryman, indeed "let the cat out of the bag" when the housewife insisted upon seeing the quality of the pig she thought of buying. Once a literal statement, we use the expression nowadays with the meaning, to disclose something that has been kept secret. Literary use of the saying is not very old, going back only about two hundred years, but in common speech it is likely that usage antedates that by another two hundred years at least.

to play to the gallery

To seek popular acclaim. The expression came from the theater, as long ago, at least, as the seventeenth century. Originally, the notion seems to have been a play that was written expressly for those in an audience thought to have been of lower intelligence and, hence, to occupy the gallery seats, rather than for the educated persons who had seats below. Later, the reference was—as it is today—to the actor or other public person who, cheapening his abilities, seeks the favor of the populace without troubling to exhibit qualities that might also win the approval of the fewer persons able to appreciate skill and artistry. In America, a synonymous expression, with the baseball diamond as its source, is "to play to the grandstand," that is, to play for applause from the grandstand; hence, to do something showy for effect.

to cut the Gordian knot

Gordius was the king of ancient Phrygia, in Asia Minor, during the times of Alexander the Great. He had, according to legend, tied the yoke of his chariot with an exceedingly intricate knot; so intricate that, by promise of the oracle, all of Asia would become the subject of whatever man could succeed in loosening it. When Alexander reached Phrygia, wishing to leave nothing undone that might inspire his army or impress enemies with his invincibility, he took his sword and, with one blow, severed the cord that tied the yoke to the chariot of Gordius. Thanks to the Roman historian, Justin, known almost only by his works, the legend has come down to us. And even now we "cut the Gordian knot" whenever we refuse to become enmeshed in a difficulty and use bold tactics in overcoming it. Shakespeare knew the term and used it in *Henry V*, Act I, scene 1. Therein, the Archbishop of Canterbury, pleased by the unsuspected virtues of Henry V, newly made king, says to the Bishop of Ely, "Turne him to any Cause of Pollicy, The Gordian Knot of it he will vnloose."

to swap horses in midstream

This homely American phrase is just our way of saying "to change leaders (generals, presidents, or what have you) during the course of an engagement (or at the height of a crisis)," and the point is always stressed that such change may lead to disaster. As a matter of literary record, Abraham Lincoln is credited with the utterance, though one historian of that period said that Lincoln quoted an old Dutch farmer, and Mencken reports the occurrence of the phrase some twenty-four years before Lincoln used it. The occasion of Lincoln's use was an informal address that he made to a delegation from the  National Union League who had called to offer their congratulations upon his renomination for the presidency, June 9, 1864. Lincoln knew that there had been considerable disaffection with the conduct of the Civil War and that many loyal Republicans felt that he had failed as the commander in chief. Hence, in his speech, he said, "I do not allow myself to suppose that either the Convention or the League have concluded to decide that I am either the greatest or the best man in America, but rather they have concluded it is not best to swap horses while crossing the river, and have further concluded that I am not so poor a horse that they might not make a botch of it in trying to swap."

halcyon days

The seven days preceding and the seven days following the shortest day of the year, believed by the ancients always to be windless and calm; hence, any protracted time of peace and serenity, rest and rejoicing. According to Greek legend, Halcyone and her husband, whom she had found drowned upon the shore, were turned into birds by the gods and were thereafter known as halcyons, or, as we call them, kingfishers. Their nests were believed to be built upon the sea, and the gods decreed that whenever these birds wished to build their nests, the sea should remain perfectly calm and unruffled. They made their nests, according to Pliny, during the seven days preceding the winter solstice and brooded upon their eggs during the next seven days. The same writer says that the nests, as they floated upon the water, resembled a kind of ball, not unlike a large sponge. The legend, of course, and Pliny's description are equally fanciful, but they were believed as late as 1398 when John de Trevisa, in translating *De Proprietatibus Rerum* by Bartholomæus, wrote, "In the cliffe of a ponde of Occean, Alicion, a see foule, in wynter maketh her neste and layeth egges in vii days and sittyth on brood seuen dayes."

to nail to the counter

It is usually a lie, a canard, or the like that one, emphatically, "nails to the counter." By this, the one who does the figurative nailing means that he declares or asserts publicly that the statement is false, definitely and wholly false. The allusion is to a former practice of storekeepers when taken in by a spurious coin. Such a coin, when found to be bad, was nailed to the counter where it could be handily compared with others of similar appearance when offered. Oliver

140

Wendell Holmes, the doctor and poet, is quoted as the first literary user of the expression in the figurative sense. In one of his serious works, published in 1842, he speaks of certain alleged facts that "have been suffered to pass current so long that it is time they should be nailed to the counter."

to read the riot act

When Bill, or even his sister, stays out too late, or drives too fast, or commits some other indiscretion which, we feel, requires stern reproof or threat of severe punishment upon repetition, we "read the riot act"; that is, we administer a severe scolding and a warning. The allusion is to the actual Riot Act decreed in 1716 by George I of England. That act, to quote *The Encyclopedia Britannica, Eleventh Edition*, "makes it the duty of a justice, sheriff, mayor, or other authority, wherever twelve persons or more are unlawfully, riotously and tumultuously assembled together, to the disturbance of the public peace, to resort to the place of such assembly and read the following proclamation: 'Our Sovereign Lord the King chargeth and commandeth all persons being assembled immediately to disperse themselves, and peaceably to depart to their habitations or to their lawful business, upon the pains contained in the act made in the first year of King George for preventing tumultuous and riotous assemblies. God save the King.' " The penalty for disobedience was penal servitude for life or for not less than three years or imprisonment with or without hard labor for not more than two years.

plain as a pikestaff

We use this now to mean thoroughly obvious, quite clear; but originally it meant bare and unadorned. The reference was to the metal-shod staff or walking stick used by pilgrims or foot travelers during the fifteenth and sixteenth centuries. That staff was for service, rather than for show, and was polished plain and smooth through use. In some localities, the expression was "plain as a packstaff," with reference to the equally smooth staff on which a peddler carried his pack. Both phrases are found at about the same time in early sixteenth-century literature.

to upset the apple cart

To ruin one's carefully laid plans; to turn things topsy-turvey; to halt a procedure as effectively as a farmer would be halted if, on his way to market with a load of apples, his cart were to be overturned. The Romans had a similar saying, minus the apples, and with the same meaning: "Perii, plaustrum perculi! (I am undone, I have upset my cart!)" Probably the expression came into English through the translation of some witty eighteenth-century schoolboy who, when called upon to read the line in Plautus' *Epidicus*, where it occurs, called it an apple cart to be more effective. If so, the new rendition became popular almost simultaneously on both sides of the Atlantic, for concurrently with the record in England by Francis Grose in 1796 in the second edition of his *Classical Dictionary of the Vulgar Tongue*, it was used in New Hampshire by the political satirist, Thomas G. Fessenden, in one of his poetic attacks on Jefferson's policies.

to cook one's goose

To frustrate one; to ruin one's schemes or plans. As far as can be positively determined, the expression with this meaning is no older than the middle of the last century. It appeared then in a doggerel current in England at the time when Pope Pius IX, sought to re-establish the Catholic hierarchy in England through the appointment of the English cardinal, Nicholas Wiseman. The doggerel, expressive of high resentment in some quarters against the action, ran, in part:

> *If they come here we'll cook their goose,*
> *The Pope and Cardinal Wiseman.*

This does not explain the origin of our phrase, however. Both in Walsh's *Handbook of Literary Curiosities* and Brewer's *Dictionary of Phrase and Fable*, it is attributed to an incident that occurred during the reign of the "Mad King of Sweden," Eric XIV, that began in 1560. Walsh's account is the more interesting because it purports to be in the wording of some anonymous ancient chronicler. It reads: "The Kyng of Swedland coming to a towne of his enemyes with very little company, his enemyes, to slyghte his forces, did hang out a goose for him to shoote, but perceiving before nyghte that these fewe soldiers had invaded and sette their chiefe houlds on fire, they demanded of him what his intent was, to whom he replyed, 'To cook your goose.' "

To my notion, however, it would be simpler to look for the origin in the old folk tale, "The Goose that laid the Golden Eggs." Here, you will recall, the couple to whom the goose belonged became so eager to amass great wealth quickly that they couldn't wait for the daily golden egg from their rare bird, so they killed her in order to lay hands more quickly upon the eggs still within her body. Their aims were frustrated, you may remember, because the unlaid eggs had not yet turned to gold. So all they had was a dead goose which, if their former habits of frugality had not been wholly lost, they undoubtedly plucked and cooked for dinner. Both literally and figuratively, their goose was cooked.

a kettle of fish

Prefaced by some such adjective as fine, nice, or pretty, this is an ironic way of saying a terrible mess. It was so used by the British novelists, Samuel Richardson, in *Pamela*, and Henry Fielding, in *Joseph Andrews*, back in 1742. The expression is assumed to have arisen from a custom of the gentry residing along the river Tweed. According to a writer who toured the region in 1785, "It is customary for the gentlemen who live near the Tweed to entertain their neighbors and friends with a Fête Champêtre, which they call giving 'a kettle of fish.' Tents or marquees are pitched near the flowery  banks of the river . . . a fire is kindled, and live salmon thrown into boiling kettles." Scott mentioned such a picnic in *St. Ronan's Well*. Probably there were times when things went awry with the kettle of fish; maybe the chowder burned, or someone forgot the salt, or maybe the kettle would overturn. In any such instance the picnic would be ruined, the "kettle of fish" would be a sad failure.

lock, stock, and barrel

Today we would say, "the whole works," and mean the same thing. The expression is of American origin and, though the earliest literary record appears to be in one of T. C. Haliburton's "Sam Slick" stories, it probably goes back at least to the American Revolution. The three items of which the expression is comprised are the three essential components of a gun—the barrel, the stock, and the lock, or firing mechanism. In other words, the entire gun; the whole thing; the entirety.

to bury the hatchet

To settle one's differences and take up friendly relations. We in America are accustomed to think of this as an Indian custom; that it was a literal action, after the cessation of hostilities against the whites or a neighboring tribe, with considerable ceremony to bury a war tomahawk. I think, however, that the practice was merely attributed to the Indian, for I have not been able to find that there was any such ritual or saying among the Indians of North America. However, a similar saying has been extant in English speech since the early fourteenth century, more than a century and a half before the discoveries of Columbus. It was, "to hang up the hatchet," and it had the same meaning as the phrase that we attribute to the Indians. The earliest record, according to Apperson, is in a political song of about 1327: "Hang up thyn hachet ant thi knyf." The substitution of "bury" for "hang" did not take place until the eighteenth century.

Catherine wheel

In some localities such a piece of fireworks as this is called a pin-wheel, because the smaller sizes may be pinned to a tree or post where they rotate merrily, giving forth showers of sparks. The large sizes used in big celebrations have the more exalted name. Little is definitely known of the girl or woman whose name is associated with this pyrotechnic device, beyond the tradition that she lived during the reign of Maximinus in the fourth century. According to legend, she was born of a noble family in Alexandria and while a young girl embraced Christianity, becoming an ardent evangelist. The emperor, antagonistic to the spread of this belief, it is said,

144

determined that her powers of eloquence be silenced; but those charged with showing her the falsity of her beliefs were themselves converted to her faith. This so aroused the emperor that he condemned them to be burned at the stake and Catherine to be torn to pieces upon an especially devised wheel, a wheel armed along its rim with curved spikes which, as the wheel revolved, would tear the flesh from its victim. But, so the legend runs, as the torture was about to begin, a bolt of lightning shattered the wheel and severed the cords by which the maiden was bound. The miracle, however, failed to sway the emperor from his course, for he then had her scourged and beheaded. She became one of the earliest of the Roman Catholic saints; numerous chapels have been dedicated to her, and statues that honor her usually show also a representation of the wheel as her symbol. This symbol, with curved spikes on the rim, appeared often in medieval heraldry; and the name "Catherine wheel" is also sometimes applied, in church architecture, to the wheel or rose window.

to bell the cat

In figurative use this means to undertake a hazardous mission that may cost one his neck or his job, as when acting as ringleader in telling the boss that the working conditions are unpleasant. It alludes to an ancient fable of mice and a cat. A family of mice, finding that fear of the cat so disturbs them that they are unable to forage for food, holds a meeting to discuss their problem and figure out some course of action. After a prolonged session it is decided that the  best solution is to get a brass bell and, in the words of Langland, in *The Vision of Piers Plowman,* "hangen it vp-on the cattes hals (neck); thanne here we mowen (we may hear) where he ritt (scratch) or rest." All agree upon the excellence of the scheme and they beam with pleasure over their cleverness. But the meeting is thrown into consternation when one graybeard steps forward, calls for attention, and solemnly asks the question, "Who will bell the cat?"

An historic use of the phrase occurred in Scotland in 1482. The king, James III, influenced by certain of his courtiers, imprisoned his two brothers. A loyal group of the nobles of Scotland determined, however, even at the risk of displeasing their sovereign, to save him from his courtiers by seizing them and turning them over to the assassin. They found that it would be necessary actually to enter the king's presence in order to apprehend the false counselors, but the Earl of Angus offered to run the grave risk and said, "I will bell the cat." The deed was accomplished, but, so history says, one of the king's brothers had already died or had been murdered, and the other had fled to France.

in the nick of time

It means, of course, at the critical or precise moment; just at the instant when our hero was saved at the last moment from onrushing death, for example. The expression is about three centuries old, formed when someone added the redundant "of time" to the older expression, "in the nick," which meant the same thing. A nick is a groove, a notch, as made with a sharp knife when one cuts a *V* in a stick of wood. Nothing could express precision more accurately than a notch so formed, especially when applied to time.

Procrustean bed (bed of Procrustes)

In Greek legend, Procrustes was a notorious robber, living on the roadside near Eleusis. Unsuspecting weary travelers who stopped at his home for an overnight rest were always accommodated. But Procrustes had two beds, one that was overly long and one that was unusually short. A tall traveler would be given the short bed, whereas a short traveler would be shown to the long bed. But to overcome these discrepancies, the inhumane bandit merely chopped off the legs of his tall guest or stretched the bones of the short one. In either case the victim died, but Procrustes had fitted his guests to his beds. Thus, in figurative use, we speak of a Procrustean bed, or bed of Procrustes, when we must use violent or arbitrary measures in an attempt to fit something to a condition with which it does not readily conform.

146

like a bull in a china shop

Like one, who, heedless of physical damage or the personal feelings of anyone, shoulders his way through delicate situations. This is another of the numerous idiomatic waifs in English literature which, like Topsy, apparently "jus' growed." One would expect a story back of the saying, but none has been found. The nearest is one from Aesop's fables, "The Ass in the Shop of the Potter," in which the Ass, pictured as clumsy and stupid, breaks most of the earthen pots in the shop, awkwardly knocking down two while trying not to bump into a third. The expression is not an old one; no earlier literary record has been found than in Marryat's *Jacob Faithful*, written in 1834—but I suspect that its origin may have been a cartoon, an illustration of  some sort poking fun at some British political event of the early nineteenth century. This cartoon, I would surmise, depicted "John Bull" in the role of the Ass and, with reference to some episode or event connected with British trade with China, threatening the destruction of a "China" shop, substituted by the artist for the potter's shop of the fable. The episode may have been the failure of Lord Amherst's diplomatic mission to China in 1816, or the events may have had to do with the termination of the monopoly by the East India Company, in 1834, of trade with China. The cartoonist may have been some such political satirist as George Cruikshank, or the earlier caricaturists, James Gillray or Thomas Rowlandson.

apple of discord

Anything that furnishes a cause for disagreement. The allusion is to an oft-told Greek legend which relates that Eris, goddess of discord, angry because she alone of all the goddesses had not been invited to the wedding of Peleus, king of Thessaly, and the sea nymph, Thetis, threw a golden apple among the guests, upon which she had written, "For the fairest." Hera, Pallas, and Aphrodite (in Roman mythology, Juno, Minerva, and Venus) each claimed the beautiful apple. Unable to settle their disagreement, they called upon Paris, son of Priam, king of Troy, to decide the issue. Hera promised him the sovereignty of all Asia; Pallas, all glory in war; Aphrodite, the fairest woman on earth as his wife. After careful deliberation, Paris made his decision in favor of Aphrodite, and as his reward claimed Helen, wife of Menelaus, King of Sparta, as his wife, bearing her off with the aid of Aphrodite. The result of the decision is amusingly told by Thackeray in *Roundabout Papers:*

"Angry, indeed!" says Juno, gathering up her purple robes and royal raiment. "Sorry, indeed!" cries Minerva, lacing on her corselet again, and scowling under her helmet. . . . "Hurt, forsooth! Do you suppose we care for the opinion of that hobnailed lout of a Paris? Do you suppose that I, the Goddess of Wisdom, can't make allowances for mortal ignorance, and am so base as to bear malice against a poor creature who knows no better? You little know the goddess nature when you dare to insinuate that our divine minds are actuated by motives so base. A love of justice influences *us.* We are above mean revenge. We are too magnanimous to be angry at the award of such a judge in favor of such a creature." And, rustling out their skirts, the ladies walk away together. This is all very well. You are bound to believe them. They are actuated by no hostility; not they. They bear no malice —of course not. But when the Trojan War occurs presently, which side will they take? Many brave souls will be sent to Hades, Hector will perish, poor old Priam's bald numskull will be cracked, and Troy town will burn, because Paris prefers golden-haired Venus to ox-eyed Juno and gray-eyed Minerva.

on tenterhooks

We use this now always in the figurative sense, "in anxious suspense." But a tenter is really a device used in the final processes of the manufacture of woolen cloth; its function is to stretch the cloth, thoroughly wetted in a previous process, in such manner as to rid it from wrinkles when dry. The olden tenter was an upright frame or railing of wood, the cloth being suspended from hooks along the upper rail and similarly attached to the lower rail, which was adjustable and could be fixed at any height by means of pegs. As an incidental note, it is interesting to observe that even in the days of

148

Richard III there were so many unscrupulous weavers who stretched their cloth so much that he had to pass laws obliging them to use none but public tenters.

Because of the construction of a tenter, especially the hooks along the upper rail, other similar devices were anciently also known as "tenters." Thus, the framework provided with hooks and used by a butcher was sometimes called a tenter. But particularly because the tenter was a stretching device and not unlike the rack in its construction, that instrument of torture was also called a tenter. And it was from this last device that we have our present-day figurative phrase, "on tenterhooks."

to peter out

The dictionaries say, "source unknown," so we'll do a little guessing. It originated in America; this much is very certain. Because it was known and used by Lincoln when he was a young man—a store in which he was a partner "petered out" when he was in his thirties —we know that it has been used more than a hundred years. It is possible that the expression originated through allusion to some certain man by the name of Peter, who, with an infinite capacity for engaging in new enterprises, never had the ability to carry any one to success; each in turn may have tapered off into failure. But I think it more likely that some irreverent American may have used it first in allusion to the apostle, Peter, with especial reference to his conduct as recorded in the eighteenth chapter of John. There, as you may recall, when Jesus was seized in the Garden of Gethsemane, Peter, flushed with devotion and eagerness, grasped a sword and rushed to his defense; but within the next few hours his enthusiasm had diminished to such an extent that before the cock crowed he had thrice denied that he even knew Jesus. At any rate, our expression could relate to the zeal shown by Peter, for in our use it means to taper off, to fail, to come to an end.

to fight like Kilkenny cats

In modern parlance, this would be an all-out fight, tooth and nail, no holds barred, a fight to the finish. There are three stories that have been advanced to explain the Kilkenny cats, and probably none of them is true. One is a legendary battle between a thousand cats of Kilkenny and a thousand selected from all other parts of Ireland.

In this battle, which lasted all night, the felines of Kilkenny were still alive in the morning, but a thousand dead cats lay on the field.

The second and more popular one refers it to a period, about 1800, when Kilkenny was occupied by a troop of Hessian hirelings. Some of these ruffians, bored by inaction, got the brilliant notion to tie a couple of cats by the tail, hang them over a clothesline, and enjoy the ensuing fight. One night, it is said, an officer heard the terrific caterwauling and started toward the barracks to investigate. Though warned of his approach, there was not time to untie the cats, so a quick-witted soldier seized a sword, cut off their tails and the cats dashed out of the windows. The officer, seeing the two tails over the line, was told that the cats had clawed each other until nothing but their tails remained.

But the third account, told by Dean Swift, is the most probable. It relates that the town of Kilkenny, lying on either side of a small stream, was populated by two warring factions in the seventeenth century—Englishtown on one side and Irishtown on the other. Friction was intense; hot tempers led to blows, and the turmoil was so constant that the town was prostrated.

"Gentlemen Prefer Blondes"

As far as is known, Anita Loos originated this expression when selecting it as the title of her book; but she may have taken the idea from an amusing book, *The New King Arthur*, which first appeared anonymously in 1885, but was written by an American poet, Edgar Fawcett. The book is a burlesque of Tennyson's *The Idylls of the King*, and in it Sir Galahad, "the spotless knight," is depicted as an insufferably vain prig. Vivien, a brunette lady-in-waiting to Queen Guinevere, desperately in love with Galahad, has sought vainly for the magical "face-wash and hair-dye," alleged to be a secret concoction of Merlin, the magician, for both she and

Galahad think that his affection would be fixed upon her if she were a "Saxon blonde." Frustrated in obtaining the concoction, she says at last:

> Sir Galahad, canst thou never love me, then,
> If I remain brunette? I promise thee
> That no brunette of more domestic turn
> Has ever lived as wife than I would prove.

To which Galahad loftily replies:

> Hadst thou been blonde . . . ah, well, I
>   will not say
> What joy has perished for all future time!
> O Vivien, wildly, passionately loved!—

Vivien: *My Galahad! Dost thou mean it?*

Galahad: *No, not now.*
> I would have meant it, wert thou only blonde.
> Farewell, by blonde that art not nor canst be
> This woful barrier lies between us twain
> Forevermore. I shall be virgin knight
> Henceforth, with one long sorrow in my soul,
> And all my dreams and thoughts to one sad
>   tune
> Set ceaselessly—"She might have been a
>   blonde!"

dog days

These are the extremely hot days that, in the Northern Hemisphere, occur during July and August. It used to be the popular belief that this hot period was given the name "dog days" or "canicular days," because dogs frequently went mad in such weather. Actually the name has an astronomical source. It is the period in which the Dog Star, Sirius, the most brilliant star in the constellation Canis Major (the Greater Dog), rises in conjunction with the sun. In ancient belief it was the combined heat of Sirius and the sun, while these two heavenly bodies are in conjuction, that brought about the sultry weather.

to flog a dead horse

One means by this to try to revive interest in an issue that appears to be entirely hopeless. "Dead horse" has long been used (for more than three centuries) as meaning something of no present value—as, "to pay, or work, for a dead horse," to continue to pay or labor for something that no longer exists, like continuing to pay the instalments on an automobile after it was smashed. The present phrase, however, dates only to the last century. It is ascribed to the British statesman and orator, John Bright, who probably used it on at least two occasions. One was when John, Earl Russell, sought the passage by Parliament of a reform measure, and the other was when his friend, Richard Cobden, was similarly seeking a reduction in expenditures. Bright favored both of these measures; both had at one time interested the Parliament, but that interest had waned. It was, as Bright said, like flogging a dead horse to rouse Parliament from its apathy.

to go the whole hog

From the evidence, this first attained popularity in the United States in the early nineteenth century, though it was not long before it was also being used in England. That is, the earliest printed use was American, in 1828, but that does not debar the possibility that it was not already well established in the common speech of either country some years earlier. From the first, the meaning has been to accept without reservation; to support wholeheartedly; to carry through to completion; to stop at nothing; to go all the way.

It is highly probable that the expression arose from a poem of William Cowper's—"The Love of the World Reproved; or Hypocrisy Detected." The works of this versatile genius were highly popular during his lifetime (1731-1800) and for many years afterward, though he is remembered now chiefly through his "Diverting History of John Gilpin." We need not here quote the whole of "Hypocrisy Detected," but the part which connects it with the theme of the present study runs as follows:

> *Thus say the prophet of the Turk,*
> *Good mussulman, abstain from pork;*
> *There is a part in every swine*

No friend or follower of mine
May taste, whate'er his inclination,
On pain of excommunication.
Such Mahomet's mysterious charge,
And thus he left the point at large.
Had he the sinful part express'd,
They might with safety eat the rest;
But for one piece they thought it hard
From the whole hog to be debar'd;
And set their wit at work to find
What joint the prophet had in mind.
Much controversy straight arose,
These choose the back, the belly those;
By some 'tis confidently said
He meant not to forbid the head;
While others at that doctrine rail,
And piously prefer the tail.
Thus, conscience freed from every clog,
Mahometans eat up the hog.

Each thinks his neighbor makes too free,
Yet likes a slice as well as he:
With sophistry their sauce they sweeten,
Till quite from tail to snout 'tis eaten.

It has been suggested that the expression had another origin, a monetary one, because, just as we speak of a dollar bill as a "buck," a shilling in England or a ten-cent piece in the United States was at one time called a "hog." Thus, a great spendthrift, one willing to spend an entire shilling or a full dime upon the entertainment of a friend in a bar, was willing "to go the whole hog."

a flash in the pan

This takes us back to the days of the flintlock musket, from the late seventeenth century until, roughly, a hundred years ago. In those muskets, sparks produced from a flint struck by a hammer ignited powder in a small depression or pan; this powder was the priming by which the charge was exploded. The process was laborious and, at the best, no more certain than, in these days, that a similar spark will ignite a cigarette lighter. Also, the powder had to be kept dry. But even when the operations worked well there was always the possibility that the priming or powder in the pan would merely burn harmlessly, just emitting a flash. Hence, anything that begins in a showy or ostentatious manner, and usually after considerable preparation, but which fails to go off in the manner expected, we still call "a flash in the pan," as our ancestors have done for several centuries.

sour grapes

Though sour grapes are mentioned in the Bible, both by Jeremiah and Ezekiel, the reference there is to the ancient proverb, "The fathers have eaten sour grapes, and the children's teeth are set on edge." Our figurative use of the expression, however, is derived from the story of "The Fox and the Grapes," in Aesop's fables. In  this fable, a fox espied some delicious looking grapes hanging from a vine. It was a very hot day and his throat was parched; the grapes were exceedingly tempting and, he was sure, were just what the doctor ordered. But, try as he would, the cluster of grapes was just out of reach. Each leap fell short by several inches, and the effort made him hotter and thirstier. Finally, when he realized that he could not spring high enough to get the grapes, he became philosophical. Even if he had been able to get them, he reasoned, he would have found that the grapes were sour and inedible, so it was just as well that they were out of reach. Hence today, we, finding that something that seems especially desirable is unattainable, may comfort ourselves with the argument that we would not have liked it anyway. To which an unkind friend may cuttingly remind us of the fable by the sly remark, "Sour grapes!"

a fine Italian hand

This expression is used to mean characteristic or individual style, and it may be in a favorable sense or an unfavorable one. Thus we may say that we see a certain artist's "fine Italian hand" in a piece of work, intending thereby to say that we are able to detect his handiwork by some characteristic feature. Or we may also detect the "fine Italian hand" of a politician who, secretly, is up to some sculduggery. But this is merely an example of how meanings are altered when the source of a phrase has been forgotten. The "Italian hand" referred to is the handwriting that was introduced into England from Italy some three hundred years ago which was "fine" in comparison with the heavy Gothic or Old English (or "black letter") handwriting of the preceding centuries. Germany was among the last of the nations to adopt the "Roman" type in printing and "Italian" handwriting, but we in America have never known any other style, except as we see it in old manuscripts or books.

to look a gift horse in the mouth

This expression or proverb is so old that its origin cannot be determined. It has been traced to the writings of St. Jerome, one of the Latin Fathers of the fourth century, who then labeled it a common proverb. The expression, or a variant proverb, occurs in French, Italian, Spanish, and other languages of Europe. The reference is, of course, to the bad manners displayed by one who receives a gift if he examines it for defects. Up to a certain age, the age of a horse can be determined by looking at its teeth; though it may appear to be young and frisky, the number or condition of the teeth may show it to be almost fit for nothing but the glue-works.

before one can say Jack Robinson

This means in a couple of shakes, two shakes of a lamb's tail, or, in plain English, immediately, with no loss of time. The expression arose during the latter part of the eighteenth century and, as far as anyone has been able to discover, it was no more than a meaningless phrase. No "Jack Robinson" nor "John Robinson" attained any prominence at that period.

a chip on one's shoulder

The expression, often in the form, "carrying a chip on his shoulder," is of American origin. It is used to describe a person who assumes an air of defiance or a truculent attitude, as if daring an adversary to strike the first blow. One cannot say when the saying originated; all we know is that it had become commonplace more  than a century ago. Possibly there was a connection between the chip that one dared another to knock off his shoulder and the chip of the ancient proverb, "Hew not too high lest chips fall in thine eye." By the late sixteenth century this admonition against peril had become something of a challenge; one who was fearless dared to look high without regard to falling chips. When transferred to America, this chip, which had become a figurative term for consequences, may have again become a real chip placed at the height of one's shoulder to warn an adversary against "hewing too high."

to go berserk (or berserker)

In Norse mythology, there was a famous, furious fighter who scorned the use of heavy mail, entering battle without armor, thus acquiring his name, Berserker, or "Bear Shirt." It was said of him that he could assume the form of wild beasts, and that neither iron nor fire could harm him, for he fought with the fury of wild beasts and his foes were unable to touch him. Each of his twelve sons also carried the name Berserker, and each was as furious a fighter as the father. From these legendary heroes the early Norse described any fierce fighter as a "berserker," especially one so inflamed with the fury of fighting that he was equally dangerous to friend and foe. So, since the nineteenth century, we have adopted the term and say of anyone in a furious rage that he has "gone berserk," using it synonymously with "run amuck."

not to turn a hair

The allusion is to a horse which, though hot, as from racing, has not become sweaty and, therefore, its hair has not become ruffled. The horsy expression saw literary use first by Jane Austen in *Northanger Abbey*. When used figuratively it means unexcited, composed, unruffled.

a song and dance

Typical of American vaudeville since the 1870s have been performers who, coming upon the stage, open the act with a song and follow it with a dance. In theatrical parlance, such performers are called "song-and-dance artists," and many stars of later life have been included among them. Because of the nature of the performance, however, the phrase has acquired two other meanings in common speech: First, thanks to the usual nonsensical patter that precedes the song, one is said to "give a song and dance," when he tells something or, especially, offers an excuse which seems to the listener to be nothing but nonsense. Second, thanks to the necessity for the accompanist or orchestra leader to start the musical accompaniment exactly at a prearranged cue, one is said to "go into one's song and dance" when, in the course of a speech or a conversation, he begins a statement or story that he has carefully rehearsed or has related upon previous occasions.

to take time by the forelock

The ancient Grecian sages, Pittacus and Thales, both of whom lived in the sixth century B.C., and the Latin writer of fables, Phædrus, who lived in the first century A.D., all advised the ambitious person to seize the opportunity or the occasion at the moment it was presented, so this saying has been attributed to each of them. It was Phædrus, however, who described "Opportunity" as having a heavy forelock but being completely bald at the back, thus implying that one could not wait until opportunity had passed before hoping to take advantage of its offers.

In agreement with Phædrus, English usage of the expression during the sixteenth century was, "to take opportunity by the forelock." The switch from "opportunity" to "time" came about through the personification by artists of "time" as an old man carrying an hourglass and a scythe, and, borrowing from Phædrus' description, bald behind, but having a forelock.

to eat crow

To abase oneself; be obliged to accept or do something extremely disagreeable. Though this homely American saying is not found in print prior to 1877, there is no doubt that it was in common use many years earlier. According to an account in an 1888 issue of the Atlanta *Constitution*, the incident which gave rise to the expression

occurred along the Niagara River toward the end of the war of 1812. During an armistice it was the practice of the opposing garrisons to go hunting. While on such an expedition a hapless New Englander crossed the river in search of larger game, but finding nothing took a shot at a passing crow and brought it down. A British officer, hearing the shot, resolved to punish the intruder and came upon him just as the Yank was reloading his gun. But as the officer was unarmed he used diplomacy; he complimented the soldier upon so fine a shot and asked to see so excellent a weapon. The unsuspecting soldier passed it over, whereupon the Britisher brought it to his shoulder, covered the Yank, and berated him for trespassing; then, to humble him thoroughly, ordered him to take a bite out of the crow. Despite all pleas, the soldier was forced to obey; then, after a warning never to cross the river again, the officer handed back the soldier's gun and bade him be gone. But when the Englishman turned to go back to his camp, the quick-witted New Englander, now having the weapon, stopped him and ordered him to finish eating the crow. The officer begged and implored, but the soldier was firm; promises of money and gold were sternly refused; the Britisher, faced with death, ate the crow.

The incident became known, the story says, because the British officer went next day to the American commander and demanded that the soldier be punished for violating an armistice, telling his own version of the affair. When the soldier was brought in, the American captain asked him if he had ever seen the Englishman before. After several attempts to speak, the stuttering Yankee finally had the wits to say, "W-w-why y-y-yes, Captin', I d-d-dined with him y-y-yesterday."

sub rosa or under the rose

Whether Latin or English, German (*unter der Rose*) or French (*sous la rose*), it means in strict privacy, utter confidence, absolute secrecy. This ancient expression it is said, came down to us from the Greeks who, seeing the Egyptian god, Horus, seated under a rose and, depicted with a finger at his lips, thought that he was the god of silence. The concept was mistaken, however, for the rose was a lotus and the infant god was sucking his finger. But the mistake survived and gave rise in turn to an apocryphal story in Latin. This relates that Cupid, wishing to have the love affairs of his mother, Venus, kept hidden from the other gods and goddesses, bribed Harpocrates (the Latin name for Horus) to silence with the first rose that was ever created. And this story is credited by some as the origin of the phrase.

It has also been said that the expression was derived from some wholly unknown Teutonic source and that, during the Middle Ages, it was translated into Latin and thus spread throughout Europe. Verification of this theory is said to have existed in ancient German dining-halls where a rose was carved upon the ceilings as a reminder that whatever might be revealed by tongues loosened with wine should not be divulged outside. The phrase was known in the English court of Henry VIII, but apparently was not then so widely known as not to require explanation, for in a letter in 1546 that became one of the state papers is the passage: "The sayde questyons were asked with lysence, and that yt shulde remayn under the rosse, that is to say, to remayn under the bourde, and no more to be re-hersyd."

a round robin

A petition or the like signed by a number of persons in such manner that the order of signing cannot be determined, usually as if the signatures were spokes radiating from a hub. This method of submitting a petition is supposed to have originated among British sailors during the seventeenth or early eighteenth centuries when presenting a grievance to the captain and officers of a ship. In those days the captain had absolute authority, when at sea, over the members of his crew and, usually, would inflict severe punishment upon any man who dared question any order or make any complaint. But a captain could not punish an entire crew who signed a petition, nor could he pick out the instigator of such a petition for punishment if he could not tell who had first signed it. The name is often supposed to have come from the French *rond ruban*, round ribbon, but the course is difficult to follow. In the sixteenth century, however, there was some device, perhaps a toy, or some trick practiced by sharpers that was known as a round robin. It is mentioned both by Miles Coverdale, in 1546, and by Nicholas Ridley, in 1555, and in association with "jack-in-the-box," which at that time was, to quote Nares, "a thief who deceived tradesmen by substituting empty boxes for others full of money." Coverdale, defending a religious ceremony, wrote: "Certayne fonde talkers applye to this mooste holye sacramente, names of despitte and reproche, as to call it Iake in the boxe, and round roben, and suche other not onely fond but also blasphemouse names." (In those days, "fond" meant foolish.) As the nature of this sixteenth-century "round robin" is wholly unknown, we cannot determine why it was so called nor the reason for giving its name to the sailors' petition.

higher than Gilderoy's kite

Gilderoy was an actual person. Just when he was born isn't certain or important; but he died, unmistakably, at Edinburgh, Scotland, in June, 1636. His real name was Patrick MacGregor; the nickname "Gilderoy" came from his red hair—"Gillie roy," a red-haired gillie, or red-haired laddie. But Gilderoy got into evil ways; he became a highwayman, and it was his proud boast that he had robbed Cromwell, picked the pocket of Cardinal Richelieu, and that he had hanged a judge. In due course he, along with five of his companions, was apprehended and sentenced to be hung. So especially heinous were his crimes that, according to the legal custom of the period, the gallows erected for him was very high, far higher than those for his fellows. "Kite" is a Gaelic word for "belly," sometimes used figuratively for the entire body. So, referring to our phrase, for anyone to be hung or to be higher than Gilderoy's body when it swung from the gibbet would mean that it would be exceedingly high.

In William Percy's *Reliques of Ancient English Poetry* is a ballad presumably sung by Gilderoy's sweetheart, one stanza of which runs:

Of Gilderoy sae fraid they were
They bound him mickle strong.
Till Edenburow they led him thair
And on a gallows hong:
They hong him high abone the rest,
He was so trim a boy. . . .

in two shakes of a lamb's tail

One who has seen a lamb shake its tail, sees readily that this saying means with no loss of time, for a lamb can shake its tail twice "before one can say Jack Robinson." Usage appears to be entirely American, going back a hundred years or longer. The probabilities are that the saying is a humorous enlargement of the older "in a couple of (or brace of, or two) shakes," a slang saying first recorded by Richard Barham in *Ingoldsby Legends* in 1840, but probably much older. This latter saying has been variously interpreted—as alluding to a double shake of the hand, two shakes of a dice box, two shakes of a dustcloth, or whatever it may be that takes little more time in shaking twice than in shaking once.

Garrison finish

A spectacular success when defeat seems inevitable. The expression is usually applied to a race, but is often used in connection with a political campaign or the like in which a candidate whose chance seems hopeless makes a strong and unexpected last-minute effort that wins the victory. Edward H. Garrison was the man to whom the term was first applied. He was a famous jockey, better known as "Snapper" Garrison, who died after a long career on the turf in 1931. Among the practices he is said to have introduced, according to an account in the New York *Herald Tribune* at the time of his death, was the so-called "Yankee seat,"—standing high in the stirrups and bending low over the horse's mane. The term "Garrison finish" was coined during 1882. In the Suburban for that year "Snapper" Garrison first demonstrated a technique that he had worked out. He held his horse in, trailing those bunched ahead, until the last furlong; then, in a superb ride, he brought his mount, Montana, past all others to win at the finish by a nose. It is said that he was unusually successful in pulling off this stunt in later races, taking a horse that appeared to be jaded to a strong finish. The first and later successes made that type of race a byword on the racetrack, from which the name spread into other applications.

on the bum

One may be feeling "on the bum" when he's not OK physically. It is an American expression, dating back fifty years or so. George Ade was the first to use it in print, but it comes from a dialectal English use of "bum," which for four hundred years has been a childish word for drink. The American phrase thus first signified the condition one is in or the way one feels after overindulgence in drink.

But "on the bum" also means itinerant, living the life of a hobo. This second American use derives from a slang term which was current in San Francisco about a hundred years ago, or during the gold rush. A "bummer" was a worthless loafer; later, during the Civil War, a deserter who lived by raiding the countryside. Maybe the word was derived from the German *Bummler*, an idler, a loafer.

catch as catch can

This is what we say these days when we mean to catch in any manner that one can devise, by hook or by crook. But six hundred years ago when the expression was new our forefathers said, "catch that catch may," or, in the quaint spelling then used, "cacche that cacche might."

to lie in one's teeth

To accuse a person of lying in his teeth is the strongest of accusations, implying that the person is such a double-dyed liar as to be unfamiliar with truth. It is very old, traceable to the early 1300s, as in *The Romances of Sir Guy of Warwick*, "Thou liest amidward and therefore have thou maugreth (shown ill will)."

to set one's teeth on edge

The full proverb, as quoted by the prophet Jeremiah, ran, "The fathers have eaten a sour grape, and the children's teeth are set on edge." The thought of the proverb was that children would suffer from the iniquities of the father, a thought denied by the prophet, Ezekiel, who quoted the same proverb. This very ancient saying has nothing to do with our use of the expression, "sour grapes," but referred rather to the physical effect from eating anything as tart as unripe grapes, a tingling that seems to disturb the very edges of the teeth. Shakespeare, in *Henry IV*, gave us the figurative meaning that anything jarring to the sensibilities, such as "mincing Poetrie," sets one's teeth on edge.

apple polishing

The term is recent; the practice was known to your grandfathers and probably goes back to the Garden of Eden. Undoubtedly the wily serpent saw to it that the apple of the tree of knowledge looked attractive before offering it to Eve. The apple polisher of today is one who offers blandishments; one who, his father would have said, uses "soft soap," or what his grandfather  would have called "soft sawder." The term got its name from the long-time practice of the schoolboy—rarely schoolgirl—of carrying a beautiful and tasty, highly polished apple to school as a "gift" to his "well-beloved" teacher. Of course, it was nothing but a bribe, hopefully offered to one whom he secretly considered a lantern-jawed harridan, with the silent prayer that she would overlook any peccadillos that day.

to burn the candle at both ends

In the figurative sense this phrase originally referred to the wasting of one's material wealth, as when a husband and wife were both spendthrifts. We still use it with that sense, but our usual application is to the wasteful consumption of one's physical powers, as when a person tries to work all day and write a book in his evenings and spare time. It is not a new saying, and was not originally English, for Cotgrave, who died in 1611, records it in his French-English dictionary, "Brusler la chandelle par lex deux bouts."

soft soap

There have been many terms devised through the centuries for flattery, many of which have been retained in the language. "Soft soap" came into vogue sometime during the early nineteenth century, probably in allusion to the peculiarly unctuous quality of the semi-liquid soap that is called soft soap. Its predecessor was "soft sawder," or "soft solder," which was a solder with a peculiarly oily feel that melted at low temperatures.

to take to the tall timber

The twentieth-century version of the nineteenth-century "to break for high timber," and with the same meaning, i.e., to decamp suddenly and without ceremony. The original notion, back in the early 1800s, seems to have been literal, to make a break for heavily timbered regions so as to make pursuit difficult. The earliest "high timber" actually mentioned was, in 1836, along the banks of the Mississippi west of Illinois.

Black Maria

This is the popular name for a police wagon or van, the vehicle sent from a police station to pick up or transport persons under arrest. The source of the name is altogether traditional, not known to be fact, but generally accepted. The name is said to be the familiar sobriquet of a Negress, Maria Lee, who ran a lodging house for sailors in Boston, probably in the early 1800s. She was a woman of huge stature and, it is said, willingly assisted the police whenever her lodgers became unruly or violated the law. If this story is true, her name must have made a deep impression upon such British subjects as fell afoul of the law when guests at her house, for the appellation "Black Maria" was first applied to a prison van in London.

gone to pot

We use the expression now to mean ruined; destroyed; disintegrated. But the earliest English usage, which goes back at least to the sixteenth century, seems to have been literal, actually gone to *the* pot, chopped up into pieces, as meat, for stewing in a pot. There seems to have been a figurative meaning, too, in early usage, for a number of writers use the phrase with allusion to death, in some instances with the implication that the person dying had been the victim of a cannibalistic feast. Thus in one of John Jackson's sermons, published in 1641, speaking of the persecution of the Christians under Marcus Aurelius, he wrote, "All went to the pot without respect of Sex, dignity, or number." And Edmund Hickeringill, in his *History of Whiggism*, in 1682, wrote,  "Poor Thorp, Lord Chief Justice, went to Pot, in plain English, he was Hang'd."

Other interesting explanations of the origin of the phrase occur. In *A Dictionary of Modern Slang, Cant & Vulgar Words*, published in 1860, the thought is advanced that the phrase comes down from the classic custom of putting the ashes of the dead in an urn. Brewer, in *Dictionary of Phrase and Fable*, says "The allusion is to the pot into which refuse metal is cast to be remelted, or to be discarded as waste." There is no literary support for either theory, however.

pope's nose

We also call it the part of a chicken that last goes over a fence; that is, the rump of a fowl. The name is said to have been applied to this tidbit during the days following the reign of James II of England when feeling was intense against the possibility that the British throne might again be occupied by a Roman Catholic. Some unnamed wit, during that troubled time, fancied a resemblance between the rump of a fowl and the nose of the pope—and the allusion stuck. But the witticism was not all on one side because, in America, at least, that "epicurean morsel," as Longfellow termed it, is just as well known as the "parson's nose," and has been so called since the early part of the nineteenth century.

namby-pamby

Henry Carey, who died in 1743, was both musician and poet. The song by which he is best remembered is "Sally in our Alley," though his original air for the song has been replaced by a tune composed by another. He is also reputed to have been the author and composer of the British national anthem, "God Save the King."

Ambrose Philips, who died in 1749, was also a poet. Both of these men were contemporaries of Addison, Steele, Swift, and Pope, living at a time when literary England was divided in allegiance between Addison and Pope. Philips, whose works were chiefly pastoral poems, received high praise from Addison, who at the same time ignored Pope's works in the same field. Hence, when Philips produced an insipid, sentimental poem addressed "to the infant daughter of Lord Carteret," Pope's scorn knew no bounds.

Now the nickname of Ambrose is "Namby." It is not certain whether Pope or Carey, who shared Pope's scorn, first hit upon the use of Philips' second initial for the reduplication, but Carey seized upon it and wrote a parody of Philips' sentimental poem under the title "Namby Pamby." Thus the term came into our language, and we still hold to the original meaning, "sickly sentimental; insipid."

bears and bulls

In stock market parlance, a bear is a speculator who sells a stock that he does not own in the belief that before he must deliver the stock to its purchaser its price will have dropped so that he may make a profit on the transaction. A bull, on the other hand, is optimistic of future rises in the value of a stock; he buys at what he  believes to be a low price, encourages a demand for the stock, and thus expects to make his profit by selling at an increased value. (Both gentlemen may get stung.) The terms have acquired additional meanings, but these are the basic senses.

We must again go to Exchange Alley, in London, (see *lame duck*) to learn how these names originated. "Bear" was the earlier of the two designations. Even back in Bailey's English Dictionary of 1720, we find the definition, "*to sell a bear:* to sell what one hath not." The allusion here is to an old proverb, so old that it is in many languages, appearing in many forms. The English version was, "to sell the bear-skin before the bear is caught." Thus, in Exchange Alley, stock sold, but not owned by one speculating on a decrease in price, was formerly called a "bear-skin," and the dealer was known as a "bear-skin jobber." Later, although still two hundred years ago, the title of the dealer was contracted to "bear."

The origin of "bull," used in this sense prior to 1720, is not positively known. It is probable, however, that it was adopted through the long association of the two words, bear and bull, in the old English sports of bearbaiting and bullbaiting.

in one's black book

This has now no more sinister meaning than a loss of favor, more or less temporarily; but at one time to have one's name entered upon an official book with a black cover was a very serious matter. The first of these historic books of ill omen was one compiled in the reign of Henry VIII. It was a report on the English monasteries, and as Henry was desirous of seizing the papal authority and revenue in England, each of the monasteries listed in the report was conveniently found to be a seat of "manifest sin, vicious, carnal, and abominable living." It was not difficult to induce Parliament, therefore, to dissolve these monasteries and, in 1536, to assign their property to the king.

The saying itself arose from that historic incident, but there were later "black books" in which records were kept of persons charged with violations of the law or of misdemeanors. One of these, in the eighteenth century, was a university list of students under censure; another, in the British army, named the officers who had committed offenses; another, begun some seventy-odd years ago and annually extended, listed the habitual criminals of England. So, although we may lightly say that we are in someone's "black book," it might be discreet to avoid the expression when a police officer is about.

Incidentally, a "black list" has a similar connotation. This is a list of persons who are under suspicion. Popular use of the expression apparently goes back to the reign of Charles II of England, with reference to the list of persons implicated in the trial, condemnation, and execution of his father, Charles I. Clemency was ultimately extended to all but the fifty-eight men who, as judges, condemned his father to death.

three sheets in the wind

This means, of course, pretty drunk, reeling from too much indulgence in strong drink, somewhat more tipsy than "half-seas over." Like many other common expressions, the phrase dates back to the times when ocean navigation was entirely by sail. But in nautical use, a sheet is not a sail, as landsmen are accustomed to suppose, but the rope or chain attached to the lower corner of a sail by which the angle of the sail is controlled. In a strong wind the sheet may be loosened, and is then said to be "in the wind," flapping and fluttering without restraint. If all three sheets are loose, as in a gale, the vessel staggers and reels very much like a drunken person.

to kick the bucket

At best, this is a disrespectful synonym for "to die." Perhaps if we used it only of animals, or especially of animals slaughtered for food we might approach a literal meaning and the phrase would lose its humorous concept. The evidence on the original meaning is slight and perhaps future etymologists will find other and stronger clues for another interpretation. This evidence is that "bucket," in this phrase, refers to a beam or yoke on which anything may be hung or carried. This evidence is supported by Levin's *Dictionarie of English and Latine Wordes*, published in 1570, and also by Shakespeare's use of "bucket" in *Henry IV*, "Swifter than hee that gibbets on the brewers bucket." Further evidence appeared in *Notes & Queries* about 1860, in which a correspondent stated that even at that time in East Anglia "to kick the bucket" alluded to the way in which a slaughtered pig is hung up. His explanation was that "bucket" referred to a bent piece of wood placed behind the tendons of the hind legs of the pig by which the animal was suspended to a hook in a beam. Probably the dying convulsive struggles of the pig became the literal origin of the phrase.

It is interesting to note that a recent correspondent to *Notes & Queries* (April 19, 1947), who signs his communication only with the initials "C.T.S.," advances the theory that the expression comes from an old custom observed in the Catholic church. He says: "After death, when the body had been laid out, a cross and two lighted candles were placed near it, and in addition to these the holy-water bucket was brought from the church and put at the feet of the corpse. When friends came to pray for the deceased, before leaving the room they would sprinkle the body with holy water. So intimately therefore was the bucket associated with the feet of deceased persons that it is easy to see how the saying came about."

a peeping Tom

When we call anyone "a peeping Tom" we mean usually that he is a despicable person with a prurient mind. ("Prurient," to spare you a trip to the dictionary, means "inclined to lewd thoughts or desires.") A peeping Tom may be a person who peers into windows with a desire to satisfy curiosity; but whatever his purpose, he is not a popular person.

We have to go back to the eleventh century, to the story of Lady Godiva and her famous horseback ride, for the origin of the name. Although Lady Godiva was a real person, who died about the year 1080, the account of her ride may be pure fiction. Her husband,  Leofric, Earl of Mercia, it is said, levied a tax upon the people of Coventry which they found oppressive. His wife asked him to repeal the tax and, probably in jest, he promised to do so on the condition that she should ride nude through the streets of the town. Because the people of the town adored her, she had full confidence that they would obey her request that on a certain day everyone would remain indoors with the windows barred; in that confidence she rode through the town "with no covering but her flowing tresses." One person only, the town tailor, could not restrain his curiosity and peeped through a knothole in the shutter of his shop. Some say that "peeping Tom" lost his life through his curiosity, others that he became blind, but in any event his name has come down down to the present time as one who was too curious for his own good.

The story was told originally by an unknown writer in the twelfth century, about seventy-five years after Lady Godiva's death, and it forms the theme of a poem by Lord Tennyson.

at loggerheads

A loggerhead, in Shakespeare's day, was a person whom today we would call a blockhead—probably derived from an old word, *logger*, meaning heavy or stupid, plus *head*. But although Shakespeare used the term in that sense, the same word had a military meaning that was very different. In this sense it applied to a ball-like mass of iron, with a long handle, which, when heated, was used to melt tar or pitch that might be poured onto the heads of a besieging party or to set fire to an attacking vessel. The historical records do not say, but it is a logical assumption that the soldiers or sailors who were in charge of these operations with tar would, if the attackers came close enough, use their "loggerheads" as formidable weapons, bashing in such heads as came within reach. We can reasonably assume, therefore, that our present-day use of "at loggerheads," by which we mean "engaged in dispute," originated from the use of a loggerhead in battle.

to be on the beam

By this very modern expression we mean "to be on the right course"; hence, right, accurate, correct. It comes from the use of directional radio beacons established along lines of airplane travel. A continuous pulsating note emitted from the beacon is heard at its greatest intensity by an aviator when he is directly upon the course along which he should be traveling, fading off to dimness if he departs from the course to one side or the other.

living the life of Riley

There is excellent reason for the belief that the gentleman who gave life to this modern expression was given the name "Reilly" by his creator, not "Riley," but as he lived only in song and the pronunciation was the same no one will cavil over the spelling. The original song which seems to have given our present meaning—living luxuriously—was popular in the 1880s. It was a comic song, "Is That Mr. Reilly?" written by Pat Rooney. The song described what its hero would do if he suddenly "struck it rich." Some of the lines ran, "I'd sleep in the President's chair," "A hundred a day would be small pay," "On the railroads you would pay no fare," "New York would swim in wine when the White House and Capitol are mine." At the close of each verse there was a spoken line such as, "Last night while walking up Broadway the crowds shouted," and then the chorus would follow:

Is that Mister Reilly, can anyone tell?
Is that Mister Reilly that owns the hotel?
Well, if that's Mister Reilly they speak of so highly,
Upon my soul Reilly, you're doing quite well.

sent to Coventry

Why this ancient town, famed for the notable ride of the Lady Godiva, should have become a synonym for a place of ostracism, has been a matter of speculation for many years. The account favored by historians is rather tame. It relates to the Great Rebellion (1642-1649) in England, the struggle between Charles I and Parliament. Citizens of the town of Birmingham, it is said, rose against some of their fellow townsmen who were loyal to the king and sent them to the nearby town of Coventry, which strongly supported Parliament, where they would be unable to aid the king. These royalists were literally ostracized, sent into exile.

But in an old issue of Chambers' Cyclopedia we find a more interesting reason for the fact that "sent to Coventry" is equivalent to having no notice taken of one. This account states that the people of the town became so annoyed with soldiers who were harbored among them that fraternization with them was forbidden. A woman, for example, who was seen speaking to a soldier would be given the cold shoulder by her neighbors. Hence, it is said, no soldier wanted to be sent to Coventry, for he knew that while there he would be ignored by the townspeople. No date was given, but the reference was likely to have been to the same historic struggle between the king and Parliament.

with a grain of salt

Because this expression of skepticism, doubt, or distrust is so familiar to us in its Latin form, *cum grano salis*, we sometimes assume that it has great antiquity. Perhaps it does, for Pliny, in telling the story of Pompey's seizure of the royal palace of Mithradates, says that Pompey found the hidden antidote against poison which, all his life, the Asian king had been obliged to master. The closing line of the antidote read, "to be taken fasting, plus a grain of salt (*addite salis grano*)." But it is likely that this resemblance is accidental and that Pliny meant the phrase in its literal sense.

Our modern saying does not appear to be more than three centuries old. Undoubtedly the original thought was in humorous allusion to the use of a little salt to make a meal more palatable. Hence, an improbable story might be more readily swallowed by the listener if taken with a small amount of salt.

not worth a Continental

This is a long way of saying "worthless." But it is a good reminder of the early days of the United States, especially of the financial status of the country. During the War of Independence and until the Constitution was adopted, or for a period of about fourteen years, the Continental Congress was obliged to issue currency in the form of notes, but was powerless to levy taxes from the several states which would give those notes an actual cash value. These paper notes, because of their origin, were popularly called "Continentals." Because they were not secured by anything tangible, people were very loath to accept them. They became, or were thought to be, worthless, not worth the paper they were made of. The saying has remained, though in these opulent days we have forgotten that there was a time when a government note of the United States had no value.

that's the ticket!

It may sound a little far-fetched, but nevertheless it's true that this expression of approval had its origin in a mispronunciation of the French word "etiquette." Try it yourself. Put the accent on the second syllable. You will get "uh-tick'ut." Someone, perhaps a schoolboy, may have jocularly made a persistent point of such mispronunciation round the year 1800 or later in saying, "that's etiquette," that's the correct thing. From "that's uh-tick'ut," it was an easy and natural corruption to "that's the ticket," and the latter phrase acquired general use, making its bow into literature about 1838.

a feather in one's cap

To tell Johnny, "That's quite a feather in your cap," is to compliment him upon an achievement; he has done something to be proud of. Five or six centuries ago the expression was a literal statement; a man who had gained a distinction, especially upon the battlefield, actually wore a feather in his cap, or his helmet, as a token of his prowess. Later, presumably beginning in England during the reign of Henry IV, or early in the fifteenth century, any member of the English nobility was assumed to be a person of distinction, and feathers on the headgear, especially ostrich feathers, became a usual part of the costume of a nobleman.

It is said that the hunter's custom of taking a feather from the first bird slain in the hunting season and sticking it in one's cap gave rise to the saying. This may have been a Continental custom, but literary evidence fails to show its early use in England. It seems more probable that the English origin of the phrase came from an early deed of valor of Edward, "the Black Prince," son of Edward III. The young prince, who was only sixteen at the time, won his spurs in the historic Battle of Crécy, in 1346, when the English forces seemed to be so hopelessly outnumbered—nineteen thousand English and Welsh

173

soldiers again sixty thousand French and allied forces. Young Edward greatly distinguished himself in the battle, and after the English victory he is said to have been awarded the crest of John, King of Bohemia, who was one of the illustrious French allies slain in the fight. This crest consisted of three ostrich feathers, and thenceforth became the badge of each succeeding Prince of Wales. From such royal precedent it is logical that subsequent valorous deeds would receive similar decorations.

to jump (or marry) over the broomstick (or besom)

The expression isn't very common now, though it is used occasionally by writers. The dictionaries are not very explicit, saying merely that it means to go through a mock marriage ceremony, in which both parties jump over a broomstick. During the times, a few short centuries ago, when marriage laws were not very stringent and not at all uniform, a man and woman might go through the formality of publication of the banns but might live together as man and wife without waiting for the sanction of the church. This, through a popular superstition of the times, was thought to be quite proper and legal if both parties jumped over a broomstick. But in Scotland, broomstick or besom now means a prostitute, and in France *rôtir le balai*—literally, to roast the broomstick—means to lead a dissolute life. So perhaps those who "married over the broomstick" did not always or long remain in wedded state.

the jig is up

As far as the word "jig" is concerned, whatever its origin it seems to have been a very old term for a gay and lively dance, probably a dance commonly known throughout all western Europe fifteen centuries or more ago. But in England, around 1600, "jig" became also a slang term for a practical joke, a bit of trickery.

When the victim of a practical joke discovers the trickery, he is no longer fooled. Nowadays he would say, "I'm on to you," or, "I'm wise." The old expression was, "The jig is up," and we have used it since with the general meaning, the trickery is exposed, the time for settlement has come.

half-seas over

This is what we say of a man when we wish to imply that he is pretty thoroughly drunk, not yet under the table and still able to get along, after a fashion, on his own two legs; not quite "three sheets in the wind." The English allusion is probably a reference to the likeness between the half canted gait of a man when intoxicated and that of a ship heeled over in the wind, with decks half awash. But there is also a theory that "half-seas over" is an Englishman's interpretation of the Dutch expression, *op ze zober*, which literally is "oversea beer," a beer from Holland that was particularly heady and strong.

as poor as Job's turkey

Judge Haliburton—Thomas Chandler Haliburton—has about vanished from the memories of most Americans as one of the earliest of our humorists; yet he was the "Mark Twain" of the early nineteenth century. Born in Nova Scotia in 1796, trained for the bar, and raised to the bench at the age of 32, he began sending a series of literary sketches to a Nova Scotian paper under the pen name, "Sam Slick." Sam, according to these sketches, was a Yankee clockmaker and peddler, with an aptitude for quaint drollery, subtle flattery (which he called "soft sawder"), and a keen insight into human nature. It is in one of these yarns that Sam Slick, finding  the need to describe someone as even poorer than Job, who, you may recall, had been stripped of all his possessions by Satan, hit upon the expression, "as poor as Job's turkey." He explained this by saying that Job's turkey was so poor that he had but one feather to his tail and had to lean against the fence to gobble.

Simon pure

We use this when we mean that an article is genuine, not an imitation but the real thing. Sometimes for greater emphasis we say, "the real Simon pure." The author of the phrase has long since been forgotten—an English female dramatist at a period when few women could make a livelihood by writing, least of all for the stage. Susannah Centlivre died in 1723; she was twice widowed before she was thirty, when she turned to literature for a living. One of her most successful plays, *A Bold Stroke for a Wife*, concerns a Pennsylvania Quaker, Simon Pure, who has a letter of introduction to the guardian of an heiress. His letter is purloined by Colonel Feignwell, who then impersonates the Quaker and marries the heiress. Later, Simon succeeds in establishing his own identity as "the real Simon Pure."

baker's dozen

This, we all know, means thirteen. But why? The answer appears to take us back to the thirteenth century, to the reign of Henry III, though it may go still further, to the reign of King John or even to the middle of the twelfth century.

A loaf of bread, like a Swiss cheese, can be made so as to contain more air pockets than solid material. This fact appears to have been known by professional bakers even in remote times. And there were some, it appears, who did not scruple to take advantage of it. Hence, bakers as a class were viewed with suspicion—suspected, perhaps rightly, of giving their customers short weight. In Constantinople as recently as the eighteenth century, it is said, a baker guilty of selling lightweight bread might be nailed by the ears to the doorpost of his shop as a punishment.

But in England, Parliament enacted a law in 1266 for regulating the price of bread by weight, though similar royal decrees had been issued earlier. The penalty for short weight was severe. But because it is likely that few bakers were able to determine accurately the weight of a loaf and did not dare risk the penalty, it became customary to distribute thirteen loaves for every dozen ordered by the vendors who marketed the product. Each vendor, in turn, cut off a piece from the extra loaf to add to the full loaf bought by a customer. This extra, or thirteenth, loaf became known as the inbread or vantage loaf, for it gave a vantage, or chance, to the bakers and dealers to obey the law, and a surety to the customer that he was getting full weight.

176

according to Hoyle

If the ghost of Edmond Hoyle were to listen to some of the heated controversies about various games of cards, all of which are settled amicably as soon as some one is able to say, "according to Hoyle, it is thus and so," he would be the most amazed ghost that ever returned to earth. Yes, Hoyle has been dead a long time—since 1769, to be exact—and the book that he wrote, *A Short Treatise on the Game of Whist*, was written in 1742, slightly over two centuries ago. But the book that he wrote was extremely popular and authoritative; it settled all the arguments over whist that arose in his day and for more than a hundred years, until Henry Jones, who wrote under the pen name, "Cavendish," brought out his *Principles of Whist* in 1862. Hoyle continued to be quoted, nevertheless, and his name became again authoritative when, in 1897, Robert F. Foster, a specialist on games of cards, brought it back into public notice with his book covering many card games which he called *Foster's Hoyle*.

to run amuck

We are likely to forget that civilization in Malaya extends further back than the founding of Rome, so when we ascribe the origin of this phrase to the Malays we must bear in mind that it is not an indiscriminate custom of the people, just isolated practice. The Malay word *amoq* means "frenzied," or, with extended implication, "engaging furiously in battle." Various causes may exist, but there seems to be an underlying temperament among Malayans that makes them peculiarly susceptible to fits of depression. Such a spell may be caused by jealousy, or by despair, and it may be aggravated by excessive recourse to opium or other drug. Its effect is to seize the victim with a murderous frenzy. He snatches a cutlas, or native *kris*, and dashes out into the road striking at any and  everyone he meets. A cry of "Amoq! Amoq!" goes up among the people, and perhaps before the madman has been able to do much damage he is himself killed.

English use of the phrase has become more figurative than literal; we may say that a person has "run amuck" when we mean no more than that he is engaging in an unreasonable attack upon the established social order.

to the manner born

That is the way Shakespeare wrote it—m-a-n-n-e-r, not m-a-n-o-r. The phrase occurs in *Hamlet*, Act 1, scene 4. The friends of Hamlet are amazed at hearing a flourish of drums and trumpets at midnight and ask him the meaning of it. He says that it is a royal drinking custom, "But to my mind, though I am native here and to the manner born, it is a custom more honored in the breach than the observance."

In other words, when you use the phrase, bear in mind that it refers to a habit or practice, a custom of the people; it has nothing to do with rank or aristocracy or high estate, as would be implied by the word "manor."

to run the gantlet (or gauntlet)

Every youngster knows that this means, nowadays, to run between two rows of one's fellows who will try to strike him, in penalty for some fault. The extended meaning is figurative, to encounter a series of unpleasant happenings. The original literal meaning, however, was sinister, often terminating in the maiming of the unfortunate man who was compelled to undergo such a form of punishment.

During the Thirty Years' War (1618-1648) the British forces observed a form of punishment used by the Germans which was said to have originated among the Swedes. In this punishment, the severity of which could be regulated, a soldier guilty of an offense was compelled to strip to the waist and run between two lines of his fellows, each armed with a whip, leather thong, or rod. As he passed, each was supposed to strike him upon the back. The lines of men might be long or short, depending upon the severity of the punishment to be inflicted.

The Swedish word for the punishment was *gatloppe*, literally, a running of the lane. This, taken into the speech of English soldiers, became corrupted into *gantlope* and was further corrupted into *gantlet* and, through similarity of sound, into *gauntlet*.

When Old World colonists began to settle in America they found that the Indians had a similar form of punishment or torture, with the difference that the victim, usually a captive, was not expected to survive the blows of the war clubs with which his assailants were armed. From its likeness to the European punishment, this, too, was called a "gauntlet" by the whites.

at sixes and sevens

This plural form of the expression is comparatively modern, dating back only a hundred and fifty years or so. The older form, "on six and seven," however, was so old and well known in Chaucer's day that, worse luck, he didn't bother to explain what it meant when, about 1375, he used it in *Troylus and Cryseyde*.

As we use it today and as it has been used for centuries, the phrase means "in a state of disorder or confusion; topsy-turvy." Explanations of its origin have been sought, but nothing certain is known. One writer tries to connect it with a Hebrew phrase that we find in Job v, 19, "He shall deliver thee in six troubles: yea, in seven there shall no evil touch thee." Another seeks an explanation in the Arabic numerals 6 and 7, which, he points out, extend higher and lower respectively in a line of figures than do the others; hence, that these two are irregular.

But it is more probable that Chaucer's use had reference to an old dicing game. From Chaucer and other old sources we know of one game in which to try a throw of a five and a six (cinque and sice were the old names) was regarded as the most risky gamble to be made. One who staked his chance on such a throw was reckless in the extreme, utterly careless of consequences. To hazard such a throw was "to set on cinque and sice," in the old wording. It is presumed that Chaucer's use, "to set on six and seven," had reference to a similar game. From heedlessness and carelessness in taking such a risk, the expression "on six and seven," later changed to "at sixes and sevens," may have come to denote general carelessness; hence, disorder and confusion.

the real McCoy

The genuine article; the person or thing as represented. The story is told, and has not been denied, that this expression had its origin in a true incident that occurred about the turn of the present century. A prize fighter who traveled under the *nom de guerre* of "Kid McCoy," showed such promise in the late nineties that the name under which he fought was also adopted by other lesser lights who lacked something of his skill and ability. It is said that a barroom frequenter, a little the worse for drink and in an argumentative mood, cast aspersions on "McCoy" as a prize fighter. Cautioned by the barkeeper that Kid McCoy was standing near, the drunk said in a loud tone that he wasn't afraid of any McCoy. When he picked himself up from the sawdust, after "The Kid" had delivered a haymaker, he is said to have amended his remarks to "any but the real McCoy."

grass widow

In modern usage, especially in America, this term is used generally to mean a woman who is separated from her husband by divorce; but this is a recent extension of an older meaning and is virtually unknown in England. Formerly, and still in England, a "grass widow" was one who was temporarily separated from her husband.

Thus, as recently as the days of the California gold rush, there were many grass widows in the eastern states, so many that they were also known as "California widows."

Various explanations for the use of "grass" in the expression have been sought. Some think that it may have had a coarse allusion to such a woman left to fend for herself, like a horse turned out to pasture. This is certainly more plausible than a fanciful explanation advanced some seventy years ago. In this "grass" was supposed to be a corruption of "grace"; that is, a grass widow was a grace widow, "a widow by courtesy." Suffice it to say that etymologists, though gravely analyzing this claim in all details, found it altogether untenable many, many years ago—perhaps one reason was because no one could find any place where anyone had ever used the term "grace widow."

But the term "grass widow" is much older than either the present British or American meaning. It goes back at least to the sixteenth century, and the meaning that it had then is still used in some of the rural parts of England. This old meaning was a woman, usually one with child, who had never been married, who never had a legitimate husband. It is supposed that, in the crude satire of peasantry, "grass" alluded to the probable bed in which the child was begotten, and "widow" to the unmarried state of the mother. This probable explanation is strengthened through analogy with terms in other languages. Thus, in Germany, Sweden, the Netherlands, and Denmark, for example, the provincial name for an unmarried mother is, by translation, "straw widow."

beyond (or *outside*) *the pale*

We use this expression now as if it had the same meaning as "on the wrong side of the tracks"; that is, socially unfit. That is an acquired sense. "Pale" means the region or district under the jurisdiction of a governing body, the part figuratively enclosed by a paling or fence. In English history, "the pale" meant those portions of Ireland, or Scotland, or France which, at various times, were under English jurisdiction. So "beyond (or without) the pale" originally meant nothing more than outside the district ruled by England. But rogues or even honest men sometimes preferred not to be under the jurisdiction of English laws and would "leap the pale," thus becoming an outlaw or, in modern usage, a social outcast.

a flea in one's ear

Taken literally, it would be most unpleasant and irritating to have a flea in the ear, and the original sense of the phrase carried, figuratively, an even greater unpleasantness. To be sent away with a flea in the ear indicated that one had received a sharp and stinging reproof or rebuff, often wholly unexpected. Modern usage has somewhat softened the force of the phrase. Now we use it to carry no greater meaning than that of warning. To drop a flea in one's ear often means merely to caution one against some procedure.

The phrase is very old. In English it has been used for at least five hundred years, and was then a direct translation from the French of that period. Modern Frenchmen say "mettre la puce à l'oreille," to put a flea in the ear. Rabelais, in *Pantagruel*, wrote it, "la pulce en l'oreille." Maybe the Greeks had a similar expression.

the $64 question

Back in 1940, in April to be exact, a new radio "quiz" program was started under the name "Take It or Leave It," with Bob Hawk as its master of ceremony. (Hawk was succeeded in December 1941 by Phil Baker.) Contestants, as usual, were selected from the studio audience, and each in turn as he appeared before the microphone had his choice of a series of topics upon which he professed a willingness to be questioned. Thus the topic of one contestant might be geography, of another music, of a third first names of famous people, and so on. The topics were divided into seven questions. If the contestant answered the first question correctly he was awarded one dollar, and he might then take his seat if he chose; but if he elected to try the second and did so successfully, the award was two dollars; if unsuccessful, he got nothing. He could stop at any time after a correct answer; but as the promised awards were successively doubled —$4, $8, $16, $32, $64—through the remainder of the questions to be asked, most contestants elected to continue, despite cries of "You'll be sorry!" from the studio audience. Each question was supposed to be a little more difficult than the preceding, and the final one, for which the award jumped from $32 to $64, was supposed to be the most difficult of all. This came to be known as "the $64 question." Thanks to the popularity of the program, the expression became well known and any question, as to a statesman, which was difficult to answer might be called "the $64 question."

to bring home the bacon

This may be used literally or figuratively; it means "to succeed in gaining the prize, or in winning one's point." Although there is still an ancient annual custom in Dunmow, England, of awarding a flitch of bacon to any married couple who can take oath that they have never once during the year wished themselves unmarried, it is not likely that our present phrase owes its origin to that scene of competition.

It is more likely that the expression has come from the rural American sport at country fairs of catching a greased pig. The lucky winner in this slippery contest is awarded the pig that he has caught; thus, literally, he brings home the bacon. But an old dictionary in my possession, the third edition of Nathan Bailey's dictionary of 1720, contains an appendix of "Canting Words and Terms used by Beggars, Gypsies, Cheats, House-Breakers, Shop-Lifters, Foot-Pads, Highway-men, etc.," and in this collection "bacon" is defined, "the Prize, of whatever kind which Robbers make in their Enterprizes." This would indicate that our present expression would at least have been understood, if it did not originate, in the eighteenth century.

It is also interesting to note that the compiler of this old collection considered that the phrase, "to save one's bacon," had a related meaning. He carries it in the same paragraph and defines it: "He has himself escaped with the Prize, whence it is commonly used for any narrow Escape." This is significant, for the phrase was not recorded before the late seventeenth century, and it throws doubt upon the theory, recently advanced, that "bacon," in the phrase, referred to the human buttocks.

like a Dutch uncle

In England, especially during the seventeenth century, the mannerisms and characteristics of the people of Holland were held in scorn. Thus *Dutch courage* came to mean cowardice; *Dutch comfort* or *Dutch consolation* meant "Thank God, it could be worse"; *Dutch bargain*, a one-sided bargain; *Dutch nightingales*, frogs. Even in America *Dutch treat* came to mean a treat in which each person pays his own bill. But the origin of the simile "like a Dutch uncle" is not clear. It seems to have originated in the United States, but whether the allusion was to the early Dutch colonists of New York or to the Pennsylvania Dutch is uncertain, for the expression did not appear in literature  until the early nineteenth century. The people in each of those sections were noted disciplinarians, however, and woe betide the unfortunate child who, having lost its own parents, was obliged to depend upon an uncle as a foster parent. The expression indicates a merciless tongue lashing, just the reverse of the discipline usually administered by an uncle.

to call a spade a spade

It means to call a thing by its right name, to avoid euphemism or beating about the bush. The saying is so old that what we have is just a translation of the original Greek. Perhaps it was old when Plutarch, in the first century A.D., used it in writing of the life of Philip of Macedon. But, although the expression is now firmly fixed in the English language, it is quite possible that the Greeks of Plutarch's time did not have the garden implement in mind in their use of the expression. The Greek words for "spade" and for "boat" or "bowl" were very similar, and it seems likely that the better translation would have been, "to call a boat a boat." Lucian, Greek writer of the second century, used the same saying, which Erasmus in the sixteenth century translated into Latin to read, "to call a fig a fig, and a boat a boat."

not worth a tinker's dam (damn)

Whichever the spelling, the intent is that the thing or matter described by the phrase is utterly worthless, of no value. In Knight's Dictionary of Mechanics (1877) we find the interesting explanation that a tinker, having a hole or the like to solder, erects a small barrier or dam of clay about the area so that his molten solder will not flow off. The clay, once its usefulness is past, is thrown aside. This explanation is ingenious, but it leaves one dubious that the practice, if true, would have been so conspicuous as to give rise to a household expression.

But we do have excellent authority for believing that the tinkers, mostly itinerant, were a knavish, drunken, and blasphemous professional class, during the reigns of the Yorks, Tudors, and Stuarts. Blasphemy was their most characteristic failing, and "damn" was probably the most frequent and most abused word in their vocabulary. From their mouths it became meaningless. Hence, to say, "I don't care a tinker's damn," or, "that's not worth a tinker's damn," merely adds a little intensive force to one's indifference.

184

fifth columnist

The expression arose in 1936, and came to mean, without regard to the numerical sense, a person who acts secretly within a city or country toward furthering the interests of an outside enemy; a secret agent. The expression is attributed to General Emilio Mola who, leading four columns of armed rebels against Madrid during the revolution in Spain, told the foreign correspondents that he had a "fifth column" within the city, meaning an army of sympathizers and active partisans waiting to assist in its overthrow.

to cut one's eyeteeth

To acquire wisdom; to learn the ways of the world. An eyetooth is a canine tooth, the third from the center in the upper jaw. The expression is somewhat literal, for the implication is that by the time a person has got his permanent set of canine teeth, has reached the age of twelve or fourteen, he has passed out of babyhood and has reached years of discretion. This wording of the saying appears to have originated in the United States, first recorded in 1870 by the essayist, Ralph Waldo Emerson, though undoubtedly long in use before that date. The British version, dating to the early eighteenth century, is "to have one's eyeteeth"  or "to have one's eyeteeth about one." The usage differs slightly, carrying the implication of alertness against chicanery; that is, to use one's knowledge and experience in one's dealings.

to take French leave

We use this now to mean to take one's departure secretly or without authorized permission; thus, a soldier may be said to take French leave if he surreptitiously absents himself from quarters. But, despite the fact that the French counterpart of the expression is, "to withdraw as the English (*filer à l'anglaise*)," the origin of the expression is attributed to a custom that originated in France in the eighteenth century. The Emily Post of that day ruled that a guest who had a pressing engagement elsewhere might with propriety leave the function which he was attending without going through the formality of seeking his host or hostess and making a ceremonious apology for his departure. The latter, it felt, might lead to a general exodus of guests and be embarrassing to the host.

right as a trivet

A trivet is just a three-legged stool or table. The name, somewhat distorted, comes from the same source as "tripod," three footed. Anything that is three legged, as a milking stool, will stand firmly on any kind of surface. So the phrase, right as a trivet, means thoroughly right, perfectly stable. From the evidence of literary use, the expression is little more than a hundred years old; but the fact that Thomas Hood used it in 1835, and Charles Dickens put it into the mouth of one of his characters in 1837 indicates that it had long been in colloquial speech before those dates.

to go up (or down) the pike

We use this so commonly in America to mean up or down the road that we never stop to inquire the source. It is not used in England and is almost unknown there, and if we were to say "up the turnpike," by which we would mean just the same thing, an Englishman would be sure that we were daffy. He might say, "turnpike road," but would wonder at our current use of "turnpike," or our shortened form "pike."

Turnpike roads were common up to the middle of the last century. They were built by private enterprise or by a community or, as the great Cumberland Turnpike (or "National Pike") between western Maryland and southern Illinois, by a state or government. They were toll roads, the cost of maintenance paid from the tolls of those using the road. But what we today call "tollgates" were then called "turnpikes," a name that itself had long ceased to have any of the original sense. The first turnpikes were really rotating constructions upon which pikes or sharpened rods were mounted. They were effective barriers until the fare of a horseman or coach had been paid, and were then probably rolled or turned out of the way.

on the nose

This current expression had its origin in the radio studio. It means exactly on time. Those who have attended the broadcast of a radio program know that the director of the program stays within the soundproof control room during the performance. Thus he is able to see each performer and, via the engineer's radio, to know just how the performance sounds to the radio audience. His especial concern is to watch the time, for the program must run with railroad-like attention to schedule. In rehearsal he noted the exact intervals for each bit of the performance, the minutes and seconds for each song or musical number, for each bit of comedy or the  like, and has the elapsed time marked on his copy of the script. His assistant on the stage watches him for signals and transmits to the performers the directions he receives. If too much time has been taken up to a prearranged point, a dozen or more lines of the script may be dropped or the performers may be notified by gesture to speed up the reading of their lines or, if ahead of schedule, to slow down the reading. Tenseness subsides, however, when the assistant or the performers see the director place his forefinger on the tip of his nose. By that sign they know that the timing has been perfect.

Another sign that originated in the control room is made with the hand held up and the thumb and forefinger pressed lightly together. This is used to mean that performance is being rendered perfectly.

to leave in the lurch

This has nothing to do with the lurching of a ship or a drunken man. But we can't do very much with it except to trace it to an old French dicing game called *lourche*, which somewhat resembled the present game of backgammon and which was played some time before the seventeenth century. The player who was left in the lurch was apparently left far behind the goal, for in later games in which the name persisted it kept that meaning, as in cribbage in which *lurch* describes the state of the player who has pegged fewer than thirty-one holes while his opponent has scored sixty-one and the game.

hitting on all six

When first coined, this was "hitting on all four." It may become, as we adjust our speech to the progress of the machine age, "hitting on all twelve" or sixteen or other multiple of two. Whatever the alteration in the numeral, it means "functioning perfectly." We get it, prosaically, from the shop mechanic who applied it to the  cylinders of the automobile. If the engine is running smoothly and efficiently, all the pistons in the cylinders, whatever their number, are hitting perfectly. We have given it a figurative sense, too, and use it, for example, in compliment to a person who, we say, is "hitting on all six" when he is giving a forceful talk or an excellent performance.

to hold at bay

Those of us who are familiar with Landseer's painting, "The Stag at Bay," know the meaning of the phrase; when facing a desperate situation, to hold it at a standstill. Despite the picture, the fact that the dogs are obviously barking or baying is just a chance double meaning of the word "bay." Our phrase seems to come instead from the French phrase, *tenir à bay*, which really means "to hold in a state of suspense or inaction; to hold in abeyance," or, literally, "to hold agape."

thumbs down

If you decide to veto a matter under discussion or to express disapproval of a person or thing, don't try to air your Latin by saying "pollice verso"; better just stick to the English "thumbs down." We know what that means and what the accompanying gesture is; but nobody knows exactly what gesture the old Romans used when they signaled a victorious gladiator to show no mercy to his opponent.

The present popular concept that "pollice verso" meant "thumbs down" is derived from the celebrated picture having that title painted by the French artist, Jean Léon Gérôme, and exhibited by him in 1873. But Latin scholars have advanced almost every other conceivable gesture except that shown by Gérôme. *Verso* just means "turned," and could mean "extended" or even "rotated." The Latin phrase has been translated, "with thumbs turned inward" and "with thumbs turned outward," in either case using the thumb as if it were a dagger pointing at oneself or thrusting into an opponent, much as we "thumb a ride" by pointing the thumb in the direction we wish to travel. The meaning, "with thumb thrust outward" has been stoutly defended.

From all these possible gestures one is reminded of the old children's game: Simon says "Thumbs up!" Simon says "Thumbs down!" Simon says "Wiggle-waggle!"

The Latin term for the reverse signal, to spare the life of the defeated gladiator, was "pollice primo," meaning "with thumbs pressed." Probably the gesture was with the thumbs folded into a fist under the fingers, and it may have signified that the dagger was to be sheathed.

on the nail (or *nailhead*)

This saying is used chiefly of money transactions, having the force of "spot cash," and we use it also to mean "now; at once." But it is so old that no one can be quite sure of the allusion. The same expression occurs in German (*auf den Nagel*) and in Dutch (*ep den nagel*). Walsh reports the occurrence of the phrase, in Latin, in a Scottish deed of 1326. These records tend to throw doubt on the claim advanced by Joyce (*English as We Speak It in Ireland*) that the expression had its origin in a custom formerly prevailing in Limerick where, he says, a pillar about four feet high, topped with a copper plate about three feet in diameter, stood under the Exchange. This pillar was called "The Nail," and a purchaser laid his cash upon the plate to seal a bargain. Probably, however, the pillar derived its name from the phrase.

An expression in French runs, *faire rubis sur l'ongle*, literally, to make a ruby on the fingernail; and it carries the figurative meaning, to drain to the last drop. Some have figured this out to mean that a wine cup is to be drained until no more remains than would make a ruby droplet on the fingernail. From this they argue, somewhat obscurely, that "the nail" in our expression meant the fingernail and that "on the nail" means fair and square.

to stand the gaff

We use this usually in the sense of "to take punishment," but often employ it for mental fortitude rather than physical, "to accept  raillery in good spirit." A gaff, of course, is a pointed hook on the end of a long rod and is used for landing large fish, or at least that is the instrument most commonly known. But there is also a Scottish and provincial English word, "gaff," which means noisy, insulting language; so it is possible that the expression, "to stand the gaff," may very literally mean "to take punishment, as from a steel hook," or "to withstand raillery, as from insulting remarks."

to spike one's guns

We use this now only in its figurative sense, to deprive one of his power, to make one's authority or arguments valueless. Its literal sense amounted to exactly the same thing, for the expression arose back in the seventeenth century and earlier when guns were fired by igniting the charge at the touchhole. If the touchhole were blocked, the gun would be rendered entirely valueless. And as the guns of that period, especially the siege guns, were extremely unwieldy affairs, almost immobile once they had been dragged into position, and had a comparatively short range, a sudden sortie by those under siege, if successful, would drive off the gunners. A nail or spike driven into the touchhole then destroyed the menace of the guns.

to pay through the nose

Legend has it that this saying originated during the Norse or Danish conquest of Ireland back in the ninth century when, it is said, the Irish peasants and nobles were compelled to pay their oppressors a stiff tribute or suffer a slit nose. We can only say, "not proven"; there is no historical record. Furthermore, the earliest

190

literary use of the expression in English is not found before the late seventeenth century. The phrase means to pay reluctantly or to pay an exorbitant price, and it is likely, though not certain, that the saying originated among the thieves in England along in the sixteenth or seventeenth century, possibly in allusion to some practice among them of compelling a victim to yield his purse.

the land of Nod

We are apt to forget that this comes from the Bible, in which "the land of Nod" is the place (Genesis iv, 16) where Cain dwelt after he had slain Abel. Jonathan Swift, famous satirist of the seventeenth-eighteenth century, turned the biblical phrase into a pun when he wrote that he was "going into the land of Nod," meaning that he was going to sleep. It appears in a work of his, little known nowadays, *A complete collection of genteel and ingenious conversation*, (usually referred to as *Polite Conversation*), written between the years 1731 and 1738.

to be in the groove

This has no connection with being in a rut, for the current crop of American young people use it to mean to be exactly right, to fit exactly the mood or spirit. It seems to be a coinage of the jazz or swing era of music and to have been derived from the phonographic records of that music; that is, to the quality of accurate reproduction of such music through a good needle traversing the grooves of a record. The phrase is not more than about ten or fifteen years old,  and, although applied generally to things that are functioning smoothly, its specific application is music.

to ride shanks' mare (or pony)

This means to walk; to use one's own legs, for the shank is the part of the leg below the knee. It has been a jocular expression for some two hundred years or so. Possibly it arose from playful allusion to a Mr. Shank who had no other means of conveyance, but more likely it was an invention of some Scottish wit.

funny as a barrel of monkeys

One monkey arouses a great deal of amusement. Two more then double the interest and amusement. If one were to release a barrelful of monkeys, we must suppose that their antics would become hilariously comical. The expression is common among children.

go to Halifax!

Most people regard this as a polite euphemism, probably American, for the blunter request, go to hell! But why Halifax? The explanation is interesting, for it goes back four centuries at least— to the manufacturing town of Halifax in northern England.

History doesn't tell us whether there were more rogues and thieves in and about Halifax than in other parts of England, but in the sixteenth century the people of that town had become so harassed by thievery that they had instituted what became known as "Halifax Law." This provided "that whosoever doth commit any felony, and is taken with the same, or confess the fact upon examination, if it be valued by four constables to amount to the sum of thirteen-pence halfpenny, he is forthwith beheaded upon one of the next market days." The instrument used for the beheading was an early form of guillotine, one that served as a model for the later Scottish "maiden."

As the seaport town of Hull, also in Yorkshire, had a reputation for being just as summary in meting out punishment to undesirable characters, these two towns became a byword among thieves as places to be avoided. They gave rise to the lines in the so-called *Beggar's Litany*, "From Hell, Hull, and Halifax, good Lord deliver us," for the three places of punishment were almost equally dreaded. Thus, in fact, our impolite order is not so much a euphemism for "go to hell," as a substitute with equal force.

to face the music

Our earliest record of this American expression is found, according to Bartlett, in the *Worcester Spy* in the issue of September 22,

1857. But a later collector of Americanisms, Schele de Vere, makes it earlier by saying that James Fenimore Cooper, about 1851, remarked that the phrase had more picturesqueness and was less unpleasant than "the Rabelais quarter." (His allusion was to the French expression, *quart d'heure de Rabelais*. Rabelais, according to the legend, traveling from Tours to Paris, had a bad quarter of an hour at a post inn when he found himself unable to pay his reckoning. He put up a bold front by accusing the innkeeper of a conspiracy against the king, and finished his trip at the expense of the terrified innocent victim.)

The source of "to face the music" is generally thought to have been theatrical parlance, referring to an actor who, however nervous, must come boldly on stage before his public; thus literally facing the music, or the orchestra in the pit below the footlights. But other explanations have been offered. Some ascribe it to military origin. If so, its first meaning may have been simply to take one's place in the line of assembly, facing the band. Or it may have referred to a cavalry mount which must be trained to show no restiveness when the band starts to play. Or it may have referred to a cavalryman dishonorably dismissed from the service who, it is said, when drummed out of camp would not only be facing the music of the drums but also would be facing the rear end of his horse.

jot or tittle

We don't hear this expression very commonly nowadays, though it crops up on occasion and we find it in the Bible, as in Christ's Sermon on the Mount. The expression as a whole means a minute particle. And that's just what it always meant.

Jot is a corrupted form of the Greek *iota*; the Greek letter *i*, in other words. The corrupted spelling, with initial *j* instead of *i*, goes back to the days before the eighteenth century when *i* and *j* were used almost interchangeably. The *iota* is the smallest letter in the Greek alphabet, scarcely requiring more than a wiggle of the stylus to produce it. And *tittle* means the dot over the *i*—a mere point. Anciently it meant any point by which pronunciation was indicated, just as we use *tilde*, a corrupted form of *tittle*, for the wavy line over an *n* in some Spanish words, like *cañon*.

So, by the expression *jot* or *tittle*, the ancients really meant something so small as to be scarcely noticed, not only the tiny letter *i*, but the even tinier dot or point over the *i*.

to get one's goat

This expression is now almost as commonly heard in England as in America, but although the first printed record of its use is as recent as 1912, one cannot say positively how it originated. It means, of course, to goad one into signs of irritation; to annoy, tease, exasperate. There has long been a French idiom, *prendre la chèvre*, (literally,

to take, or seize, the goat; figuratively, to take offense), but the American phrase does not appear to come from that source. The tale that the expression derived from the one-time custom in the shanty neighborhood of Harlem, in old New York, of keeping goats, to the annoyance of the more aristocratic residents, fails to satisfy. There were too many other sights and sounds and smells in that neighborhood.

In my opinion, the more logical source is the small boy and his known habits of ridiculing whatever he may regard as an affectation. Turn back in your photograph album to the family portraits of 1890. Most of the adult males, you will notice, are wearing full beards. "Beavers," we would call them today. Now turn on to around 1900. Most of the full beards have disappeared; but now and then among your male relatives you will see that some were reluctant to part with all the facial adornment, needed something to stroke reflectively, and so retained a more or less neat tuft on the chin—a goatee, so called because it resembles the beard of a goat.

If you looked like a cow would your temper be unruffled if, from discreet distances as you passed, you heard, "Moo-oo"? That wasn't the sound your uncles heard; they heard, "Naa-aa-aah!"

to a T

We use this expression very commonly in the sense of minute exactness, perfection; as, the coat fits to a T; the meat was done to a T.

It is easy to dismiss the origin of the expression, as, I am sorry to say, some of our leading dictionaries do, by attributing it to the draftsman's T-square, which is supposed to be an exact instrument, but the evidence indicates that the expression was in common English use before the T-square got its name. "To a T" dates back to the seventeenth century in literary use and was undoubtedly common in everyday speech long before any writer dared to or thought to use it in print. But it is likely that the name of the instrument, "T-square," would have been in print shortly after its invention, yet the first mention is in the eighteenth century.

The sense of the expression corresponds, however, with the older one, "to a tittle," which appeared almost a century earlier, and meant "to a dot," as in "jot or tittle." Beaumont used it in 1607, and it is probable that colloquial use long preceded his employment of the phrase. Then as now Englishmen took pleasure in employing abbreviations and contractions, and I have no doubt that someone thought that "to a T" had a more amusing sound than "to a tittle," and thus introduced our current expression.

dead (deaf, or dumb) as a doornail

This expression means very dead, of course (or deaf, or dumb)— completely and absolutely non-responsive. It is very old, has been traced back to 1350 in literary use and was therefore probably used in common speech long before that, possibly for several centuries. But just why our remote ancestors conceived a doornail to be very dead, or deaf or dumb, is something that has never been satisfactorily explained. Todd, who published a revision of Johnson's English Dictionary in 1818, advanced the notion that the ancient doornail was a heavy stud against which the knocker was struck. If such a nail was used for that purpose, perhaps some old-time wit proclaimed that it had been struck on the head so often as to be dead; or another, after pounding vainly upon it without response from within, proclaimed it to be deaf or dumb. I don't know—nor have I anything to support Todd's theory. The earliest usage, as far as the records show, was with the adjective "dead." When "dumb" first appeared, in 1362, it related to the door only; as in Langland's *Piers Plowman*,

"As doumbe as a dore." "Deaf" did not show up until the sixteenth century, when it was applied indiscriminately either to the "doore" or the "doore nayle."

to fly off the handle

This Americanism first got into print about a hundred years ago, meaning, as it does today, to lose one's self-control suddenly, or, in popular parlance, to loose one's head. The latter was the literal meaning, for the allusion was to the head or blade of a woodsman's ax, which, if loose upon the helve, was likely to fly off dangerously at a tangent anywhere along the swing of the ax.

John Neal seems to have been the first to record the forerunner of the present expression, for the earlier usage was just "off the handle." Neal, a novelist from Portland, Maine, visited England when he was thirty, and while there published, in 1825, the novel, *Brother Jonathan; or the New Eng-landers*. In this, speaking of a surprise attack upon an Indian village, one of his characters says, "How they pulled foot when they seed us commin'. Most off the handle, some o' the tribe, I guess." Our old friend, Judge Thomas C. Haliburton, who has already been quoted several times as the first to record some American expressions, has again the honor of being the first to use the full line, "to fly off the handle." This appeared in another of his "Sam Slick" tales, *The Attaché, or Sam Slick in England*, published in 1844.

forlorn hope

Things are not always what they seem, and this is one of such. What we have in this expression is really an English spelling of a Dutch phrase, not at all a translation. The Dutch spelling is *verloren hoop*, which sounds very much like the English "forlorn hope." But *hoop* doesn't mean "hope"; it means "troop" or "band." And *verloren* doesn't quite mean "forlorn"; it means "abandoned" or "wasted."

The Dutch term is of military origin; it designated a small band of soldiers, usually volunteers, who undertook some perilous expedition, such as heading an attack against the foe, or rushing forward the scaling ladders to breach a fortress. In modern military parlance they would be called "shock troops." But because casualties were very high and the chance of success always doubtful, "forlorn hope" has now the non-military meaning, "an enterprise having little prospect of success."

Philadelphia lawyer

Sometimes the phrase is embodied in a simile: "as smart as," or "as tricky as," or "as shrewd as a Philadelphia lawyer," or in such form as, "it would take a Philadelphia lawyer to figure that out." But always the "Philadelphia lawyer" is an exceptionally astute person and, nowadays, the implication is that he is given to somewhat shady practices.

Originally, however, to be compared to a Philadelphia lawyer was high praise. Prior to 1800 and for some time thereafter the City of Brotherly Love was the most important and the most beautiful city in America. It held, until 1800, the seat of the new federal government and was the financial center of the country. It was also the center of literature and intellect. Naturally the city attracted the best legal brains of the country, men constantly obliged to sharpen wits against others equally sharp and more than a match for other men with lesser opportunity. But when wits become too sharp, practices are likely to become less scrupulous, so what had been praise turned to satire as lawyers began to become less honorable.

all around Robin Hood's barn

Robin Hood (or "Robert of the wood," as some have explained the name) may have been altogether a legendary figure or may have actually existed. No one knows. The earliest literary reference to him is in Langland's *Piers Plowman*, written about 1377. He may have lived, according to some slight evidence, toward the latter part of the twelfth century.

But Robin Hood's house was Sherwood Forest; its roof the leaves and branches. His dinner was the king's deer; his wealth the purses of hapless travelers. What need had he of a barn, and how was it laid out if to go around it means, as the use of the phrase implies, a rambling roundabout course? The explanation is simple. He had no barn. His granary, when he had need of one, was the cornfields of the neighborhood. To go around his barn was to make a circuitous route around the neighboring fields.

a fly in the ointment

This modern version suggests that something unpleasant may come or has come to light in a proposition or condition that is almost too pleasing; that there is something wrong somewhere. The older version was "a fly in the amber," meaning merely that something is as unexpectedly out of place as the fly that one occasionally finds embedded in fossilized amber. Possibly the substitution of "ointment" for "amber" may have been through association of ideas, for "amber" was originally used in the sense of "ambergris," and ambergris is used in some perfumed ointments.

from pillar to post

This means back and forth monotonously; from one thing to another; hither and thither. It is a very old saying, perhaps as old as the game of tennis—court tennis, that is, not lawn tennis. We who are familiar only with the rather new game of lawn tennis forget that it was invented as recently as 1874, whereas court tennis was certainly played in the thirteenth century and perhaps earlier. There is little resemblance between the two games, other than that both are played on marked courts, with a ball and, nowadays, with rackets; but lawn tennis is usually played outdoors, whereas court tennis is necessarily played indoors in a building especially designed for it. Rackets were not introduced until about the time of Henry VIII; previously, the game was played by striking the ball with the palm of the hand. The game was very intricate, even in recent times; the court laid out into side and end "penthouses," the roofs of which had to be struck by the ball, and there were "galleries," "grilles," "tambours," "*dedans*," and other structures involved in the game. Many modifications took place in the method of play, and at some time prior to the fifteenth century one feature of the game lay in some form of volley which, at the time, was called "from post to pillar," apparently referring to a post that supported the net (though a rope was used in those days, rather than a net) and one of the pillars that supported the galleries. No explanation now exists of the nature of that volley; but, because of the popularity of the game at the English court, the name of the volley passed into a common saying—always "from post to pillar" until the sixteenth century when, the original allusion having been forgotten, it gradually became reversed to the present usage, "from pillar to post."

Another explanation of the phrase has been offered. It ascribes the origin to the old-style riding academy, the pillar being the center of the ring and the posts being upright columns placed two and two around the circumference of the ring. The explanation seems groundless to me, and one is left to imagine a possible reason for having the pupils of such an academy ride endlessly from the center pillar back and forth to the surrounding posts.

to mind one's p's and q's

To take pains; to be careful and precise. More conjectures have been advanced to explain the original meaning of this phrase than upon any other equally obscure. Each has a certain degree of plausibility. The simplest explanation is that it was an incessant admonition among pedagogs to their young charges, warning them to note the right-handed knob of the p and the left-handed knob of the q. But if such admonitions were given to youngsters just learning to print the alphabet, why was there not a like warning to mind their b's and d's in which the knobs are also reversed? Another, of the same category, is that it was a warning to young apprentice printers who might be readily confused in picking out type, because the face of a type letter is just the reverse of the printed character. But here, again, the explanation is weak because the reverse of p is d, not q.

Another, and more likely explanation is that the expression originated in the old inn or alehouse. A customer, bent upon a convivial evening, would have his accounts chalked up against his final reckoning, so many pints (*p*'s), so many quarts (*q*'s). A little carelessness on the part of the barmaid might spoil his whole evening.

But other less plebeian explanations have been offered, dating back to the courtly etiquette of the seventeenth and eighteenth centuries when men wore queues. One of these refers to the probably frantic efforts of French dancing masters to instruct young gentlemen in the stately steps and deep courtesies of the minuette. The young men had indeed to mind their *pieds* and *queues* (feet and pigtails) to avoid loss of balance and to keep the pigtail from bobbing over the head or to lose entirely the huge artificial periwig.

Another associates *p* with the old word "pee," a kind of coat worn by men in the fifteenth to seventeenth centuries, now surviving only in the word "peajacket." This account would have it that "to mind your *pees* and *queues*" was a wifely admonition to avoid soiling the jacket from the grease or flour of the queue or pigtail. This explanation seems the least likely of the various ones that ardent delvers have offered.

to thumb a ride

This, like a number of other current expressions, is recorded in this volume for the convenience of future generations. You and I know that it means to obtain a lift toward one's destination by requesting it in dumb pantomime. It originated after the automobile had become so commonplace, around 1920, that pedestrianism almost ceased. If one wished to go a mile, ten miles, fifty miles in either direction along almost any road in the United States, all one had to do was to take up a wistful stand at the side of the road and point with his thumb toward the direction he wished to go. Sooner or later an obliging driver would be overcome with pity toward one so unfortunate as not to have his own car. In the long depression after 1930, many persons were reduced to this form of locomotion, and in World War II it became a virtue to share one's car and one's gasoline with others unable to get tires or whose rationed gasoline had been exhausted. By the end of World War II men in uniform were also sometimes able "to thumb a ride" on airplanes.

to cook with gas

This expression, at the time this is written, is classed as slang. It is included here because almost every other phrase in this book was, at one time, slang and eventually passed into literary use. Perhaps this will too. Currently it is used to mean to be strictly up to date, or even a little ahead of the procession, not out of date, as cooking with wood or coal would imply. Just why the expression should imply ultramodernity is not clear, other than that the use of gas is supposed to make a faster, hotter fire than wood or coal; but electric current as used in stoves is more modern than is gas.

to go haywire

Although this expression is wholly American in origin and use and is comparatively recent—*i.e.*, has gained popularity within the past thirty or forty years and is not found in literary use earlier than 1910—no one knows who coined it nor from what section of the country it first came to mean to be perversely unright, messed up, snarled, crazy, at sixes and sevens, makeshift. People who have never seen a piece of haywire now use the phrase freely and easily, as if it had always been in the language.

For the benefit of the uninitiate, when hay is to be shipped it is usually tightly compressed into a cubical bale, roughly two by two by four feet, and tied securely by single strands of soft, pliable wire about half the thickness of a matchstick. This wire is now generally called "haywire," rather than the former non-descriptive term, "baling wire." It must be removed before the hay is fed to horses or cattle and the best way to do so is by a sharp blow with a hatchet; the wire is then tossed aside.

Now with three or four strands of wire to each bale it isn't long before the farmer, liveryman, dairyman, or rancher has quite a mass of haywire on his place. He uses it for a thousand purposes, wherever or whenever a piece of wire may come in handy, or even in place of string or rope. He uses it to repair a broken implement of any sort, to wrap the handle of a split hayfork, to hold a broken strap together, to replace a broken chain link, to mend temporarily a piece of farm machinery, to guy a sagging stovepipe, to replace a broken section of wire fence, and so on and so on.

H. L. Mencken, in *Supplement One, The American Language*, advances his own theory of the origin of the present meaning of the phrase. He says, "No one who has ever opened a bale of hay with a hatchet, and had the leaping wire whirl about him and its sharp ends poniard him, will ever have any doubt as to how *to go haywire* originated." But with the highest respect in the world for Mr. Mencken's philological parts, and with first-hand experience with the diabolical punishment those leaping ends can give to a tyro, I think he has the wrong slant on the origin of the expression. It would partly account for the sense of perversity or craziness implied by the expression, but not the sense of disorder, derangement, general confusion, and hodge-podge that we also associate with the phrase.

Most farmers tolerate the use of haywire for temporary repairs only. They know that it rusts quickly, not only becoming unsightly but having little permanent value. But there are many farmers, loggers, ranchers, miners who are shiftless, who once having used haywire to hold a thing together, use it over and over again and never get around to making a permanent repair. Their machines, their tools, fences, gates, barns, sheds, and houses are patched with rusted haywire, more haywire often being added to a piece that has rusted out; haywire used to hold the paintless jalopy together; masses of tangled rusty haywire lying around anywhere. Such a disorderly, deranged, shiftless place has "gone haywire," and this, from observation of numerous such places in Colorado mining camps, Wyoming ranches, and Idaho, Utah, and California farms, I believe, gave rise to our expression.

THEREBY HANGS A TALE

Stories of Curious
Word Origins

To

B. M. F.

Who patiently and often has listened to many of these tales, this book is lovingly dedicated.

PREFACE

THIS book is the outcome of a collection of material that has been slowly accumulating over the past thirty years or so, since the time when, under the guidance of the late Dr. Frank H. Vizetelly, I began to work as his associate in the editorial department of the Funk & Wagnalls New Standard Dictionary. The ancestry of most of the words that we now use glibly or find in books or other current literature, is prosaic. We can trace their lines of descent back to Old English, or Old French, or Latin, or Greek, or other ancient source, but beyond the bare bones supplied by etymologists, which indicate those sources, and the steps by which they became English words, the dictionaries tell us little—for there is little more that can be told. The ancient Roman or Greek, say, who may have been the first to use a word that has strayed on to us, perhaps could have told the story of its origin. It may have been picturesque, based upon some historic episode, like the word *anecdote*; it may have come from a tale in some older language, for the languages that we consider ancient were themselves based upon still more ancient sources, but that story, if any, cannot now be determined. Thus what we know about the origins of the great majority of the words in our present language can be found in an unabridged dictionary or in a work dealing with etymologies, such as that compiled by W. W. Skeat about seventy years ago, or the one more recently prepared by Ernest Weekley.

But there are in our current language a number of fairly common words—some old, some new—which were born, or grew, or acquired their meanings in an unusual manner. They came, as our language has, from all sources—sources of which the dictionaries, for lack of space, can rarely supply more than a clue. These are the tales that I have been collecting and which are offered here. A number of them may be already familiar to some readers, such as the origin of *tantalize*, from the Greek legend of the punishment

207

meted out to Tantalus by the wrathful Zeus, or *echo*, from the fate of the perfidious nymph of that name. Such tales, though familiar to some, are included here for the benefit of those to whom they may be new. But I have found that few but scholars in the language know how the word *clue*, which was just used, acquired its present meaning; that the Portuguese gave us *coconut* because, to their sailors in the sixteenth century, the nut resembled a *coco*, "a grinning face"; that *sylph* was a coinage of that master charlatan or genius, depending upon the point of view, the sixteenth-century alchemist, Paracelsus; that we owe our terms *chapel* and *chaplain* to the cloak or cape worn by the fourth-century monk, St. Martin; that the name *Easter* was taken from a pagan goddess, and that the names of the days of the week denote dedication to ancient pagan gods.

Whenever it has been possible, the stories are historical; that is, for example, facts in the life of St. Martin are briefly stated to explain why his cloak was venerated; the occasion for the coinage of *sylph* by Paracelsus is summarized; a brief account tells why *magenta* commemorated a battle; short sketches of the invasions of the Vandals and Tatars account for such words as *vandal, tartar,* and *horde*; highly abridged biographies of such persons as the Scottish engineer, John L. McAdam, the Scottish chemist, Charles Macintosh, and others, tell why their names were adopted into the language; an explanation is deduced why the French general, Martinet, became a byword in English, but not in French; the historical circumstances that introduced the word *nepotism* are related, and so on, and so on.

To the best of my knowledge, no similar collection of tales accounting for such a number of English words has yet appeared. The facts have been drawn from numerous sources and have been carefully checked. It would be impossible to list all the authorities that have been consulted during the years through which the material has been collected; they have been numerous, embracing many languages. Murray's *A New English Dictionary on Historical Principles*, usually referred to as the *Oxford English Dictionary*, has been an invaluable aid and has supplied clues to many older references; the various encyclopedias, not only English, but also French, German, and Italian, brought other information to light; considerable source material was obtained from Sir William Smith's *Dic-*

tionary of Greek and Roman Antiquities, checked against later findings, which sometimes gave occasion for variant stories; the files of the British *Notes & Queries*, as well as the American *Notes & Queries*, were frequently consulted, as well as a number of volumes dealing with medieval life and customs. With few exceptions, the stories as written are entirely my own, and those exceptions have been duly accredited to their authors. I am indebted to Robert (Bob) Burns for the account, by letter, of his creation of the term *bazooka*; to Mr. R. W. Henderson, also by letter, for his findings on the word *tennis*, and to Mr. H. L. Mencken, and his publisher, for permission to reprint his conclusions, in which I concur, on the origin of *yankee*.

Sometimes, because of the relationship existing between some of our words, it has seemed advisable to group several words together to avoid repetition. Thus, for example, *augur* and *inaugurate* are related, and a common story suffices for each; so are *money* and *mint*, *eliminate* and *preliminary*, and various others. Similarly, though in different manner, is there relationship between such divergent words as *grotesque* and *antic*, *matinee* and *noon*, *monster* and *prodigy*, *foreign* and *denizen*, and others. These also have usually been grouped into common stories. Hence, although the book is alphabetical in general arrangement and no index is therefore essential for the main list of words, an index is provided at the end of the book to show under what heading other words may be found. Thus: *augur*, see *inaugurate*; *mint*, see *money*; *grotesque*, see *antic*, and so on. The index also includes the names of the persons, mythological characters, and places directly associated with a word-story, as well as those persons to whom the author is indebted for material. Thus: *David*, see under *Abigail*; *Mencken, H. L.*, see under *Yankee*; *Theseus*, see under *clue*, etc.

Rarely, in this work, has an attempt been made to follow the various alterations in the form of a word from its ancient source. Although that has sometimes been done for the purpose of clarification, such lines of development have been left generally to etymologists. It may be well, however, to review with extreme brevity the general outlines of the main sources of our language for the benefit of those to whom the subject is new. With few exceptions, our commonest words—the prepositions, the pronouns, the conjunctions, the auxiliary verbs (do, may, can, have, be, etc., and their derivatives), and the common objects pertaining to domestic and agricultural life—have descended to us from the period known as Old English, sometimes referred to as Anglo-Saxon. Such words are usually of Teutonic origin, surviving from the early centuries of the Christian Era when England was conquered, overrun, and settled, its earlier occupants wiped out, by Angle, Saxon, and Danish invaders from regions now embraced by Germany and Denmark. The language introduced by these invaders, intermixed with each other and absorbing some of the older tongue, became standard speech until the eleventh century. It was chiefly a spoken language and there were few scholars to preserve its integrity. Consequently, through the centuries, the forms of the original words often became greatly altered and corrupted in common speech. Spelling in this period was usually phonetic, according to the values placed upon the alphabet that was then in use.

In the year 1066, William, duke of Normandy, with a well-armed force of sixty thousand followers, entered England, defeated Harold II, the Saxon king, at Hastings, seized the throne and became the lord of the country. During the next two centuries, the English, or Saxons as they were called, were reduced almost to servitude by their conquerors. Norman-French became the language spoken by all except the common folk, and even they were driven to become somewhat familiar with it to understand the speech of their masters. All royal proclamations and the proceedings of all law courts were also in that language. Thus, through that period, many Old French words were grafted upon the language. And again, through the general illiteracy of the people, these in turn were corrupted in the common speech of a folk unaccustomed to French speech—like the French *naperon*, being first *a napron*, and then further corrupted to *an apron*.

But Old French was itself, to a considerable extent, an outgrowth of Latin. That is, just as William the Conqueror imposed his language upon the people of England, so, in the days of the emperors of Rome, had Latin been imposed upon the people of the conquered country that later became France. But it was largely the Latin of the Roman soldier quartered upon the country—a debased Latin— that became further corrupted when adopted into the native speech.

210

Many of our words thus trace back through Old French to a former Latin source.

Preceding the flood of Old French after the Norman Conquest by several centuries, and continuing steadily side by side through it and until at least the sixteenth century, our language was being enriched through another channel. That increment came through the form of Latin that we call Low or Medieval Latin and Late Latin, used by the fathers of the Christian Church and by the later priests and monks in their devotions and intercourse with one another. It was a development from classical Latin and formed a language common to all Europe, enabling the clergy to travel anywhere. It was also used in the church services of England. Hence, though some of the words became incorporated into our language without much change, others were sadly misunderstood by the illiterate listeners and were altered into strange meanings. Thus, for example, we have *patter* from *pater noster*, *dirge* from the funeral chant with the opening word, *dirige*, direct, *anthem* from *antiphon*, and so on.

This stage in the development of the language, in which Old French and Medieval Latin were mingled with the corrupted remnants of Old English, is referred to as Middle English. The works of Geoffrey Chaucer furnish an example of its later form. Spelling was, in a measure, phonetic, employing the Roman alphabet. But the sounds of words were often unlike those we now give to the same words, thus accounting for many of our modern spellings, such as *thought, eight, once*. There were no rules to guide one in spelling; each man spelled according to the way words sounded to him. Hence, any uniformity that may have existed was accidental.

Finally, without considering here the immense number of words that we have constantly borrowed from every language with which English-speaking people have been in contact, we owe a large volume of our words to the period that we call Modern English, beginning, roughly, with the sixteenth century. Scholarship, previously limited largely to the clergy, was opened to all, and the study of classical learning became a fetish. Writers and thinkers sprang up from every walk of life, and did not hesitate to cull their words from the Latin of Cicero, or Horace, or Ovid, or Seneca. Many also went to the Greek of Æschylus, or Plato, or Plutarch to derive their words. It is thus chiefly through these writers and their unceasing stream of successors that the great bulk of words derived directly from Latin and Greek ancestry and meanings have entered our language. From this practice also has descended our present custom of looking to one or another of those languages for the formation of new words, especially those of scientific nature.

At the beginning of this last period, the old dialectal pronunciations continued to influence the spellings of the older language. Many of those pronunciations, in fact, were carried along in cultured speech until the seventeenth century or later, and continued in the common speech for at least another hundred years. With the advance of learning, our spelling, though continuously subjected to fads and mistaken notions, has gradually assumed a certain degree of uniformity. Because it still retains many of the sixteenth-century forms, however, it cannot be called phonetic. But it is highly probable that the unwieldy forms that we have inherited will disappear one by one in course of time, as the people find it more convenient to drop them.

THEREBY HANGS A TALE

*Stories of Curious
Word Origins*

abet

The so-called sport of bear-baiting was widely known among the Teutonic countries a thousand years ago, but it became nowhere more popular than in England, especially after the fourteenth century. For the pleasure of the spectators, a bear, freshly caught and starved enough to make it vicious, was fastened to a stake by a short chain or, it might be, was turned loose in a small arena. Then dogs were set upon it, fresh dogs being supplied if the first were maimed or killed. In the end, of course, after perhaps hours of sport, one of the dogs would succeed in seizing the exhausted bear by the throat and worry it to death. The man or boy who urged his dog to attack was said to *abet* it, using a contracted Old French word— *abeter*, meaning to bait, or hound on. The early French, in turn, had taken a Norse word, *beita*, which meant to cause to bite. So, though we now use *abet* in speaking of persons—chiefly of persons who encourage others in wrongful deeds—the word traces back to an Old Norse command to a dog, an order to attack, equivalent, perhaps, to the modern "Sic 'em!"

abeyance

When anything is in *abeyance* now we mean that it is in a state of inaction, that the matter, whatever it was, is dormant, although some action is expected to occur eventually. It was that expectancy that gave us the word, for it came as a law term, after the Norman Conquest, from the Old French *abeance*, a state of expectancy. The term referred especially to the condition of a property or title while, after the death of the former possessor, often by foul means in those days, his successor could be determined from among various claimants. The Old French word was derived from the verb *beer* (modern *bayer*), to gape, to expect, perhaps because of the gaping expectancy with which the settlement of an estate was awaited either by the rightful heir or by a hopeful usurper, none too certain that his claim would pass scrutiny.

abhor

When the hair stands up from fright or dread, we have the literal meaning of *abhor*. The Latin source of our verb was *abhorreo*, from *ab*, away from, and *horreo*, to stand on end, to bristle. Thus the literal meaning was to shrink back from with horror, but, though the verb still expresses great repugnance, it no longer conveys the notion of shuddering dread or fear that its use indicated to the Romans.

abigail

We must turn to the Bible to see why this feminine proper name started to become a synonym for servant. In the First Book of Samuel, the twenty-fifth chapter tells how David, in return for past favors, made a peaceful request to the wealthy Nabal for food for his followers. Nabal rejected the request and David was about to take by force what had been denied. But *Abigail*, Nabal's wife, heard of the affair. She learned, first, that the request was reasonable, then taking more food with her than had been requested, she went to David to turn away his wrath. She was just in time. Her abject apologies for the churlishness of her husband fill the next eight verses of the chapter; in them, to show her great humility, she refers to herself six times as David's "handmaid." The association of name and occupation was further fixed in men's minds by the dramatists, Beaumont and Fletcher. When writing the play, *The Scornful Lady*, in 1609, they gave the name *Abigail* to the very spirited lady's maid who had one of the leading parts. This character, or the actress who played the part, made so great an impression on the audiences that the later writers, Congreve, Swift, Fielding, Smollett, and others began to use the name as that of any lady's maid.

abominable

The Romans were intensely superstitious. Any chance event or chance remark that occurred on the eve of an undertaking was carefully examined to determine whether it might indicate good luck or bad luck. Thus Cicero tells us that Crassus, when about to embark upon his ill-fated expedition against the Parthians, should

216

have turned back. At the harbor, a man selling dried figs from Caunus, gave the cry, "Cauneas!" to signify the source of his wares. This to the Romans sounded like "*Cave ne eas,*" meaning, "Beware of going," which Crassus should have taken to be a sign of bad luck, an evil omen. Crassus had not heeded the warning, however, and was treacherously slain by the Parthians. Any such omen as that was considered to have been a clear portent of doom, amply warning one to avoid whatever undertaking he had in mind. For that reason it was described as *abominabilis*, from *ab*, away from, and *omen*. The early sense of the term, "direful, inspiring dread, ominous," came through association of ideas to mean "loathsome, disgusting," because it was usually loathsome things that were taken as omens of evil.

abound, abundant

When things are in such profusion as to be like the waves of the sea overflowing the land, we may properly say that they *abound*. Literally, that is what the word means. It comes to us from the Latin, *abundo*, to overflow, from *ab*, from, and *unda*, wave, billow, surge. Our words *abundant* and *abundance* have the same poetic source.

aboveboard

Card-playing has been known in Europe since about the middle of the thirteenth century, but it is not known how soon thereafter the players discovered ways to cheat their opponents. But by the late sixteenth century, at least, the players had learned that cheating was more difficult, more easily detected, if the cards around the table were all kept in open sight—literally, "above the board." This expression was used so frequently among card-players that it became contracted in the early seventeenth century to *aboveboard*.

academy

Helen, who later became noted as the owner of the "face that launched a thousand ships," was the fabled Grecian queen whose abduction by Paris brought on the Trojan War described by Homer almost three thousand years ago. As a little girl in Sparta her beauty was even then so remarkable that, according to legend, the Athenian prince, Theseus, was so affected by it when he saw her dancing that he seized and hid her, intending to hold her until she was old enough to become his wife. But her mother, Leda, sent her sons, the twins Castor and Pollux, to find their sister. When they reached Athens, the story goes, they found someone who could help them, an Athenian named Academus. It was through his assistance that Helen was recovered and returned to Sparta. The Spartans were so grateful, according to one account, that they purchased a grove on the outskirts of Athens and presented it to their benefactor. In later years, this spot became a public garden, known as the Grove of Academus.

About the year 387 B.C., the Athenian philosopher, Plato, took up his residence upon a plot of ground that he owned, which directly adjoined this grove. It then became his habit, when the young men of Athens came to pursue their studies under him, to walk and talk with them along the paths of this peaceful spot. Plato continued this mode of instruction during the rest of his life, or for about forty years, as he was about eighty when he died, so it is not surprising that among the Athenians the school that he conducted was called the *Academia*, after the name of the grove. And when he died, it was found that he had made arrangements, according to the customs of that day, for his own estate to be converted into a religious foundation sacred to the Muses, for in that way his school could be perpetuated as an institution of learning. Thus, through Plato's chance use of a grove that had been the legendary property of an obscure Athenian countryman, we have obtained our word *academy*.

accost

The early sense was nautical, so much so that it was often written *accoast*, as if the meaning were "to lie along the coast of." The original meaning was not far from that, because the word was derived from the Latin prefix *ad*, to, plus *costa*, which, though actually meaning "rib," was extended to "side." So the nautical meaning was "to lie alongside," almost, as it were, rib to rib. Later the meaning became less exact, "to approach for the purpose of addressing," and now we use it most frequently just in the sense of "to address."

acre

The Old English word was *æcer*. In the Middle Ages, however, it was adapted to the Latin of the period and became *acra*, which gave rise to our present spelling. The word originally meant unoccupied country, whether field or woodland. But through increased interest in agriculture, the meaning became limited to land that could be cultivated. And by the time of the Norman Conquest, the extent of that land had become limited to the area that a yoke of oxen could plow in one day. Through the course of the next two centuries that method of measurement was seen to be unfair, the land allotted to a tenant depended not only upon the condition of his oxen, but upon the kind and condition of the soil to be plowed. A good yoke of oxen on level ground and rich light soil could plow twice as much as an ill-conditioned yoke on hilly, stony ground. In the reign of Edward I, therefore, the acre was fixed as a piece of land 40 rods in length by four rods in width. (A rod measures 16½ feet.) The practical farmer of those days took this to be thirty-two furrows of the plow, a furlong in length. But it has been many centuries since the acre was necessarily rectangular; now it may be of any shape, though its area is still fixed at 160 square rods or 4,840 square yards, as in the days of King Edward. (See also FURLONG.)

acrobat

From time immemorial, perhaps as proof of our relationship with the ape, man has amused himself by performing feats of daring upon ropes—ropes hanging from trees or high structures, or ropes tautly or loosely stretched high between two trees or other supports. In ancient Greece, skill in such feats became highly developed, though, like most paid entertainers of that era, the reputation of the performers was not above suspicion. Any such performer was known as an *acrobat*, one who walks aloft, from Greek *akros*, aloft, and *batos*, climbing or walking. (The full Greek term, *akrobatos*, is translated by some to mean walking on tiptoe.) Today we would call such a man a rope-walker or rope-dancer. But, although all the performers were classed as acrobats, among themselves or other well-informed persons they were separated into their several skills. The *neurobat* was at the top of the profession; considered among them as the true *acrobat*, for, as the name signified—*neuron*, sinew —this aerial dancer exercised his skill upon tautly stretched cords the thickness of catgut. So slender was the cord that, from a slight distance, he appeared to be dancing lightly upon air, sometimes playing the flute as he danced. The *schœnobat*—from *schoinion*, rope twisted of rushes—performed upon a thick rope, suspended from aloft, climbing it to dizzy heights, as a sailor does, tumbling about it held by a foot or knee, and showing his great strength and agility.

admiral

Abu-Bekr, the first successor to Mahomet, who died in A.D. 632, had been his faithful follower for many years. Upon taking the new title, *Caliph*, or "successor," he relinquished his former title, "The Faithful." This latter title was then taken by Omar, the man appointed to succeed him, who announced himself to be "Commander of the Faithful," or *Amir-al-muninin*. The title, "Commander," or *Amir* became increasingly popular after that. The Caliph himself was *Amir-al-Umara*, "Ruler of Rulers"; the minister of finance became *Amir-al-Ahgal*, and finally there came *Amir-al-Alam*, "Commander of Banners," and *Amir-al-Hajj*, "Commander of Caravans to Mecca."

Christian writers of the period naturally assumed that *Amir-al* was a single word, *amiral*. Later English writers then assumed that this word beginning with "am" was just another queer foreign way of spelling Latin words that began with "adm." But, though they now changed the spelling of the Moslem expression to *admiral*, they retained the original meaning, ruler, or prince, or commander. Italy, France, and Spain, however, began to follow the Saracen lead with a "Commander of the Sea" (*Amir-al-Bahr*). England also, not to be outdone, appointed such an officer for the British fleet in the late fourteenth century, and gave him the title *Admiral*. Thus when we say "Admiral Smith," we are using an Arabic expression which, if the literal meaning were observed, would be "Commander of the Smith," *Amir-al-Smith*.

afraid

Scarcely known nowadays, except in stories laid in olden times, is the verb *affray*. Its ancient meaning was "to startle out of one's rest," as by a clap of thunder or other sharp noise. That is, one who was *affrayed* was one who was alarmed. From alarm to fright was a natural development in meaning, so *affrayed*, in the sense of "frightened," had come to be common usage in the fourteenth century. Thanks to lack of uniform spelling before the eighteenth century, it has come down to us in the form *afraid*.

agony (antagonist)

Although we have since extended the meaning of this word to include intense physical suffering, such as we experience when in great pain, its original meaning in English referred to intense mental suffering or anguish, specifically that experienced by Christ in the Garden of Gethsemane, for it was in the English translation of the Bible in the fourteenth century that our word first appeared. This meaning was taken from the Greek *agonia*, but the way in which the Greek word developed that meaning is peculiar.

As far back as the days of Homer, *agon* denoted an assembly, a meeting of the people, usually for the discussion of public affairs. Hence, as time went by, any meeting of the Grecian people for any purpose came to be called an *agon*, especially one of the meetings devoted to games or contests. These contests might be athletic, such as the Olympic games, comprising foot races, wrestling, jumping, throwing the discus and the spear, or they might be musical, or for poetic competition, or for other competition in which one man or group might vie with another. From the place of the assembly, the *agon*, any such contest was an *agonia*.

Each *agonia* was, of course, a struggle between competitors, whether a physical combat between wrestlers or a mental combat between two dramatists. It was from the mental struggles of the latter group that *agonia* acquired its figurative sense of mental anguish, thus giving rise to our term, *agony*.

Incidentally, since it is derived from the same source, it might be noted that one of the rivals in the Greek *agonia* was an *agonistes*.

His opponent was therefore called an *antagonistes*, from *anti*, against, thus giving us the word *antagonist*.

aisle

One wonders how we acquired such a curiously formed word. By way of answer, we shouldn't have it. The spelling is the result of confusion; its present common meaning—a passageway, as in a church or theater—arose from still another confusion. The English word was originally *ele*, borrowed from the French in the fourteenth century; and that, in turn, came from the Latin *ala*, a wing, the original meaning of the word. It applied to the part on either side of the nave of a church, usually separated from the nave by a row of columns. But, as with many other words, *ele* had many spellings during the fifteenth and sixteenth centuries, of which *ile* was the most common. But *ile* was also the common spelling for a body of land surrounded by water; so when the latter word was given the spelling *isle* in the seventeenth century, the term relating to church architecture followed suit and also became *isle*. Changes in the French spelling of *ele* were taking place as well, and the French term had become *aile* in the meantime. English writers of the eighteenth century, in desperation, unwilling to have their readers think they were writing of "islands" in a church, threw the French and English spellings together into our present anomaly, *aisle*.

The French *aile*, however, had become confused through the centuries with *allée*, alley. So along with the union of *isle* and *aile* into *aisle*, the English word acquired, as well, an additional meaning, "passageway," and it is this meaning that has become the more common.

alarm

The Norman-French military call when, for example, a sentinel spied an enemy force approaching, was "*As armes! as armes!*" That summons was introduced into England where it was used for a while, but eventually it was translated into the equivalent English, "at arms!" which became the modern "to arms!" Similar calls were employed at the same period elsewhere in Europe. That used in Italian armies was "*all' arme!* (to arms!)" This became the popular call among other armies; but in every case the words that were called soon became the name of the cry or the name of any kind of signal to indicate danger. Italian *all' arme!* (to arms!) became *allarme*, French *alarme*, and English *alarm*, meaning "a warning sound," and lost its strictly military use. The word *alarum* arose from mispronunciation of *alarm*, for the same reason that causes many people to sound "film" as if it were spelled "fillum."

alcohol

From very early times the women of Oriental countries, desiring to enhance their beauty, have stained their eyelids with a very fine dark powder. This they call *koh'l*. The cosmetic is usually obtained from antimony. English writers of the sixteenth and seventeenth centuries in describing this cosmetic, thinking the definite article to be part of the word (*al-koh'l*), wrote it as *alcohol*. Early chemists then took this name and applied it to any extremely fine powder, so fine that one could not feel the separate grains. Thus, as one example, powdered sulfur was known as "*alcohol* of sulfur," a name that it retained into the nineteenth century. In the next step, the notion of similarly complete refinement began to require the name *alcohol* for liquids which seemed to have reached the superlative of refining. Such, in the late seventeenth century, seemed to have been attained by a wine which chemists and distillers spoke of as "*alcohol* of wine," and the term *alcohol* has since applied to liquids partly or wholly of the composition of that wine.

alert

Literally, *alert* means "on the watchtower." It came from an Italian military expression of the sixteenth century, *all' erta*, in which *all'* is a common contraction of *alla*, on. The original phrase was *stare all' erta*, "to stand on the watchtower." As conditions changed, the phrase merely meant "to stand watch." Ultimately, with the omission of the verb, it came into English in the seventeenth century further contracted to *alert*, and with its meaning altered to signify "on watch; vigilant."

alimony, aliment

Someone has said that *alimony* is no more than a telescoping of "all the money." It may seem so to a man who has little left after his former wife has received the monthly allowance awarded to her. Actually, however, the Latin *alimonia* was just a new-fangled spelling, two thousand years ago, of the older *alimentum*. Both of them, in those days, had the same meaning—nourishment, sustenance, provisions. From the first has come *alimony*, from the other, *aliment*. Thus the real intent of the word *alimony* is an allowance that will provide *aliment*, or a means of living.

alkali

Like our mathematics, we owe much of the early study of chemistry to Arabic scholars of the so-called Dark Ages. Thus the word *alkali* is but a transliteration of the Arabic *al-qalīy*, which means "the ashes of saltwort." Saltwort is a marine plant used in the production of sodium carbonate, formerly called soda ash. As chemists learned that other salts than sodium carbonate possessed some properties in common with it, *alkali* became a term common for all.

alligator

English writers of the sixteenth century correctly called this American creature a *lagarto*, for that was the Spanish name for this huge saurian—"lizard." But because Spaniards, like Arabs, are accustomed to put the definite article *al* before a noun—*al lagarto*, the lizard—careless English writers assumed that this was a single word—*allagarto*. This became further corrupted in the seventeenth century to *allegator*, and the present spelling became established in the early eighteenth century.

alone

One who is *alone* is distinctly "one," not two or more. And that was the original intent and use of the word. It was formed from *all one*, wholly one, and was used as two words until the fourteenth century. In those days and until about the end of the seventeenth century the word *one* was pronounced just as we pronounce "own" today. This pronunciation survives in "only." (See also ATONE.)

amazon

Before the days of the Trojan War, according to the legendary tales of Homer, there was a tribe of fierce warriors living near the Caucasus Mountains. They were ruled by a queen, it was said, and they had waged war against other tribes in Asia Minor and had even invaded Greece. But the peculiar thing about this tribe was that all its members were women; there were no men among them. Once each year they met a neighboring tribe of men, but any boys that might be born from such a union were either killed or sent over the hills to their fathers. The girls were kept and were trained for warfare and the hardships of military life. These strange women were called *Amazons*, a name that the Greeks believed came from the two words, *a*, without, and *mazos*, breast, because, as Homer explained, in order that they might be more skilled in the use of bow and arrow, the right breast of each woman had been removed. Many paintings and some statuary of this warlike race have been preserved which, though they do not support the explanation that was given for the origin of the name, do show that the Greek artists believed the Amazons to have been large and powerful women of noble proportions. It is in this sense in which *amazon* is now used. The large river in South America received its name from the Spanish explorer, Orellana, who, in his first descent of the river in 1541, was attacked by a tribe of natives, among whom the women fought alongside the men. He thought them to be another tribe similar to that known by ancient Greeks, and gave them the name *Amazon*.

ambiguous

In the Latin language, it was the custom to do about as we do today; that is, to give a verb a particular meaning by using a preposition along with it. Thus, with our verb "to walk," we may say "to walk in," meaning "to enter"; "to walk up," meaning "to ascend"; "to walk down," meaning "to descend," and so on. The Romans, however, placed their prepositions before the verb, and usually combined the two words into one. The preposition *ambi*, which means "around" or "roundabout," was one of those usually combined. And when combined it was often shortened into *amb*, or into *am*, or even changed into *amp*. Our English word *ambiguous*, from the Latin *ambiguus*, was thus originally formed from the Latin verb *ambigo*, which came from the two Latin words *ambi*, roundabout, and *ago*, to drive. So the verb meant to drive roundabout, or in a wavering or uncertain manner—as a charioteer might drive if he weren't certain of the road or if the way were indistinct. At a time when there were few roads it was a common experience to wander hesitantly about the countryside when seeking a strange place, so the verb came to denote any kind of wandering or uncertain moving, and it is thus that *ambiguous* acquired the meaning "uncertain, vague."

ambition

Roman candidates for public office who wore a white toga (see CANDIDATE) were not content simply to be seen whenever they happened to be outdoors. They knew that if they wanted many of the voters to notice their glistening white togas they would have to go about from place to place where the voters were, talking with them—canvassing for votes, as we would say. Now the Latin word for "to go about, to move round," was *ambio*, from *ambi*, about, and *eo*, go. In time this verb acquired the extended meaning, "to go about for the purpose of soliciting votes." Thus the noun *ambitio*, from which our noun *ambition* was formed, formerly meaning "a going about," now denoted "a soliciting of office; a canvassing for votes"; and a person who was *ambitiosus—ambitious* is our word— was one who went about with the obvious intent of courting favor, seeking by his manner to obtain votes.

What had been originally a harmless practice of walking about to exhibit one's white toga generally, began to acquire a sinister meaning; an *ambitious* person was suspected, and was often guilty, of using underhand methods to obtain votes. In fact, so definite did the practice become and so identified in the Roman mind with *ambitio*, that the word *ambitus* was coined to designate bribery by office-seekers. In 181 B.C., the first of many laws was enacted against it. But when *ambition* and *ambitious* came into our language, through French, back in the fourteenth century, men were usually appointed to public office by kings. The words then lost the flavor of political crookedness; the chief meaning of each, as today, implied no more than eager desire for advancement or power.

ambulance

Until late in the eighteenth century any soldier wounded in battle was likely to lie where he fell until nightfall or until the battle was over. Even then his chance of surgical attention was slim unless a comrade carried him to the rear, for surgeons did not reach the battlefield until the next day. But toward the end of that century there was introduced into the French army a rather crude system for bringing quicker aid to the wounded. A vehicle, equipped to carry the injured, and furnished with bandages, tourniquets, and the like to stop the flow of blood, moved behind the lines to pick up and transport the wounded to the hospitals. Such a vehicle was called *hôpital ambulant*, traveling hospital, from the Latin *ambulo*, travel, walk, move. They had been devised at the instigation of a young surgeon, Dominique Jean Larrey, later created baron by Napoleon in appreciation of his services. For a time the vehicles were called *ambulances volantes*, literally "flying travelers." The name was shortened in England to the present *ambulance*, literally, thus, "a traveler."

amethyst

Among the many superstitions of the ancient Greeks was one concerning the wearing of a certain rare stone. To be effective, this stone had to be clear and very like the wine of the grape in color; that is, a clear purple or bluish violet. The possessor or wearer of such a stone, it was believed, would not become intoxicated, no matter how much wine he might drink. So the Greeks named this precious charm against intoxication, *amethystos*, not drunken, from the negative prefix *a*, and *methy*, wine. It is in dim remembrance of the ancient belief that this stone, the *amethyst*, has been favored by men, worn in a ring or as a watch fob.

ampersand

Back in the Middle Ages, when only a few people could write, and those usually priests, most of the writing was in Latin. But in those days, just as with us now, one of the words that occurred very frequently was "and." The Latin word for "and" is *et*. In part because of the script then used, and in part because of frequent use, this Latin word came to be generally written "&." Later, English began to replace Latin, and the character which we generally see now (&) began to replace the older one.

Now, when children were learning the alphabet in those early days, they were taught to distinguish between the letter "a" and the word "a"—that is, to see that in "a boy," "a" is a word. So the word was described as "*a per se*," in which the Latin *per se* means "by itself." Sometimes it was written "*a-per-se*," sometimes, "*A-per-se-A*"; the meaning was, "*a* taken by itself makes the word *a*." The pronoun "I" was also so distinguished—"*I-per-se-I*." And at the very end of the alphabet, after the letter "z" in their "A-B-C books," the children were taught to recognize the common character "&." This, in similar manner, they called, "*and-per-se-and*." That is, the old monks who first taught them said, "*and-per-se-and*," but children's ears in those days were no more acute than in these, so it was repeated as *ampassy-and*, *ampussy-and*, and even as *amsiam*. The least corrupt of the forms, however, came down to us as *ampersand*, which is now recognized as the name of the character, &.

anecdote

Justinian, emperor of the Byzantine Empire from A.D. 527 to 565, was one of the few really great emperors of that division of the old Roman Empire. He is noted especially for the framing of the legal code, since known as the Justinian Code. Among the attendants at his court was the historian, Procopius, who, when he had completed a history of the wars waged during the reign of his emperor, wrote also an account of the many structures erected by his master. Now Justinian, though professedly a Christian monarch, indulged in or permitted many of the vices and excesses common to Oriental courts of the period, and Procopius had an observant eye and a satiric pen. He knew the inside lives of the persons of the court, and he was moved to indulge his satire and to write brief accounts of some of the incidents he had observed concerning the emperor, his wife, Theodora, and other eminent persons. Some of his tales were witty and pleasant, but most of them were indecent or absurd. Possibly he did not intend that the tales should ever be published, because he gave them the title, *Anecdota*, a Greek word meaning "unpublished, kept secret." The manuscript was published, however, and the term thereafter meant a brief true story about someone or some event. Early *anecdotes*, like those of Procopius, related to persons or events connected with court life, but the term is now used for any short story assumed to be fact.

228

anthem

Originally this was the same word and had the same meaning as *antiphon*, a response, sung or chanted. Introduced into Christian worship, the Greek *antiphon*, in the speech of the priests, became Old English *antefne*. Then and for many centuries thereafter it referred to a composition for two voices or two choirs sung or chanted alternately. The Old English word gradually altered to the present *anthem*. Later, when the meaning of *anthem* was extended to embrace sacred music generally, whether for solo, duet, or choral singing, the Greek term *antiphon* was reintroduced to provide for the original meaning.

antic (grotesque)

Back in the early sixteenth century, some Italian archeologists, in Rome, were digging about in the ruins of the huge structure now known to be the Baths erected by the emperor Titus. Unexpectedly running across some chambers that had long been buried, they found that the walls were covered with paintings. These paintings were of a strange composition, hitherto unknown among the painters of the Christian Era. They showed fantastic representations of human, animal, and floral forms, curiously intermixed and compounded— heads of beasts upon the bodies of men; centaurs, satyrs, tritons, as well as shapes and fancies designed by the artist about such figures; flowers and vines of unknown kinds, impossibly supported figures seated among them. Because these paintings were ascribed to the ancients, the Italians described them as *antica*, antique. In the spelling of England at that time this became *antike, anticke, antick*, and finally *antic*. Hence, though first pertaining to the ancient and comic type of decorative art, the meaning gradually became also synonymous with ludicrous, and referred especially to an absurd gesture, pose, or trick that excited laughter, such as those shown in the ancient Roman paintings. The Italian name for these curious paintings, however, and for the equally fantastic sculptured forms sometimes found, was *grottesca*, a name formed from *grotte*, the grottoes or excavations in which the curious figures were discovered. This Italian term was later borrowed by French scholars in the form *grotesque*, and the French name ultimately reached England, though not until a century later than *antic*.

antimacassar (tidy)

Our ancestors were just as vain as we are, and, like ourselves, were always searching for ways to make the hair more attractive. Early in the nineteenth century a new unguent for the hair was produced which, its makers vowed, possessed marvelous properties. This oil, they said, came from the Dutch East Indies, from a district named Macassar on the Island of Celebes. Lord Byron, in 1819, referred to this preparation in *Don Juan*:

> In virtues nothing earthly could surpass her,
> Save thine "incomparable oil," Macassar.

The preparation retained its popularity for a long period, but housewives found it to be a source of serious annoyance. The oil left its stain upon the back of their brocaded chairs, and could not be removed. They could do nothing more than cover the spot with a cloth until the chair could be reupholstered; but as use of the grease persisted and they could not constantly have chairs recovered they had to seek ways to prevent the damage. They solved this by a lace or crocheted piece of fancy-work hung over or pinned to the back of the chair. It protected the chair and could be easily removed and washed when soiled. Because of its purpose it was called an *antimacassar*, from *anti*, against, plus *Macassar*. It was also less pretentiously called a "tidy," for it was intended to keep the chair tidy. Both names have been extended to include similar coverings for chair-arms.

apron (adder, auger, umpire, orange)

Strangely enough, even as recently as the fifteenth and sixteenth centuries, our ancestors were accustomed to speak of this protective garment as "napron." The word was adapted from the French *naperon*; in modern French, *napperon*, now meaning "napkin." But our forefathers were careless, even as we are, and "*a napron*" became slurred in speech into "*an apron*," and so it remained. Other similar corruptions were "*an adder*" (snake) from "*a nadder*"; "*an auger*" from "*a nauger*"; "*an eft*," formerly spelt *ewt*, from "*a newt*,"

230

though both forms have survived, and *"an umpire"* from *"a num-pire,"* taken from the Old French *non*, not, and *per*, peer. Our word *orange* was adapted from the Italian *arancia*, which itself had suffered a like alteration from *"una narancia."*

arena

The amphitheaters of ancient Rome were structures that resembled in many respects the stadiums in many of the colleges and cities of the United States. The structures, both ancient and modern, were erected so that spectators could easily see and enjoy the contests in the large open spaces which they surrounded. But the great difference lies in the nature of the contests. In the stadium a contestant is injured only by accident; but in the amphitheater the crowds of spectators expected to see bloodshed—gladiators fighting one another to death with swords or other weapons, or infuriated wild animals turned loose upon poorly armed or defenseless human victims. Therefore, because the hard-packed ground of the old amphitheaters would not soak up the quantities of blood spilled upon it in a contest, it was always liberally covered with sand. And it was this sand by which the place of combat became known, for *arena* is the Latin word for "sand."

arrant (errant)

We use it now to mean downright, out-and-out, unmitigated; as, an *arrant* coward, an *arrant* scoundrel. But it was formerly just another spelling of "errant," and it meant wandering, vagabond, nomad. Thus a "knight errant," in the Age of Chivalry, was a knight, usually young, who roamed the countryside, seeking an opportunity to win an accolade through good deeds. In similar style a bandit or highwayman five or six centuries ago was termed an *"arrant* thief," meaning one who wandered over the countryside, holding up persons whom he might encounter.

arrive

If we were to use this word only with regard to its source and original sense we would use it exclusively when the destination was reached by water. That was the usual application until about four

231

centuries ago. The source was the Latin *ad*, to, and *ripa*, land or shore. Its meaning was "to come to the shore; to reach land."

assassin

Late in the eleventh century, Hassan ben Sabbah, forced from his studies in Cairo, returned to his home in Persia. He then acquired a mountain fortress in the southern part of the country, and made it the seat of a new religious organization. Though the principles were mainly those of one of the leading sects of Mohammedanism, he determined that the head of the organization itself should be an absolute ruler. During the two centuries in which it flourished, the new sect wielded great power, not only throughout Persia, but also in all of Asia Minor, because of the terror it inspired. The hereditary title of its chieftain was Sheik-al-Jebal, known among the European Crusaders as "the Old Man of the Mountains," a name that caused the bravest among them to tremble.

The lowest order and the most numerous of its members was a body of young men known as the *Fedahvis*, "the Devoted Ones." The most absolute obedience was required of them, even, if ordered, to embrace death without question or hesitation. And it was this group that caused the terror in which the sect was held, for it was the duty of its members to kill any person whom the chieftain might designate. That person would be killed. If the first youth were slain in the attempt, another, or another, or another would fulfil the order. The score of murder in Persia, Syria, and Arabia was high during those centuries.

But before these young men were sent out on their tasks, they were induced to partake liberally of hashish. This is the Oriental equivalent of marihuana, but is more powerful. The young votaries, under the stupefying influence and ecstatic effect of this drug, were not only utterly fearless, but eager for the bliss of Paradise. In the Arabic language, they were *hashashin*, or, "eaters of hashish." Travelers from Europe understood the word to be *assassin*.

assets

When a person dies the immediate concern of his heir or the executor of his estate is to determine whether he left sufficient property to pay his debts and legacies. In England, after the days of William the Conqueror, this was known by the Anglo-French legal term, *aver assetz,* from *aver,* to have, and *assetz,* sufficient, hence "to have sufficient (to meet the claims)." In the French of today this would be *avoir assez.* Thus *assets,* stripped of meanings that it has acquired through the years, rightfully means nothing more than "sufficient."

atlas

One of the oldest of the Grecian myths tells of the struggle for supremacy between Zeus and the Titans, the sons and grandsons of Uranus and Gæa. The leader of the Titans was the powerful Atlas. And when the Titans were overcome, Atlas, in punishment, was obliged thereafter to bear the weight of the heavens upon his shoulders throughout all eternity. (Later legends say that he was transformed into a mountain, which bore the heavens upon its peak. This legend accounts for the name of the Atlas Mountains in northwest Africa.) Ancient artists, in picturing the scene, showed the heavens as a huge globe of tremendous weight that Atlas supported. A copy of one of these pictures was used in the sixteenth century by the Flemish geographer, Mercator, as a frontispiece to his first collection of maps. Such a picture was deemed so happy a selection for a volume of maps that similar ones were carried by all succeeding map makers. Thus through constant association of the Greek hero with a volume of maps, the book itself began to be known by his name.

atone

Nowadays when we are in full agreement or have a fellow-feeling with another, we say that we see eye to eye, or that we are hand in glove with him. Back in the thirteenth century and for the next several hundred years, the saying was to be *at one,* or to set *at one* with the other. The expression was so commonly employed, especially in sermons—"to set *at one* with God"—that by the fifteenth century, it was frequently written as a solid word, *"atone."* (The word "one" was pronounced in those days as we pronounce "own.") The change in meaning of the solid word was gradual. Thus, when Shakespeare wrote, in Richard II, "Since we cannot *atone* you," he meant, "Since we cannot set you at one." From this notion of reconciliation came the idea of expiation; that is, to become reconciled

233

with another by making amends for a fault, or by settling differences. The noun *atonement* developed in similar manner from *at onement*, the condition of being *at one*. (See also ALONE.)

atropine

Three goddesses were in control of all human destinies, according to ancient Greek belief. They determined when a man should be born, what his activities should be during his life, and when and under what circumstances he should die. These three beautiful sisters were known, therefore, as the goddesses of Fate, or the Three Fates. Clotho, the first of the sisters, controlled the time and place of birth; Lachesis laid out the course of life, and Atropos, the dark-haired one of the three, cut the thread of life. Thus, because Atropos had in her power all the agencies which might cause man to die, according to this ancient thought, the name of this goddess was fancifully given by botanists to one of the genera of deadly plants of the nightshade family, the poisonous *Atropa*. And chemists in their turn have still further commemorated the death-disposing goddess by the name *atropine* given to the poisonous drug extracted from this plant.

auburn

Strangely enough, when this first came into the language, after the Norman Conquest, it was used as a perfect description of the color of the flaxen hair of the Saxons, a yellowish hue. The Old French spelling was *alborne* or *auborne*. But after being taken into English the spelling began to vary, taking a number of different forms. Thus in the seventeenth century it moved from *abron* to *abroun* and *abrown*, and because of this latter spelling the meaning of the word shifted into that which we still give it, a reddish brown. Our present spelling, however, is a compromise of the eighteenth century.

August (July)

In the name of this month we still commemorate the first emperor of the Roman Empire, more than nineteen hundred years after his death. His real name was Caius Octavianus, which was also his father's name. His mother, Julia, was the sister of Julius Caesar, the great Roman general. The young Octavianus, better known as

234

Octavius, was but nineteen when the news of the murder of Caesar reached him in Spain in 44 B.C. Upon returning to Italy immediately thereafter he learned that his late uncle, who had always treated him as a son, had previously adopted him secretly and had willed him his entire property. Octavius then took as his official name, Caius Julius Caesar Octavianus. Trained both in the science of war and the art of statesmanship by his uncle, he became immensely popular with the army and with the people, his successes in the field increasing his popularity at home. Egypt fell before his armies in the year 30 B.C., and both the Roman senate and people vied with each other to heap additional honors upon the young general. Already a consul for the fifth successive year, he became the actual ruler of the Roman Empire in 29 B.C. and, two years later, was declared *Augustus* by the senate, a title equivalent to that of "imperial majesty." As a further honor, because the fifth month of the year (see JANUARY), previously called *Quinctilis*, had been renamed *Julius* (*July*) in honor of Julius Caesar, the senate decreed that the sixth month, previously *Sextilis*, should be renamed *Augustus* (*August*). And, so that the two months would be of equal length, a day was taken from the last month of the year, February, and added to the sixth month. Octavius Augustus, the name by which he is known in history, ruled his vast empire wisely until his death at the age of seventy-five in the year A.D. 14.

auspice

Ancient peoples held the firm belief that future events and the purposes of their gods were revealed by certain signs. These signs, however, could be understood only by the very devout, especially trained to observe and to interpret. Different nations had different beliefs in the way these signs were delivered, but among the forerunners of the Roman people, and by the Romans also, the signs or omens were thought to come through the birds, which, flying in the heavens, could readily be guided by the gods on high. Hence, among the ancient Latin peoples, certain men were appointed to watch the flights of birds, to determine what kind of birds they were, to note the quarter of the sky in which they appeared and the direction of their flight, and, in some instances, to listen to their songs and to observe the food which they ate. Such a man was called an *auspex*, a word derived from the Latin *avis*, bird, and *specio*, to see. (In later times the *auspex* was replaced by the *augur*. See IN-AUGURATE.) The services of the auspex were called upon when anything of importance was under consideration. It was his function to say whether the signs were or were not favorable. That function was termed an *auspicium*, a term that was later applied to the prophetic token itself, to the omen or sign. This latter meaning was retained in the English *auspice*, but with a favorable sense especially. Thus when we use the phrase, "under the auspices of," we mean that our undertaking is under the benevolent protection or patronage of the named person or body. And when we say that such and such a moment, or occasion or event is *auspicious*, we express belief in its success, as if the gods were approving the undertaking.

babbitt

When still a young man, Isaac Babbitt produced the first of several inventions by which he became famous. He had been apprenticed as a youth to a goldsmith in Taunton, Massachusetts, where he was born, and it was in this employment that he acquired an interest in metallurgy. Hence, in 1824, when he was but twenty-five years old, he turned out the first Britannia ware that was produced in the United States. This metal is an alloy of copper, tin, and antimony; its successful production led the young man to further investigations with the same three substances, with the result that, in 1839, he produced a metal which, when used for machine bearings, was found to be far better than anything yet discovered at that time for reducing friction. Mr. Babbitt received a grant from Congress for this invention, which is still widely used in mechanical operations and still carries the name *babbitt* or *babbitt metal*. There are also many housewives who are familiar with the soap, *Babbitt soap*, that he manufactured. (Isaac *Babbitt* did not furnish the model for the fictitious character, George Follansbee *Babbitt*, described by Sinclair Lewis in his novel, *Babbitt*. The latter name has also taken its place in the language as a descriptive term for a type of American businessman, ambitious and smugly satisfied with the outward show of prosperity, but totally lacking in culture and refinement.)

babel

Every Sunday School scholar knows that we got this word from the high tower which the descendants of Noah started to erect, "whose top may reach unto heaven." The name of the tower and of the city which was also being built was *Babel*. But the Lord, according to the eleventh chapter of Genesis, did not approve of the presumption of these men, and brought their purpose all to nought by causing each to speak in a tongue unknown to any of the others. No one could understand anyone else. Probably, as we do to this day on like occasions, each thereupon shouted the louder. Hence, any such confusion of voices we refer to as *babel*.

baffle

Little is known of its source, but *baffle*, in the sixteenth century, was thought to be a Scottish term. We use it now when we mean "to flabbergast, confuse, frustrate, foil"; but in those days it meant "to disgrace publicly." It seems to have referred especially to the manner in which a knight who had forsworn his oath was held up to ridicule and ignominy. For, in the earliest record, we are told that the Scots would "baffull" such a man. This, says the account, was done by painting a picture of him, in which he was shown hung up by the heels. Edmund Spenser describes it in *Faerie Queene*:

> He by the heels him hung upon a tree
> And bafful'd so, that all which passed by
> The picture of his punishment might see.

bailiwick

A *wick*, in olden times, was a village—from the Latin, *vicus*, village. (It survives now chiefly in place names, often as *wich*, as in Warwick, Greenwich, Norwich.) And the bailie, whom we now call *bailiff*, was the administrative officer. Thus a *bailiwick* was actually the district over which a bailiff had jurisdiction. We use the term figuratively now to mean also any place that one regards as one's own.

baize

Back in the sixteenth century, during the period when Spain had given the cruel Duke of Alva complete authority over the Netherlands, more than 100,000 Dutch Protestants were forced to flee the country. Many of them went across the channel to England, and of these, many were weavers. Textile weaving had long been a staple industry in England, but these Dutch weavers, as well as similar emigrants who fled from France, were welcomed because they introduced a number of fabrics that had not previously been made in England. Among these was a woolen fabric, light and fine in texture and, originally, of chestnut color. Because of its color, this material was known among the foreign weavers by its French name, *bai*, though more commonly under the plural form, *bais*. English spelling was most erratic in those days, so the French *bais* became *bays* (often with a second plural *bayses*), *bayes*, *baies*, *bayze*, and *baize*. This last artificial form has persisted, but the material, of any color nowadays, would not now be recognized by the early Dutch weavers.

Bakelite

Leo Hendrik Baekeland was born in Belgium in 1863, studied and taught chemistry in his native land, but then, at the age of twenty-six, emigrated to the United States. There, for the rest of his life—he died in 1944—he engaged in industrial research. His earliest invention was the photographic paper, "Velox." But the invention for which he was best known is a plastic, valuable as a nonconductor of electricity and as a heat resistant. This was given the registered name *Bakelite*, formed from the name of its inventor.

ballot

Originally, this meant "little ball," contracted from the Italian *ballotta*. It may be easy to recall this original meaning if we remember that, formerly, the method of voting was through the use of a small ball—white or black, according as one voted affirmatively or negatively—dropped secretly into a receptacle. The method, still used in some organizations, is extremely old. In ancient Athens it was employed by the judges, or dicasts, in giving their verdicts, except that small shells or beans or balls of metal or stone, variously colored or marked, were used as the ballots. From the frequent use of beans in Athenian elections, a politician was sometimes humorously called a "bean-eater."

baluster (banister)

Probably because they could be turned out more easily on a lathe, the short upright columns for supporting a handrail were made, in the Middle Ages, in circular section and a doubly curved outline, a narrow neck above, swelling into a pear-shaped bulge below. These columns strongly resembled the shape of the flower of the wild pomegranate. The Italian name of this flower, taken from the Latin and thence from the Greek, is *balaustra*, and this then became the Italian name of the column. French architects adopted the column because of its beauty, but spelled the name *balustre*, which, in turn, became *baluster* in English. Thanks to careless speech and to indifferent hearing, the form *banister* began to be used shortly after the new word *baluster* was introduced. The corrupted term has been frowned upon and condemned by purists ever since, but it has taken a firm position in the language and is now more commonly used than *baluster*.

balloon

Back in the late 1500's and early 1600's the young men of England had a game of football that seems to have borne some resemblance to the later game of rugby. The player might either kick the ball or strike it with his arm or hand, though the inflated ball was so large and so heavy that the players were obliged to wear a bracer of wood strapped to the arm and hand to prevent injury. Both the game and the ball with which it was played were named *balloon*, a name derived from the French *ballon*, meaning a large ball. The next step in the history of the word came in the early 1630's. Some unknown genius discovered a way to stuff pyrotechnics into a cardboard ball which, shot from a mortar, made a wonderful display of fireworks when the ball was high in the sky. This was also a large ball, and so, naturally, was called *balloon*. But a far larger ball was devised by the Montgolfier brothers of France in 1783. This was a huge bag which, when filled with hot air, ascended above the earth. This too, obviously, was called *balloon*. It was the forerunner of that which we now know by the name.

bandanna

When Portuguese explorers in India, back in the sixteenth century, began to learn about the various beautiful cloths produced in the country, they saw that one owed its interesting appearance to the curious manner in which it was prepared for dyeing. The cloth was tightly knotted before it was dipped into the dye, and thus some portions of the cloth retained the original color. The Hindus called this method of dyeing, *bāndhnu*, a word that, coming through the Portuguese, has given us the English *bandanna*. The original material in India was silk. The process was later applied to cotton, and chemical means have been substituted to obtain the former effect produced by knots.

bankrupt

From time immemorial there have been money-changers. These were men who, for a premium, calculated the value of currency received by a merchant dealing with foreign countries and exchanged it for domestic money. Their business was conducted in some public place, such as the market place in Athens, the forum in Rome, or the temple in Jerusalem. There they set up a small table or bench for the convenience of their customers. In later times, as in the cities of Florence and Venice, which were the chief trading centers of the Middle Ages, such a table or bench had the name *banca*, the source of "bank," for these money-changers corresponded in some degree with our modern bankers.

Although the principal occupation was changing money, these men sometimes took money from wealthy patrons which, with their own, they lent to others at a profit—a rate of interest that would be considered usury now. But there was always a risk involved in such a loan—the borrower might lose his life, his goods, and his ship through some disaster. A succession of such misfortunes could cause the failure of the banker, unable to repay his own creditors. The laws of ancient Rome, though perhaps never exercised, permitted creditors actually to divide the body of a debtor into parts proportionate to their claims. However, the penalty was less severe in the Middle Ages. The creditors of such a banker or his fellows in the market place merely broke up his table or bench, thus showing

240

that he was no longer in business. This, in Florence, was designated *banca rotta*, broken bench. Italian bankers of the sixteenth and seventeenth centuries carried this expression of business failure into England, but the Italian *rotta* gradually gave way to the Latin word for broken—*ruptus*—and *banca rotta*, altered to *banca rupta*, became corrupted to our present term, *bankrupt*.

barbarous

To the ancient Greeks the sound made by two foreigners talking together was as if they said "bar-bar-bar-bar" to each other. So they called any unintelligible speech, *barbaros*, and applied it to any language that was not Greek. Later on, the Romans borrowed the word, changing it to *barbarus*, and had it apply to any language that was neither Roman nor Greek. The sense then became extended to embrace anything of any nature that was foreign to either Greece or Rome. That included the people. So great was the feeling of superiority among Greeks and Romans that they considered customs which differed from their own and all foreign persons to be necessarily crude, uncultured, and uncivilized. Although *barbarous*, which we in turn have borrowed, still retains this latter meaning, we no longer apply it indiscriminately to all foreign ways and persons.

barbecue

The Spaniards, when they took possession of Haiti shortly after its discovery by Columbus, saw many customs among the natives which were strange to them. Among those for which they could readily see the reason was an elevated framework upon which to sleep. This was a protection against marauding beasts. A similar framework, with a fire beneath, was used for drying or smoking fish and meat. The natives, as nearly as the Spaniards could understand, had a general name for such an elevated framework, regardless of its use. They called it *barbacoa*. Thus when the Spaniards themselves roasted meat upon a spit over an outdoor fire, they fell into the habit of using the native name, calling the frame upon which the meat was roasted, *barbacoa*. The name was carried to various Spanish colonies, and was thus introduced into the colonies of North America, slightly corrupted into *barbecue*. (See also BUCCANEER.)

241

Barmecide

This occurs usually in the expression "Barmecide feast" or "Barmecide banquet." It comes from the "Story of the Barber's Sixth Brother" in *Arabian Nights*. A poor man who had been without food for several days, it relates, begged for bread at the door of the rich Persian noble, Barmecide. To his amazement he was invited to the table. Servants brought in golden platter after golden platter, and his host urged him to help himself bountifully. But there was nothing upon any of the platters, though the beggar, entering into the spirit of the jest, pretended to pile his plate full and to eat heartily. Finally the wine jug was brought. It, too, was empty, though the beggar pretended to fill his goblet frequently and to become quite drunk. Then, seeming to be intoxicated, he boxed his host heartily on the ears. This and the good nature of the poor man so delighted Barmecide that a real banquet was brought upon the table. Hence, in modern literature, a *Barmecide* is one who offers an unreal or disappointing benefit, and a *Barmecide feast* is either nothing at all or a meal that leaves much to the imagination.

barnacle

It was firmly believed by our ancestors, even so recently as in Shakespeare's time, that the goose which we still call *barnacle goose* came out of the shell of a nut or tiny gourd growing upon certain trees along the seashore. Some thought that the immature birds were attached to the trees by their bills, but the more general belief was that the birds did not develop until the nuts fell into the sea, where they became small shellfish and attached themselves to any floating object until the birds were ready for flight. That is to say, the small shellfish or *barnacle* which we find attached over the face of a rock in the sea or upon the bottom of a ship, or the like, was formerly believed to have begun its life as the nut of a tree and to be itself capable of developing into a kind of goose. The legend developed because the breeding habits of the barnacle goose were long unknown. Always some fable was invented, in olden times, which would account for the unknown.

basilisk

Although we apply this name now to a South American lizard, which grows to a length of about two feet, this harmless animal only faintly resembles the fabulous reptile that terrified the people of medieval and ancient times. The name was originally Greek, *basiliskos*, little king, from *basil*, a crown, because the monster was said to have a spot on its head that resembled a crown. (The South American basilisk has a crest which it can erect.) The mythical *basilisk* came, it was believed, from an egg laid by a cock; it lived in the deserts of Africa; its hissing was so powerful that all other serpents fled from it; its breath was fatal and so fiery as to kill off all vegetation. The very sight of it, according to some writers, was enough to kill a man. (See also COCKATRICE.)

batiste

Among the weavers of Kameric, the old Flemish name of Cambrai, was one who was able to produce upon his loom a linen fabric that was even softer and finer than that produced by any of his neighbors. Nothing is known of this man beyond his name, Jean Baptiste. But English merchants, having already given the name "cambric" to the general products of Kameric, needed a name for the newer and finer material which they began to import in the seventeenth century. Therefore, they decided to call it by the name of the weaver and, indifferent to French spelling, wrote it *batiste*. The material was originally of linen, but the name is now often applied to sheer cotton or silk fabrics, and to thin, lightweight wool.

battering-ram

Long before the days of Alexander the Great some military genius hit upon a scheme for entering the walls of an opposing city. He ordered a group of his soldiers to take a long log and swing it repeatedly against a vulnerable spot in the wall. In later improvements, the beam, sometimes eighty, a hundred, or even a hundred and twenty feet in length, was hung by chains from a frame under a protective canopy and operated by a hundred or more men. No wall could be built in those ancient times, according to one chronicler, that could withstand such battering if long continued. To protect the head of the beam and to make its blows more effective, it was at first shod with iron. The machine was already called a *ram* (Latin, *aries*), in allusion to the butting propensities of the male sheep. Hence, to make the allusion even more fitting, the ancient artisans fashioned the head into the form of a ram's head. The Roman military machine remained in use among European armies until the invention of gunpowder. Its English name, *ram* or *battering-ram*, is no more than a translation of the name used in the days of Caesar.

bazooka

Bob Burns, radio humorist, in a letter to the author, says that he coined this term to fit the alleged musical instrument that he has made familiar to radio listeners. His explanation follows:

I started taking mandolin and trombone lessons when I was six years old in Van Buren, Arkansas. When I was eight, I started playing the mandolin in the school string orchestra, and when I was nine, I was playing the slide trombone with Frank MacClain's "Van Buren Queen City Silvertone Cornet Band." In 1905 our string band was practicing in back of Hayman's Plumbing Shop in Van Buren, and while we were playing "Over the Waves" waltz, I broke a string on the mandolin. With nothing else to do, I picked up a piece of gas pipe, inch and a half in diameter and about twenty inches long. And when I blew in one end, I was very much surprised to get a bass note. Then, kidlike, I rolled up a piece of music and stuck it in the other end of the gas pipe and found that sliding it out and in like a trombone, I could get about three "fuzzy" bass notes. The laughter that I got encouraged me to have a tin tube made that I could hold on to and slide back and forth inside the inch-and-a-half gas pipe. Later on I soldered a funnel on the end of the tin tube and a wire attached to the funnel to give me a little longer reach.

No doubt you have heard the expression, "He blows his bazoo too much." In Arkansas that is said of a "windy" guy who talks too much. Inasmuch as the bazooka is played by the mouth, it's noisy and takes a lot of wind. It just seemed like "bazoo" fitted in pretty well as part of the name. The affix "ka" rounded it out and made it sound like the name of a musical instrument—like balalaika and harmonica.

Mr. Burns adds that the proudest moment of his life was when he learned that the rocket gun, used by American soldiers in World War II, had been named *bazooka* after his instrument. According to a letter from the Ordnance Department, he says, when the new gun was being demonstrated in the presence of General Somervell a captain in the group of officers gave the gun a surprised look and said, "That damn' thing looks just like Bob Burns' bazooka." There was general laughter, in which General Somervell joined, and from then on the gun became known as a *bazooka*.

bedlam

Back in the time when Henry VIII was king of England, that is, back in the first half of the sixteenth century, there stood in London a structure known as the Hospital of St. Mary of Bethlehem. It had been erected three hundred years earlier, in 1247, as a priory for the sisters and brethren of the religious order of the Star of Bethlehem. One of its functions was to serve as a place of rest and entertainment for visiting dignitaries of the Order, for that is what the word "hospital" indicated in those days. But sick people were also sometimes received at such places, and by the year 1400 the Hospital of St. Mary of Bethlehem was one of the few places in Europe where insane persons were occasionally cared for.

In 1536, after Henry VIII had brought about a severance of the Church of England from the Roman Catholic Church, he ordered that most of the monasteries in England should be dissolved. He had little better reason for this act than to display his power. The religious order of the Star of Bethlehem was among those affected, so the Hospital of St. Mary of Bethlehem passed into the possession of the corporation of London. It was then entirely converted into an asylum for the insane, with fifty or sixty lunatics confined in it.

In those days, it must be remembered, insane persons were treated more like animals than like human beings. If violent, they were chained to the wall, and, as recorded by Samuel Pepys and others, they were often exhibited to visitors and made sport of, like wild beasts in a cage. And the confusion and din created by these wild, crazed people must have been indescribable.

Now, the name of the hospital had long previously been shortened to "Bethlehem." People in those days were even more careless in their speech, however, than those of today, so "Bethlehem" had been further contracted to "Bethlem," and this in turn was commonly pronounced and often spelled "Bedlam." Thus *Bedlam* became the common name for the hospital after it was converted into an insane asylum. From that time to this, therefore, anything that compares with the din and confusion in that ancient madhouse is described as *bedlam*.

beggar

Because proof is lacking, the dictionaries play safe by saying that this is probably just a derivative of *beg*, which in turn may have come from an unusual Old English term, *bedecian*. But some scholars flout that theory; they believe that *beggar* was first in the language, with the verb, *beg*, derived from it, and that neither term was in use before the thirteenth century. They explain the origin thus: About the year 1180, a priest of Liège, Lambert le Bègue, founded a religious sisterhood, the members of which, from his name, were known as *Beguines*. They devoted themselves to a religious life and to chastity, but were permitted to leave the order for marriage. At a subsequent date, probably in the early thirteenth century, a similar order for men became established. These members were called *Beghards*. But the organization of the brotherhood was very loosely drawn; it was possible for thieves and mendicants to go about the country, professing to be Beghards, and even before the end of the thirteenth century the order was held in low repute and its members persecuted. But the name was already attached to such men, whether religious or not, who lived by asking for and receiving alms, to mendicants. Thus, it is explained, the *Beghards* of the Low Countries became, by natural phonetic spelling, the *beggars* of England.

belfry

While besieging a fortified place, in the early Middle Ages, German soldiery sometimes protected themselves under the shelter of a movable wooden tower. This protection they called a *bergfrid*, literally, shelter shed. The device was soon borrowed by the armies of other countries, and the soldiers probably thought that they were still using its German name. But by the time it reached England, in the early fourteenth century, the name was spoken and written *berfrey*. Within another hundred years this had become *belfroy* and *belfrey*, winding up as *belfry*. The name resulted from mispronunciation, for there was then no association with bells. Along with altered name, the structure began to acquire a different military use and to become a formidable mechanism of offense. It was made of sufficient height to enable archers, sheltered by its roof, to overlook the fortified place under siege and fire directly at persons within. But when gunpowder replaced arrows, these cumbersome wooden towers were no longer of use in military operations. Probably at first, then, because there was no other use for them, it was found that they did serve as excellent watchtowers, when hauled within the walls of a city. A watchman stationed within could sound an alarm upon the approach of danger. For such purposes these towers were then provided with bells. Ultimately, as we know, the towers were attached to church buildings, sometimes erected to great heights; the bells, except at rare times of great public peril or celebration, serve only to summon the populace to worship or to announce the passing time.

berserk

In Norse mythology there was a famous, furious fighter who scorned the use of heavy mail, entering battle without armor. His only protection was the skin of a bear fastened over one shoulder. From this he became known as *Berserk*, or "Bear Shirt." It was said of him that he could assume the form of a wild beast, and that neither iron nor fire could harm him, for he fought with the fury of a beast of the forest and his foes were unable to touch him. Each of his twelve sons, in turn, also carried the name *Berserk*, and each was as furious a fighter as the father. From these Norse heroes, it came to be that any person so inflamed with the fury of fighting as to be equally dangerous to friend and foe, as was that legendary family when engaged in battle, was called *berserk* or *berserker*.

bessemer

Henry Bessemer, though of English birth, was the son of a French artist, and was dependent almost entirely upon himself for his education. Metallurgy was his chief interest, and while still a young man he invented a highly successful machine to replace the former cumbersome hand method of reducing gold and bronze to powders. Later, he became interested in the metallurgy of steel. In the preceding century great strides had been taken in steel making, after the introduction of the first blast furnace in 1714, the latest, in 1830, being the employment of the hot blast. Even so, the output of steel was slow, the English production being only about fifty thousand tons a year. In 1856 Bessemer, then forty-three years old, revolutionized the industry. Basically it was through the use of molten pig iron in his converter, through which a blast of air was forced. The process has since been greatly improved, but after its introduction the English output of steel per year was tripled. *Bessemer*, for whom both process and product have since been named, was knighted for his services in 1879.

Bible

Though our word traces back to the Greek *biblia*, little books, the Greek word was itself derived from *byblos*, which was the name for the particular kind of papyrus from which ancient books were made. Such books, of course, were not bound into pages, but were long rolls or scrolls of paper, each scroll containing an entire book, closely written. Probably during the third century of the Christian Era it became customary among the Church Fathers to speak reverently of the Holy Books as *ta biblia*, the books. In such fashion *biblia* came to refer especially to the collection of books sacred to Christians. The term was early anglicized to *Bible*.

bigot

The origin of this word has been greatly disputed. About all that is certainly known is that it was used in France, before the beginning of the thirteenth century, as an opprobrious name for the Normans. Some scholars believe that the French borrowed it from the old Teutonic oath, "*bi got*." They quote a legend circulated in the twelfth century that when Charles the Simple, in 911, granted the lands of Normandy to Rolf, which that wily Norse chieftain had already seized, Rolf refused to perform the usual courtly act of kissing the royal foot with the indignant words, "*Ne se, bi got* (No, by God!)" The saying became historic, they believe, and was later applied by the French to anyone obstinately set in his opinions, beliefs, or mode of life.

248

billingsgate

The gates in the old walled city of London were known by the names of those who had constructed them. Thus the one below London Bridge has been known as *Billingsgate* since time immemorial, probably so called from a man named Billings, although a map of 1658 ascribes it to "Belen, ye 23th Brittish Kinge." A pier was built alongside this gate in 1558 as a landing place for provisions and, later, as an open market for fish. In each instance, the shops or stalls were conducted by women, wives of the sailors or fishermen. Through the coarse tongues of these viragos the place became noted for its vituperative language—"the rhetoric of *Billingsgate*," as one wag described it.

blackguard

Four or five centuries ago it was not so easy as it is today to move from one's winter residence to his place in the country for the summer and to make the reverse move in the fall. Today, the very wealthy may have a retinue of servants at each place, and the actual change of residence may be accomplished by automobile or airplane with little inconvenience in a matter of a few hours. But in the sixteenth century even the king was compelled to shift his entire retinue—and the retinue of the royal house or of any of the noble houses ran into large numbers. The more important members went before on horseback. Huge springless wagons carried the linens and the multitudinous boxes of raiment. Bringing up the rear were the unsightly but necessary men and women of the kitchen, the lowest menials of the household, the scullions and knaves who performed the needful dirty work of the smoky kitchen; they, with their black and sooty pots and pans, had one large wagon to themselves, or rode on mules or traveled on foot, loaded with their clattering greasy implements. In playful allusion to the appearance and most unmilitary equipment of these tailenders, they were called "the black guard." In later years, whether or not these kitchen menials were drawn from or became loafers and criminals, the name became attached to that class, and still later, as at present, *blackguard* came to denote a low, vicious person, addicted to or ready for crime.

blackmail

Farmers and small landholders along the border counties of England and Scotland, until roughly a century and a half ago, lived in constant dread of being raided by robbers and outlaws in that poorly protected area. Some of them, however, escaped those depredations by paying a regular tribute to the principal robber chieftain of the neighborhood in exchange for protection. Such tribute was called *blackmail*. "Mail" in Scotland, has long been the term for rent. And rent, according to the terms of a lease, might be paid in cattle or grain, or in silver. If paid in silver, white in color, the rent was known as "white mail"; if in cattle for grain or the like, it was "*black mail*." It was the latter which was demanded by robber chieftains, who had their men and horses to feed. Consequently, *blackmail* came to be known along the Scottish border as the tribute the landholders were forced to surrender.

blarney

Blarney Castle, in County Cork, Ireland, was built about 1446 by Cormac McCarthy. Its name was derived from that of a little village nearby. When Queen Elizabeth appointed Sir George Carew Lord President of Munster, something over a hundred years later, it became his duty to obtain, by peaceful means if possible, the surrender of all the castles and strongholds in the region to the crown. However, the owner of Blarney Castle, descendant of its builder, was unwilling to agree to this plan, but did not wish to appear wholly rebellious. So, by blandishment, it is said, he kept putting off the actual surrender, using vast powers of persuasion to delay the event from month to month. The repeated postponement finally became a joking matter among the associates of the Lord President, and *blarney* became a byword for soft speech, cajolement, or persuasive words to gain an end. (Sometimes this legend is attributed to an earlier period and to the original builder of the castle.) To commemorate the achievement, it is said that a certain stone set high up on the wall of the castle, accessible only with great difficulty, has such potency that if one can succeed in kissing it, he too will become gifted with all the soft speech and persuasiveness that served the lord of the castle in such good stead centuries ago.

blatherskite

During the Revolutionary War the American soldiers, gathered about their campfires, of course sang all those songs that any of them could recall. Among the favorites was the Scottish song, *Maggie Lawder*, one verse of which ran:

> O wha wadna be in love wi bonny Maggie Lawder,
> A piper met her gaun to Fife, and speir'd what
>   was't they ca'd her;
> Right scornfully she answer'd him,
>   Begone ye hallen shaker,
> Jog on your gate, ye bladderskate,
>   My name is Maggie Lawder.

Bladder skate is the Scottish name for a skate that is able to inflate itself. Thus it became a fitting term for a person who is full of empty vainglorious talk. The song dropped out of memory in the years after the war, but the term, altered to *blatherskite*, stayed in the language.

blizzard

Nobody knows when or how this American word originated. Its earliest occurrence in print was in 1829, but it may have been well known in frontier speech long before that. According to the collection, *Americanisms*, published by Schele de Vere in 1871, the usual western meaning was a stunning blow, as by the fist. But in 1870, as recorded after extensive research by Allen Walker Read, in the February, 1928, issue of *American Speech*, an obscure editor of an obscure newspaper in Iowa, in telling his readers some of the effects of an unusually severe snowstorm, accompanied with high wind and intense cold, mentioned it each time as a *blizzard*. The storm had occurred on March 14, 1870, and was of such severity that it was long known locally as "the great *blizzard*." The editor of that small paper continued to use *blizzard* in referring to similar storms in subsequent years; other newspapers in the state began to adopt it, and when much of the country experienced a succession of heavy snowstorms and gales in the winter of 1880-81, *blizzard* had become

251

so widely known as to be employed, not only in mid-West papers, but also in those of New York and Canada.

bloomers

This article of feminine attire, as someone has said, was named after a woman who "did not invent it, was not the first to wear it, and protested against its being called by her name." She was Amelia Jenks Bloomer, wife of Dexter C. Bloomer, of Seneca Falls, New York, whom she married in 1840. Her husband was the proprietor and editor of a small magazine, in which she became interested. But in 1849 she started a small journal of her own, *The Lily*, chiefly devoted to temperance, woman's suffrage, and dress reform. None of these notions originated with Mrs. Bloomer, however. They had long been advocated by others. In fact it was through the well-known suffragist, Elizabeth Cady Stanton, that she first learned of the garment that was to bear her name. Mrs. Stanton, who was also living in Seneca Falls at that time, was visited in 1850 by her cousin, Mrs. Elizabeth Smith Miller, daughter of the very wealthy philanthropist and abolitionist, Gerrit Smith. It was Mrs. Miller's costume, of her own designing, which Mrs. Bloomer described as "sanitary attire" in the February, 1851, issue of *The Lily*. Later, Mrs. Bloomer herself adopted the costume and appeared in it upon the lecture platform. Today, it would seem extremely modest, but in that day of multiple heavy skirts, dragging on the ground, it was daring. These skirts, in Mrs. Miller's costume, were replaced by a single short skirt over long loose trousers which were gathered round the ankles—very similar to the bathing dress seen at our beaches in the early twentieth century. Although Mrs. Bloomer constantly denied credit for the garment, the public persistence in giving it her name introduced *bloomers* into the language.

bluestocking

About 1750 some of the ladies in the upper circles of London society got thoroughly tired of the empty life which they led, with its constant card-playing and incessant idle chatter every evening of the week at one house or another. So, under the leadership of Lady Mary Montagu, they decided upon a different kind of social diversion. Lady Mary, herself an author, had been an intimate friend of Joseph Addison and Alexander Pope, and was well known among the literary men of the later day. The ladies, then, meeting at the houses of one another, filled their salons with the eminent and the aspiring men of letters. Sumptuous evening dress was not a requisite at these affairs; in fact, to put at ease those who could not afford costly raiment, the ladies themselves dressed simply. Because of this simplicity, the group was held in ridicule by the social circle which they had deserted. And when it was observed that one of the regular attendants of the literary evenings, Mr. Benjamin Stillingfleet, habitually wore his ordinary blue worsted stockings, instead of the black silk stockings usual among gentlemen at an evening affair, merriment was unbounded. "The Bluestocking Club," the set was promptly dubbed by some wit, said to have been Admiral Edward Boscowan, and the ladies were thenceforth *bluestockings*. The epithet was subsequently applied to any lady of literary bent.

blurb

In 1907 the gifted humorist, Gelett Burgess, added to his list of whimsical writings with the small book, *Are You a Bromide?* The book was such a success that the dictionaries were obliged, not only to add in their pages a new definition of "bromide," but also, as a by-product, to add a new word to their lists. The word was *blurb*. The story of its creation was told by Burgess' publisher, B. W. Huebsch, in the summer, 1937, issue of the publication, *Colophon*. Mr. Huebsch wrote, in part:

It is the custom of publishers to present copies of a conspicuous current book to booksellers attending the annual dinner of their trade association, and as this little book was in its heyday when the meeting took place I gave it to 500 guests. These copies were differentiated from the regular edition by the addition of a comic bookplate drawn by the author and by a special jacket which he devised. It was the common practise to print the picture of a damsel—languishing, heroic, or coquettish—anyhow, a damsel, on the jacket of every novel, so Burgess lifted from a Lydia Pinkham or tooth-powder advertisement the portrait of a sickly sweet young woman, painted in some gleaming teeth, and otherwise enhanced her pulchritude, and placed her in the center of the jacket. His accompanying text was some nonsense about "Miss Belinda *Blurb*," and thus the term supplied a real need and became a fixture in our language.

bogus

The origin of this American term has not yet been traced. According to a letter to the editor of the *Oxford English Dictionary*, in the earliest appearance of the word in an Ohio newspaper, it was applied to a kind of mechanism used in making counterfeit coins. The date given to that paper was 1827. Whether *bogus* was used earlier than that, and in what sense, is not known. But thereafter it acquired general use in the United States as a substitute for counterfeit, sham, false, spurious.

bombast

Probably the use of cotton for padding started when men wore armor during the Middle Ages. A chunk of soft cotton where a hard metal joint chafed the skin would relieve the pain. But in the sixteenth century such cotton padding began to be used for another purpose, to stuff into the linings of the large doublets which the men of the court wore. In England this was done in servile flattery of Henry VIII, who was naturally very broad across the shoulders and chest. Such padding was known by the French word for "padding," *bombace* or *bombase* (from a Late Latin word *bombax*, cotton). The thing padded was at first said to be *bombast*, past tense of the verb *bombase*, to pad. But then *bombast* gradually replaced *bombace* as the name of the padding itself. It was not long before this word of fashion came to be applied to any kind of talk which could be recognized as nothing more than padding, the sense in which *bombast* is known today.

It is sometimes said that the word came from the real name of the fifteenth-century German physician, Theophrastus Bombast von Hohenheim, who is best known under his assumed name, Paracelsus. This physician was actually several centuries in advance of his time, so far as his theories and practice were concerned. But he was also a great talker, especially about himself. For these reasons he was held to be a quack and a charlatan by all the medical practitioners of his own and later generations. Because of his arrogance and vanity, it is possible that his own name, Bombast, was used by his enemies to hold him up to ridicule. But the identity of the name is actually nothing more than coincidence.

bonfire

We know very little of pagan times in England. A number of early customs have survived which originated, undoubtedly, before Christianity was introduced, but in the absence of written records the sources of some of those customs cannot be determined. Thus we know that annually upon a given day in midsummer all the bones that had been collected throughout the year, especially the bones of cattle and sheep, were gathered up and burned in a huge outdoor fire. Whatever its pagan significance, the custom continued to be observed generally throughout England. By the sixteenth century, however, the celebration had been transferred to the eve of St. John's Day (June 24) in order to give it a Christian significance. Such literal "bone-fires" were made in certain parts of Scotland until about the nineteenth century. But the name *bone-fire*, later corrupted to *bonfire*, was also applied in the literal sense after the sixteenth century to any funeral pyre upon which a corpse was cremated. And the term was further used then for a fire heaped about a heretic, condemned to be burned at the stake. Probably from early times, however, other things than bones were consumed in these ceremonial fires. At least there is written record that by the sixteenth century *bone-fire* or *bonfire* had also become a term for any large fire in the open air.

book

In Rome, the inner bark of certain trees furnished the material that was used for paper. This inner bark was called *liber*, a word that furnishes us the root of "library." In England, and other Gothic countries, it was the inner, thin bark of the beech tree which the scribes used. The word for this tree was, in Old English, *boc*; so the name of the writings upon the bark came to be known by the same word, which, after many centuries, became *book*.

boulevard

There came a time, in the city of Paris, when the walls of the city were no longer useful. The ramparts were broad, but when gun-

255

powder came into military operations they were of little value for defense. So the ramparts fell into disrepair, until some engineer, seeing that they encircled the city and were broad and flat, thought that a wonderful promenade could be made of this abandoned structure. The Parisians called this promenade *le boulevard*. There was then only one. English visitors took it to be a fashionable name for "path," or, because of its width, for a wide road. Thus the French term *boulevard* came to signify, especially in America, a broad highway which, in the aspirations of its namer, has greater social distinction than "avenue" or "street." Paris is now full of boulevards, though rightly there should, perhaps, be no more than one, because the actual meaning of the French term is "bulwark, rampart."

bowdlerize

Now and then someone comes along who, just like the heroes of mythological times, does something that causes his name to be perpetuated. Sometimes his action is altogether innocent, with no thought that it will bring him lasting glory; sometimes his name becomes noted because the action was held to be especially ridiculous or arbitrary. Thus, back in 1818, the Scottish physician, Dr. Thomas Bowdler, had no other thought than the favor he was conferring upon conscientious British families when, at great pains, he brought out a new edition of the works of William Shakespeare. The value of this edition, he thought, lay in the fact that he had so edited it that all "words and expressions are omitted which cannot with propriety be read aloud in a family." But it is a risky business for a publisher to decide how the works of a famous writer may be improved, and Dr. Bowdler found himself being held up to ridicule. From his name, *bowdlerize* became a symbol for the arbitrary expurgation of words from famous literary works.

boycott

By 1879 the effects of the land laws had driven the people of Ireland to a state of desperation. Most of the land was held by absentee landlords and, through several years of crop failures, tenants unable to pay their rents were being evicted. Home rule had long been demanded from the British Parliament. Now, in that year, under the

256

leadership of Charles Stewart Parnell, a National Land League was organized with an aim to force Parliament into the passage of bills that would, at least, ameliorate existing conditions. Parliament was slow to act. In September of 1880, speaking before a gathering of tenants, Parnell advocated that anyone who took over the land from which a tenant had been evicted should be punished "by isolating him from his kind as if he was a leper of old." This policy was accepted and its scope immediately enlarged. In County Mayo occurred the most notable test. The tenants upon the estates of the earl of Erne, unable to pay the rents charged to them, set up a lower scale which, if accepted, they felt that they could pay. The manager of the estates, however, Captain Charles Cunningham Boycott, would not accept those figures. In retaliation, the tenants applied the measures advocated by Parnell, but with more intense force. Not only did they refuse to gather the crops, but they forced his servants to leave him, tore down his fences so that cattle might enter, intercepted his mail and his food supplies, hooted him in the streets, hung him in effigy, and even threatened his life. He was but the first to be subjected to such treatment; others received it soon after. But the intimidation practiced against Captain Boycott became so famous that within two months the newspapers of England were using his name to identify any such practices. The term *boycott* became not only a new word in our own language, but was speedily adopted in the French, German, Russian, and Dutch languages.

braille

Though not born blind, Louis Braille, born in 1809, lost his eyesight when he was only three years old. When he was nine he was left a homeless waif and was taken to the Paris Institute for the Blind. Here he developed great talent in scientific studies and in music, becoming an instructor for the blind when he was nineteen. At the age of twenty he developed a marked improvement in the so-called "point system" for the printing and writing of raised characters for the use of the blind. It is this system, modified through the experience of time, which, known by his name, is chiefly used in correspondence with blind persons, and in books and music prepared for them.

bribe

Where it came from, no one knows; but in France, six hundred years ago, *bribe* was the alms or the food that one gave to a beggar. When the word reached England it meant, as Chaucer used it, to steal or extort, as well as the thing stolen or extorted. But in the sixteenth century that which was extorted was ironically regarded as a voluntary offering by the person from whom it was taken as an inducement to act in the interests of the giver. The irony thus suggested in the word *bribe* at that time has now been lost. In our present use it has a sinister sound. The giver of the *bribe* expects or demands something in return; the taker, however reluctant, upon his acceptance agrees to the terms, whatever they may be.

broker

We think of a broker these days chiefly as one who, acting for another, buys and sells stocks and bonds for a commission, though there are, of course, other kinds of brokers; as cotton brokers, tea brokers, insurance brokers, and by no means least, pawnbrokers. The last differs from the others in that he advances money upon security, for a premium, rather than acting as an agent who handles the money of others. But *broker* comes from precisely the same Anglo-French source as our word *broach*, and the broker of old was actually a broacher of casks, a tapster, one who drew off wine to sell it at retail to his customers. It was through such retail sales that the term gradually changed its meaning, for it then became applied to any retail dealer, to one who bought either new or secondhand commodities to sell over again. From that its meaning became further extended to the senses in which we use it today.

buccaneer

Explorers from Spain, Portugal, and France of the sixteenth century found many strange customs among the people whom they encountered along the coasts of South America and on the islands of the Caribbean. Some of these they were able to adopt to their own advantage. One of the latter was a simple method for drying or smoking meat. In this, four posts were set in the ground, with a wooden grating or grid for the meat set over the top, at sufficient height to be above the flames of a fire beneath. It was, no doubt, similar to the structure which the natives of Haiti called *barbacoa* (see BARBECUE). French explorers then picked up the name, perhaps from the natives along other shores, as *boucan*. The device was easy to build and convenient to use. So French navigators, hunters, and explorers took to it quickly. Those who used it called themselves *boucaniers*. But when French pirates began to replace the earlier navigators in the seventeenth century, *boucanier*—which had already become *buccaneer* in English—was the innocent name which they adopted for themselves. It was through these *buccaneers*, sea rovers, or pirates, that western Haiti was wrested from Spanish control in 1697.

budget

When this first came into use back in the fifteenth century, it meant a little wallet or purse, from the French *bouge*, purse, or *bouget*, little purse. The diminutive sense died out, and *budget*, the anglicized word, was used for a purse of any size, especially for a purse made of leather. It is a trait of our language, however, that the name of a container is often transferred to the thing contained, so *budget* shortly acquired another meaning also—the contents of a bag or wallet, including whatever papers it might contain. Thus, in the eighteenth century, when the English Chancellor of the Exchequer "opened his *budget*," as the Parliamentary phrase became, he was in effect opening his wallet or bag to extract papers pertaining to the public finance. And when, in our own family circles, we make up our *budget* for the year, we are really examining the family purse to see how much it will receive during the year and how much of that we can spend.

bug, bugbear, bugaboo (bogy)

The people of Cornwall and Wales, seven or eight hundred years ago used to frighten their children with tales of fearful hobgoblins or specters. We don't know what those ancient tales were nor how they described those imaginary creatures which became very real beings to the children. The Welsh term for specter is *bwg*. The English in telling about the Welsh specter called it *bug*, for the original meaning of that word was "specter" or "ghost." The word hasn't been used in that sense for several centuries, however, except in *bugbear* and *bugaboo*, but became another term for "beetle," some varieties of which resemble a hideous specter. In *bugbear*, the thought may have been a ghostly bear of very frightening appearance, but the concluding syllables of *bugaboo* were apparently meaningless, possibly resulting from nothing more than alliteration. *Bogy*, or *bogey*, which now has the original meaning of *bug*, was probably a dialectal form of the older word.

bugle

In Roman days the forerunner of this musical instrument was originally made from a horn. It was not, however, made from any horned creature, but from one particular kind. That was a bullock, a young bull. The Latin name for such an animal was *buculus*. The name later became *bugle* in French and English, and was long retained as the term for a bullock. In all that period the musical instrument made from its horn was properly called a *bugle-horn*. The name was often shortened to *bugle*, and when that term for a bullock fell into disuse, the musical instrument took full possession of the name. It has been many centuries, however, since the instrument was actually made from the horn of a bullock. Even in Roman times metal was often used for the purpose.

bulldozer

After the American War between the States and the abolition of slavery, there was a natural tendency for the newly enfranchised Negroes of the South to vote for the political party represented by their emancipator, Abe Lincoln. Southern whites objected. Violence and threats of violence sprang up toward the eve of all elections, continuing for many years. In Louisiana especially, the terrible bullwhack, bullwalloper, or bullwhip, as it was variously called, was employed to intimidate the Negro voters. This was a long, heavy, leather lash, fixed to a short wooden handle, and used chiefly by Texan drovers to keep strings of cattle from straying off the road. An expert could lay open the flesh of a bull's hide at a distance of twenty feet. It is a matter of dispute whether the whites were the first to threaten refractory Negroes with "a dose of the bull," or whether Republican Negroes, spurred on by northern carpetbaggers, used the threat against such of their own brethren as were suspected of an intent to vote Democratic; but in either case the victim was first warned and then flogged, "given the *bulldose*," as it was called. The term was spelled both *bulldose* and *bulldoze*. From it was developed *bulldozer*, a bully, one who wields the *bulldose*, who intimidates through superior power or strength. Thus, because of its great power, the mechanical *bulldozer* of today inherited the name.

buncombe, bunkum, bunk

Back in 1820 the petition of the residents of the Territory of Missouri for admission into the Union as a state came before the Sixteenth Congress. Immediately the question of slavery came into discussion, for even then, forty years before the Civil War, there was strong feeling among the northern states against any further extension of slaveholding rights. Debate became furious and bitter, with representatives from the southern states supporting the cause of the many slave-owners in the Territory. Finally a compromise was reached—the historical "Missouri Compromise." It provided that, although Missouri should be admitted as a slave state, slavery would thereafter be prohibited north of 36° 30'. Before a vote could be taken, Representative Felix Walker, from Buncombe County, North Carolina, took the floor and asked permission to speak. He then proceeded to deliver a long oration. It did not have much bearing on the question before the House; in fact, it did not have much bearing upon anything. The weary members began to take up the cry of "Question," but the representative calmly continued his address until it finally came to an end. When he was asked to what purpose he had taken up the time of the House, he replied, it is said, that his constituents expected him to make a speech of some sort in the Congress, that he had carefully prepared one, that this seemed as good a time as any to deliver it, and that he was not speaking so much for Congress, "he was only talking for Buncombe." *Buncombe*, later frequently spelled *bunkum* and contracted eventually to *bunk*, was first, then, any political claptrap or political expedient that was expected to win the favor of one's electors. The term was eagerly seized by the press of the United States and later, of England as a fitting term for such measures. We have since broadened it to include any kind of empty talk or humbuggery believed to be for effect only.

burke

In England and Scotland an intense interest in the study of anatomy had been aroused among young medical students in the last half of the eighteenth century through the researches of Dr. John Hunter. Such study, however, was badly cramped by the laws of the period. For, according to law, none but the bodies of persons executed for murder could be placed upon the dissecting table. Plenty of persons were being executed in those days, but the number executed for murder was comparatively low. There was thus greater demand for bodies than there was a legal supply. In consequence, a new profession sprang up—grave-robbing, or, as it was called, body-snatching. The men who supplied bodies by such means came to be called "resurrection men" or "resurrectionists." Despite the risk, for detection might result in heavy fines and deportation, the grave-robbers found their profession highly lucrative. At the peak of the demand they received as high as £14 for a single body. Students of anatomy did not ask questions as to the source of supply.

In 1827, two Irishmen living in Edinburgh, William Burke and William Hare, happened upon an easier way to obtain corpses than grave-robbing. Hare was running a lodging house, in which Burke had a room. One of the other tenants, an old army pensioner, died, but instead of having him buried, Burke suggested that they sell his body to an anatomist. This was done so readily and for so handsome a price— £7, 10s—that they contrived a scheme for supplying other bodies. Successively, then, they enticed various obscure travelers into Hare's lodging house. It was not difficult to ply them with drink and then suffocate them, being careful to leave no marks. The bodies brought from £8 to £14, and it was subsequently estimated that fifteen victims were thus disposed of. The police eventually became suspicious and the two men were brought to trial. Hare turned king's evidence, but Burke was found guilty and hanged in 1829. The crimes brought such notoriety that even to this day a strangler is said to *burke* his victim, and *burking* has become a synonym for strangling. Partly as a result of these crimes the laws

262

were greatly modified, so that anatomists did not have to resort to illegal methods for pursuing their studies.

bus, (omnibus)

In the spring of 1662 a new conveyance appeared upon the streets of Paris. They were large coaches or *carosses* with places for eight passengers and, under decree of Louis XIV, they were authorized to run upon fixed schedules, whether filled or empty, to extreme parts of the city. Their great virtue was in the low cost of transportation, five sous per person. This made it possible for persons in modest circumstances to ride; the cost of carriage hire at that time might come to thirty or forty times such a fare. However, though expressly designed for the conveyance of infirm and needy persons, it was not long before the coaches catered almost exclusively to the wealthy or to those well able to provide themselves with other transportation. But Dame Fashion is notoriously fickle; it became unfashionable to ride in these coaches, and the socially elect abandoned them to the common herd. They, in turn, would now have nothing to do with the cast-offs of society, and the enterprise failed.

Nevertheless, these coaches, running upon regular schedules over established routes and at fixed low fares, were the forerunners of a system of passenger transportation which has become universal. A century and a half passed after the initial failure, when, again in Paris, larger coaches with places for fifteen to eighteen persons appeared upon the streets in 1827. These bore the inscription along the sides, *Entreprise générale des Omnibus*. The venture became successful immediately, for the word *omnibus*—a Latin term meaning "for all"—was assurance that anyone who could pay the fare was acceptable as a passenger. Two years later, when a similar system of transportation was introduced into London, its promoter, Mr. George Shillibeer, wisely adopted the name already generally used in France and called his larger coach, drawn by three horses and carrying twenty-two passengers, an *omnibus*. Within three years Londoners had familiarly lopped off the first two syllables and, in speech and writing, said that they were traveling by *bus*, the term now ordinarily employed.

butcher (buck)

The *butcher* of today may rarely see a living cow, sheep, or hog, or may never be called upon actually to slaughter anything larger than a turkey or goose. Most of the killing and dressing of animals destined for food is now done in large packing houses, and the word *butcher* is often applied to one who merely handles portions of the dressed carcass. But, unlike the tradesman to whom the term was anciently applied, he deals with meat of all edible kinds. The early *butcher* of France and Italy, slaughtered and sold only goat's meat, according to the name of his occupation. For the name is the Old French *bochier*, one who deals in goat's meat, from *boc*, whence our word *buck*, a "he-goat."

cab, cabriolet (hansom, taxi)

It would seem awkward to say, "Call a cabriolet," rather than "Call a cab," but *cab* is merely a contraction of *cabriolet*, just as *taxicab* is a doubled contraction of *taximeter cabriolet* further shortened to *taxi*. The original cabriolet, or *cabriole*, as it was also called, was built in France in the latter part of the eighteenth century. It was a light two-wheeled affair drawn by a single horse, and had a large hood, usually of leather, and a leather apron to protect the legs of the one or two passengers from the mud of the roads. The springs which supported the body of the vehicle were probably designed for the heavier chaise of the period, for, in combination with the uneven roads of that day and the trotting of the horse, imparted through the shafts, the springs gave the light carriage an elastic bounding motion which reminded someone of the capering of a young goat. In French, *cabri* means a kid, and *cabriole* describes its frolicsome leaps, both from the Latin *caper*, a goat. So *cabriole*, sometimes *cabriolet*, became the descriptive name of the vehicle. In England, where the vehicle was introduced in the early years of the nineteenth century, its more common name, *cabriolet*, was shortened to *cab* within twenty-five years; *cabriolet* became obsolescent and was not revived until an automobile with a similar type of body received the name in the early twentieth century. The *hansom cab*, or, in shortened form, *hansom*, which has all but disappeared from our streets, was so named for its inventor, Joseph Aloysius Hansom,

264

who died in 1882. The first appearance of this improved vehicle was in 1834; its twofold popularity came from its greater safety, provided by a low-hung body, and the privacy afforded to the passengers, for the driver's seat was upon a dickey behind the cab.

cabal

There has long been a popular notion that this word was formed from the initials of the name of five of the members of the English ministry who were particularly given to intrigue during the reign of Charles II, especially during the period from 1667 to 1673. There were indeed five such men, and because of them the word *cabal* did acquire additional prominence. Their names were Clifford, Ashley, Buckingham, Arlington, and Lauderdale. But the word did not arise from their initials; it had been in the language before their time. These five men were not the only ministers who met for secret intrigues, in fact, and they were not likely to meet often with such a purpose. Two of them usually met with one cabal or set of connivers and the other three with another. These five, nevertheless, were those who signed the infamous and secret Treaty of Alliance with France in 1672, without sanction of Parliament, and thereby plunged the nation into war with Holland in defiance of existing treaties.

Cabal actually comes, however, from *cabbala*, sometimes written *cabala*. This was the name used by the Jews for their traditional and occult interpretation of the Old Testament. Thus the word came to apply to anything that was hidden or secret. In English use it became contracted to *cabal* and came to mean a secret or conspiratorial intrigue.

cabbage

The ordinary cabbage which grows in the garden fittingly comes from the Old French word *caboche*, meaning a head, derived from the Latin *caput*, a head. But we use *cabbage* also when we mean "to steal," and this has nothing to do with a head. The origin of the word in this sense isn't positively known, but it is interesting to know that back in the seventeenth century, when it first appeared, it referred to the small pieces of leftover cloth that a tailor appropriated after making a garment. He *cabbaged* them, though they belonged to his patron. The poet, Robert Herrick, spelled the word

265

either *carbage* or *garbage* as the fancy struck him. One place in his *Hesperides*, he wrote:

> Pieces, patches, ropes of haire,
> In-laid *garbage* ev'rywhere.

But in another, these lines appear:

> . . . His credit cannot get
> The inward *carbage* for his clothes as yet.

cad, caddie

A dishonorable word from an honorable source, it is little more than a hundred years old, and came, in roundabout manner, to its present form and meaning from the French word *cadet*. Back in the sixteenth century, and at present, a cadet was a younger son, or younger brother, of the head of a family, and this remained the chief sense of the word when it was taken into English use in the early seventeenth century. Then, in both England and France, cadet became also applied to any such younger son who entered into the military profession, one of the few professions that a young gentleman could enter, in those days, without loss of social standing. (In democratic United States, where brains are more honored than family, cadet applies to any military, naval, or aeronautical student undergoing training to become an officer.) Those young men had no commissions and received no pay. They were dependent upon their families, and, as a result, were usually hard up, probably willing to accept chance employment by an officer.

That may or may not be true, but English *cadet* was usually pronounced and often spelled *caddie* in those days. This at first retained its earlier meaning, but eventually came to be applied to any young fellow on the lookout for chance employment—ultimately, to carry a golfer's clubs. Such fellows, around Oxford University, came to be familiarly designated as *cads*. And thus, because a man who hangs around awaiting a chance job is likely to be ill-bred and vulgar, the term *cad* came to have a meaning opposite to that of its origin.

cadre

It may help, in recalling the military usage, to remember that, although this came originally from the Latin *quadrum*, a four-

266

sided thing, it came to us from the French, in which language a *cadre* was a picture frame or a framework. Thus a military *cadre* is the framework or skeleton organization of officers and men upon which a complete unit may be built.

cajole

We cannot do more than speculate about this word. It was borrowed from the French *cajoler* in the seventeenth century, but it is not certainly known how it originated. Its French meaning, at the time, was to babble or chatter, like a jay or magpie in a cage. That may have been a slang or secondary meaning, because the word was also used as we now use it, to wheedle, or coax by flattery or false pretenses. Perhaps the strident tones of the jay and magpie reminded some French joker of the shrill voice of his querulous wife, demanding that he do some favor for her. He may have ironically termed it *cajolery*, in likeness to the insistent chatter of a jay.

cake

Outside of Scotland, the original sense of this word applied to something edible occurs chiefly in combination, as pan*cake*, hoe*cake*, fish*cake*. That is, back in the days of Chaucer (and still among the Scots), a cake was distinguished from a loaf by its appearance and the manner of its baking. The cake was flattened and, usually, small and round or oval in shape, was generally baked hard, ordinarily being turned over in the process. In Scotland, such cakes have long been made of oaten flour, and the predilection of the people for these oatcakes caused the country to be banteringly nicknamed the "land of Cakes." But English cooks began to experiment, adding other ingredients, such as sugar, spices, raisins, or the like, to their batter, and did not always bake it hard or turn it over while baking. In fact, except by its rounded and flattened shape, it did not greatly resemble the cake of old. This modified and more tasty concoction is what we in America understand by the word today.

calculate (abacus)

The *abax* of ancient Greece, used as a counting board, was found to meet fully the needs also of later Roman mathematicians, who changed its name to *abacus*, a name that we still employ. Wooden

267

beads, or the like, strung upon wires, are used on modern boards. But in ancient times the board was divided by partitions into the number of compartments that might be wanted, and small pebbles were used for the counters, such pebbles being moved from compartment to compartment as the reckoning might require. The Latin name for a pebble was *calculus*. One who *calculates* is, therefore, one who, in ancient times, moved pebbles about upon an abacus for a mathematical reckoning.

calico

Nowadays in America this applies to a printed cotton cloth of plain weave, though in England it is unprinted. But originally, back in the sixteenth century, the name applied to cotton cloth of various kinds which might be stained, dyed, printed, or plain, for it then referred to any of the various cloths that were imported into England from the seaport city of *Calicut*, India, from which it got its name.

caliph

After the death of Mahomet in 632, the question immediately arose among his loyal adherents who should serve as his representative. The leading spirit among them was Omar who, as a young man, had opposed the Prophet, but who later was to be one of his ablest supporters. Omar decided, however, that the honor should first be bestowed upon the man who had been Mahomet's sole companion in the flight from Mecca (the Hegira) and who subsequently became his father-in-law. This was Abu-Bekr, long known as "the faithful." Abu-Bekr thus became the first "successor," a word that, in Arabic, is rendered *khalifah* and which in English became *caliph*. (See also ADMIRAL.)

calliope

Among the Muses, honored by the Greeks as goddesses of poetry and song, the ninth was the silver-toned *Calliope*. Her name was derived from the two Greek words, *kallos*, beauty, and *ops*, voice, and she was assumed to preside over the arts of eloquence and epic poetry. About a hundred years ago, however, an inventive genius by the name of Lax took the older steam organ and made some improvements upon it—possibly making its whistles louder and shriller. This new and strident musical device he graced with the name of the goddess, calling it a *calliope*. Mounted upon a circus wagon, as it usually was, its blatant tones could be heard a mile or more. In later construction its tones have been softened and made more pleasing.

calumet

While the English were doing little more than talk about the colonies they hoped to establish in North America, Frenchmen were busily engaged in exploring the vast reaches that stretched along either side of the great St. Lawrence River, making friends with the tribes of Indians whom they met, observing their customs, and building up a large trade in furs. Wherever they went they found one unchanging custom: after being convinced that the mission was peaceful, the chieftains, in solemn conclave, would pass a lighted pipe of tobacco from one to another and to their guests as a supreme proof of hospitality. Each took a few brief puffs of smoke from it. Acceptance of the pipe was a sign of friendship; refusal was a grievous affront. Because the practice of smoking was new or as yet unknown to the early French explorers, these pipes were of great interest. The bowl was often made of an easily carved red stone, later found to have come from a region in South Dakota near Big Stone Lake. But it was the stem of the ceremonial pipe that was chiefly honored. This was of reed or of slender hollowed wood, highly decorated with the quills of an eagle or of the porcupine, and often further ornamented with beads made of shell. These stems, usually about two and a half feet in length, reminded the French of the reed upon which the shepherds of their own country evoked soft music. Such a reed, in Norman speech, was called a *calumet*, and it was thus that *calumet* became the name of the American Indian ceremonial pipe.

cambric

Weaving in France and the Low Countries, was the chief industry of the Middle Ages. Each town prided itself upon the nature and quality of its products, vying with one another. Astute buyers, just as in parts of Persia, India, and China, were able to recognize the textiles of one community from those of another. Thus, a little Flemish village (now in northeastern France) was noted for the fine, white linen fabric woven upon its looms. The material was admirably adapted for the making of luxurious shirts, ruffs, neckbands, and when introduced into England in the early sixteenth century, king and courtiers demanded use by their tailors. It was then the English custom to call an importation by the name of the place from which it came; hence, merchants gave this cloth the name *cambric*, for that is how the Flemish name sounded in their ears, though the Flemish spelling was *Kameric*. (This village is now the town of Cambrai, and the fabric is more often of cotton than of linen. See also BATISTE.)

camellia

A humble Moravian Jesuit is honored by the name of this beautifully flowered plant. He was George Joseph Kamel, who was born in 1661 and died in 1706. He took the name Camellus, a Latinized form of his name, after his entry into the religious order of his choice, and was sent on missionary work to the Philippine Islands. There he found a fascinating interest in the plants and animals of the islands, and wrote extensive accounts of them. Among the plants was a beautiful flowering member of the tea family, previously unreported. So when Linnæus, the eminent Swedish naturalist of the eighteenth century, was obliged to find names for many of the formerly unknown plants of the world, he chose the word *camellia* for that first reported by the priest, Cammellus.

camera

So long ago that no one can say when, it was discovered that if one were in a room shuttered so as to be quite dark, except for the light entering a small hole, say, in the shutter, an image of any object in the sunshine and directly facing that hole would be projected in reverse position upon the opposite wall of the room. This phenomenon was apparently known to Aristotle, and down through the later centuries. It seems to have been known to Roger Bacon in the thirteenth century and to Leonardo da Vinci in the fifteenth. In the latter part of the fifteenth century several experimenters found ways to show the image in a natural position by the use of a mirror to reflect the rays, or by inserting a small lens in the aperture through which the rays passed. But it was not until the early seventeenth century, when the German astronomer, Johannes Kepler, was finding practical use for the plaything in his observations on the size of the sun and moon, that it acquired a name. He called it *camera obscura*, literally, "dark chamber." The later British physicist, Robert Boyle, found that it was not necessary to darken an entire room, but that a small box, fitted with a lens at one end, would serve the purpose admirably. Paper stretched across the opposite end received the image. The *camera obscura*, or *camera* as it was then sometimes called, made little advance during the next hundred years or so, except by an occasional use of additional lenses or a reflecting mirror. In 1802, however, Thomas Wedgwood announced to the British Royal Institution that he had been able to find "a method of copying paintings upon glass and of making profiles by the agency of light upon nitrate of silver." From that time the *camera obscura* became the *camera* that we know today.

camouflage

Slang can rarely be traced with any certainty, and this, prior to World War I, was Parisian slang. It was the smoke blown into a person's eyes, in fun or seriously, to blind him from observing what was going on around him. Thus, in reverse, it was a kind of smoke screen. And, in World War I, it may have been that the term was first applied to a smoke screen, a screen of smoke emitted by a vessel to conceal its movements from an enemy or to make difficult the determination of the distance between them. But it was found that a ship painted in varicolored designs was likely to escape detection entirely, and thus *camouflage* came to embrace any kind of disguise. It is probable that the word came from an earlier French military term, *camouflet*. This was applied to a kind of bomb which was discharged, by countermining, within the mine of an enemy. It was filled with a powder which, when discharged, would emit dense fumes that would asphyxiate the enemy's mine crew.

canard

The French have an old saying, *vendre un canard à moitié*, literally, to half-sell a duck, for *canard* means "duck." But, so the explanation goes, one cannot half-sell anything, let alone a duck flying in the sky, and when one says that he has half-sold a duck, he is, of course, trying to make a fool of the person to whom he is talking. Thus, more than three centuries ago, one who related false stories or circulated false reports became known, in France, as one who delivered ducks, or, that is, uttered *canards*.

canary

A few years after the death of Julius Caesar, or about 40 B.C., the chieftain of an extensive region in northwest Africa, then called Mauritania, set out upon a sea journey of exploration. On clear days, about sixty miles off the coast of the southern stretches of his country, the peaks of small islands could be seen. Juba, the Mauritanian chieftain, determined to explore those islands. An account of his explorations was preserved by Pliny the Elder. The islands are believed to have been known long before this time, however, for somewhere to the west of the "Pillars of Hercules"—by which ancient mariners meant the Strait of Gibraltar—lay the mythological "Fortunate Islands," or "Isles of the Blest." By old Greek legend, this was the abode of such mortals as had been saved from death by the gods. The climate was idyllic and food was abundant. These are thought to have been the same islands seen and explored by Juba. One of the islands, Juba found, had its peaks—which were above eleven thousand feet in elevation—covered with snow. To this he gave the Latin name, "*Nivaria*," or "The Snowy Island." But the impressive feature of another of the larger islands was the multitude of large dogs which roamed over it. For that reason he named it *Canaria*, or "The Island of Dogs," from *canis*, dog. This last name was kept by later explorers and colonists—becoming *Canary* in English—and was the name by which the entire archipelago was known. Spain took possession of the islands in the fifteenth century, but it was another hundred years before the most widely known of the products of the islands, the songbird, was domesticated and carried to all parts of Europe. We call the bird a *canary*; the dogs from which the name originated have long been extinct.

cancel

The learned monks of the Middle Ages, and perhaps the less learned scribes who copied their writings, were just as likely to find errors in the things they wrote as we of today find in our own. But they had no erasers, and parchment was too precious to risk the removal of ink with a knife, so they merely crossed out the matter in which an error had occurred by drawing lines obliquely across it. To the monks such criss-cross lines looked like lattices, so they called them *cancelli*, the Latin word for lattices. This gave rise to the French verb *canceler*, modified into the English *cancel*.

candidate, candid, candor

The Latin source, *candidatus*, originally meant "clothed in white." But the whiteness indicated by this word differed from ordinary white, for which the Romans used *albus*, because it meant a glistening or shining whiteness, the whiteness of newly fallen snow in brilliant sunshine; hence, spotless purity, stainlessness.

Now it was the custom in ancient Rome, from three or four centuries before the days of Cæsar until a similar period after his death, that a man who aspired to one of the high offices—consul, edile, pretor, tribune—should declare his intent to seek that office and should make public appearance clad in a pure white toga, one in which the natural whiteness of the cloth was intensified by applications of chalk rubbed into its fabric. By implication, that man publicly declared that his character was as pure as the stainless snow; that, through this array, the voters might be assured that he sought public office with none but the highest of motives, and that he was the soul of honor and integrity.

From the color of the robe traditionally worn upon such occasions, the name *candidatus* became transferred to the person seeking office. Our English derivative, *candidate*, no longer carries the implication of stainless purity that its source conveyed, although office seekers and their adherents often try to give us such an impression. The English word is comparatively recent; it is not recorded until a dozen years or so after the death of Shakespeare in 1616; he knew neither this word nor the related words, *candor* and *candid*, in which honesty, frankness, and fairness are still implicit.

cannibal

Christopher Columbus, when he landed in Cuba, inquired of the natives how they were named. In their dialect they said that they were *Canibales*, or people of *Caniba*. Because Columbus thought that he was in Asia, however, he took this to mean that the people were subjects of the Great Khan, or Great Can, as the name was sometimes spelled. Actually, however, *Caniba* was no more than a dialectal form of *Caribe*, and the Cuban natives were Caribs. Later explorers used either name, *Canibales* or *Caribes*, in referring to any of the people of the West Indies. They learned also that all of these people were very fierce. Some were known to be eaters of human flesh, so within less than a century after the voyages of Columbus all Europeans, hearing the name *Canibales*, promptly associated it with man-eaters, or anthropophagi, until at last that became its accepted meaning. The change in English spelling to *cannibal* took place in the seventeenth century.

canopy

The Greeks were bothered by mosquitos, just as we are—and so were the Egyptians before them. So, taking the idea from Egypt, the Greeks draped a mosquito curtain about their couches at night to have some unmolested sleep. From *konops*, mosquito, the Grecian name for such a protected bed was *konopeion*. Romans, who found similar beds afforded great relief from the pesky insects breeding along the Tiber, borrowed its Greek name also and called it *canopeum*. Thus *canopy*, by which we now mean almost anything in the way of an overhead covering, was originally a mosquito-protected bed.

canter

In 1170, Thomas a Becket was murdered near the altar of the Cathedral of Canterbury, of which he was archbishop. He had defied King Henry II and was slain when he refused to retract. But Becket was canonized two years later and the anniversary of his death, December 29, was set by the pope as his feast day. His bones, however, remained in the crypt in which they had been hastily interred for a period of fifty years. Then, in 1220, King Henry III had them placed in a splendid shrine in the cathedral. For the next three hundred years this shrine became an object of peculiar veneration among English people and, as related in Chaucer's *Canterbury Tales*, the aim of countless pilgrimages. These pilgrimages were as often for a summer excursion as for actual piety, but they served for a leisurely journey along roads and to a place where well-kept inns and pleasant companionship could be found. Many of the pilgrims rode, but in the pleasant summer weather no one was in a hurry, and the usual pace was a leisurely amble. This became so common a sight to farmers and others along the roads leading to Canterbury that the style of riding became spoken of as a *Canterbury pace*, or, depending upon the speaker, a *Canterbury trot*, or *rack*, or *gallop*. Eventually it became customary to call it just a *Canterbury*. Even this shortened form was ultimately found to be too long, and thus the name of the leisurely pace became further abridged to *canter* some two hundred years ago.

canvas, canvass

Strangely enough, *canvas* and *canvass* sprang from the same source, the Latin word, *cannabis*, hemp. In fact, they were identical words. It is only within the past century or so that we have been using different spellings to indicate their different meanings. *Canvas* was originally made of hemp, which accounts for its name. It has always been of various weights or thicknesses, depending upon the purpose for which it was needed. Thus, five or six centuries ago, it was sometimes woven sufficiently fine to be used as a bolting cloth, that is, for sifting flour after it was milled. From that use of the cloth, the word *canvas* came to be used as a verb, meaning to sift, examine, or scrutinize. Then it was not long before it began to be used in a figurative sense, as in speaking of the need for examining or sounding out voters and discussing the qualifications of a candidate. Thus we find that by the middle of the sixteenth century, it had passed to the next step, meaning to solicit support for a certain cause, or to solicit votes. Then, because both meanings were just as commonly spelled one way as the other, it was decided that the textile should be spelled *canvas* and that the term pertaining to scrutiny should be *canvass*.

caper, caprice, capricious

Men, women, and children will stand for hours watching the antics of goats enclosed in a pasture. The goats will nibble the grass contentedly and soberly, until suddenly, as if pricked with a thorn, one or another will bound away for a short distance, perhaps prance a bit, or playfully butt another, and then with the utmost composure fall to nibbling grass again. The young kids indulge more frequently in these sudden outbursts of exuberance and are, therefore, more amusing to watch, but the antics of the older ones are more unexpected. Now the Latin word for goat is *capra*. Thus, from the unaccountable leaps upward, forward, or sideward of these animals has come our word *caper*. And when, through a quirk of the mind, one indulges in something unexpected, we call such an action a *caprice*, and one is *capricious* when, through whim, he turns from one thing to another. (See also CAB.)

cardigan

The Crimean War, 1854 to 1856, with England and France fighting against Russia, might have left little impression upon the people of the United States, except for two notable features connected with it. It was the great suffering of the British soldiers in battle and during the terrific winter of 1854-55 in Crimea that enabled Florence Nightingale to overcome opposition and establish well-equipped hospitals, staffed with women trained in nursing, as a part of the military unit. And it was the Crimean War that furnished the incident, in 1854, which was made famous through Tennyson's *Charge of the Light Brigade*. The leader of this charge and the first man to reach the strongly intrenched Russian guns was James Thomas Brudenell, 7th Earl of Cardigan, who was an English major general at that time. Whether the charge was a tactical mistake or not was a matter of debate for many years, but no one questioned the heroism of Lord Cardigan and his prompt obedience of orders, though two-thirds of his brigade were left on the battlefield. He became the hero of the hour. It is not known how many things may have been named in his honor, but the only one bearing his name that has survived is the knitted woolen jacket, still referred to as a *cardigan*.

carnival

The real meaning is "the putting away of flesh (as food)," for it comes, through Italian, from the Latin *carnem*, flesh, and *levare*, to put away. Originally it pertained to the day preceding the beginning of Lent, to the last day when, for a period of forty days, one would again be permitted to eat meat, to the French *Mardi gras* and to the English "*Shrove Tuesday.*" This was, therefore, a day of feasting and revelry. In some countries, especially during the Middle Ages, the period of riotous amusement began on the previous Sunday and extended through Tuesday, some places it lasted a week, and in England a general period of festivity and entertainment began the day after "Twelfth Day," January 6, and lasted through Shrove Tuesday. But, three and a half centuries ago, *carnival* began to be used as a term to denote any period or occasion for gay festivity, revelry, or riotous sport, and the modern affair rarely has any connection now with the Lenten period or abstinence from meat.

carol

In the Middle Ages, a *carol* was not a song, but a dance—one probably performed by a ring of men and women, or boys and girls, holding hands and dancing round to the music of a lute. The poetic thought has been expressed that Stonehenge, that mystical circle of stone monoliths in southern England, was originally a group of gay maidens who, dancing a carol on Sunday, were turned to stone for breaking the Sabbath day. It is thought that the word *carol* is related to the Latin *chorus* and Greek *choros*, each of which denoted a band of dancers.

carousel

In Italy, during the late Middle Ages, when jousts and tournaments and feats of archery had given way by a century or more to the more deadly and impersonal bombard and cannon, the courtiers made up a pageant to commemorate the olden days. Grouped into sets of four, each set distinguished by similar old-time costume, and mounted upon gaily caparisoned horses, they engaged in harmless and picturesque tournaments, mainly exhibiting equestrian skill. Such a pageant was called a *carosello*. When introduced into France, in the early seventeenth century, the Italian name was altered to *carrousel*, from which the English term was derived. Other features were added to the pageantry in France, the most popular being to run with a lance at the pasteboard head of a Turk or Moor. The *carousel* of the United States, which we usually call "merry-go-round," retains the gaily caparisoned galloping horses, though they are now of wood and move mechanically up and down on steel posts, and the Turk's head at which they charged is replaced by an arm containing, now and then, a brass ring that permits the lucky young "knight" to mount his trusty steed for a free second joust.

carpet

This was not always a floor covering. In fact, back in the thirteenth century, it merely designated a rather thick, wooly cloth which, in certain religious orders, was used as a garment. However, it was more commonly used as a cover for beds or as a tablecloth. It was the latter use that gave rise to the expression, "on the *carpet*," meaning under consideration at the council table. But some fine lady of the fifteenth century discovered that these thick bedspreads were an excellent protection under foot against the chill of a cold stone floor. Her modified use soon became general, and the earlier use of a *carpet* for a bedcover or tablecloth is all but forgotten.

cartridge

Back in the sixteenth century, when pistols, like the small cannons or curtalls, were loaded through the bore, the powder and shot were poured first into little paper cornucopias, to be ready for use. Because these were identical in shape, though not in size, with the paper horns which grocers used for the goods which they sold at retail, the French gave the military cornucopia the same name, *cartouche*. Both the device and its name were borrowed by the English army. Then English soldiers began giving their own versions of the pronunciation of the word, calling it *cartage*, *cartalage*, *cartrage*, and, later, *cartredge* and *cartridge*, among a variety of other forms. For no good reason, the form *cartridge* was adopted by the majority of writers in the eighteenth century, and became the accepted spelling.

caterpillar

Pilare is the Latin for "to grow hair" and gives an adjective *pilosus*, meaning "hairy." From this and their own word *chat*, a cat, the French formed *chatepelose*, "hairy cat," which may be compared to "woolly bear," the common name by which English children refer to the same fuzzy creature, the *caterpillar*. The French word, *chate-*

pelose, was in due course taken into English; but the significance of the latter part of the word was not recognized. It was actually confused with the stem of the old English word "to pill," meaning "to strip or plunder," the idea being that the caterpillar strips the bark off trees. This is the reason why the spelling of the word has departed so far from the French form.

caucus

A group of men, meeting in Boston in colonial Massachusetts for political purposes, called themselves the "*Caucus* Club." Very little is known about this Club beyond a statement made by the historian, William Gordon. Gordon had lived in Massachusetts for sixteen years, returned to England in 1786, and then wrote a four-volume *History of the Rise and Independence of the United States.* In part, his statement reads:

More than fifty years ago Mr. Samuel Adams's father and twenty others, one or two from the north end of town, where all the ship-business is carried on, used to meet, make a caucus, and lay their plans for introducing certain persons into places of trust and power. . . . By acting in concert, together with a careful and extensive distribution of ballots, they generally carried the elections to their own mind. In like manner it was that Mr. Samuel Adams first became a representative from Boston.

Mr. William Adams, father of Samuel Adams, died in 1747, and it thus seems probable that the Club existed ten or more years before that date, as Mr. Gordon implies.

If Mr. Gordon was correct in his spelling of the name of the Club, as our leading dictionaries believe, the name seems to have been taken from the Algonquian term, *caucawasu,* which means advisor, or counselor. This derivation, however, is doubted by some scholars. They point out that Mr. Gordon, an Englishman, might have heard the name of the Club incorrectly; they argue, on the basis that some of the members were "from the north end of town, where all the ship-business is carried on," that the name might have been, "Calkers' Club," that is, a club composed of those whose profession it was to calk ships. And in the *Dictionary of American English* another theory is advanced. It is brought forth that in 1745, at least, one section of Boston was known as "West Corcus"; hence, presumably, another section was "Corcus." Thus the Club may have been named from a geographical region, the "Corcus Club." And more recently, according to H. L. Mencken in *The American Language: Supplement I*, Dr. L. C. Barret, in 1943, announced the discovery of some papers which John Pickering, the philologist, received from a correspondent, later than 1816 undoubtedly, in which it was alleged that the word *caucus* was derived from the "initials of six men, viz.: Cooper (Wm.), Adams, Urann (Joyce, Jr.), Coulson, Urann, Symmes." Mr. Mencken points out, however, that at least one of the persons named could not have been more than twelve or fourteen years old in 1736 when, presumably, the Club was already active.

chancellor

The term from which this word was derived originally applied to an individual whose duties were no more onerous than to stand at the railing of a court, back in the days of the Roman Empire, to protect the court from the press of the people. He was just an usher. His title came from the place where he stood, at the railing or latticework. *Cancelli* was the name of that railing, hence the usher was known as *cancellarius*. At the breakup of the Roman Empire, the functionary represented by the title became of great importance in the Roman-German Empire and the kingdoms of the West. In England—where the title was first *canceler*, and ultimately became *chancellor*, through French influence—it became the title of the highest judicial officer of the crown.

chaperon

As a part of their costume, French nobles of the late Middle Ages wore a kind of hood, not unlike the hood that is a part of the academic gown of today. It somewhat resembled the mantle, *chape*, worn by priests and others of that period, and for that reason the hood was called a *chaperon*, little mantle. In England, when Edward III founded the Order of the Garter, in 1349, the *chaperon* was a part of the full-dress costume worn by the members. Except by these members, however, this hood was not worn by men after the fifteenth century. It was then taken up by ladies, especially by those of the court. Ultimately, but not before the eighteenth century, the term acquired its present general sense, which has thus been explained: "When used metaphorically (it) means that the experienced married woman shelters the youthful *débutante* as a hood shelters the face."

chapel, chaplain

In the early part of the fourth century a young soldier in the army of the Eastern Roman Empire became converted to Christianity. His name was Martin. It is said that, while a soldier, young Martin passed a beggar shivering in his rags one bitterly cold day. Moved with compassion, the soldier took his own cloak and, with his sword, cut it in half. Keeping half for himself, he wrapped the other about the poor beggar. Some years after his discharge from the army he founded a monastery in Gaul, with the aid and advice of the great St. Hilary, over which he presided until 371. Then, with reluctance, he agreed to leave his peaceful monastery to become Bishop of Tours. There he was credited with many cures of the sick and with many miracles. So great became his fame for saintliness and miracles that he was again obliged to take refuge in a nearby monastery, where he died in A.D. 400. A later biographer listed more than two hundred miracles wrought by him after death. But St. Martin of Tours, as he was subsequently known, became the patron saint of France. The Frankish kings preserved his cloak, or *cappella*, as a sacred relic, bearing it before them in battle, and keeping it otherwise within a holy sanctuary. This sanctuary thus became known as a *cappella*, and those under whose charge the cloak was placed were known as *cappellani*. These terms became *chapele* and *chapelain* in Old French, and thus yielded the English *chapel* and *chaplain*.

chapter

Even in its Latin form, *capitulum*, the extended meaning among Romans was "a division of a book," and this remained a familiar usage in the Christian Era, especially with reference to a division of one of the books of the Bible. But in the days of Saint Augustine, in the fourth century A.D., a custom was introduced which led to a further extension in the meaning of *capitulum*—and the much later English word *chapter* formed through French corruption of *capitulum*. That custom, established in monasteries, was the reading of one of the chapters of the Bible to the assembled canons or monks of the establishment. Later a chapter from the Rules of the Order was sometimes substituted. Thus through this custom it became the familiar practice to refer to the assemblage which met for the reading as a *capitulum* or *chapter*. And from this usage arose the further development in which *chapter* referred also to the members of one branch of a monastic order, the members of one house, or, later, of one branch of a fraternal order of whatever nature.

charity

Saint Jerome, who translated the New Testament into Latin in the fourth century, sought to avoid the use of the ordinary Latin word for "love," *amor*, because of the distinctly worldly associations attached to that word. It did not agree with his interpretation of *agape*, in the original Greek, which denotes more nearly brotherly love or the deep affection between close friends. So he substituted, wherever the Greek text would naturally have required *amor*, one or another rather colorless word, one of them being *caritas*. Its meaning is "dearness," but, being colorless, it was capable of taking the color of its biblical surroundings and thus came to mean, specifically, Christian love of one's neighbor, and especially of the poor. The English word *charity*, derived from it, perhaps owes its sense particularly to the great passage in I Corinthians, chapter 13, which begins: "Though I speak with the tongues of men and of angels, and have not *charity*, I am become as sounding brass, or a tinkling cymbal."

chattel (cattle)

Under the feudal system, one's "capital" consisted in what was considered to be his personal property, that is, in such possessions that could be moved, whatever the form of those possessions. To an English peasant of the Middle Ages, such possessions were largely restricted to his livestock, to the oxen, cows, sheep, that the tenant on an estate might have. These were his "capital"; they were his chief and principal holdings, as the Latin word *capitale* implies. But Latin was a stumbling block to the common man, and *capitale* was a difficult word for him to master. It became corrupted in ordinary speech to *catel*, or to a dozen other spellings having similar sound, and finally wound up as our present word, *cattle*. In France, similar difficulty was found with the Latin *capitale*. Eventually, in French speech of medieval times, it became *chatel*, and this term found its way into England after the Norman invasion. Its meaning was at first the same as the English *catel*, movable property of any sort, including goods and money, as well as livestock. Hence, in due season, *cattle* meant only "livestock" to the common Saxon serf, who had no other possessions, while the aristocratic Norman-French *chattel* became the legal term for all personal property, including such livestock as the Norman conquerors might possess.

chauffeur

In the struggle between the Vendeans and the Republicans in France from 1793 to 1795, a band of brigands sprang up, pillaging and firing the countryside. They entered such houses as they suspected of holding treasure, demanding that the owner turn over his gold and silver to them. Their chief leader was one called *Schinderhannes* or *Jean l'Ecorcheur*, "Jack the Scorcher," who introduced ways of enforcing their demands. If a householder refused or was thought to have concealed some of his valuables, he would be bound to a chair and his feet thrust into the fire on the hearth. For that reason these brigands became known as *chauffeurs*, firemen, from the French verb *chauffer*, to heat, to stoke. Later, after the introduction of steamships, locomotives, and so on, the term was more honorably applied to stokers and firemen. The name was logically transferred to the mechanic employed to tend an automobile (later its driver) because the early automobile, which operated by steam, required a stoker.

chauvinism

Nicolas Chauvin was one of Napoleon's soldiers, wounded seventeen times, it is said, in the cause of his emperor. He retired with a pension of two hundred francs a year—and for the rest of his life talked to all who would listen of nothing else but the glory, majesty, and generalship of Napoleon and the greatness of France. He became a laughingstock in his village, but it is likely that he would have remained unknown to the rest of France had it not happened that the two dramatists, Charles Théodore and Jean Hippolyte Cogniard, brothers, heard of him and his boasts. They used Chauvin as a character in their first successful comedy, *La cocarde tricolore*, produced in 1831. In the play they represented him as an almost idolatrous worshiper of Napoleon, which was literally true. Because of the popularity of the play, the name then appealed to the popular fancy, and *chauvinisme* (*chauvinism* in English) was coined to typify this kind of extreme hero worship or national adoration.

check, checkmate, chess, checkers, (exchequer)

Chess is an exceedingly old game. No one knows how old, but it appears to have been played in Hindustan in remote times, and was probably taken from there to Persia where the Arabs acquired a knowledge of it. The Arabs then introduced the game into Spain in the eighth century. Thence it spread into all Europe. The main piece in the game is the king. The Arabs, taking the name of this piece from the Persians, called it *shah*, and when the king had been maneuvered by an opposing player into a position from which it could not be extricated, thus ending the game, they said, "*Shah mat* (The king is dead)." In Old Spanish this became *xaque mate*; in Old French *eschec mat*, and this in turn produced the Middle English *chek mate*, coming down to us as *checkmate*. And when a player notified his opponent that his king was exposed, the Arabian *shah*, through the same process, became the English *check*. (All other uses of our word *check* and of the British *cheque* have been extensions of this original sense.) When the game had reached France it became known by the Old French name, *eschès*, a plural of *eschec*. And when this term reached England the first syllable was dropped, like many other similar words of French origin. Thus was produced the name by which we know the game, *chess*. So, if we go back to original sources, "chess" is another word for "kings."

The game of *checkers* (British *chequers*) was originally a modification of chess, and its name came from the same source. (In England, the game is preferably known as "draughts.") And the *Court of Exchequer*, an English department of government connected with the public revenue, is believed to have taken its name in the twelfth century from the square table which was laid out into square spaces, like that of a chessboard, for convenience in making calculations in the system of accountancy then in use.

chevaux-de-frise

During the long struggle for Dutch independence from Spanish rule, in the latter part of the seventeenth century, the people of the Low Countries were greatly handicapped by a lack of adequate cavalry or, especially, by lack of protection against cavalry charges. They might, to some extent, flood their lands by opening dikes, but that often hampered their own movements on foot more than it impeded the opposing cavalry. In this dilemma, some Friesian military engineer devised a kind of movable abatis which, when rolled into position, could be linked with others of like construction with heavy chains. The device consisted of a log or heavy beam, some twelve or more feet in length, with sharply pointed stakes or steel tipped lances mounted radially about its sides, each stake about six feet or so in length. A series of these devices chained together thus provided an effective barrier. Because they were first used as substitutes for the cavalry that the Dutch did not have, they were known by the French name, *chevaux-de-frise*, or, literally, "horses of Friesland," each unit being a *cheval-de-frise*.

chivalry, chevalier (cavalry, cavalier)

When William the Conqueror sailed from Normandy with 60,000 men to bring England under his subjection, he took with him many mounted men, their horses, and their armor. These men were knights, for it was then not likely that any lesser man than a knight had the means to own a horse and its caparison. In the literal sense, that mounted knight was a *chevalier*. That is, from the French word *cheval*, meaning horse, he was a rider. Thence, because a knight had taken an oath to bear himself with bravery and honor and to be at all times courteous and gallant, *chevalier* became an equivalent of a knight, or a term for a man of knightly deportment.

A body of *chevaliers*, in William's day, was *chevalerie*, literally a collection of mounted men. This became *chivalry*, in English. Then, because "the *chivalry*," or group of mounted knights, was composed of *chevaliers*, the term *chivalry* came to denote the conduct or the ideals of those upon whom it depended.

The Age of Chivalry passed before the invention of gunpowder, but then, in the seventeenth century, came the military need for

285

greater numbers of mounted horsemen than those gallant gentlemen of earlier times could have supplied. This later body took its name also from the Latin *caballarius*, horseman, which had been the source of French *chevalier*, but came instead through Italian *cavalleria* into all of western Europe. It was readily accepted in England in the form *cavalry*. *Cavalier* had already come from Spain (Old Spanish *cavallero*), from the same Latin source, to denote a gay and courtly military equestrian. It was applied ironically to the partisans of Charles I, both military and political, by their Parliamentary opponents during England's Civil War, because those who followed the king in his fight against Parliament, were held to be nothing but riffraff, far removed from courtliness.

clerk

We do not now necessarily impute scholarship to the person whom we call a *clerk*, but such was the original significance of the word and is still assumed to be the case in many instances of its use. The term was originally a slurred pronunciation of *cleric*, and it designated a clergyman, one who was ordained to the ministry of the Christian Church. Scholarship, in medieval times, was rarely found outside of the religious orders, so the *cleric* or *clergy* was called upon for most of the secretarial work of the period. Gradually, as learning became more general, the early significance faded, except in certain long-established legal and clerical titles.

climate

Contrary to general impression, the fact that the earth is a sphere was accepted by Greek geographers more than two thousand years ago. Their writings and theories, however, were denounced as heresy and contrary to biblical interpretation by the Christian Church of the fourth century A.D., and thus remained sealed books for more than a thousand years. An earlier Greek belief, before the spherical shape was advanced, was that the earth sloped from the equator to the north. (The Greeks knew nothing of the southern hemisphere.) The slope at the equator, they thought, was slight, but it became steadily steeper toward the north. Thus, for geographical purposes, they conceived the earth to consist of seven equal broad belts, parallel with the equator, each belt having its own degree of slope. The Greek word for "slope" being *klima*, the successive belts were referred to as first *klima*, second *klima*, and so on northward. Cities and other places were thus said to be in such and such a *klima*. With increased learning and the discovery that the earth was a globe, other methods of geographical location became essential. It had long been known that the farther one went toward the north, the longer the summer daylight lasted. So a new method was worked out on that basis. Daring navigators were sent out into the Atlantic Ocean, and expeditions were made southward along the coast of Africa probably to the Gulf of Guinea, and northward probably to the northern tip of the British Isles. These navigators were to determine, among other things, the length of the longest day of the year. From these data Greek mathematicians worked out a new series of *klima*, as they continued to call the belts, based on half-hourly differences in the longest day of the year. Thus the first belt or *klima* or *climate* (to give the term its English form, derived through Latin) ranged from the equator, where the longest day was twelve hours, to a line parallel with it where the longest day was twelve hours and thirty minutes. This first *climate* was eight degrees and twenty-five minutes in width. Each belt or *climate* became progressively narrower. Thus the tenth *climate*, along the British coast, ranging from a longest day of 16 hours to 16 hours, 30 minutes, embraced a belt less than three degrees wide. The half-hourly *climates*, as worked out by the Greeks, extended to the Arctic Circle, and were 24 in number. In those days, then, "a change of climate," had the expression been used, would have meant nothing more than a change of latitude, that is, to a place nearer to or farther from the equator. But observations began to reveal that there was a direct relationship between distance from the equator and average atmospheric conditions, such as temperature, humidity, etc. These differences then began to be embraced in the term *climate*. Hence, when time belts gave place to more accurate means for determining location, *climate* was retained in the language with the extended meaning in which we now use it.

cloak, clock

It may seem odd to combine these words, but they are closely related. The *clock* got its name from the bell that sounded its hours; the *cloak* from its resemblance, in the early Middle Ages, to the shape of a bell, to its form when hung over the shoulders. Both words descend from a common Medieval Latin word, *cloca* or *clocca*, which was probably formed by early Christian priests from an earlier Celtic or Teutonic source. The Dutch *klok*, the Norwegian *klokka*, the the German *glocke*, and the Welsh *cloch*, each meaning "bell," all bespeak a common source. But it must be remembered that early bells showed little resemblance to the church bells of today. They were little larger than our modern hand bells, and, made up from thin plates of hammered iron, riveted into quadrangular shape, they looked something like the modern cowbell and were about the same size.

clue (clew)

Several thousand years ago, the large island of Crete, in the eastern Mediterranean, was at the height of its glory. Explorations show that its culture, about two thousand years before Christ, must have rivaled that of Egypt at its best and was far more advanced than that attained in Greece for many centuries. But among the legends of ancient Greece that have come down to us, one of the most interesting, possibly based upon an actual form of animal worship in early Crete, is the slaying of the Minotaur by the Greek hero, Theseus. Minos, legendary king of Crete, had offended one of the gods. In retribution, his wife became captivated by a sacred bull and gave birth to a creature of ferocious appetite that had the head of a bull and the body of a man. This creature was given the name "Minotaur." Because of its ferocity, Minos had it confined in a vast labyrinth of so intricate a design that any person entering was unable to find his way out. Here, the Minotaur, roaming at will, was fed upon criminals who were thrust within the maze. But, every ninth year, its fare was supplemented by a tribute of seven youths and seven maidens exacted by Minos from Attica on account of the murder of his son in that country. When the time for the third of these mournful tributes approached, Theseus, son of the Athenian king, offered himself as one of the victims, believing that he could slay the monster and thus free Athens from the terrible tribute. This he was able to do; but he and his companions would have wandered hopelessly within the labyrinth, except for the aid given by Ariadne, daughter of Minos. She had fallen in love with Theseus and secretly gave him a ball of yarn, one end of which, when he entered the labyrinth, he tied to the portal; then, unrolling it as he went, he and the others were able to follow it back to the entrance and make their escape after the Minotaur was slain.

Now, in the time of the English poet, Geoffrey Chaucer, a ball of yarn was called a *clew*, a word still used with that meaning in Scotland and parts of England. And it was this word that Chaucer used when, in his *Legends of Good Women*, he told the tale of Ariadne:

> By a clewe of twyn as he hath gon
> The same weye he may returne a-non
> ffolwynge alwey the thred as he hath come.

This episode and the popularity of Chaucer introduced among other writers a figurative use of "clew of thread" as an expression for any guidance through a perplexity or difficulty. Later, when the spelling of *clew* changed to *clue*, in conformity with that which changed "blew" to "blue" and "trew" to "true," the newly formed *clue* came to have as its prevailing sense the idea based upon the legendary tale of Theseus—that which serves as a guidance to the solution of a problem or mystery. The older spelling is still sometimes used in this sense, but is generally retained for certain other meanings of nautical nature.

coach

In a little town in Hungary, back in the fifteenth century, there lived an obscure carriage builder, destined to make his village known throughout Christendom, though his own name is unrecorded. Possibly the king, Ladislaus Posthumus, or his successor, Matthias Corvinus, for the date is uncertain, wished something more elaborate or larger than the usual state carriage for his personal use while traveling. Or maybe the carriage builder had dreams and wished to offer something new in carriages. Whatever the cause, he built a heavier and larger vehicle which, over the unpaved roads of those days, provided greater comfort to the passenger than was found in the earlier springless carriages. It may have been a closed vehicle, though that is not known. That new vehicle, however, was so successful an innovation that, within the next hundred years, it was copied all over Europe. But wherever it was built it still retained the name of the Hungarian town where its first maker had lived. Like the "Conestoga wagon" of the United States a hundred years ago, so called because built originally in Conestoga, Pennsylvania, it was, in Magyar, a "*Kocsi szeker,*" or "wagon of Kocs." Each country, of course, adapted the pronunciation of the Hungarian town to its own spelling. Thus, because of the sound of the name *Kocs*, the name became *coach* in English, when the first of these vehicles was built in England in 1555.

cobalt

According to old German folklore, every cottage had its own guardian spirit. This was a *kobold*, a name probably derived from *kobe*, cottage, and the stem of *welten* (English *wield*), to rule; thus, "the ruler of the household." In later times this familiar spirit came to be associated with mischievous pranks, thought to be responsible for curdled milk, fractious cows, kettles tipped into the coals, and other mishaps that vex housewives. Their misdeeds came gradually to be associated especially with matters affecting miners. Hence, when the German miner suffered in health (probably from some such disease as miner's worm or miner's phthisis), he blamed his misfortune upon the *kobold*, whom he had come to regard as a malignant demon. In the same manner, certain ores which looked to be metallic failed to yield any metal when they were smelted. The miners tossed them aside contemptuously, muttering, "*Kobold* (Goblin)." So common had this designation become that it was retained when the true nature of the ore was determined by Georg Brandt in 1735. The German name became *cobalt* in English.

coconut

The slang reference to one's head as a "coconut" is, of course, familiar to everyone, so familiar that we may not even wince when we hear the term contracted to "nut." The slang use isn't amazing, for, after all, the shape of the head does somewhat resemble that of the nut. In fact, that is just what Portuguese explorers thought when, in their successful attempt to reach India in the late fifteenth century by sailing around the southern tip of Africa,

290

they found this fruit growing upon islands of the Indian Ocean. Not only was the nut about the shape and size of a small head, but the base of it, with its three dark holes, strikingly resembled a grinning face. And that is what led the Portuguese to call the nut a *coco*, for in their language that means "a grinning face."

cockatrice (ichneumon)

Like the basilisk, with which it was sometimes identified, this fabulous creature was formerly supposed to be able to kill man or animal just by a glance from its deadly eyes. The actual existence of such a creature was believed even into the seventeenth century. It was then thought to be a kind of serpent; so considered by Shakespeare (in *Romeo and Juliet*) and by the translators of the King James Version of the Bible (in the Psalms and in Jeremiah). It could be killed, people said, by the sound of a crowing cock, so travelers were wont to carry a rooster with them when going through regions where they were thought to dwell. The only mammal unaffected by the baneful eye of the creature and which could attack it successfully was the weasel, because this animal could cure its own injuries by rue, the one plant which the cockatrice could not wither. Like the basilisk, the cockatrice was believed to hatch from an egg laid by a cock, a belief probably influenced by the first part of the name. But *cockatrice* is actually a corruption of the Latin *calcatrix*, and this, in turn, was a translation of the Greek *ichneumon*. This was and still is an Egyptian quadruped resembling a weasel. It is a mortal enemy of the crocodile, devouring its young and searching for its eggs. Hence its name, for *ichneumon* means "a tracker." It was anciently believed that when the ichneumon found a crocodile asleep, it would dart into its open mouth, into its stomach, and kill it by eating through its belly, but this is not true. So little was actually known of the creature that any fantastic story was accepted by credulous persons.

coin, coign, (quoin)

Although the minting of metals into currency has sometimes been done by casting—that is, by pouring molten metal into molds—the general practice has been to stamp the metal. Nowadays, as it has been for some centuries, the stamping is done by powerful presses.

Formerly, it was done by hammering, with little change in method back to the times of ancient Rome. The Roman practice, after blanks of uniform size had been procured, was to place the blank upon a die which carried the design of the reverse side. A wedge-shaped tool, with the design of the obverse face upon its small end, was then used to receive the blows of the hammer. Now this wedge-shaped tool was called a *cuneus*. In Old French, this Latin word became corrupted first into *cuigne*, then into *coing*, and finally into *coin*. The last form, though variously spelled, was carried into England. By that time, however, *coin* meant not only the wedge-shaped tool used in the minting of currency, but it was also a general name for currency produced by stamping. The old sense of a wedge has since died out in English usage. But it is interesting to observe that the old Roman meaning of *cuneus*, a wedge, is still retained in our architectural terms *quoin* and *coign*, both of which words developed along the same lines from the same Latin source.

collation

From its Latin source, *collatio*, the basic meaning of this is "a bringing together, a conference." It is from the participle, *collatum*, of the verb *confero*, confer, compare, collect. Most of its present various meanings are directly derived from the Latin meanings, but there is one use of *collation* that has come to us in a curious fashion. Back in the fifth century there lived a French priest, Joannes Cassianus. He is especially noted as being one of the first to introduce monastic orders into western Europe; he himself founded two large orders in Marseilles, one for monks and one for nuns. Little was known in France at the time about the proper conduct and way of life of those who took monastic vows, but Cassianus had lived for many years in several of the monasteries of Palestine and Egypt. He was requested, therefore, to write a memorandum which should serve as a guide to those who followed him. One of the most notable of the treatises that he then wrote had the title, *Collationes Patrum in Scetica Eremo Commorantium* (Conferences with the Fathers Dwelling as Hermits in Egypt). This was a series of twenty-four dialogues. Subsequently it became the custom in Benedictine Orders at the close of day to read aloud from the passages of these *Collationes* or from passages of the

Scriptures and to confer over them. After the reading or conference it became a further custom to have a light supper. This supper or light repast thus being associated with the reading from the *Collation,* as the treatise was called in England, or from the conferences that attended this or similar readings, became itself referred to as the *collation.* This usage was then extended to any light repast served at any time.

colonel

Our spelling of this word comes from Italian, from the "little column" or company of infantry which this officer formerly led at the head of a regiment. Such a little column was, in Italian, a *colonello,* or later in France, *colonelle.* The French word, however, became corrupted to *coronel,* and it was in this form that the word was introduced into England in the sixteenth century. The spelling was corrected to *colonel* within the next century, and strenuous efforts were made to reform the pronunciation also to accord with the reformed spelling. But the early influence was too great. Even by 1780 the pronouncing dictionaries had given up the battle and showed *colonel* to be pronounced like the former word *coronel,* that is "kurnel," just as we say it today.

colossal, Colosseum

Ancient sculptors were accustomed to make their statutes somewhat more than life size, especially those which were to be mounted upon high pedestals or as architectural ornaments upon lofty buildings. Thus, when viewed from the roadway, the figures appeared in proper proportions and the fine details of the artist's handiwork were not lost through the distance. Any such enlarged statue, however little it exceeded man's ordinary size, was, in Rome, a *colossus;* in Greece, *kolossos,* though no one knows the earlier source of the word. But some of these *colossi* were of such vast proportions that they would be notable objects of interest even in our present day of eye-filling skyscrapers. The most famous was the celebrated statue of the Sun, created in bronze by Chares of Rhodes, most widely known as "The Colossus of Rhodes." Its size was so great that the statue became counted as one of the seven wonders of the ancient world. This famous statue gave rise to our present interpretation of *colossus* as something of huge or vast proportions, and *colossal* like something vast, huge, tremendous, immense. From ancient descriptions, the statue was 105 feet in height; it stood at the entrance to the harbor at Rhodes, and was completed, after twelve years in the erecting, in 280 B.C. But it stood only about sixty years before it was destroyed by an earthquake. The broken fragments remained on the ground for more than nine centuries and were finally sold by the Turks. Nine hundred camels are said to have been required to transport the load. Another famous *colossus* was a statue of Nero, executed by Zenodorus and 110 feet in height. It stood near the huge amphitheater subsequently erected by the emperor Vespasian, and because of the proximity to the statue, the amphitheater got the name *Colosseum*.

comedy

Comedy among the early Greeks was for men only. In fact there were but few occasions when women were permitted to attend any of the public festivals or to appear outside of their homes. But the early comedy, or *komodia*, derived from *komos*, revel, and *oide*, song or ode, was a type of drunken revelry alongside of which the modern burlesque would be rather tame. The jokes and witticism were of the coarsest nature. Persons of important position were caricatured and lampooned freely. The utmost license prevailed, and the participants, who might include anyone, were careful only that their faces were concealed by masks or stained with wine to avoid discovery of their identities. In later periods much of the license and vulgarity disappeared from the Greek comedy. The term was retained, but the earlier festivities were replaced by well-written plays which were light and amusing and by eminent writers.

commando

Although it was the Portuguese who were first to colonize South Africa, no extensive development of the region took place until the Dutch East India Company founded Capetown in the latter part of the seventeenth century. Dutch settlers immediately began to have difficulties with the natives. The Hottentots, first to be encountered, were either enslaved, slain, or driven out, but as the colonists extended their settlements within the next hundred years they

294

came against the more hostile and warlike Bushmen. Here, adopting a strategy of the earlier Portuguese, they organized their military parties into small units or commands capable of effecting quick raids against Bushmen villages. It is said that within six years they thus killed or captured more than three thousand Bushmen. The name of such a military unit, *commando*, meaning a party commanded, was also borrowed from the Portuguese, and came into English knowledge when the British began to establish colonies in southern Africa in the early nineteenth century. The British revived the term in World War II and applied it to each of various military units specially trained to effect quick raids into enemy-held country, usually at night, either to secure information, to destroy some menace, or to engage in some military undertaking involving great risk and requiring unusual courage, skill, speed, and initiative.

company, companion (accompany)

When we speak of, say, "John Smith & Company," we do not think of a body of men sitting down and partaking of bread together, but, in its original sense, that is precisely what the word *company* indicated. It, and its associated word, *companion*, though originating in France, were derived from the Latin *con*, together, and *panis*, bread, thus conveying the notion of friendship so true as to share bread, each with the other. And the derived word, *accompany*—from the Latin *ad*, to, plus *company*—had the original meaning, to go along with one and share bread together.

complexion

Back in the Middle Ages a person's disposition or temperament was thought to be dependent upon the proportions of the four humors which were combined in his body (see HUMOR). It was this combination that was said to determine his *complexion*, a word formed from the Latin *con*, together, and *plecto*, to braid. Thus if a man's countenance were ruddy and he was of an active nature, it was thought that blood was the predominant "humor" or liquid in his system, and his *complexion* was therefore said to be "sanguine." Or the combination of the four qualities—cold or hot, and moist or dry—might determine the *complexion* of a substance. Thus, in olden medical practice, gristle was said to be of cold and dry *complexion*, while flesh was of a *complexion* hot and moist. That is, formerly *complexion* was the habit or temperament revealed by the natural color and appearance and quality of the skin (especially of the face); the "braiding together" of those qualities was thought to indicate disposition.

comrade

We borrowed this word, three and a half centuries ago, from Spain. There, in the form *camarada*, it was used chiefly by soldiers to mean one who shares one's sleeping quarters or, as we would say, a roommate. It came originally from the Latin *camera*, chamber, room.

constable

When the Roman Empire was divided upon the death of Theodosius the Great, in A.D. 395, the eastern part had its court at Byzantium, a city that was later named Constantinople and is now called Istanbul. This empire, sometimes styled the Byzantine Empire, the Eastern, the East Roman, or the Greek Empire, lasted a thousand years. But its emperors were usually weak and vacillating; the court was torn with palace intrigues, feuds, and conspiracies. In course of time the emperors began to confer titles upon some of their young attendants of noble birth in order to retain their services, though the duties attached to those titles were often nominal. One of these titles was *comes stabuli*, two Latin words that meant simply "master of the horse, head of the stable." Eventually the head of the stable, however, like his underling, the groom of the horse (see MARSHALL), became a great officer of state, one of the most important in the retinue of the emperor, literally the leader of the king's troops. This title, along with those of other officers of the court, was embodied in the Theodosian Code of A.D. 438, and thus passed to the Roman Empire of the West at Rome. Hence, when France broke away from Roman domination in 486, the *comes stabuli* became one of the officers of its first king, Clovis I. This functionary gradually assumed increasing powers. The imperial master of the horse became the principal officer of the imperial household. From that office he rose to commander in chief of the army. In the meantime, the Latin spelling of his title had given way to the Old French single word *conestable*, and in this form it was introduced in England after the Norman Conquest, ultimately becoming *constable*. The Constable of France and the Lord High Constable of England are both now defunct offices, though both were once of great importance. In England, as in America, the title survives only to denote an officer of the peace.

copesetic

In a letter to the author, the noted tap dancer, Bill Robinson, stated his belief that he had coined this word or expression when a boy in Richmond, Virginia. Each morning the patrons of his little shoe-shining stand, he said, would say, "Well, Bill, how do you feel this morning?" To which he would respond, "Oh jes' copesetic, boss; jes' copesetic!" By which he intended to convey to them that he was feeling just fine and dandy, that all was right with him. The expression is one that he continued to use on the stage and which became almost his trade-mark.

But when that statement was published some years ago in the department, "The Lexicographer's Easy Chair," of *The Literary Digest*, a number of Southerners or persons of southern descent, perhaps a dozen in all, voiced their doubt of that origin. They had themselves heard it, they wrote, before Bill Robinson was born, or when a child, had heard it used by a parent or grandparent who could not have known Bill Robinson and who had never been in Richmond. The probability is, therefore, that the term, of unknown origin, was an expression current in some family, maybe a hundred or more years ago, and thus became familiar among acquaintances and friends of that family. Bill Robinson may have heard it as a youngster; its orotund polysyllabism may have stuck in his mind, and, unconsciously, he may have appropriated it, perhaps ascribing to it a meaning of his own.

copper

Because of its extensive occurrence throughout the globe in native form and the ease with which it can be hammered or drawn into a desired shape, this metal was known and used by the human race in remote periods of time. Alloyed with tin into bronze, it was the first metallic compound, so commonly employed before the days of recorded history that an extensive period of early civilization is known as the Bronze Age. The Greeks called it *chalkos*; the Romans named it *aes* and used it from early times for the manufacture of coins. The Roman supply came chiefly from the island of Cyprus, in the eastern Mediterranean, though this island did not come under the control of Rome until 58 B.C. To distinguish it from other sources, supplies of the metal from Cyprus became known as *aes cyprium* or, eventually, just *cuprum*, because the Greek letter *y* was equivalent to the Roman *u*. We still retain this Latin form in scientific terminology, but in the speech of the common man in the Dark Age of the early English people it became corrupted to *coper* by the time of Chaucer, finally assuming the present *copper* in the sixteenth century.

cornucopia

When Zeus was about to be born, according to ancient Greek tradition, his mother was anxious to save him from the fate of all his brothers and sisters who had been swallowed by their father, Cronus, at their birth. So she gave birth to him in a cave, concealing him there, and gave the father a stone wrapped in a cloth which he swallowed, believing it to be the child. The infant, according to one of several accounts, was then given to the care of the nymph Amaltheia, who fed him with milk from a goat and honey from the bees. When the goat once broke off one of its horns, Amaltheia took the horn and filled it with fresh fruit and herbs for the child. The horn thereafter always replenished its supply of such food, no matter how much might be taken from it. The Greek artists of old often depicted this horn in their paintings, calling it the horn of Amaltheia. Roman artists, taking the same theme, gave it the name *cornu copiae* or *cornucopia*, from *cornu*, horn, and *copia*, plenty.

coroner

Back in the twelfth century, when this English office was established, the full title of the person who held it was the Latin phrase, *custos placitorum coronae*, guardian of the pleas of the crown. His duties were to record all criminal matters occurring within his province, primarily with the view of securing to the king his proper fines and dues. His office, next to that of the sheriff, was the highest in a county. But the only one of the duties which survives about as it was in olden times is that of holding an inquest, with a jury, over the body of a person who has died by violence or in an unaccountable manner. The original Latin word, *coronæ*, "of the crown," became early corrupted to *coroner* in the common speech of the people, and has so remained.

credence

From the time of its first use in English, *credence* has had as its prime meaning, confidence, belief, trust—from the Latin *credo*, believe. But there has also been a secondary meaning which arose from a cautionary measure back in the Middle Ages. In those days, when the preservation of meat was unknown and the food might readily become tainted and poisonous, or deliberately poisoned, it was the custom for the servants of a royal or noble house to carry the prepared dishes from the kitchen and place them on a small side-table in the dining hall. There, under the observation of the master and his guests, one of the servants or an official of the household tasted each dish before it was served at the table. (See also SALVER.) That tasting or assaying of the food and, by transference, the table at which it was performed, were known as *credence*. (A side table or buffet is called *crédence* in France, *credenza* in Italy, to this day.) In later days, when the needs for such precautions had passed, the name of the table was retained and applied, in Roman Catholic and Episcopal churches, to a small table near the altar which holds the bread and wine previous to consecration.

criss-cross

Our ancestors treated learning with reverence and respect—possibly because most of the teaching, three and four centuries ago, was performed by men trained for the ministry. So it is not amazing to find that when children learned the alphabet, the little "hornbooks" from which they studied were almost invariably decorated with a cross. Sometimes there was just one cross, preceding the letter "A." Sometimes there was one at the beginning of the alphabet and another at the end, and sometimes the alphabet itself was arranged in the form of a cross. The cross was itself referred to as *Christ-cross*, to distinguish the figure from the letters that followed, and the row of letters forming the alphabet came to be known as *Christ-cross-row*. Along with the pronunciation of Christmas, Christian, Christopher, *Christ-cross* was always sounded *criss-cross*, and was often so spelled. Ultimately, in this form, it took on the special meaning which we now give it, a series of crossing lines.

culprit

The story that is sometimes told to explain the origin of this word is that it was formed in the last quarter of the seventeenth century from two legal abbreviations. It is said that when a prisoner stood for his trial and pleaded "Not guilty," the Clerk of the Crown, using Anglo-French legal phraseology, contradicted by saying, "*Culpable: prest d'averrer nostre bille*," that is, "Guilty: (we are) ready to prove our charge." This became a court formula and was entered on the roll in the abbreviated form, "*Cul. prit.*" The story is entertaining and may be correct, but has not been proved. All that is certain is that in the earliest record it appears that *culprit* was first used when the Earl of Pembroke was on trial for murder, in 1678. When he had pleaded "Not guilty," the Clerk responded, "*Culprit, how will you be tryed?*"

curfew

In the medieval towns of Europe, fire was an ever-present danger. The houses were of timber, usually with thatched roofs, and the household fire, in a hole in the middle of the floor, sent out its smoke and sparks through an opening in the center of the roof. Naturally, the danger was greatest at night. Therefore, the authorities of each town had a signal sounded, usually a bell, at about the time that folks were about to go to bed, to warn them to take care of their fires for the night. In many places of Europe this signal was known by the Latin words *pyritegium* or *ignitegium* (from *pyra* or *ignis*, fire, and *tego*, cover), but in olden France the signal was called *cuevre-feu*, cover-fire. The custom was taken from France to England several centuries before the Norman Conquest, and the people undoubtedly thought they were still speaking its French name when they called it *curfew*.

curmudgeon

It may be said at once that the source of this word is unknown. It is of interest, however, because of the several speculations that have been made of its source. In his *Dictionary of the English Language*, back in 1756, Dr. Samuel Johnson said that an "unknown correspondent" had suggested the French *coeur méchant* as a possible source. This, amusingly, was wholly misread by John Ash, twenty years later, who said, in his *New and Complete Dictionary of the English Language*, that *curmudgeon* came from the French *coeur*, unknown, and *méchant*, correspondent. Actually, of course, *coeur* means "heart" and *méchant* means "avaricious" or "evil," and it is not impossible that this may be the true origin. The renowned etymologist, Walter W. Skeat, in 1882, dismissed this possible source and gave it as his opinion that the original word had been *corn-mudging*. He based this upon a translation of Livy, in 1600, in which the Latin *frumentarius* was rendered *cornmudgin*, in a passage that speaks of fines paid by "certain cornmudgins for hourding up and keeping in their graine." The second element of the word he believed to be derived from an old French word, *muchier*, to hide, conceal. Thus, *corn-mudging* would be explained as "corn concealing," a miserly concealing of corn. But Skeat did not know that *curmudgeon* had been in literary use twenty-five years before this translation of Livy appeared, nor did he reckon with the fact that no one other than this one translator, Philemon Holland, ever wrote the word as *cornmudgin*.

currant

The plants which we grow in our gardens under this name, as well as the berries produced upon them, are really sailing under false colors, for the name *currant* should never have been given to them. The real currant is the dried seedless fruit of a certain variety of grapevine; a raisin, that is, but a particular kind of raisin. The grapevine from which it is produced came originally from Corinth. For that reason the dried fruit from these vines were known, in the thirteenth century, as *raisins de Corauntz*, raisins of Corinth. Gradually, the delicacy became known chiefly from its source, and the name of that source, already transformed to *Corauntz*, passed through many forms, becoming *currants* in the sixteenth century and settling into *currant* in the seventeenth. But the plant which we call "currant" is a bush, not a grapevine. When this bush was introduced into England in the sixteenth century, it was popularly but erroneously thought to be the source of the fruit that, in dried state, came from the eastern Mediterranean.

cynic

Among the students of Socrates was one named Antisthenes, a man who, as time went on, never abandoned the teachings of his master, but, rather, extended them and applied them to a philosophy of his own devising. But because his mother was not an Athenian by birth, Antisthenes was obliged to meet his own students in a gymnasium outside the city of Athens, known as the Cynosarges. He was not popular; he never had many pupils, although the celebrated Diogenes remained steadfast among them. Furthermore, the philosophy which he taught required too great an asceticism to be pleasing. It required a contempt for sensual or intellectual pleasure, holding that virtue was the ultimate goal in life. Ultimately, therefore, his followers became noted for insolent self-righteousness. It may be that originally the followers of Antisthenes were called *Cynics* through some reference to the gymnasium at which he taught, but the name early became associated with the habits that became outstanding characteristics of his disciples. These were a doglike insolence, a doglike disregard of social customs, a doglike use of tubs or kennels for sleeping, and a currish insistence upon one's own opinion. It may have been a coincidence that the Greek word for "doglike" is *cynikos*.

cynosure

Zeus, according to one of the many traditions surrounding his infancy, desired especially to honor the nymph to whose care he had been entrusted when a babe. (See CORNUCOPIA.) So he placed her in the sky and made one of the stars which form her constellation of great brilliancy and to be stationary in the heavens, so that all other stars and constellations appear to rotate about it. But to the more practical minds of Greek mariners, the last three stars in this constellation seemed to have the curve and upward sweep of the tail of a dog, so they gave the entire constellation that name, Dog's Tail or, in Greek, *Cynosura*. And the brilliant star, the one that appears to be the center about which all others rotate, they also called *Cynosura*, from which we get our figurative sense of *cynosure*, something which is the center of attention. The constellation is more familiar to us under the name *Ursa Minor* or Little Bear, and the star as *Polaris*, the Pole or North Star, still the guiding star of mariners in northern seas.

dædal

Among the traditions of the ancient Greeks the earliest developments in the arts of sculpture and architecture were accredited to the legendary personage, Dædalus. However, it is said, he was obliged to flee from Athens at the very peak of his genius when, jealous of a skill that threatened to surpass his own, he killed his nephew and pupil, Perdix. Dædalus fled to Crete where the wife of Minos gave him her patronage. When she gave birth to the monster Minotaur, half bull and half man, Dædalus built the labyrinth in which the creature might be kept. (Compare CLUE.) But this so enraged king Minos that Dædalus was again forced to flee. Unable to take a ship, he constructed wings for himself and his son, Icarus, attaching them to their shoulders with wax. But the young Icarus flew too close to the sun, the story runs; its heat melted the wax from his wings, and he plunged to his death in the sea below. Dædalus made his flight in safety and continued to exercise his skill in various lands about the Mediterranean. He was said to have originated carpentry and to have invented the tools essential to that trade, the saw, the ax, the gimlet; he invented the mast and yards for sailing vessels; in sculpture, he was the first to give an appearance of life to his figures, showing them with opened eyes and with hands and limbs extended; he built a reservoir and an impregnable city in Sicily, a temple at Memphis, and his sculptures were said to have abounded among all the coastal towns. So skilled an artist and workman was he that our poets continue to use *dædal* in describing workmanship which, in cunning, invention, or variety might be compared with that of Dædalus.

damask, damascene

Although Chinese weavers had long engaged in the production of beautiful woven designs in their silken fabrics, it remained for the weavers of Damascus, in the eleventh or twelfth century, to outstrip all other countries in the creation of silken textiles of unusually rich and curious design. These fabrics, sometimes with colors woven into the pattern, became the choice possessions of such nobles and others as could afford them, and were carried by traders to all parts of Europe. English merchants, after their usual practice of describing each cloth by the name of the city or town from which it came, gave this the name *damask*. The name has continued in use, although fabrics bearing it are now rarely of silk and do not often come from Damascus.

Damascus was formerly also noted for a certain beautiful and blush-colored rose. This, too, was called *damask* when introduced into England, and poets, Shakespeare among them, told of fair ladies with *damask* cheeks.

But the city was, as well, the habitat of many artificers in fine metal. Some of them possessed the rare skill of beating steel and iron together into a combination of curious elasticity and fine temper. Swords of such metal were especially prized; the best could be bent without injury until the point touched the hilt and could be used, with a powerful blow, to cut through an iron bar. Such steel, or a blade produced from it, was also known as *damask*. Other workers in metal created a type of beautiful inlay known only in Damascus. First, making fine incisions in the surface of the steel or other metal to be decorated, the workman would then beat a silver or gold wire into the depression until it became firmly united. By the use of both gold and silver, or gold of varying shades, skilled artisans were able to produce masterpieces of delicate elegance. Again, from the city of its source, such figured surfaces were said, in England, to be *damascened* or *damaskeened*.

damson

The damson plum was one of the fruits which the Crusaders of the twelfth and thirteenth centuries tasted on their weary travels in the lands bordering the eastern shores of the Mediterranean, found to be good, and took back with them for cultivation in their own countries. Because it was one of the products obtained from the gardens about Damascus, it was first known as *damascene* or *damesene*, when introduced into France and England. In the common speech of the countryside of England, however, the name underwent various changes and *damson* emerged as the one to be finally retained. Other fruits from Asia Minor, introduced to western Europe by returning Crusaders, included the orange, lemon, citron, apricot, and melon, some of them adaptable to the warm climates of southern Europe. Hence, although the several Crusades failed ultimately in the attempt to restore Jerusalem to Christian control, they did widen the knowledge of the western countries to the products of the East and were an important step in the establishment of extended commerce. (See also DAMASK.)

daphne

Old Greek and Roman writers tell of a chaste nymph, Daphne, who was so beautiful and graceful that the god Apollo, when he saw her, fell in love with her charms and would have taken her for himself. But she, fearing that he would harm her, fled from him. Apollo pursued, but as he was about to catch her, she prayed to the earth goddess, Gæa, to rescue her. Gæa heard the prayer and opened the earth to receive the frightened maiden. Then, to appease Apollo, she caused to grow from the spot a flowering bush that was thereafter sacred to him, the laurel, which in southern Europe is still known as *daphne* from the name of the nymph. The leaves of this plant were made into a garland by the young god and worn by him in memory of his lost love.

debauch

In the Middle Ages it was no more difficult to persuade a man to leave his work, perhaps for conversation or a convivial drink, than it is today. The French of that period had a word for that. It was *desbaucher*, literally, to lure from one's place of work or from one's duty to a master. The French meaning altered in the course of years, and by the time the word entered England, where it was eventually spelled *debauch*, it had acquired the meanings with which we use it now.

debut

Literally, when this was two words in French, *dé but*, it meant "from the mark." It was used just as we say, "your first stroke," in billiards, "your lead," in cards, or "your first throw," in dice. In other words, it signified the opening move or play in a game. From that expression, a French verb was coined, *débuter*, to lead off in a game. This meaning was then extended into to make one's first appearance (upon the stage, into society, or the like). The French verb and the noun created from it, *début*, retain the original and the extended senses, but we borrowed the noun only, now Anglicized to *debut*, and retained only the extended senses.

defalcate

In its original sense *defalcate* meant "to cut off by a sickle." Its Latin source, *defalco*, was formed from the preposition *de*, off, and *falx*, sickle, and that was the literal sense in which the word was employed in Medieval Latin. After its introduction into English speech, however—possibly from the notion that grasses cut with a sickle are then to be taken away—*defalcate* was used in the extended sense, "to take away." This has become its usual meaning, chiefly applied to the embezzlement of money.

delirium

The ancients employed figures of speech just as we do. Thus, if a person in the days of Cæsar wished to say that another was suffering from vertigo or was wandering in mind or speech, he might use the Latin verb *deliro*. The literal meaning was "to stray from the furrow," *lira* being "furrow." Naturally, no farmer in his senses would deliberately turn his oxen aside from the furrow previously plowed or the row that he was harrowing, and the term therefore came to be applied to anyone not in his senses, to a person suffering from a disordered mind.

demijohn

Possibly, back in the seventeenth century, there was in France a buxom barmaid of such portliness and jollity that her fame spread throughout the countryside. Her name, it would appear, was

Jeanne, known to all as *Dame Jeanne*. We may further surmise that at this period some wine merchant of the region began to use flasks of an unusual size for bottling his wine, bottles that would hold 20 liters or so. Some wag, it would seem, seeing these large bulging bottles encased in rush and with rush-work handles at the sides, was reminded of the neighborhood barmaid in her peasant costume with arms akimbo. Struck by the resemblance, he shouted, "Dame Jeanne!"

That story is entirely conjectural. All that is certainly known is that the bottles were known by the name *dame-jeanne* in France in the late seventeenth century and are still so called. The Spanish name is *dama-juana*; the Italian, *damigiana*, both meaning "Dame Jeanne." When introduced into England, they were first known by the French name, *dame-jeanne*, which, thanks to the English difficulty with French pronunciation, became corrupted to our present *demijohn*. (See also JUG.)

demon

The Greek verb *daiein*, which meant "to divide," had the special sense "to distribute destinies." Thus *daimon*, which is probably connected with it, meant "a divine power." It was nearly always used in a good sense; Socrates, for instance, spoke of his *daimon*, meaning very much what we should call "guardian angel." But when the worshipers of the old gods became Christians, they could not grasp the idea that their former deities had never existed; yet at the same time they were taught that they must cease to worship them. So they tended to compromise, regarding the *daimones* as real enough, but spirits of evil. Hence the deterioration of the meaning of *demon*.

denizen (foreign)

In the days of William the Conqueror, the French distinguished between a person living within a city and one living without. They described them as *deinsein* and *forain* respectively—the first word being an Old French corruption of the Latin *de intus*, from within, and the second from Latin *foras*, without. Both words were brought into England within the next few centuries and both meanings were at first retained. Later, under the influence of "citizen" the old *deinzein* became altered to *denizen*, and its meaning enlarged to include any inhabitant of a place, whether native-born or an alien entitled to the privileges of residence. The original *forain* became, at first, *forein*; then some one in the sixteenth century, probably an ignoramus thinking to exhibit great learning, stuck a meaningless *g* in the word, mistakenly influenced by "deign" and "reign," perhaps. Thus it has come down to us as *foreign*. We still use it in the original sense, but more generally apply it to a person or thing of another nation or another country than our own.

derrick

The device must have been new about the year 1600, although no historical account of its use or appearance has yet been found. Whatever its nature we do know its purpose, because it was named for the man who used it. His name is recorded as Godfrey *Derick* or *Derrick*. His profession was that of hangman at Tyburn, that place of public execution formerly just outside of London, where many famous and infamous persons were executed between the fifteenth and eighteenth centuries. Possibly, because the gallows generally used at that time had three posts set in triangular form, connected by crossbars at their tops, the hangman Derrick extended and slanted one of the legs and suspended a pulley from its top, thus constructing in rude form the mechanism since known by his name. The most famous of those executed by Derrick was Robert, Earl of Essex, the young and handsome nobleman who, after enjoying for fourteen years the favor and protection of Queen Elizabeth, presumed once too often upon her affection. He was condemned for treason and hung at Tyburn in 1601. By chance Essex had himself previously pardoned Derrick for an offense, an act long remembered in a ballad of the times called *Essex's Good Night*. In this, while on the gallows, the Earl is represented as saying:

> Derick, thou know'st at Cales I saved
> Thy life lost for a rape there done;
> . . . .
> But now thou seest myself is come,
> By chance into thy hands I light;
> Strike out thy blow, that I may know
> Thou Essex loved at his good-night.

derring-do

Chaucer, when writing *Troilus and Criseyde* in 1374, used the language of his day in describing his hero as "in no degre secounde in *dorrying don* that longeth to a knyght." He meant that Troilus was second to no one in "daring to do" that befitting to a knight. But a succeeding poet, John Lydgate in 1430, who borrowed extensively from Chaucer thought that *dorrying don* was some manly quality, and said that Troilus was a second Hector in *dorrying do*. At least he wrote it *dorrying do*, changing it slightly from Chaucer's *dorrying don*. But greater mischief was done when Lydgate's book was reprinted after his death, because the printer changed it still further to *derryinge do*. The poet Edmund Spenser completed the misinterpretation in 1579. Relying upon the language of Lydgate's reprint, not only did he use *derring doe*—the reformed spelling of his time—in the text of *The Shepheardes Calendar*, but he told, in a glossary, what he understood it to mean, "manhood and chevalrie." That is the sense in which our poets and romanticists still use it, though arrived at deviously from what Chaucer wrote.

despot

Nowadays when we apply *despot* to a person, we mean to imply that he, whoever he may be, uses his position or power in an oppressive or tyrannical manner. We don't like him—or her, as the case may be—and we don't want to be subject to his domineering authority. But this meaning is one that has developed within the past few centuries. The original Greek, *despotes*, meant merely master, lord. During the Byzantine Empire, *despot* was used as a title of the emperor and, later, was a title bestowed upon princes or rulers of dependent countries. A bishop or, especially, a patriarch of the Eastern Church was also addressed as *despot*. The word carried no connotation of tyrannical mastery. But because the old Greek master of a household usually had absolute authority over his slaves and his family, *despot* began to carry the notion of tyrannical power some two hundred years ago. Its frequent use in that sense during the French Revolution led to our present ordinary interpretation.

desultory

Expert horsemen have been greatly admired through all the ages. Even in the days of Homer there were some who, in their skill, could vie with those we see in our modern circus rings. Those of the greatest skill were those who, with three or four horses at full gallop, could skip nimbly from the back of one to the back of another. Usually, however, especially in the Roman circus, these equestrians used but two horses and rode them sitting, because such exercises were a part of military training. A soldier supplied with two horses was able, when one became wearied, to vault to the other, losing no time in the chase. In the circus, greater interest was evoked by charioteers who, driving two chariots abreast, would expertly leap from one to the other. Each such performer, horseman or charioteer, was known as a *desultor*, that is, a leaper, from the Latin *de*, from, and *salto*, to leap. Because these equestrians stayed but a moment upon each horse or chariot, seeming to flit like the butterfly from one aim to another, the word *desultory* acquired its present meaning.

deuce

This is the expletive, as in "What *the deuce!*" It has come to be synonymous with "the devil," and is often used euphemistically for the stronger expression. But there is every reason to believe that originally it meant the throw of two at dice, the lowest throw that one can make. In Low German that would be *de duus*. A player after a series of such unlucky throws might become sufficiently irritated to exclaim, "*De duus!*" or "*Wat de duus!*" The English expletive, "the *deuce*," now three hundred years old, is believed to have come from this Low German exclamation.

devil

The Hebrew "Satan," which appears in the Old Testament as the name of the enemy of mankind, means literally "adversary." When the Old Testament was rendered into Greek the translators looked for a word to reproduce this literal meaning. They hit upon *diabolos*, the noun from *diaballein*, which was compounded of *dia*, across, and *ballein*, to throw. *Diaballein*, from meaning "to throw across," had

310

come to mean "to slander or accuse"; and *diabolos*, therefore, meant "accuser." Accordingly, the *Devil*, whose name is derived from *diabolos*, is properly to be regarded as the accuser of the soul.

diadem

When Alexander the Great, ruler of Greece, defeated Darius, king of Persia, in 331 B.C., he became thereby the ruler of all Persia. Until his death in Babylon eight years later, it was then his ambition to unite East and West into one world empire with Babylon as its capital. To that end he founded many cities throughout his new empire, habiting them with Greek settlers. And he himself began to adopt Persian and Oriental customs, persuading his officers to follow his example. To please his new subjects, Alexander also affected the costume of a Persian monarch, especially the fillet about the head that was a symbol of royalty. This fillet was a white band trimmed with blue, which encircled the head, its two ends descending to the shoulders. The Greeks called this a *diadema*, literally, a binding over, from *dia*, through, and *deo*, to bind. This same emblem of sovereignty was later assumed by rulers of the Western world and affixed by sculptors to their statues of the Greek and Roman gods. For further decoration the *diadem* became enriched with gold and gems and at length was transformed by the monarchs of Europe into a rich crown of gold, ornamented with gems, and worn especially as a symbol of royal dignity.

diaper

Although this has been the name of a textile fabric from its earliest introduction into western Europe, the fabric was not always intended to be converted into breechcloths for babies. Quite the contrary. In the earliest Greek reference to the cloth, in the tenth century, the fabric was probably made in Byzantium and woven of silk, its surface flowered with gold threads, though its name, from Greek *diaspros*, would indicate that originally it was "pure white" throughout. The material was then used for ecclesiastical robes. In England, however, from the fourteenth century, *diaper* was applied to a fabric, usually of linen, so woven that its main lines when viewed under reflected light formed innumerable small lozenges. The fabric was then employed chiefly as a cloth for the table. Later a similar fabric was made of linen and cotton, and eventually of cotton alone. Because of its softness and absorbency, it then became generally used for and its name transferred to, babies' breechcloths.

dicker

When we attempt to obtain a bargain by *dicker*, we have no thought that a unit of ten is involved in the transaction, nor do we remotely conceive of a bundle of hides in connection with the bargaining. But such, nevertheless, is the history of the word. In European languages its various transliterations still show such connections. It comes from the days after the Roman legions had conquered the German tribes and demanded regular tribute. The chief items which these barbaric races could supply as tribute were furs and skins. For convenient reckoning, the Romans demanded that such skins be in bundles of ten. Such a unit of anything was, in Latin, a *decuria* (from *decem*, ten). But among the Germans, who corrupted the word first to *decura* and eventually to the present *decher*, it meant only ten hides. This was its meaning also when, in the form *diker* or *dyker*, the German term came into English use about the thirteenth century. The British later applied it to any group, set, or bundle of ten or even twelve, such as dishes, knives, necklaces, etc. But when English colonists began to settle in America and to trade with the Indians, the old sense of the word was brought back into use, because skins and furs were commodities which the Indians had and which the colonists wished. So they began to bargain for *dickers* of skins, offering beads or cloth or knives in exchange. The notion of bundles of ten became lost through the years, and American traders among the Indians started our present use of *dicker*, treating it as a verb and equivalent with barter, or, especially, with haggle.

diploma, diplomatic, diplomacy, diplomat

During the days of the Roman Republic and of the later empire a person upon whom certain rights or privileges were conferred received an official document, signed and sealed by the consuls and senate or, later, by the emperor or such magistrate as he might designate. This document or state letter consisted of two leaves, either two tablets of wax or a folded sheet of writing material, and it was therefore known by the Greek name for such a twofold sheet, *diploma*, from *diploos*, double. Public couriers especially, on errands to foreign cities or countries, carried these tokens of authority. Because a *diploma* was essentially a state document, the term carried that meaning among the scholars of Europe.

Therefore when a German writer of the seventeenth century undertook to compile a collection, in the original texts, of the important public documents between the eleventh and fifteenth centuries, he coined the Latin adjective *diplomaticus* to indicate the nature of his collection. This provided us with the English adjective, *diplomatic*, which, though it first pertained to original official documents, came to refer to documents relating to international affairs, the usual nature of such official documents. From the adjective in its revised sense came the noun *diplomacy*, the art of conducting affairs between nations. Then, but not until the early nineteenth century, the nations found it expedient to rely upon persons who possessed certain skills in handling foreign relations, and the term *diplomat* was created. The original notion of a state paper is retained by all these terms. We are more accustomed to the use of *diploma*, however, as an indication of scholastic attainment; but here, too, it was originally a state paper, and is still issued under the license of the state.

dirge

Among the customs coming down through the ages has been that of chanting or singing a mournful or memorial song at the funeral service for the dead. In the Roman Church, from the Middle Ages, the response to the chant that was so used was based on the eighth verse of the fifth Psalm. In English, the words are, "Guide, O Lord, my God, my way in Thy sight." But the service was sung in Latin. The line was, accordingly, *"Dirige, Domine, Deus meus, in conspectu tuo viam meam."* Through the frequent repetition of the line, the service became known by its first word. The early English pronunciation of that Latin word gave us *dirge*.

disheveled

Nowadays we speak of a person being *disheveled* whose clothing is disarranged or very untidy or whose hair is badly disordered and uncombed, and such a person is more than likely to be a woman. In Chaucer's day, however, though it might apply to either man or woman, it referred more correctly only to the state of one's hair. Chaucer used it to mean either bareheaded or baldheaded, if a man, or with hair flying loose, if a woman. (He wrote it *discheuel, discheuelee, disshevely*, or as the spirit moved him.) The word was borrowed from the Old French *deschevelé* (modern French, *déchevelé or échevelé*), meaning stripped of hair, bald. It was formed originally from the Latin *dis*, not, and *capillatus*, having hair.

dismal

Two accounts have been advanced to explain the origin of this word. Both are plausible, and neither is absolutely certain; therefore the dictionaries usually content themselves by saying, "probably thus and so," or "origin uncertain," or the like. One account connects it with an early English phrase, "in the *dismal*," meaning "in the blues, depressed," and believes it to be derived from the Old French *disme*, meaning "a tenth," from Latin *decem*, ten. It would thus refer to the practice of feudal lords in exacting one-tenth of the harvest produced by their vassals, just as tithes were demanded by the church. Thus the phrase, "in the *dismal*," would indicate such depression as that experienced by people compelled to submit to the cruel extortionate measures of feudal barons at the time when these tithes were to be paid.

The second account ascribes its source to the Latin *dies mali*, evil days, of the medieval calendar. Such unpropitious days were also known as "Egyptian days," because their occurrence, it was believed, had been computed by Egyptian astrologers. These days of misfortune or gloom occurred on January 1 and 25, February 4 and 26, March 1 and 28, April 10 and 20, May 3 and 25, June 10 and 16, July 13 and 22, August 1 and 30, September 3 and 21, October 3 and 22, November 5 and 28, and December 7 and 22. It was considered unlucky to begin any new enterprise upon any one of those days. In Old French these days were called *dis mal*, and some scholars contend that it was from this that English *dismal* was formed.

divan

The countries of western Europe borrowed *divan* from Turkey, which in turn borrowed it from Arabic or Persian. In early times it signified a collection of written leaves, such as a compilation of

314

poems or even a register of persons. It thus came to denote an account book or an office where accounts, especially accounts of state, were maintained. Eventually, in Turkey, *divan* meant a council of state, or the hall in which this council met. (In India, a minister of finance or a native prime minister is known as *dewan*, from another form of the same word.) But European visitors to the Turkish council chamber were impressed by the long, low seat or step, furnished with cushions, which ran around the walls of the chamber and upon which the councilors sat. This seat afforded ease for meditation and deliberation. To the western mind, *divan* thus became associated with easy comfort. Hence, though the Turkish meaning was also retained, the western countries adopted *divan* as a somewhat grandiloquent name for a deeply cushioned couch or sofa.

doily

We shall probably never know anything more than his surname, and we cannot even be sure that he spelled it *Doily*, *Doiley*, *Doyley*, or *Doyly*. He lived, however, in the latter part of the seventeenth century and we are told that he was the proprietor of a linen shop in the Strand, in London. His chief claim to popularity through the early part of the eighteenth century resulted from his introduction of some form of lightweight fabric for summer clothing, fabric which, as one writer for the London *Spectator* put it, was at once cheap and genteel. Probably this material was a loosely woven woolen cloth which could be converted into garments for men or women. But it seems to have been fabricated especially for his shop and for that reason to have been known as *Doily*. However, Mr. Doily did not limit his genius to the production or selling of material for clothing. He also put before his patrons a small table napkin for use when serving desserts. These were fringed and perhaps otherwise ornamented. At first, the purchasers proudly referred to them as "*Doily* napkins," but in the course of frequent use the name became abridged to *doilies*, by which we know similar articles today. The name of the clothing fabric has long been in disuse.

dollar

Silver was discovered in the valley of the Joachim, a few miles west of Prague, in 1516. This valley was then part of the vast estate owned by the Count of Schlick and, as was then the custom, the Count decided to mint his own coins. The first of the coins was produced in 1518 and was intended to have the value of the gold florin then in circulation. Because the valley, and the town within it, had been named in honor of St. Joachim, the new coin bore a picture of the saint upon its face. For that reason the coin could be readily identified and, from the name of the valley where it was produced, was known as *Joachimsthaler*, literally, "of the valley of Joachim," from *thal*, valley. The name was contracted to *thaler*, and this in turn became *daler* in some of the German dialects and in the speech of the Low Countries. Thus the name came to England as *dollar*. Forgetful or ignorant of the source of the term—that it meant "of the valley"—and thinking of it only as the name of a coin, the English used it to designate the Spanish *peso duro*, better known to us as "piece of eight" because of the large figure 8 on its face. This silver coin was widely circulated in colonial America, and thus the name *dollar*, already familiar, was applied to the unit of value in the United States when the first currency was minted in 1787. Our common expression, "two bits," meaning 25 cents, or "four bits," meaning 50 cents, is a survival from the time when pieces of eight were in circulation. One-eighth of that coin was the equivalent of the English shilling and was commonly known as a "bit." The value of a "bit" was thus 12½ cents; of "two bits," 25 cents, and so on.

dragon, dragoon

In the *Iliad* Homer describes a reptile of huge size, of blood-red or dark color shot with changing hues, and sometimes with three heads. This monster he called a *drakon*, which became *dragon* in English. Agamemnon, leader of the Greeks in the Trojan War, according to this ancient story, bore a shield with a picture of this creature painted upon it. But belief in dragons was not confined to the Greeks. They are pictured in the ancient art of China and Egypt, and even the Norse Vikings, in their day, carved dragons' heads on the prows of their ships. Generally, but not always, dragons were thought to be huge four-legged monsters with large fan-shaped wings extending on either side; sometimes from their wide jaws they shot a blood-red and venomous forked tongue against an attacking foe, and sometimes their nostrils breathed out fire.

Or again they attacked an enemy with their sharp claws, or struck at him with long and scaly forked tail. Some had but one head; others two or even three. Many legends describe how heroes of old fought and killed such a fabulous monster to rid the neighborhood of his baneful presence. In English history the most renowned is the legend of the holy knight, St. George, who became the traditional patron and protector of the English nation. He was supposed to have been a prince of Cappadocia, who, passing by, rescued the lady Aja from the jaws of a fierce dragon and slew the dread creature. The Crusaders of the twelfth and thirteenth centuries were so impressed by this heroic deed that, likening the dragon to their Mussulman foes and themselves to St. George, they felt themselves safe from danger if their banners pictured St. George killing the dragon.

In later years, after firearms were invented, the early muskets were called *dragons* because of the fire and smoke they emitted. In English spelling the term became *dragoon* and, like "lancer" for men armed with a lance, the name was also applied to those who carried the weapon.

dumbbell

Some two hundred and fifty years ago someone noticed that bell ringers attained a remarkable muscular development of the chest, shoulders, and arms, thanks to repeated exercise in pulling the ropes which put the great weight of the bells in motion. Whoever the person was, he figured out a scheme for erecting a device which would simulate the bell ringer's gallery, but without the bells. This device could be installed in the corner of a room or in the attic. The English essayist, Joseph Addison, had one in his room. The rope was probably attached to weights suspended over a pulley from the ceiling. A wooden bar, knobbed at the ends to keep the hands from slipping, was knotted to the other end of the rope and hung just within the reach of the exerciser. He could thus duplicate the physical activity of the bell ringer and, by regulating the weight, get whatever degree of exercise he might wish. Because there was no bell attached to this apparatus, it became known as a *dumb bell*. Later on someone else discovered that one could get much the same kind of exercise by dispensing with most of the cumbersome contrivance, using only the wooden bar or a heavier one of metal. This simpler device, because originally a part of the earlier equipment, continued to be known as *dumbbell*, though no longer associated otherwise with the art of bell ringing.

The modern *dumbbell* of American slang does not get its meaning from either of the above devices, other than by a play upon words. It was applied originally only to females, to the belle of the beautiful-but-dumb type.

dunce

John Duns Scotus was one of the greatest philosophers and scholars of the Middle Ages. He was still a young man when he died, suddenly, in 1308, though the year of his birth and the place where he was born, Ireland or England, are both unknown. He had attained great renown as a teacher at Oxford University before being appointed regent of the theological school at Paris in 1307. A member of the Order of Franciscans, his career was largely spent in contradicting the arguments advanced by the Dominican Order, especially those of Thomas Aquinas a quarter of a century earlier. So successful was he that his works on theology, logic, and philosophy became the accepted textbooks in the universities of the fourteenth century. His followers, called "Scotists," continued to dominate scholastic learning for two hundred years after his death. In the early fifteenth century, however, the Scotist system began to be attacked, first by argument and then by ridicule. The methods of the Scotists were condemned as sophistry, and the "Dunsmen" or *Dunses*, as the adherents of Duns Scotus were now termed by their foes, were said to be hairsplitters and stupid obstructionists. Eventually, after a long and bitter struggle, the cause of the reformers was victorious, but not until the term *dunce*, the ultimate spelling, had become a synonym for a blockhead incapable of learning.

dungeon (donjon)

If one looks at a picture of an ancient castle of medieval days, it can be seen that one of the towers, usually the central one, dominates all the others and the countryside around. It was also the strongest part of the castle, the part where the defenders, if forced back, might withstand a long siege or regain their strength. For this

318

reason, this tower was often called a "keep" in England, meaning a place that could be held or "kept" against attack. But in France, and sometimes in England, the tower had its name from its dominant position and was known as a *donjon*. *Donjon*, in Old French, was a corruption of a Medieval Latin word, *dominio*, which meant dominion or mastery; in England, the spelling was usually *dungeon*. Moreover, because of its impregnability, the *dungeon* or "keep" served as a lodgment for prisoners, who were kept in the dank, gloomy vaults beneath the massive structure. To them and to all who feared such cheerless confinement, *dungeon* meant a dark, underground cell, rock-walled and comfortless. It is this meaning that has survived, and the archaic *donjon* is now used to designate the tower above.

easel

In all countries people have been wont to bestow the name of some animal upon a tool or implement which in some way resembled it. Thus tailors of old, seeing that their heavy smoothing iron, with its curving handle, somewhat resembled the heavy body and curved neck and head of a familiar barnyard fowl, called it a "goose." The housewife saw a resemblance to a wildfowl standing on one foot, its other leg stretched behind, in the upright iron rod alongside her hearth, its leg swinging over the coals, and called it a "crane." The old-time fire-"dog" or andiron looked somewhat like the short-legged hunting dogs of the English peasant. And of course, the bench commonly employed by the carpenter takes little imagination to see in it a "horse." Dutch painters familiarized English artists with a similar word from their own language. It was the stand upon which their canvas rested while they were painting. In those days this framework was not unlike a smaller copy of the carpenter's horse. They likened it to an ass. Accordingly they called this stand an *ezel*. Perhaps the English ear would have been hurt had English painters translated the name into "ass." But instead the Dutch name was adopted, modified into the English spelling, *easel*.

Easter

Early Christian missionaries, spreading out among the Teutonic tribes northward of Rome and Italy, found many pagan religious observances. Whenever possible, the missionaries did not interfere too strongly with the old customs, but quietly transformed them into ceremonies harmonizing with Christian doctrine. Thus they found that all the Teutonic tribes did homage about the first of April each year to the goddess of spring. Her name among some of the tribes was *Ostara*; among the Angles or Saxons she was known as *Eastre*. The day was one of great rejoicing; old and young celebrated with dancing, feasting, and games. Bonfires were lighted. Children gathered eggs, which they colored, and searched for newly born hares, both of which were ancient offerings to the goddess of spring. Christian missionaries were quick to see that the occurrence of this festival corresponded with the time of the observance of the Paschal feast, and that its occasion could be readily altered into one of rejoicing over the rebirth of Christ. The old customs remained unchanged. Thus, in most of the Teutonic countries, it happens that the name of this long forgotten pagan goddess— *Oster* in Germany, *Easter* among English-speaking people—is still given to the day that commemorates the Resurrection of Christ.

echo

One of the stories of old Greek legend relates that the great god Zeus was fond of the society of a certain group of nymphs. His wife, Hera, however, tried to keep him devoted to her alone. Through jealousy she followed him wherever he went. To outwit her, Zeus arranged with a nymph named Echo to waylay Hera when he sought the others and to hold her in conversation. This ruse succeeded on a number of occasions, but eventually Hera saw through the scheme. In her wrath, then, because Echo was such a chatterer, she condemned her forever to wander over the earth, but unable to speak until someone else had first spoken, nor to remain silent when another had spoken, and then to repeat only that which had been said. Echo wandered long and mournfully over the hills, repeating only what others might chance to say in her hearing, but not otherwise able to converse with them. One day she saw the beautiful young Narcissus admiring his reflection in a pool. She fell deeply in love with the lad, the story goes, but her love was not returned. In sadness the poor nymph pined away until nothing was left of her but her voice. It is this voice, according to this tale, which we still hear coming back to us in certain spots. We still call it *echo* in memory of the lovelorn nymph.

egis (ægis), (titanic)

It was a part of Greek belief that Zeus, when an infant, had been suckled by a goat, or, in some accounts, had been raised upon the milk of a goat (compare CORNUCOPIA). At least Zeus was believed to feel that he had been especially protected by a goat. For that reason, therefore, when Zeus and his brothers arose in rebellion against the Titans in rulership over the universe, again he looked to the goat to make him impregnable. The struggle lasted for ten years; all the gods on each side of the conflict loosed all of their weapons against their adversaries, to the extent that nature itself seemed involved in the fray. The ferocity of the battle and the magnitude of the efforts put forth by the Titans have since been signified by our word *titanic*. But Zeus was eventually victorious. For his own escape he gave credit to the shield of goatskin with which he protected himself from the thrusts of the enemy. This shield was said to "flash forth terror and amazement" among the foe. The name given to it was *aigis*, a word of uncertain origin, but thought by the Greeks to mean "goatskin." The Latin transliteration was *ægis*, a form often used by English writers, although *egis* is now more common. Of all the other gods Athena alone was permitted to carry an *egis*, which she wore as a breastplate. We owe our present interpretation of the word to the English writers of the eighteenth century who assumed, poetically, that the *egis* of Zeus or Athena—or their Roman counterparts, Jove and Minerva— shed its protection to all who might come under its influence.

eldorado

Within twenty-five years after Spanish captains had begun to explore the northern coasts of South America, they began to hear tales of a marvelous king who ruled over a great and wonderful city somewhere in the interior. The streets of this city, it was said, were paved with gold, the roofs of its buildings shone from afar with their surfaces of gold; the king controlled vast golden treasures and wore robes glittering with gems and golden threads. No one knows when the legend was started nor how it was spread, but it came to be firmly believed. The Spaniards, avid for gold, sent out expedition after expedition. One lieutenant, in 1531, claimed to have seen the city and to have been entertained by its king, but was unable to lead others to it. Other parties, led by unwilling natives, either died from exhaustion, hunger, or disease, or with decimated ranks returned with tales of the utmost hardship. Among the Spaniards, the fabulous king became known as *El Dorado*, "the Golden One." The natives spoke vaguely of a city somewhere in the interior which they named Manoa or Omoa, though none knew its whereabouts. Search for the elusive city, to which the name *El Dorado* had been transferred, led subsequent parties to explore much of the interior of northern South America. Even as late as 1595 Sir Walter Raleigh headed an expedition into interior Guiana in a vain attempt to discover the mysterious city. From this sixteenth-century dream, *eldorado* has come to mean any place of untold richness or, figuratively, of untold opportunity.

electric

We may sometimes think that the word *electric* and its derivatives are of recent coinage, perhaps no older than Ben Franklin's experiments with his kite and lightning, but they are much older. They were in use three hundred years ago. Probably as far back as the seventh century B.C., it had been known by the Greeks that amber, after being rubbed, acquired the property of attracting extremely light substances, such as the dried pith of reeds. The Greek name for amber was *electron* (Latin *electrum*). Hence, in 1600, when the English physicist, William Gilbert, published, in Latin, his researches on magnetism which were based upon experiments with amber, it was natural that he should use the Latinized word *electricus*. Through his own later lectures in English this he translated as *electric*, and the agency through which magnetism was effected he named *electricity*.

elixir

We are indebted to the Arabs for the beginnings of the science of chemistry, starting perhaps in the seventh century. Their knowledge was extremely limited, however, and was based on the theory that all the metals are composed of mercury and sulphur in different proportions. It was this theory that found its way into Europe, through Spain, and which, under the name of alchemy, flourished through the Middle Ages and until the sixteenth century. Gold was the pursuit of all the alchemists. It was the one perfect metal, they held, all others being inferior. But since gold itself was basically composed of the same elements as the lesser metals, there must be something, they argued, many times more perfect than gold which entered into its composition. Therefore, this unknown substance was the chief object of their search. If found, they believed, it could be mixed with any of the other metals in proper proportion, drive out their imperfections and turn them into gold. This mysterious substance was named by the Arabs, *el iksir*, or *elixir* by the alchemists of Europe. Its Arabic meaning was "the philosopher's stone," because the olden alchemists regarded themselves as philosophers. Some of the later alchemists believed that this undiscovered substance might be a liquid or a powder and, when found, that it would also have the property of prolonging life. This accounts for the present use of *elixir* in denoting a medicinal preparation.

emancipation

In Roman law part of a formal contract of sale consisted in the buyer's actually taking hold of the thing that he was purchasing. Such a purchase was called *mancipatio*, from *manus*, hand, and *capio*, take. The proceeding was carried out even in the purchase of a slave, and the owner's power over that slave was almost as absolute as over any other purchase. Similarly, a Roman father's power over his son was like that of a master over a slave, but the son could be released from it by legal process when he became of age. The father took his son solemnly by the hand, as if he were buying him as a slave, and then let go. This was ceremonially performed three times to complete the release. It was termed *emancipatio*, the letting out of the hand, with the prefix *e* meaning out.

enchant (incantation)

From earliest times and among all primitive people the solemn chanting of songs has been supposed to have magical properties, to influence the gods, to avert evil, to cast spells, to bring sunshine or rain, to cause or remove disease, to foster the growth of crops or to ruin them, or to bring success in love or war. In fact, every mortal function, it was believed, could be favorably or adversely affected by the repetition of some poetic formula. Traces of these ancient superstitions still linger among civilized people, as when children chant over and over, "Rain, rain, go away. Come again some other day." For ordinary singing, among the Romans, the verb *canto*, was used, but when the song was intended to work magic against another, they used *incanto*, literally "to sing against." This verb, through French, became our term *enchant*. The song, such as attributed to sirens in luring men to harm, or in averting or bringing about evil, thus became an *incantatio*, from which comes our word *incantation*. *Enchant* we now use chiefly in a pleasant sense, as of rapture, though we no longer associate the term with song. But *incantation* still carries a suggestion of muttered rhythm and is usually associated with witchcraft and evil.

enthusiasm

Annually, in ancient Athens, groups of play-writers, poets, musicians, and other skilled artists competed with one another among their group for the plaudits of the populace. In their day the men of greatest renown thus had their work reviewed by the great throngs attending these festivals. A successful contestant or one who showed remarkable attainment was said by his admirers to be *entheos*, that is, to have a god (*theos*) within, or to be *enthousiazo*, inspired or possessed by a god. Thus our English word, *enthusiasm*, if used in its purest sense, which is rarely the case, would denote a God-given fervency, divine inspiration.

epicure

The Greek philosopher, Epicurus, who was born in 342 B.C., held that pleasure constitutes the highest happiness. He argued, however, that pleasure was not a transitory or momentary sensation; it was rather something lasting and imperishable. It was attained chiefly by pure and noble thoughts. Freedom from pain and from all influences which disturb the peace of one's mind resulted in happiness, and his teachings were directed to the attainment of such peace of mind. After the death of Epicurus in 270 B.C., his pupils and disciples maintained his school, under fourteen masters, for more than two hundred years, despite violent attacks upon his theories by later philosophers. Some asserted that his theory provided an excuse for the greatest debauchery and sensuality. And it was from these distorted notions that some men, who had devoted their lives to such vices, called themselves Epicureans. Cicero was one who held such a mistaken thought. It is therefore largely through him that *epicure* came to denote, rather than a true follower of Epicurus, one given over to sensual pleasures, especially gluttony. (We do not now imply gluttony in our use of the term, but rather one who shows a refined taste in his eating and drinking.)

ergot

Sometimes, as many farmers have observed, a seed of rye becomes diseased and is transformed into a fungus growth of dark purple color, in shape strongly resembling a cock's spur. The condition was noted by French farmers many centuries ago, and because of the shape they gave this fungus the name *argot*, cock's spur. In modern French this has become *ergot* and was thus borrowed by us.

escape

As the dictionary says, this is from the Latin *ex*, out, and *cappa*, cape. In olden days the meaning was literal. One slipped out of his cape or threw it aside in order to free himself for running, or, it might be, he left it in the clutch of a would-be captor and made away from the spot. One is reminded of the young man mentioned by St. Mark who, when the servants of the high priests attempted to seize him by the garment he was wearing, "left the linen cloth, and fled from them naked."

esquire

In the Age of Chivalry—that is, in the period between the tenth and fourteenth centuries—young men of gentle birth who aspired to be knights were accustomed to attach themselves to the services of the knight of their choice and attend him in his travels. The chief duty of such a voluntary servant was to act as shield-bearer. Because of this duty the young man was called an *esquire*, a word of French origin, but tracing back through the Italian *scudiere*, shield-bearer, to the Latin *scutum*, shield. In later days the title was transferred to men of gentle birth, such as the younger sons of a peer, who ranked immediately below a knight, and ultimately became a courtesy title to any man who, through birth, position, or education is considered to be a gentleman.

etiquette

Elsewhere it has been shown how the expression, "That's the ticket," arose from a mispronunciation of *etiquette*.* But the French word itself means "ticket," among other things, and in Old French was used to designate the ticket that prescribed a soldier's lodging place, his billet. Just how the sense became transferred to prescribed conduct is not known.

eureka

The Greek mathematician, Archimedes, who was born in Syracuse in 287 B.C., was so far in advance in the practical application of geometry to mechanical devices that he may be called the Thomas Edison of his day. It is hard to comprehend that more than two thousand years after his death we are still making use of his discoveries and inventions and have done little more than effect improvements upon them. Faced one time with the problem of determining the amount of silver a dishonest goldsmith had used in making a crown for the king which had been ordered of pure gold, Archimedes hit upon the solution one day when he stepped into his bath. The bath was full and a certain amount of it overflowed. This suggested to him what is now known as a law of hydrostatics, that a body surrounded by a fluid is buoyed up by a force equal to the weight of the fluid which it displaces. Thus by weighing out an amount of gold equal to the weight of the crown and by putting them separately into a basin full of water, the difference in the weight of the overflow would denote the amount of alloy. It is said that Archimedes was so excited by his discovery and so eager to test its proof that, forgetting his clothes, he sprang from the bath and rushed home, shouting to astonished passers-by, *"Eureka, eureka!* (I have found it, I have found it!)"

* See the author's *A Hog on Ice, and Other Curious Expressions.*

explode (applaud, plaudit)

The Roman populace expressed their opinion of the abilities of their actors in manners that were unmistakable, and their ways were not unlike our own. If they liked an actor's performance, they clapped their hands at the end of his lines, when the action permitted; if they liked the entire play, they continued to clap after the performance closed. But if an actor gave a poor performance, he was literally clapped off the stage; that is, the clapping and hissing, begun at each appearance on the stage, continued until he was forced to retire. These judgments, all accompanied by clapping, were all based on the word *plaudo*, to clap. They were *applaudo*, from *ad*, to, thus meaning "to clap to," which became our word *applaud*. The second came through appeal by the actors—*Plaudite!* Please clap!—which has given rise to our English word, *plaudit*, acclamation. The action of disapproval was expressed by *explaudo*, from *ex*, off, meaning "to clap off," especially with a loud noise. Our English word, *explode*, derived from that, was still used, though rarely, with the Latin sense into the nineteenth century. The sudden burst of loud noise and the ejectment of the actor brought about a figurative usage, applied to anything that burst forth suddenly and with noise, and this in turn led to our present usages of *explode* and *explosion*.

expunge

In old Roman days, when a soldier had retired from service and his name was to be carried no longer on the lists, the fact was indicated by a series of dots or points pricked over or beneath his name. In this manner it was said to be "pointed out." The Latin term for "to point or prick out" is *expungo*. In English use *expunge* carries the sense of deletion by erasure, blotting, omission, or striking out in any form.

extravagant

Formed from the Latin words *extra*, outside, and *vagor*, to wander, *extravagant* has the literal meaning, "tending to wander outside the usual path; hence, astray, roving." Such were the senses of the term in Shakespeare's time. But it soon became extended in meaning, and "straying beyond reasonable bounds" became the usual intent of the word. Thus one who is *extravagant* with money or in statement goes beyond the bounds of reason.

fad

In certain regions of England, the local people, when they fondle or caress a child, or make a pet of it, say that they "faddle" it. That word has been known and used for three hundred years. From it, about a hundred years ago, the curtailed word, *fad*, was formed and used to indicate a pet project, something that one took up as a hobby. It is not known who originated the contraction.

fake

Until a hundred years ago this was one of the words frowned upon by the schoolmasters. It was slang. Not only that, but it was the slang used by thieves and gypsies, not by reputable speakers and writers. The true history is therefore unknown, but some suppose it to have been picked up long before by English soldiers during the Thirty Years' War (1618-48) when they were in long contact with German allies. If so, the German source was *fegen*, to clean, sweep, or, in a slang sense, to take the contents of something, such as a purse. But it seems more likely to me that *fake*, obsolete for many centuries in literature, came directly from *faken*, a term used in England until the fifteenth century, meaning fraud, guile, dishonesty.

fan

In the popular sense of an enthusiast, a *fan* is a follower or devotee of a sport or special interest, or an ardent admirer of some person. One of my elderly friends, an early baseball *fan*, insists that the term originated through the fact that the spectators at baseball games, back in the 1880's, seated in the hot sunshine, usually carried with them common palm-leaf fans with which to cool themselves. Players and reporters, he says, constantly reminded of the spectators by their large waving fans, began to refer to the spectators as *fans* for that reason. His account is plausible, but no proof of the theory has yet been found. Another entertaining theory is that *fan*, in this sense, was a contracted form of "the fancy," an expression which, a hundred years ago, was a popular term for those people who followed some sport or interest, such as prize fighting, dog breeding, or the like. This theory also lacks proof. The accepted opinion, therefore, is that *fan*, in this sense, is a contracted form of *fanatic*.

fanatic

It is said that Sulla, while leading the Roman army in Asia Minor against Mithradates in the early part of the first century B.C., was visited in a dream by a goddess. She appeared to urge him to return to Rome to forestall enemies who were plotting against him at home. He followed the advice and was in time to save his reputation. In gratitude, Sulla caused a temple or fane to be erected to this goddess, who, like an old Italian goddess, was named Bellona. He brought priests and priestesses from Asia Minor to establish the rites sacred to her and conduct services in her worship. At the annual festivals these rites were peculiarly grim. All the priests were clad in black robes from head to foot, but some among them, inspired by religious frenzy, would tear their robes aside, seize a two-edged ax, and gash themselves about the arms and loins, scattering the blood upon the spectators. These priests were believed to be inspired into excessive zeal by the goddess or by the fane or temple at which she was worshipped. Such zeal, accordingly, was said by the Romans to be *fanaticus*, from which our *fanatic* was derived. Its literal meaning is, therefore, "inspired by the fane."

farce

In the churches of medieval France and England, back in the thirteenth century, it became customary to insert various phrases in the litanies sung by the monks between the words *Kyrie* and *eleison* in the supplication, *Kyrie eleison!* "Lord have mercy!" Such an insertion, borrowing a term already used in cookery, was called a *farce*, from Latin *farcio*, to stuff or pad. (The cookery term survives in present use, slightly altered, in "forcemeat," finely chopped meat used for stuffing.) Later, when religious dramas, such as the mystery plays, became so popular, the actors who had comic parts began to introduce impromptu ludicrous gags into their lines to fit some local event or condition. Because these inserted remarks also padded out the lines of an actor, to his amused audience his buffoonery became known, in turn, as a *farce*. It was but a natural sequence then that any short dramatic work which had the production of laughter as its sole object should be given the same name, and that we should carry the term still further to apply to any sham or piece of mockery.

farm

The history of this word, especially of its change in meaning, is curious. It is derived, through the French *ferme*, from Latin *firmus*, fixed, settled, and when first used in England, as in France, it denoted the fixed annual rental, tax, or revenue payable by a person, town, or county to the overlord. A *farmer* was then the person who collected such payments. In France, even up to Revolutionary times, the *fermes générale* or "general farmers" grew inordinately wealthy by pocketing the difference between the annual sum paid by them in advance into the royal treasury and the sum subsequently collected by them through taxes and customs levied upon towns and individuals. In England, however, *farm* commonly designated the fixed annual rental paid by a tenant upon a tract of land leased for agricultural purposes. Most of such tracts were not, and still are not, owned by the persons who operate them. Later, but not until the sixteenth century, the meaning of *farm* was transferred from the rental upon land to the modern sense of a tract of land devoted to agricultural purposes. In England a *farm* is still held under lease, but in the United States it may be operated by the person who owns it.

faro

In the early eighteenth century various card games which became popular at the gambling tables were introduced into England from France. Little is now known about some of these, and others, such as basset (or bassette) and lansquenet, lost their popularity many years ago. But among these was the game now known as *faro*, although the name of the game, when first brought into England, was correctly spelled *pharaoh*, a translation of the French name, *pharaon*. The reason for the original name is not positively known, but the assumption is that the name was taken from one or all of the king cards in the deck which bore a likeness to the Egyptian monarch

330

upon its face. Possibly that likeness appeared only upon the king of spades. *Pharaoh* means "king," and it is customarily the spade suit, beginning with the king, which is reproduced upon the painted cloth upon which the game of *faro* is played.

fascinate

From earliest times, and even today among superstitious people, it has been believed that certain persons, if so inclined, have the power to injure or even kill other persons or animals or to destroy crops or commit other injury by no more than a malignant glance. Such a person is held to possess the "evil eye." In ancient Greece, the power of the evil eye was called *baskania*, in Rome *fascinatio*. Because no one knew who that he might meet had the power and the wish to do him injury, it was an almost universal custom, in olden times, to wear an amulet of some kind which was believed to protect the wearer. Even the cattle were sometimes so adorned. Children were thought to be especially susceptible to the power of the evil eye, and no Roman mother, in classical days, would permit a child of hers to leave the house without first suspending from its neck, under the robe, a certain amulet called *fascinum*. Actually, therefore, our word *fascinate*, when first brought into English use, meant to cast the evil eye upon one, to put one under the spell of witchcraft. We use the word rarely now in such a literal sense, but employ it rather to mean to hold one's attention irresistibly or to occupy one's thoughts exclusively by pleasing qualities.

February

Among the oldest of the annual festivals of Rome was that known as the Lupercalia. It was celebrated on February 15 in honor of Lupercus, an ancient Italian god of fertility, sometimes identified with Pan or Faunus. He was the god of shepherds; thus the festival was connected with Romulus and Remus, the kings of shepherds, and thence introduced into Rome. In the ceremony, goats and dogs, noted for strong sexual instincts, were sacrificed by the priests. Two youths of noble birth were then touched upon the forehead with a sword smeared with the blood of the goats. Other priests then wiped the foreheads clean with wool dipped in milk. Whereupon the two youths were then obliged to shout with laughter. After that the priests, all of whom were of patrician birth, cut the skin of the goats into strips and, holding the strips in their hands and clad only in a loincloth of goatskin, they ran through the streets of the city touching or striking all persons whom they met. Women sought the runners eagerly, because the thongs were thought to be charms against barrenness. These thongs were called *februa*, purifiers, derived from *februo*, to purify, and the day upon which the festival occurred was called *dies februatus*, day of purification. From this most important festival in its period, the name *februarius*, month of purification, was given to the month. Thence our term, *February*. (See also JANUARY.)

ferule

In southern Europe there is a perennial plant which, though not a true fennel, is called "giant fennel" because it somewhat resembles the fennel and belongs to the same order. Unlike the fennel, which runs about three or four feet in height, this plant sometimes reaches a height of fifteen feet. Its Latin name is *ferula*. The old Romans prized it, as do their descendants, because the dried pith of the stem made an excellent tinder. But the *ferula* had other uses. The plants were plentiful, the stalks were pliable, and they were early found to be handy switches for the punishment of small boys. Such rods came to be known as *ferulæ*, from their source, and the schoolmasters of Shakespeare's time turned the name into *ferule* for the rod or flattened piece of wood they used to chastise refractory scholars. (*Ferule* and *ferrule* should not be confused. The latter is the name of the metal ring about the end of a cane or the like; it is corrupted from an earlier *verrel*, which goes back to the Latin *viriola*, little bracelet.)

fiasco

This Italian word means, in its literal sense, a flask or bottle. But at some time there became current among theatrical people of Italy the expression, *far fiasco*, which, though it actually means nothing more than "to make a bottle," was used with exactly the same meaning that we convey when we say, "to make a mess of; to fail," or in popular speech, "to pull a boner." So *fiasco*, in English use, came to mean complete and ignominious failure, but not even the most profound scholar in Italy can explain why "bottle" became a synonym for "flop."

fib

"Fable," from the earliest appearance of the word in English, six hundred years ago, not only meant a pleasant narrative, but also meant a downright lie, and we still use the word in either sense. Some three or four hundred years ago, however, an unknown parent thought to soften the word, probably, by accusing her small child of telling a "fibble-fable" when she caught him (or her) in a story which she knew to be nonsense. At any rate, this expression caught the popular fancy at about that time as a term for a slight falsehood. But, according to best conjecture, the expression proved to be too long a name for a slight sin, and soon became shortened to *fib*.

fife

Back in 1515, when Francis I of France was leading his army against Milan, he found twenty-five thousand Swiss soldiers, the bravest in Europe at that time, drawn up against him ten miles north of the city. They had been hired by the Milanese government to assist in defending the city. The brave Swiss, however, armed with their old-fashioned pikes, were no match against the new arquebuses with which the French troops were then supplied. Hence, though they fought by the light of the moon until midnight, only three thousand of their number were left to escape, as best they could, after the second day of battle. Milan fell. But this battle, aside from proving the superiority of the firearm over sword and pike, introduced a new instrument into military music. The drum had long been used, but with it the Swiss also used a kind of flute having a loud and brilliant tone. German musicians of the period, to distinguish it from the shrill pipe (German *pfeiff*) which it somewhat resembled, called it *Schweizerpfeiff*, Swiss pipe. The instrument soon became generally popular in army use because its tones carried well, and it is believed to have been carried to England by German musicians of the sixteenth century. The English, unable to pronounce *pfeiff*, called it and wrote it *phife, phyfe, fiphe*, or *fyfe*, and finally, in the seventeenth century, settled upon *fife*. (See also MAGENTA.)

filibuster (freebooter)

Piracy flourished in the seventeenth century, probably more successfully and openly than ever before or since. Spain had secured all of the rich new countries bordering the Caribbean Sea, and, although nominally at peace with the other maritime nations of Europe—France, Holland, and England—rigidly excluded those nations from establishing colonies in her domain. Her own American colonies, moreover, were supposed to trade with Spain alone, a trade that was usually extortionate, and she ruthlessly seized any vessel caught within the "Spanish Main" to enforce her rule. Such a condition could not be tolerated by Dutch, English, and French shipmasters, who knew the wealth that awaited them among the colonies. Their governments conveniently looked elsewhere while they armed themselves and set sail to capture Spanish ships, sink any that might interfere, and bring back wealth from New Spain. Ultimately such a captain or a member of his crew, of whatever nationality, became generally known as a "buccaneer," but one from Holland was first called a *vrijbuiter*, literally, a "free robber" or corsair. This, because of its sound and its resemblance to "free" and "booty," became "freebooter" in English. In French, however, it became first "fribustier" and then *flibustier* (the *s* probably inserted to show that the preceding vowel was long). These French forms were rarely used by English writers, who favored "freebooter" or "buccaneer" in telling of the pirates of the sixteenth and seventeenth centuries. But the French term passed into Spain, and there it suffered another alteration into *filibustero*. It was but natural, then, that the American adventurer, William Walker, of the 1850's should have been called a *filibustero* by Central Americans, a term that was shortened to *filibuster* in English. Walker, it may be recalled, was the young fellow who, in 1853, led an expedition of American adventurers in an attempt to capture the State of Sonora, Mexico. The attempt failed, but two years later a similar expedition against Nicaragua succeeded to such an extent that he was able, briefly in 1857, to proclaim himself president. Driven out of the country later in the same year, he then attempted to capture Honduras in 1860, but was caught and shot by the Honduran government. Our modern use of *filibuster* in legislative halls is harmless by comparison. At least it doesn't involve piracy or acts of violence. It probably arose through a mild comparison of the actions of legislators seeking to block a bill with the actions of Walker who sought to block international law.

flapper

It is perhaps just as well that this slang term for an adolescent young woman, the equivalent of the later "bobbysoxer," has just about disappeared. It was never complimentary, even if, as some think, the name was borrowed from the hunters' term for a young wild duck in ungainly flight. But there was an earlier slang use of *flapper* which preceded the twentieth-century use by only a few decades, and which was more probably the direct antecedent, somewhat altered in meaning. The late nineteenth-century slang meant an immoral young woman. Immorality was not implied in the later slang.

fork

The ancient Romans ate with their fingers, conveying food with such grace as they could master from plate to mouth. So, for that matter, did all European people until about the eleventh century A.D. The Roman *furca* (from which *fork* is derived) was an agricultural implement with two tines, like the hayfork of today, and it was used for various similar purposes. An instrument of punishment was also called *furca* because, shaped like an inverted V, it resembled the farm tool greatly enlarged. This device, of heavy wood, was hung over the neck of the person to be punished, usually a runaway slave, and his hands were fastened to the two ends. The inventor of the table fork is unknown. The implement is said to have been introduced into Vienna in the eleventh century by a Byzantine princess, who may have had it designed for her. Like many of the forks of today, it probably had but two tines. The Viennese promptly dubbed it *furca* from its resemblance to the agricultural implement which had descended to them. The rest of Europe was slow to adopt this novelty, and even as late as the sixteenth century its use in France was ridiculed. Forks came into use by English nobility early in the seventeenth century, though even at the close of that century few nobles possessed as many as a dozen. The English name *fork* came from the Old English corruption, *forca*, of the Latin word.

fortnight (sennight)

The Angles and Saxons who conquered Britain in the fifth and sixth centuries A.D. had not yet fully adopted all of the Roman devices for marking the passage of time. Thus, though it is probable that they had already accepted the Roman method of naming the days of the week, modified to honor corresponding Teutonic gods, it is not certain that "week," as we use it today, was understood by them to mean a period of seven "days." They clung, instead, to the ancestral practice of referring to such a period as "seven nights," because, with them, night, when the world was dark and men were asleep, marked a distinct division of time. Their term became *seofon nihta* in Old English, and this, through the centuries, became corrupted to *sennight*, now almost entirely out of use. The more convenient term for a two-week period, roughly half a month, is still in current use in England, though not often heard nowadays in America. In Old English it was *feowertene nihta*, fourteen nights, which became contracted into *fortnight*.

foyer

In these days of comfortable living we are likely to forget the discomfort that our ancestors took as a matter of course. The theater of today, regardless of outside winter temperature, is pleasantly warm, both for audience and performers. Such was not always the case. Even so recently as a century ago, no matter how warmly dressed, the audience welcomed the intermissions between acts to walk about and get the blood back into circulation; those especially cold retired to the lobby or entrance hall of the theater where a large fire burned upon the hearth. The actors congregated about a similar hearth in the greenroom. In France, the name for hearth is *foyer*, and the sense of this word gradually came to include the large hall or room in which the hearth was located. The need for the hearth and the hearth itself vanished long ago, but the name was borrowed into English usage for both the greenroom and the lobby.

336

franc

After the battle of Poitiers in 1356, John II, king of France, sometimes called "John the Good," was taken prisoner by the British. He remained a prisoner in London until 1360. Then, upon a promise to cede certain French provinces to the British crown and to pay a ransom of three million gold crowns, he was permitted to return to France to evolve ways of raising this huge sum. His attempt failed and he returned to England voluntarily to resume a not too onerous captivity. During his brief period of freedom, however, which was spent largely in debasing the currency in order to raise money, he caused a new gold coin to be struck. It was actually equivalent in value to the livre then in use, merely having a new legend and new design upon its face. The design was presumably an effigy of King John on horseback; the Latin legend read, *Johannes Dei gracia Francorum rex*, "John, by the grace of God, King of the Franks." Because of the legend and the effigy, this coin became popularly termed *franc à cheval*, "a franc with a horse." The term was given additional impulse when Charles V, successor of John II, issued another coin of the same value bearing an effigy of himself standing upright. This became *franc à pied*, "franc on foot." The new name for the livre persisted, and from then on French writers used *franc* or *livre* indiscriminately until, in 1795, the gold coin was superseded by the silver franc and the livre was dropped from currency.

frank

In the late sixth and early seventh centuries A.D., a warlike German tribe living along the lower stretches of the Rhine, moved steadily southward. The Roman legions had at one time conquered this tribe and had used its forces as honored allies, but now the Roman power had become weak and the tribe finally occupied all the coastal country north of the Pyrenees. The members of this tribe were known to the Romans as *Franci* (plural of *Francus*), after the javelin with which they were efficiently armed. The English equivalent is *Frank*, and the tribe is referred to in English accounts as the *Franks*. After their conquest of the country the Franks imposed their own laws, subjugating the natives and arrogating all the privileges to themselves. Thus they became the only free people in the land. Hence their name, having lost the old Roman meaning, came to be used as meaning "free." And because of this and their power, they scorned the use of subterfuge in their dealings among themselves or with others. Thus the Franks became noted, not only for their freedom, but also for integrity. Hence, *frank* came to denote the characteristics attributed to these people, straightforwardness and candor. Part of the country which they occupied still honors this old free tribe by the name it bears, *France*.

Frankenstein

In 1818, Mary Wollstonecraft Shelley, second wife of the romantic young poet, Percy Bysshe Shelley, published her first piece of writing. It is said that she had undertaken such authorship two years before when she, Shelley, and Byron had agreed that each was to undertake to write a tale dealing with the supernatural. Mrs. Shelley was the only one to complete the task. Her tale bore the title, *Frankenstein, or The Modern Prometheus*. The story tells about a Swiss student, Victor Frankenstein, who found a way to create life artificially. After making the discovery he visited dissecting rooms and graveyards and constructed a body in human form and endowed it with life. The soulless monster thus created had muscular strength and animal passions, but was shunned by all other living creatures. Made frantic by its unsatisfied desires and by Frankenstein's unwillingness to create a mate for it, the monster revenged itself upon its creator. After committing many atrocities, including the murder of Frankenstein's friend, brother, and bride, it finally slew Frankenstein himself. The book became very popular, and the term *Frankenstein* came into the language as indicating any person whose work brings about his own ruin. Unfortunately, Mrs. Shelley did not give a name to the monster, with the consequence that *Frankenstein* has often been misapplied to the monster itself, and, thus, to the agency that brings about the ruin of its creator.

Friday

When the Egyptian system of a week of seven days was adopted by the Roman Empire during the reign of Constantine, the sixth day of what is now our week was named *dies Veneris*, day of Venus, in honor of the planet that was presumed to influence that day, according to Egyptian astronomers. But the Teutonic tribes of the north, when adopting the seven-day week, knew nothing of the planetary reason for naming the days, and, supposing the Romans to have merely honored their chief gods and goddesses, gave to this day the name of their own chief goddess, *Frigg* or *Frigga*. She was the wife of Odin (or Woden); she presided over marriages and over the skies, and knew the fate of all men. Later myths, however, introduced a new goddess among some of the Teutonic tribes, a goddess of similar name. This was *Freya* or *Freyja*. She, with her brother, Frey, were the children of Njord, the god of the winds and sea. Freya was the goddess of love, and therefore corresponded more closely with the Roman goddess, Venus, than did Frigg. In Old English literature her name appears as *Freo*, of which the possessive is *Frige*. Consequently, because of this similarity, some scholars believe that *Friday*, which appears as *Frigedæg* (Freo's day) in Old English, also honors the goddess of love, just as, by way of the planet, the Romans did with *dies Veneris*. (See also SATURDAY.)

fudge

There is, unfortunately, no certainty about the origin of this word. But Isaac D'Israeli (the father of the statesman, Benjamin Disraeli), in *Curiosities of Literature*, published in 1791, quoted a story that went the rounds of the British navy in 1700 which was then thought to explain the source. The quoted explanation ran: "There was, sir, in our time one Captain Fudge, commander of a merchantman, who upon his return from a voyage, how ill-fraught soever his ship was, always brought home his owners a good cargo of lies, so much that now aboard ship the sailors, when they hear a great lie told, cry out, 'You *fudge* it.'" The story may be true, for there was a real Captain Fudge living in the seventeenth century, and he was said to have been known by some as "Lying Fudge," but the explanation is not generally accepted as the source of our word.

fun (fond) (fondle)

We know that "son" is pronounced as if spelled "sun," so it is not surprising to learn that *fun* was spelled *fon* back in the days of Chaucer. The meaning of *fon*, however, was not quite the same as that which we give to the later spelling. It meant "a fool," and when the word was revived in the early part of the eighteenth century in the present sense and spelling, *fun*, after two centuries of disuse, the learned Dr. Samuel Johnson called it "a low cant word." In the early use, *fon* was also a verb, meaning "to act the fool; become foolish." Its past participle, though sometimes spelled *fonned*, was then usually spelled *fond*. So when Shakespeare and earlier writers speak of "fond old men" or "fond maydens," they actually described foolish or silly old men or maids. This past participle didn't fall into disuse, as did *fon*, but its meaning gradually altered from "foolish" to "foolishly tender," and finally to "tender and sentimental," although fond young men, and especially fond old men, still often look and act foolish. Toward the eighteenth century someone felt the need of a verb to indicate the action of being fond, and thus created *fondle*. Sometimes it, too, carries back to the original *fon*, for a doting grandmother sometimes acts foolish when fondling a grandchild.

furlong (mile)

Before the days when Edward I ruled England (1272-1307), an acre of land was understood to be such amount of tillable land as a yoke of oxen could plow in a day. The size was indefinite, just as was the Latin *ager*, field, from which *acre* is derived. It was several times the size of our present acre, usually ten times the size, because in some regions at least the extent was measured as the amount which a team of eight oxen could plow in a day. This latter ideal field was a square which measured an eighth of a Roman mile, or a *stadium*, in each direction. The furrows were therefore each a stadium in length and, with the primitive plow then used, there were probably 320 furrows across the field. The length of a furrow thus became a convenient measure of distance—a *furlang*, it was called in Old English, from *furh*, furrow, and *lang*, long. But for the sake of standardization, the size of the acre was reduced under the statutes of King Edward. Thereafter it denoted an area which measured forty rods in length by four rods in breadth, although neither the rod nor the yard upon which it was based were of standard size. Then when the Roman mile of a thousand paces (*mille passus*), or about 1,618 yards, was replaced by the standard English mile of 1,760 yards, and the length of the yard became a standard measure, *furlong* became merely a term for a unit of distance an eighth of a mile or 220 yards in length, no longer equal to the Roman *stadium*. (See also ACRE.)

galvanism

Luigi Galvani was only a young man of twenty-five when in 1762, through the merit of his studies in medicine, he was appointed professor of anatomy at the University of Bologna, Italy. One day, a few years later, it is said, while his wife was watching him dissect a frog, she saw something that astonished her. She saw the skinned leg of the frog twitch as though alive when, accidentally, the scalpel which her husband had just picked up from the table came into contact with an exposed nerve. She called it to his attention. Upon investigation they found that the scalpel had become charged by an adjacent electric machine. Further experiment showed that the phenomenon was repeated as long as the nerve remained fresh at every such contact with a charged instrument. Galvani continued this new line of experimentation for some twenty years before publishing his findings. His conclusions—that the nerves are sources of electricity and that the scalpel or other metal served only as conductors—were subsequently proved to be wrong by Volta, but his experiments opened up a new line of electric research in the development of electricity by chemical means, and the name of the Italian physician has been perpetuated through the name given to the process, *galvanism*.

gamut

Guido of Arezzo was the greatest musician of medieval times. He lived in the eleventh century, although few details of his life are known. He is credited with the first systematic use of the lines of the staff and the spaces between them, but is now chiefly remembered from the names that he gave to the notes of the scale, six of which are in present use. It is said that when teaching his choristers the hymn addressed to St. John the Baptist he was struck with the regularly ascending sounds of the opening syllable of each hemıstich in the first three verses. These verses, separated into hemistichs, were:

Ut queant laxis	*re*sonare fibrıs
*Mi*ra gestorum	*fa*muli tuorum
*Sol*ve polluti	*la*bii reatum

The hymn closed with "Sancte *I*ohannes," the initials of which—*si*—provided the seventh note of the scale when, in later days, the heptachord of seven notes replaced the hexachord of six notes used by Guido. The first syllable, *ut*, has been replaced by *do* in English-speaking countries, but is still used in France. In his written music Guido used the Greek letter *gamma* (Γ) to indicate the note one tone lower than A, which from classical times began the scales, and this note was accordingly designated *gamma ut*. It became contracted to *gamut*, and ultimately became the name by which the entire "Great Scale" of Guido's invention was known. Because this scale was intended to cover the entire singing range of both bass and treble, *gamut* early acquired a figurative usage denoting full range or entire sequence—such as we say of an actor who may be able to assume expressions that run the full *gamut* of emotions.

gantlet (gauntlet)

During the Thirty Years' War, which lasted from 1618 to 1648, the English forces observed a form of disciplinary punishment used among their German allies. It looked highly effective, so it was not long before it was adopted by English disciplinarians. The Germans said that it had originated in the Swedish army, in which it was known as *gatloppe*, literally, "a running of the lane." In this punishment, the severity of which could be regulated, a soldier guilty of an offense was compelled to strip to the waist and run between two lines of his fellows, each armed with a lash or rod. As he passed, each was supposed to strike him across the back. Depending upon the severity of the punishment to be inflicted, the lines of men might be short or long, and the lashes might be knotted for maximum severity. The Swedish word became corrupted into *gantlope* by the English, but was later altered to *gantlet* or *gauntlet* because of the resemblance of the word to the name of the glove.

gardenia

Alexander Garden was born in Charleston, South Carolina, and went to Scotland to study medicine. He returned to Charleston in 1755 as a young physician of twenty-five. He was also a profound student of botany, as a young man, and it was in his honor that the Royal Society, in 1760, gave the name, *gardenia*, to a newly discovered tropical shrub. Throughout the Revolutionary War, Dr. Garden remained a Tory, and was still opposed to the formation of an independent country when the war closed. Accordingly, in 1783, he emigrated to London where he again took up the practice of medicine. His estates, confiscated during the war, were returned to his son Alexander, a volunteer in the American army, serving with distinction under General Lee and General Greene.

gargantuan

When the great French writer of the sixteenth century, François Rabelais, wished to satirize the extravagances of the French court of his period, he chose to do so by allegory. This he wrote in the form of an account of the life of an enormous giant, whom he named *Gargantua*, taking the name from that of a legendary giant of the Middle Ages. At birth, he explained, the huge infant required the milk of 17,913 cows. For his education he rode to Paris on a mare as large as six elephants, and about the mare's neck he hung the bells of Notre Dame as jingles. The mare's tail was as great as the bell tower of San Marco, and when stung by wasps near Orleans, the mare swung it so furiously as to knock down all the trees in the neighborhood. *Gargantua* was so huge that he combed his hair with a comb 900 feet long; his shoes required eleven hundred cowhides for the soles alone. His appetite was prodigious. To this day our expression, "a *gargantuan* feast," refers to the occasion when *Gargantua,* being hungry, made a salad from lettuces as big as walnut trees and, inadvertently, ate up six pilgrims who had taken refuge among them.

garret

If one recalls the French expression so commonly heard during the recent World Wars, "*C'est la guerre!*" a clue may be seen for the origin of the word *garret*. The ancient French spelling was *guerite*, and the term meant a watchtower or place of observation, as under the roof of a building where a sentry could be on the lookout for an approaching enemy. Taken to England by the Norman conquerors, its original meaning became altered to our present sense and its spelling, thanks to similarity of pronunciation, transformed to *garret*.

gas

Until about the end of the sixteenth century chemists, or alchemists more properly, still held to the theory of Aristotle that the four primary properties of matter were fire, air, water, and earth. At that period, however, some such experimenters as Galileo, Harvey, and others were beginning to discard the old theories, and the alchemists themselves were finding flaws in their ancient beliefs. Among the critics was the Belgian physician, Jean Baptiste van Helmont, born in 1577. Although he believed that he had himself transmuted mercury into gold with a small piece of the "philosopher's stone," he was obliged to fall back upon supernatural agencies to find an explanation for certain phenomena that he discovered in his other experiments. He observed that when he applied heat to certain things, water especially, a vapor would arise. He believed this vapor to be fundamentally water in ultrararefied form, and, as he says, "for want of a name, I have called that vapor *gas*, not far disassociated from the *chaos* of the ancients." Thus, although van Helmont had no more than a vague understanding of the nature of gases, we are indebted to him for the word.

gazette

Back toward the early part of the sixteenth century there circulated in Venice a small coin of low value, made chiefly of tin. Probably it was worth no more than half a cent in our currency. The Venetians called it a *gazzetta*. This name may have been a diminutive of *gazza*, a magpie, or, as some scholars believe, a diminutive of *gaza*, which denoted the treasure of Persian kings. If the latter, the Venetian *gazzetta* was an extremely small treasure. Be that as it may, the Venetian government began to issue official leaflets, about the middle of the sixteenth century, which dealt with battles, games, elections, and other matters of general interest. (Some of the material was supplied by merchants returning from foreign ports. Much of the information was based upon unreliable rumor and hearsay.) The price set upon this paper—or for the privilege of reading it in such public places as it was displayed—was one *gazzetta*. The leaflet itself thus became known as a *gazzetta*. This term was brought into England in 1598 by John Florio in his Italian-English dictionary. He described the contents of the paper as, "running reports, daily newes, idle intelligences, or flim flam tales that are daily written from Italie, namely from Rome and Venice." Our present spelling came about through French influence.

gerrymander

Elbridge Gerry, born in 1744, was a member of the group of the American patriots who stirred the townspeople of Boston into active opposition toward the Acts of George III, resulting in the War for Independence. Subsequently he was a member of the Continental Congress and a signer of the Declaration of Independence. He continued to serve in this Congress until 1786, and was elected to the First and Second Congresses after the adoption of the Federal Constitution in 1788. Twice he was elected governor of Massachusetts, but was defeated when running for the third time in 1812. Instead, however, he was elected vice-president of the United States in that same year and served in that capacity until his death in 1814. But despite this honorable record, Gerry's name has come down to us in association with one dishonorable episode in his career. While running for his third term as governor of Massachusetts, he permitted the state legislature, in accordance with customs of the times, to divide the electoral districts of the state into new districts in such manner that the strength of the opposing party was concentrated into a few districts. A map of one of the districts thus arbitrarily created was seen by the painter, Gilbert Stuart. Stuart saw in it a resemblance to the body of an elongated animal. With a few strokes he added a head, claws, and wings, and remarked, "That will do for a salamander." "Better say a *gerrymander*," growled the editor in whose office the map was hanging.

gin

Credit for the introduction of the juniper berry into wine in the sixteenth century is given to the Count de Morret, one of the illegitimate sons of Henry IV of France. The beverage, subsequently known as juniper wine, was found to be pleasing and it led others to try the effect of the berry when added to spirit distilled from fermented liquors. Previously, ginger, pepper, and other aromatic ingredients had been used. The addition of the juniper berry, however, was found to be far more agreeable, and the older experiments were dropped. The new beverage became known in France by the name of the berry—*genevre* (in modern French, *genièvre*). In Holland, where manufacture was largely centered during the following century, the name became *genever*. The English, who marketed vast quantities of the liquor, altered this to *geneva*, after the Swiss city of that name. It was not long, however, before they shortened the general term *Holland geneva* into *Holland gin* in accordance with the customary British penchant for contraction, and this then soon became more commonly further shortened to *gin*.

glamour

Until the seventeenth century there was no necessity for anyone to speak of "Latin grammar," because that was the only kind of grammar that was taught. Anyone who knew his "grammar" necessarily knew Latin. Even in these days, among untutored folk, any learned person is regarded with something akin to awe. But in those days, when few men in any community could read or write, one who was so learned that he could read and speak Latin was believed, by common folks, to possess occult powers, to be capable of witchcraft or of working magic spells. Accordingly, in the speech of England, such a person was said to have *gramary*, that is, ability to effect charms through a knowledge of grammar. In Scotland he had *glamer*, a corruption of the same word and with the same meaning. Various Scottish writers, spelling it *glamer*, *glamor*, or *glamour*, used the term in that sense, but it was Sir Walter Scott who explained it and brought it into English usage slightly more than a century ago. Since then we have extended the earlier sense by glorifying the enchantment, though we no longer imply that one possessing *glamour* is necessarily learned.

gorgon

Three hideous sisters, according to Greek mythology, lived in the region of Night at the extremity of the Western Ocean. They were known as *gorgons*; their separate names were Stheno, Euryale, and Medusa. The latter, the only one of the three who was mortal, had once been a beautiful girl, but having had the misfortune to enrage the goddess Athena, her aspect was changed so that she became even more fearsome and deadly than her sisters. The sisters are described as being girded with winged serpents which had brazen claws and enormous teeth which they gnashed viciously. The hair of Medusa was changed by Athena into writhing serpents, which gave her head so fearful an appearance that anyone who looked at it was changed into stone. According to other tradition, the *gorgons* were formidable animals with long hair, and of such frightful appearance as to paralyze anyone seeing them. In modern usage, a *gorgon* repels more by a forbidding manner than by repulsive appearance.

gorilla

In the fifth or sixth century B.C., a Carthaginian navigator, Hanno, set out upon a westward voyage along the north coast of Africa, through the Pillars of Hercules, which we now call the Strait of Gibraltar, and thence southward along the west coast of Africa. He wrote an account of his voyage in a small book called *Periplus*. It is not now possible to identify the points at which he touched nor to determine the actual extent of his expedition, though he is supposed to have reached what is now Sierra Leone. He says that an object of the trip was to establish Carthaginian colonies along the way, and that he took with him 30,000 men and women for the purpose. That number, however, is probably an exaggeration introduced by translators when the book was circulated in Greece. Among the strange things that he encountered on the trip was a wild creature which he believed to be a large hairy woman. This he called *gorilla*, using the native name. It is probable that the creature described by Hanno was either the chimpanzee or the baboon, however, for it is not believed that he traveled far enough to the southward to encounter the fiercer creature that we now call *gorilla*.

gospel

A missionary to any heathen country must first learn the language of that country. He then tries to deliver his message in that language, translating the words that are familiar to him into new words that will carry the same meaning. Thus the Latin *evangelium* was turned into *god spell*, good tidings, when Roman missionaries came to England, for that was the literal translation. These were two separate words, *gōd* and *spell;* but through carelessness or ignorance early writers began to join the words into *god-spel* or *godspel*, the literal meaning of which was thereby altered to "God story." In speech and eventually in writing, this became *gospel*, though the true meaning of the missionaries is still to be found in such titles as "The *Gospel* (Good Tidings) according to Saint Matthew."

gossamer

The story of St. Martin is briefly told under CHAPEL, originally the sanctuary in which his *capella* or cloak was preserved. He became the patron saint of France, but was also honored elsewhere in Christendom. In Germany his festal day, November 11, was especially celebrated with eating, drinking, and merrymaking, probably, in part, because it replaced the old pagan festival of *vinalia*, noting the time when wines had reached their prime, and in part because it occurred in November when, through long custom, fat roast goose was the favorite dish, goose being then in season. In fact, the period was so given up to the consumption of roast goose that the month itself, in Germany, was called *Gänsemonat*, goose month. This Teutonic association of the goose with St. Martin was carried into England, to the extent that "St. Martin's summer" was also called "goose summer" in olden times. At such a period of unseasonably warm weather, which in America is called "Indian summer," finely textured cobwebs may be found on the grass or floating in the calm air. Such a delicate web, which we call *gossamer*, is now generally believed to have taken its name from the period—"goose summer"—in which its occurrence was most marked. From "*goose-summer* webs," the term was eventually corrupted to *gossamer*.

348

gossip

Sponsors for infants in the rite of baptism were, at one time, held to contract a spiritual kinship with the infant in whose name they took the vows. We still observe that kinship by the terms we use for sponsors—"godparents," parents in God; "godfather," "godmother." Such godparents thus were held to be spiritually related to the other members of the family. Hence, in a family containing several children, there would be a number of men and women who, though not related to each other by blood, could claim kinship through their ties with this family. Such folks were said to be *godsib* in olden times, that is, "related in God," for *sib* means "related." That gave them the privilege of talking with each other about the family to which they were mutually akin, and about its various members—probably also about such of their own number as might be absent. Undoubtedly they exercised the privilege—to such an extent, in fact, that *godsib* became a term for anyone who entertained others with rumors, idle talk, and tattletales. And, just as *gōd spell* became corrupted to "gospel" through assimilation of the letter "d," so *godsib* became corrupted to *gossip*.

graham

Sylvester Graham was born in Connecticut in 1794 and, after studying at Amherst College, entered the ministry in 1826. Within a few years he became an ardent advocate of temperance and of vegetarianism. He held that the two were related, for it was his belief that one who followed a diet composed wholly of vegetables would have no desire for alcohol. Along with his dietary principles he favored the use of unbolted wheat flour in the making of bread, and had this flour especially prepared for him. Others tried the product upon his recommendation and created a demand for it. His name thus became inseparably associated with the flour and any of its products. One may buy *graham* crackers or *graham* bread in any grocery in the country.

Greenland

We know little about the character of Eric the Red except what can be judged from episodes in his life related in the sagas of Iceland.

He must have been hot-tempered. His father and he fled from Norway to Iceland after killing a man. But in Iceland Eric was so continually in trouble with his neighbors and involved in other killings that he was finally obliged to flee from that country as well for a term of years. He had heard of a country lying further west and determined to sail for it. After he found it he explored the coast until he discovered a place that was habitable, spending three years in the search. He must have been a humorist also, because when he returned to Iceland and sought to persuade others to help colonize the new country, in 983, he called it *Greenland*. He gave it this name, he said, because "people would be more willing to go there if it had an attractive name." He did, in fact, start a colony and helped in the foundation of others. These grew until, according to estimates, there were four or five thousand people living in them at the height of the prosperity of the country in the twelfth or thirteenth century.

gregarious (aggregate, segregate, congregate, egregious)

Among any primitive people the care of one's livestock is, next to oneself, the most important duty. Such people therefore become very familiar with the ways of their livestock and, naturally, compare the actions of their fellowmen with the actions and habits of dumb creatures. So it was among the Romans, and so did they pass down to us words with meanings for which we must search among farm animals in explanation.

The Latin word for herd, whether sheep, goats, or cattle, was *grex* (the root of which is *greg-*). Hence, when a band of men joined together into a military company, the people saw that this band, when grouped together, looked like a herd of sheep; so they called the military company *grex* also. The way the men flocked together, they said, was *gregarius*, the way of a herd. This has become *gregarious* in English, and we still use it to describe a person who is not happy unless with a number of other persons.

The same root has given us the verb *aggregate* (from Latin *aggrego*, to add to a herd), which means to collect into a total; and the verb *congregate* (from Latin *congrego*, to assemble into a flock or herd), which we use to mean to assemble into a body; and the verb *segregate* (from Latin *segrego*, to set apart from the flock or herd), which has come to us with little change in meaning.

From the same root we have also the word *egregious*. The Latin word, *egregius*, with the literal meaning, "surpassing the rest of the flock," was always used in a favorable sense. This was also the sense in which it was first employed in English, but it then became ironical and is now usually employed in a bad sense; an *egregious* blunder is one that tops all other blunders.

grenade (garnet, grenadier, pomegranate)

Granum is the Latin word for grain or seed, and is the source of a number of the words we now use. Not only *grain* and *grange* and *granary*, but also *garnet*, *grenade*, and *pomegranate*. The latter words came from the Latin adjective, *granatus*, "having many seeds." Anyone who has eaten a pomegranate will readily see why the Romans called it *granatum*, for it is certainly filled with seeds. They also called it *Punica granatum* and *malum Punicum* (Punic apple), believing it to have originated in Carthage. (Our present name, *pomegranate*, from *pomum*, fruit, apple—hence, fruit of many seeds—was of later formation.)

The pulp of this fruit has a deep, transparent, reddish color, very similar in appearance to that of the gem, garnet. Either because of the color or because of the general resemblance between the seeds of the fruit and the crystals of the gem, the precious stone was called *granaticus* by the Romans. This became *grenat* in Old French and, when taken to England, *gernat*, *gernet*, and, ultimately, *garnet*.

After the invention of gunpowder, experimentation began with various explosive missiles. One of these used by the English army in the late sixteenth century was a small bomb, shot from a gun or thrown by hand into a cluster of the enemy. This missile was facetiously called a *granate* or *granade*, perhaps because it was about the size of a pomegranate and was filled with "seeds" or grains of powder. The name became fixed as *grenade*. Later, a company in each regiment or battalion was specially trained in the handling and hurling of grenades and, quite properly, each member of such a company became a *grenadier*.

grog

In 1738, the British House of Commons was stirred by a story related by one Robert Jenkins. Jenkins, a master mariner, said that he

351

had been peacefully trading in the West Indies when his vessel had been boarded by a Spanish guard, his hold had been rifled, and as a crowning indignity one of his ears had been lopped off. So many incidents of Spanish aggression had occurred that the government decided that it should be suppressed. Thus occurred what is sometimes called, "The War of Jenkins' Ear." As the first step, Vice Admiral Edward Vernon—whose name was later given by Lawrence Washington, who served under him, to his estate in Virginia, Mount Vernon—was sent to the West Indies. In 1739 Vernon captured the small and poorly defended garrison at Porto Bello, in what is now Panama and, though his subsequent encounters with the Spaniards were failures, he was given a great ovation in London upon his return in 1743. Vernon was not popular with his crew, however. They called him "Old Grog," in allusion, it is said, to the grogram cloak that he habitually wore. He was a stern disciplinarian, as were most naval officers of the period, and, historians say, he was arrogant and self-conceited. His popularity was not improved among those under his command by an order issued by him in August, 1740. Previously, according to long custom, all sailors received a daily ration of undiluted rum or brandy. Summarily, Vernon ordered that after that date the rum should always be diluted with equal parts of water before it was served. The incensed sailors contemptuously called this piffling watered beverage, *grog*, taking the name from the nickname they had bestowed upon the admiral.

guillotine

Joseph Ignace Guillotin did not invent the machine that bears his name, nor did he die by it, although both statements are sometimes made. He was a physician, born in 1738, and was practicing in Paris at the outbreak of the French Revolution. He then became a member of the National Assembly. In 1789, three years before the beginning of the Reign of Terror, the Assembly was considering the matter of capital punishment. Dr. Guillotin, who had probably seen one or another of the beheading machines used in other countries, proposed that all executions in France should be on some similar machine, which he described. His ideas gradually took hold, and the method that he had suggested was adopted in 1791, after Dr. Guillotin had retired from the Assembly. The machine that was built was actually designed by Dr. Antoine Louis and built by a German named Schmidt. The first execution by it was that of a highwayman, in April, 1792. At that time it was known as a *Louisette*, after the name of its designer, but the public, remembering the man who had first proposed the machine, insisted upon calling it a *guillotine*. Dr. Guillotin died in 1814, fifteen years after Napoleon had suppressed the Revolution.

guinea

In 1663, the Royal Mint of England made a special gold coinage of twenty-shilling pieces "in the name and for the use of the Company of Royal Adventurers of England trading with Africa." These coins, and others of the same value afterward coined for general use, were called *guineas*, because the trade of the "Royal Adventurers of England" was actually along the coast of Guinea. At this period in English history the standard of value was not gold, but silver, and the silver coinage was in bad state owing to the activities of "clippers," who mutilated coins by paring the edges. The value of the gold guinea therefore increased to more than twenty-shillings' worth of silver coin, or more than its face value. Accordingly, in 1717, its value was fixed at 21 shillings. After the establishment of the gold standard in 1816 no more guineas were coined.

guy

In early November, 1605, a plot, long under preparation, was about ready to be put into execution. It was to blow up King James I of England and the entire House of Parliament when the king was to address the opening session of that body on November 5. The gunpowder, covered with faggots to fire it, was in readiness in the cellar of the building, and the man selected for resolution and bravery was stationed in the cellar ready to light the fire. He was provided with a slow match which, it was hoped, would allow him to set the fire and make his own escape before the explosion. The plot—later called the "gunpowder plot"—would undoubtedly have succeeded had not one of the conspirators recalled that a dear friend would be among those killed. So he wrote that friend an unsigned note, urging that he absent himself from that first session and giving an inkling of what was about to happen. The friend immediately took steps to start an investigation, with the result that late in the evening of November 4, the plot was discovered and the man charged with setting off the gunpowder was arrested. That man was Guy Fawkes. He was later tried, with some of his fellow conspirators, and all were hanged. "Guy Fawkes' Day," as November 5 has since been known in England, is celebrated by carrying grotesque effigies of Fawkes clad in ragged garments through the streets. From these effigies, any person faintly resembling them in dress or appearance became referred to as a *guy*.

gymnast, gymnasium

Among the Greeks a sound body was considered to be equally as important as a sound mind. Thus physical training was as much a part of the general education of boys and young men as was mental training. Buildings were set aside for the purpose and officials were especially selected for their fitness in supervising all athletic activities. But that their charges might receive the best instruction for the proper development of their bodies, as well as have the greatest freedom of movement when exercising, all the young athletes were naked while undergoing this training. "Naked," in Greek, is *gymnos*; "to train naked" is *gymnazo*. Thus, in its literal sense, a *gymnast* is one who is naked while exercising, and a *gymnasium*, from the Greek *gymnasion*, is the place where such exercises are held. The terms lost those literal senses, however, before being adopted into our language.

halcyon

Greek legend relates that Halcyone, whose name sometimes occurs as Alcyone, threw herself into the sea when she found the drowned body of her husband. She was one of the demigods, a daughter of Æolus, but had married a mortal. The couple were blissfully happy and their wedded life had been compared with that of Zeus and Hera. Hence, after their tragic death the gods changed both husband and wife into birds, thereafter known as *halcyons* by the Greeks. These are the birds that we call kingfishers. The ancients believed that these birds built their nests upon the sea and that the sea was charmed by them into calmness while they brooded upon and hatched their eggs. The times chosen for building the nests and hatching the eggs were supposed to be the seven days preceding and the seven days following the winter solstice. This period became known, therefore, as "*halcyon* days," an expression now referring to any period of peace and tranquil serenity.

halibut

In Old English the common name for any of the flatfish—skate, turbot, plaice, flounder, or whatever—was "butt." The most highly regarded of all, however, the one that was reserved for eating upon holy days, was the largest of the flatfishes, so large that fish weighing three and four hundred pounds are not uncommon, running up to seven or eight feet in length. This they named the *haly butt*, for *haly* was the old-time spelling of *holy*. The consumption of the *halibut* is no longer limited to feast days of the Church, despite our designation of the fish as "the holy flounder."

halloween

The thirty-first of October was the last day of the year, according to old-time Celtic reckoning. Ghosts walked until the midnight of that evening, and all witches held their annual festivals, riding to them on their broomsticks in the company of their black cats. Many of our present customs and sports in observance of the day trace back to the time when it figured as the Celtic New Year's Eve. But with the introduction of Christianity, New Year's no longer was observed on November 1 and belief in witches was discouraged. However, as with other pagan observances in old England, the Church transformed the occasion of celebration into one of sacred character. Instead of celebrating "all witches," as in the past, the occasion was transformed into one for celebrating "all saints." Thus, because *hallow* was the term used in England for "saint," or "holy man," until the fifteenth century, the celebration became *All Hallows' E'en*, literally, "All Saints' Evening." The contraction to *hallowe'en* followed as a matter of course.

handicap

Gamblers of the fourteenth century had a sport which they called "Newe Faire." Three players were required, one of whom served as umpire. All three put some forfeit money into a cap held by the

355

umpire. Then one of the other two offered some article that he had in exchange for something held by the other. It was then the umpire's duty to appraise the two articles and state how much should be offered to boot for the better article. The two other parties then reached into their own caps or pockets, in which there were loose coins, and drew out their hands. If both drew out money, the exchange was effected, and the umpire took the forfeit money for himself. If neither drew out money, the umpire again took the forfeit money, though the exchange was not made. But if only one drew out money, he was entitled to the forfeit money, even though again the exchange was not made. The game later became known as "hand in the cap" or "hand i' cap," whence *handicap*. The game was later modified and transferred to horse racing, probably in the seventeenth century.

hangnail

Here is an instance of a word being formed first, through mispronunciation, and a meaning then devised which would account for the word. Anciently the English word on which this was based was *angnægl*, which then meant "a painful corn or wart on the foot." It was literally, "a painful nail," because at that time *nægl* or "nail" meant not only the ordinary metal nail with rounded head, but anything that resembled it, such as a corn or any other hard, rounded growth upon the skin, as well as a fingernail or toenail. But the spelling gradually became *agnail*, and its meaning was enlarged to include a whitlow, or painful swelling about a fingernail or toenail. In British dialects, however, the older pronunciation still lingered, "angnail." Then, like many another English word, an "h" was added and a new word was born, *hangnail*. This required explanation; so *hangnail* became a term for the small strip of skin that occasionally breaks away or "hangs" from the epidermis covering the root of a fingernail. *Agnail* was then reserved for the older meaning for a while, but then it embraced the new meaning also, although *hangnail* is the more usual term.

harvest

The Old English word from which this was derived, *haerfest*, had the same source and original meaning as the present German word *herbst.* Its meaning, that is, was the season in which crops were ripe. It was the name of the season, the third quarter of the year, the season now known by the later name, "autumn." That original English sense has now almost passed out of use, and now *harvest* usually covers, not only such crops as ripen in autumn, but also those that may be gathered at other seasons, such as fruit and vegetables that may ripen in the spring.

hazard

This term originated as the name of a gambling game which, at least in its later form, somewhat resembled the American game of craps. The name itself is from the Arabic *al zahr,* the die. This became *hasard* in Old French, and the English borrowed both game and name shortly after the Norman Conquest, it would seem. The game became very popular and was played for extremely high stakes in some of the most famous gaming halls of London. The chance of great loss associated with *hazard* thus caused its name to become synonymous with peril, risk or danger.

hearse (rehearse)

After he had plowed, the old British agriculturalist raked his land with a "harrow." The Norman invaders of England in the eleventh century called this implement a *herse,* a term which had come down in French from the Latin *hirpex,* rake. This was a heavy, triangular affair of wood, with spikes projecting from the lower side. When this instrument was overturned, it closely resembled the framework for holding lighted tapers used in certain religious ceremonies, with the tapers taking the place of the spikes. Consequently, the ecclesiastical device came also to be called, in France, a *herse,* a term that was later brought into England. The framework, though still called a *herse,* began to assume greater elaboration. More candles were added than the original thirteen used in Holy Week, and the structure was placed over the bier during the funeral services of distinguished persons. Such structures went out of use in England in the sixteenth century or shortly thereafter, but the name, which folks were beginning to spell *hearse,* was now applied to the vehicle that transported the coffin at a funeral.

Our word *rehearse* more nearly retains the sense of the Old

French *herse*, a harrow or rake. The act of repeating something that had been previously said was likened to the act of raking a field previously raked; hence, "to *herse* again," or *rehearse*.

hectic

The Greek physician Galen, who lived in the second century B.C., discovered that the cheeks of certain of his patients were continuously flushed as if by fever. He described that condition as *hektikos*, which meant "habitual." Later the condition was recognized as a disease, and the physicians of the fifteenth century, using Galen's term, called it *hectic fever*, though we now call it consumption from the fact that the disease gradually consumes the tissues of the body. (The broader term, tuberculosis, is more accurate.) Doctors use the term *hectic fever* nowadays, however, for a type of fever which, though usually associated with tubercular disease, also accompanies some forms of septic poisoning. An accompanying symptom of this fever is a nervous excitability in the patient, the appearance of which is heightened by flushed cheeks and abnormally bright eyes. In consequence of this air of excitability, the ancient medical term, in recent years, has acquired a meaning that would astonish poor old Galen. He would find it difficult to believe that a term meaning "habitual" could have had its meaning so distorted as to be used in place of "wild, reckless, excitable."

hector

In Homer's *Iliad*, the chief hero and champion among the Trojans was Hector, the son of their king, Priam. He was described as being an ideal son, husband, and father, loyal to his friends, and a man of the highest courage and bravery. He was feared by the Greeks above all others among their Trojan enemies. But when Hector, taking advantage of Achilles' withdrawal from the Greek camp, drove the Greeks back to their ships, which he almost succeeded in burning, and killed Patroclus, the friend of Achilles, the wrath of Achilles knew no bounds. He returned to the conflict, armed himself, routed the Trojans with fearful slaughter, and sought out Hector in single combat. Hector's courage failed him and, hotly pursued, he fled three times round the walls of Troy. But Achilles caught and slew him, and to complete his revenge dragged the body

358

of Hector from his chariot once more about Troy. The story became a familiar one to the Romans, who looked upon themselves as descendants of the Trojans, and in due course *Hector* took his place in the minds of English schoolboys as a paragon of valiant courage. In the seventeenth century, however, the name came to be applied less worthily to a set of bullies who frequented the streets of London. These *Hectors* are described as swashbucklers or swaggering ruffians who, traveling together, insulted wayfarers, broke windows, and, in general, behaved with the utmost insolence. It is from their actions rather than from the Trojan hero that we owe our present use of *hector*.

helpmeet

Although this is another word for "helpmate," it was formed through a misunderstanding. If one turns to Genesis 2:18, one reads, "And the Lord God said, It is not good that the man should be alone; I will make him an help meet for him." The meaning of *meet* in this passage is "suitable, fitting, proper." Hence the biblical intent was "a suitable helper for him." But the two words were consistently read as one, many years ago, and resulted in an unneeded word.

hermetic

The ibis-headed god Thoth, in Egyptian theology, was the god of wisdom, science, magic, religion, and art. The Greeks identified him with Hermes, and he was therefore often known as Hermes Trismegistus (Hermes Thrice-greatest). He was the reputed author of the 42 books that constituted the sum of Egyptian learning, books which were therefore known as the "*Hermetic* Books." Because they dealt largely with the occult sciences—magic and alchemy—*hermetic* acquired the significance of "secret, hidden," and, in one usage, "airtight."

hobby, hobbyhorse (morris dance)

Among the amusements in England of the fifteenth and sixteenth centuries, especially in the May-day celebrations, was one known as the morris dance. Its original name had been "Moorish dance," and some of the features, probably borrowed from the Moors of

Spain, were long retained. Thus, although the group of characters costumed for the dance always included a Robin Hood, a Maid Marian, and a Friar Tuck, others, fantastically arrayed, were intended to represent Moorish dancers, some garbed as clowns, some with bells dangling from long hoods, and some with bells on their ankles. Usually also one of the Moors was represented as riding on an Arabian steed. The "steed" was a figure made of wicker, covered with hide or cloth to resemble a small horse, but actually fastened about the waist of the person supposed to be riding it. Its "rider" pranced about to show off the spirited nature of the steed. This make-believe steed became known as a *hobbyhorse*, probably because *hobby* had long been the term for a small horse, just as "dobbin" indicated a farm horse. From the use of the hobbyhorse in the morris dance, someone got the notion to convert it into a plaything for a child. Thus, since the sixteenth century some such imitation, variously constructed, has been a childhood favorite. Sometimes a child gets such enjoyment from his toy horse as to abandon all other playthings, and whenever awake, will furiously ride his *hobbyhorse* or *hobby*, which early became the shortened name. This favorite pastime was likened, even in the seventeenth century, to the devotion some men exhibit to a subject or an occupation that was at first taken up for amusement. Thus *hobbyhorse*, later shortened to *hobby*, came to denote any pursuit which is of great interest to an individual, though followed only for pleasure.

hobo

Little more may be done with this word than to repeat the several theories that have been advanced to explain its origin. Any one of them might be true, but there is no proof as yet.

Slightly less than four centuries ago the French musical instrument, the *hautbois*, came into English use. Its name was literal, from *haut*, high, and *bois*, wood, for the instrument was made of wood and its tone was high. (Later, from Italian spelling, it came to be called, as at present, the "oboe.") The English, as they frequently did with French words, corrupted the spelling into *hautboy* or, often, into *hoboy*, giving it the latter pronunciation in either case. There are, therefore, many people who think that our term *hobo*, which is of American origin, came somehow into use through itinerant players of the *hoboy*. Jack London, who had a lot of first-hand experience among tramps and vagabonds and who wrote much about them at the turn of the century, gave this theory the stamp of his approval.

Another explanation credited the source to the lumber camp. French-Canadians, they say, when felling a tree, instead of giving the shout, "Timber-r-r!" would cry, "*Haut bois!*"— literally, "high timber." From this cry, which might be rendered "*ho bo*" in English, it has been suggested, the itinerant Canadian lumberjack came to be called a *hobo* by his English-speaking fellow workers.

Another theory, advanced by a recent authority, is that the word may be derived from an ironic use of the word "beau," together with the word of greeting, "Ho." Thus, "*Ho, beau!*"—just as, in present popular speech, we hear, "Hi, fella!"

It is my own thought that the source might go back three hundred years. There is record of a slang term in use about that time applied to a man engaged in the most menial of all labor—one whose work it was to go about London at night and clean latrines. Such a man was called a *hoboy*. Possibly the name was of gypsy origin, as was much of the underworld slang of that period and some that is still alive. It is therefore possible that *hoboy* persisted among gypsies, changing to *hobo* through the years, and applied either to a tramp or to a migratory worker.

hollyhock

Because the name is actually a corruption of *holy hock*, in which *hock* is an old name for mallow, an ingenious scholar of the past century (Hensleigh Wedgwood) made the statement that it "was doubtless so called from being brought from the Holy Land, where it is indigenous." This statement has been repeated by others, but it lacks foundation. It is much more probable that the affix *holy* came about through an early association of this plant with some holy man. The plant has also been known as "St. Cuthbert's cole," thus warranting the inference that its later name was derived in some way either from that holy man, or from the island, Holy Island, off the northeast English coast which he made his retreat in the seventh century.

horde

Genghis Khan, great leader of the Mongols, died in 1227. He left his vast empire to his sons and grandsons, dividing it among them. To one of the grandsons, Batu Khan, fell the leadership in 1235 of the Mongol invasion of Europe. Without meeting much resistance his armies crossed the Volga River, where one part turned northward toward Moscow and Poland and the other southward into Bulgaria and Hungary. City after city fell before the invaders, was burned and leveled and the inhabitants massacred. An historian, writing of the taking of the Bulgarian capital in 1237, says: "The inhabitants, without regard to age or sex, were slaughtered with the savage cruelty of Mongol revenge; some were impaled, some shot at with arrows for sport, others were flayed or had nails or splinters driven under their nails. Priests were roasted alive, and nuns and maidens ravished in the churches before their relatives." Similar fates were met by those of other cities until, in 1241, satisfied with his conquests, Batu retired to the Volga to set up his capital. Wherever he had camped he had set up his own gorgeous tent, richly covered with embroidered silk and gilded leather. His followers called it the *sira ordu*, or "silken camp." The Poles put an initial *h* on the second element, making it *horda*. From this the name "Golden Horde" was applied to the tent or camp of Batu. This name in turn came to include the entire army of the Mongols. Thus, because of the great terror inspired throughout eastern Europe by this vast Mongolian army, *horde* became a general term for any Tatar tribe, and ultimately was applied to any large group of persons, savage in appearance or actions, or to a pack of fierce animals, likened to the savage and brutal Mongols.

hoyden (hoiden)

The most interesting story of the probable source of *hoyden* is the one that connects it with *heathen*. Formerly the word did not apply chiefly to a boisterous or ill-mannered girl, as it does now, but denoted an awkward lout, an ignorant boor of either sex. Persons of such uncouthness, in olden days, were commonly those who dwelt far from the villages and towns and had little contact with persons of refinement. Such were the folks who dwelt far from neighbors upon the heath; they were the last to hear of new things, and, thus, being the last to learn of Christianity, gave rise to our word *heathen*. (See PAGAN.) Now the former Dutch word for *heathen* was *heyden*. Thanks to the nearness of Holland to the English coast, it is likely that the Dutch word, slightly altered in pronunciation, passed over to England. There, although still applied to the rustic clown, male or female, who haled from the lonely heath, it became *hoyden* or *hoiden*.

humor (choleric, melancholic, phlegmatic, sanguine)

Ancient physicians—Hippocrates, Galen, and others, and even the physicians of the Middle Ages—believed that the body was governed by four primary fluids, or *humors*, as they said, using the Latin term for "fluid." These four fluids were the blood, the yellow bile, the black bile, and the phlegm. The nature of the four fluids was supposed to be hot and sweet, hot and dry, cold and dry, and cold and clammy, respectively, the Latin terms for these (some taken from the original Greek) being *sanguineus, cholericus, melancholicus* (from Greek *melas*, black and *chole*, bile), and *phlegmaticus*. The meanings of our words *sanguine, choleric, melancholic*, and *phlegmatic* accordingly trace back to those original senses. Thus, in olden days, a person said to be of *sanguine humor* was of ruddy countenance and had a courageous, hopeful, and amorous temperament; one of *choleric humor* was bilious and jaundiced, and of irascible temperament; one of *melancholic humor* was characterized by sullenness, sudden outbursts of anger, and fits of depression; and one of *phlegmatic humor* had a marked inclination toward indolence and apathy.

By a natural extension, *humor* thus became a synonym for temperament or disposition. In the sixteenth century the meaning of *humor* was further extended to unreasoned preference, capricious fancy, and at this period it became one of the most overused words in the language. Shakespeare poked great fun at this tendency to run the word into the ground when, in *Merry Wives of Windsor* and in *Henry V*, he has the character, Corporal Nym, interlard almost every sentence with "*humor*." From this use developed the further extension that we understand chiefly by *humor* today, the

363

quality of being amusing or of perceiving that which is droll or whimsical.

hyacinth

Once there was a Spartan youth, son of a king, who possessed such extraordinary beauty as to win the affection of the god Apollo. The name of this remarkably beautiful lad, according to Greek legend, was *Hyacinthus*. But he was also beloved by the West Wind, Zephyrus. And one day, when Apollo and Hyacinthus were playing quoits, Zephyrus in jealousy caused the heavy disk thrown by Apollo to stray from its course and strike Hyacinthus upon the head, with such force as to kill the lad. Great was the remorse of Apollo, but he could not restore the life of his friend. In grief, therefore, he caused a flower to spring from the blood-soaked earth, thereafter called *hyacinth* in memory of the handsome lad. It is believed, however, that the Greeks included several flowers under this name, especially the iris, the gladiolus, and larkspur. It is otherwise difficult to account for the variety of colors ascribed to the flower by various Greek writers.

hydraulic

About the year 200 B.C., an inventive genius, named Ctesibius, lived in Alexandria. He is supposed to have conducted experiments upon air pressures, but his chief invention was a water organ or clypsydra. It is not certain how this organ was operated, but it is likely that water served to regulate the air pressure within the tubes of the organ. The instrument was named *hydraulis*, or *hydraulikon organon*, from Greek *hydor*, water, and *aulus*, pipe. Later instruments operated by water power or through the utilization of water became thus classed as *hydraulic* by virtue of this first invention.

hymeneal

There is an ancient Greek legend of a youth of such delicate beauty that he might have been taken for a maid. His name was *Hymen* or *Hymenæus*. The girl with whom he fell in love spurned him, but in the disguise of a girl he followed her into the country to a festival. On the way he and all the real maidens in the gathering were carried off by a group of brigands to a foreign shore. But upon landing, the weary robbers fell asleep, whereupon Hymen, throwing off his disguise, seized a weapon and slew all of them. Then, leaving the maidens, he returned to Athens. There he got the promise of the citizens that his own beloved should be given to him in marriage if he were to bring the maidens back to Athens. The request was granted gladly, and he soon restored the girls safely to their homes. From that time onward Hymen was praised in the bridal or marriage songs of the nation, thenceforward described as *hymeneal* songs in honor of his exploit.

iconoclast

The word means "a breaker of images," from Greek *eikon*, image, and *klastes*, breaker. It originated in a great struggle within the Christian Church, beginning in the eighth century and lasting for one hundred and sixteen years. For a number of generations there had been discussion over the appearance of works of art—pictures and statuary—within church edifices. Some held that they should be excluded, because they were reminiscent of idol worshiping; others held that they merely increased the spirit of reverence in the mind of the beholder. Among the latter was Pope Gregory the Great, who had said, "What those who can read learn by means of writing, that do the uneducated learn by looking at a picture." But the emperor of the Eastern Roman Empire, Leo III, took the opposite view. He was a zealot, of such decided views that he had forcibly baptized all Jews and Mohammedans within his empire. In 726, therefore, he decreed the abolishment of all paintings and images from the churches of the realm. The ensuing struggle, carried on even more aggressively in the reign of Constantine V, who succeeded his father in 740, assumed the proportions of a crusade. In 765, images and relics were destroyed on a great scale throughout the Eastern Empire. The tide changed with succeeding monarchs, but the issue was not finally settled until 842 when the patriarch of the Eastern Church, assisted by clergy and court, solemnly restored the images in the church of St. Sophia in Constantinople. The term *iconoclast* is now usually employed figuratively, and is applied to one who destroys cherished illusions or declares the falsity of long-credited beliefs or superstitions.

idiot

When we say that *idiot* is derived from the Greek *idiotes*, it must be understood that the Greek term had no such meaning as we give to *idiot*—not remotely. Its stem—*idio*—is the same as that which gives us "idiom," one's own personal or individual language, and "idiosyncrasy," one's own personal or individual characteristics. So the Greek word originally meant nothing worse than a private person, an individual, a person occupied in his own affairs as distinct from one holding public office. It acquired an extended meaning from this—one who lacked professional knowledge, whether of politics or other subjects; a layman—but in Athens there was no reflection upon one's mentality when referred to as an idiot.

When the Romans borrowed the term, giving it the form *idiota*, they gave it a slight stigma, however. In their view, a man who failed to take enough interest in the affairs of state as not to hold any public office, must be one who lacked the brains for the job. They held that contact with public life was indispensable for the full development of the intellect, and thought that none but a weak-minded person would refuse an opportunity for such service. So, to the Romans, an *idiot* was a person who, through lack of mental ability, was unfit for public office; hence, an ignoramus. Early English writers were somewhat confused as to the meaning when *idiot* was introduced into our language. Some used it in its Greek sense and some gave it the Latin meaning, but others went further than the Romans had gone and gave it just the meaning that we give it today—a person so deficient in mental powers as to be incapable of reasoning or of self-protection.

ignoramus

Literally, this is a Latin plural, meaning "we do not know." The term was introduced into the courts of law in England in the sixteenth century. When used by a grand jury it was written across the back of an indictment presented to the jury if the members thought the evidence was too weak to warrant prosecution. The term might have been confined to legal usage if, in 1615, it had not been for a play written by George Ruggle. He gave the play the title, *Ignoramus*, after the name of his chief character, a lawyer. It was a satire written "to expose the ignorance and arrogance of the common lawyers" of his day. The wits of the period took up the name of the character and thus spread the application of the term to ignorant persons, regardless of profession.

imp

In the days of King Alfred—that is, in Old English—an *imp* was a sapling or offshoot of a tree. This meaning gave rise to a figurative use, the scion of some noble house or, especially, a male child. Then, in due course, probably because most male children are mischievous, *imp* became synonymous with a young demon. Thus since the sixteenth century an *imp* may be a mischievous child, a young demon, or one of the petty fiends of hell. The original meaning has passed completely out of use.

impede (expedite)

Those who were slaves in ancient Rome were usually left unfettered, their hands and feet unbound for the better performance of work. Severe and sometimes barbarous punishments for those who attempted to run away, involving scourging, mutilation, or even death, were generally sufficient to make it unnecessary for the owners to chain them. It was customary, nevertheless, to employ fetters or chains when the nature of the work was such as to make escape fairly possible. Thus the slave whose duty it was to attend the door of a Roman house was chained to his post, and those who worked in the fields or woods were compelled to have their feet in fetters. The Latin word that meant "to put fetters on the feet" was *impedio*, from *in*, on or upon, and *pes*, *pedis*, foot. Thus, because one who has his feet shackled together is hampered in his movements, *impede* came to signify "to check the motion of; to hinder." But a Roman slave who had been placed in chains, either at the time when he was taken into captivity, or in punishment, or at his work, found that he could move actively, apparently even with greater ease than ever before, when his fetters were removed. Therefore our word *expedite*, from the Latin verb *expedio*, literally "to release the feet, as from fetters or a trap," came to mean more broadly, "to hasten the progress of; to accomplish more rapidly."

inaugurate (augur)

When the twins, Romulus and Remus, decided to found a city along the banks of the Tiber, according to ancient Roman legend, they disagreed upon the hill on which the city should be laid out. Romulus preferred the hill later called the Palatine, Remus the Aventine. They agreed, however, to leave the decision to the gods, and each passed the night upon the hill of his choice to learn their will. Remus, it was said, saw six vultures as the day began. This was thought to be highly propitious. But just as Romulus received the information, twelve vultures flew over his head. The omens, therefore, appeared to favor him. Remus was unwilling to yield the decision, however, and in the struggle that followed, he was killed. Accordingly Romulus was the sole founder of Rome.

In those days and for many centuries thereafter, no important matter was undertaken by the Roman people until it was learned whether the gods favored the enterprise. This was often determined by watching the birds, for it was believed that they were the messengers of the gods. Certain men, wise and highly devout, were given the responsibility handed down to them by Romulus, and were thought to be able to read those messages. These were interpreted from various signs—the kinds of birds, their numbers, their appearance in certain quarters of the sky, the direction of flight, their songs in flight, and so on. A man able to make such interpretations was called an *augur*, a word partly derived from the Latin *avis*, bird, and *garrio*, to talk, or chatter. The interpretation that he made was called *augurium*, from which our word *augury* was derived. The verb *inauguro* meant, at first, "to consult the birds before undertaking an enterprise"; later it carried the meaning, "to consecrate (an official) by the ceremony of consulting the birds." Our word *inaugurate* comes from this verb; hence, when we use it we imply an accompaniment of special ceremony. (See also AUSPICE.)

incubus (succubus)

In the Middle Ages any woman who gave birth to a witch or sorceress was supposed to have been visited, in her sleep, by a male demon or evil spirit. The name given to this spirit was *incubus*, from the Latin *in*, upon, and *cumbo*, to lie. It was also supposed to be the

368

cause of nightmare. The feminine counterpart of this demon, bringing nightmares to men, was called a *succubus*, the first element from *sub*, under. The existence of such demons was recognized in those days by both church and state, but has long been known to be entirely imaginary, except perhaps by highly superstitious persons. It is because of the feeling of great pressure or heavy weight upon one who is ridden by the supposed *incubus* that the term is now used figuratively for an oppressive load.

indent, indenture

To prevent the likelihood of alteration in deeds and other contracts between two parties, a certain practice was introduced into the England of the late Middle Ages. The contract was written out in duplicate upon a sheet of parchment or paper, with a blank strip between, and then the two documents were cut or torn apart in such manner as to leave a notched or wavy edge. At any time thereafter the genuineness of either document could be proved by matching the cut edge with that of the other. One was said to *indent* the contract, from Latin *in*, in, and *dens*, tooth. The contract itself was, and still is, called an *indenture*, from that original means of identification. It was this form of contract that existed between an apprentice or a servant and his master; the apprentice or servant "took up his indenture" when he had completed his service. Thus, many of the early settlers of the American colonies, lacking the money for their transportation, voluntarily became "*indentured* servants" in order to get to America. Usually after seven years such a servant was table to "take up his indenture" from the master who had bought it from the ship owner. (Compare KIDNAP.)

indolence

When Cicero coined the term *indolentia*, from *in*, not, and *doleo*, suffer, he meant it to be the equivalent of the Greek word *apatheia*, lack of sensibility to pain or passion, indifference. And this was the sense in which *indolence* was first employed by the philosophers of the seventeenth century. But because indifference is usually accompanied by a disinclination to invite trouble or to disturb oneself, *indolence* passed out of use in its initial sense and came to be synonymous with laziness.

infantry

The literal meaning of *infant*, from the Latin word *infans*, is "one unable to speak." Though that literal sense actually applies only to the first year or two of babyhood, both under Roman law and those of our own country a person is referred to as an infant until he has reached such age as he may legally enter into certain forms of contract. That is, extending the literal sense, a person remains an infant until fully able to speak for himself in all matters. In Italy, some centuries ago, much as we today apply the word "maid" to any female servant, there began the practice of calling a personal attendant of a knight, or a foot soldier, or other similar retainer an *infante*. Possibly, though it is not known, the practice came about through the youthfulness of the early retainers. A collection of retainers or foot soldiers became *infanteria*, a term that, passing through French, produced our *infantry*.

ink (encaustic)

Artists of ancient Greece, employed in the painting of murals, sometimes used a process that is no longer fully known. As described by Pliny, the colors were mixed with wax and resin. The mixture was heated in a brazier and was then applied as needed to the wall or other surface with a spatula, which was also heated. Somehow the chemicals that were used and the application of heat caused the colors to sink into the surface of the stucco of the wall. The Greeks said that they were "burnt in," using the word *enkauston*, from *en*, in, and *kaio*, burn. Such *encaustic* paintings, as we now call them, from the Greek term, had remarkable life; one upon an open portico, *Stoa Poikile*, in Athens, was said to have retained its colors for more than nine hundred years. Others, protected by the ashes of Pompeii, are still visible after nineteen centuries. Because of that longevity the process was thought to be worthy of use by Roman and the later Greek emperors for their signatures upon royal documents. A purple dye was used for this purpose, and the dye in turn was called *encaustum* in Latin, *enkauston* in Greek. Through the Roman colonies in France, the Latin word became corrupted to *enche* or *enque* in Old French, giving rise to *enke* or *inke* in medieval English, and our present *ink*.

insolent

In its truest sense, *insolent* would mean "unusual, not according to custom." Its source was the Latin *in*, not, and *soleo*, to be accustomed. But even the Latin writers realized that one who violates custom is usually willing to offend and is, indeed, likely to be offensive. So they used *insolens* also to mean haughty and arrogant. It is thus from the latter use that our meaning of *insolent* is derived.

insult

The literal sense of the Latin *insulto*, from which *insult* is derived, was to leap at or spring upon a person or thing. A wild beast might spring upon its prey, ready to tear it apart; a soldier leap at his foe, prepared to take his life. But the ancients realized that they could tear a person apart, in a figurative sense, by a torrent of abusive words, or kill him with scorn and abuse, and thus *insulto* acquired such a figurative meaning, giving rise to the sense in which we use *insult*.

interloper

About the middle of the sixteenth century a group of British merchants formed a company for the carrying on of trade with Russia. The company, under the name of the Russia Company, was highly successful through the next thirty or forty years. Perhaps too successful, because toward the end of the century some Spanish traders operating from Holland, and other bands of Englishmen, began to break in upon the monopoly of the English company through bribes to Russian officials. The interference was settled within a few years, perhaps with adequate counterbribery, but the incident brought a new word into our language. The trespassing traders were called *interlopers*; the source of the new coinage being the English *lope*, to run, and the Latin *inter*, between.

intoxicate (toxic)

In ancient times some armies equipped their archers with poisoned arrows. Greek and Roman writers referred to it as a practice of barbarians, and, in order to describe it, the Greeks had to distort the meanings of some of their own words. Thus the Greek word

371

for an archer's bow was *toxon*, and accordingly that which pertained to a bow was said to be *toxikos*. From that connection the poison with which an arrow was smeared, thus making the arrow ready for the bow, was called *toxikon*. The term was taken into Latin in the form *toxicum*, and in the Middle Ages this came to be a general term for poison of any kind, no longer connected in any way with the archer's bow. Hence, *toxic* now means "poisonous," and our verb *intoxicate* originally meant "to poison."

intransigent

After Queen Isabella of Spain was deposed in 1868 the country was without a ruler for some years. Members of the royal families of Europe declined to accept the vacant throne, but at last, in 1870, Prince Amadeo of Savoy accepted the offer. Three years later, however, he was glad to resign. Thereupon one branch of the party favoring a republic, made up, it was said, of the dregs of society, though calling themselves "volunteers of liberty," attempted to establish a form of communism within Spain. They were termed *los intransigentes* (from the Latin *in*, not, and *transigo*, to come to an agreement), because they refused every attempt to reconcile their political views with those of others. The press of England and America took up the name as *intransigent*. The party was put down in 1874 under force of a temporary dictator who ruled the country until Isabella's son, Alfonso XII, revived the monarchy in 1875.

investigate (vestige)

Hunters through all the ages have known that their game could be found by following its footprints or the traces that it left of its passage. Roman hunters used the word *vestigium* for footprint or trace—whence our word *vestige*, trace—and thus *investigo* meant to trace or track out, as a dog scents game. Our word *investigate* is not quite so literal in meaning, but the term does imply the thoroughness of search similar to that of a dog on a cold trail.

italic

Aldus Manutius was the Latin name of the noted Italian printer, Teobaldo Mannucci, who was born in 1450. He received an excellent education before establishing himself as a printer in Venice in 1490. There he surrounded himself with other scholars and set out to make Venice the center of literature, especially in the printing of Greek, Latin, and Italian classics. Aside from the merit of the works printed by the Aldine press, as his establishment had been named, was the excellence of the type that was used. Aldus experimented with various faces, cut either by himself or under his direction. The one type to which we are still indebted to his genius is that which he named *italic*, thus honoring his native land. Until this invention all type was erect, called "Roman" from the erect letters of the ancients. The first book to utilize the new type was an edition of Vergil, printed in 1501.

jade

A few hundred years ago it was believed that one need merely wear this stone to be free of colic or of disorders of the kidney. It was sometimes called "colic stone" or "nephrite" (from Greek *nephros*, kidney) for that reason. The Spaniards, who found much of the stone in Peru and Mexico in the sixteenth century, called it *piedra de ijada*, literally "stone of the colic," and the French, taking only the last part of the Spanish name, rendered it first as *l'ejade*, and later as *le jade*. From the French it was a natural step to the English name *jade*. (The homonym, *jade*, a term for an old horse or spiteful woman, is from Old Norse *jalda*, a mare.)

janizary

Turkey became an independent monarchy in the year 1300. Its army, however, was too feeble and poorly organized for the wars of aggression that the political leaders wished to wage against neighboring states. Hence, in 1330, it was suggested that a band of Christian youths be taken from their parents each year, and that this band be specially trained in the arts of warfare and maintained in the strictest discipline. The first levy was a thousand of these lads. They were enrolled as *yeni chéri*, or "new army," this term being ultimately corrupted into English *janizary* or *janissary*. The army was increased until it numbered 20,000 of these professionally trained soldiers, and this remained the normal strength until the sixteenth century. The janizaries received little pay, but had so many privileges that service in the organization ultimately became sought. Acceptance of Mohammedanism was not required, but the faith was regularly taught to them. After the sixteenth century the number became larger and larger until in 1825 there were 135,000 janizaries in the army. In that year this band thought it had the power to defy the government, against which it had been staging acts of violence for many years. But the sultan was in readiness with troops of Moslems that had been drilled. The struggle was short and bloody. In its course every janizary was massacred.

January

This month derived its name from the ancient Italian god, Janus— *Januarius* being the Latin name, which signified "the month pertaining to Janus." How old the worship of the god may have been cannot be determined, but it undoubtedly dated back prior to the foundation of Rome. Janus was the tutelary deity of doors and gateways—*janua* is Latin for "door." He was therefore always represented as having two faces, so that, it was explained, he might guard both entrance and exit. Upon one of the hills of Rome— named Janiculum, in his honor—the gateway of a temple to him was always open in time of war, according to legend, in order that the defending soldiers might not be delayed in seeking refuge, if in danger of defeat, or of marching into the city triumphantly, if victorious. Prior to the reign of Augustus, it was said, the gates had been closed but once in seven hundred years, at the close of the first Punic War, 241 B.C., when Rome was briefly at peace.

It is sometimes thought that January, being the first month of the year, was so named because Janus was also the god of beginnings. That is not so, however. In the oldest of the Roman calendars the year had only ten months, thus accounting for the names of the last four months in our present calendar—September (seventh), October (eighth), November (ninth), December (tenth). Some seven hundred years B.C., the calendar was readjusted and two months were added to the year. The names given to them were *Januarius* and *Februarius*; they were, respectively, the eleventh and twelfth months, and they were so named because the first contained a feast day in honor of Janus, and the second included the Roman festival of purification (*februum*). March continued to be the first month of the year until long after the Christian Era had begun and March 25th, because that date coincided with the vernal equinox (the beginning of spring) in the Julian calendar, was the day upon which the civil year began.

It was not until the adoption of the Gregorian calendar that January was accepted in all countries as the first month of the year and that January 1st was generally observed as New Year's Day. This calendar was prescribed by Pope Gregory XIII in 1582, to correct errors in the Julian calendar, but it was not adopted in England and its colonies until 1752. Hence, in England, the confusion that had existed through many centuries in matters of chronology was finally cleared away, for the popular practice and the practice of historians from the twelfth century or earlier had been to date the year from January 1 (or sometimes from Christmas), though in civil and church practice March 25 had been the beginning of the year.

jeep

It is regrettable that the story of the word *jeep* is not complete. In 1937 the cartoonist, E. C. Segar, began to use an animal in his comic strips about "Popeye," which he called "Eugene, the Jeep." This creature was described as being able to move at will between the third and fourth dimension, being invisible while in the latter, and being able to answer all questions about the future. Because of the popularity of this comic strip, the term *jeep* was somewhat in the public mind at the beginning of World War II. But the Willys-Overland people, although maintaining that the term *Jeep*, designating a type of vehicle prominent in that war, was first applied to the vehicle actually produced by that company, have been entirely unable to trace the reason for the application. In a small book, *Hail to the Jeep*, by A. Wade Wells, from which I am privileged to quote, the first use of the name is credited to Irving (Red) Hausmann, test driver for the Willys-Overland plant in Toledo, Ohio. Hausmann does not claim credit for originating the name. He drove the test model to Baltimore, for Army test and approval, and is quoted as saying:

Shortly after our arrival the Ford Motor Co. also sent their ¼-ton vehicle in for test. Some distinction had to be made as to a name for our vehicle. I took a lot of pride in the vehicle we had developed, and I didn't like people confusing it with the others and calling it a "Bantam," "Bug," "Midget," "Blitz-Buggy," a "Ford G.P.," "Quad," or "Peep," so I picked up the name "Jeep" from the soldiers who were tossing it around among themselves. I started calling our model a Jeep and called it Jeep at every opportunity.

Upon his return to Toledo, it is said, others in the Willys-Overland plant took up his use of the name. But in late 1941 when, as a lexicographer, I was investigating the word *Jeep* for dictionary inclusion, neither Army nor maker was able to satisfy my interest in its source. The best guess was that the name had been formed from the sound of the initials "G.P.," which indicated the "general purpose" for which the vehicle was designed, although proof is lacking that the design was ever so designated.

jeopardy

In the game of chess, as played in England until about the beginning of the sixteenth century, a problem which posed an even chance of winning or losing was known as a *iuparti*. This was from the Old French *iu parti*, meaning "divided chance" or "even game." The term was also introduced into other games in which certain positions offered an even chance of winning or losing, and thus came into general use for any situation in which safety hung in the balance, for any position of peril or possible harm. The initial letter, despite numerous variable spellings of the word through the centuries, seems always to have been consonantal, and so when the letter *j* came into general use in the seventeenth century the form changed from *ieopardy*, as Lord Francis Bacon wrote it, to our present *jeopardy*.

jeroboam (jorum)

Someone with a sense of humor, back near the beginning of the nineteenth century, must have remembered his Bible when he first beheld a huge brandy bottle. He was reminded of the verse which says, "And the man Jeroboam was a mighty man of valor" (I Kings 12:28), and the one, also about Jeroboam, "who did sin, and who made Israel to sin" (I Kings 14:16). This unknown wit thereupon christened this large bottle, *Jeroboam*, a name by which it is still

376

known. It may have been the same man who gave the same name to an unusually capacious bowl or goblet at about the same time. Through confusion with a later biblical king, the latter vessel is also called a *jorum* or *joram*.

jitney

Usually a slang term baffles those who search for its source. By the time it has become popular, the person who invented it and the occasion leading to the invention are forgotten and cannot be located. *Jitney* acquired popularity throughout the United States in 1914 and 1915 as a slang term for a five-cent piece, a nickel. The meaning was then transferred to the passenger vehicle, other than a streetcar, for which the fare was, originally, five cents. A correspondent of the late Dr. F. H. Vizetelly, quoted by him in his *A Desk-Book of Idioms and Idiomatic Phrases*, suggested that *jitney* might be a corruption of *jetnée* in a catch song of the French-speaking Louisiana Negro:

> Mettons *jetnée* dans li trou
> Et parcourons sur la rue—
> Mettons *jetnée*—si non vous
> Vous promenez à pied nu!

Which is freely translated thus:

> Put a *jitney* in the slot
> And over the street you ride;
> Put a *jitney*—for if not
> You'll foot it on your hide.

The explanation is plausible, and *jetnée* itself may be a corruption of the French *jeton*, a token, counter.

joke

Like our words *bus* and *mob*, contracted by humorists of bygone years from the more pompous Latin terms *omnibus* and *mobile vulgus* respectively, *joke* came into our language in the seventeenth century as a contraction by some unknown wit of the Latin *jocus*, a jest. The legend that John Milton originated the contraction cannot be proved, for the word does not appear in any of his writings. He had the wit to have done so, however, as shown by his various facetious poems.

journey, journal

Through the fact that French *jour* means "day," it is not surprising to find that Old French *journée* meant the space of a day, or that which was accomplished in a day, such as work, employment, travel, or the like. It was the sense of day's travel, however, in which the word was carried to England. Thus at first a *journey* was usually understood to be a distance of twenty miles, or what a man could walk in a day, and greater distances were spoken of as *two journeys, ten journeys*, or sometimes as *two days' journey, ten days' journey*. Also from French *jour*, day, it is readily seen that *journal* was originally a record of the day. As first employed in England, however, a *journal* was a record of the ecclesiastical services for each hour of the day. In strict accuracy, in this sense of a written or printed record, the term should still apply to the occurrences of a single day, though many technical publications, perhaps issued not oftener than once a month, contain the word *journal* in their titles.

jug

From the early sixteenth century, in England, a popular nickname for anyone with the name Joan or Joanna was *Jug*. Especially was she called by that name if she were a servant or of unattractive appearance. No one knows why, any more than one can explain why the name "John" became altered to "Jack" as a nickname, or "Margaret" to "Peg," or "Mary" to "Molly" or "Polly." Be that as it may, it was during the same century that potters began to turn an earthenware vessel somewhat similar to, but larger than, a pitcher. Perhaps the squat shape of these early vessels reminded some wag of a popular barmaid named *Jug* who was of similar shape; or perhaps it was just because other drinking vessels were already known as *jack* and *jill*, from the nicknames of John and Gillian. The fact cannot be determined. The full name, Joan, which would be Jeanne in French, suggests the possibility that "Dame Jeanne" (demijohn) might have been a French translation of *jug*.

378

juggernaut

A huge grotesque image of the god Vishnu has been worshiped for the past eight centuries or more at Puri in Orissa, India. The local name of the god is *Jagannath*, a name which sounds to Occidental ears as *Juggernaut*. There are several curious customs connected with the worship of this god. Among them is that each summer he is taken from his temple to his "country house," a distance slightly less than a mile. The god is therefore placed on a large cumbersome wagon about thirty-five feet square and having sixteen wheels, each about seven feet in diameter. The god towers about forty-five feet in the air. Ropes are attached to the wagon, and to those carrying the images of his brother and sister which accompany him. Thousands of willing pilgrims drag the huge conveyances on their way. The path is so sandy and the weight so great that, despite the short distance, the journey requires several days. Early travelers, seeing this annual spectacle, brought back strange tales. Perhaps, seeing some weak or aged pilgrim faint under heat and exhaustion while pulling the ropes, he thought the man had thrown himself under the slow-turning wheels as a deliberate sacrifice. His report of one such victim, which may have been accidental, was magnified by later travelers. Some of these Occidental travelers, then, not knowing that even the accidental shedding of blood in the presence of the god is a pollution, reported that many devotees threw themselves each day beneath the wheels as the car moved slowly toward its destination. Thus, through these exaggerated tales and mistaken interpretation, brought about by ignorance of the real purpose of the journey, the "car of *Juggernaut*" became a literary symbol of relentless self-sacrifice to which one devotes himself blindly, and *juggernaut* was adopted into English speech as a figurative term for any powerful force that relentlessly moves to destroy all in its path.

June

One of the most prominent of the families in ancient Rome was that to which the members of the clan Junius belonged. Their ancestor, Lucius Junius Brutus, drove out the last of the Tarquin kings, 510 B.C., and was elected the first consul of Rome. We owe the name of our sixth month, *June*, to the name of this clan or gens, or, more likely, to the first consul who may have decreed that his name be thus honored.

junket

Originally this was a creel, a basket of woven rush in which to catch or carry fish. The Norman-French word was *jonket* or *jonquette*, from *jonc*, a rush. But even before the Normans invaded England some housewife had discovered that the same basket, before being contaminated with fish, could be used in preparing a kind of cheese. This cheese then became *junket*. Incidentally, when served with a dressing of scalded cream, the dish is known as "curds and cream" in some parts of England. The rush basket also suggested, to our forefathers, the meal that could be carried in it, with the result that *junket* came to denote a sumptuous repast or merry feast. We in the United States have carried that notion still further, and that which originally denoted a rush basket now embraces a picnic or, especially, a pleasurable excursion.

kaleidoscope (stereoscope)

Sir David Brewster, when a young man, had intended to follow his father's career in the ministry, but found within a few years after entering that field that his greatest interest was in science. Hence, at the age of twenty-seven he had become an editor of the *Edinburgh Encyclopedia*, writing upon scientific subjects. The study of optics was most fascinating to him—the reflecting powers of mirrors and the magnifying powers of lenses. But it was purely as a scientific toy that, in 1816, he devised an arrangement of mirrors within a tube, which would show by reflection a shifting pattern, multiplied symmetrically, as the tube was rotated. Because of the beauty of the patterns, when bits of colored glass were reflected, the toy was named *kaleidoscope*, from the Greek *kalos*, beautiful, *eidos*, form, and *skopos*, watcher. A few years later Brewster, with some associates, devised another type of optical instrument, consisting of two lenses, so ground that when mounted upon a rack before two identical pictures, the two pictures would blend into one, creating an effect of three dimensions. The name given to this instrument,

380

which became very popular with advances in the art of photography, was *stereoscope*, from the Greek *stereos*, solid, and *skopos*.

kangaroo

A great controversy arose about the name of this Australian animal, a controversy that now may never be settled. Captain James Cook, the British explorer, and his shipmate, the noted naturalist, Sir Joseph Banks, both trained observers, understood that the Australian natives called this strange animal a *kangaroo* (which each of them subsequently spelled *kangooroo*). They saw the animal near Endeavour River, Queensland, while their ship, "Endeavour," was undergoing repairs on its northward voyage of exploration along the eastern coast of Australia in 1770. Later explorers within the next fifty years were unable to find any tribe along the coast that used this name, and concluded that the natives with whom Cook and Banks had tried to converse were actually saying, "I don't know," in their language. They reported that various other names were used by the different tribes, though none resembled *kangaroo*. Now, however, all the natives have adopted the English name, regardless of the name by which they had previously known the animal.

ketchup (catsup)

Manufacturers will continue to spell it *catchup* and *catsup*, but the spelling here shown is that which best resembles its source, the Chinese term, *ke-tsiap*. The Dutch, who were heavy importers of this Asiatic condiment in the eighteenth century, spelled it *ketjap*, indicating a pronunciation very similar to *ketchup*. The original importation, however, was a sauce composed from the juices of edible fungi, chiefly mushrooms, salted for preservation and spiced.

khaki

The British army borrowed both the material and its name from India, where the army first used it. The Indian name means "dusty," and the original material was a stout cotton drill of the color of dust. For clothing it served a twofold requirement. It was adapted to a warm climate, and its color was an admirable camouflage. It was first word in 1848 by the Guide Corps, a mixed regiment of frontier troops. Military use of today does not confine the material to cotton and permits the color to range from tannish-brown to olive-drab.

khan

Europe first heard this term in the year 1222. A strange band of invaders from the east had pushed across the Volga and the Don, and was threatening Galicia and Bulgaria. (See HORDE.) The Russian princes who opposed this invading force were destroyed with all their armies, and the inhabitants of towns and villages were massacred. This, Europe learned, was the army of the Mongolian emperor who became known to the West as Genghis *Khan*—that is, Genghis the Ruler, or King, or Emperor. The title became much more familiar to Europeans generally, however, in the latter part of the same century when the great Venetian traveler, Marco Polo, returned from his long expedition into China and wrote his memorable account of his travels and of his long stay at the court of the Great Khan, Kublai. This ruler was a grandson of Genghis, and therefore retained the title which his grandfather had been the first to assume.

kidnap

We like to think that all those who flocked to North America from England after the founding of Jamestown and Plymouth came eagerly and of their own accord. That was far from the case. Many of the early colonists, especially those in Maryland and Virginia, flocking into the country which, they were told, offered such great opportunities, were unaccustomed to manual toil and needed servants and agricultural workers. Craftsmen, skilled in trades greatly required by their fellows, needed more apprentices and labor than the villages could supply. To meet this varied demand for unskilled help, British shipowners began to offer free transportation to the new colonies in return for an agreement to work without wages for seven years. Many thousands accepted these offers. These were known as "indentured servants." (See INDENT.) After the seven years of service their master was required to supply them with certain agricultural implements, some clothing, and some seed, and the colony usually gave them fifty acres of land. There was nothing debasing in such indentured service and many of these settlers were

382

well educated and later became honored citizens. But the demand for labor exceeded this willing supply. Some shipowners then began to obtain passengers by unscrupulous measures. At first they induced young homeless waifs from the slums of London to board their vessels, with great promises for a future in America. But later their gangs ranged the streets of English towns and cities and, using a term of the times, "spirited" the youngsters away. In the reign of Charles II (1660-85) when this crime was at its height, the term *kidnaping* was coined to describe it. This was composed of the slang *kid*, a child, and *nap*, to steal. The full number of these unwilling colonists probably exceeded one hundred thousand. One *kidnaper* confessed in 1671 that in the previous twelve years he had himself annually transported an average of five hundred youngsters. Another admitted that he had kidnaped eight hundred and forty in a single year. In theory all of such kidnaped children had become voluntary indentured servants, but in 1682 the London Council forbade any person under fourteen (the age of consent at that time) to be bound into service unless with the knowledge and consent of his parents.

knave

The history of this word is similar to the slow change we are witnessing in the meaning of the word "boy," now often applied to servants and grown men. Originally, back in Old English times, a *knave* was a boy in a literal sense—a male child. It had the same meaning as the German *knabe*, to which it was closely related. Then people began to apply it to a boy who was employed as a servant, one who might be apprentice to a cook or to a groom, or who served as a potboy in a tavern or in any such form of work as a boy could perform. In those olden days, however, the life of any menial was hard; that of a boy was doubly so. His sleeping place might be the stable or a drafty garret, without mattress or blanket; his clothing any castoff garment that he could tie upon him; his food any scraps that might be tossed to him from his master's table. It is not surprising, therefore, that these boys, still called *knaves* as they became older, developed a high degree of rascality. They had to become crafty in order to survive. Thus the meaning of the term gradually came to apply only to such a person, boy or man, who practiced dishonesty.

knickerbockers

Some time in the latter part of the seventeenth century, probably about 1682, a gentle Dutch farmer from Holland settled with his family near the site that was to become Albany, New York. There he prospered greatly and left sizable properties to his seven children. His name was Harmen Jansen Knickerbocker. The eldest of his children, Johannes Harmensen Knickerbocker, acquired additional property north of Troy, along the river Schaghticoke, and this estate and the great manor upon it descended in due course to his grandson, Harmen, born in 1779. This man, great-grandson of the original Harmen, entertained lavishly, for he had inherited great wealth. He became known as "the prince of Schaghticoke." But it is likely that he would have had little more than a local notoriety had it not been for the satirical writer, Washington Irving. Intending at first merely to burlesque a pretentious guidebook to New York written by Dr. Samuel Mitchell, Irving got carried away with his theme. He could not resist playing up the characteristics of the phlegmatic Dutch burghers, and wound up with a richly humorous book, *A History of New York from the Beginning of the World to the End of the Dutch Dynasty.* The two-volume *History*, published in 1809, was ascribed by Irving to "Diedrich Knickerbocker," a thinly disguised alias for the "prince of Schaghticoke," who, of course, had actually had nothing to do with the matter. The most popular edition of *Knickerbocker's History*, as the book came to be called, was illustrated with pictures showing Dutchmen clad in seventeenth-century costume, wearing knee breeches buckled just below the knee. These costumes were copied, especially for boys' wear, during the 1850's. The trousers, because of the distinctive cut and the buckle or button at the waist and knee, became immediately known as *knickerbockers*, a term now often shortened to *knickers*.

lace

Properly, as it was of old, a *lace* is a noose, a cord or the like with which to snare game or a victim. It was so used in the time of

Chaucer. The word comes to us from the Latin *laqueus*, noose, which in popular spelling was *lacius*. The latter term became *las* in Old French, and came in that form into the English language. The development into our present meaning came progressively. Because garments were formerly held together by loops, the cord that was used for the purpose was termed a *lace*, a meaning that survives with us in the word *shoelace*. Then when it became fashionable to decorate garments with fanciful nooses or loops of gold or silver wire or cord, these were in turn described as gold *lace* or silver *lace*. The further substitution of threads for the earlier cords into an intricate network was the final stage, an elaborate multiplication of nooses.

laconic

Spartan youths were all trained with the utmost rigor. But in addition to the activity, vigilance, endurance, and cunning which were practiced in all the land, those dwelling within the province of Laconia were also taught modesty of deportment and conciseness of speech. The Laconians thus became so noteworthy for their short and pithy way of speaking and writing that such a style became characterized as *laconic*, from the land where it was the native practice.

lady

It is a far cry from the woman of Old England from whom this title descended to the one who often calls herself a lady today. That remote woman was proud to be known as the breadmaker, *hlæfdige*, a word subjected to many changes, becoming *levedi* in the thirteenth century, *levdi* and *ladi* in the fourteenth, and *ladie* and *lady* in the sixteenth. By present standards of usage *lady* is a term of courtesy applied to any woman, but no longer necessarily implies an ability to make bread.

larva

Many years ago it was the popular belief that the caterpillar concealed within itself the complete butterfly in perfect form. It was then thought, that is, that the caterpillar served as a mask for the butterfly. For that reason it was called *larva*, Latin for "mask."

leech

From early English antiquity a physician has been called a leech, and from equally early times physicians have used the aquatic blood-sucking worm, known as *leech*, for bloodletting under certain conditions. It is impossible to tell which was first to receive the name. Etymologists believe, however, that present identity of spelling is accidental and that, originally, the words were different, although of similar form. They think also that through the use by the early physician of the worm for bloodletting, the name of the latter became altered to that of the physician through association.

legend

Toward the end of the thirteenth century the Archbishop of Genoa, Jacobus de Voragine (James of Viraggio), brought forth a book upon which he had long been engaged. It was, largely, a collection of the stories told about a number of the Christian saints within the several churches with which they were chiefly connected. The actual title was *Legenda Sanctorum*, literally, "things to be read of the saints," but the title by which it was and is generally known is *Legenda Aurea* or "Golden Legends." The book became exceedingly popular and was translated into many languages. The data were chiefly historical, although through the years the original facts had become somewhat magnified and distorted. Subsequent stories of the lives of saints, following the model set by this book, became more and more fanciful and imaginative. The consequence was that all these stories were viewed with skepticism. Hence the word *legend*, originally "something to be read," came to denote a story that, though apparently historical, was actually traditional and lacking in authenticity.

lethal, lethargy

There was a river in the lower world or the region of Hades, according to Greek mythology. Its name was *Lethe*, which signifies forgetfulness or oblivion; its water was believed to possess such properties that one who drank of it totally forgot all of the past. Shades of the dead, entering into the pleasures of Elysium, drank of the water and forgot all their mortal sorrow and suffering. Hence,

386

from the likeness between this state of obliviousness and that of a deep slumber, ancient Greek physicians gave the name *lethargia* to a certain disease characterized by extreme drowsiness. From this has come our *lethargy*. The Romans took the meaning of the myth more implicitly and, reasoning that total and lasting forgetfulness came only with death, coined the adjective *lethalis*, whence our *lethal*, to signify deadly or fatal.

libel, liber, (library)

In legal use, a *libel* must be published. Otherwise the damaging statement may be slander, but not *libel*, although the latter word is often popularly used when "slander" should be employed. The legal interpretation emphasized the source of the word, for *libel*, from the Latin *libellus*, originally meant a "little book." Thus a *libel*, in its early English use as well as the Latin source, denoted written matter, especially matter that was shorter than that constituting a book. The basis of the Latin *libellus* was *liber*, which was actually the name for the inner bark of a tree. This inner bark was found to furnish an excellent surface upon which to write; hence, by transference *liber* came to denote "book." This Latin term is still used in reference to legal books and is the source of *library*, a collection of books.

libertine

In ancient Rome, *libertinus* denoted a slave who had been liberated, a freedman, and this was the meaning of *libertine* in early English use. But, just as a schoolboy released from irksome confinement of school is likely to break all bonds in his exuberance, so it was found that those released from slavery were likely to show no restraint in the observance of moral laws. Thus it came to be expected that a *libertine* would lead a life of unbridled license, and it was in this manner that the term came to refer to anyone, whether ex-slave or not, who lived such a life.

livery

Livery formerly corresponded exactly with our word "rations," except that it denoted the rations allotted to servants and retainers. The term, from Old French *livrée*, delivered, was taken to England by the Norman conquerors, and was meant to include food, clothing, or other provisions "delivered" to the servants. (In time it came to include allowances for the feed of horses; hence, *livery stable*.) Eventually, as the feeding of one's servants became a matter of course, *livery* was largely restricted to the clothing allotted to one's retainers or servants. Such clothing, in olden days, was marked by badge, color, or cut in some manner as to render it distinctive, so that anyone in the service of a prominent person could readily be identified when appearing in public. Well-informed persons with social pretenses prided themselves upon the number of such *liveries* they could place. Today the term is used for the uniform style of costume worn by the pageboys in a hotel, waitresses in a restaurant, elevator operators in a building, or the like.

lord

Just as "lady" was gradually formed through alterations in the pronunciation of the Old English original *hlæfdige*, so was *lord* formed from *hlaford* or *hlafweard*. The forms in which it appeared were also numerous, including the twelfth century *laford, leverd, lauerd*, and the fourteenth century *louerd, lhord*, and *lorde*. And just as the original meaning of "lady" was "breadmaker," so was the original meaning of *lord* "keeper (*weard*) of the loaf (*hlaf*)." The significance of the title was that he who was the keeper of the bread was master of the household. His servant, in those ancient days, was known as *hlaf-æta*, literally, "loaf-eater."

lottery, lotto

From remote antiquity disputes have been settled, ownership agreed upon, priority established, leadership determined, or the like, by casting or drawing lots. The emperors of Rome introduced a novelty into the old practice when, during the Saturnalia, or feasts to Saturn in mid-December, they awarded elaborate gifts to the person fortunate enough to hold or draw a winning lot. Similar customs were observed by European rulers during later centuries. Eventually the thought occurred to someone that people should pay for the chance to hold or draw a winning lot. So far as is known the earliest of these latter events was held at the city of Bruges in 1446. It may not have been until the following century, however, that a drawing held in Florence in 1530 was the first to be called by the Italian term, *lotteria*. The first *lottery* in England was a state affair for the purpose of raising money, in 1569, for the repair of harbors. The Virginia Company held another in 1612 for the benefit of the distracted colonists of Jamestown. Thereafter lotteries were frequent in England and throughout Europe. In Italy a numerical lottery was invented in 1620 by the Genoese, and was called *lotto di Genova*. It had been devised originally for the election of counselors, with wagers upon the outcome. But later the names of candidates were replaced by the numbers from one to ninety, with wagers, according to the ability of the gambler, upon the five numbers that were drawn. There were four different kinds of chances in this *lotto*, the lowest returned fourteen times the stake and the highest forty-eight hundred times the amount of the stake. This form of Italian lottery was transformed into a game, called *lotto*, often played for stakes, which became popular in France and England in the eighteenth century.

lounge

The story of this word is not certain; all that we can say is "perhaps." The name of the centurion who pierced the side of Jesus with a spear as He hung upon the cross, was said to be *Longinus*, according to the apocryphal gospel of Nicodemus (7:8). This Longinus, by later legend, became converted and, in German and English calendars, was honored as a saint, his day being March 15. In medieval times his name was usually written *Longis*, and was popularly supposed to be derived from the Latin *longus*, long. Hence we may infer that in casting the characters for mystery plays dealing with the Crucifixion, the part of the centurion was given to a tall man. That this character was also depicted as slender and exceedingly indolent is highly probable, because Cotgrave, in 1611, thus defines *longis*: "A slimme, slow backe, dreaming luske, drowsie gangrill (a slim, indolent, dreaming sluggard, a drowsy toad); a tall and dull slangam (lout), that hath no making to his height, nor wit to his making, one that being sent on an errand is long in returning." If a person of that description were cast in the role of *Longinus* (or *Longis*), it is likely that, in the coarse humor of the period, he would be shown leaning indolently upon his spear, or sprawled upon the coat of Jesus. Thus, *lounge* is supposed to have been suggested by the attitude of *Longis*. The story cannot be proved.

lumber

Originally, the Lombards were a Teutonic people whose earlier name, *Langobardi*, long beards, was traditionally derived from the appearance, before the god Wotan, of their women with their hair combed over their faces. Startled, as he awoke from sleep, Wotan asked, "Who are these longbeards (*longobardi*)?" They were a warlike tribe, and in the year A.D. 568, with their families and possessions, moved southward into Italy where they occupied the plains at the head of the Adriatic, a region that became known as Lombardy. In the fourteenth century, enterprising traders and merchants from Milan and other parts of Lombardy (see also MILLINERY), found it profitable to move westward into England. There, through ingenuity, they became bankers, money-changers, moneylenders, or pawnbrokers. (The three golden balls, still marking a pawnbroker's establishment, are from the coat of arms of the Medici family, long the chief family of Lombardy.) They were so successful in these various enterprises, which then did not greatly differ, that the establishments themselves were popularly called "Lombards." From the various spellings employed in the early days, however, the name was usually pronounced *lumbard* or *lumber*. The latter became not only the usual pronunciation but also the usual designation of a Lombard pawnbroking establishment, sometimes also called *lumber-house*. Thence, because articles placed in pawn often consist of furniture or other cumbersome items that take up space, *lumber* assumed the meaning, "disused household furnishings." Thus *lumber-house* and *lumber-room* became places for storing such odds and ends. The reason for the American use of *lumber* instead of "timber" is difficult to determine. Possibly it derives from a practice of early settlers of storing rough timbers in the lumber-room for drying or until ready for use, although the *Dictionary of American English* says it "undoubtedly arose from the fact that ship-masts, sawed timber, barrel staves, etc., as important but bulky commodities, once blocked or *lumbered* up roads, streets and harbors of various towns."

lyceum

Among the epithets borne by Apollo was Lycean, an epithet of such antiquity that it has never been determined whether it was derived from the root *luce*, light, or *lyco*, wolf. In the one case it would refer to the god as the giver of light; the other as the wolf-slayer. Either explanation could be readily supported. Be that as it may, the Athenians dedicated an enclosure to Apollo, which was known as the *Lyceum*, in its Latin form. It was decorated with buildings and sculpture by the leading artists and was a favorite place of exercise by Athenian youths. But its significance to us lies in the fact that it became also the favorite walk of the most noted Athenian philosophers, especially Aristotle, who taught his followers most readily while strolling through its paths, and it was this practice that caused the term to be adopted for certain of our lecture halls or meetings.

lynch

Dispute has waged during the past century over the identity of the man who achieved the doubtful honor of adding this name to our language. Was it Colonel Charles Lynch, or was it Captain William Lynch? The case for each has been stoutly maintained. Both were Virginians and each was an officer of militia in the Revolutionary War. They lived in adjoining counties, Colonel Charles in Bedford (his brother, John, was the founder of Lynchburg), and Captain William in Pittsylvania, and each was a justice in the court of the county in which he resided. The description of the manner credited to each in meting out justice, and the causes therefore, are almost identical. At that period, the concluding years of the Revolutionary War, Williamsburg was the seat of the only court in Virginia in which certain felonies could be tried. But Williamsburg was some two hundred miles from Bedford County, and the difficult roads led through country held by the British or controlled by Tories. Many of the offenders brought before Colonel Charles Lynch and his three fellow magistrates were Tories; in any event they could not securely be transmitted to Williamsburg for trial. After due and deliberate consideration of the conditions, these four magistrates—Charles Lynch, James Callaway, William Preston, and Robert Adams—set up a court and, observing all of the practices of a regular court, tried such cases as came before them. In no instance save one, a case of proven manslaughter, did a convicted prisoner receive greater punishment than fine or whipping. Their actions were subsequently reviewed by the Virginia legislature which found them "justifiable from the imminence of the danger." It is likely that Charles Lynch was the leader of this group as he was a man of considerable prominence in his community. He had been a member of the House of Burgesses and had served in the Virginia constitutional convention in 1776.

The case for Captain William Lynch of Pittsylvania County rests largely upon the testimony of one man, and the attending circumstances of that testimony combine to make it of doubtful value. In *Harper's Magazine* for May, 1859, there appeared an article by one who signed himself "Cohee." This person related that, following some recent incident, he had had occasion to use the term *lynch law* in some conversation. Among the hearers was an old man, Richard Venables, who had "long been in feeble health, and often sat for hours to all appearance unconscious of what was said or done in his presence." This very old man was aroused by the expression, "lynch law," and said that as a young man he had known the "Mr. Lynch" for whom this form of justice had been named. Thereupon the author persuaded the old man to give him further information, but the remainder of the article is chiefly concerned with the activities of a gang of Tory horse thieves under one, "Captain Perkins," who was a sample of the villainy that "Mr. Lynch" tried to suppress. Nowhere in the article is the first name of "Mr. Lynch" given; in one place Mr. Venables is quoted as saying, "Our flourishing town of Lynchburg received its name in compliment to his worth." All in all, therefore, there are grounds for a suspicion that the account related by the aged Mr. Venables, if worthy of credence at all, might properly have been intended to refer to Colonel Charles Lynch. Perhaps some future historian may find additional proof to support the William Lynch claim.

macabre

This is often written *danse Macabre* and is sometimes Anglicized into "Dance of Death," in allusion to the common representations of the dance in paintings. The origin of *macabre* is disputed. Some think it to be merely a French corruption of the Arabic *makbara*, funeral chamber. Others think that it was the name of the first artist to depict the allegory. The paintings, or occasional sculptures, which first appeared in the fourteenth century, represent Death presiding over or in the midst of a group of dancers of all ages and conditions. For that reason some think the allegory to have been based upon the terrific plague, the Black Death, which swept over Europe in the middle of the fourteenth century, wiping out an estimated two-thirds of the population. The basis for that belief was provided by the fact that, almost literally, during that plague, man, woman, or child, aglow with health in the morning, might be stricken with the disease and be dead before night. But others, now the majority, hold the opinion that *macabre* is an Old French corruption of *Macabé*, the French equivalent of *Maccabee*. In this view the "Dance of Death" is thought to have been taken from an old morality play. Death and his victims, representing all walks of life—old and young, rich and poor, clown and scholar, male and female—have a long series of debates, in which each victim hopes to obtain a reprieve of Death's sentence. Death wins each argument, and the play ends in a weird dance, with Death escorting his victims off the stage. The dance is supposed to have received its name from, and to have been inspired by, the account in the second book of Maccabees, an apocryphal book of the Old Testament. The sixth and seventh chapters describe the torture and death inflicted upon the followers of Judas Maccabeus in his revolt against the laws of Antiochus IV which required all Jews to worship the Greek gods. The "seven brothers of the Maccabees," their mother, and the venerable scribe, Eleazar, were horribly tortured, under the king's orders; in the morality play they were especially prominent participants in the dialog with Death.

macadam

Although born in Scotland, John Loudon McAdam went to New York in 1770, at the age of fourteen, to work with an uncle. He returned to Scoltand when a young man of twenty-seven and bought an estate in Ayrshire. There he became interested in the improvement of roads. The French had been experimenting with the use of small broken stone as a surfacing material for some twenty years, spreading it to a thickness of ten inches upon a sublayer of large stones set on edge. The completed road was excellent, but its construction was costly. After considerable experimentation and study Mr. McAdam concluded that a base of heavy stone was unnecessary, that if drainage were good nothing was required but a layer of small broken stone, six to ten inches in depth. Appointed surveyor-general for the roads of Bristol in 1815 he was able to develop his ideas. The results were so satisfactory as to lead to general adoption, not only in England but for new roads built in France. From these "McAdam roads" came the general term *macadam* for any road surface constructed along the principles of this Scottish engineer.

mackintosh

In the early years of the nineteenth century numerous chemists and inventors were trying to find satisfactory ways to utilize the baffling substance known as "rubber." The substance got that name because the one thing for which a use had been found for the stuff was to "rub" out lead-pencil marks. The most notable success was achieved in 1823. In that year a 57-year-old Scottish chemist, already the inventor of various other chemical processes, found that rubber could be dissolved by the action of naphtha. The resulting solution could then be spread upon cloth, he discovered, and would produce a fabric that was absolutely waterproof. This new invention was immediately seen to be highly practical in the making of waterproof outer garments. Coats so made, taking their name, slightly altered, from that of the inventor, Charles *Macintosh*, gave us our present name for the garment, *mackintosh*. (Compare RUBBER.)

Machiavellian

The late fifteenth and early sixteenth centuries produced a great Florentine student of political affairs. He lived at the time of the Borgias and de Medicis and it is undoubted that his chief work, *Il Principe*, was greatly colored by his knowledge of the practical politics played by those two unscrupulous families. He was Niccolo Machiavelli. Actually Machiavelli was an ardent advocate of a united Italy and a sincere believer in political freedom, but, oddly enough, his book was heartily condemned some years after his death, in 1527, through the erroneous belief that it was intended to instruct tyrants in the art of oppression. Much of what he advocated toward obtaining good government is now in general acceptance, but his defamers alleged that he proposed duplicity in statecraft and that he justified the adoption of any means, however vicious, to obtain a desired end. Thus was formed *Machiavellian* to characterize political craftiness, cunning, or treachery. So heartily was this political writer condemned that perhaps the historian, Thomas Macaulay, was right when he wrote, "Out of his surname they have coined an epithet for a knave—and out of his Christian name (Niccolo) a synonym (Nick) for the devil."

maelstrom

This now means any strong power that seems to influence one irresistibly, especially a power composed of conflicting forces which seem to engulf one. That meaning is figurative. It is derived from the name, *Maelstrom*, which means whirlpool, given to a certain strong tidal current found near the island of Moskenes off the coast of Norway above the Arctic Circle. This current, under certain tides and winds, attains great force because of the vast mass of water that rushes past the island every twelve hours out of and into West Fjord. Differences in the depth of the channel also produce powerful eddies which, with the violent seas, cause the destruction of small vessels that may attempt passage. The entire current was formerly thought to be one vast whirlpool of such irresistible force, according to old fables, as to engulf whales and to suck into its depths any ship that might venture too close to its rim.

magenta (fuchsin)

On the morning of June 4, 1859, in the series of wars for a unified Italy, the French and allied Italian armies, though of inferior strength, fell upon the Austrian army defending Milan in the vineyards and mulberry groves about the small town of Magenta. (See also FIFE.) This battle, which subsequently was known by the name of the town, was momentous and a great victory for the French and their allies. It had a side effect, however, in a direction quite remote from warfare. In the field of chemistry a new aniline dye had recently been discovered. It produced a beautiful purplish-red color, not unlike the color of crushed unripe mulberries, and this new dye, though sometimes called "aniline red," had not yet received a distinctive name. When news of the battle in northern Italy reached the French chemists, the name *magenta* struck them as an excellent label for the dye in celebration of the victory. (The dye is now preferably known as "fuchsin," a name given to it because the color is like that of the blossom of the fuchsia.)

magnet (lodestone)

Homer and Plato knew about the magnet. The ancients, that is to say, had discovered a peculiar stone native to the neighborhood of the town of Magnesia, in Thessaly, which had the power of attracting small pieces of iron. They called it *magnes*, from the name of the town, or more frequently, *lithos Magnetis*, stone of Magnesia, whence our term *magnet*. There is no certainty, however, that the Greeks put the peculiar properties of this stone to any use; in fact, the first European record of the use of the directive properties of the magnet is not found before the end of the twelfth century A.D. This record, made by Alexander Neckam, foster brother of Richard I of England, makes it certain, however, that the mariner's compass, which depends upon the magnet, had long been familiar to English navigators. Perhaps in some mysterious way the knowledge had been brought from China, for the Chinese are thought to have made such use of the stone many centuries earlier. Through the use of the compass this "stone of Magnesia" or *magnes*, as it was also called, came to be known as a *lodestone* because, like the lodestar, it pointed the way (from the Middle English word *lode*, way). Many curious beliefs were attached to the magnet or lodestone. William Gilbert, who, in 1600, was the first to produce a scientific study of magnetism, related some of the "figments and falsehoods" which had once been taught. People were told, he says, that "if a lodestone be anointed with garlic, or if a diamond be near, it does not attract iron"; "if pickled in the salt of a sucking fish, there is power to pick up gold which has fallen into the deepest wells"; there were "mountains of such stones and they draw to them and break ships that are nailed with iron"; the stone could be used as a "love potion" and also had "the power to reconcile husbands to their wives, and to recall brides to their husbands."

mandrake

The plant was formerly known as *mandragora*, which is still its scientific name. Five or six hundred years ago, however, although actually of Greek source, this name was thought to be a combination of *man* and *dragon*. But at that time a dragon was commonly known as *drake*; so *mandragora* became *mandrake* in common speech. Because the plant is poisonous and because the root sometimes bears an uncanny resemblance to a diminutive man, all sorts of fantastic beliefs have been associated with the plant from remote times. Thus in the Bible (Genesis 30) we find that the plant was anciently thought to be able to cure barrenness in women; nevertheless, as Josephus records (*History of the Jewish War*, Book vii, chapter 6), it was exceedingly dangerous to dig up the root. The safest way, he says, was to remove most of the soil about the root, taking care to avoid touching it, then with a cord tied with one end about the stalk of the plant and the other to a dog, the dog could be lured to drag the root from the ground. The dog would die, but thereafter anyone could handle the plant harmlessly. Josephus called the plant *baaras*, but probably referred to the mandrake. He thought that its chief virtue lay in the power that it possessed to cast out demons from sick persons. The plant, even in the times of Shakespeare, was supposed to shriek when drawn out of the ground, and to cause madness, or sometimes death, to any who might taste of it. Sometimes the roots were thought to have a female form. Such were supposed to have especial potency when concocted into a love philter for men.

manure

This was originally a verb, its origin the Old French verb *manouvrer*. Thus, in the fourteenth century, it meant "to work by hand; especially, to work the soil by hand; to cultivate the soil." From that came the noun, which at first meant "that which may be worked by hand; the action of cultivating the soil." Our present meaning was a later extension.

March

This, the name of the third month in our calendar, denoted the first month in the Roman year before the reforms made under Julius Caesar. (See JANUARY.) We commonly think of the Roman god *Mars*, for whom the month was named, as their god of war, equivalent to the Greek god Ares, and think it peculiar to associate his name with the advent of spring. But in remote times Mars, who bore the surname of Silvanus, was worshiped by early Italians of the tribe of Sabines as the god of agriculture; sacrifices were offered to him for the success of crops and herds. The later Romans considered Mars to be the father of their race and the god of war as well as the patron of agriculture. As the latter they worshiped him under the name *Mars Silvanus*, but under the name *Mars Gradivus* as the god of war. The Roman calendar, however, was supposed to have been established by Numa, the second legendary king; and, because Numa was a Sabine, he would have thought of Mars as Silvanus, the god of forests, fields, and crops. It was for that reason that the advent of spring was dedicated to this god.

marmalade

In theory, at least, this delicacy should always be made of or contain quince, for such is implied by the name. Or to be even more exact, if the fruit were available, it should be a "honey-apple," which was anciently obtained through grafting some kind of apple upon the quince stalk. The Greek name for the resulting fruit was *melimelon*, literally "honey-apple." It was known in Latin as *melimelum*. From the latter the Portuguese name for "quince" became *marmelo*, and the preserve made from it they called *marmelado*. English housewives later discovered that other fruits, especially the orange, could be used for making a similar preserve, and this, regardless of the inherent meaning of the word, they proceeded to call by the already familiar term *marmalade*.

marshal

Just as in the Roman Empire of the East the master of the stable, *comes stabuli*, became count of the stable, his title eventually altered to *constable*, so in the West was the history of our word *marshal.* Under the kings of the Franks the *mariscalcus*, to use the Latin form of the old Teutonic title, was no more than a groom of the stable. (Even after the term became altered to *marshal*, this was still one of its meanings in England.) But the term gradually assumed greater importance. Cavalry, in the eighth century, again became of great value in the armies of Europe after a long period of decline, and both the offices of constable and of marshal, the lesser functionary, rose in dignity. In England, the two officers also served as judges in the Court of Chivalry, the marshal serving alone after the office of constable was virtually abolished in 1521. In warfare he was the esquire of the king and commanded the vanguard. From this his functions became extended to embrace full command of the armed forces. The *field marshal*, a title that arose in Germany, was originally a subordinate of the marshal. In warfare he was one of several officials who selected the camping sites and assigned locations to the knights and lords. In France the field marshal is still subordinate to the marshal in rank, though above all others, but in England the title denotes the highest military rank. In the United States, where a *marshal* is an officer of the civil court, the title has descended from one of the duties attending the office in thirteenth-century England. At that time, and thereafter until the eighteenth century, the marshal was an officer of the civil court and had custody of prisoners. In certain ceremonial functions the title is borne by the man in charge of the proceedings, reminiscent of the *marshal* of the Age of Chivalry.

martinet

When the young king of France, Louis XIV, decided to take the reins of government into his own hands in 1660, after the death of Mazarin, the former minister, he appointed as his war minister a youthful military genius, François Michel le Tellier Louvain. The young minister—he was only nineteen at the time—promptly set about to reorganize the army. Previously, in time of war, a nation hired most of its army, a regiment being in the employ of its colonel and a company in the employ of its captain. The units of an army had thus been independent, and discipline was lacking. Louvain decided to change this, to have an army in the employ of the state and constantly available for duty. The Royal Regiment, commanded by Colonel Jean Martinet, exhibited the kind of infantry training which, he thought, would be needed for such an army; so Louvain gave Colonel Martinet the responsibility for devising the system of drill which was to be used. Voltaire, in his *Siècle de Louis XIV*, says of the result, "The exact discipline which was kept up in the army made it appear in a different light from any that had yet been seen." Eventually all the nations of Europe adopted Louvain's scheme of a standing army, and eventually they copied or modified the drills and discipline invented by Martinet. But in England the matter of discipline was at first ridiculed. Few could see any point in an exacting discipline. The result was that *Martinet* became an epithet, in England, applied to any officer who was a stickler for military precision or a stern disciplinarian. In France, the name never acquired that connotation; the French still attach more importance to the small copper boats or pontoons that this officer invented than to the military drill that he established.

match

It isn't a certainty, but it is the belief that *match*, referring to the article with which we make fire, is a descendant from the Greek word *myxa*, which meant mucus from the nostril. This may seem far-fetched, but the course is reasonably straight. Greek *myxa* gave rise to Latin *myxus*, which by metonymy was used as the name for the nozzle of a lamp, the ancient lamp, the flame of which came from a wick projecting from the spout or nozzle. It is highly probable that the Italian *miccia*, a lampwick, came from either the Latin or the Greek word, getting its meaning through association of ideas, the lampwick from the spout suggesting mucus from the nose. Our word *match*, formerly written *macche*, comes from the Italian word by way of several altered French forms. Originally it, too, meant lampwick. Our present meaning developed after guns were invented, from the use of lampwicks for igniting the gunpowder. The wicks, or similar cords, were impregnated with saltpeter and sections were cut to the length desired. Guns fired by such slow-burning *matches* were called "matchlocks." It was a natural step to apply the name "matchwood" to splinters of resinous wood that burned slowly or evenly, and thus to give the name *match* its present application.

matinee (noon)

"Noon" did not always refer to the middle of the day, as we always understand it now to mean. It formerly meant three o'clock. That is, in the Roman system of reckoning, the day began at sunrise, or six o'clock, as the average time of sunrise. The principal meal of the day—dinner—was served at the ninth hour—*nona hora*—from sunrise, which would be at three o'clock in our present reckoning. Certain ecclesiastical services held at the ninth hour in Christian churches were also called *nona hora*, a term corrupted to *nones* in English usage. This latter term, *nones*, became not only the name of the services held at the ninth hour (subsequently observed earlier in the day), but also the name of the dinner hour. The spelling later became altered to "noon." "Noon"—that is, three o'clock—continued to be the dinner hour in England and France until the fourteenth century. "Morning," which is *matin* in French, was thus understood to extend from sunrise until three o'clock. The noon meals in most of the baronial halls of the period were bountiful, and the lords of the manors usually had guests whom they delighted to entertain for an hour or two before dinner. Therefore, strolling troubadours, jongleurs, jugglers, and other entertainers were careful to plan their journeys so as to arrive in ample time to delight the lord and his guests with their tricks and accomplishments before they sat at table, sometimes during the meal as well. Such a show, thus held in the "morning" of that period, was known as a *matinee*. When customs decreed that dinner should be served at six o'clock and that "noon," no longer either the ninth hour or the dinner hour, should denote midday, social usage still permitted "morning" to embrace all the period before dinner. This usage is still reflected in the names "morning coat" and "morning dress." The term *matinee* is a similar holdover, but is usually still applied to a show or entertainment that begins before three o'clock.

maudlin

The search for word origins takes us into some strange places. Here, we look into the miracle plays, as they are called, of Old England, and we must learn something about their production. These crude plays flourished for about three hundred years, from the late thirteenth century to the late sixteenth century at least. They were based on some miracle described in the Bible or that had occurred in the life of some saint. And originally they were produced by one or another of the religious houses of England. By the late thirteenth century, however, the productions were taken over by the various craft guilds of a city, though still with religious sanction.

Each play was actually a series of pageants in regular sequence, and each pageant was staged by one or another of the guilds of the city. For the performance, a pageant somewhat resembled a scene from a play, mounted upon a platform or stage on four wheels. The first pageant (or scene) was played before the doors of the abbey, and was then hauled off to its next position in the city. The second pageant then succeeded the first—and so on, until all the pageants, in due order, had traversed the appointed settings throughout the city. Thus all the people were given an opportunity to see each play. These plays did not vary from year to year and they were shown annually at least. Consequently, the townspeople became very familiar with all the plays and with the characters in them.

Favorite among the subjects were those plays that presented the life of Christ. In all of these one of the chief characters was Mary Magdalen. And when we recall that Mary Magdalen, at that period, was supposed to be the same person as Mary, the sister of Lazarus, and as the sinner who washed the feet of Jesus with her tears, it is evident that she appeared in a number of the pageants. Thanks to the pronunciation of the French name, *Madelaine*, the English "Magdalen" was formerly always pronounced and frequently spelled "Maudlin"—Magdalen College, Oxford, and Magdalene College, Cambridge, are still so pronounced. So when we bear in mind that in almost every pageant in which Mary Magdalen appeared—at the death of her brother, Lazarus; when washing the feet of Jesus, and during the scenes of the Crucifixion and Resurrection—she was in tears, and when we remember that each of these pageants went from one street to another and that, therefore, all day long the actors who played that part had to be shown constantly in a state of tearful affection, it is not at all amazing that, during the course of many years, *maudlin* was taken into the language to signify a state of sentimental and tearful affection.

maundy

The Christian Church early laid stress upon humility. There were various instances in the New Testament to show that this was a basic precept. Perhaps chief of these was the washing of the feet of His disciples by Jesus before the Feast of the Passover. This, because of the example of great condescension, is observed to this day by Christian churches, celebrated the evening before Good Friday. The ceremony itself was formerly solemnly observed in all churches. In England, until the time of James II, it was the custom that the king also receive on that evening as many poor men as he was years old and personally wash their feet, after which money, food, or clothing was distributed among them. The charitable gift became known as *maundy*, for a curious reason, and the day, which of course fell on Thursday, is still known as *Maundy Thursday*. This came about from the fact that, in church, the celebration of the washing of feet was always followed by a discourse which opened with the words of the thirty-fourth verse of the thirteenth chapter of the Gospel according to John: "A new commandment I give unto you." In the French spoken by the clergy of England after the conquest of that country by the Normans, *mandé* was the word used for "commandment." Its pronunciation at that period sounded to the English as *maundy*, and this later became the recognized English spelling. Thus the day before Good Friday became known as *Maundy Thursday*, for it was the day upon which *maundies* were said and the day upon which *maundy money* or *maundy gifts* were distributed.

mausoleum

There was once, in Asia Minor, a small kingdom known as Caria. In the fourth century B.C., its inhabitants were mostly Persians, although those dwelling in the two principal cities, Halicarnassus and Rhodes, were mainly Greeks. The Persian king at that time was not outstanding and had done nothing that would particularly commend him, but he was greatly adored by his wife, Artemisia, who, in the peculiar customs of the time, was also his sister. The king's name was *Mausolus*. When he died in 353 B.C., his wife was inconsolable. She was said to have had his ashes collected and to have added a portion of them to her daily drink until she died of grief two years later. But Artemisia also gathered together the best architects and sculptors before her death and caused them to begin to erect at Halicarnassus a sepulchral monument to her husband. This sepulcher was called *mausoleum* in memory of his name. It was completed after her own death and was long regarded as one of the seven wonders of the world. Ruins of the building were excavated in 1857 which showed that the area of its base had been about 230 by 250 feet and that it was cased with marble. Fragments of numerous statues were found, including a statue of Mausolus, now in the British Museum. The edifice was standing at the time of the Crusades, but was left in ruins by the knights of St. John of Jerusalem, who occupied Halicarnassus in 1402 and used much of the material from the tomb in building their castle.

May

The month of May is believed to have been named in honor of a goddess *Maia*, but it is not certain which goddess was thus honored. Among the Greeks the divinity so named was regarded as the mother of Hermes, whose father was Zeus. It would have been strange, however, for the Romans to have placed the name of a Greek goddess in their calendar. Late Roman writers, who may have been right, explained that *Maia* was the ancient name of Fauna, daughter or sister of Faunus, and that she was therefore the goddess of spring. The Roman months were presumably named by Numa who was traditionally the successor of Romulus and who aided him in the founding of Rome. Numa was a member of the neighboring tribe of the Sabini, and he may have used the old Sabine name, *Maia*, later called *Fauna* by the Romans. Some think that the ancient name was one of the various appellations of the great goddess whom the Romans usually referred to as *Bona Dea*, "the good goddess."

meander

There is a river in the western part of Turkey, Asia Minor, now called Menderes, known in ancient times as Mæander. The nature of the stream has greatly changed in the centuries since it was described by Herodotas, Xenophon, and other writers. In those days, however, although the river was not remarkable for length or

404

width, it was especially notable for the number of twists and turns it pursued through low, flat country on its way to the sea. Perhaps such windings amazed the Greeks because, living in a mountainous country, they were accustomed to streams that flowed rapidly and directly to the sea. But the extremely tortuous *Mæander* was so unusual to them that its name became a term which they applied to anything that deviated frequently in its course or pursued a labyrinthine pattern. The altered spelling *meander* is a variant that has now become generally accepted.

meerschaum

Because of its whiteness and softness, and because it was often cast up along the shores of the sea, the ancients thought this light, soft mineral actually to be the foam of the sea turned into stone. Hence in all languages it was named "sea foam." Little practical use was found for the mineral until German artisans began to carve it into pipe bowls and cigar holders, seeing that it would readily absorb nicotine from the tobacco and acquire a beautiful, warm brown color. Thanks to this German application we have accepted the German name, from *meer*, sea, and *schaum*, foam. The scientific name is "sepiolite," from Greek *sepia*, cuttlefish, and *lithos*, stone, because the mineral resembles the bone obtained from those animals. A more appropriate name for us to use than German *meerschaum* would have been "aphrodite," from Greek *aphros*, foam. This would have honored the goddess Aphrodite, supposed to have been created from sea foam. Unfortunately, however, the name is now applied to another mineral of similar composition.

mentor

When Odysseus left Ithaca to participate in the siege and capture of Troy, according to Homer's *Odyssey*, he entrusted the care of his wife, Penelope, and his infant son, Telemachus, to his great friend, *Mentor*. Homer does not develop the character of the loyal friend to any extent, but twenty years later the young Telemachus, we are told, started out to try to find his father, accompanied, as he thought, by his old tutor. Actually, however, the form of *Mentor* had been assumed by Athena, goddess of wisdom, who gave the young man the benefit of her counsel and advice. The story was taken by the French author, Fénelon, archbishop of Cambrai, as the basis for the political novel, *Télémaque*, which he published in 1699. In this he assigns the role of adviser and counselor of the young hero entirely to the aged tutor, *Mentor*, and makes him second only in importance to the chief character. The book received great acclaim. Voltaire called it "a Greek poem in French prose." From the wisdom and counsel displayed by this fictional companion, *mentor* became one of our common words for any person who serves as a counselor to another.

mercerize

John Mercer was born in Lancashire, England, in 1791. He became a calico printer. When he was fifty-three years old he discovered a chemical process by which cotton fabric became thicker and softer and its affinity for dyes greatly increased. He patented the process in 1855, but no practical use came of the discovery for another forty-five years. The difficulty was that the fabric shrunk from 20 to 25 per cent in the process. This loss, plus the cost, was then considered prohibitive for the results obtained. But in 1895, taking advantage of intermediate discoveries, Messrs. Thomas and Prevost found that the shrinkage could be almost eliminated by treating the material under tension and that, at the same time, a permanent silky luster was imparted to the fabric. Mercer, who had died in 1866, had merely spoken of his process as "sodaizing," with reference to the caustic soda that he used. But in view of the original discovery made by him, the revised process became known as *mercerization*, and the operator is said to *mercerize* the cloth.

mesmerism

In 1766 a young Austrian physician of 32, Friedrich Anton Mesmer, published a thesis in which he argued that, through the diffusion of some invisible vapor, the heavenly bodies affect the nervous systems of all living beings. The argument did not receive the attention which the young physician had hoped, so he went to Vienna to extend his theory. There he identified his invisible force with magnetism, and began to attempt to cure patients by stroking them with magnets. When he learned that a rival practitioner was effecting cures by manipulation alone, however, he discarded his magnets and proclaimed his ability to cure disease by what he called "animal magnetism." This claim he began to demonstrate in Paris in 1778. There he made many converts and made a fortune for himself through gifts from grateful patients. His methods were spectacular. In a dimly lit room Mesmer, garbed in the robes of an astrologer, would receive a group of patients. He formed them into a circle, with joined hands, and then to the accompaniment of soft music he passed from one to another, fixing his eyes upon and touching each one in turn. Many cures were alleged, and there were some reputable physicians who supported his claims. Upon the demand of others, nevertheless, a government commission was appointed to investigate. The commission, which included Benjamin Franklin among its members, rendered an unfavorable report, deriding Mesmer as a charlatan and an imposter. He removed himself then to Switzerland, where he died in 1815. His process, subsequently called *mesmerism*, after its claimant, was later identified as a form of hypnotism.

milliner

From early in the sixteenth century traders from Milan flocked into England with the products of their city and of Lombardy. Steel work was a large part of the manufactures they brought, but their chief articles of commerce were textile fabrics. Milan bonnets, Milan gloves, Milan lace, Milan ribbons were in great demand. The English pronunciation of the name of that foreign city, however, was not that which we use today; they rimed it then with "villain." In fact, the English often spelled the name "Millain." Merchants from Milan were naturally called Milaners, pronounced as if spelled *milliners*, and thus *Milliner* actually became the general spelling. Hence, subsequently, any person dealing with products similar to those that had once come from Milan became known as a *milliner*. Restriction of the term to women's headgear and the like is recent.

miniature

Important writings or manuscripts in the Middle Ages were often decorated or illuminated with "minium." This was the name then used for the color that we now call vermilion, taking the name of the Latin *minium*, red lead. Thus the monks or scribes who illuminated those manuscripts were said to "miniate" the parchment, because the decorative color was chiefly red. Sometimes the decorator was called upon to illuminate a manuscript further with a picture. This required fine workmanship because of the small space allotted to the artist. The picture thus obtained was term a *miniature* because it was done by "miniating." Strictly speaking, it could have been of any size and would still have been a *miniature* if done by that process, but owing to the fact that there was invariably a *minimum* of space for the picture, *miniature* acquired by association a significance of a picture on a small scale.

miscreant

Through its origin, *miscreant* was at first used only in a theological sense. Its source was the Old French prefix, *mes*, badly or wrongly, and *creant*, believing. Hence a *miscreant* in olden times was a heretic, an unbeliever. But through the fact that an unbeliever is one who is likely to violate the code of morals set up by believers, the term *miscreant* lost its original limited sense long ago and was applied instead to any such depraved person as a robber, a thief, or evil-doer of any sort.

mob

It used to be called a rabble. Then some Latin scholar of the seventeenth century recalled that the Latin phrase for a "fickle rabble" was *mobile vulgus*. This was picked up by others who shortened it to the one word, *mobile* (pronounced "mobilly" at that time). But even this was too long, and before the end of the century, much to the disgust of the purists of the period, it had been further shortened to *mob*.

money, monetary (mint)

According to legend, during a war when the Romans were hard pressed for the means to carry on their campaign they appealed to the goddess Juno for aid. They were told that their cause was just and therefore that their resources would be replenished and made ample for their needs. In grateful appreciation for the victory that followed, we are told, the Romans then erected a temple to Juno, giving it the name *Moneta*, "the advisor." It was in this temple, according to historical records, that in the year 269 B.C., silver coins were first produced by the Romans. These coins, from their place of coinage, were henceforth commonly given the name *moneta*, to distinguish them from the earlier copper coins. And it is from this word, through corruptions in sound and spelling in Old French, that we have obtained both our terms *money* and *mint*. From the uncorrupted Latin *moneta* came the Latin *monetarius*, "pertaining to the mint," from which we have derived our word *monetary*.

monster (demonstrate) (prodigy)

Any sign thought to have been given by the old Roman gods, that is, any strange incident or wonderful appearance, was taken as a warning, a belief that the gods were provoked. The sign prophesied the approach of a calamity or misfortune, of public nature or to the nation as a whole, rather than to an individual. Such a foreboding omen or portent was variously called. The term most frequently used was *prodigium*, though this might also denote, rarely, a favorable portent. This, when borrowed into English use in the form *prodigy*, continued at first to mean something of extraordinary nature taken as an omen, but is now applied especially to a person or animal above the ordinary in some skill or talent or mentality. Another term was *monstrum*, which always, from the nature of the strange incident, denoted the approach of some catastrophe. The term was derived from the verb *monstro*, to show, point out, familiar to us in the derivative, *demonstrate*. But through the dread inspired by the term *monstrum*, that word also came to be applied to whatever was the fearful thing, the strange appearance of unusual and frightening form, that had been taken as an omen of evil. Thus, even among the Romans, *monstrum*, which became *monster* in English, was used also for anything abnormally large, or of unusual or frightening appearance.

morphine (somnolent)

The Roman poet Ovid found a need for a new god while writing the poem, *Metamorphoses*, a series of stories written by him a few years before his banishment in A.D. 8. This series is devoted largely to the adventures of the gods in their amatory pursuits of nymphs and the daughters of mortals. While writing, the poet's fancy took him into the realms of dreams, which he felt to be apart from sleep. There was a god of sleep, the Greek Somnus, from whom "somnolent" and related words were derived, but there was no god of dreams. So, taking the Greek word *morphe*, "shape" or "form," he coined the name *Morpheus*, whom he described as being the god of such dreams as include human shapes or forms. Later poets accepted the name as if there had actually been such a god among those of the Greeks or Romans. In more recent times, however, the god of dreams has been confused with the god of sleep, and *Morpheus* is popularly supposed to have been the name of the latter. The result has been that some of our modern terms, such as *morphine*, which actually pertain to sleep, rather than to dreams, have received their names from Ovid's fictional god.

mortgage

Literally this Old French expression, introduced into the law courts of England after the Norman Conquest, meant a "dead pledge," from *mort*, dead, and *gage*, pledge. The reason for calling the legal instrument a "dead pledge" was given by the great English jurist of the seventeenth century, Sir Edward Coke, in these terms:

It seemeth that the cause why it is called mortgage is, for that it is doubtful whether the Feoffor will pay at the day limited such summe [sum] or not, & if he doth not pay, then the Land which is put in pledge vpon [upon] condition for the payment of the money, is taken from him for euer [ever], and so dead to him vpon condition, &c. And if he doth pay the money, then the pledge is dead as to the Tenant, &c.

mountebank

Much of the business of Italian cities of the Middle Ages was conducted upon benches placed in the streets or public squares, especially in Venice. The Italian word for bench, *banca*, accounts for our English word "bank." Usually the business thus conducted in public was of the ordinary serious nature, but there were also itinerant quacks in those days, just as there are today. Such men knew, as others had known from the beginning of time, that the best way to get folks to buy their wares was to attract a crowd, and the best way to attract a crowd was to put on a show. Juggling was the favorite performance, but in order to be seen to better advantage, the

410

juggler would, of course, step up upon a bench if one were nearby, perhaps at the shouted request of someone in his audience. The Italian for such a request is "*Monta in banco* (Climb upon a bench)." Quacks soon realized that it was to their advantage to have a bench nearby upon which to mount, and even to get on it before being asked. Hence they came to be known as *montimbancos*, altered to *mountebank* in England. Sometimes the quack was assisted by a professional clown, or by a rope-dancer, or an acrobat, or a ballad singer, and sometimes in their wanderings the mountebanks would accumulate a considerable show, somewhat on the order of a traveling vaudeville. The majority, however, traveled alone or with one or two assistants. Some English writers in the seventeenth century tried to bring the Italian term *saltimbanco* into the language. This, from the Italian *saltare*, to leap, was applied especially to the charlatans who performed upon their platforms or benches by dancing, leaping, or tumbling.

mugwump

John Eliot, so-called "apostle to the Indians," had many difficulties when, in the middle of the seventeenth century, he was translating the Bible into the Indian language. There were so many words for which the Indians had no equivalent. Hence, when he came to the thirty-sixth chapter of Genesis, he lacked a word for "duke," which occurs forty-three times in that chapter. He decided upon *mukquomp*, an Algonquian term sometimes used to mean a chief or great man. Perhaps other New Englanders picked the word up at that time and used it jokingly of someone who thought himself a great man. We do not know, but we do know that it had already been modified to *mugwump* and was so used in the early nineteenth century, especially of those who thought themselves rather superior. So in 1884, when quite a number of Republicans bolted from the party and supported Cleveland for the presidency, rather than Blaine, the New York *Evening Post* derided them as *mugwumps*, people who thought themselves too good or too superior to vote for Blaine. But the men who were thus sneered at turned the tables and adopted the term themselves, saying that they were independent voters and were therefore proud to call themselves *mugwumps* or "great men."

muscle (mussel)

Our ancestors had a good sense of humor. With one accord, no matter in what part of Europe they lived, they agreed that the Romans had properly described a muscle by the name given to it. All, with variations arising from language of course, adopted that name. It is *muscle* also in French, *muscolo* in Italian, *músculo* in Spanish, and *muskel* in German, Dutch, Danish, and Swedish. The Romans named it "a little mouse"—Latin, *musculus*. Perhaps they were thinking of the biceps of some Casper Milquetoast of ancient Rome, or the muscles of the arms and legs of most of us. It is more likely, however, that the intent was just the opposite. The Romans were great lovers of beauty and great admirers of physical perfection. Some poet among them, seeing the smooth rippling play of muscle in the arms, shoulders, back, or thigh of a well-developed athlete, may have seen how the muscles resembled little mice appearing and disappearing in their play. His whimsy may have taken the popular fancy and may have thus been perpetuated to this day. Similarly, the marine bivalve, though we spell it *mussel*, was also known to the Romans as a "little mouse" or *musculus*, but that was doubtless because of the size and color.

museum

Today it seems rather far-fetched to associate this word with the nine Muses of ancient Greece, for we do not usually think of these beautiful nymphs in connection with collections of paintings, furniture, insects, curios, or the like. Nor do we connect the term with any one of them, nor with the art over which each presided— Clio, history; Calliope, epic poetry; Polyhymnia, sacred music; Euterpe, the music of the flute; Terpsichore, the dance; Erato, love poetry; Melpomene, tragedy; Thalia, comedy; Urania, astronomy.

But shrines to the Muses were common among the cities influenced by Hellenic culture. Such a shrine was known as a *mouseion*, or, in Latin, a *museum*. Hence about 285 B.C., when Ptolemy Soter erected his widely famed temple of learning at Alexandria, which was dedicated to the Muses, it became properly known as the *Museum* at Alexandria. Under that name it flourished for about seven hundred years and was the forerunner of our present universities. When it was destroyed by fire in the fourth century, however, the name became merely a memory and the word dropped almost completely out of use.

Then about three hundred years ago some scholar dug the word out of the dusty past and thought that *museum* would apply to any room or building which provided a "home for the Muses," such as the library or study of a learned man. From this careless use, *museum* came to be thought of as a home for anything pertaining to learning; hence, to collections of scientific curios or of antiquities. The first of these latter *museums* was the Ashmolean Museum, a collection of scientific material presented by Elias Ashmole to Oxford University in 1683. It is thus seen that the Muses do preside over our modern museums.

musket

Early types of artillery developed in the fifteenth and sixteenth centuries were usually named after the venomous serpent or swift bird of prey to which they were likened. Most of these names are now archaic, along with the artillery, and we are no longer familiar with the names of some of the animals. There was the *basilisk*, a fabulous serpent whose name was applied to a large brass cannon; the *culverin*, originally a small handgun, named for a snake called *coulevrine* in French; the *falconet*, a small cannon named from the falcon, a bird of prey; the *saker*, slightly larger than the falconet, named for the saker, a species of falcon, and the *musket*. This was originally a matchlock weapon, fired from a rest which the *musketeer* stuck into the ground before him. The French, who named the weapon, called it *mousquet* from the sparrow hawk, known to them by that name.

mystery

Ancient nations, like fraternal orders of our day, always kept some of their religious rites and ceremonials hidden from the eyes of the multitude or from those not yet initiated. To preserve that secrecy the rites were sometimes observed at night or within some sanctuary. These were the secret parts of the worship, in which the participants had undergone some form of initiation and were sworn never to

413

disclose them to others. The Greek term for such a secret rite, ceremony, or sacrifice was *mysterion*. The *mysterion*, or *mystery*, often consisted in the recital of legends, and sometimes this was accompanied by a dramatic representation in which certain holy things, including symbols and relics, were revealed. In many cases a symbol—very like a fraternal button, pin, or token in our times—was openly displayed, but the meaning of the symbol was known only to those initiated.

nabob (nawab)

The great Tamerlane invaded India in 1398, looting its treasures at will, but making no attempt to add it to his empire. But, in 1526, Baber, the fifth in descent in this illustrious line of eastern rulers, led another expedition southward. From this invasion India came under the rule of a long line of Mogul emperors, lasting until the country came under the British crown in 1858. Among the customs during the Mogul Empire was the delegation of authority in the various subdivisions of India to men who acted as governors or vice-regents. The native title of these men was *nawwab*, or Arabic *na'ib*, meaning "deputy." In theory, the provinces or districts under a *nawwab*, corrupted by Europeans into *nabob*, continued to pay tribute to the central government in Delhi, but some of these districts grew so wealthy and powerful that the tribute did not pass beyond the nabob. Thus they grew fabulously wealthy and, with the further decline of central government, the office became hereditary. Through the wealth of these officials, Europeans acquired the habit of referring to any wealthy man as a *nabob*, especially such a person as had obtained his wealth in India. The custom spread to England, and we now use the term to include any influential person of great wealth.

namby-pamby

In 1725-26 the English poet, Ambrose Philips, chiefly noted for his pastoral poems, published some simple pieces addressed to the infant children of his friends, Lord John Carteret and Daniel Pulteny. These little poems, though charming, would probably have attracted little attention had it not been for Alexander Pope. Some years earlier Pope and Philips had become bitter enemies, and Pope, with his gift for satire, lost no opportunity to hold Philips up to ridicule. On this occasion, however, it was a friend of Pope's, the poet Henry Carey, who opened the attack. Philips' poems were, perhaps, somewhat sentimental. Carey seized upon that feature and wrote a parody upon the verses that he thought most insipid. His title, "*Namby Pamby*," he took from "Amby," the diminutive of Ambrose, with the initial of Philips suggesting the alliterative. Pope carried the name further into the language when he republished his *Dunciad* in 1733. Through the wide popularity of the latter, *namby-pamby* came to denote anything, especially of a literary nature, that was sweetly sentimental.

narcissus, narcotic

After the nymph Echo was permitted to speak only when she heard another voice and could then repeat only what she heard, (See ECHO.) it was her further misfortune to fall in love with the youth, Narcissus. This young man, according to Greek mythology, was exceptionally handsome. There are several stories that account for his ultimate fate. In one it is said that he was wholly untouched by the feeling of love, and when Echo pined away in grief over her unrequited love she prayed that he might fall in love with himself. And this, when Narcissus chanced to see his own beautiful face reflected from a pool, is what he did. As he was unable to approach his own image, he in turn perished with love. One account says that he melted away into the pool in which he saw his reflection. In another tale, in which Echo plays no part, it is said that Narcissus had a twin sister as fair as himself and with identical features. His love for her was so great that, to recall her image to him after her death, he sat and gazed constantly at his own reflection in a pool until he himself died with grief. In all the stories it is further related that after the death of Narcissus his body was changed by the gods into the flower that bears his name. The Greeks considered the *narcissus* to be sacred to Hades and a symbol of death. Varieties of the plant contain properties that induce sleep; hence, *narcotic* and other derivatives are based upon the same term.

necklace

In the sixteenth century, when this word was introduced, its meaning was exactly that indicated by its two components, lace for the neck. But lace was not then what we usually consider it today. (See LACE.) Its meaning had expanded from a string or cord (still preserved in our word "shoelace") and, in the sixteenth century, had come to include ornamental braid of gold or silver. Such gold lace or silver lace, made of wire, was usually sewn on garments, but was sometimes further ornamented with precious stones and worn about the neck and was then called *necklace*.

neighbor

In the early days of our language, in the times that we call Old English, this was a compound word, made up of the two elements, *neah* and *gebur*. These separately have descended to us as "nigh" and "boor," and that is exactly what *neighbor* originally meant—a nearby rustic or peasant, a husbandman dwelling nearby. From the origin it would appear, therefore, that the term applies only to countryfolk and to small villages, but it was early taken into the towns and cities and applied to anyone who lived nearby.

nemesis

Not all of the Greek gods were kindly. There was one, according to mythology, whose duty it was to sit in judgment upon men. Her name was *Nemesis*, thought to have been the daughter of Night. She measured out happiness and unhappiness, and saw to it that any who were too greatly or too frequently blessed by fortune were visited in equal measure by loss or suffering. From this last she became looked upon as the goddess of retribution, as a goddess of vengeance and punishment.

nepenthe

When Paris abducted Helen from the home of her husband, Menelaus, in Sparta and fled with her to Troy, he wanted her to forget her family and former home. To that end, according to Homer, he gave to her an Egyptian drug, believed to allay grief and induce forgetfulness. This drug was known as *nepenthe* or *nepenthes*, and was probably some form of opium. We use its name now to indicate any agency that may bring about freedom from mental pain, but we owe the name to Homer's story.

nepotism

One after the other of the popes of the fifteenth and sixteenth centuries, upon ascending the papal throne, used its great power to further his own ambitions. To do so it was first advantageous to have important offices filled by men who would be tied to him. There were none better for that than members of his own family. Best of all were his own illegitimate sons who, by courtesy, were referred to as "nephews." Perhaps the most notorious of these political popes was the Spaniard, Rodrigo Borgia, who, as Alexander VI, reigned at the turn of the century. His son Giovanni became duke of Gandia; his son Cesare was created an archbishop at 16 and was elected cardinal at 17; his nephew Giovanni also received a cardinal's hat, and other members of the family received similar important honors. Such favors as these to nephews by courtesy and nephews in fact, as well as to other relatives, all accompanied by great gifts of land and wealth from the resources of the Church, brought a new word into the languages of Europe. In English, it was *nepotism*. The original source was the Latin *nepos*, which meant "a descendant," such as a grandson, or, especially, a nephew. The detractors of the popes of that period gave the new term a slightly larger range, including not only nephews and descendants, but also all members of the family who received undue preferment over other qualified persons.

newt (eft)

Solvers of cross-word puzzles may sometimes wonder why *newt* and *eft*, such different words in appearance and sound, are apparently used interchangeably. When is a newt an eft, they may ask. The answer is that a newt is an eft in the United States, sometimes, and in some sections of England, but the usual name of this curious little relative of the salamander is newt in both countries. Actually even the names are one and the same. The ancient word was *efeta*, in which the f was sometimes voiced and sometimes voiceless. When voiced, the spelling became changed to *eveta*. Then, because the

417

letters *v* and *u* were used interchangeably in writing, this word was often written *eueta*. The next change to *ewte* probably came about after the introduction of the letter *w* and through the fact that the combination *ue* (such as *due*) was usually pronounced like *ew* (*dew*). At about that time also, just as with "nickname," the *n* of *an* (in *an ewte*) was transferred in common speech to the word that followed, producing *a newte*, which eventually gave us *newt*. While these changes were going on there were other lesser sections of England in which the original word was undergoing another modification. These were the sections in which the *f* of *efeta* was voiceless. (In *of* the *f* is voiced; in *often*, voiceless.) In this speech the form of the word gradually changed into *eft*. For many years both *newt* and *eft* were used according to whim, many writers using both words to make sure that the reader would understand. But gradually *newt* has become the more common form, *eft* becoming obsolescent.

nickel

German miners looking for copper were often baffled by an ore which, though it had an appearance of copper, yielded none whatsoever when it was tediously excavated, brought to the surface, and treated. Time and time again they were fooled by this stuff. They thought it must be that a demon or sprite had entered into ore that had been copper and had changed it into worthless stuff. For that reason they called it *kupfernickel*, copper nickel, in which *nickel* was an old Teutonic name for demon. But in 1751 the Swedish mineralogist, Axel F. Cronstedt, succeeded in treating the ore and in isolating the metal from it, although in an impure form. To name the metal thus obtained he went to the name given to the ore in disgust by German miners and called it *nickel*. (Compare COBALT.)

nickname

From early times men have been in the custom of giving to their acquaintances some name considered to be more fitting than the name given by the parents. It is an added name, one in addition to the name already borne. In olden England, when *eke* meant to "add," such an added name became known as *an ekename*. Many words which began with a vowel became altered at that period through the transference of the *n* from the indefinite article *an*, thus producing "a nox" for "an ox," "a negge" for "an egg," "a napple" for "an apple," and so on. Most of these alterations were temporary. But *ekename* when altered to *nekename*, like "eft" when altered to "newt," also speedily suffered a change in pronunciation which served to disguise the earlier form. Thus *nekename* changed in sound to *nickname*, and the original *ekename* dropped from memory. (Compare APRON.)

nicotine

The French ambassador to Lisbon in 1560, Jean Nicot, became curious about some seeds that he saw. They had been brought from the new continent of America a year or two earlier and were said to be seeds from the curious plant that the Spaniards called "tobacco." Some of the seeds were courteously presented to Nicot, who then sent them back to his queen, Catherine de' Medici. The seeds were planted and thus produced the first tobacco, it is said, to be raised in Europe. Through the services of Nicot in obtaining the seed, the scientific name of the plant became *Nicotiana*, and, many years later, the oily liquid contained in its leaves became known as *nicotine*.

Nimrod

Now these are the generations of the sons of Noah, Ham, Shem, and Japheth . . . And the sons of Ham; Cush and Mizraim, and Phut and Canaan . . . And Cush begat Nimrod: he began to be a mighty one in the earth. He was a mighty hunter before the Lord: wherefore it is said, Even as Nimrod the mighty hunter before the Lord.

Thus, from the tenth chapter of Genesis, *Nimrod* has come to be a nickname for anyone noted as a hunter.

nostrum

The plague that beset England in 1563-64 terrified the populace. A thousand people were reported to have died from it each week in London alone, while everyone feared that it might reach the terrific toll of the Black Plague of the fourteenth century when two-thirds or more of the population of the entire country was wiped out. The later plague was not so devastating, but there were several sporadic recurrences, probably new epidemics, which developed in London and elsewhere through the remainder of the century and into the following, with great loss of life. The culmination was the Great Plague of 1665-66, with a death total during 1665 alone of about sixty-nine thousand persons in London only. Medical science was helpless during that period, either to prevent infection or to cure the victim. The result was an influx of quacks from Holland, charlatans from France, mountebanks from Italy. Each proclaimed loudly the virtues of the secret concoction that he alone could produce. This, to make his claim the more impressive, he labeled *Nostrum*, thereby displaying his learning in the Latin tongue. The term thus became a general name for any quack medicine or, in later years, for a patent medicine. But the Latin meaning of *nostrum*, however, is merely "Our own"—that is, "our own preparation."

omelet

Oddly enough, *omelet* comes to us from the Latin word *lamina*, a plate, by virtue of several modifications in passing through French. The Romans had earlier created *lamella* to denote "a small plate." This became *la lemelle*, the thin plate, in French, and—in manner very similar to the alteration of English *an ekename* to *a nickname*—the *a* of *la* was prefixed to the word that followed, thus *la lemelle* became *l'alemelle*. Early French cooks must have prepared eggs in some manner by which, when whipped, seasoned, and fried, the resulting dish resembled a thin plate. At least it was this dish which they called *alemelle*. The next change in the word was the alteration of the ending *-elle* into *-ette*, in accord with the usual diminutive suffix, a change which produced *alemette*, as well as *alumette*. Next came a simple transposition of *l* and *m*, resulting in *amelette*. Possibly each of these alterations came about through the speech of illiterate cooks and were put down upon parchment by literate writers who, knowing nothing about cooking, wrote what they heard. This last form was thence introduced into England, and was in turn variously written. From the sound of the French speech the more common form was *omelet*, which ultimately became preferred. And this in turn has been accepted in France in the form *omelette*.

one

Here we have a curious pronunciation. As seen from the words *alone* and *atone*, which are really compounds formed from *all one* and *at one*, an early sound of *one* was identical with our present word "own." Our word "only," once written "onely," still preserves the old pronunciation. There were variances, of course, but that remained the standard sound until the eighteenth century. In certain dialects, however, there became a tendency in the fifteenth century to sound an initial *w* before some words beginning with *o*. Thus "oats" was sounded and sometimes spelled "wotes"; "oath," "wothe"; "oak," "woke"; "old," "wold." This tendency, occurring only when the initial vowel was long, was not general and did not persist. But in the words *one* and *once*, which were sometimes spelled *won* or *wone* and *wons* or *wonus*, the tendency was persistent. Apparently this tendency toward sounding these words as if spelled with initial *w*, and in which they were then pronounced *wun* and *wunce*, became increasingly common. Grammarians did not recognize them, but they had become so generally used by the seventeenth century as to be the only pronunciations of the two words (except, perhaps, the colloquial "*un*," as in "He's a good un,") to be brought to America. They were standard pronunciations in England by the eighteenth century.

oracle

The ancients would not think of entering upon any important undertaking without first consulting the will of the gods. (See also AUGUR.) Perhaps this was partly curiosity as to the outcome of future events, but more probably it arose from a deep reverence for their gods and a belief that nothing should be undertaken without their approval. Although Zeus was regarded as the father of all gods and men, they did not often approach him directly, because he was believed to be too remote from mortals to be concerned with their individual actions. Instead they made their usual supplications to the lesser gods and goddesses. The questions, accompanied by prescribed gifts or sacrifices, were asked of the priests of the god whose favor was sought, and it was through these priests that the will of the god was then revealed. The replies or prophecies that finally came from the lips of the priests, often in verse form, were usually of so obscure a nature that the supplicant could interpret them as he chose. Sometimes, however, the replies showed great judgment. The temple or place where prophecies were sought, as well as the answer that was received, was known in Greece as *manteion* or *chresterion*. In Rome, where the gods were consulted in similar manner, the more simple term was *oraculum*, from *oro*, pray, which has come to us as *oracle*.

ordeal

To this day in parts of the world, as among some African tribes, persons suspected of a crime are tested with a red-hot iron. He who can have it pressed against his flesh without a blister forming is adjudged innocent; he upon whom a blister forms is guilty. Such a test, or one of similar nature, has been known among primitive races from early ages. Among Teutonic tribes an accused person might be compelled to walk barefooted and blindfolded among a number of red-hot plowshares. He was declared innocent if, by chance, he did not step against one. Or the test might be that he was compelled to step on each of the plowshares, or to carry a glowing iron bar a certain distance; his innocence was thought to be clearly proved if he were uninjured. Sometimes an accused person was tested by having his arm thrust into boiling water. Or the test might be with cold water; a guilty person would float, rejected by the water; the innocent would sink. Among the Germans of old, any such test was called *urdeli*. The Saxon term became *ordel* in Old English, and ultimately *ordeal*. Many of these ordeals were carried into Christian times and adopted by the clergy. Persons accused of witchcraft were sometimes compelled to undergo the ordeal of cold water. She thus adjudged was first stripped, rendered powerless by having her right thumb tied to her left toe and the left thumb to the right toe, and was then tossed into the water. If a witch, she floated. In the ordeal of the bier, known in England until the seventeenth century, a person suspected of murder was obliged to approach or touch the body of the victim. If the wounds bled at his touch, or if foam appeared at the mouth, or if the body altered its position, the accused was declared guilty.

ostracism

When Athens adopted the constitution, in 508 B.C., that was intended to make it an ideal democratic state, unique provision was made that no one should again be able to exert his wealth or power and seize the reins of government. Each year, at a stated assembly of the populace, the question was asked whether anyone had reason to suspect that such an attempt was being made, or that a citizen was acquiring dangerous power. No one was named, and there might be several persons under suspicion, so if an affirmative answer was given, the senate gave notice that the matter would be voted on at a special meeting of all the citizens two months later. Each citizen came to this second meeting with his ballot prepared. If he thought that the charge was well founded and that some man (or men) was endangering the state, the name of that man (or those men) was written upon his ballot, but if he did not think so, he cast a blank ballot. He was expected to be very conscientious, because if a majority of the ballots named one person, it meant that that person would be banished from the state for the next ten years. The man thus sent into exile would not lose his property and would regain full rights of citizenship upon his return, though his other losses might be great. On the other hand, the state sometimes lost the services of some of its wisest counselors, as when such men as Aristides, Themistocles, and Thucydides were banished.

Ordinary voting, in Athens, was by show of hands or by other device in which a simple affirmative or negative opinion could be expressed. The vote of banishment, however, had to be written, but because paper, or papyrus, was rare and costly, the ballot was written upon the most common article to be found about any household of that period—broken pieces of pottery or pieces of tile. Any such piece of baked clay was called *ostrakon*, a name first applied to the shell of an oyster, which it somewhat resembled. Thus, because a vote to send a man into exile was commonly written upon a piece of broken pottery, the Greeks gave the name *ostrakismos* to the banishment itself. Our word *ostracism* is taken directly from this, but we use the term more frequently now to denote social banishment, such as the barring of a person from one's social contact, and the decision is reached by common agreement, rather than by ballot.

oscillate

Perhaps to frighten birds away, or perhaps to propitiate the gods, it was the custom of ancient Roman vintners to hang little images of the face of Bacchus upon their vines, to be swung by the breeze and turned in all directions. The supposition was that in whatever direction the faces were turned about, the crops would increase in fruitfulness in that portion of the vineyard. Now the Latin word for face is *os*; for a little face this becomes *oscillum*, and it is true that little masks such as these were used as described. Some of the older etymologists concluded, therefore, that the Latin verb *oscillo*, which means to swing, was derived from the motion imparted to these *oscilla* by the breeze. However, the majority of present-day scholars doubt this explanation, and prefer to say merely that our word *oscillate* is derived from *oscillo*, without attempting to decide the source of the Latin verb.

ottoman

In the last half of the thirteenth century a small band of Moslems moved eastward out of Persia into western Asia Minor. Their leader took them into the service of a local ruler, but after the death of that leader his son took the remnants of the band into territory still further to the west. There he set up an independent nation. The name of that young leader was Othman, sometimes spelled Osman. The nation that he established is known to us as Turkey, but is also known, from the name of its founder, as the *Ottoman* Empire, and its citizens call themselves *Osmanli*. In time it prospered, and in time it became noted for the luxurious fittings of its court and its palaces. Some of these Oriental fittings and comforts were greatly admired by visitors from western lands, and astute merchants saw to it that western markets then became supplied. Velvets, silks, and carpets were in greatest demand, but when it became the fashion in France under the Bourbons to invest an apartment with couches and divans from Turkey, another article of Turkish source was also introduced. This was a smaller couch than the divan, and, although backless, was intended primarily as a seat for one or two

424

persons. The Oriental name was not brought to the western market, but, coming from the Ottoman Empire, the French dubbed it *ottomane*. The English, first calling it *ottoman sofa*, also finally settled on *ottoman*.

pagan (heathen)

The story of *pagan* and *heathen* can best be told in the words of Archbishop Trench (1807-86) in his *Study of Words*:

You are aware that *pagani*, derived from (Latin) *pagus*, a village, had at first no religious significance, but designated the dwellers in hamlets and villages, as distinguished from the inhabitants of towns and cities. It was, indeed, often applied to all civilians, as contradistinguished from the military caste; and this fact may have had a certain influence when the idea of the faithful as soldiers of Christ was strongly realized in the minds of men. But it was mainly in the following way that it became a name for those alien from the faith of Christ. The Church fixed itself first in the seats and centers of intelligence, in the towns and cities of the Roman Empire; in them its earliest triumphs were won; while, long after these had accepted the truth, heathen superstitions and idolatries lingered on in the obscure hamlets and villages; so that *pagans*, or villagers, came to be applied to all the remaining votaries of the old and decayed superstitions. . . . Heathen has run a course curiously similar. When the Christian faith was first introduced into Germany, it was the wild dwellers on the heaths who were the last to accept it, the last probably whom it reached.

palace

Chief among the famous seven hills upon which Rome was built, and most central of the seven, was the Palatine Hill—*Mons Palatinus*, as it was known, named for the Sabine goddess, Pales. According to tradition, this hill, selected by Romulus upon which to build the city, was ever the seat of government, and upon it Augustus Cæsar caused a large residence to be built for him when he became emperor, in 27 B.C. This edifice, occupied by his successors as well, was not only of great size, but was also of great magnificence, fitting for the emperors of Rome. Because of its location upon the Palatine Hill, the building was referred to as the *Palatium*; and when other wealthy Romans later built similar grand structures in and about Rome or her dominions, each strove to follow the elegance of the emperor's residence and termed his own also a *palatium*. This word degenerated into the Old French form *palais*, and was introduced into English speech in that form. Our present spelling, *palace*, was an alteration from that.

palaver (parable)

The Greek term for "parable" was *parabole*; literally, "a throwing beside," from *para*, beside, and *ballo*, to throw. But the Greek meaning of the compound word was "a placing beside"; hence, "a comparison," and this is, of course, what we mean by parable—a comparison, in the form of an allegorical story, by which some moral is taught. The recorded teachings of Jesus were often in the form of parables, for it was a favorite Hebrew device; the Book of Proverbs contains other examples. The term passed into Latin as *parabola*, and thence into the languages of the West. Its Portuguese form was *palavra*, but when Portuguese traders carried the term to Africa in the fifteenth or sixteenth century, they extended its meaning to include the lengthy powwows with the chieftains that the native conventions required. It was there, in the eighteenth century, that English traders encountered the word, though they understood it to be *palaver*. We continue to use it with the meaning it acquired in Africa.

pale

Originally, *pale*, from the Latin *palus*, stake, meant just that, a stake to be driven into the ground. It had an especial meaning, also—a stake to be driven into the ground along with others, so as to form a fence. From the latter it came to mean a definite limit or boundary, and this was further extended so as to signify a territory outside the area of, but under the control of a nation. Thus the *English pale* once denoted an area in France on either side of Calais which, until 1558, was under English jurisdiction. Most notably, however, the *English pale* was that portion of Ireland—the present counties of Dublin, Kildare, Louth, and Meath—which was under English domination from the twelfth century until the subjugation of the entire island in the reign of Elizabeth. The name *pale* was not applied to it, however, until the fourteenth century. (The adjective "pale," of whitish appearance, is from Latin *pallidus*, pallid.)

Pall Mall

Although now the name of a popular cigarette and of a street in London, the names were both derived from an old outdoor game. The original game and its name were of French origin, literally a game of ball, *palle*, and mallet, *maille*. The game was popular in France in the sixteenth century and, when introduced in the reign of Charles I (1625-49), became popular in England. The boxwood ball used in the game was about the size of the modern croquet ball, and the mallet, also of wood, was similar to the croquet mallet, except that the head was curved and the two faces sloped toward the shaft. The game was played on an alley of considerable length, from the starting point at one end to an iron ring suspended at some height at the other end. The player was winner who took the fewest strokes to drive his ball through the ring. The most noted alley in London in which the game was played was that near St. James's, now bearing the name of the game. The French name was long retained, but because of its pronunciation the spelling was altered by some to *pell-mell*. Others, however, recalled that the Latin sources of the French words were respectively *palla* and *malleus*, and therefore insisted upon the spelling *pall-mall*, which; nevertheless, is still pronounced in England either as if spelled "pell-mell" or like the first syllables of "pallet" and "mallet" respectively.

pamphlet

In the thirteenth century there appeared in France a few leaves containing a poem of love with the title *Pamphilus, seu de Amore*. The story became very popular, so popular that the small work became familiarly known as *Pamphilet*, just like the small book of Aesop's Fables had been familiarly named *Esopet*. Hence, the English, because French was still the court language, also referred to the poem as *Pamphilet*, although later spelling it *Pamflet*, *Pamfilet*, or eventually *Pamphlet*. Because of the few pages which were required to hold this old poem, any other treatise that occupied approximately the same few pages came also to be known as a *pamphlet* even by the fourteenth century. It became an extremely popular term during the period of the Reformation in the sixteenth century, when numerous religious tracts were circulated as *pamphlets*, their writers designated as *pamphleteers*.

pandemonium

When writing *Paradise Lost* Milton's imagination led him to suppose a place that would serve as the capital of Hell, a place that would be inhabited only by the demons and which would be the meeting place and council chambers of all the evil spirits. He coined a name for this imaginary place and called it *Pandemonium*, from the Greek *pan*, all, and *daimon*, demon. The name passed later into general use as a polite substitute for "hell," and through the popular notion that hell is a place of great noise and wild confusion, *pandemonium* now denotes also any scene of great tumult and uproar.

pander

English readers of the fourteenth century were treated to a great story told by two different great writers. It was the story of the love of the Trojan prince, Troilus, for the beautiful Chryseis or Cressida. Boccaccio told the story, in Italian, in his *Filostrato*, basing it upon two legendary accounts of the siege of Troy written by men who were reported to have then lived within the city. Chaucer retold the story in English later in the century in greater detail, using all of the earlier writings and adding to them his own vivid imagination. English readers thus became acquainted with the plight of the brave and handsome Troilus and how, in his desperation, he called upon his great friend Pandarus, kinsman of Chryseis, to aid him in his suit for her love. The story thereafter is chiefly filled with the plots devised by Pandarus to arouse the interest of Chryseis (called Criseyde, by Chaucer) in the Trojan prince and to stimulate that interest into affection. Thus Pandarus became a familiar character to the readers of these two romances, and because the name, for the purpose of rime, was often written Pandare by Chaucer, later writers adopted the designation *Pandare* for anyone who acted as a go-between in love affairs. This was later corrupted to *pander*.

panic

The Greeks ascribed many things to their demigod Pan; among them, the power to inspire great fear or terror in one who saw or heard him—"*Panic* fear," it was called. Through such unreasoning fear, it was said, the Persians were put to flight at the battle of Marathon, when Pan took up the cause of the Athenians. And the same terror affected men who, hunting in the forests of the mountains, heard fearsome noises which, they thought, were produced by Pan. It is not strange that the superstitious Greeks were frightened by this god and derived the word *panic* from him, for they pictured him in a terrifying form. As described by ancient Greek writers, he was a monster, half man and half beast. His head and torso were those of a man, except that such of his face as could be seen was fiery red. His nose was flat, two short horns grew from his head, and his face and body were covered with thick hair. He had the legs, thighs, tail, and feet of a goat. He was said to have been the son of Hermes and a nymph, and his appearance at birth was so frightening that his nurse fled in terror. He dwelt, it was believed, among the mountains or in the forests. One good thing, however, has been accredited to Pan—the invention of a musical instrument, the so-called "pipes of Pan," or panpipes, hollow reeds of graduated length, bound together side by side, to be played on by the mouth, like a harmonica.

panjandrum

The Irish actor, Charles Macklin, retired from the London stage in 1753 at the age of fifty-four and opened a tavern near the Drury Lane theater, the scene of many of his successes. It became his custom, in his new role of innkeeper, to serve dinner personally. Then afterward he would deliver a lecture to such as would listen. A debate invariably followed. Macklin was rather pompous, and the younger actors who frequented the place loved to lead him into making the assertion that he had so trained his memory that he could repeat anything after he had once heard it. Upon one such occasion the witty young actor, Samuel Foote, thereupon composed the following nonsense lines to expose the old man's folly:

So she went into the garden to cut a cabbage leaf to make an apple pie; and at the same time a great she-bear, coming up the street, pops its head into the shop, "What! no soap?" So he died, and she very imprudently married the barber; and there were present the picninnies, and the Joblillies, and the Garyulies, and the Grand Panjandrum himself,

429

with the little round button at top, and they all fell to playing the game of catch as catch can, till the gunpowder ran out at the heel of their boots.

The lines became a grand test for anyone's memory, but were no more than that until Edward Fitzgerald, best known for his translation of the *Rubaiyat*, took *panjandrum* a hundred years later and applied it humorously to a self-important local official, whom he designated "the Grand Panjandrum." Since then, it has become a term of disparagement applied to any pompous individual.

pannier

When introduced from France in the thirteenth century, *pannier* denoted nothing more than a basket, originally for the carrying of bread—whence its name, from the Latin *panarius*, bread basket. But it had also come to mean a fish basket or, if of larger size, a basket for the carrying of provisions of any kind. When someone in later centuries conceived the brilliant notion of balancing two of these larger baskets across the back of a donkey, these too became *panniers*. It was but a step, then, to transfer the name to the basketlike frames which, at the demand of fashion, women affix beneath skirts to extend the size of the hips.

panorama (cyclorama)

In 1788 a Scottish portrait painter, Robert Barker, succeeded in carrying out in practical form an idea that had previously been suggested by a German architect named Breissig. This was to produce and exhibit on canvas the effect of the continuous scene that is open to anyone who turns himself completely around at one spot. To achieve the desired effect, he erected a rotunda, about sixty feet in diameter and reached by stairway, with a continuous painting mounted upon its cylindrical inner wall. Ceiling and floor were blended into the painting to suggest sky and ground. At first Barker called his invention, "*La Nature à coup d'Œil* (Nature at a Glance)," but later he coined the more euphonious name, *panorama*, from Greek *pan*, all, and *orama*, view. Robert Fulton, more noted then as artist than as engineer, was one of those greatly attracted by Barker's invention, and introduced the *panorama* into Paris, where he was staying, in 1799. Nowadays *panorama* also embraces a complete natural view in all directions, and the term *cyclorama*, from Greek *kyklos*, circle, and *orama*, view, is used for the artificial scene.

pants, pantaloons

A hundred years ago the witty poet, Oliver Wendell Holmes, wrote the delightfully humorous *Rhymed Lesson*, in which he sought to correct various bad habits. Among them was the use of the word *pants*, which, he wrote, was "A word not made for gentlemen, but 'gents.'" There are still some people who agree with him, but most Americans think its use is now as legitimate as the well established "cab," for "cabriolet," or "bus," for "omnibus." *Pants* is, of course, a contraction of *pantaloons*, a contraction that sprang up in America almost as soon as the garment itself reached our shores in the last years of the eighteenth century. So our story must be of *pantaloons*. This takes us back to a character in fifteenth-century Italian comedy, to a part that was always played by a lean and silly old man, always representing a foolish old Venetian and always wearing spectacles and slippers. The most characteristic part of his attire, however, was his nether garment, a pair of trousers that, skintight about the thin shanks, flared out above the knees like a petticoat. This character, in the comedy, always bore the name, *Pantaleone*, possibly because of some allusion to an early Christian martyr of that name especially honored by Venetians. The comedy, played as a pantomime, was popular throughout Italy and was played by strolling bands of actors in many other countries. Always *Pantaleone* —*Pantalon* in France, *Pantaloon* in England—appeared in his extravagant trousers. From that Italian character, then, any unusual kind of trousers, especially one covering both the upper and lower legs, was immediately described as *Pantaloon*. But it was in France, during the Revolution at the close of the eighteenth century, that the *pantalon* became popular. In the early days of that terrible struggle the Revolutionary army was composed chiefly of poor and ill-clad volunteers. The aristocrats called them *sans-culottes*, "without breeches," because the trousers which they wore were so tattered as almost to be no clothing at all. Later, however, when the Revolution had succeeded, the Revolutionaries took this as a term of honor, and repudiating the aristocratic knee breeches, adopted the *pantalon* as the masculine garb of republicanism. The well-cut, stylish garment of the period following the Revolution, the garment first imported to England and the United States in the earliest years of the nineteenth century, fitted tightly from thighs to ankles, with buttons or laces below the calves of the legs to assure a snug fit. Almost from the first, in America, they were popularly called *pants*, and, regardless of change in cut, style, length, and purpose, the abbreviated name has persisted despite all efforts of purists and pedagogs.

paraphernalia

In ancient Greece, as well as in some modern countries, a bride-groom received some gift or dowry—money, cattle, or other property—along with his bride, usually from her parents. This dowry then became his, to dispose of as he might wish. But the bride might also bring with her certain personal property, such as slaves or jewels, for example. These, under Greek law, her husband could not touch. They were distinctly her own possessions, and were known as *parapherna*, from *para*, beyond, and *phero*, bring; that is, belongings brought beyond those specified in the marriage contract. In present-day legal usage the Latinized term, *paraphernalia*, carries the same general interpretation, varying somewhat in our different States. The term is also used more broadly to designate any sort of miscellaneous equipment possessed by any individual or group.

parasite

Originally, in ancient Greece, there was nothing derogatory in referring to a man as a *parasite* (Greek *parasitos*, from *para*, beside, and *sitos*, food). It then referred to a class of priests, probably, who feasted together áfter a sacrifice. At an early date, however, it was applied to one who, as a guest, ate at the table of a friend. But, just as today a perfect guest does not insult a host, in those far-off times it was then customary for the perfect guest to choose his words even more carefully and to make nothing but complimentary remarks to his host. The more complimentary the remarks, the greater the chance that invitations would be repeated, for human nature hasn't changed very much in that respect. In time, therefore, a *parasite* came to be known contemptuously as one who lived entirely at the expense

432

of another, feeding him with servile flattery in return for food and drink for one's own stomach.

pariah

In prehistorical times much of southern India was occupied, apparently, by a black-skinned race of primitive people. Some time after the Aryan invasion, which may have been as early as 2000 B.C., these people were subjugated and forced into menial positions. Gradually, after the caste system was introduced, they became separated into different lowly classes. Among these people was one class known as *Pariah*, which, from the name, indicates that at one time they were the hereditary beaters of the drum (*parai*) at various festivals. Eventually they became agricultural laborers and, among the British, household servants. They are not the lowest caste, but are regarded by the Brahmans as "untouchable." Among the British, therefore, *pariah* became a general term for anyone of low caste, but especially for the lowest of the low, or for those of no caste at all. Hence, although the application is not strictly correct, any person (or animal) who is an outcast among his kind has become known as a *pariah*.

pasquinade

In the year 1501 a mutilated old statue was dug up in Rome near the palace of Cardinal Caraffa. The statue was not identified, but the Cardinal, nevertheless, had it set up in the roadway at the corner of the palace. Opposite the spot where the statue had been found there had lived an old man with a sharp wit, said to have been either a tailor, a cobbler, or a schoolmaster, whose name had been Pasquino. Accordingly, as soon as it had been set up on its pedestal, the statue was promptly dubbed "Pasquino." Thereafter, on St. Mark's Day, it became the custom for the young men of a nearby school to dress "Pasquino" in various garments and to salute him with mock solemnity in passing and ask him for advice. It was not long before such requests were put into writing and posted or hung upon the statue. Then the written matter took the form of witty and satirical lampoons upon prominent persons and especially upon the papal government. The citizens of Rome began to enjoy these squibs, referring to them as *Pasquinata*, from the name given to the statue. A printed collection of them appeared in 1509. The name became *Pasquinade* in English, because the fame of these sharp little squibs had spread throughout Europe. Popular enjoyment was enhanced when another old statue was discovered and placed near "Pasquino." This was given the name "Marforio," because it came *a Martis foro* (from the forum of Mars). The lampoons then often took the form of dialog, with "Marforio" propounding questions for the caustic "Pasquino" to answer. The authors were numerous and their identities were never revealed, although the successive popes, against whose private and public conduct the lampoons were generally directed, would have taken harsh measures against them. The statue "Marforio," the recumbent figure of a man, was removed to the Capitoline Museum in 1784, but by that time the former pungency of the pasquinade had largely disappeared and these lampoons had become infrequent.

patrol

The Old French source of the verb was *patouiller*, and it then meant "to dabble in the mud." The supposition is that French soldiers detailed to guard a camp at night found that their duty seemed to consist of nothing but tramping interminably back and forth in the mud, and thus adopted this word to express in a slang sense the nature of the duty. The spelling was altered to *patrouiller* in modern French, and it had then become an accepted military term, meaning, "to go the rounds, as the guard of a camp." England, which adopted many French military practices, took over this term also, but further altered it to *patrol*.

patter

The Lord's Prayer was recited in the Middle Ages in very much the fashion that one often hears it today, especially by children—with great rapidity and with no shadow of understanding of the words. The difference is that in the Middle Ages the recitation was in Latin, so that few people knew what they were saying. Instead of opening with the words, "Our Father," therefore, it opened with "*Pater noster*"—thus giving rise to the word *paternoster* as a general name for the Lord's Prayer. It was because of this glib and indistinct utterance, then so commonly heard in church, that the slang word *patter* was formed, taken from the first word of the prayer.

pavilion (tavern, tabernacle)

The Roman military tent was often called *taberna*, a term that usually denoted a shop, because, like the shop, it was generally constructed of boards. (This word was also the source of *tavern*, since many Roman shops sold wine and served as inns. It is also the source of *tabernacle*, which, as Latin *tabernaculum*, meant a little tent, a hut.) But for non-military purposes in which a structure of less permanent nature was needed for protection against sun or rain, the Romans were accustomed to stretch a many-hued cloth, somewhat like an awning, over upright poles. Under it, in hot weather, they sometimes ate the morning or midday meal. This brilliant cloth structure, when fully spread, looked not unlike a mammoth butterfly with outspread wings; so they named it *papilio*, the Latin name of that pretty creature. Through later centuries such temporary structures found increasing use in France; its name was corrupted to *pavilon*, however, and in this form it passed into England. Our present spelling, *pavilion*, arose in the seventeenth century.

peculiar

From the same source as *pecuniary*, the Romans coined the adjective *peculiaris*, which, though originally referring to one's property in cattle, acquired a broader reference to personal property in general. From this, even in Roman days, *peculiaris* took on the more specific meaning, "one's own; belonging particularly to one's self." Thus, a Roman slave, although the absolute property of his master, was sometimes able to save some money in one way or another. This the master could not legally touch; it was *peculiares servi*, strictly belonging to the slave. Hence, without taking into consideration the shades of meaning that *peculiar* has acquired in English, its general sense pertains to character, qualities, abilities, or the like that are unshared with any other person, that are distinctly one's own.

pecuniary (impecunious)

Back in olden times, just as in many rural regions today, a man's wealth was measured, not by the money he might have in the bank nor the land that he held, but by the cattle that he owned; that is, the number of sheep, cows, or goats that he had. Now the Latin word for such a general collection of farm animals was *pecus*. Therefore, it followed that *pecus* also came to mean personal wealth or riches. But in later times, when property began to consist of other forms of wealth, the Romans altered the term slightly into *pecunia*, a word broad enough in meaning to include money as well as other riches, but which ultimately meant money in particular. From this was formed our adjective *pecuniary*, which we use to mean pertaining to money or wealth. The prefix *im-* "without" or "lacking," gives us *impecunious*, without or lacking wealth —or, in the older Roman meaning, pertaining to a person who has no cattle.

pedagog

In the Grecian family there was one slave, especially selected for his prudence, whose duty it was to attend the sons of the family during boyhood. One of these duties was to accompany his charges when they went upon the public roads, to and from the gymnasium, or elsewhere. From the nature of his duties such a slave was known, in Greek, as a *paidagogos*, literally a leader of boys, from *pais*, boy, and *agogos*, leader. Sometimes the *pedagog*, as the term became in English, was himself a man of high learning, unfortunate enough to have been captured in warfare and subsequently sold as a slave. In such instances he also served as a tutor to the boys of the family. It is from the latter that the term has come to signify a school-teacher.

pedigree

This is a distorted spelling of the French words from which it is said to have originated, *pied de grue*. Some of the many English forms the word has taken since its introduction into the language in the early fifteenth century, were *pee de grew*, *petiegrew*, *pytagru*, *peti degree*, *pedicru*, to show just a few of them. The French phrase means "foot of a crane," and the reason for giving this peculiar name to the genealogical table that shows one's line of descent is explained thus:

Back in the Middle Ages, people were just as proud of their ancestry as many are today; in fact, numerous instances in the Bible, especially the First Book of Chronicles, show that such pride is very ancient. It exists among all races. But in England, the study of genealogy began to assume undue importance in the fourteenth century when, after the Norman Conquest, matters of inherited rights came into question. Scholars, usually monks, were employed to trace back the lines of descent claimed by noblemen, or to prove that some remote relative was the legitimate heir to an estate or title after all the direct descendants had died or been killed in battle. Hence, just as among scholars of our day certain signs or symbols have acquired particular significance—as the asterisk (*), the dagger (†), the double dagger (‡)—so did the genealogists of the Middle Ages also employ certain conventional significant symbols. Thus, it appears, the line of descent that one was engaged in tracing was marked by a symbol that was easy to make—a caret or inverted V having a straight line extending from slightly above the apex down through it to the base (⅄). Some monk, probably, knowing the tracks that birds make in mud or snow, must have seen the resemblance between this symbol and the track made by a crane and, French being the court language, called it *pied de grue*. The name of the mark was retained, and, marking the lines of descent, the line itself came to be called *pied de grue*, eventually corrupted into the English spelling, *pedigree,* under the influence of the French pronunciation.

pen, pencil, penicillin

In spite of the fact that these names apply to writing instruments which, nowadays, look something alike, and despite the fact that the three letters of one form the first syllable of the other, the sources of the two words are unrelated. *Pen* is derived from the Latin *penna,* a quill, feather, because, until the invention of steel pens late in the eighteenth century—and long thereafter, until the quality was improved and the price cheapened—sharpened quills had been in use since about the eighth century A.D. As the point became dulled with use a new point could be made with a sharp knife; hence the term *penknife.* Before the unknown inventor discovered that a *penna,* or goose quill, could be sharpened for use, the chief writing implement had been the *calamus* or sharpened reed, dating back to classic Greek use.

The term *pencil*, however, was first employed by artists and referred especially to the finely sharpened brushes that they used. Its source was the Latin *peniculus*, meaning "a little tail," because painters' brushes were first made from hairs from the tails of oxen or horses. The name was borrowed for the lead pencil when the latter device was invented, about the middle of the sixteenth century A.D., probably because of the softness of the graphite that was first used in them and the resemblance thereby to the soft little brush of the artist. The medicinal drug, *penicillin*, was so named because the mold from which it was first obtained resembled numerous tiny brushes.

person

Greek and Roman actors almost invariably wore masks in every dramatic appearance. Such a mask covered the entire face and was made with highly exaggerated features so as to be readily distinguished by the remote spectator. Thus, an actor, donning the proper mask, could assume any character that the drama called for. In a Greek tragedy, for example, a pale mask with hollow cheeks and floating fair hair invariably denoted a sick young man, whereas if the hair were black, mixed with gray, and the mask were pale, the character would be recognized as a man of about forty who was suffering from sickness or wounds. The gods, who appeared in most tragedies, were each also represented by a particular mask. Every character could thus be recognized from the mask. Now the Roman name for "mask" was *persona*, and *persona* thus came to signify a particular character in a play. From that, *persona* came to mean the player who wore the mask, and eventually a human being. The old senses, along with the new, still prevailed when Old French *persone* was first brought into England and altered to the present *person*.

petticoat

The early *petticoat*, or "little coat," was worn by men. In fact, men continued to wear petticoats until the eighteenth century, although the garments were then usually called waistcoats. But the small coats worn by men of the fourteenth and fifteenth centuries were actually coats, not skirts, and were worn under the doublet.

438

phaeton

Helios, in Greek mythology, had charge of the chariot of the sun. It was his duty to drive it each day from the ocean of the farthest east across the heavens and to the ocean of the farthest west. (Thence, it was believed, Helios, his chariot, and the four horses that drew it were wafted in a golden boat during the night along the northern rim of the earth back to the east again.) Helios had a young son, it was said, whose name was Phaëton. The lad, as boys will, tremendously admired the shining chariot and the wonderfully speedy horses, and constantly begged the privilege of driving it. His pleas fell on deaf ears, until, finally, he persuaded his mother, Clymene, to add her petitions. Thus, one day, Helios yielded against his better judgment, and the young lad set forth proudly. But as the morning wore on young Phaëton's arms grew weary from the strain of controlling the four dashing steeds, and he became unable to keep them upon the straight course. The chariot was sometimes pulled high into the sky, when, exerting all his strength, the lad brought it back so close to the earth that the ground scorched. Zeus, watching the erratic course of the chariot through the sky, feared that both heaven and earth would be set afire. To stop it he drew a thunderbolt from his shaft and hurled it at the boy, whose lifeless body then fell into the Eridanus, a mythical river subsequently thought to be the Oder or the Vistula. His weeping sisters rushed to the spot, mourning his death. There the sympathetic gods transformed them into poplars, their tears into amber, a formation later found abundantly at the mouths of those two rivers. It was to this ancient legend that the British alluded in the sixteenth century when they called any reckless young driver dashing along the roads a *Phaeton*. The sound of the word was pleasing, so the name was transferred later to the vehicle which, drawn by two horses, became fashionable in the eighteenth century.

phantasmagoria

Today we have television. Before that we had motion pictures, or cinema. Earlier was the stereopticon, and before that the magic lantern. But in 1802 a man by the name of Philipstal introduced a device that was considered a great improvement upon the older

439

magic lantern. In part the difference was that the figures to be projected, instead of being on transparent glass, were themselves painted in transparent colors, the rest of the glass slide opaque. Thus it was the image only that was projected upon the screen. Such slides were later adopted in all magic lanterns. But the chief feature of the new invention was the means that Philipstal devised for creating optical illusions. His screen, of thin silk, was mounted between the lantern and the spectators and could be moved imperceptibly forward or back. Thus the images appeared to advance or recede, and, by separate device, could be made to fade from one into another or disappear entirely. These are common illusions in the motion picture of today, but were then considered marvelous. Philipstal coined a mouth-filling name for his invention and named it *phantasmagoria*, probably devising it from the Greek *phantasma*, phantasm, and *agora*, assembly. We now apply his term to any dreamlike fancy in which figures fade or shift into others.

philopena (fillipeen)

How old the German custom might be, no one knows. It was probably brought to America in the early eighteenth century, but that is entirely a guess because the earliest written record is not until a century later. The custom was that if, in the eating of almonds, hazelnuts, or other like nut, one were to find twin kernels within the shell, the contents were shared—a lady sharing with a gentleman, a gentleman with a lady. The next time these two persons met, the one who was first to say, "*Guten Morgen, Vielliebchen* (Good morning, sweetheart)," would receive a present, perhaps previously agreed upon, from the other. American youth, ignorant of German but almost catching the pronunciation, appreciated the custom, especially if the reward were a kiss, but corrupted the German *Vielliebchen* into the sound *fillipeen*. But because that was not a known word, it was often altered in print to *philippine*. Both game and name have been varied, but the name is now usually written either *philopena* or *fillipeen*.

photography

Cameras and the production of pictures upon paper or glass had been made before the nineteenth century, but the first to produce permanent pictures by these means was Joseph Niepce of France, with the cooperation of his fellow countryman, Louis Daguerre. The process was first called *héliographie*, later dropped in favor of *daguerreotype* when the process was further improved. In January of 1839, however, an Englishman, W. H. Fox Talbot, described a further improvement made by him which he called *photogenic drawing*. This has been called the first of the processes for printing pictures. A few months later, in March of the same year, Sir John Herschel announced yet another advance in the rapidly expanding new field, and brought us the name that has now become standard, *photography*, which, it is supposed, he coined from the first element of Talbot's *photogenic* and the last element of Niepce's *héliographie*.

piano

Unknown to each other, several men were working simultaneously upon the same problem in the early years of the eighteenth century. The harpsichord had been developed two centuries earlier from the older clavichord, a distinct improvement; but the instrument, with its tones produced by the action of quills plucking the strings, was still too soft for concert work; it could be heard only in a small room, and composers were demanding a greater volume of sound. The first to reach the goal was Bartolomeo Christoforo, a maker of harpsichords in Florence, Italy. In 1709 he produced the instrument that he called *piano e forte*; that is, in Italian, "soft and loud," because the instrument, with hammers striking its strings, could be played with great volume or, by damping the strings, with the softest of tones. The name was promptly contracted to *pianoforte*, and this is still the correct name technically, though it is commonly further abridged to *piano*. England had its claimant for the invention in the person of Father Wood, who made a similar *pianoforte* in 1711. A German claimant, Christoph Gottlieb Schroter, delivered a differing device to the Elector of Saxony in 1717.

pompadour

Jeanne Antoinette Poisson was born in Paris in 1721 of poor parents, but was early taken into the home of a wealthy financier and educated as if she were his daughter. She was extremely beautiful and received every social advantage. At the age of twenty she married the nephew of her benefactor, Lenormant d'Etoiles, and became the queen of fashionable Paris. Three years after her marriage, however, she met the king of France, Louis XV. From that time until her death in 1764 her life was devoted to the king, who was equally attached to her. In 1745 he established her in the court of Versailles and, a few years later, bought for her the estate of Pompadour, giving her the title "Marquise," later "Duchesse" de Pompadour. She became a person of great power in the court, where she retained her leadership of Parisian fashion. Various innovations of style and costume were attributed to her. One in particular was a mode of hairdressing that she affected in which the hair was swept upward high above the forehead. That style, somewhat modified, is still known as *pompadour* after the famous mistress of Louis XV.

poplin

From 1309 to 1376 the papal see was located at Avignon in France. Clement V, pope from 1305 to 1314 never entered the Vatican in Rome. He was French, and so were the five popes who directly followed him. After Gregory XI transferred the seat of papal power again to Rome, Avignon continued in importance because first one and then a second antipope assumed the papacy and resided in the city until expelled in 1408. Avignon was also noted at that period for a certain textile fabric made by its weavers. Made with a silk warp and a weft of worsted yarn, it was in demand both as a dress material and for upholstery. Fabrics at that period were usually identified in some unmistakable manner with the place at which they were made. Thus, because Avignon, sold to the papacy in 1348, remained a papal town until 1791, the term *papeline*, papal, was applied to it. English merchants, attempting the French pronunciation, reduced the name of the material to *poplin*.

post, posthaste

Marco Polo is responsible for our use of *post* in connection with mail. It was after his return from his long sojourn in China in the thirteenth century, when he described the Great Khan's system for receiving and sending messages from and to all parts of his vast empire. Large stations, housing many horses and men, were placed at twenty-five-mile intervals along all the great roads, and messages were thus quickly relayed to their destinations. The system was not unknown in Europe; Augustus Caesar had such a system, and so had the Persian king, Darius the Great. But in describing the Khan's system, Polo used the term *poste* (from the Latin *positus*, placed) for the "station" at which each of the relays of men and horses were kept. Hence, when European traders established a similar system, in later centuries, for sending messages to and from their agents, Polo's term was adopted. In England, the station for men and horses became a *post*house; the rider, a *post*boy, and we still recall the speed of horse and rider in *posthaste*.

potato

Shortly after the West Indies were discovered, Spanish navigators must have learned of the plant, new to them, with its tuberous roots which the natives used as a food. But the first mention of these plants in European accounts appears to have been in 1526. The name, in Haiti, was *batata*, and it was under this name that the plant was first known in Europe. This plant, however, was what we now call the sweet potato. It was cultivated only as a curiosity for some time after its introduction into Europe; its edible qualities were viewed with suspicion. When the Spaniards reached Peru and began to explore its resources, they found another tuberous plant with white tubers which the natives of that region also ate. Although the local name appeared to be *papas*, the Spaniards took it to be another variety of the West Indian plant and called it *batata* also, though the two are unrelated. The latter plant, described in 1553, may have been brought to Spain before 1580, but that is the earliest recorded date. It was then independently cultivated in Italy, France, and in Germany before the end of the century. And, although the plant is not a native of Virginia and Sir Walter Raleigh was never in that colony, it was stated that Raleigh introduced the plant from Virginia into England in 1596. The early *batata* was corrupted in Spain to *patata* and was altered to *potato* when first described in England. They also called it the Virginia or common potato to distinguish it from the earlier sweet or Spanish potato. Except in Ireland, such cultivation as it had was as a food for cattle, rather than for human consumption. There, from early in the seventeenth century, it became so staple an article of food and was so largely cultivated that the common name of the white potato has become "Irish potato," or, humorously, "Murphy." The colloquial American name "spud" arises from the narrow, spadelike tool of that name used in digging potatoes.

precipitate, precipice

The Latin source of both is *præcipito* which, in early use, meant "to cast down or fall headlong," as if from a high place. It is from *præ*, before, and *caput*, head; hence, literally, "headforemost." The term was used many times by Roman writers when referring to criminals executed by being cast from the Tarpeian Rock in Rome, or to those who, by similar means, committed suicide, and *præcipitium* (English *precipice*) was applied to such a place or such a fall. Later writers extended the meaning of *præcipito* to have it mean "to rush headlong," as if down a steep grade, and thus *precipitate* has come to mean to take hasty action of some sort, action so hurried as to appear rash.

precocious

Were we to reserve this for its ancient Latin meaning, we would use it now instead of "precooked," for that was the original literal sense. It was derived from *præ*, before, and *coquo*, cook or boil. But *præcoquo* came early to mean "to ripen fully," and from that sense its participle, *præcoquus* or *præcox*, was applied to fruit "ripening before its time; prematurely." We continue to use *precocious* in this latter sense, but we also apply it especially to children who develop prematurely, either mentally or physically.

preposterous

When the Romans had occasion to express the notion that we have in mind when we use "putting the cart before the horse," they did it by the compound word *præposterus*. Freely translated, that means "the before coming after," from *præ*, before, and *posterus*, following. The exact meaning of our *preposterous* is, therefore, "inverted; in a reversed order"; but because things reversed or turned upside down are contrary to the natural order, *preposterous* has also taken the meaning "nonsensical, utterly absurd."

pretext

The principal outer garment of the Roman citizen, in olden days, was the toga. This outer cloak was variously marked to distinguish the rank of its wearer. That worn by various high magistrates, and by freeborn children until the age of puberty, was marked in front by a border of purple. It was known as a *toga prætexta*, or more commonly as *prætexta*, the name being derived from *præ*, before, and *texo*, weave. But, just as our word "cloak" has come to mean a cover or shield which conceals one's real purpose, so did the Romans use *prætexta* in precisely the same figurative sense. Hence, when in the form *pretext* the term came into English, it was the figurative meaning only that persisted.

prevaricator

If a cowboy had been seen in the streets of Rome in the days of Caesar it is likely that a spectator, seeing his bowed legs, would have called him a *prævaricator*. That is what the term meant—a bandy-legged person, a straddler with crooked legs, one who, because of his distorted legs, cannot walk in a straight line. The term was used especially in the Roman law courts where it was applied to a prosecutor who, though supposed to represent one party, made a secret agreement with the opposite party and betrayed his own client. He did not walk straight; he straddled the issue. It was, therefore, a false defense (or a false accusation) that was formerly meant by *prevarication*, and it was that type of crookedness and falsehood which marked a *prevaricator*.

procrastination

We have a saying, "Never put off till tomorrow what can be done today." The ancient Romans condensed such an action into a single word—*procrastinatio*. Its literal meaning is "a putting off to the morrow." It was formed by joining the preposition *pro*, for the benefit of, to the adverb *crastinus*, tomorrow.

Procrustean

According to Greek legend, there lived in the days of Theseus a highwayman named Procrustes who dwelt on the road toward

Eleusis. Travelers, it was said, seeing his house by the roadside, sometimes stopped to seek accommodation for the night. Procrustes never turned any away. But he had two beds, one a short one and the other quite long. If the traveler was tall, Procrustes showed him into the room having only the short bed, a short traveler saw only the long bed. But Procrustes always had a remedy. He chopped off the feet or legs of the tall guest or stretched the bones of the short one. In either case the traveler died, and the bandit stole his wealth. According to another account of the legend, Procrustes, who was also known as Damastes or Polypemon, used but one bed, but fitted his guests to that in the same manner. In either story the villain was eventually slain by Theseus. His method of fitting something by arbitrary methods to a condition which it does not meet is called *Procrustean*, often in the phrase, "*Procrustean* bed."

profane

In certain rites of the ancient religions of the Greeks and Romans none but men who were fully initiated into the mysteries were permitted to participate. Those sacred ceremonies and sacrifices, the objects of worship, and the traditions, with the interpretations of all of these, were disclosed only to those admitted into the body of the initiates. All others were, as the Romans put it, *profane*, that is, not admitted into the innermost secrets of the temple. The word is from Latin *pro*, which here means "outside," and *fanum*, temple. Such was also the original sense of *profane* when it was brought into English use, but it was applied particularly to persons or things not belonging to the Christian religion. Then, because of the contempt held by nonbelievers, *profane* came to be associated with irreverence and blasphemy.

Promethean

Among the traditions of the Greeks was one of an ancient hero whose name, Prometheus, signified "forethought," and his brother Epimetheus, whose name meant "afterthought." It was Prometheus who stole fire from Zeus and brought it to mortals, and who taught them in all the useful arts and sciences. It was Epimetheus who, against the advice of his wiser brother, became flattered by the charms of Pandora and prevailed upon her to open the box from which then escaped all the evils that have since plagued mankind. But the tradition chiefly relates the punishment inflicted by Zeus upon Prometheus for stealing the divine fire. He was caused to be chained to a rock upon the side of a mountain, and there, defenseless, he was attacked every day by a huge bird, an eagle or a vulture, which feasted upon his liver. Each night his wounds were healed, only to be subjected to the attack of the evil bird the following day. This continued until after eons of torture, Zeus relented and permitted Heracles to kill the bird and break the chains of Prometheus. Our adjective *Promethean* may thus be connected with recurring ills, reminiscent of the punishment of this mythical hero, or with any of the many skills and arts credited to his beneficence.

purple

Hundreds of years before the Christian Era the Phoenicians who dwelt along the coast of the Mediterranean Sea near Tyre discovered a curious shellfish attached to the adjacent rocks. This shellfish or mussel was found to yield a minute quantity of fluid which imparted a dark crimson color to cloth. It is said that the stain was first observed about the mouth of a dog which had crushed and eaten one of the mussels. The Greeks called this shellfish *porphyros*, because the color it yielded resembled the red volcanic rock, that we call porphyry, then quarried in Egypt. The name was altered to *purpura*, in Latin, further corrupted in English to *purple*. The dye that was thus discovered became greatly desired because of its scarcity. The mussels were found only along shores nearby Tyre, and there was but a tiny amount in each mussel. None but emperors or men of great wealth could afford "Tyrian *purple*," as it was called. The dye, used only in the finest cloths, became the distinguishing mark of the dress of emperors and kings. Thus, the expression, "born to the *purple*," still denotes a person of royal birth.

pygmy

Travelers in southern Egypt brought tales to ancient Greece of a fabulous race of dwarfs who lived along the upper Nile. These dwarfs, it was said, were so small that they were in constant battle with the cranes, constantly on guard against being seized and swallowed. Greek historians, at a loss for a name for such a dwarf, invented the descriptive name *pygmaios*. This was because the people were said to be no taller than the length of a man's arm from the elbow to the knuckles, and *pygme* was the term for that unit of length, the English ell. The form of the word was gradually altered to *pygmy* after its introduction into our language.

python

The oracle of Apollo at Delphi was the most celebrated of all the places in ancient Greece where the will of the gods was sought. But, by some traditions, this oracle had not always been sacred to Apollo. Its chasm, from which mysterious smoke arose, was believed to have first been an oracle of the goddess Gea and to have been guarded by a fearsome dragon known as *Python*. This dragon was said to have pursued Leto, mother of Apollo, when she arrived at Delos in search of a resting place to give birth to her son. Four days after his birth, the infant Apollo pursued the dragon and slew it in revenge, and thus acquired the oracle for himself. The large snake of India and Africa which we now call *python* received the name of this mythical monster only a hundred years ago, when zoologists determined that it was a separate genus of the family of boas.

quack

The duck makes the same sound regardless of the country she is in and, with her waddle, she reminds one always of a pompous person, strutting along, and eternally quack-quacking to himself. That is what the Dutch thought of the charlatans and mountebanks parading around through plague-ridden Europe in the sixteenth century, each proclaiming loudly the virtues of his salve or nostrum. Accordingly the Dutch named them *quacksalvers*, ducks quacking over their salves. Neighboring countries thought the term so apt that it was borrowed by Germany, Sweden, and England. The English, however, soon shortened it to *quack*, and applied it to any pretender of medical learning and skill.

Quaker

The members of the Society of Friends sometimes use the name *Quaker*, but have never officially adopted it. The term is said to have been first applied to the founder of the Society, George Fox, according to Fox himself, in 1650 by Justice Bennet of Derby. Fox was being arraigned before two justices in Derbyshire and was exhorting them to "tremble at the word of God." This Judge Bennet sarcastically interpreted as "quaking," and thus sneeringly referred to those who practiced it as *quakers*. The term was picked up as a humorous appellation for the new sect, although it was later the belief of many that the name had reference to some practices thought to be a result of the religion. Thus a writer in the late seventeenth century, referring to the Friends, said that they "do not now quake, and howl, and foam with their mouths, as they did formerly."

quarry

Hunting dogs of the Middle Ages were as well trained as those of today and held their prey at bay until the hunters had arrived for the kill. As a reward for this restraint it was the custom to give the dogs certain parts of the animal, which was usually a stag. These parts were placed on the skin of the animal, and it was this which gave the feast its name. "Skin," in Old French, was *cuiree*. This became *quirre* in Middle English and was ultimately converted into *quarry*. But that which had originally denoted the skin of the animal and then the part of the animal placed upon that skin as a reward to the dogs, became in turn the entire live animal which the dogs sought as their prey, and was then applied also to any animal or human chased by hunters. (The term *quarry* which designates an excavation for stone blocks is from the Latin *quadratus*, square.)

quisling

Perhaps the term will not survive; few other names of traitors to their country have become part of the language of their owner, let alone being adopted into our speech. But the circumstances that made *quisling* a synonym for "traitor," and *quisle* to mean "to betray one's

449

country," have warranted the inclusion of both terms into several recent English dictionaries. These were the circumstances: Vidkun Abraham Quisling was born in Norway, July 18, 1887. He received a military education and entered the Norwegian army in 1911, taking the oath of allegiance both to country and king. Seven years later he served as military attaché to his country's embassy at Leningrad, and from 1919 to 1921 in the same capacity at Helsingfors. Through promotions he was commissioned a major in the Norwegian army in 1931. But two years later, within four months after Adolf Hitler became chancellor of Germany, Quisling organized a Fascist Party in Norway, imitating the German organization of Hitler and becoming an ardent admirer of that leader. Hence, when word was received in the winter of 1939-40 that the German army, already having overrun most of western Europe in the first few months of World War II, was contemplating an invasion of Norway, Quisling, then on the retired list, and his small party of Fascists got themselves in readiness. The invasion surprised all Norway and Europe; it occurred, partly by sea and partly by air, on the night of April 8-9, 1940. The government refused to yield to German demands for surrender, and ordered a full mobilization of its army. But Quisling and his followers seized control of the Oslo radio station and countermanded the orders. King Haakon and his loyal ministers fled northward and eventually escaped by sea to England, where a government-in-exile was set up. After the king's flight, Quisling was named the head of government by the German commander, a position that he occupied briefly. But in the following September he was again given the title, and thereafter carried out all the orders of his German overlords until the German military collapse in April, 1945. Immediately, then, Quisling was placed under arrest by orders of the legal government, charged with treason, murder, and theft. The murder charge was based upon his responsibility for the deaths of a thousand Jewish and a hundred other Norwegian civilians. He was convicted on all counts in September, 1945. The verdict, a sentence of death, was the first of such extreme penalties given by a Norwegian court in many years, for criminal execution had long been abolished under the laws of the country. However, the Supreme Court promptly upheld an act passed in October, 1941, by the government-in-exile re-establishing that penalty for convicted traitors, and Quisling was shot by a firing squad at the Akershus fortress in the early hours of October 24, 1945. Because of the great contempt in which his actions were held by the peoples of all nations fighting against Germany, his name became a hateful byword applied, especially during the war, to anyone whose actions were traitorous.

quixotic

Cervantes, in writing his most famous work, *The History of Don Quixote*, in 1605, stated that its "fabulous extravagances" should be interpreted as "only an invective against the books of chivalry" which had been riotously produced in Spain. There is reason to doubt the sincerity of that statement, however, because the books he referred to had already been out of fashion for fifty years. But he created the characters of the decayed nobleman, Don Quixote, and of his stout serving-man, Sancho Panza, in burlesque imitation of the valiant knights and faithful squires of earlier writers. He made the elderly Don on his ignoble steed the very epitome of chivalry in its purest form, inspired by high ideals and filled with enthusiasm, but pitifully and ludicrously unaware of the false and visionary nature of his dreams. The book became immensely popular and, though Cervantes died in great poverty a dozen years later, it was translated into most of the languages of Europe. It added the word *quixotic* to our language, expressive of lofty but impractical sentiments resembling those of the foolishly romantic hero, Don Quixote.

quorum

The literal meaning of this Latin word is "of whom." But, like other of our words, such as "patter" and "omnibus," *quorum* was once part of a Latin phrase—in this instance, a legal phrase. Originally, that is, it was a custom, among English justices of the peace, to name one, or perhaps two or three, of especial knowledge or prudence and without whose presence the other justices would be unwilling or unable to proceed with the business of the court. Thus the wording of the commissions naming such a justice or justices, contained the Latin expression, "*quorum vos*, William Jones, (or *vestrum*, William Jones, John Smith, etc.) *unum* (*duos*, *tres*, etc.)

esse volumus, of whom we will that you, William Jones (or you, William Jones, John Smith, etc.), be one (two, three, etc.)." The abbreviation, *quorum,* was thus first applied to specified persons who were required to be present before a session could be opened, and it ultimately developed the meaning in which we now employ it, a prescribed number of the members of a group whose presence is necessary before business may be transacted.

raffle

Raffle was a game of chance in Chaucer's time, played with three dice. Every player in turn strove to throw a triplet, but if no one made that lucky cast, the winner was he who threw the highest pair. The game and its name were of French origin.

rake

The dissolute man whom we now speak of as a *rake* was said to be a *rakehell* four hundred years ago, and we still sometimes use the older word. The original term was cynical and figurative. It came from the thought that one would have to *rake hell* to find a person so vile as the dissolute scoundrel whose character was under consideration.

rapt, rapture

In its earliest use, *rapture* meant "an abduction," especially the forcible kidnaping of a woman. It was formed, in analogy with "capture," from *rapt,* at a time when *rapt* meant "abducted." The Latin source was *rapio,* to snatch, seize, which became *rape* in English, and the Latin participle *raptus,* seized, was shortened to *rapt.* The latter word, however, acquired a theological usage; it was applied to such personages as Elijah, Elisha, Enoch, and others who were said to have been *rapt*—that is, snatched—into heaven. From this theological use it acquired further extension into the senses now current, "carried into realms of emotion or deep thought." The course of *rapture* was similar, from "abduction" to "transportation into heaven," hence "mental or emotional transport."

recalcitrant (refractory)

Sometimes a stubborn horse or mule is content to let fly a few kicks without doing much damage, and let it go at that, but at other times he does not stop until he has broken up the cart to which he is hitched or has injured the driver. On the first occasion the animal is most fittingly described as *recalcitrant*, which literally means "kicking back," from Latin *re*, back, and *calcitro* (from *calx*, heel), to kick. He may, of course, do damage. A *refractory* animal or person, however, if the word is taken literally, is not content with being obstinate or stubborn; he breaks something. The word, from Latin *refractarius*, is derived from *refringo*, to break up.

record

In the days when few could read and fewer still could write, *record* was used in its literal sense, "to get by heart; fix in the memory." Its remote Latin source was *re*, back, and *cor*, heart, thus denoting that anything back in the heart was fixed in the memory. The more immediate Latin was the verb *recordor*. With the increase of knowledge of reading and writing, things that theretofore had been repeated from memory or fixed in the mind through repetition were reduced to writing, and *record* thus took on its present meanings.

reefer (peajacket)

Midshipmen, in the sailing vessels of a century ago, were often familiarly called "reefers," because, to quote an authority of that period, "they have to attend in the tops during the operation of taking in reefs." That duty, especially in cold weather, would prevent the midshipman from wearing the long topcoat of an officer, but as the midshipman was next in line to the lowest commissioned officer it was beneath his dignity to wear a sailor's peajacket. Accordingly he wore a close-fitting, heavy woolen coat. It was properly described as a "reefing jacket," but, because worn by a "reefer," it too was dubbed a *reefer*, and this became the common term for the garment of similar cut adopted by landlubbers. The "peajacket" of the sailor, incidentally, took its name, not from the garden vegetable, but from the Dutch word for "woolen," *pij*, identical with "pea" in sound.

remora

This strange fish, which attaches itself to moving objects by a curious sucking-disk along the top of its head, was known to ancient

453

Roman navigators. The fish would attach itself to the bottoms or sides of their slow-moving sailing vessels, and it was believed that they acted as a drag to the vessel, holding it back or even stopping its progress. It was for that reason that the Romans gave it the name *remora*, which means that which holds back, a delayer.

remorse

Our own language once contained an exact synonym of this—*ayenbite*, "again bite." There was a fourteenth-century English book under the title, *Ayenbite of Inwit*, literally, "Again-bite of Inner Wit," but which we would understand better if translated, "Remorse of Conscience." *Remorse* came to us, through French, from the Latin *remordeo*, and its literal meaning was exactly that of Old English *ayenbite*, "to bite again." Its use, however, was generally figurative, expressive of the inner bitings of one's mind, just as we use it now.

requiem

To many persons this term merely denotes a dirge played or sung at a funeral service. Its source, however, is found in the opening word of the solemn mass sung, in Latin, in Roman Catholic churches for the repose of the dead. The first line is, *Requiem æternam dona eis, Domine* (Give eternal rest to them, O Lord), in which *requiem* means "rest."

retaliate

This, in its Latin form, *retalio*, might be said to have been the equivalent of the English response, "And the same to you!" after an uncomplimentary remark. The source was *re*, back, and *talis*, such. *Retalio* thus meant "to give tit for tat, to return like for like." In legal usage it meant "to inflict punishment similar and equal to the injury that had been sustained." When introduced into the English language in the seventeenth century as *retaliate*, a new meaning was added, "to return good for good." That meaning is still recorded, but in general the verb has returned to the Latin sense.

reynard (renard, bruin, chanticleer, monkey)

Some time—probably in the tenth century, but that is not certain—there began to develop in France or Flanders a series of stories about animals. They were somewhat like the Uncle Remus stories of our present age, but the chief character was a fox, instead of a rabbit. The name given to the fox was *Renard* or *Renart*, in Old French, usually altered to *Reynard* in English. The tales became exceedingly popular and traveled by word of mouth all over western Europe, translated into the common speech of all races. Probably gifted story-tellers added new episodes to the narrative, for it became eventually a lengthy epic and the versions of one country did not wholly agree in detail with those of others. This folk tale dealt chiefly with the adventures of "Reynard the Fox" and the sly tricks that he played on separate occasions upon the other beasts. Like the fox, each of the beasts had its nickname. Several of the names thus bestowed became so familiar that they have since become synonymous names for the animals to whom they were applied. Thus our word *bruin* came from the tale which concerned "Bruin the Bear," *chanticleer* from "Chanticleer the Cock," and of course, *reynard* from "Reynard the Fox." Other names were "Noble the Lion," "Tybert (or Tibert) the Cat," "Isengrim the Wolf," "Kyward the Hare," etc. Our word *monkey* may also have originated in this epic, but that is not certain. It does not occur in the first printed English version, published by Caxton in 1481, but it does appear in a Low-German version of the same period in which the son of "Martin the Ape" is called *Moneke*. A similar version may already have been known in England, because the epic was familiar long before Caxton's time, or it may be that *moneke* was carried to England by German showmen. The ultimate sources of these nicknames is not known; they may have been inventions of the unknown "Uncle Remus" of a thousand years ago.

rhubarb

The plant was known to the ancient Greeks, and it was they who named it. The general theory explaining its source is that the plant was native to the regions along the river Volga, then known as the Rha. This, of course, was territory foreign to the Greeks, and was therefore classed as "barbarian." The plant, then, was described as *rha barbaron*, "from the barbarian (foreign) Rha." Its later Latin name was *rhabarbarum*, which, by elision, corruption, and partial restoration, passed into English *rubarbe* and, with Greek characteristics partly restored, *rhubarb*.

rigmarole

The reason is not known, but back in the fourteenth century a list or roll of names was called a *rageman*. Later this was altered to *ragman*, and the list itself was generally called *ragman roll*. Perhaps because, like in a dictionary, the subject matter in a list or roll changes frequently, *ragman roll* became equivalent to a series of disconnected statements. In the process its own name became altered, by the eighteenth century, to *rigmarole*.

rival

The Latin *rivalis*, whence our *rival*, referred to one who lives on the same stream with another—it came from *rivus*, a brook. That would make any such two persons neighbors, of course. But the ancients had many things in common with men of today. Two people who share the same stream are inevitably at odds. Each wishes to use the water in his own way, and is constantly contending with the other. If one uses the stream for irrigation, the other has no water for his cattle. In such fashion, *rival* came to mean one who contends with another for the same object.

road (raid, inroad)

In the early days of the English language, *road* meant the act of riding, a journey upon a horse. The horseback journey itself was made upon a "highway," if upon the principal way between two cities, or upon a "way," if a lesser path were used. At that time *road* had a sinister meaning also. Because of the fact that a group of mounted men often betokened a hostile intent, *road* sometimes signified a foray by mounted men, an attack upon some person or district. The Scottish word *raid*, which Sir Walter Scott brought into English usage, is now often used to convey that meaning, and the old sense is still present in our word *inroad*. In reality *road* and *raid* are merely different spellings of the Old English *rad*, but the Scottish development went no further than the hostile foray. Through association of ideas, probably, the act of riding a horse was carried over to the act of riding the waves; hence, *road* also came to mean a place where ships may anchor with safety, a roadstead. This sense, wherein space and security were implied, seems to have affected the development of *road* into its present chief use, a public thoroughfare. Strangely enough, this use which is now so common to us, was unknown much before the time of Shakespeare.

roam

It is traditional that *roam* was derived from *Rome*, and that it referred originally to the roundabout course taken by English pilgrims of the Middle Ages to that holy city. Language experts through the past hundred years, however, have searched for proof of that tradition and have been unable to find it. All that can thus far be said is, "source doubtful." The tradition is strengthened, however, by the fact that other countries, from which pilgrimages were also made to Rome, had similar words. Thus, in France, *romier* meant a pilgrim to Rome; in Spain, *romero*, a wanderer; in Italy, *romeo*, a wayfarer, wanderer.

robe

Some notion of the extreme poverty of the common people of Europe in the Middle Ages may be obtained from a treatise written by Sir John Fortescue. Though written (in Latin) in the latter part of the fifteenth century, his description would have served equally well in the preceding three or four hundred years. He says, in part, to quote from a translation made in the following century, that the French common people

be so impoverishid and distroyyd, that they may unneth lyve [barely live]. Thay drink water, thay eate apples, with bred right brown made of rye. Thay eate no fleshe, but if it be a litill larde, or of the entrails or heds of bests sclayne for the nobles and merchants of the land. They weryn no wollyn, but if it be a pore cote under their uttermost garment, made of grete convass, and cal it a frok. Their hosyn be of like canvas, and passen not their knee, wherfor they be gartrid and their thyghs bare. Their wifs and children gone bare fote.

457

Under conditions such as these the common people, little better than beasts, were reduced to treachery, thievery, and every sort of rascality. Footpads abounded. The readiest victims were wayfarers, especially such as traveled with few or no servants in inclement weather. The servants were usually dispersed easily by a gang of footpads, and it took but a quick hand to throw the traveler's cloak over his head and thus blindfold him. Lucky the traveler who was able to slip out of his cloak, or cape, and take to his heels (see ESCAPE). But the victim's cloak was almost as greatly prized as his purse, for it provided protection and warmth. It was through this latter association—of the cloak with the robber—that the cloak came to be called a *robe*, the thing "robbed."

rostrum

In this word we commemorate an event in Roman history dating back to 338 B.C. It happened off the coast of Antium, a spot of Italy that will again be long remembered under its present historic name, Anzio. The inhabitants of the region in those days had long been guilty of acts of piracy against Roman traders and of direct acts of aggression against the Roman people. It was determined, therefore to suppress them conclusively, and the consul, Mænius, was sent against them. He was wholly victorious, and brought back with him to Rome the bronze prows or beaks of six of the ships that he captured. These prows were attached to a platform, previously erected in the Forum, which was used by orators. That platform then became known as *rostra*, or "the beaks." The singular, *rostrum*, has become preferred in English use, although the plural, *rostra*, is historically correct.

rubber

The material which we call rubber was not known in Europe before the voyages of Columbus. The first probable mention occurs in the account written by that discoverer after his second trip, in which he tells of the "bouncing balls" with which the people of Haiti amuse themselves. But, although the Spaniards of the seventeenth century attempted to use the gummy substance to produce a waterproof canvas, no really satisfactory use had been found for "elastic gum," as it was then called, until near the end of the eighteenth century. The chemist, Joseph Priestley, then found that it possessed one useful quality—it did serve as an extremely satisfactory medium for rubbing out pencil marks. Because of that quality, the name "elastic gum" was dropped and the material has been called *rubber*, or *India rubber*, ever since.

sabotage

Nobody knows just when the French began to use the word *sabotage*. Probably it was formed a number of years ago when children found to their delight that, clattering together in their clumsy wooden sabots, they could drive their teachers or their parents to distraction. At least, in some such manner, *sabotage* came to signify any kind of nuisance that might or would bring about a desired end. But in 1887 it acquired a more sinister meaning. In that year the French General Confederation of Labor adopted *sabotage* as an instrument of industrial warfare. It was to include any kind of malicious damage that would injure an employer in any way—the disablement of machinery by dropping sand in its bearings, the destruction of tools, destruction of belting, spoilage of raw material—anything at all that was calculated to force an employer to yield to a demand by labor. The term came into English use by journalists in describing a long and disastrous strike upon the railway lines of France, at which time all the principles of *sabotage* were put into practice.

sacrament

All Roman soldiers, at the beginning of any military campaign, took an oath of allegiance. The usual method was that one soldier in each legion was called forward by its tribune and asked if he would swear that he would obey the commands of his generals and execute them promptly, that he would not desert, and that, in battle, he would not leave the ranks except to save the life of a Roman citizen. After that oath was taken, each of the other soldiers, in answering to his name, then said, "*Idem in me* (The same for me)." This oath was termed *sacramentum*, literally, an action of sacred nature. Its violation by any soldier was sufficient cause for the general to order his death without trial. The term was also used in courts of law, applying to the sum of money deposited by the contestants of a suit. But perhaps because of the formal nature attending the ceremony of *sacramentum*, the term was taken by Christian writers of the third and later centuries to be the equivalent of the Greek *mysterion*, a term originally applied to the secret rites attending the worship of Greek gods, but in Christian use applied to the rites connected with Christian worship. The term *sacrament* continues to apply to those rites observed in Roman Catholic and Protestant churches, whereas *mystery* is the term for similar rites in the Greek Orthodox Church. (Compare MYSTERY.)

sacrifice

Among most early religions based upon the worship of supernatural beings, the thought persisted that evil might be averted or some purpose achieved if something treasured were offered in exchange. The greater the treasure or the more it was cherished, it was thought, the greater the chance that the desired end might be obtained. When the religions became formalized, as they did in Egypt, Greece, and Rome, it was customary for the priests to indicate the treasure that would be most acceptable to the god for the particular occasion. Usually the offering was something that might be eaten, such as fruit, cakes, or farm animals, which were thought to be pleasing to the gods. When the offering had been determined, the person offering it first washed his hands and then, with clean hands to avoid pollution, carried or led it to the temple. Then, if the priest found the offering to be without blemish, for only such things were acceptable, it was declared sacred. Such an offering thus became, in Latin, *sacrificium*, literally, a thing made sacred, from *sacer*, sacred, and *facio*, make. The term, which became *sacrifice* in English, although chiefly retaining a religious sense, has also become loosely used for a surrender of anything that is valued, with or without a gain that may offset the loss.

sacrilege

Because it was the custom in ancient Rome to offer cakes, or fruits, or even pots of cooked beans upon the altars of the gods as tokens of gratitude, there was an always present temptation before the poor people of the city to steal and eat of these when no priest was in sight, or to conceal them in their clothing and make off with them.

Or if an animal had been offered up in sacrifice, bits of its charred flesh might sometimes be found clinging to a bone. But whatever the temptation to steal these or any other of the things that had been consecrated to the gods, the penalty exacted of any who were caught in such a crime was expected to deter all but the most daring or the most desperate. Such theft was called *sacrilegium*, literally, from *sacer*, sacred, and *lego*, to pick, the picking up of a sacred thing. If committed by a member of the lower classes, the penalty was always death. The victim might then be thrown to the wild beasts of the circus, or crucified, or burned alive as a public spectacle. Or under certain conditions his life might be permitted to drag out a few years longer by work in the mines. If the criminal were a person of higher class, he was deported. In later times, as recorded by Cicero, *sacrilege*, to use the English form, embraced not only the crime of stealing sacred objects, but also the act of profaning anything held sacred.

salary

The ancients knew that of all the things required for the support of human life salt was the most essential. The Romans called this element *sal*, and whenever the Roman soldier was sent to a foreign land he was given, over and above his regular pay, an amount of money for the purchase of salt. This was called his *salarium*, salt money. The amount varied, because salt might be hard to get and expensive in one country, but cheap and plentiful in another. Later, after the days of Augustus, *salarium* denoted the sum of money which a military officer or a governor of a province or a like official received at intervals, in addition to various supplies in kind. And still later, by the end of the third century A.D., all connection with the original notion of salt money had passed away and *salarium*, or *salary*, carried no more than the present meaning, "monetary payment at stated intervals."

saltcellar

This container for salt has nothing in common with the cellar of a house, except its spelling. And the spelling is a mistake. It should be, and originally was, *saler*. If we returned to that spelling, however, it would be redundant to leave *salt* in front of it, because *saler* itself denoted a saltcellar. The old word, used in the fourteenth and fifteenth centuries in England, was derived from the Latin adjective *salarius*, "pertaining to salt." The early English container was commonly of pewter, but was made of gold or silver for noble or wealthy persons. In the houses of the great, the position of the *saler* on the table separated the honored guests from those unhonored. Those whom the host honored, he placed "above the salt," or toward the end that he graced. All others sat "below the salt."

salver

Poison was the favored medium for getting rid of one's enemies in olden times, and was especially popular in the Middle Ages. Placed in the wine cup or the food, the victim had it swallowed before its presence was detected, and cook or servitor could be bribed to put the poison into the plate or cup. The real murderer might thus remain undetected—perhaps a near relative or, ostensibly, a friend. Because of the constant danger, wealthy men or men of high position kept a servant standing by his place at table whose duty it was to drink of the goblet and partake of the meat before his master touched them. After a due interval, if the servant were not taken sick, the master thought it safe for him to drink and eat. The Spanish term for such precautionary measures—for such attempted murders were especially frequent in Spain—was *salva*, derived from the Latin *salvo*, to save, protect. Then, eventually, because the master's food was invariably served and tested upon a separate tray, the term *salva* included the tray, as well as the victuals to be tasted. Under stricter laws, the need for this protection subsided. The tray, however, continued to retain the name. In England, perhaps in analogy with "platter" from "plate," or from resemblance to "silver," of which the tray was usually composed, *salva* was altered to *salver*. (See also CREDENCE.)

sandwich

For the entire duration of the American Revolution, or until March of 1782, the first lord of the British admiralty was John Montague, 4th Earl of Sandwich. He was exceedingly unpopular, and the period of his tenure of office was notorious for graft, bribery, and general mismanagement. The personal life of the Earl was also corrupt. Although married, he kept as his mistress a Miss Margaret or Marth Reay, by whom he had four children. (She was murdered by a rejected suitor in 1779.) And he was an inveterate gambler. It was in his honor, because he was first lord of the admiralty at the time of their discovery, that the Hawaiian Islands were first called and long known as the Sandwich Islands. But the misdemeanors of the Earl have now been forgotten and he is remembered only for his introduction of the convenient quick lunch composed of two slices of bread with a slice of meat or other filling between them. It is said that this repast, called a *sandwich* in his honor, was devised at his direction during an exciting all-night session at cards when he did not wish to leave the gaming table for a full meal. But, unfortunately, no record has been found of the date of the occasion. The sandwich cannot be said to have been invented by the Earl, however, because the Romans had a similar slight repast, called *offula*, many centuries before his time.

sarcasm

The Greeks loved metaphor. They loved to compare human emotions and human tendencies with the actions or traits exhibited by animals. And, because dogs were ever at hand for purposes of comparison, the ways of the dog served as convenient and well-understood metaphor. Thus they took the word *sarkazo* and gave it a figurative meaning. Literally it meant "to tear flesh" after the manner of dogs, to snap and rip. The physical effect upon the animal or person thus attacked by a fierce dog was so similar to the mental effect resulting from a sharp and stinging taunt or gibe that *sarkazo* seemed perfectly fitted to the latter meaning also. The caustic remark became *sarkasmos*. Altered by Latin *sarcasmus*, this ultimately became English *sarcasm*.

sarcophagus

Generally the ancient Greeks disposed of their dead very much as do we of the present age, either by burial or by cremation. But there were some who adopted a burial custom found in Egypt. In place of the ordinary coffin of baked clay or the elaborately carved stone tomb, a stone coffin was procured from a special region in Asia Minor. The stone of that region was almost pure lime and,

463

according to Pliny, a coffin made of it had the power to completely destroy a body interred in it within forty days. Because of its properties, such a coffin was called *sarcophagus*, the name being derived from Greek *sarx*, flesh, and *phagos*, eating.

sardonic, sardonyx

There grew on the island of Sardinia, according to ancient Grecian folklore, a plant that was to be shunned above all others. It had a fearful effect upon anyone so unfortunate as to eat it. The mouth and face became horribly drawn up as if in scornful laughter. The victim was fortunate if he did not die. Because the Greek name of Sardinia was Sardo, this appearance of laughter was called *Sardonios gelos*, Sardinian laughter. This then led to the transfer of *Sardonios* to any laughter that was scornful or mocking, and, hence, to any scorn or mockery. The Greek *Sardonios* was first altered in English to *Sardonian*, but French development had led to *sardonique* which, altered to *sardonic* in English, eventually replaced the earlier form. The name of the semiprecious stone, *sardonyx*, bears only an accidental resemblance. Its name is really composed of the two elements, *sard* and *onyx*, because the stone itself consists of layers of onyx alternating with layers of sard.

Saturday

Egyptian astronomers believed that there were only seven planets and that these all revolved about the earth. From the most remote they were successively Saturn, Jupiter, Mars, the Sun, Venus, Mercury, and the Moon, using our present names. These planets were held to preside in the same order over the twenty-four hours of the day, and the day of the week was accordingly named after the name of the planet which presided over its first hour. As Saturday (the day of Saturn) began the Egyptian week, its first hour and each successive seventh hour—the eighth, fifteenth, and twenty-second hour, respectively—was presided over by the planet Saturn. The twenty-third hour was then governed by Jupiter, and the twenty-fourth by Mars. The first hour of the next day was therefore presided over by the Sun, the next in order, and the second day of the Egyptian week received the name of that planet. In the same manner of reckoning, the Moon presided over the third day, Mars over the fourth, Mercury over the fifth, Jupiter over the sixth, and Venus over the seventh, when Saturn again took over the first hour of the beginning of the next week. Although the Egyptians regarded the week as beginning with the day of Saturn, the Hebrews regarded that day as the last day of the week, because, it is said, of their hatred toward their Egyptian oppressors when they fled from the country. The week of seven days was not adopted in Rome until the reign of Constantine, A.D. 324-37. For lack of a better system of nomenclature, probably, the days continued to be named after the planets, following the ancient pagan Egyptian system, though with Saturday (*dies Saturni*, the day of Saturn) as the seventh day. Teutonic mythology did not embrace a god equivalent to the Roman god, Saturn, god of harvests, after whom the planet was named, so, in Old English, a partial translation of the Latin *dies Saturni* became *Sæternesdæg*, which has descended through many shifts into our present *Saturday*.

savage

Most plants and animals growing or living in forested country are wild. For this reason the Romans spoke of all such things as *silvaticus*. The term was really equivalent to our word "sylvan," of or pertaining to forests, being derived from *silva*, forest, but was transferred to mean the plants and animals found in such places, especially the animals. Thus *silvaticus* acquired the meaning, "wild." The popular sound of the word was *salvaticus*, and this, through the general alteration of Latin words occurring in France, became *salvage* in Old French and *sauvage* in later French, in which form it was carried to England. Gradual change brought it to the present form, *savage*, and its use to apply especially to persons or animals thought originally to dwell in forests, hence of ferocious nature.

scapegoat

And he (Aaron) shall take the two goats, and present them before the Lord . . . And Aaron shall cast lots upon the two goats; one lot for the Lord, and the other lot for the *scapegoat*. And Aaron shall bring the goat upon which the Lord's lot fell, and offer him for a sin offering. But the goat, on which the lot fell to be the *scapegoat*, shall be presented alive before the Lord, to make an atonement with him, and to let him

465

go for a *scapegoat* into the wilderness . . . And Aaron shall lay both his hands upon the head of the live goat, and confess over him all the iniquities of the children of Israel, and all their transgressions in all their sins, putting them upon the head of the goat, and shall send him away by the hand of a fit man into the wilderness.

The quotation is from the sixteenth chapter of Leviticus, in the King James Version of the Bible. Thus, *scapegoat* entered the language and has become applied to one chosen arbitrarily or at random to receive the punishment merited by a group.

scavenger

It was the custom in London and some of the other cities of England, during the late Middle Ages especially, to inspect the wares and collect a fee or toll from foreign merchants who might exhibit their wares for sale. The Old English law called such a toll a *sceawung*, "showing," but after the Norman invasion the Anglo-French form *scawage*, later *scavage*, was adopted. The man authorized by the city officials to collect these tolls was, of course, a *scavager*, which later became modern *scavenger*. (Similar alterations are found in "messenger" from "message," "passenger" from "passage," "porringer" from "porridge," etc.) But the duties of the scavenger as inspector and collector of tariffs in the early days could not have occupied his full time, because as early as the fifteenth century we find that he was also expected to keep the streets clean. This latter duty the *scavenger* has retained, even though his original office, showing the source of the name, has long been abolished.

scepter

The *skeptron* of the Homeric period of Greece was a walking-stick, a cane or staff for the aged or infirm. But such a staff was also carried by foot travelers as a weapon of defense, or perhaps of offense. Either as cane or weapon, however, it received ornamentation and embellishment, and was handed down from father to son in token of transfer of authority. It became enriched with gold or silver studs, and perhaps adorned with gems for persons of high rank or leadership. In time this simple staff, transformed into a jeweled rod of gold and known to us as *scepter*, became a symbol of the authority of the leader of an empire, a monarch.

466

school

The Greek *scholē* which was the original source of *school*, once meant just the opposite from what the schoolboy of today thinks of that institution. It meant vacation, leisure, rest. The education of a Greek boy was by private teachers in reading, writing, arithmetic, singing, and gymnastics. But no man ever considered his education to be completed. His leisure time was spent in listening to the discussions of learned men, and thus this product of leisure, this use of one's spare time came also to be called *scholē*. Eventually the Greeks used the term for the lectures or discussions themselves, and ultimately it included as well the place wherein the instruction was given. It was the latter sense which descended to English use.

schooner

Captain Andrew Robinson, of Gloucester, Massachusetts, is credited with being the builder of the first vessel of this type. It was completed in 1713, according to evidence, and attracted a good deal of notice. Its launching was attended with much interest. When the blocks were knocked away and the vessel slid gracefully into the water, an excited bystander, according to the story often told, is said to have exclaimed, "Oh, how she *scoons*!" Captain Robinson overheard the remark and, not having decided what to call the new type of vessel, spoke up and said, "A *scooner* let her be." The subsequent spelling, *schooner*, was probably due to the influence of "school." The source of the bystander's *scoon* may have been the Scottish word *scon*, "to make flat stones skip over the water."

scot-free

In olden times, although the source is uncertain, a *scot* was the amount that one owed for entertainment, usually the amount of one's share in that entertainment, as for the drinks in a tavern. *Scot-free* thus described one whose debt was assumed by others or whose drink was "on the house." From that beginning, the meaning of *scot-free* came to be freedom from other kinds of payment, as taxes or tolls, and from that it became extended to freedom from punishment.

467

scruple

Anyone whose shoe has worn thin enough for a nail to press through into the foot can have some sympathy for the sufferings constantly threatening the old Romans. They were not troubled with nails coming through the soles of their sandals, but there was every likelihood of picking up a sharp pebble—and no stocking even to protect the tender foot. The word for such a pebble or pointed bit of stone was *scrupulus*, from which our *scruple* developed. It is easy to see how the uneasiness one would feel from a pebble in the sandal gave rise to the figurative use of *scrupulus* for an uneasiness of the mind. The small apothecaries' weight, *scruple*, came from the same Latin source. And our adjective, *scrupulous*, which denotes extreme caution and carefulness, suggests the care that the old Romans would take in traversing a road described as *scrupulosus*, "full of tiny sharp pebbles."

senate

In the republics of Greece and Rome the government was divided between the popular assembly and a group of men selected for their wisdom. But because it was considered that full wisdom came only with advanced years, all members of the latter group were persons of advanced age, old men. For this reason the Roman group was *senatus*, a council of old men, from *senex*, old. Thus, to be literal, a member of our own *senate* should be an old man, an age set by our Constitution, however, as not less than thirty.

Septuagint

There were really seventy-two of these men, according to the story, although the Latin *septuaginta* means "seventy" only. The story was supposed to have been told by a man of Cyprus, Aristeas by name, in a letter to his brother Philocrates, some time during the reign of Ptolemy II, 285 to 247 B.C. It relates that the king had been requested to have a copy of the laws of the Jews translated into Greek. The king agreed, and the chief priest of the Jews was asked to appoint six learned men from each of the twelve tribes to perform the task. These seventy-two men were lodged in a

468

house on the island of Pharos, the letter went on to say, and there they completed their difficult task within the space of seventy-two days. Modern scholars do not wholly accept this story. They agree, however, that the Jewish laws were translated into Greek in Alexandria and at the time stated, but do not believe that it was done at the request of Ptolemy. Nor by seventy-two men in seventy-two days. They think it more likely that the translation was made solely for the benefit of the Greek-speaking Jews who lived in Alexandria. The remainder of the Old Testament was later translated. Nevertheless, this earliest Greek version of the Old Testament, traditionally ascribed to seventy-two (or, in round numbers, seventy) Jewish scholars, has become known as the Septuagint, often expressed by the Roman numeral, "LXX."

shagreen (chagrin)

The skill of the metal workers of Damascus and Arabia was gradually acquired by European artisans after the Crusades. Along with that skill the new workmen also copied many of the practices which the Orientals had learned through long centuries of experience. Thus it had long been known that nothing was better for rubbing and polishing fine metal than the hard and rough leather from the rump of a horse or ass. The Arabian term for such leather was *saghri*. Both the practice and the name were borrowed by Europeans, but to the Venetian worker it became *sahgrin*. The French, taking it from the Venetians, called it *chagrin*. Some English workers may then have retained the French spelling, but the majority, influenced by the sound of the French word, called and spelled it *shagreen*. The leather that we now know by this name may derive from any one of several land or marine animals. It is generally dyed green, probably after the color the old-time leather assumed after long use in polishing gold, silver, or copper. The French term, *chagrin*, also acquired a later figurative meaning, and was borrowed in this sense by the English. Because of the rough surface of the leather, which gently abraded the metal, *chagrin* came to be applied to cares and worries which fret the mind. From this our present sense arose, a feeling of disappointment, vexation, or humiliation which frets the spirit.

469

shambles

In its earliest sense in our language a *shamble*, although then spelled *scomul*, meant a stool. (By a roundabout course it had come from the Latin *scamellum*, a little bench.) From stool, *shamble* became the name of the bench, table, or stall where meat was sold. Then, although after the fifteenth century always spelled in plural form, through the constant association of *shambles* with the blood of meat, the meaning was extended to cover the place where animals were slaughtered for meat. From this its meaning was further extended figuratively to any place of bloody slaughter, especially a place of widespread carnage, such as a battlefield. But, because battles are usually accompanied by wholesale destruction, the word *shambles* acquired a still further figurative sense in World War II, when it was often used to designate the scenes of destruction brought about by the bombing of cities. In the latter application blood or bloodshed is no longer essentially attached to the word, as it was for many centuries.

shibboleth

This Hebrew word actually means "ear of grain" but, because of the odd use to which the word was put on one occasion, it has taken on an altogether different meaning. This meaning arises from a bit of history told in the Bible, in the twelfth chapter of the Book of Judges. It is related, in this chapter, how the men of Ephraim rose against Jephthah and his army, but the latter were victorious in the fight that followed. In their victory they seized the passages over the river Jordan where the fleeing Ephraimites must cross to save their lives. But Jephthah had posted guards at the fords and had given them a catchword by which they could tell friend from foe. That word was *shibboleth*. Jephthah knew that an Ephraimite "could not frame to pronounce it right," but would say, "Sibboleth." All the Ephraimites were thus detected and slain, to the number of "forty and two thousand." Hence, *shibboleth*, regardless of its original meaning, has come to refer to any catchword or slogan or pet phrase, such as one used by a political party.

shrapnel

The inventor, for whom this missile was named, was Henry Shrapnel. He was born in Wiltshire, England, in 1761, entered the army when a young man, and began the study of hollow projectiles as a young officer of twenty-three. He was a colonel, however, before the most notable invention resulting from his studies was accepted by the army. The official name of the invention at the time of its adoption was "*Shrapnel's* shot" or "*Shrapnel's* shell," and it was not long before *Shrapnel* had become the customary abridgment. The first actual test of the new shell in combat came in 1803 when the British seized a portion of Surinam from the Dutch and established British Guiana. In the Peninsular War of 1808 to 1814, in which England fought against Napoleon to free Portugal and Spain from French domination, the *shrapnel* was proved to have high military value. The inventor died in 1842, and had then attained the rank of lieutenant general.

shrew, shrewd

Many centuries ago in Old England the name *shrew* (Old English *screawa*) was applied to a common small animal about the size and appearance of a mouse, though having a long sharp snout. The source of the name is unknown. The animals, living chiefly in the woods and feeding upon insects, grubs, and the like, were not destructive, and for some peculiar reason the name by which they were once known dropped into disuse for five or six hundred years. But the little animals had one characteristic and were thought to possess another which seem to have caused their name to be used in another manner. They were found to be exceedingly pugnacious. Two would fight over a morsel of food until one was killed; the fallen would then be eaten by the victor. They were also thought to be venomous, and, in popular superstition, if one were to run over the leg or body of a farm animal, that animal was then believed to be poisoned. It might be cured if a live shrew were imprisoned in a hole bored into an ash tree, and then twigs of that ash gently brushed over the affected parts of the animal. Because of the pugnacity and suspected venomosity, the term *shrew* was transferred to either a man or woman whose character was evil or malignant, especially to one, usually a woman (now always a woman), whose disposition was to nag, scold, or rail. This led to the formation of the verb *to shrew*. Its past participle was *shrewd*, and this, in its early sense, meant evil-disposed, vicious, dangerous, but has passed into sharp or acute, or into astute or keen-witted.

silhouette

France was ill prepared when, at the outbreak of the Seven Years' War in 1756, Louis XV plunged his government into the conflict. Under the domination of his mistress, Madame de Pompadour, the government had become completely corrupt and on the verge of bankruptcy. Both Canada and India, partly French possessions at the time, speedily fell to the British through lack of competent generals and adequate support. In 1759, hoping for a miracle, Madame de Pompadour induced the king to replace the French minister of finance with a man of her own choice, a man of fifty who had made a small name for himself by the publication of studies on governmental finance. His name was Étienne de Silhouette. Immediately upon assuming office the new minister imposed systems calling for the most rigorous economy. These appeared to be directed especially against the nobility, whose members found the restrictions placed upon them extremely irritating. They might endure the conversion of their table plate into currency, but they poked fun at regulations calling for coats without folds and snuffboxes made of wood. At this time, by chance, there had also been revived the ancient art of profile drawing; that is, drawings made by tracing the outlines of shadows cast by a light—an art said to have been invented by the daughter of Dibutades, in ancient Corinth, who traced the outline of her lover's face as thrown in shadow on the wall. The revival became popular. But, because they replaced costly painted portraits, these drawings too, along with the snuffboxes, the coats, and other petty economies, were sneeringly referred to as "*à la Silhouette*, according to Silhouette." Through popular clamor, perhaps also because of incompetence, Étienne de Silhouette was obliged to relinquish his post after nine months. His name, however, had become permanently attached to the profiles which are so easily drawn.

simony

In the eighth chapter of Acts in the New Testament, we are told of the conversion of a magician to Christianity by the Apostles. That is, the magician professed to be converted, but it soon turned out that he was not. He had himself been skilled, and was able to perform marvelous tricks. Hence, when he saw the miraculous cures effected by Peter and Philip simply through the laying on of hands, he thought it to be a new kind of sorcery, one that he could use to advantage. So he sought out the Apostles and offered them money to teach him these tricks. "But Peter said unto him, Thy money perish with thee, because thou hast thought that the gift of God may be purchased with money." The name of this sorcerer was Simon—sometimes referred to as "Simon *Magus*," that is, "Simon the magician." From his name and the sin that he committed, the purchase or sale of ecclesiastical position is now described by the word *simony*.

sincere

It has been often said that *sincere* came from two Latin words *sine*, without, and *cera*, wax. This fanciful source was explained as arising from the alleged practice by Roman artisans of using wax for filling cracks or holes in furniture, whence *sine cera* would mean "without flaw; pure; clean." Modern scholars, however, do not accept that dubious account. The present belief is that the Latin *sincerus*, which became *sincere* in English, came from *sine*, without, and some lost word that was akin to *caries*, decay. It would thus be synonymous with the Greek *akeratos*, without taint.

sinecure

This began as a church term, part of the Latin phrase *beneficium sine cura*, a benefice without care (of souls). It was a practice of the Church of England, developing in the seventeenth century, upon occasion to reward a deserving rector by alloting to him a parish in which he did not reside and for whose parishioners he had no responsibility. Such a benefice was highly desirable, for it entailed no work in return for the good living that it brought. The actual work of the parish was performed by a vicar, though his absent superior got the better pay. The ecclesiastical practice was abolished in 1840, but the expression—at first *sine-cura*, eventually *sinecure*— had long since become a term for any office or position which the incumbent might fill with a minimum of labor, or none at all, in return for a fixed income.

sinister

Roman augurs, when studying the heavens for signs which, it was believed, would indicate the will of the gods, faced toward the south. The eastern heavens from which favorable omens were expected, were therefore upon the left; unfavorable omens in the west or toward the right. Thus among the Romans, *sinister*, which means left or left-hand, meant lucky, favorable, or auspicious, and *dexter*, which means right or right-hand, meant unlucky or inauspicious. But Greek augurs faced the north when looking for signs from the heavens. The eastern or favorable omens, accordingly, appeared on the right side, and the unfavorable ones upon the left. Roman poets, who almost invariably aped Greek customs, followed the Greek thought in this field as well. Hence, because the writings of the Roman poets were popular in the literary world of England in the sixteenth and seventeenth centuries, *sinister*, although a Latin word, has come down to us in the sense ascribed by the Greek augurs to the left or western side of the heavens; hence, of evil aspect.

siren

When Odysseus was nearing the end of his long homeward journey after the Trojan War, according to Homer, he was told one evening by the sorceress Circe of some of the perils that yet awaited him. The first would be the sweet-voiced sea nymphs, the *Sirens*. These, she told him sang the most beguiling songs of all the world. But woe betide any passing sailor who heard them. In his enchantment he would leap into the sea to join the nymphs, and nevermore see his home and loved ones again. Circe counseled Odysseus to seal the ears of all his companions with wax before passing that shore, and have himself bound most securely to the mast, his men warned to tie him even more tightly if he signaled them to unbind him. Thus

474

Odysseus and his crew safely passed this danger, but it is because of the dulcet lure anciently thought to have come from the throats of those beautiful nymphs that the name *siren* has been applied to various warning signals of penetrating tone.

sirloin

The story is told of various British monarchs. Henry VIII was the first to receive credit. That would be some time between 1509 and 1547, although he did not receive the credit until 1655. Next, in 1732, Jonathan Swift bestowed the credit upon James I, who reigned from 1603 to 1625. The last to be credited, in 1822, was Charles II, ruler between 1660 and 1685. In each tale the monarch was supposed to have been so delighted with the quality of a roasted upper portion of a loin of beef, upon some special occasion, that he drew out his sword, touched the beef with it, and said, "Hereafter thou shalt be dubbed 'Sir Loin.'" Aside from the profusion of "dubbers," the only trouble with the tale is that it is utterly fictitious. The only story in the word is that some time about 1600 it began to be misspelled. For many years this cut of meat had been known as *surloin*, which, from *sur*, over or above, meant nothing more than the cut over the loin. This correct spelling persisted, but after the foregoing stories began to be taken seriously, everyone began to shift to *sirloin*.

size (assize)

Here we have a word passing through a great shift in meaning. The parent word, which became *assize*, was borrowed from France after the Norman Conquest and meant "a sitting," as of a legislative body or court, a meaning that it still retains. *Assize* also began to embrace the regulations established at such sittings, specifically those relating to weights and measures and, thus, to quantity and dimension. In all these senses, however, the word *assize* was taken by many people, especially by those untrained in law, to be merely "a size." And because it was the common people who were most affected by quantity and dimensions, *size* became the common term for all standards of measurement or specified quantities and, ultimately, for dimensions or magnitude of any sort.

skeptic (sceptic)

Schools of philosophy in ancient Greece were almost as plentiful as the philosophers. Thus, in the third century B.C., came the philosopher Pyrrho who carried some of the earlier theories a stage further and thereby provided a new name for his followers. His thesis, in the main, was that human judgment is liable to uncertainty, for no one can be absolutely certain that that which seems to be is exactly what it seems. This thesis he extended into ten topics of argument, as recorded by one of his disciples. His followers came to be called the *skeptikoi*, the hesitants, or philosophers who would assert nothing positively, but only thought. Through later extensions of this philosophy, *skeptic* reached its present senses.

slave

Prior to the Christian Era little was known of the people living north of the Carpathian Mountains, in the vast regions now embracing, in particular, Poland and adjacent areas. The names of a few tribes had been mentioned by some Roman and Greek historians, but few travelers or even military expeditions had penetrated those lands. By the sixth century A.D., however, the northern tribes along the Baltic began pressing to the west against their more warlike neighbors, the Germans, along the banks of the Elbe. The Germans called them *Sclavs*. In the inevitable conflicts that followed, the fierce Germans found these people no match for their arms and were able to take many captives. Some were sold into serfdom to willing Roman and Greek buyers of the south, and others were held in bondage by their captors. In time the entire population of parts of their land were reduced to servility by their Teutonic neighbors, and *Sclav* or *Sclave* became a term of contempt applied to anyone of servile character or actually in bondage. Later it became a synonym for the latter condition only. When it came into English use, the term retained the initial *scl-* until the sixteenth century, then our present form, *slave*, began to appear.

smog

London has been troubled throughout its history by occasional blankets of fog, so dense that traffic becomes dangerous. The condition is aggravated, especially during the heating season, by the vast volumes of black smoke rising from the soft coal used by householders and industries and in public buildings. The result is almost total darkness at those times. Many other cities suffer from similar combinations of smoke and fog, although possibly none to the same extent as London. In 1905, according to the London *Globe* in its issue of July 27 of that year, "at a meeting of the Public Health Congress Dr. Des Voeux did a public service in coining a new word for the London fog, which was referred to as *smog*, a compound of 'smoke' and 'fog.'" Adoption of this portmanteau word has been slow, although it is recognized in all the dictionaries.

snob

No one knows the origin. It may be related to an Old Norse word that means "dolt," but in the late eighteenth century *snob* was a British slang term for a shoemaker. Students at Cambridge took up the term and applied it somewhat more broadly to any townsman, to one not attending the university. Perhaps some Cambridge citizens, to impress their acquaintances, began to ape the speech and mannerisms of students or lecturers at the university. It is not known. But for some such cause, *snob* became applied to one who affects to be what he is not, in birth, wealth, or breeding, or to one who seeks unduly the society of persons possessing those qualities.

sock

The professional comedian of ancient Rome, he who acted in comedy, took every precaution when he stepped upon the stage to have no one mistake him for other than a comic actor. Of course he wore the grinning mask which, by its hair or beard, complexion or wrinkles, or other well-known markings would indicate whether the character he was portraying was old or young, sick or well. (See PERSON.) But in addition he wore upon his feet a pair of loose leather slippers, slippers of a type that, in Rome, were worn only by women or by effeminate men. These were in sharp distinction from the *cothurnus*, worn by actors in tragedy, which laced high up the calf of the leg. The soft, low slipper—*soccus*, it was called—of comedy was shaped somewhat like the modern pump, but loosely covered little more than the toes and heel. These light shoes were the forerunners of our *socks*. Romans carried the name *soccus* to Germany, whence, abridged to *soc*, it traveled to England. There, even until recent times, the name—*sock*, by that time—still meant a light slipper. But, many years ago, *sock* also came to be applied to any soft covering for the foot, worn inside of a boot or shoe. Neither hose nor stocking then covered the foot, for these were coverings for the leg. Eventually foot and leg covering were attached, and *sock* then became the term for a short stocking, extending to the calf of the leg.

solecism

There was anciently a colony in the province of Cilicia, Asia Minor, known as Soli. The colony had been settled by Grecians, and the inhabitants thought they spoke Greek. But the ears of fastidious Athenians were greatly offended by the barbarous, uncouth speech of these outlanders. Words were mispronounced; speech was slurred, but most prominent were the terrific mistakes in grammar. To the Athenian, such speech was an unpardonable offense. He called it *soloikismos*, the speech of *Soli*; hence, incorrectness. Through the Latin, this has become *solecism* in English.

soldier, solidus

It may be that the members of the far-flung legions of the Roman Empire sometimes wearied of waiting for their pay. That may have been the reason, we do not know; but at some time during the first or second century A.D., they began to refer to the *aurum*, the gold coin used in paying them, as "solid," perhaps because it was better than promises. The term they used, of course, was *solidus*, and this term was later generally employed when speaking of military pay. The *solidus* was a fractional part of the silver pound, *libra*, and was further divided into other fractional coins called *denarii*. (These names were subsequently adopted for British currency, thus giving rise to the initials, £, s, d, now referred to as pound, shilling, pence.) Among members of the Roman military outposts, where Latin was mingled with native speech, *solidus* became corrupted in France to *solde* or *soude* or similar variant, and the person who received military pay became a *soldior* or *soudiour* or the like. The name had many other spellings when it passed into English, but ultimately became *soldier*.

spinnaker

The facts are not ascertainable. Apparently no one kept a record. But from such evidence as there is it would appear that some yacht owner in the 1860's devised a new sail for his racing vessel. It was rigged at right angles from the vessel's side and extended from the masthead to the deck, ballooning far out to get full advantage of all the breeze. The name of the vessel carrying this unusual sail is said to have been *Sphinx*. Its crew had great difficulty in pronouncing that name. "Spinnicks," was as near as they could make it. They spoke of the new great sail devised for this yacht as "Spinnicker's sail," and, so the story goes, *spinnaker* the name became.

spoonerism

The Reverend William A. Spooner of New College, Oxford, England, who was born in 1844 and died in 1930, was one of many of us who, when speaking, accidentally transpose the initial sounds of two or more words, sometimes to one's own great embarrassment and the hilarity of one's audience. Such slips are usually the result of nervousness, sometimes from too great an effort on the part of a speaker to say a difficult combination of words correctly. Such transposition of letters or sounds is known in rhetoric as "metathesis." To their horror, radio announcers have been known to make some that were extremely amusing to their listeners. But the Reverend Mr. Spooner constantly made these unintentional transpositions. Thus, upon one occasion, when he intended to say that something was "a half-formed wish," he convulsed his listeners with "a half-warmed fish." Upon another he was heard to refer to "our queer old dean," when he meant to say, "our dear old queen." He is said to have chided a student who had "hissed my mystery lecture." But perhaps the most notable of his numerous slips was the hymn that he announced: "When Kinkering Congs Their Titles Take." From his affliction, this type of metathesis is now often called *spoonerism*.

spruce

Anything from Prussia or native to that region was said to be *Pruce*, in England of the Middle Ages. Thus there was "Pruce beer" from the "Pruce tree," and "Pruce leather," and the country itself was

"Pruceland." Gradually, through the fourteenth and later centuries, *Pruce* absorbed an initial "s" and became *Spruce*. This in turn was applied to the products of Prussia—or "Sprucia," as it was now sometimes called. There was then "Spruce beer" from the "Spruce tree," "Spruce leather," and so on. Then, during the sixteenth century especially, men of fashion began to ape, in their dress, the manners of particular countries. Thus in the reign of Henry VIII and for some time thereafter it was the style for courtiers to affect the garb of the nobles of Prussia, in doublets of crimson velvet, cloaks of satin, silver chains hanging from the neck, large, broad-brimmed hats with flowing feathers, and other fanciful attire. Men thus gaily and smartly appareled were said to be *spruce*.

staple

The term that now means the chief commodity of a place, once had a quite different meaning. The German word *stapol*, which had once meant a post or pillar, developed into the English word *staple* which came to mean a U-shaped pin or rod to be driven into a post or pillar or the like as a fastener. We still attach such a meaning to the word. But through another line of development the German term came also to designate a place, specifically the place where the judgment of a king was administered. Thence, borrowed by the French in the form *estaple* (modern *étape*), its meaning was altered to specify a market place, emporium. By the thirteenth or fourteenth century, the French *estaple*, transformed to *staple* in English, especially designated a town appointed by the king in which the merchants had a monopoly on the purchase of certain goods for export. Thus, for example, as long as the port of Calais was an English possession, that is from about 1390 to 1558, that city was the *staple* for the export of all English wool. Its merchants had the exclusive right to purchase wool for export. Other important cities enjoyed similar privileges. Gradually the meaning of *staple* underwent reversal. From the place where certain wares could be bought, it came to have the present meaning of the chief wares to be found at a certain place.

steelyard

Royal permission was granted, in the thirteenth century, to merchants of Hamburg, Lübeck, and Cologne to set up a trading association, a hanse or branch of the Hanseatic League, in the city of London. These merchants took a place of business near London Bridge on the north bank of the Thames, and designated it, *Stalhof.* The name merely signifies a "courtyard" (*Hof*) in which a "sample" (*Stal*) may be inspected or tested. Suspended in the courtyard there was one of the old-style Roman balances for the weighing of goods, a balance with a short arm or beam from which an object is hung at the end, and its weight determined from a counterpoise slid along the opposite and much longer beam. But the German *Stal*, sample, has exactly the same sound as the German *Stahl*, steel, and the latter word was much more familiar to Londoners. Hence, *Stalhof* began to be translated, "Steel yard," as if the German name were "*Stahlhof*," and this locality was long known thereafter as "Steel yard." At the same time it became customary to refer to the old Roman balance in the courtyard as the "*Steel-yard* beam," a name shortened later to *steelyard.*

stentorian

Among the Greeks at the siege of Troy, as recorded in Homer's *Iliad,* was a herald named *Stentor.* Homer described him as having "a voice of bronze" and with a cry "as loud as the cry of fifty men." His name passed into a Greek saying, "to shout louder than *Stentor*," whence *stentorian* became an English synonym for "extremely loud-voiced." Greek legend says that *Stentor* died, however, as the result of a vocal contest with Hermes, herald of the gods.

stigma

Greek slaves, on the whole, were treated leniently. But they were usually captives taken as a result of warfare, and it was but natural that escape was eagerly sought. If they did not succeed, however, they were returned to their owners and, to make further attempts to escape more difficult, they were branded upon the forehead, usually by a hot iron, but sometimes with a tattooed mark. Such brand or mark was called *stigma*, a word borrowed by the Romans for a similar mark. The Greeks used the letter "phi" (ϕ), initial of *pheutikos*, fugitive; the Roman mark was the letter "F," which might designate either *fur*, for a slave branded as a "thief," or *fugitivus*, for a "fugitive." Sometimes a black coloring substance was put in the wound to make the mark more prominent. In Rome, a person so marked was said to be *literatus*, that is, "lettered," a term that later designated a person well educated. From the practice of branding slaves the meaning of *stigma* extended to embrace any mark or sign of shame or disgrace.

stoic

About three centuries before Christ, the Greek philosopher Zeno founded a new sect. Various principles were expounded by the founder, but the supreme duty of the wise man, he maintained, was complete and serene submission to divine will. The doctrines were taught by Zeno in the corridor on the north side of the market place in Athens, a place usually referred to as *Stoa Poikile*, "the Painted Porch," from the frescoes representing scenes of the Trojan War which adorned it. (See also INK.) Consequently, from the place where lectures on the new philosophy were given—the "Stoa"—the followers of this school became known as *Stoics*. And through the fact that the most notable of the doctrines was that true wisdom is superior to passion, joy, or grief, both *stoic* and *stoicism* came to be regarded as indifference to feelings of pleasure and pain.

succinct

The Roman tunic, like the Greek chiton, was a simple garment worn by all classes of people. In its early form it was a wide woolen sheet, folded across the body and pinned over one shoulder, sometimes with a hole on the opposite side for the other arm. This garment was thus sleeveless and entirely open down one side. A girdle or *cinctura* just below the chest held it in place, however. But the later tunic was made very much like a long shirt, and usually with short sleeves. It extended just above the knees, and was also kept in place by a *cinctura*. For freedom of movement, it was common practice to loosen the garment above the *cinctura*, thus having a fold of the tunic over the girdle. And for still greater freedom, as when one was at work, the tunic was shortened still more, tucked still higher under the girdle. Thus from the two words *sub*, under, and *cingo*, **to** gird, was developed *succingo*, to tuck up; hence, to shorten. The participle, *succinctus*, shortened, produced our adjective, *succinct*.

supercilious

Actually the Latin source, *supercilium*, means the eyebrow, from *super*, above, and *cilium*, eyelid. But the haughty man who looks contemptuously at those whom he regards as inferiors, inevitably looks at them with his eyebrows raised. The old Romans were aware of this characteristic lifting of the brows in expression of scorn, and even with them *superciliosus* denoted an air of disdain.

superman

The German philosopher of the nineteenth century, F. W. Nietzsche, used the German term, *übermensch*, to describe his notion of the ideal man evolved from the present type. This, by literal translation, would produce the English "overman" or perhaps "beyondman," but neither of these terms seemed agreeable to the ear of George Bernard Shaw when, in 1903, he sought to extend the earlier philosophy. Hence, using the Latin prefix for "over," he coined *superman*, when writing his work, *Man and Superman*.

surplice

The age of this liturgical vestment is not precisely known, but it dates at least from the eleventh century. At that time and probably earlier, but certainly for a number of centuries after, lack of heat in the churches necessitated that the clergy wear warm garments as a protection from the cold dampness of those stone buildings. Hence it was the custom to wear a robe of fur. But this necessitated an overgarment of white. Its name is therefore derived from its function —*surplice*, corrupted through Old French from the Latin *super*, over, and *pellicia*, fur garment.

sybarite

In the eighth century B.C., some people from Thessaly in central Greece crossed the Ionian Sea and established a colony on the shores of the Gulf of Tarantum in southern Italy. They named the colony Sybaris. The land was found to be very fertile and it was not long before the city that sprang up became large and prosperous, with citizens from all quarters. But its opulence proved to be the undoing of the colony; its people turned toward greater and greater luxury

483

and effeminacy. Thus its name became a byword among the Greeks, a *Sybarite* denoting any person given over to luxurious living or sensuality, a meaning retained to the present day. The life of Sybaris was short, however. Its inhabitants became so soft and pleasure loving that, when attacked by the army of the nearby city of Crotona in 510 B.C., the city fell an easy prey. Its enemies razed the city to the ground and diverted the river Crathis to engulf the ruins.

sycophant

Various attempts have been made to explain the original intent of this word. Its source is the Greek *sykophantes*, which came from the two words, *sykon*, a fig, and *phaino*, to show. Because the Greeks themselves used *sykophantes* to mean "an informer," the general supposition is that the early "one who shows figs" was one who informed against persons who were attempting to export figs from Attica. A person against whom such an accusation was made was subject to a stiff penalty. The Greeks also used *sykophantes* to mean "a false accuser," so it is probable that many a false accusation was made against an unpopular person. English usage originally followed the Greek sense, "an informer," after the term was introduced into the language in the sixteenth century, but the object of the informer was soon inverted. From being a person who bore tales against a person in high position, it came to designate one who bore tales to that person and otherwise fawned upon him.

sylph

The great German alchemist of the early sixteenth century, best known under his assumed name, Paracelsus, collected a vast amount of information and made many important contributions to medical and chemical knowledge. The science of the times, however, compelled him to sail some uncharted seas, and we might today laugh at some of his theories. Thus the title of one of his writings is *Liber de Nymphis, Sylphis, Pygmæis, et Salamandris et Cæteris Spiritibus* (Book concerning Nymphs, Sylphs, Pygmies, and Salamanders and Other Spirits). His intent was to account for and describe the four elements of the alchemists, water, air, earth, and fire. The *nymphs*, in his system, were the spirits of water (later disciples called them *Undines*); *sylphs* were spirits of the air; *pygmies* (later called *gnomes*) were spirits of the earth, and *salamanders* were spirits of fire. The term *sylph* was coined by Paracelsus. He regarded these elemental spirits of the air as being in all respects like man, though able to move with greater agility and speed, and having bodies more diaphanous than man. Probably through the influence of Pope's *Rape of the Lock*, in which the term appeared, the concept of *sylph* became altered to apply only to a girl or woman of graceful form and movement.

symposium

Greeks of old did not customarily drink with their meals. Instead, after a dinner was finished, the host and his guests—and perhaps some guests who had not attended the dinner—were served wine to the extent that might be desired. This drinking party was called *symposion* (taken into Latin as *symposium*), derived from *syn*, together, and *poton*, drink. These occasions, enjoyed by men only, were accompanied by music, dancing, games, or other amusements, or sometimes merely by agreeable conversation. It is through the latter diversion that, nowadays, we regard a *symposium* as a discussion by several persons upon a given topic, often in writing. But drink, although the essence of the original word, is no longer necessarily an accompanying feature.

tabloid

In 1884 a British manufacturer of medical and pharmacal supplies, Messrs. Burroughs, Wellcome & Co., registered a trade-mark for a name that the Company applied to certain of its products. These were, generally, chemical drugs compressed into tablets. The name which the Company had devised was *Tabloid*, a name which, by process of registry, was then legally restricted to the preparations made by that firm. But the Company succeeded better than it had supposed in acquainting the public with its trade-mark. *Tabloid*, instead of denoting only the compressed tablets of Messrs. Burroughs, Wellcome & Co., came to be applied to various things other than drugs which appeared to be compressed or concentrated. The Company made many efforts in the law courts of both England and America to stop other use of the term, but is now protected only to the extent that the name may not be legally applied to products which interfere with its trade rights.

talent

In the biblical parable of the man who, before going on an extensive journey, left certain amounts of money with three of the servants whom he wished to test, the amount in each instance is referred to as *talents*. The source of the word is the Greek *talanton* which, like the English word "pound," was used both as the name of a weight and as the name of an amount of silver of that weight. The weight varied among different peoples and at different times, so it cannot be determined how great was the value of the talent in the biblical story. If it were the Roman talent, the value might have been no more than $500 of our money; if the Attic talent, about $1,200, but if the Babylonian talent, the equivalent value might have been $2,000. The point of the parable, however, lies in the passage that the amount received by each servant was allotted "according to his several ability." Consequently the theologians of the later Middle Ages began to give *talent* a figurative meaning, to use it as if it meant "natural ability." The figurative usage became predominant, and has so extended that the original ancient sense, "a weight," is forgotten.

tally

For a number of centuries the British Exchequer kept its accounts by a system that now seems fantastic. A stick of willow or hazel, about one inch square and twelve inches long, represented each transaction, the nature of which was written on two opposite faces of the stick. The sum of money involved, as, for example, a loan to the royal crown, was indicated by notches cut across the other two faces, the character, size, and depth of the cuts accurately representing the amount of the transaction in pounds, shillings, and pence. After the account was thus marked by characteristic notches, the stick was then split in half lengthwise across the cuts, each half thus having the entire series of notches. One half was given as a form of receipt to the person making the loan and the other was retained by the Exchequer. Each party thus had a record of the transaction. The stick was called a *tally*—*talea* being the Latin for "stick." The system was completely abandoned in 1826 and the great accumulation of the wooden tallies was then used as fuel for the stoves in the houses of Parliament. In October of 1834 so much of this dried wood was piled into the stoves that they became overheated, thus setting fire to and burning down the houses of Parliament.

tantalize

One story accounting for the severe punishment administered to Tantalus was that he had stolen nectar and ambrosia from the table of the gods to give to his friends. Another was that, receiving a golden dog, stolen by someone else from the temple to Zeus, he later denied that he had received the dog. And another was that, seeking to test the wisdom of the gods, he had cut his own son Pelops into pieces, boiled them, and served them to the gods with their meal. The crime was discovered, however, and Pelops was restored to life. But the most popular account was that Tantalus, a great favorite of the gods, betrayed some confidences which Zeus had entrusted to him. Whatever the crime he was punished by being placed in the lower world in the midst of a lake with clusters of fruit hanging over his head. Whenever he stooped to drink of the lake, however, the waters receded, and whenever he stretched up his hand for the fruit, the branches drew away. Thus, though water and fruit were apparently plentiful to relieve thirst and hunger, he was forever in torment by the withdrawal of that which he desired. *Tantalize*, formed from his name, commemorates the nature of his punishment.

tarantula, tarantism, tarantella (St. Vitus's dance)

Along about 708 B.C., a body of Greeks from Sparta moved across the Adriatic Sea and established a colony on a favorable spot upon a seacoast in southern Italy. Under the ancient name, *Tarentum*, the colony prospered, vying briefly with Rome for greatness in the third century B.C. The present city, its name altered to Taranto, is now an important naval base. But the region about ancient Tarentum harbored a species of fearsome-looking, hairy spiders capable of inflicting a painful, if not dangerous, bite. This spider, from the place

487

of its discovery, was called *tarantula*. Sometime during the Middle Ages, a strange disease broke out in various parts of Europe. It manifested itself by a twitching or jerking of the limbs of the person afflicted, and was accompanied by an almost uncontrollable impulse to dance. In Italy, the superstition grew that the disease was caused by the bite of the tarantula. From that erroneous belief, the disease became known as *tarantism*, though it is now called "chorea," from Greek *choreia*, dance. Through the spread of the epidemic, accompanied by a form of hysteria, and perhaps religious mania, a dancing mania seized much of Europe, recorded in Germany first in 1374. In southern Italy the dance, if done in rapid measure, was thought to be beneficial to victims of the disease and, by the fifteenth century or earlier, such a dance had been developed and standardized. It, too, was named from the supposed source of the disease—*tarantella*. Children afflicted with tarantism were taught, in olden days, to offer up their prayers to the child martyr, Saint Vitus. This young saint, martyred under Diocletian in the fourth century, was firmly believed to be able to cure them. It is for that reason that chorea among children, especially, is still called "Saint Vitus's dance."

tariff

Some books that may still be in circulation account for this word in an interesting fashion. The story is plausible, but unfortunately is not true. It runs thus: For many centuries the Moors had strongholds on either side of the Strait of Gibraltar. Thus their vessels were able to intercept all merchant craft sailing into or out of the Mediterranean and exact tribute. On the European side, the Moorish pirates had their quarters in a town nestling at the foot of the Rock of Gibraltar, the name of which was Tarifa. That much of the story is true. There was such a Moorish town, named in the eighth century from the Moorish invader, Tarif, and the Moors did use it for piratical raids until the end of the thirteenth century. But, although our word *tariff* is Arabian in source, it was not derived from the name of the Moorish village, Tarifa, as the story concludes. The real source is humdrum by comparison. The Arabic term for "inventory" is *ta'rif*. This became *tarifa* in Spanish and *tariffe* in French, from which it became English *tariff*.

tartar

Chief among the Mongols ruled over by Genghis Khan were the people known as Ta-ta Mongols. Through their warlike qualities they had extended his dominions, before his death in 1227, to embrace all China, had successfully invaded northern India and Persia, and had crossed the Caucasus Mountains, penetrating as far westward as the Volga and Dnieper rivers. But it was under the successors of "the Great Khan" that these fierce warriors left their memory upon European countries for all time. Known as *Tartars* (later more correctly spelled *Tatars*), these bloodthirsty hordes of the thirteenth century swept as far westward as Poland and Hungary, and into Palestine to the south. They massacred all who opposed, leaving smoking ruins behind them. (See also HORDE.) From their early name *tartar* became synonymous with "savage," and is still applied to any person of violent temper, or, if to a woman, to one who is notably shrewish.

tattoo

Various military and naval expressions made their way into our language through the long contacts in past centuries of English soldiers and sailors with Hollanders, either as their foes, fighting on Dutch soil, or as their allies. One expression in particular became well known. It was that used by Dutch tavern keepers when the bugler or drummer sounded the nightly call for all to return to their quarters. The tavern keepers said, "*Tap toe*," meaning, "The tap (or bar) is to (or closed)." To the English soldier that sounded like *tattoo*. Hence, from the cause of its utterance, the term was adopted and transferred to the signal itself. (The term *tattoo* as applied to patterns marking the skin, is entirely unconnected with the foregoing word. It was adapted from the Polynesian name for the practice, *tatau*.)

tawdry

The story of this word takes us back to an Anglian princess of the seventh century. In early records her name appears as either Etheldreda or Æthelthreda, but in Norman times it was altered to Audrey. Her father, it is said, had married her to a neighboring king against her wishes, and she fled from him to the Isle of Ely in the river Ouse, a few miles north of Cambridge, England. Here, after purchasing the island, she established a religious house, of which she became abbess, and here, in 679, she died and was buried. Some sixty years later, the Venerable Bede wrote of her in his *Ecclesiastical History*, and said that her death had been caused by a growth in her throat, which, according to the abbess herself, was in punishment for a vain fondness in her youth for wearing golden chains and jewels about her neck.

The monastery continued to grow after her death, becoming, many years later, the Cathedral of Ely. A town grew up around it, and it then became the custom to hold annual fairs upon the day, October 17, sacred to the memory of St. Audrey. "Trifling objects," as they were called in old records, were sold at this fair. Especially treasured were those that in some way commemorated the foundress of the establishment. Naturally enough, among the most popular of the souvenirs was a golden chain or band of lace to be worn by women about the neck; and this trinket became yet more popular when, sometime in the sixteenth century, a noted preacher drew attention to the custom and repeated the story told by the Venerable Bede of St. Audrey's vanity.

Thereafter, everyone who went to the fair at Ely was beset by the cry of hucksters: "St. Audrey's lace; St. Audrey's lace!" And as the quality of the chain or lace began to become less through the years, so did the cry of the merchants become less distinct. "Saint Audrey's lace" became "Sin t'Audrey lace," and by the time it had become "*Tawdry* lace," the necklace might retain its charm no longer than until its wearer reached home. By association of ideas, other objects of gaudy ornamentation and inferior quality have since been described as *tawdry*. (Compare LACE and NECKLACE.)

tea

If it were not for the Dutch, it is not likely that we would have had *tea*. Instead we might have had *cha*, which is another name for the same thing. The leaf was first brought to Europe in the sixteenth century by the Portuguese, the first to reach China by sea. They introduced it with the Cantonese name, *cha*. Dutch merchants of the next century, however, were more successful in selling the chief ingredient for the beverage, calling it by the name used in Amoy or Formosa, *te* or *thee*, altered by the English to *tea*.

tennis (racket, racquet)

The source of this game and of its name has long been conjectural. Until recent years the most prevalent theory was that the name *tennis* was derived from *tenez*, the imperative of the French *tenir*, to hold. The historical authority on various ball games, Robert W. Henderson, chief of the main reading room of the New York Public Library, did not agree with that theory. The game, in his opinion, was too old to have been known by a French name. He had reached the conclusion that both name and game were of Arabic origin. A letter from Mr. Henderson, which the author is privileged to use, supplies the material for the rest of this article.

The first to suggest an Arabic source was Lady Wentworth who, under the pen name "Antiquarius," in an article in *The Field*, November 10, 1927, wrote: "We find its origin in the Arabic word meaning to leap, and we get further Arabic variants in *t'nazza*, to strive against one for superiority or glory; and to twang string, *t'nazzi*, to make a thing bound, *tenziz*, in constant movement." (Lady Wentworth omitted the main Arabic word, *tanaz*, to leap, bound.)

"In 1932," Mr. Henderson writes, "I collaborated with the late Malcolm D. Whitman in a book *Tennis: Origins and Mysteries*. In previous research on the game of tennis I had learned of a fine fabric, *tissus de tennis*, which was manufactured at Tinnis, an island at the Nile Delta. Tinnis was famous for its fine fabrics, and also as a health resort. It sank into the sea sometime about the eleventh century. Because early tennis balls were sometimes made of rolled fabrics, I considered it possible that a ball made of fine linen, such as the *tissus de tennis*, might have been desired by the best players. Hence it may have given the name to the game. I wrote this up for the book, and Whitman accepted it. But long before publication, because of objections raised by Albert de Luze, tennis historian of Bordeaux, I abandoned the theory as untenable. Whitman, however, clung to it, and insisted that it go in the book."

Mr. Henderson publicly renounced his theory in the March, 1934, issue of *Squash Rackets and Fives*. But in the meantime Mr. Whitman had discussed the theory of light balls made from fabric of

Tinnis with a friend, Philip K. Hitti, professor of Arabic at Princeton University. Professor Hitti accepted the theory, and, perhaps unaware that its author had renounced it, offered it as the true source of the word *tennis* in the Second Edition of *Webster's New International Dictionary*. After the appearance of that dictionary in 1934, Mr. Henderson says that he wrote to Professor Hitti, "asking if he had any evidence that the Tinnis fabric had been used to make tennis balls, but he could produce none."

Mr. Henderson has supplied further historical information of general interest. He says that, far from the word *tennis* having been introduced by crusaders in various places in Europe, "only one early continental reference is known, that in the *Cronica di Firenze* of Donato Velluti, written 1367-70. The form used is *tenes*. The commonly stated derivation of *tennis*, that it comes from the French *'Tenez!'* a cry supposedly used by French players when ready to serve, started with John Minsheu's *Ductor in Linguas*, 1617. But there is absolutely no evidence that such a cry was ever used, in ancient or modern times. The game of tennis undoubtedly had its origin in ancient Egyptian-Arabic religious rites. (See Henderson's *Ball, Bat & Bishop*.) Several of the terms used are of Arabic origin. Racquet, for instance, is from *ruqat* or *raqat*, a patch of cloth tied around the palm of the hand, the earliest form of the racquet."

Mr. Henderson concludes: "The best conjecture to date is that *tennis* is derived from the Arabic *tanaz*, on the grounds that the game is from Egyptian-Arabic sources and that the earliest use of the word in English, *tenetz* (about the year 1400), approximated the sound of the Arabic word."

termagant

At a time when legends of the Saracens were popular subjects of poetry and drama in Europe—that is, after the Crusades of the eleventh and twelfth centuries—Mohammedan characters began to be added to some of the mystery plays. But so little did the writers of these plays know about the Mohammedan faith that some of the characters had to be invented. Thus they created two deities whom the Saracens were supposed to have worshiped. The names, Old French *Mahum* and *Tervagan*, may have been taken from the eleventh-century poem *Chanson de Roland*. The name *Mahum*, which became *Mahoun* or *Mahound* in English, is readily identified as *Mohammed*, thought by Christians to have been worshiped as a god. But the identity of *Tervagan*, in the French poem and French mysteries, is still undetermined. In English plays his name was variously written, *Tervagant*, *Termagaunt*, and *Termagant*. He was always represented as a boisterous, blustering swaggerer of outrageous violence and ferocity. In due course the name was thence transferred to any person, man or woman, of similar temperament, although it is now rarely applied to other than a brawling woman.

terminus, term

Numa, the second king of Rome, was traditionally believed to have decreed that every one of his subjects should mark the boundaries of his land by monuments consecrated to the god *Terminus*, and that fitting sacrifices should be made to the god annually. The monument was sometimes merely a post or a stone, garlanded upon the occasion of the annual festival, and with a rude altar, upon which were offered sacrifices of cake, meal, or fruit or, later, of lambs or pigs. Sometimes the monument was a statue of the god, by which he was represented as a human head, sometimes with a torso but without feet or arms, to intimate that he never moved from his place. The annual feast, or *Terminalia* as it was called, was on the 23rd of February. At that time the owners of adjacent lands met for offering their sacrifices. Through the passage of time the monument itself came to be regarded as the *terminus*, which thus acquired, even in Roman times, the meaning, an ending-place. It was contracted in Old French to *terme*, with similar meaning; the English form *term* has acquired various extended meanings.

thug

Among the religious fanatics of India there was one highly organized band which specialized in murder, murder in a particular manner—by strangling. The band is believed to have been wiped out now, because the British hung about four hundred of them in the 1830's and transported or imprisoned for life almost a thousand others. No one knows when the association originated nor how it came about, but it was in existence as far back as A.D. 1290. The correct name of the members was *p'hansigars*, stranglers, although

493

they were more commonly known to the British as *Thugs*, a term of Sanskrit source meaning "cheaters" or "rascals." The Thugs believed that they were divinely delegated to strangle a selected victim and that the deed was wrought in honor of the goddess Kali, wife of Siva. The murder was therefore entirely a religious duty, unaccompanied by any remorse. The victims were invariably of the wealthy class, because plunder, both for the goddess and for the association, was the main object. Three or four selected Thugs might follow an appointed victim for many days or many miles before an opportunity presented itself to slip a noose about his neck. Through practiced skill the sacrifice was usually dead before he struck the ground. The assassins were also bound by their beliefs to bury their victims. For this reason, as well as to escape detection while committing the crime, an unfrequented spot was usually selected for the murder.

Thursday

In Norse mythology, as related in the Icelandic sagas, Thor was the most popular of all the gods. He was the son of Odin and Frigg (see WEDNESDAY and FRIDAY), and was represented as a man of middle age with red hair and beard, and of enormous strength. The chariot in which he rode was drawn by he-goats; the rolling of this chariot caused the thunder. Thor was armed with a terrible magic hammer, Mjölnir, the smasher, which he hurled at his foes and which then returned to his hand, for the gods were always at war with the forces of evil which sought constantly to destroy them. But Thor was the friend of man whom he aided, guarding him against evil spirits and disease. He was looked upon, especially, as the god of agriculture and was most widely worshiped for that reason. Accordingly, although Odin (or Woden) was the god most nearly the counterpart of the Roman Jove (or Jupiter), it was Thor who was selected from among the Norse and early English gods for honor by having his name replace the Roman *dies Jovis* (day of Jove) in naming the fifth day of the week. His name, among the early English, was sometimes given as *Thur* and sometimes as *Thunor*, so the Old English name of the day was sometimes written *Thursdæg* and sometimes *Thunresdæg*. The first was the one that survived, giving us *Thursday*. (See also SATURDAY.)

tinsel

Originally this was a much dressier word, the Old French *estincelle* —modern *étincelle*—and its meaning was also smarter. It denoted "brilliance; sparkle," and the name was applied to a cloth of silk or rich wool in which strands of gold or silver were woven. Such cloth made up into robes or gowns sparkled in the sunshine and attracted the notice of all eyes. And of course, those who could not afford such richness found ways to imitate it. In English speech, the Old French spelling became cropped to *tinsel*. Along with the loss in the elegance of the word, its meaning also lost refinement. Copper threads look not unlike gold; brass and tin spangles sewn upon cloth in plentiful profusion glitter even more brilliantly than gold and silver, and if these threads and spangles be attached to a gown of cheap net, the cost becomes trifling. Silk may be worn beneath. In such fashion, *tinsel* lost its elegance and came to denote cheap but brilliant finery, decorations, or other material showy in appearance but of little value.

toady

The makers of nostrums still loudly proclaim and advertise the remarkable curative powers of their remedies, sometimes claiming that they will cure anything from falling hair to ingrown toenails. The charlatans and quacks of the seventeenth century were no less modest. In fact, they went further. It was sincerely, though mistakenly, believed at that time that anyone so unfortunate as to eat a toad's leg instead of a frog's leg would surely die. Toads were thought to be deadly poison. Charlatans, taking advantage of that superstition, sometimes employed a helper who, under compulsion, would eat (or pretend to eat) a toad, whereupon his master would promptly demonstrate the remarkable properties of the remedy that he sold and, ostensibly, save the life of his helper. Such a helper became referred to as a *toad-eater*. And because anyone who would eat such a repulsive and dread creature would needs be wholly subject to his master, both *toad-eater* and its diminutive form, *toady*, became terms for one who fawns upon or is subservient to another.

Tory

The story of how this word of Irish origin—Englished to *tory* from Irish *toruidhe*, robber—became a political term was told in 1711 by Daniel Defoe in his journal, *The Review*. The events he mentions occurred during his own lifetime. Titus Oates, to whom he refers, had been trained for the Protestant ministry, but spent his time hatching up malicious plots aimed against the Catholics, which cost the lives of thirty-five innocent, but alleged conspirators. Defoe's account, in part, is as follows:

The word *tory* is Irish, and was first used in Ireland at the time of Queen Elizabeth's war, to signify a robber who preyed upon the country. In the Irish massacre (1641), you had them in great numbers, assisting in everything that was bloody and villainous: they were such as chose to butcher brothers and sisters, fathers, the dearest friends and nearest relations. In England, about 1680, a party of men appeared among us, who, though pretended Protestants, yet applied themselves to the ruin of their country. They began with ridiculing the popish plot, and encouraging the Papists to revive it. . . .

These men were those who, as falsely charged by Oates, were plotting the murder of the king, Charles II, in order to set upon the English throne his Catholic brother, James. Also included were all royalists who opposed any act of Parliament that would exclude James from accession to the throne. On account of someone saying, Defoe added, "that he had letters from Ireland, that there were some *tories* to be brought over hither to murder Oates and Bedloe (a colleague of Oates), the doctor (Oates) could never after this hear any man talk against the plot or witnesses but he thought he was one of these *tories*, and called almost every one a *tory* that opposed him in discourse; till at last the word *tory* became popular. . . ." The term as applied to a political faction thus came to include, at first, all the considerable number of men, including many Protestant churchmen, who favored the legitimate right of James, the duke of York, to succeed to the crown. The name came to stand for any adherent to constituted authority of Church and State, and thus eventually superseded the former designations, "Royalist" and "Cavalier," of a political party. The name was dropped about 1830 in favor of "Conservative."

town

In many parts of Europe it is still unusual to find a farmer who lives upon his farm. Generally he lives in a nearby village and walks each day to his fields. The custom is a survival from olden times when, for the sake of mutual protection at night, men slept within call of others. Their group of houses in those days was surrounded by a tight hedge or fence through which no marauding wild animal could gain access. In Old England this hedge was known as *tun* (pronounced "toon"). Later, *tun* indicated any kind of enclosure, especially, a wall; and eventually it referred more specifically to the place enclosed by such a wall, a walled village. Thus a *town*, of early and Medieval England, was distinguished from a hamlet or a village by virtue of the wall that then surrounded it.

tragedy

Like comedy, the original intent of the Greeks in naming this type of play cannot be determined. It is derived from the two words *tragos*, goat, and *ōdē*, song, ode. Thus the Greek *tragodia* was apparently a "goat-song." The reason for the name has been variously conjectured. One thought is that the members of the introductory chorus were clad in goatskins, which may have been symbolical of the serious nature of the play, something like the masks worn by actors to indicate the age or nature of the character to be impersonated (see PERSON). Or the goatskins may have been in honor of *Dionysus*, god of wine, to represent the satyrs who followed him. Another thought is that a goat may have been sacrificed when the play was presented. And another that a goat was offered as a prize to the successful writer of a tragedy. The name for the performance was so old that even the later Greeks could not explain its source.

trapezium, trapezoid

When Euclid wrote his work on geometry, about 300 B.C., he used the word *trapezion*, "little table," as a name for any four-sided figure except the rectangle, rhombus, and rhomboid. The name was later Latinized to *trapezium*. Many centuries later, in the fifth century A.D., the geometer Proclus added certain refinements to Euclid's work which have since become part of the study of geometry. Proclus limited the meaning of *trapezium* to any four-sided figure which had two parallel sides, and introduced a new term, *trapezoeides*, "resembling a table" (our term *trapezoid*), to designate a four-sided figure having no two sides parallel. These remained the standard descriptions of the two names throughout Europe. But in 1795 an English mathematician, Charles Hutton, in his *Mathematical and Philosophical Dictionary*, got the two descriptions just reversed. Hutton's error, unfortunately, was subsequently adopted not only in his own writings, but by other British and American mathematicians. British usage has gradually returned to the original meanings indicated by Proclus, but the usage of the United States still follows that of Hutton.

travail, travel

The nature of the instrument of torture cannot be determined. Possibly it was employed by the Roman soldiery in outposts far from Rome at some period of the Dark Ages, because its name survives in all the Romance languages. It was the torment of the "three poles," or, in Latin, *trepalium*, from *tres*, three, and *palus*, pole. The French term for the verb, to be submitted to such torment, became *travailler*, and, perhaps when the form of torture had fallen into disuse, the sense of the verb became extended into those of harass, vex, weary; hence, to vex or tire oneself, to work hard, or, further, to be in labor. These were the meanings when the French *travailler* followed the Normans into England. In England, however, it acquired a further extended meaning. The notion of wearying oneself became akin to the wearying of oneself by journey. Thus the same term came to mean "to make a journey." All meanings passed through many forms of spelling before we separated them into *travail* and *travel*.

treacle

It used to be called *theriac* or *theriacle*; the Romans called it *theriaca*, and the Greeks knew it as *theriake*. But the substance and its purpose were then quite different from the *treacle* of today. The ancients were, rightly enough, extremely fearful of the bite of wild animals. Unaware of the causes of infection, they assumed that many more creatures were venomous than are now known to be. But from

498

remote antiquity it was believed that every venomous animal carried within itself the antidote to the poison which it transmitted by its bite. Consequently, curative salves for the bite of vipers or other poisonous creatures were thought to contain no virtue unless the flesh of the vipers were employed in preparing the concoction. Such a salve the Greeks called *theriake*, which—from *ther*, a wild animal —meant an antidote against poison from an animal. Hence, though *treacle* was originally a salve, the charlatans of the sixteenth and seventeenth centuries, vying with one another, altered its nature to that of a medicinal compound, which they began to sweeten. Ultimately the sweetening agent itself, usually molasses, became known as *treacle*. The common sixteenth-century interpretation of *treacle* to mean a medicinal salve or lotion brought about one use that is now considered amusing. The word "balm," corrupted from "balsam," was not very well understood at that time. Hence, when translating the Latin Version of the Bible made by St. Jerome into English, the translators were at a loss for a satisfactory term to use in Jeremiah viii, 22, which now reads: "Is there no balm in Gilead; is there no physician there?" John Wyclif and others had used "rosin" or "gumme," but neither of these satisfied the group of bishops who, in 1568, brought out the so-called Bishops' Bible. In this, the word *treacle* was substituted, spelled by them *tryacle*, the passage then reading, "Is there no *tryacle* in Gilead?" For this reason the Bishops' Bible is now humorously referred to as the *Treacle* Bible.

tribulation

For threshing grain and cutting the straw the old-time Roman farmer used a heavy board to which, on the underside, were affixed sharp pieces of flint or iron. The driver added his weight or loaded the board with stones, and it was then dragged over the grain by oxen. The device was called *tribulum*. The Latin term *tribulatio*, accordingly, meant the act of separating grain from the husks by the aid of this crushing and cutting instrument. Some early Christian writer—probably the third-century writer, Tertullian, was the first —saw in this a metaphorical likeness to the kernel of spiritual faith which emerges from the harrowings of grief and hardship. Hence, he took this homely term, *tribulatio*, and applied it to human trials and afflictions. This gave us *tribulation* in its present sense.

trivial

Some of the customs of ancient Greece and Rome were undoubtedly very much like those of today. Among them was the custom of meeting and loafing at street corners in idle conversation. In fact, there was additional justification in olden times, because there was undoubtedly at the junction of the road a statue or other representation of either the god Hermes or the goddess Hecate, which one might worship. Such statues were exceedingly commonplace; so much so that Hecate was known as *Trioditis*, or, in Latin, *Trivia*, signifying "one who is worshiped where three roads meet." The latter term was from the Latin prefix *tri-*, three, and *via*, way. Statues of Hermes were even more numerous. It is not likely, however, that the statues of the gods were more than excuse. Nevertheless, through such meetings and gossip at the street corners, *trivia* came to signify things of little importance, things so commonplace as to be found or heard where three roads meet.

trophy

After a victorious battle it was a custom of the Greeks of early days to take from the field the arms of the enemy and hang them up on the stump of a tree in such manner as to imitate an armed man, the helmet on the top, breastplate about the stump, and shield, sword, and spear attached to branches left for the purpose. Such a monument was named *tropaion*, literally, "a turning point," for it signified the turning point of a battle, the place where the enemy had been put to flight. If the enemy permitted the monument to be erected, it was a confession of defeat. The Greek term became *tropæum* among the Romans, who followed a similar custom, but was later altered to *trophæum*, from which our term *trophy* is derived.

Tuesday

When the Teutonic peoples attempted to render the Latin name for the third day of the week, *dies Martis*, day of Mars, into a name that would honor one of their own gods, they chose *Tyr* as the one who most nearly resembled the warlike Mars. At one time Tyr was probably one of the foremost gods in Teutonic mythology, but little is known of this early prominence. In Norse mythology he appears as a son of Odin, and is the bravest of all the gods. The story is told that a wolf monster, Fenrir, threatened the destruction of all the gods. They sought to bind him, but he broke their chains easily until, on the third attempt, Tyr, who had befriended the creature, put his hand into the wolf's mouth as a pledge of good faith. The third chain was too strong for Fenrir to break, but in his struggles he bit off Tyr's hand. In a later battle among the gods, the one-handed Tyr was slain by Garm, a hound of hell, at the same moment that he killed the dog. Old English mythology gave this god the name *Tiu* or *Tiw*. The day which gave honor to him was *Tiwesdæg*, descending to us as Tuesday. (See also SATURDAY.)

turnpike (pike)

Comparatively few of our roads could now rightly be called turnpikes. The Merritt Parkway in Connecticut; the Skyline Drive in western Virginia; the Pennsylvania Turnpike stretching more than a hundred and fifty miles between Harrisburg and Pittsburgh, and a few other roads in the United States could properly be so termed, but the onetime great National Road, begun in 1835 and running from Maryland some eight hundred miles across Ohio and Indiana and into southern Illinois, although locally still called "turnpike," is one no longer. That is, a *turnpike* is really a road for the use of which a traveler pays a toll; actually a tollroad. But even so, our English ancestors four or five centuries past would have found it difficult to understand how *turnpike* could be construed to mean "road." To them it had a literal meaning; it denoted a series of pointed rods—pikes—so mounted about a beam as to prevent the passage of a foot traveler or mounted man across a bridge or along a path until the array of pikes was rotated or turned aside, a form of chevaux-de-frise. (Compare CHEVAUX-DE-FRISE.) It was probably similar to the mechanism that we now call "turnstile." In a later period, when communities or private persons began to maintain roads and bridges that would accommodate vehicles as well as horsemen and foot travelers, the devices were so placed, with keepers to operate them, as to compel a toll from travelers. Our ancestors properly called such a road a *turnpike road*, a name that continued when the original device was replaced by a gate or beam or other barrier that could be opened only by the keeper. Roads and bridges were maintained and improved through this revenue. The descriptive term was too long; hence it was commonly shortened to *turnpike*, to distinguish the improved road from others. In common speech even this shortened form was then often further abbreviated to *pike*, and both this and *turnpike* loosely applied to any road, especially an improved road.

tweed

Sometime about the year 1830 a weaver in the south of Scotland shipped a quantity of his woolen fabric to a London merchant. The material was twilled and with a rough surface, but there was nothing otherwise unusual about the shipment. The merchant who received it is said to have been James Locke, although in a book by Locke, *Tweed & Don*, published in 1860, he did not acknowledge the story told by others. That story relates that, following the Scottish custom, the word *twill* was written *tweel*, and the weaver had billed the merchant for so many yards of *tweel*. Thanks either to careless handwriting, however, or to a careless clerk, the word was read, not *tweel*, but *tweed*. The assumption was, therefore, that the weaver, who lived near the river Tweed, had used the name of the river as a trade name for his product.

ultramarine (lapis lazuli)

The pigment that we know by this name was formerly obtained only by extracting it from the mineral *lapis lazuli*, or "azure stone" (from Latin *lapis*, stone, and Arabic *lazward*, azure). The pigment was known in the eleventh century A.D., at least, and may have been used at an even earlier date. It was then very costly, literally worth its weight in gold, for only a small amount of pigment was obtainable from the mineral and the mineral was itself imported, probably from Persia. It was to the fact that the mineral came from a foreign country that the pigment received the name *ultramarine*. That is, for many years after importation was begun, it was simply referred to by the Latin phrase, *azurrum ultramarinum*. The meaning is "azure from over the sea." The English translation reduced it to *ultramarine*, literally meaning, "over the sea."

urchin

When the Normans invaded England they brought with them their name for the hedgehog, an animal that we do not have in America but which is related to the porcupine. The Norman name was *herichon*, from the popular Latin name, *hericion*. English attempts to master the French name produced forms variously spelled *hurcheon*, *irchin*, and ultimately *urchin*. Popular superstition had it that these creatures were not always what they appeared, but sometimes disguised an elf or goblin who had assumed the form of the innocent animal for concealment. Thus it came about that a mischievous child, likened to an elf by his conduct, has had the name of the hedgehog, *urchin*, applied to him.

utopian

Sir Thomas More was a contemporary of Christopher Columbus and of Amerigo Vespucci and was well informed upon the discoveries of the former and the alleged discoveries of the latter. Accordingly, in a book published in 1516, he represents that the island which furnished the setting for his story was an actual western island, described to him in 1514 by its discoverer, a supposed companion of Vespucci. It was, he said, a place of ideal charm, but especially was inhabited by a people who had perfected an ideal social, political, and economic system. More called this wonderful but nonexistent island, *Utopia*, and Greek scholars had no difficulty in discerning it to mean "no place," from *ou*, not, and *topos*, place. His book, first published in Latin, achieved great popularity and was soon translated into the chief languages of Europe. The name of the fictitious island is now applied to any place where life appears to be ideal, and *utopian* now describes anything regarded as ideal but visionary.

valentine

Legend has it that there were two Christians, each named *Valentine*, and both of whom suffered martyrdom on the same day. The day was February 14, and the martyrdom is supposed to have occurred during the reign of Claudius II, or about A.D. 270. One was a bishop, the other a priest; both were subsequently canonized. The bishop is sometimes said to have been so exceptionally distinguished for love and charity that his friends inaugurated the custom of selecting his day, February 14, upon which to designate one's choice of a sweetheart. Another theory is that the custom was altered and put one day forward from an old practice in the ancient Italian observance of the Lupercalia (see FEBRUARY). This festival occurred on February 15, and it included among its ceremonies the custom of putting the names of young women into a box from which they were drawn out by the young men. Old customs were hard to stamp out after the advent of Christianity, and the priests of the early Church sometimes did no more than to transfer innocent pagan practices to a festival of Christian flavor. Thus the latter theory is probably correct; if so, connection of the customs with either Saint Valentine is accidental, and the practices of the day actually commemorate the Italian pagan festival, the Lupercalia.

vandal

In the fifth century A.D., a remarkable group of Teutonic tribes crossed the Rhine, descended southward through lands occupied by the Franks, fighting their way as they went, crossed the Pyrenees, lived for twenty years in Spain, and then, upon invitation from the Roman count of Africa, Boniface, crossed the Mediterranean into Africa. Eighty thousand persons were said to have made that crossing. The group, although including various tribes, was called *Vandals*. Their leader, at the time of the crossing, was Genseric, a man naturally endowed for war and dominion. In October, 439, he led his forces against Carthage, third largest of the cities of the Roman Empire and the last in Africa to fall before him, and made it thenceforth his own stronghold. In the year 455 he sailed across to Italy and took, without much difficulty, the city of Rome. This city he sacked completely, his ships loaded with plunder when he returned to Carthage. The son of Genseric, Hunneric, who succeeded him in 477, was noted for even greater rapacity than the father, but spent it chiefly in persecution of Christians, extorting from them by cruel torture and death all the treasures and sacred vessels of their Church. The remnants of the Teutonic tribes were finally subdued, captured, or scattered in A.D. 536, and the Vandals disappeared from history. Their name lives as a reminder of willful or ignorant destruction or mutilation of things beautiful, sacred, or historical.

vaudeville

In the early fifteenth century there lived in Normandy a notable fellow, a fuller by trade, who achieved local fame for his satirical, but rollicking drinking songs. His name was Olivier Basselin; his home in the valley of the Vire. The songs that Basselin composed took off the follies of the day and eventually attracted notice far outside his humble valley. *Chansons du Vau de Vire* (or *Vaux de Vire*, for there were two valleys) became popular all over France. Songs of similar nature, always with topical satiric verses and sometimes accompanied with country allusions or sayings, were composed by others and introduced into the music halls. Gradually the name of the valley was forgotten or was corrupted, so that *Vire* became *ville*, town. The change into *vaudeville* was fully effected by the eighteenth century.

vie (envy)

Originally it was a contraction of *envy*, formed by lopping off the first syllable. But *envy*, in the sense in which it was thus employed, was a gambling term in the sixteenth century, meaning to invite, to challenge; the contraction, *vie*, was the more popular word at the gaming table. One *vied* or made a *vie* by putting up a stake on the strength of a hand at cards. Hence, *vie*, meaning to contend or strive against another at cards, later embraced any kind of contest.

volume

Most of the written literature of ancient times was on continuous sheets of parchment or papyrus. For convenience these sheets were wound into fairly tight rolls about sticks, one stick at either end of the roll. In reading, the scroll was thus unwound from one stick and, as the reading proceeded, wound upon the other. The Latin term for the rolling of the scroll was *volvo*, to roll. For that reason the thing which was rolled was anciently known as *volumen*, a derivative of *volvo*. When books were no longer rolled into scrolls, *volume* continued to be used, especially for a book of considerable size. Further, from this notion of a book of considerable size, *volume* then acquired a second meaning, "any large quantity, any considerable amount."

Wednesday

Chief among the gods of the Scandinavian peoples was Odin. It was he, with the aid of his two brothers, who created the world out of chaos and who ruled the heaven and earth. His throne was in Valhalla. There, as the god of war, he received all those who were slain in battle, and there they fought and feasted according to the pleasures they had most enjoyed on earth. Odin was also the god of wisdom and learning, which he had obtained, at the sacrifice of one eye, by drinking from the fountain of Mirmir. His wife was Frigg, goddess of marriage. In the Icelandic sagas, from which most of our knowledge of Scandinavian and Teutonic mythology is derived, Odin is represented as an old man, whose greatest treasures were his spear, known as Gungner, which never failed to hit its mark, his eight-footed steed, Sleipnir, swift as the winds of heaven, and his broad ring of red gold, Draupnir, made in the form of a snake, from whose mouth, every 'ninth night, a similar ring was dropped. In the early mythology of England, the name of this god was Woden. In naming the days of the week after the Roman system, his name was substituted for the Roman *dies Mercurii* (day of Mercury) as the name of the fourth day. In Old English, accordingly, the name was *Wodensdæg* (day of Woden), which has gradually shifted to our present Wednesday. The pronunciation, "wenzday," is a survival from the fourteenth and fifteenth centuries when the word was variously spelled, *Wensday, Wenysday, Wonesday,* and *Wanysday*. (See also SATURDAY.)

Whig

All the Presbyterians of Scotland bound themselves by a covenant, in 1638, to resist all attempts to alter their form of worship and to maintain the Presbyterian doctrine as the sole religion of their country. This oath was taken because Charles I, king of England, was then employing every device to bring Scotland into the fold of the Church of England. Hence, it was not difficult to enlist the support of the Scots against him when the English Parliament finally rebelled against the king's autocratic rule. Charles was eventually taken prisoner in 1646. Many throughout England and Scotland, however, had opposed him only to secure better government, not to do harm to the person of their monarch. Hence, in 1648, when it appeared that the English captors under Cromwell might try and condemn the king for treason, a number of those loyal to the British throne and to the House of Stuart resumed arms in an attempt to rescue him. These Royalists included many Scotch Presbyterians, a large force of whom were led into England, under the Duke of Hamilton, in support of the king. There were other Scots, however, who were greatly incensed by this act. It seemed treachery to them, and they banded themselves into an opposing force. They called themselves *whiggamores*, a word of uncertain origin, and marched upon Edinburgh with the insistent demand that their own parliament stand firmly against the king. Cromwell suppressed the attempted rescue, and Charles I was tried and beheaded in 1649. But the term *Whig*, shortened from *whiggamore*, remained in the language in memory of those Scots who had risen up in wrath against the wealthy and powerful Royalists who would support a king whom they could not trust.

yacht

The original craft from which this vessel derived its name was not used for pleasure. Its early Teutonic name, *jaght*, indicates that it was intended as a hunter; its modern German descendant, *jagd*, is "a hunt." Thus, along the shores of the North Sea, the *jaght* of the sixteenth century was a speedy vessel which had undoubtedly been originally designed for piracy. In that and the following century, however, British seamen had learned that vessels of that type were also ideal for pleasure. More and more of them were designed for wealthy British patrons, especially for the royal family. But the spelling of the Teutonic word was as varied as the number of the craft built. That which probably most nearly represented, in English spelling, the sound of the foreign word was *yaught*. The form that finally became standard, *yacht*, probably represented the German pronunciation, even though the average British tongue has been content to call it "yaht."

Yankee

One of the great mysteries, for two hundred years, has been the source of this word. Some have thought that it came from the mispronunciation of the word "English" by the Indians of Massachusetts. Others, that its source was in the name of a Dutch captain whose name was Yanky. And still others, more reasonably, credited it to *Janke*, diminutive of the Dutch name, *Jan*, John. But in 1945, H. L. Mencken, that indefatigable delver in Americanisms, in his *The American Language: Supplement One*, presented some additional findings in substantiation of an earlier theory. His statement,* which he has authorized me to use, follows:

The etymology adopted in *The American Language, Fourth Edition*, to wit, that *Yankee* comes from *Jan* and *kees*, signifying *John Cheese*, is not approved by the DAE (*Dictionary of American English*), but it has the support of Dr. Henri Logeman of the University of Ghent, and it seems likely to stand. In its original form the term was *Jan Kaas*, and in that form it has been a nickname for a Hollander, in Flanders and Germany, for a great many years. In the days of the buccaneers the English sailors began to use it to designate a Dutch freebooter, and in this sense it became familiar in New York. Presently the New York Dutch, apparently seizing upon its opprobrious significance, began to apply it to the English settlers of Connecticut, who were regarded at the time as persons whose commercial enterprise ran far beyond their moral scruples. A little while later it came into general use in the colonies to designate a disliked neighbor to the northward, and there was a time when the Virginians applied it to the Marylanders. In the end the New Englanders saw in it a flattering tribute to their cunning, and so not only adopted it themselves, but converted it into an adjective signifying excellence. The DAE's first printed example of *Yankee*, then spelled *Yankey*, is dated 1683, at which time the term still meant a pirate, and was applied as a proper name to one of the Dutch commanders in the West Indies. By the middle of the Eighteenth Century it had come to mean a New Englander, and by the Revolutionary period the English were using it to designate any American. During the Civil War, as everyone knows, the Southerners used it, usually contemptuously, of all Northerners, and in consequence its widened meaning became restricted again, but in World War I it underwent another change, and since then, though they objected at first, even Southerners have got used to being called *Yankees*, *e.g.*, by the English.

HEAVENS TO BETSY!

And Other Curious Sayings

TO MY WIFE

Who has most unmistakably been at my side "through sickness and health" during the preparation of this volume

FOREWORD

LONG BEFORE I began to prepare for publication the collection of sketches in the little volume, *A Hog on Ice and Other Curious Expressions,* brought out in 1948, I had been greatly interested in certain other sayings or expressions, equally curious, but about which I had not yet been able to learn anything. Why, for instance, did my father and others of his generation speak of Abraham Lincoln as a typical example of a man who had "lifted himself by his own bootstraps," or people of my own generation use the same saying of the Negro scientist, George Washington Carver? Why did my wife's father, a Massachusetts country doctor, so frequently during his lifetime say of a person who seemed uninterested in what was going on that he "just sat like a Stoughton bottle"? The reasons for these omissions I shall shortly explain.

There were, as well, a considerable number of other sayings, some in daily use and some that we encounter chiefly in literature, that justified further investigation or that I had omitted for one reason or another. And, to be frank about it, having no complete list of all the numerous sayings we employ in our speech, many did not occur to me at the time; interested readers of *A Hog on Ice* have subsequently called scores of them to my attention. In addition, in a few instances I have run across pertinent supplementary information about some expressions discussed in that book, usually through the courtesy of its readers, or, occasionally, I have wished to correct a statement or alter an opinion.

For these reasons, influenced also by the gratifying reception given to the earlier book, the publishers suggested that I prepare the present collection rather than to revise and greatly enlarge the former one. This I have done. The book stands alone, however;

513

its contents are independent of the previous book—at least, in the terms of a popular soap advertisement, "ninety-nine and 44/100 percent" independent. My nephew, Tom Funk, well known for his humorous drawings in many of our popular magazines, has again exercised his imagination in illustrating the text, which, I fear, is often in need of his lightsome aid.

The sayings that I have included owe their origins to all levels of life and take us back through virtually all periods of English and American history. A number had their origins in early translations of the Bible; others have come to us from the translations made in the classroom by ebullient young students of Greek and Latin in the days when those languages were an essential part of one's education. Many came from the everyday activities of men and women engaged in homely labor on the farm. Some are from the circus and the theater. Some are from the gambling table with cards or other games of chance. Some, chiefly used by political orators, are traceable to American frontier life. Many were undoubtedly slang expressions that were current at the period cited. Some— a very few, I've no doubt—were the carefully developed and deliberately phrased utterances of their creator.

The general formula that I have followed is that of the previous book—to give each curious saying the figurative meaning that it has acquired, to show, whenever possible, how that meaning came about, and to make an approximate estimate of the time it came into use in English speech, usually by quoting the one who, so far as records indicate, was the first to employ it in his writing. In such instances I have often gone back to the records themselves to summarize the occasion leading up to the writer's use of the expression, to say, for instance, why the diarist, Samuel Pepys, used the saying "to put one's nose out of joint," to relate the events leading up to Homer's use of "on the lap of the gods" in the *Iliad*, to give the circumstances that caused Mrs. Wiggs, in Alice Hegan Rice's *Mrs. Wiggs of the Cabbage Patch*, to say of her boarder that he was now "on the water-cart." Very rarely, of course, do I credit the actual coinage of these sayings to the writers quoted; with few exceptions, no doubt, these writers deserve nothing more than credit for passing along to posterity the popular sayings of their

514

own day. We can no more determine who was the individual who first said that something was "as scarce as hen's teeth" than we can say with any certainty who, of modern times, was the first to say of some girl that she was "as cute as a bug's ear."

Who can predict what chance happy conversational phrasing may strike a listener as worthy of repetition? Who would think to record anywhere the original speaker? Who, not very long ago, first said of someone that he "took it on the lam"? who that so-and-so had "taken a powder"? Or, to go back a hundred and fifty years, what story brought into existence the metaphor, "Everyone to his taste, as the devil said when he painted his tail sky-blue"? Or to go back three hundred years, to the period of the English Protectorate, who had the happy thought to describe something as being "as tight as Dick's hatband"?

That is to say—or to confess—that very, very often in these pages I could do no more than to trace a saying back through the years or centuries to its earliest appearance in written literature, telling in the process any historical fact or other item of interest that might have a bearing on the origin. Thus, for example, though we know much of the legendary story of the medieval heroes, Roland and Oliver, it is little more than guesswork that can be offered to explain why "a Roland for an Oliver" means "tit for tat." Whenever possible, however, I have given exact sources of sayings that have come into common or literary use. It was the Cervantes hero, Don Quixote, who first "tilted at windmills"; it was the French poet, Sainte-Beuve, from whom we got our current meaning of an "ivory tower." Coming down to the present day, it was the comic-strip artist, Arthur ("Pop") Momand, who brought "Keeping up with the Joneses" into our popular speech, and his own story of its origin on pages 141 makes very interesting reading. So also does the account by Caswell Adams on page 197 telling how any of a certain group of Eastern colleges has come to be known as a member of the "Ivy League."

My search for sources of certain sayings, however, was attended by an inordinate amount of trouble, leading me at times into wholly unforeseen twists and turns. The title selected at the very outset for the book itself turned out eventually to be completely unsolvable. I am tempted to paraphrase Shakespeare: "Who is Betsy? what is she, That heaven itself commends her?" The exclamation is in daily use in all parts of the United States. Countless people, men and women—north, south, east, west—have said to me, "Why, I've used that all my life!" But not an inkling have I been able to find that would lead to a positive source. The expression, I am told, is not used in England, which eliminates any probability of connection with Queen Elizabeth of bygone years —known familiarly as "Bess" anyway, rather than "Betsy." Nor have I found any definite clue to the age of the saying. My friend, the historical novelist Kenneth Roberts, in one of his whimsical letters wrote:

I remember "Heavens to Betsy" from my earliest days in my grandmother's New Hampshire home—always spoken in a gently derisive sort of way, as was the remark, "Well, I snum!" . . . I think there's no doubt whatever that if I had sat down with her for an hour or so, I could have worked her around to hazarding a guess, and the guess would have run something like this: Our family originated in Auvergne, lit out when things were being made rough for Huguenots, settled in Salisbury, England, then in Godalming near Stratford-on-Avon. . . . I think there's no doubt that I could have persuaded her that "Heavens to Betsy" was nothing but a corruption of the words *Auvergne betisse,* meaning "What won't they think of next!" But she, alas, died fifty years ago.

Mr. Roberts fortified his belief in the age of the exclamation by an enclosed note from an elderly friend, Florence A. Redd, which read in part: "When I was about ten (I am now eighty-six) we had a hired girl whose favorite expression was 'Heavens to Betsy.' In fact she used it so often that we always referred to her as 'Heaven to Betsy.' " And in a subsequent note he called my attention to a passage on page 494 of his novel, *Oliver Wiswell,* in which Oliver, in 1777, says of the young Marquis de Lafayette, "He was the politest young man imaginable, and was forever smiling, kissing his finger tips to denote enthusiasm, or jumping from his chair to bow with his hand on his heart. I always knew when the little marquis arrived, because of Mrs. Byles' muffled artificial exclamations of 'Oh mercy me!' and 'Heavens to Betsy!' "

Well, though I don't doubt that "Heavens to Betsy!" is a hundred years old—it would almost have to be to have become so widespread before the days of rapid dissemination by radio, movies, or newspaper—I can't overlook the fact that *Oliver Wiswell* is fictional and was published no earlier than 1940. Possibly the phrase was known in Revolutionary War days, but I doubt it. Nor do I think, as some friends have suggested, that it pertained in any way to the maker of the first American flag, Betsy Ross. It is much more likely to have been derived in some way from the frontiersman's rifle or gun which, for unknown reason, he always fondly called Betsy. However, despite exhaustive search, I am reluctantly forced to resort to the familiar lexicographical locution, "Source unknown."

Almost as baffling was the saying we have used for generations, both in England and America, when speaking of (a) a person who, attempting the impossible, "might as well try to lift himself by the bootstraps," or (b) a person who, by determination and perseverance, laboring against almost impossible odds, succeeds in "raising himself by his bootstraps." Here I encountered the incredible fact that all dictionaries, from Randle Cotgrave's *Dictionarie of the French and English Tongues* of 1611 to and including the great *Oxford English Dictionary,* completed in 1933, had somehow managed to miss any definition of *bootstrap,* and that no dictionary nor other repository of idiomatic sayings contained any mention of this familiar phrase. Accordingly, as related in my discussion of the saying on page 51, the best that I have been able to do is to establish a fairly definite date before which the expression could not have existed.

But before I could establish even that time limit I was led into learning something of the history of boot-making, hence into consulting dozens of books and other references on boot- and shoe-making, as well as books on costume—none of which, incidentally, mentioned a bootstrap. Ultimately, as the most likely source for the information I sought, I wrote to the Northampton Town (England) Footwear Manufacturers' Association, representing the center of English boot- and shoe-making since the early seventeenth century. My inquiry was, to my good fortune, turned over to Mr. John H. Thornton, M.A., F.B.S.I., Head of the Department of Boot and Shoe Manufacture, Northampton College of Technology, a gentle-

517

man long interested in all phases of shoe history and a collector of historical items connected with the industry. The seventeenth-century Cromwellian boot, of which a sketch appears on page 51, is one of a pair from his collection. When worn by its original owner it had a spur held in place by a spur-leather over the instep, but these are missing. Heavy riding boots, according to Mr. Thornton, were the first to be made with bootstraps, and such boots did not come into use much before the end of the sixteenth century. The bootstrap, accordingly—or "strap," as then called—had not been known long when Shakespeare mentioned it in *Twelfth Night,* written in 1601.

The search for the mysterious Stoughton bottle, of the old New England saying, "to sit (or rarely, to stand) like a Stoughton bottle," which I had been quietly pursuing for a dozen years ultimately became fascinating and, I might say, fantastic. The definition given in *The New Standard Dictionary,* written in 1913 by some person unknown to me, reads:

Stoughton-bottle: A stupid person; figurehead; dolt; as, they stood there like stoughton-bottles: from the black or dark-green bottles of Dr. Stoughton's bitters, shaped like a log cabin and used in the Presidential campaign of 1840.

Though I had no material fault to find with the definition, I knew enough through hearsay and reading about the so-called "log cabin bottles" used in the wildly enthusiastic "Tippecanoe and Tyler, too" —William Henry Harrison and John Tyler—campaign of 1840 to mistrust the attached explanation. First, those bottles contained whisky (under the guise of hard cider, the only beverage, it was said, that Harrison knew in his youth). Second, and more decisive, just about every distiller in the country climbed aboard the band wagon by adopting for his product one or another bottle, colored or not, that somewhat resembled the appearance of a log cabin, the intent being to honor Harrison's alleged humble origin. That is to say, there was nothing so distinctive about one make of log-cabin bottle as to make it more doltish, more stupid in appearance than another.

The popularly called Webster Dictionary—*Webster's New International Dictionary, Second Edition,* by its full title—brought out in 1934, carried for the first time a definition of the bottle, thus:

518

Stoughton bottle. (After a Dr. Stoughton, the maker.) A bottle containing Stoughton's Elixir, a tincture of wormwood, germander, rhubarb, orange peel, cascarilla, and aloes, once widely used as a flavoring for alcoholic drinks and as a tonic.

to sit, stand, etc., *like a Stoughton bottle.* To sit, stand, etc., stolidly and dumbly.*

The inference is that "Dr. Stoughton" made the bottle as well as the elixir, though I doubt that such was the intent. However, no clue is offered as to why this particular bottle was so unique as to convey so definite an impression, nor why it must have been once so common that one hearing the phrase would immediately comprehend the meaning.

The Dictionary of Americanisms, published in 1951 by The University of Chicago Press, gave me no further information along those lines either, though its very friendly and helpful editor, Dr. Mitford M. Mathews, has written to say that "Stoughton bitters" received mention in American literature in 1847, ten years earlier than the date shown in his dictionary. Let me say here also, for the benefit of any doubting Thomas, one will find no further mention than I have given here of "Dr." Stoughton, Stoughton bitters or elixir, nor the Stoughton bottle in any encyclopedia or dictionary, American or English, not even in that monumental compendium of information, the *Oxford English Dictionary* nor its *Supplement.*

Now American bottle makers have turned out and are still turning out thousands of distinctive bottles, some so distinctive and familiar that, for example, any American traversing a hillside in Korea might point to a Coca-Cola bottle and say, "Well, I see I'm not the first American here." But in all our history the "Stoughton bottle" is the only one to have passed into a household expression. We can gather that it must have been squat in shape; that it must have appeared stolid; it must have looked stupid, or at least uncommunicative; it must have been fairly conspicuous; it certainly must have been a familiar object, and it must have been well known by name, especially in New England where the expression was best known.

Though the bottle described in the dictionary might conceivably

* By permission. From Webster's New International Dictionary, Second Edition, copyright, 1934, 1939, 1945, 1950, 1953, by G. & C. Merriam Co.

meet some of those conditions—as also the two square bottles described in the book, *Bitters Bottles* by J. H. Thompson, published in 1947, early in my search—none met all. So I then began to inquire at every "antique shoppe" in which, on one pretext or another, we entered on our annual sojourns in New England, to make inquiries at New England museums, to make deliberate inquiry at country auctions, to hunt up people named Stoughton—a not uncommon patronym in New England. I drew nothing but blanks.

Eventually I sent letters telling of my search to several newspapers, and then began to get results—though not many, of course. My initial, and reasonable, assumption that the "Stoughton bottle" of the saying was glass was most obviously the opinion also of the majority of those who replied to my appeal, directly to me or through the newspapers—those who owned a bottle with the name "Stoughton" imprinted on its face or who owned a bottle which, by family tradition, was a "Stoughton bottle." Including those of which I had previous descriptions, I now had descriptions of eleven glass bottles—no two alike! Some letters were accompanied by sketches, of which six are shown here. The one in outline at the right was part of the following letter from the Bay State (name and address omitted):

Hi There—

Saw ad in Mass Papper where you Inquired about the Stoughton Bottel—That was an old whiskey Bottle Shaped like this [sketch] havent seen one in years will Enquire at Salem when get to town. That is this what you are looking for answer. That was made in New England glass works, not in Exsistence now. let me hear from you.

520

Sketches that contained dimensions showed the tallest bottle, the one of which only "ought" is visible, to be nine inches tall; the small pear-shaped bottle and the one shaped like a water carafe, each also bearing the name "Stoughton," were six and three-fourths and seven inches tall respectively.

Just possibly a person gifted with the imaginative powers of the Greek who named the heavenly constellations might be able to fit one or two of the necessary attributes to one or another of these bottles, but the very fact that there was such a variety made it impossible to accept any.

As I had been previously assured that the saying had never been known in England, I had also assumed that "Dr." Stoughton and his famous bitters were American, though the records of the United States Patent Office from 1790 to 1873 failed to indicate any patents to anyone named Stoughton for either bitters or bottle. My search was thrown into another direction at this point, in part from some other letters that replied to my newspaper inquiries, and in part from a statement made in an item in the "All Sorts" column of the Boston *Post,* conducted by Joe Harrington. Through subsequent correspondence with Mr. Harrington, the Library of the Boston Athenaeum, and the Carnegie Free Library of Allegheny (Pittsburgh), I now learned that the bitters—or more properly, elixir—contained in the mysterious bottle was a concoction of one Richard Stoughton, an apothecary of Southwark, London; that Stoughton began to publicize his "Great Cordial Elixir" in 1712—a century earlier than I had supposed—and that his preparation was the second medicine for which letters patent were granted in England, as stated in both *Chronicles of Pharmacy* by A. C. Wootton (1910, Macmillan, London) and *Four Thousand Years of Pharmacy* by C. H. LaWall (1927, Lippincott, Philadelphia). For other data concerning the elixir I am indebted to *The Quacks of Old London* by C. J. S. Thompson (1928, Brentano, London).

Stoughton's advertising bill makes various assertions as to the virtues and properties of his medicine, but the statement of interest to me was this: "The Elixir has twenty-two ingredients unknown to any one but me, and has now obtained a great reputation throughout England, Scotland, Ireland and the plantations beyond the Sea."

Well, I have no doubt that New England was included among "the plantations beyond the Sea." And I have no doubt further that so great were the real or acclaimed virtues of this elixir that shortly after the American colonies broke away from parent England, when "letters patent" were no longer a restraint, more than one American apothecary began to concoct his own version of this celebrated elixir.* They used such bottles as struck individual fancy. Some went so far as to have "Stoughton" impressed in the glass; others used printed labels. All retained the original maker's name, but though some may have sold their product as an "elixir," the more common American name appears to have been "Stoughton bitters." The use was primarily for flavoring an alcoholic beverage, though it was also sometimes recommended as a tonic. Quite likely also, some American distiller may have adopted the name and produced a "Stoughton whisky."

Some responses to my newspaper inquiries, however, directed my consideration into channels other than *glass* bottles. This part of the story is given more fully on page 33 in the discussion of "to sit (or stand) like a Stoughton bottle." The explanation necessarily involves a certain amount of deduction, because it may not now be possible to trace back to pre-Revolutionary times and determine the facts. That is, to a number of persons "Stoughton bottle" meant a kind of stoneware jug used—almost invariably—"in my boyhood (or girlhood) days by my grandmother as a bed-warmer." Inquiry among a number of my elderly acquaintances also now residing in Florida confirmed that statement. And, to my surprise, some of these of Canadian or English birth recalled a "Stoughton

* After this foreword was in type I received corroborative support for this surmise from Dr. Glenn Sonnedecker, Secretary, American Institute of the History of Pharmacy, whose letter says, in part: "There is evidence that 'Stoughton's Bitters' was being rather extensively used in the early 19th century. We have in our collection, for example, a manuscript 'Order Book' of a Philadelphia wholesale druggist—probably Jeremiah Emlen. This shows a number of entries during 1815 and 1816 for sales of 1 to 5 dozen 'Stoughton's Bitters,' at $1.25 per dozen (size of unit unspecified)."

A later letter from Dr. Sonnedecker adds further support. He says: " 'Stoughton's Elixer [sic] Magnum Stomachicum' is listed in the *Catalogue of Drugs and Medicines* [etc.], *imported, prepared, and sold by Smith and Bartlett, at their Druggists Store and Apothecaries Shop, No. 61, Cornhill, Boston,* Manning and Loring, Boston, 1795, p. 18."

bottle" put to the same use in their childhood days. This confirmed a letter from a New England nurse who said that in her probationary days in a London hospital forty-odd years ago her early duty had been to fill some thirty "Stoughton bottles" three or four times a day as foot warmers for the patients.

It is my belief, therefore, though I cannot prove it, that for safety in transportation "throughout England, Scotland, Ireland, and the plantations beyond the Sea," the Great Cordial Elixir concocted by Richard Stoughton was shipped in stoneware containers or "bottles" which, because of convenient size and heat-retaining qualities, were prized by grandmother's great-grandmother and, when empty, were filled with hot water on cold winter nights and used as foot warmers in bed or in a sleigh, and in summer were filled with sand and used as doorstops. In shape, appearance, conspicuousness, and familiarity the year around these distinctive bottles, of which several designs are shown on page 36, fulfil all the requirements.

The works that I have consulted, often futilely, in the preparation of these "where we got it" sketches would run into many hundreds, if I were able to list them. They would embrace the dictionaries of many languages, encyclopedias, volumes on customs and fashions of bygone generations—Greek, Roman, English, American. They would include histories of England and America, and the biographies of many men. Dictionaries of slang have been helpful—American, by Berrey and Van den Bark; English, by Partridge, as well as Farmer, and older works. But the collection could not have been presented in the manner chosen had it not been for the excellent research material available in the *Oxford English Dictionary on Historical Principles* and its *Supplement,* the *Dictionary of American English* and the more recent *Dictionary of Americanisms,* both of which are also on historical principles. To the editor of the last-named tome, Dr. Mitford M. Mathews, I am especially indebted for his ready response to numerous requests. For assistance from England in times of need I owe thanks in particular to Sir St. Vincent Troubridge, whose name will be found more than once in the following pages, and to Ivor Brown, whose books, *A Word in Your Ear* and *Just Another Word,* have delighted many readers. I am indebted also to various other individuals in both countries for aid on one or another single item, and I have been impressed repeatedly by the willingness of librarians in my peregrinations north and south to offer suggestions and dig out musty references—Springfield (Vermont), Dartmouth University, New York Public Library, University of North Carolina, University of Florida, Mount Dora (Florida), and especially Maureen J. Harris of the Alderson Library, Orlando, Florida.

HEAVENS TO BETSY!

And Other Curious Sayings

to play cat and mouse with one

Everyone has seen the way a cat acts with a mouse that she has caught. The poor little animal, half dead with fright or injury, waits with beating heart until the cat has apparently forgotten it or gone to sleep, and then may get halfway to its hole or other place of

safety, only to be pounced upon and again tossed around. Figuratively, then, when sweet and capricious Susan "plays cat and mouse" with lovesick Peter, she is by turns seemingly indifferent to him or mercilessly possessive if he dare cast an eye at another maid. She has him on a string. The expression came into popular use in England in 1913 during the suffragette agitation.
Women, arrested for disturbing the peace, resorted to the hunger strike, thus endangering health. To get around such voluntary martyrdom Parliament passed an act called the "Prisoners' Temporary-Discharge-for-Ill-Health Act," which promptly became known as the "Cat-and-Mouse Act." Namely, it provided that a hunger striker could be released, but was subject to re-arrest to serve out the remainder of a sentence whenever danger to health was removed.

at the eleventh hour

With not a moment to spare; at the latest time possible; just under the wire. This is of Biblical origin, Matthew xx,1–16: "For the kingdom of heaven is like unto a householder, which went out early in the morning to hire labourers into his vineyard. And when he had agreed with the labourers for a penny a day, he sent them into his vineyard. . . . And about the eleventh hour he went out and found others standing idle, and saith unto them, Why stand ye here all the day idle? They say unto him, Because no man hath hired us. He saith unto them, Go ye also into the vineyard; and

527

whatsoever is right, that shall ye receive." But at evening all received the same payment. Despite the protests of those who had "borne the burden and heat of the day," those who came at the eleventh hour received a penny, just as those who had come early in the morning.

a tempest in a teacup

Of course, the old Romans had neither teacup nor tea, but they did have a saying so like ours as to be usually translated in our wording: *excitare fluctus in simpulo*. The literal meaning is "to stir up a tempest in a small ladle"; hence, to storm about over trifles, to make much ado about nothing. In our literature the "teacup" analogy did not appear before 1872, but as long ago as 1678 small affairs were compared with great affairs as "but a storm in a cream bowl," and, in 1830, as "a storm in a wash-basin."

for crying out loud

An ejaculation, usually indicating complaint or astonishment; as, "For crying out loud, why did you do a thing like that?" Many of the users of this expression would be shocked to learn that it is in the category known as a minced oath; that is, a substitute based on, but slightly differing from a profanity. The expression is a high-school adaptation of about twenty-five years' standing of the profane ejaculation, "for Christ's sake."

a rift in the lute

It is the poet, Alfred Lord Tennyson, to whom we are indebted for this saying, and he expressed its meaning in the lines from *The Idylls of the King* (Merlin and Vivien, 1870) in which it appeared:

> Faith and unfaith can ne'er be equal powers:
> Unfaith in aught is want of faith in all.
> It is the little rift within the lute,
> That by and by will make the music mute,
> And ever widening slowly silence all.

a hair of the dog that bit you

This stems from the ancient medical maxim, Like cures like—
Similia similibus curantur. Thus, even in the *Iliad* we find the Greek
belief that a wound caused by the spear of Achilles could be healed
by an ointment containing rust from that same spear. And to this
day there are men and women who sin-
cerely believe that the best cure from the
bite of a dog is some of the hair from that
dog applied to the wound. In England,
they say, the hair should be burned before
it is applied. But, generally speaking, when
men get together, "a hair of the dog that
bit you" means another little drink. If the
conviviality of last night's sessions has resulted in a morning's hangover, the "hair"

is supposed to be a pick-me-up, a little whisky to clear the head.
This was the meaning among gentlemen four hundred years ago, as
recorded in John Heywood's *Prouerbes in the Englishe Tongue*
(1546): "I pray the leat me and my felow haue / A heare of the
dog that bote us last night."

in the dumps

Feeling blue; depressed; dejected; low in spirits. People felt this
way and so expressed themselves four hundred years ago, though no
one knew then (or now, for that matter) just what "dumps" meant.
Sir Thomas More, in *A Dialoge of Comforte against Tribulation*
(1534), has: "What heapes of heauynesse [heaviness], hathe of
late fallen amonge vs alreadye, with whiche some of our poore
familye bee fallen in suche dumpes."

to strike while the iron is hot

To act at the most fitting moment; to seize the most favorable
opportunity. It was, of course, the blacksmith who was originally
so exhorted. If he failed to swing his hammer while the metal on
the anvil was still glowing, nothing would do but to start up the
forge again and reheat the iron. His time was lost; the opportunity

for effective work had passed. Figurative use is very old. It is found in Chaucer's *Canterbury Tales,* "The Tale of Melibeus," (1386): "Right so as whil that Iren is hoot men sholden smyte."

A-number-one (A No. 1)

Superior, first class, the best of its kind. An American nautical classification of British ancestry, both of which referred originally to sailing vessels. The British term, usually written "A 1," was thus described in Lloyd's Register: "The character A denotes new ships, or ships renewed or restored. The stores of vessels are designated by the figures 1 and 2; signifying that the vessel is well and sufficiently found." The American term had a slightly different sense, as described in *Goodrich's Fifth School Reader* (1857): "Vessels are classified according to their age, strength, and other qualities. The best class is called A, and No. 1 implies that the Swiftsure stands at the head of the best class of vessels."

Charles Dickens was the earliest writer to give the British phrase a non-nautical use. In *Pickwick Papers* (1837), the faithful valet, Sam Weller, wants to know what kind of "gen'l'men" already occupy the prison room in which Mr. Pickwick is to be confined. The turnkey, Roker, describes one who "takes his twelve pints of ale a-day, and never leaves off smoking even at his meals." "He must be a first-rater," says Sam. "A-1," Roker answered.

And Harriet Beecher Stowe, in *Dred, A Tale of the Great Dismal Swamp* (1856), has the distinction of being the first to introduce the American phrase into literary use. She has Father Bennie, the preacher who buys and sells slaves as a sideline, ask a dealer, "You got a good cook in your lot, hey?" "Got a prime one," the dealer answered, "an A number one cook, and no mistake."

a bone to pick

A difficulty to be solved; a nut to be cracked; a complaint, dispute, misunderstanding or the like to be settled. The original idea was something to mull over or to occupy one as a bone occupies a dog. The Germans had the same idea but used a different simile, *ein Hünchen zu pflücken,* a bird to pluck; the French said, *une maille à partir,* a knot to pick; and in ancient Rome it was *scrupulum alicui injicere,* a pebble to throw.

An anonymous newspaper columnist recently said that this expression "started in Sicily where the father of a bride would give the bridegroom a bone to pick clean of meat as a symbol of the difficult task of marriage that he was undertaking." His statement of the Sicilian custom may be true, but any connection between that custom and our English expression of more than four hundred years is beyond credibility.

The related expression that we use commonly nowadays—"to have a bone to pick with one," to have a complaint to settle with one—is much more recent, dating back scarcely a hundred years.

to crack a crib

This is not modern slang. In the cant of thieves, "crack" has meant "to break open" since the early eighteenth century or earlier, and "crib," meaning "a house, shop," was known to Charles Dickens when he wrote *Oliver Twist* in 1838, and was used by the underworld thirty years or more before that date. Henry Kingsley used the full expression in the novel, *Ravenshoe,* in 1861.

rich as Croesus

Croesus succeeded his father and became king of Lydia, a country of Asia Minor, in 560 B.C. Through successive wars he greatly increased his dominions and, by such means and through trade within his own realm and with neighboring kingdoms, he became enormously wealthy. Probably his wealth was not actually as great as it was reputed, for the figures were fabulous. It became proverbial in his day, and is still used metaphorically as denoting great wealth. He died, however, in 546 B.C., after his kingdom had been overcome by Cyrus.

skeleton at the feast

An element of gloom or depression; an omen of misfortune; a reminder of possible disaster in the midst of pleasure. The allusion is to a custom in ancient Egypt as related by Plutarch (*c.* A.D. 46 to 120) in his *Moralia.* He tells us that at the conclusion of a feast a household servant carried a mummy into the banquet hall as a reminder to the guests that all men are mortal. However, our present phrase did not arise in English literature before the middle of the nineteenth century. It is best known, perhaps, from Longfellow's "The Old Clock on the Stairs," stanza 5:

In that mansion used to be
Free-hearted Hospitality;
His great fires up the chimney roared;
The stranger feasted at his board;
But, like the skeleton at the feast,
That warning timepiece never ceased,—
"Forever—never!
Never—forever!"

to take under one's wings

"O Jerusalem, Jerusalem, thou that killest the prophets, and stonest them which are sent unto thee, how often would I have gathered thy children together, even as a hen gathereth her chickens under her wings, and ye would not!" This passage from Matthew

xxiii, 37, was the source of our present expression. The metaphorical protection like that of a mother bird over her young appears also in Psalms lxiii, 7—"Because thou hast been my help, therefore in the shadow of thy wings will I rejoice." However, some of us may be more familiar with the saying from the lines of the Gilbert & Sullivan operetta, *The Mikado,* sung by Ko-Ko:

The flowers that bloom in the spring,
    Tra la,
Have nothing to do with the case.
I've got to take under my wing,
    Tra la,
A most unattractive old thing,
    Tra la,
With a caricature of a face.

532

one's cake is dough

One's plans have miscarried; one is disappointed. The proverb was old in the time of Shakespeare. In *Taming of the Shrew*, Act I, scene 1, he has Gremio saying to Hortensio, both suitors of Bianca, "Their love is not so great, Hortensio, but we may blow our nails together, and fast it fairly out; our cake's dough on both sides." Apperson reports the occurrence of the expression in the *Prayers* of Thomas Becon, 1559: "Or else your cake is dough, and all your fat lie in the fire." The allusion is obvious: when an oven does not reach a baking heat, one's plans for a cake have miscarried.

to speak by the card

The sense of this is nicely shown by Shakespeare's use of it in *Hamlet*. There, in Act V, scene 1, he has Hamlet himself use it in his conversation with the grave-digging clown who takes everything that Hamlet says in its most literal meaning. Finally Hamlet turns to his friend, Horatio, and says: "How absolute the knave is! we must speak by the card, or equivocation will undo us." He realized, that is, that he would have to express himself precisely, or he would get some such answer as Gracie Allen gives when she takes any remark literally. Shakespeare, the first on record to use the expression, undoubtedly alluded to the mariner's card, which may have been either the sea-chart or card, the nautical map indicating the position of rocks, sandbars, capes, and so on along a coast, or the circular card of stiff paper with the points of the compass upon it. In either case, "by the card" would denote absolute precision.

to call the turn

Let's quote some passages from Hoyle's rules for the game of faro: "The cards are shuffled and placed in a dealing box, from which they can be withdrawn only one at a time. . . . The dealer pulls out two cards, one at a time, the first card being laid aside, the one under it being placed close to the box; and the next one left showing. . . . The banker pays even money on all bets but the last turn. When only three cards remain, all different, they must come in one of six ways and the bank pays four for one if the player can call the turn. . . ." Thus, you see, if one can guess correctly, in the game of faro, how the last three cards will appear, or if one can guess correctly how any transaction or affair will develop, he "calls the turn."

to chew the fat (or rag)

Back in the fourteenth century, in Wyclif's time, they "chewed the cud"—and we still do, in imitation of the reflective appearance of cows as they lie patiently working their jaws. But to chew the fat, or rag, does not necessarily involve meditation; it usually involves nothing more than working the jaws in complaint, disputation, idle speech, vain argument, or just gossip. "Rag (or fat) chewing" we have had since the early 1880's. It was then classed as American Army slang, in Patterson's *Life in the Ranks*. To my notion, although either expression may have been adopted into army lingo, both are much more likely to have alluded to ladies' sewing circles—to the "rags," or cloth, upon which they worked while tongues clattered, or to the "fat," or choice morsels of gossip, upon which they could feast.

to cash in (hand in, or pass in) one's checks (or chips)

Whichever the phraseology, it adds up to the one result—to die. The allusion is to the American game of poker, in which a player may at any time drop from the game and turn in (hand in, or pass in) his chips or checks to the banker in exchange for cash. Perhaps on some few occasions, in the wild and woolly West, a man withdrew from an unfinished game only on pain of death, but our metaphorical usage had no such sinister general meaning at the time of its birth.

Charley-horse

A paragrapher in *Ladies' Home Journal* (Vol. LXX, No. 12) asserted without hesitation that this term for muscular stiffness came about thus: In the 1890's, a horse (named Charley) which drew a roller in the White Sox ball park in Chicago had a peculiar limp. Hence, the fans applied the name "Charley-horse" to any player afflicted with a muscular stiffness or lameness.

I can't deny that there may have been such a horse; however, if so, he must have performed his duties and to have had his name applied to such an injury some time before the 1890's. The term was used by a Cincinnati paper early in 1889, telling why a ballplayer had withdrawn from the game in 1888, and inasmuch as the nature of the injury was not described, it is obvious that "Charleyhorse" was well understood by baseball fans, at least, even outside of Chicago, before this latter date. Regrettably, we must continue to say "Origin unknown," despite much and varied speculation.

white-collar worker

Anyone who performs non-manual labor; a professional person, such as lawyer, doctor, banker, clergyman, etc.; specifically, an office worker, rather than a shop worker. An anonymous newspaper columnist recently stated that the expression started "when medicine became a respected profession and doctors began to wear white collars as part of their uniforms." The statement is an absurdity on the face of it. Medicine was "a respected profession" in the time of Galen and, though it may have fallen into some disrepute in the Middle Ages, it has certainly regained respect since the seventeenth century, long before the era of the white collar. Actually the label is recent and wholly unrelated to medicine or to uniforms of any sort. Originally it was the counterpart of the British "black-coated worker," a clerical employee, that is. The term originated during World War I.

the admirable Crichton

There was actually an individual who was so called, though not during his brief life. His real name was James Crichton, a son of Robert Crichton, lord advocate of Scotland. He is believed to have been born in 1560, and to have died at the early age of twenty-two, but his learning and athletic attainments were most remarkable—if the reports of Sir Thomas Urquhart and Aldus Manutius are to be credited. Urquhart, who wrote seventy years after Crichton's death, says that he held a dispute one time in the college of Navarre in twelve languages, and the next day won a tilting match. Aldus, who was a contemporary, is slightly more modest in his claims for his hero, but says that he spoke ten languages, could compose

Latin verse on any subject, was a mathematician and theologist, was extravagantly handsome and with the bearing of a soldier. The epithet, "the Admirable Crichton," was applied by John Johnston in his *Heroes Scoti* (1603), and is now sometimes bestowed upon any man of unusual grace and superior accomplishments.

to make no bones about (a matter)

To speak frankly; to come out flat-footed; to talk straight from the shoulder; hence, to have no scruples; to show no reluctance, also, to make no mistake (about it), to count on (it). *The Paston Letters* (1459) contain the line, "And fond [found] that tyme no bonys in the matere," and the poet, John Skelton, in *The Tunnyng of Elynour Rummyng* (1529), wrote, "She founde therein no bones," wherein in each case "to find no bones" was equivalent to "to find no difficulty; to have no hesitation." Accordingly, it seems evident that the allusion in the earliest form of our present expression was to the actual occurrence of bones in stews or soup; "no bones" would be indicative of no difficulty or no hesitation in the swallowing. The change to today's expression is shown in the translation by Nicholas Udall (1548) of *Erasmus's Paraphrase of Luke:* "He made no manier bones ne stickyng [no scruples nor hesitation], but went in hande to offer up his only son Isaac." Many writers since that date have "made no bones" about employing the phrase.

cheek by jowl

In early usage, six hundred years ago, when anyone wanted to express close intimacy, he said (or wrote), "cheke bi cheke." But some two centuries later someone thought it would be more picturesque to substitute the Frenchified "jowl"—variously written *jowl, joul, joll, jole, geoul, chowl*—for the second element, and this has been our choice ever since. It still means "cheek by cheek."

cute as a bug's ear

On the theory that the smaller they come the cuter they are, this modern American metaphor epitomizes the acme of cuteness, for if a small ear is cute, the ear of a bug—if bugs have ears—must be the cutest thing imaginable. Sometimes the expression is paraphrased into "cute as a bug in a rug," but this is a poor foist of new upon old. "Snug as a bug in a rug," the utmost in contentment and comfort, dates back two hundred years.

to lead by the nose

To dominate; to have control over; to have the whip hand or under one's thumb; to hold under submission. The expression is a common one in European languages, and both Romans and Greeks of old "had a word for it." The allusion is obvious: From the time

when beasts of burden were first domesticated, even as the oxen of the present time, it was found that they could be controlled and led by chain or cord attached to a ring through the septum of the nose. In the Roman Circus, trainers of wild animals sometimes thus led beasts that they had captured around the arena. Through the Middle Ages and even to recent times, bears have been so displayed. For Biblical reference we have Isaiah xxxvii, 29: "Because thy rage against me, and thy tumult, is come up into mine ears, therefore will I put my hook in thy nose, and my bridle in thy lips, and I will turn thee back by the way by which thou camest."

to know chalk from cheese

There was a time when coloring matter was not used in the making of cheese. Consequently, chalk and cheese were of the same whiteness. Such, at least, was the state of affairs in the fourteenth century. Perhaps, too, an unscrupulous tradesman would now and then take advantage of an innocent young housewife and sell her a piece of chalk which he had carefully shaped to resemble a cheese. At any rate, comparisons of chalk with cheese began to crop up at every opportunity. John Gower, in *Confessio Amantis* (1590), wrote, "Lo, how they feignen [counterfeit] chalk for chese." Such comparisons carry on to the present time from habit, though for several centuries the two substances no longer have had even a superficial resemblance.

to back and fill

To shilly-shally; to be vacillating or irresolute; to assert and deny, hem and haw; not to know if one is on one's head or heels. Originally this was said of ships, of sailing ships especially, attempting to negotiate a narrow channel when wind and tide were adverse and there was no room for tacking. Under such conditions a vessel may be worked to windward by keeping it broadside on to the current in mid-channel by counter-bracing the yards or keeping the sails shivering—that is, alternately backing and filling the sails. The progress of the ship is thus alternately backward and forward, in herringbone pattern; hence, anything that appears to do nothing more than to recede and advance, to vacillate, is said to back and fill.

between the devil and the deep blue sea

On the horns of a dilemma; between equally perilous dangers. I was reminded by a correspondent (whose signature, regrettably, I have been unable to decipher) that I had not gone far enough in my discussion of this expression in *A Hog on Ice*. "Devil," in this phrase—as also in "the devil to pay"—is a nautical term. In the days when hulls were of wooden construction, the term was applied to a seam between two planks which, because of its location or of its length, was especially accursed by sailors. In this instance, "devil" probably referred to the seam on a ship's deck nearest the side; hence, the longest seam on the deck, extending on a curve from stem to stern, and, from its location, a most dangerous one to calk or fill with pitch. Anyone between the devil and the deep (blue) sea had a very narrow footing, a narrow margin for choice.

"Devil" was also applied to the seam that was at, or just above, the water line of a ship's hull. Here again space was narrow and the margin of safety was negligible.

538

not worth a hill of beans

Beans, like straw, have long indicated small value. "Not to care a straw" means that the speaker has little more than the slightest concern over that of which he speaks, no more than the value of the straw trampled upon by householders of old. And the bean has long had no higher regard. ("Hill" is American hyperbole, inserted about a hundred years ago for exaggerated emphasis.) The expression is one of the oldest in the language. We find it used by Robert of Gloucester back in 1297 in his *English Chronicles,* page 497:

> þe king of alimayne sende specialliche inou
> To king Ion þat he wiþdrowe him of is wou
> & vnderuenge þe erchebissop & holichurche al clene
> Lete abbe ir franchise & al nas wurþ a bene.

We don't speak or write that way now, thank heavens, but freely translated it reads: "The king of Almain [Germany] sent [a message] especially to king John to forget his hurt, and receive the archbishop, and let Holy Church have her franchise, clear and clean; altogether not worth a bean."

to sit (or stand) like a Stoughton bottle

To sit (or stand) dumbly apathetic, stolidly, without expression, stupidly, like a bump on a log. I know well its meaning, as my wife's father, a New England country doctor, used it frequently during his lifetime in referring to anyone, member of his family or not, who appeared to be thus blankly uninterested in whatever was being said or done. Furthermore, the expression has been defined similarly in the *Funk & Wagnalls New Standard Dictionary* since 1913 and in the *Merriam-Webster New International Dictionary* since 1934. But it did not occur to me to ask my father-in-law, until too late, why a Stoughton bottle—presumably a bottle containing a tonic or bitters originally compounded at some undetermined time by a "Dr." Stoughton—acquired such a metaphorical meaning.

The lengthy search for a bottle, which by dictionary account was of glass, that would meet the conditions indicated by the figurative meaning is related in the foreword. It entailed much correspondence. The mysterious "Dr. Stoughton" turned out to be an English apothecary of Southwark, London. I had been seeking an American; our metaphor is of New England origin, wholly unknown in England. Stoughton's compound was the second medicine to be granted "letters patent" in England. That was in 1712, a hundred years earlier than I had supposed. Its full name was Stoughton's Great Cordial Elixir. In the early advertisements, according to *The Quacks of Old London* (1928), by C. J. S. Thompson, to which I owe this information in part, this elixir was a remedy "for all distempers of the stomach"; fifty or sixty drops of it "more or less as you please" were recommended to be taken "as often as you please" in a glass of "Spring water, Beer, Ale, Mum, Canary, White wine, with or without sugar, and a dram of brandy." (Can you not see how our great-great-grandsires would welcome this tonic for "distempers of the stomach"?)

The prospective purchaser was further told: " 'Tis most excellent in Tea, in Wine, very pleasant and proper, and in Beer or Ale, makes the best Purl in the world, and Purl Royal in Sack, giving all of them a fragrant smell and taste, far exceeding Purl made with wormwood and now used to drink in their wine at Taverns." (Purl was a spiced malt beverage popular at that period.) Then Stoughton added, the elixir "has now obtained a great reputation throughout England, Scotland, Ireland and the plantations beyond the Sea," and he concluded his bill with the offer, "If any Captain or Seaman, Book-seller, Stationer, Coffee-man, or any keeping a Publick House, wants any quantities to dispose of or sell again, they may be furnished with good allowance by letter or otherwise."

It would appear that New England was one "plantation beyond the Sea" where Stoughton's elixir had "obtained a great reputation," and that some unknown Captain, Seaman, or, most likely, a keeper of a "Publick House" profited favorably from its importation and resale. But it is not remotely probable that glass bottles of any size, nature, or description were used in the eighteenth century for shipping this liquid, either by sailing vessels or by carts that may have carried it throughout England and Scotland. On the contrary, it is almost certain that the bottles were glazed earthen- or stoneware, of the same nature as the pottery bottles in which

Holland gin has been shipped until recent years. And just as these latter bottles are spoken of as "Holland gin bottles" because of the original contents, so must the older bottles have been known as "Stoughton bottles."

I do not know either the shape or the size of those eighteenth-century bottles nor whether any may have been preserved in any collection of ceramics. But they were evidently of sufficient size to justify the housewife or grandmother in saving them when empty. In the unheated bedrooms of both England and America they made excellent foot warmers, when filled with hot water and stoppered well. And in summer, filled with sand, they were again useful as doorstops. In one capacity or another a Stoughton bottle was always in evidence. Even when not in use it probably stood in a corner somewhere, and it is likely that the housewife had several of them. It never talked back nor participated in any activity. Whether standing on its unglazed end or lying (sitting) on its side it was expressionless, stupid, apathetic.

It may be that production and importation of the famous elixir died with Richard Stoughton—the twenty-two ingredients, according to his advertisement, were unknown to anyone but him. Or it may have been that events following the Revolutionary War shut off its importation. But so persistent was the repute of this elixir that an American product, under the general name "Stoughton bitters," began to appear, probably about the turn of the century. And as neither the name nor the ingredients were now protected, I have no doubt that several makers produced their own versions of the compound and put them on sale in glass bottles of their own selection, thus accounting for the wide variety of bottles described in the foreword.

Moreover, the stoneware bottles also ceased to arrive from England. However, that was not long a matter of concern. American potteries began to supply that want of the housewife and to turn out foot warmers of better design—and these, because of long association, were still called Stoughton bottles. I do not know to what extent these American "bottles" may have differed from those that formerly had come from England. Of the first two shown in the accompanying illustration, the one on the left, bearing no label nor maker's name, was lent to me by its present owner, Mrs. Elizabeth H. Brown of Vermont, who, after purchasing it at an auction, was told by a nurse that it was a Stoughton bottle. From the evidence of other letters and various persons to whom I have shown it, I think bottles of this type were the more common. Note the broad flanges on the lower side to check the bottle from rolling, also the firm base on which it may be stood. The bottle in the center, with decorations baked in, labeled "Boss Foot Warmer" and

made in Portland, Maine, was presented to me by Kenneth Roberts and comes from other ancestral relics in the cellar of his home in Maine. The stopper, also stoneware, screws into the filler opening upon a rubber washer. The third bottle, of which detail drawings were sent to me by Russell Thornquist of Palmer, Massachusetts, whose sister owns it, was made or sold by P. L. Pride, Worcester, Massachusetts, and is of unusual design, as shown by the right-hand sketch. This bottle, also known as a Stoughton bottle, may be called a modern version, for it was purchased for use in the Rutland, Massachusetts, sanitarium as recently as 1926. Each of these three bottles is eleven or twelve inches in length and fifteen inches in circumference. The knob at the end of each was for convenience in lifting or carrying. A fourth bottle, which its present owner says was just called a hot-water jug, but does not describe, was made, according to imprint, by "Dorchester Pottery W'ks, Boston." A fifth one, described only from girlhood recollections, was said to have been twenty-four inches long, though only fifteen inches in circumference, resembling "a very large piece of bologna."

I have not been able to obtain a description of the Stoughton bottles which, until recent years at least, were in use in England. Information concerning use there is from isolated sources—Yorkshire, Northumberland, London—but details are lacking.

Incidentally, if the reader is seized with an urge to own a Stoughton bottle, he stands a better chance of success if, in browsing around a New England antique store, he asks the dealer if he happens to have a stoneware "pig."

to give (or get) the third degree

One who is a member of a Lodge of Freemasons knows so well the original meaning of this common expression that he will see little occasion for its inclusion here. But there are many who use it freely, however, who suppose it to have some connection with criminal law. Thus, in the United States, a murder that is deliberate is called murder in the first degree; one that is unintentional is murder in the second degree. Wrongly, therefore, it is supposed that some form of crime is in the third degree.

Actually the term "third degree" has no connection with criminality or brutal treatment or mental torture. It refers to the third and final stage of proficiency demanded of one who seeks to become a Master Mason. In each of the two preceding stages or degrees certain tests of proficiency are required, but before the candidate is fully qualified for the third degree he must undergo a very elaborate and severe test of ability, not even faintly injurious, physically or mentally. It is from this examinaton that "third degree" became applied to the treatment of prisoners by the police, and it was through the fact that the police sometimes did employ brutality in efforts to extort confession or information that our present expression obtained its common modern meaning.

dark and bloody ground

A title sometimes given to the state of Kentucky, so called because of the numerous raids by Indians upon white settlers in the early days of colonization. Very little was known about the region before 1752, and the first white colony was not established until 1774, at Harrodsburg. Few Indians, mainly Chickasaws near the Mississippi, inhabited the region, but it was claimed as hunting grounds by tribes from Tennessee and from southern Ohio. Despite treaties, therefore, bands of Indians would descend upon isolated farms or even villages to kill and burn. This was especially true under British instigation during the Revolutionary War, when the settlers were neglected by Virginia, in whose territory the country then lay, and were compelled to attempt to defend themselves. John Filson was the first to record the title in his history, *Kentucke* (1784): "The fertile region, now called Kentucke, then but known to the Indians, by the name of the Dark and Bloody Ground, and sometimes the Middle Ground." Filson erred on his translation, however, though the true meaning of the Indian name, Kentucky, is still not positively known.

to be caught flat-footed

In American usage, one is "caught flat-footed" when he is unprepared, asleep at the switch, inattentive, or surprised. In *A Hog on Ice,* page 57, I said that the expression probably arose from the American game of football, "for it applies most pertinently to the player who, having received the ball on a pass, is caught by an opposing player before he has moved from his tracks." My friend, Sir St. Vincent Troubridge, insists, "This is without doubt at all from horse-racing, quite solidly established in this country [England] from the reign of Queen Anne." In further correspondence he added: "In this country horse races are not started from stalls as with you, but by the horses advancing in line to a 'gate,' or barrier of tapes and webbing, which is raised by the starter by means of a lever when he is satisfied that the horses are in line. It will be clear that any horse which is 'caught flat-footed'—i.e., with all four feet on the ground, instead of dancing forward on his toes, so to speak, when the 'gate' rises—is at a disadvantage and will lose many lengths at the start. *Mutatis mutandis* the same would apply to men at the start of a foot-race, who are normally right forward on their toes awaiting the pistol shot."

dead as a herring

Very, very dead. Any dead fish soon acquires an exceedingly ancient odor if left exposed for only a few hours, but the odor of a dead herring becomes twice as noticeable. That is the reason herrings are used, by dragging them over a trail, in the teaching of young dogs to follow a scent. The expression probably started as a

544

variation of "dead as a doornail" (see *A Hog on Ice*, page 195) back in the sixteenth century. Shakespeare used both. He put the present one into the mouth of Doctor Caius, in *Merry Wives of Windsor*, Act II, scene 3. Jealous of the curate, Sir Hugh Evans, who also seeks the hand of Mistress Anne Page, Caius threatens to kill him in a duel, which the two parties, assembled in different fields, are not likely to have:

Caius (to his second, Jack Rugby): Vat is de clock, Jack?

Rugby: 'Tis past the hour, sir, that Sir Hugh promised to meet.

Caius: By gar, he has save his soul, dat he is no come; he has pray his Pible well, dat he is no come: by gar, Jack Rugby, he is dead already, if he be come.

Rugby: He is wise, sir; he knew your worship would kill him if he came.

Caius: By gar, de herring is no dead so as I vill kill him.

to keep one's eyes skinned (or peeled)

To be very observant or extremely alert; to keep a sharp lookout. No record of this American expression has been turned up

earlier than 1833, but the fact that it then appeared in a newspaper (*The Political Examiner,* of Shelbyville, Kentucky) is a fair indication that it was already well known to any reader. The meaning was not explained. The passage read: "I wish I may be shot if I don't think you had better keep your eyes skinned so that you can look powerful sharp, lest we get rowed up the river this heat."

deaf as an adder

"The wicked . . . go astray as soon as they be born, speaking lies. Their poison is like the poison of a serpent: they are like the deaf adder that stoppeth her ear; Which will not hearken to the voice of the charmer, charming never so wisely." Psalms, lviii, 3–5. Or, in the language of the *Early English Psalter* (about 1300),

"Als of a neddre als-swa yat [that] stoppand es his eres twa." The allusion is to the ancient Oriental belief that certain serpents were able to protect themselves against being lured by the music of charmers by stopping up one ear with the tip of the tail and pressing the other firmly to the ground.

to go to the dickens

This is nothing more than a polite—or if not polite, at least euphemistic—way of saying "go to hell," or to perdition, or to the devil, or to ruin in some uncomfortable manner. It has nothing to do with the novelist, Charles Dickens, for "dickens," in this sense, was known to Shakespeare. He used it in *Merry Wives of Windsor,* Act III, scene 2, where Mrs. Page, in answer to Ford's, "Where had you this pretty weathercock," referring to Sir John Falstaff's page, Robin, replies, "I cannot tell what the dickens his name is my husband had him of."

But when and how "devil," or whatever the original term may have been, became distorted to "dickens" has not yet been determined. One conjecture is that the original term may have been "devilkins," little devil, which by frequent usage may have worn down to "dickens." We have many words in our present language derived through such a process, so this one sounds plausible—but, alas, no such use of "devilkins" or "deilkins" has turned up.

every dog has his day

The time will come to each of us to chuck one's weight around; to exhibit a period of ostentation, influence, or power. It may be long in the coming, but, according to this old proverb, everyone will at some time, at least once, be able to emulate the dog that, servile and cowed all its life, one day turns and snaps at its tormentor, or, perchance, struts proudly at the head of a ragamuffin procession. No one knows how old the proverb may be, nor, if not of English origin, from whence it came. It is found in *A Dialogue Conteynying Prouerbes and Epigrammes* (1562) by John Heywood —"But as euery man saith, a dog hath a daie"—and was used by Shakespeare: "The Cat will Mew, and Dogge will haue his day," in the words of Hamlet.

546

anvil chorus

The collective critical comments of those opposing any measure, political or otherwise; as, "Any proposal made by Franklin Roosevelt met with a resounding anvil chorus of Republican senators." The term has a musical background, referring originally to the cacophony of anvils or cymbals and timpani beaten rhythmically in the accompaniment of the so-called "Anvil Chorus," based on the "Gipsy Song" in Verdi's *Il Trovatore*. This familiar chorus runs:

> Proudly our banner now gleams with golden luster!
> Brighter each star shines in the glorious cluster!
>   Hail, liberty forevermore!
>   And Peace and Union
>   And Peace and Union
> Throughout our happy land.

to bite off more than one can chew

To attempt more than one can accomplish; to try to do more than one has time for, or the ability for. A very human failing; one that is often quite praiseworthy, but also one that is often quite exasperating. The former could be said of a student, for  example, who, in the laudable desire to learn all he can, takes on more courses than he can find time to keep up with, and thus flunks several; the latter could be said of my more-than-willing yardman, Lou, who cannot say no to anyone seeking his services and, accordingingly, never turns up at an appointed date. The homely American expression has been traced back some seventy-five years, but is undoubtedly much earlier. It could have had a literal beginning with a small boy who took such a big mouthful as to be unable to do more than roll it around in his mouth; but more likely it started with a greedy person, say a Scotsman, who, borrowing a plug of tobacco, bit off too big a chunk to enjoy. (P.S. Lou isn't with me any more.)

pork barrel

According to the *Dictionary of American Politics* there was a time, on Southern plantations, back before the Civil War, when "the opening of a barrel of pork caused a rush to be made by the slaves." Mebbe so, though I doubt it. At any rate, even if so it had nothing to do with the present-day political implications of our phrase. Pork is fat, and "fat," for hundreds of years, has meant plenty, abundance—"Ye shall eat the fat of the land." Thus, anything especially lucrative or richly rewarding became "fat," and—a hundred years ago, especially in the halls of Congress—by simple transference became "pork."

Primarily, however, political "pork" in the luxuriant aftermath of the Civil War was any favor, distinction, or governmental money allotted to a district on no other basis than patronage. Later, roughly fifty years ago, when Congressmen began to seek larger appropriations to impress their constituents, as for river or harbor improvements, public buildings, or the like, such an appropriation became a "pork barrel."

even steven

With no advantage to either; as, to swap knives "even steven." Sometimes written with a capital, "Steven," and sometimes appearing as "Stephen." We've had the phrase as colloquial American for at least a hundred years, in print since 1866, but that is about all one can say of it. It is quite likely that it is nothing more than one of the numerous rhythmical reiteratives in the language, such as dilly-dally, shilly-shally, hodgepodge, 'ods bods, hocus-pocus, ding dong, hell's bells, and so on.

lame duck

'Way back in Revolutionary times, perhaps earlier, there was a woodsman maxim, "Never waste powder on a dead duck." From that, "dead duck" became popular slang, still in use, for anything —person or article—that is no longer worth a straw, that is done up, played out. Some bright wit a hundred years ago, probably a political writer with that slang term in mind, saw a chance for an apt modification. By the law that then existed (revised by the Twentieth Amendment, February 6, 1933), members of Congress who might fail of re-election in November, nevertheless still held office until March 4th following. Such outgoing "ducks" were not yet "dead," merely "lamed"; they could still, if sufficiently numerous, pass or propose legislation embarrassing to an incoming administration.

ham actor

One who is pretty far down the scale in acting ability. Sylva Clapin, in *A New Dictionary of Americanisms* (1902), defines such an actor, or the variant *ham:* "In theatrical parlance, a tenth-rate actor or variety performer." Why such a term was so applied was long a matter of speculation, but it is now generally accepted that *ham* was an abbreviated form of the earlier appellation, *hamfatter,* a term that was especially applied to an actor of low grade, such as a Negro minstrel, back around 1875 and later. The early name derived from the fact that, for economic reasons, these actors used ham fat, instead of cold cream, to remove the necessarily liberal applications of makeup. The term *ham* is now also applied to third- or fourth-rate pugilists, ball-players, and other poorly skilled athletes or entertainers, and, though with no contempt, to the large army of well-equipped amateur radio operators, probably because, in the early days of radio, these operators were fumbling novices.

I declare to Betsy!

An ejaculation expressing positive affirmation, surprise, close interest, or similar emotion; equivalent to "Well, I do declare," etc. I am afraid that this Betsy, as also she of "Heavens to Betsy," was a homeless waif of no particular parentage. Like Topsy, she just "growed." "I declare to goodness," the bald "I declare," and the slightly stronger "Well, I declare" date back perhaps two or more centuries in the usage of England. "Declaring to goodness" savored too strongly of sacrilege to God-fearing American ears, but the innocuous Betsy was at hand, ready and willing.

three cheers and a tiger

The three cheers are self-explanatory, but why the "tiger"? It is, to be sure, a vociferous yell or howl added with utmost enthusiasm at the close of the cheering, perhaps emulating the roar or yowl of a genuine tiger. Well, here's the story, retold from Bartlett's *Dictionary of Americanisms* (1859):

The Boston Light Infantry visited Salem, Massachusetts, in 1822 and encamped in Washington Square. While there the soldiers indulged in some rough-and-tumble sports, probably playing to the gallery, and one of the young lady spectators called out, "Oh, you tiger!" to one of the most brawny of the young men. On the way back to Boston, some of the vocalists struck up an impromptu song, "Oh, you tigers, don't you know," to the tune of "Rob Roy McGregor, O!"—and the name stuck. In 1826 the Infantry visited New York where, at a public festival, the men concluded some maneuvers with the howl, the tiger's growl, that they had been rehearsing for four years. Thereafter, " 'three cheers and a tiger' are the inseparable demonstrations of approbation in that city [New York]."

on the cuff

On credit. I surmise, but can't prove, that this phrase and its interpretation originated in the barroom, the saloon of old. The bartender, short of convenient paper for keeping records of amounts due, but having starched white cuff and pencil handy, just wrote "John Jones—30" on his cuff, transferring the record to something more permanent when business was slack. *The American Thesaurus of Slang* (1947) says that the phrase also means "arranged; scheduled." I have never heard it so used.

to go hog wild

To become highly enthusiastic; especially, to become wildly excited, as hogs become when aroused; to run around like a chicken with its head cut off; hence, to become very angry, to get all het up;

also, to become profligate, to spend money like a drunken sailor. Both of my parents were born and reared in agricultural communities, and I am almost certain that this Americanism was familiar to each of them in all its senses. If so, that would take it back to the 1850's or 1860's. I am sure, however, that it was a familiar colloquialism to them in my early childhood, as I have known and used it all my life in each of its varied meanings. Nevertheless, the earliest printed date takes it back only to 1904, to a definition that appeared in *Dialect Notes,* with the single example: "I never saw such an excitement over a little thing in Arkansas as there was over that debate. They went hog wild." Perhaps some reader can cite an instance of earlier usage in print.

a stiff upper lip

Courage, or stoicism, which one keeps or carries. The significance of the idiom is well indicated by one of its earliest appearances in print—John Neal's *down Easters* (1833): "What's the use of boohooin'? . . . Keep a stiff upper lip; no bones broke—don't I know?"

"The die is cast!"

According to Plutarch's *Life of Julius Caesar,* this was the remark made by Caesar when, in 49 B.C., he decided to march toward Rome to protect himself against the machinations of Pompey. His words, of course, were in Latin—*"Alea est jacta!"*

Pompey, also a great Roman general, sharing with Caesar the control of the territories of Rome, wished to become sole dictator. To do so, he conspired first to destroy Caesar, then encamped for the winter, 50–49 B.C., with a portion of his army, beyond the northern boundary of Italy. Through faithful friends, Caesar learned of the conspiracy, made his fateful decision, and in January "crossed the Rubicon," the small river bordering Italy on the northeast. As he marched southward, city after city opened its gates in warm greeting, and Rome itself, with Pompey in flight, soon declared him sole dictator.

in the doldrums (or dumps)

Nowadays we say in the dumps, blue, low-spirited. Nobody knows what a *doldrum* was originally, but possibly the word itself was derived from *dull,* "stupid," or from the Middle English word *dold,* which had the same meaning. At any rate *doldrum* referred originally to a dull or sluggish person, a dullard. Literary use of the expression has been traced to less than a hundred and fifty years only, but I have a hunch that colloquial use goes back much further. We speak of a ship being "in the doldrums" when it is becalmed. This nautical usage, however, is of later vintage.

praise from Sir Hubert

The epitome of commendation; approval to the nth degree. The original Sir Hubert was a character in the eighteenth-century play, *A Cure for the Heartache,* written by Thomas Morton and first produced in London in 1797. Sir Hubert Stanley, in the play, was a kindly gentleman, filled with such gentility and beneficence that he was contantly in financial straits. However, he was noted for his sense of fairness to others regardless of his own circumstances, always prompt in rewarding merit, even though, as was often the case, it was verbal only. Our expression, slightly modified through the years, comes from the last scene of the last act. Sir Hubert says to Young Rapid, son of the tailor: "Mr. Rapid, by asserting your character as a man of honor, in rewarding the affection of this amiable woman, you command my praise; for bestowing happiness on my dear Charles, receive an old man's blessing." Young Rapid replies, "Approbation from Sir Hubert Stanley is praise indeed."

to have up one's sleeve

To have (something) in reserve in case of need; an alternative. Usually it is some bit of testimony, evidence, argument, plan, or project, or the like, that one has up his sleeve in readiness to spring or act upon if or when the original proposal turns out unsuccess-

fully. Or, in a bad sense, it may be that the villain in the play may have a scheme up his sleeve ready to spring and cause one's undoing. The allusion traces back to the costumes of the fifteenth century. In those days a man's garments were not made with the numerous pockets that modern man considers indispensable; in fact, there were none. Though some essential items were commonly hung from a belt, it was a godsend when some genius found that by making his often detachable sleeves slightly fuller between elbow and wrist he could tuck various necessities into those new-found pockets. The fashion went to ridiculous extremes, of course, with capacious sleeves sometimes almost scraping the ground. But while it lasted, until new styles came in with Henry VIII, man could conceal any variety of things up his sleeve.

to box the compass

To make a complete turn; also, to adopt successively all possible opinions on a question. Of course, any mariner would say that is all stuff and nonsense, and in his way of thinking he would be right. With him the phrase has just one meaning; to recite in order the thirty-two points of the compass, starting from north around through east, south, west, and back to north. But, of course, in doing so one describes a complete turn. The figurative sense has been with us since at least the beginning of the nineteenth century.

let sleeping dogs lie

To let a matter or person which at the present is at rest stay at rest, rather than to create a disturbance by bringing the matter up

553

again or arousing the person. Chaucer wrote this in just the reverse form—"It is nought good a slepyng hound to wake" (*Troylus and Criseyde,* 1374)—and it was still so recorded some two hundred years later by John Heywood (*A Dialogue Conteynyng Prouerbes and Epigrammes,* 1562), "It is ill wakyng of a sleapyng dogge." But by the time of Charles Dickens (*David Copperfield,* 1850) it had been turned about into the order of today's usage.

no ifs, ans, nor buts

No back talk; no impudence; no argument. Our British cousins, from all that I can gather, limit this expression merely to "ifs and ans," as in the meaningless doggerel that my brother and I used to recite,

> If ifs and ans
> Were pots and pans,
> There'd be no use for tinkers.

—a slight variant, I believe, of an overseas doggerel. The older expression just means "if"; hence, a supposition. But our American expression is a negation and of much stronger force. A parent who uses it does so to end all argument: there'll be no *if* (no supposition), no *an* (an archaic form of *and,* hence, no condition), and no *but* (no exception).

love me, love my dog

Whatever my faults, if you love me you must put up with them. Regrettably, sometimes one's dearest friend or son or daughter construes this saying literally and thinks himself or herself quite at liberty, because of that friendship, to bring the hugest and smelliest Saint Bernard or flea-bitten pooch, shedding hair on rug or couch, into one's living-room. Perhaps some maiden fair did say it in a literal way to her gallant in the days when knighthood was in flower, but it is certainly not so meant nowadays. It is very old. Apperson found it in the writings (Latin) of Saint Bernard of Clairvaux (twelfth century): *Qui me amat, amat et canem meum,* and it occurs in the works of various English writers of the fifteenth and sixteenth centuries.

to carry the ball

To be responsible; to be in charge. The allusion is to the American game of football, to the player to whom, on a given play, the ball is assigned. Transference from literal to figurative usage became, at first, commercial lingo probably around 1925.

to tilt at windmills

To wage battle with chimeras; to take up the cudgels against an imaginary wrong or evil. The saying and its meaning take us to the redoubtable knight, Don Quixote, in the book of that name by Cervantes in 1605. The eighth chapter, Vol. I, begins: "At this point  they came in sight of thirty or forty windmills . . . and as soon as Don Quixote saw them he said to his squire, 'Fortune is arranging matters for us better than we could have shaped our desires ourselves, for look there, friend Sancho Panza, where thirty or more monstrous giants present themselves, all of whom I mean to engage in battle and slay, and with whose spoils we shall begin to make our fortunes; for this is righteous warfare, and it is God's good service to sweep so evil a breed off the face of the earth.'" Whereupon, despite the protestations of his squire, the resolute knight couched his lance, urged forward his good steed, Rosinante, and hurled himself at the arms of the nearest windmill. Clinging to the lance, he was lifted by the sail, until he dropped with a shattering thud to the earth—and had nothing but his pains for the effort.

double entendre

Those who use this term may find themselves scorned or held in ridicule by one who is really familiar with French. He will scoffingly say, "There is no such French expression. What you mean is *'double entente.'*" The latter is, in fact, present French usage, but, nevertheless, back in the seventeenth century, as recorded by Littré, the French did say *"double entendre,"* and that was the term used in England by John Dryden during the same period and by later and present English and American writers. Our dictionaries give it some such definition as, "Double meaning; a statement or phrase so worded as to be capable of either of two interpretations, one quite innocent and the other, usually, of doubtful propriety."

hanged, drawn, and quartered

To be subjected to the direst penalty; originally a judgment rendered upon a criminal sentenced to death, but now often jocularly threatened to a person in mild reproof. The original sentence was anything but a joke. Prior to the fifteenth century it meant that the person so sentenced for a major crime was to be drawn at a horse's tail or upon a cart to the scene of execution, there to be hanged by the neck until dead, and his body then to be cut into four quarters and scattered into various parts of England. In later times a further penalty was allotted; the victim was first briefly hanged, then, while still living, he was disemboweled (*drawn*), then beheaded and quartered.

playing with loaded dice

Having little chance; playing a game of chance or engaging in any undertaking in which the odds are rigged against one. Obviously the expression derives from a game of dice in which the player who is discriminated against is given dice cleverly weighted which give him little or no chance to win. Thus *The Saturday Evening Post,* in an editorial, "Should America Remain in a Red-Operated UN?" (August 7, 1954), has the lines ". . . even if this were a game, who would go on playing after learning that the dice were loaded?"

time is of the essence

No doubt those who are accustomed to think of "essence" as being connected only with extracts of one kind or another, as essence of turpentine, essence of roses, find themselves at a loss when encountering this expression. But some eighty years ago—especially in the phrase "of the essence"—it was a legal term, and its meaning was virtually that of "essential." Hence, when you sign a contract containing the term, "time is of the essence," it would be well to understand that time is of the utmost importance in the fulfilment of that contract.

to set (persons) together by the ears

To involve them in a quarrel; set them at variance; create ill-will among them. The original ears were those of quarrelsome animals, those of cats especially, which tore at each other's ears when fighting. Thus Laurence Tomson in his translation (1579) of *Calvin's Sermons on the Epistles to Timothie and Titus* wrote, "When we be together by the eares like dogs and cattes."

to lift (or hoist or pull up) oneself by the bootstraps

You may travel all over the United States, North, South, East, or West, or in any part of Canada or England, and find almost no one who isn't familiar with one form or another of this expression. It is hardly necessary to say that by its use we mean to raise oneself

through one's unaided efforts above one's former cultural, social, or economic level. And yet, beyond being able to state positively that the expression cannot be more than three hundred and fifty years old, I cannot say in what English-speaking country it originated, or even whether it dates back to the time of George Washington and George the Third of England, though I am almost certain that it is considerably older. That is, I myself have not been able to turn up any printed use or record of this common expression at any date earlier than about ten years ago. It occurs on page 456 of *The Beards' Basic History of the United States* (1944) by Charles A. and Mary R. Beard. Undoubtedly it has appeared earlier, but no dictionary nor other reference work has made note of it. Yet I have seen it in print several times since that date.

In fact, I cannot even tell you nor hazard a guess as to how old the compound word *bootstrap* may be. The earliest printed record, so far as I have been able to discover, is in the *Funk & Wagnalls Standard Dictionary*, 1894 edition; and there it appears only in the definitions of two related words—*boot-hook* and *strap*. The first definition of *bootstrap* to appear in any dictionary is in the 1934 *Webster's New International Dictionary, Second Edition,* covering the familiar loop at the top of a boot.

But this strap was known to Shakespeare. In *Twelfth Night,* (1601), Act I, scene 3, Sir Toby Belch makes the comment: "These cloathes are good enough to drink in: and so bee these boots too; and they be not, let them hang themselues in their owne straps."

In an attempt to learn when such straps appeared on boots, I was referred eventually to Mr. John H. Thornton, M.A., F.B.S.I., Head of the Department of Boot and Shoe Manufacture, Northampton College of Technology, Northampton, England—a town where footwear has been made continuously since the thirteenth century and now the center of such manufacture in England. In the course of our correspondence Mr. Thornton wrote: "In my collection of boots and shoes I have a pair of Cromwellian riding boots c. 1653 and these have the loops (or the remnants of them) inside, so it is quite evident that boot-straps are as old as heavy riding boots themselves, which, as far as I can judge, came into use towards the end of the 16th century." Mr. Thornton also sent me photographs of one of those boots, side view and top view, from which the accompanying drawing was made.

Although, as another English correspondent seemed certain, this exploit of lifting oneself by one's own bootstraps is in line with other extravagant achievements of the eighteenth-century hero, Baron Munchausen, this feat is not to be found among the list. Did the expression not exist in 1785 when the book was written? or, as I think more likely, did the author, Rudolph Erich Raspe, not happen to think of it?

If an explanation is warranted, the expression alludes to the struggle from early date to late date in inserting one's foot into a well-fitting boot. The space at the right-angle turn from shank to sole is just not quite large enough for one's heel and ankle to slide through. The bootstrap was devised to give the would-be wearer a better purchase. Then came the boot-hook as illustrated, another early invention. But even with those aids he striving to wear the boot is sometimes uncertain whether he is trying to shove his foot downward or lift himself upward.

to hang on by the eyelashes

To be just barely able to retain one's hold on something, literal or figurative; to be in a precarious condition. Our ancestors, back in the seventeenth century "hung (something) by the eyelid," rather than the eyelashes, indicating that they meant to keep that thing or subject in suspense. Later, about a hundred years, "to hang by the eyelids" came into vogue with the meaning of our present expression. One fighting to retain a spark of life, or one barely able to stave off financial disaster is, with equal impartiality, "hanging on by his eyelashes."

to have many (or too many) irons in the fire

To undertake many things or have many activities under way at one time; also, to have alternate plans for gaining one's purpose; or, if we say "too many" rather than "many," to be engaged in more activities than one can properly manage; to bite off more than  one can chew. The allusion in any case is to the blacksmith. He who has many irons in his forge wastes little time. His well-trained apprentice maintains such control of the bellows and the placement of the irons that each is ready in turn at the anvil and hammer. Or if, perchance, an armorer were engaged in forging a suit of armor, he would be ready, if skilled, to take whatever piece of steel came from the forge and shape it to best advantage, whether for greave, cuirass, vambrace, or gauntlet. "Too many irons in the fire" would mark an inefficient smith or one with an unskilled apprentice. Figurative use of either saying takes us back only to the middle of the sixteenth century.

to paint the lily

Yes, that's the way Shakespeare wrote it; not as one so often hears it, "to gild the lily." It's to be found in *King John,* Act IV, scene 2. The king who seized the throne unjustly after the death of his brother Richard in 1199 believed toward the close of his reign that a second coronation might strengthen his position and bolster the waning affections of his subjects. Lords Pembroke and Salisbury, among others, thought that to be an altogether superfluous gesture, and Salisbury added:

> Therefore, to be possess'd with double pomp,
> To guard a title that was rich before,
> To gild refined gold, to paint the lily,
> To throw a perfume on the violet,
> To smooth the ice, or add another hue
> Unto the rainbow, or with taper-light
> To seek the beauteous eye of heaven to garnish,
> Is wasteful, and ridiculous excess.

full of prunes (or beans)

Each has the same meaning—peppy, lively, energetic, in high spirits, feeling one's oats, rarin' to go. "Beans" was the first, and was originally said of horses after a feeding of beans raised for fodder—"horse beans," so called. Undoubtedly the spirited state of a bean-fed horse was observed in remote times—Romans also used beans as fodder—but I find nothing equivalent to the current expression before its own rise less than a hundred years ago. ("Full of beans" is now also used slangily to mean foolish or silly, possibly because a person in high spirits often permits his superabundant energy to express itself ridiculously.) The substitution of "prunes" came into use at least seventy years ago, but a satisfactory reason for it is difficult to determine. Perhaps the dietary effect of an overindulgence in this comestible may have had something to do with it. I am reminded, at least, of a mother who urged her son, training for scholastic track events: "Eat plenty of prunes, Jimmy; they'll make you run."

Lucullian feast (or banquet)

A feast of inordinate magnificence; a terrific spread. L. Licinus Lucullus was a great Roman general in the early part of the first century B.C., and was at first famous for his victories over Mithridates. His victories brought him great wealth, and after his retirement he embarked upon an unprecedented scale of living and sensual indulgence. "A single supper in the hall," according to Smith's *Dictionary of Greek and Roman Mythology and Biography,* "was said to cost the sum of 50,000 denarii." Such prodigality, especially when frequently repeated, was notable even in a period marked by magnificence. Thus, though his military prowess is almost forgotten, his name still lives in the language through his reputation as a glutton.

to take forty winks

Though I'm not saying that the reading of the Thirty-nine Articles has an actual bearing on the "forty winks" or short nap that is likely to succeed that reading—or interrupt it—such a sequel could be inferred. The Thirty-nine Articles, for the benefit of the unenlightened, are the articles of faith of the Church of England which the clergy are required to accept. Adoption became legal by parliamentary action in 1571 in the reign of Elizabeth I. Needless to say, the perusal of these articles is likely to be considered most dreary. At least they led a writer in *Punch* (November 16, 1872) to say: "If a . . . man, after reading through the Thirty-nine Articles, were to take forty winks"—and that is the first literary record of this precise number of winks.

fit (or fine) as a fiddle

In fine form or condition; in splendid health. Although "fiddles" were known in England back at least in the early thirteenth century, it was some four hundred years later, evidently, before their shape, form, tone, and other qualities became so pleasing as to invite complimentary applications to humans. "To have one's face made of a fiddle" was to be exceptionally good looking. "To play first fiddle" was to occupy a leading position, and one "fit as a fiddle" or "fine as a fiddle" was beyond further need of improvement in health or condition. Apperson traces the metaphor to Haughton's *England for My Money* (1616), "This is excellent, i' faith; as fit as a fiddle."

not to care a fiddlestick

To be wholly unconcerned; to care nothing at all. Although our ancestors, some three hundred years ago, had high regard for the fiddle, they seemed to think of the fiddlestick, without which the fiddle could not be played, as a mere trifle, a bagatelle, something so insignificant as to be absurd. Thus, Grose, in his *Classical Dictionary of the Vulgar Tongue* (1796) defined *fiddlestick's end* as "Nothing." Washington Irving, in *Salmagundi* (1806–1807) is credited with the introduction of the present phrase into the literary language.

on the fritz

Out of order; gone haywire; on the kibosh; not in good health or in good condition. According to my best recollections and those of others whom I have consulted, this expression entered the American language about the turn of the century, though it seems to have escaped the notice of recorders of the language. Who the "Fritz" was whose fame thus became immortalized is now, alas, lost to memory dear. To be sure Fritz of the Katzenjammer twins had even then begun to grace the pages of the New York *Journal*, but, though guilty along with Hans of every mischief in the calendar, he was ever in abounding health—definitely not the source of this commemoration.

a shot in the arm

Somewhere I read that this was derived from the hypodermic injection of a drug administered by a physician for the prevention or cure of a disease or the alleviation of pain. To be sure, the expression is used with such meaning, but I don't think that the original "shot" was with such purpose. It was administered by a hypodermic syringe, all right, but with a "Quick, Watson, the needle!" intent— the injection of any drug that would induce exhilaration. In my opinion, that is, the expression, which is not more than about forty years old, was derived from drug addiction, though it is applied now, not only to medical injections as for vaccination, etc., but also to the taking of any stimulant, such as coffee, a "Coke," or an intoxicant—in the latter instance replacing the older "shot in the neck."

rag-tag and bobtail

First, away back in the sixteenth century, it was "tag and rag," or sometimes just "tag," always meaning the rabble, the common herd, the riffraff of society, the people generally held in low esteem. Thus we read: "To walles they go, both tagge and ragge, their Citie to defende" and "Huntyd, and killyd tage and rage with honds and swords." And this remained the usual order for the next two hundred years. In the time of the diarist, Samuel Pepys, however, the expression was further intensified by "bobtail," a term that had originally applied to the tail of a horse, cut short, and later used alone as a synonym for "tag and rag." Thus Pepys wrote (1660), "The dining room . . . was full of tag, rag, and bobtail, dancing, singing, and drinking." Early in the nineteenth century, probably for greater euphony, the first two terms became reversed, usually written as in the heading here, though from a grammatical view we should write "rag, tag, and bobtail."

the fat is in the fire

The mischief is done and unpleasant results must be faced; an irretrievable blunder has been made and ill consequences will follow; some dire act has been committed which will undoubtedly provoke an explosion of anger. No one knows how old this saying may be, and the beginning can only be guessed. It was recorded in John Heywood's *A Dialogue Conteynyng Prouerbes and Epigrammes* (1562), and, accordingly, must have long been in use before that time. But in those days the saw meant that some project had failed and one must cut his cloth accordingly. Heywood wrote, "Than [Then] farewell riches, the fat is in the fire." One may surmise, probably correctly, that the original allusion was to a chunk of fat meat which, thrust through by a spit on the hearth to roast, caught ablaze and fell into the fire to the dismay of the cook.

root hog or die

Get to work or suffer the consequences. Although the earliest printed record of the Americanism so far exhumed dates only to 1834—"We therefore determined to go on the old saying, root hog or die": *A Narrative of the Life of David Crockett*—it probably goes back to colonial times or, at least, to early frontier days. And, probably, its origin was literal—an admonition to hogs or pigs when crops were scant to forage for themselves in order to survive. In fact, the expression sometimes appears as a command as given to a hog: "Root, hog, or die!" The way it appears in each of the seven stanzas of the folk song under that title in the Archive of the American Folk Song Society, Library of Congress, each of which closes with the line, is:

> Oh, I went to Californy in the spring of Seventy-six,
> Oh, when I landed there I wuz in a terrible fix.
> I didn't have no money my victuals for to buy,
> And the only thing for me was to root, hog, or die.

to cut (or split) a melon

This is a delightful procedure, both for the cutter and for him who receives a portion of the melon. He, or more likely they, in charge of the cutting is delighted that there is something to cut, and the receiver always has had a mouth watering for the taste. In other words, this was originally Wall Street jargon meaning to distribute dividends—especially extra dividends—to the stockholders of an enterprise. As such, the term came into use about 1906. Nowadays we also use it to mean to distribute profits of any kind to any entitled to receive them—usually the heads or principal officers of an organization, the employees, the financial backers, etc.

skeleton in the closet

What started this expression, no one knows. Perhaps it was an actual incident; perhaps a real skeleton was found walled up in the closet of some country house concealing some long-hidden family shame or sorrow. At any rate, *The Oxford English Dictionary* says

that this expression and its meaning are known to have been in use before 1845, though it was in that year that the earliest printed usage was recorded. That was by William Makepeace Thackeray in one of his contributions to the magazine, *Punch*. But the expression undoubtedly struck his fancy, as he used it again as the heading of Chapter LV, "Barnes's Skeleton Closet," in *The Newcomes* (1855). However, the "skeleton" in Sir Barnes Newcome's closet would not receive much consideration in any but a highly sensitive family. It was merely that he, though "the reigning prince" of the Newcome family after his father's death, was not well received by the townfolk and country gentry of Newcome, because of his own arrogance, along with a bullying attitude toward his wife. The chapter relates, in the author's words, "Some particulars regarding the Newcome family, which will show that they have a skeleton or two in *their* closets, as well as their neighbours."

Johnny-come-lately

A newcomer; one recently arrived; an inexperienced person. Apparently this was originally, in the early quarter of the nineteenth century, the American sailor's version of the British "Johnny Newcome," any recruit aboard any of His Majesty's vessels. Our earliest instance of usage appears in *The Adventures of Harry Franco* (1839), by the journalist, Charles F. Briggs: " 'But it's Johnny Comelately, aint it, you?' said a young mizzen topman."

to dance Juba

Just as Cuffee (or Cuffy), back in the days of slavery, was the name often given by Negroes to a boy born on Friday, so Juba was the name of African origin frequently given to girls born on Monday (see Hennig Cohen in *American Speech,* XXVII, 103–04). But, unlike the white child born on Monday who, in the old folk rhyme, is "fair of face," the black girl child was, presumably, a natural-born imp of perversity and had, repeatedly, to be switched. Thus, "to dance Juba," which, in the early days of minstrel shows of the 1830's, meant to dance in a rollicking manner with hands, feet, and head all in motion, appears to have had its start in the animated dancing performed involuntarily by a child being switched in punishment for some kind of naughtiness of deviltry. Such, at least, is the interpretation of Dr. Mitford M. Mathews (in *American Speech* XXVIII, 206), speaking from personal experience of his boyhood in Alabama about 1900.

like greased lightning

Lickety-split; like a blue streak; like a bat out of hell; with extreme rapidity. Although this has the appearance of typical American exaggerated hyperbole, nevertheless the earliest printed record of use is in the *Boston, Lincoln, and Louth Herald,* published in Lincolnshire, England, the issue of January 15, 1833: "He spoke as quick as greased lightning." We must have taken it to our own bosoms shortly after its coinage, however, for it flourisheth here like the green bay tree.

Main Liner

If you are one of these, in or around Philadelphia, then you really belong. You are a member of the Upper Crust, one who can look down your nose at any other class of persons in Pennsylvania, at least, and perhaps elsewhere—except, possibly, a person from Boston's Back Bay or an F.F.V. (First Family of Virginia). That is to say, by way of explanation, you live along the "main line" of the Pennsylvania Railroad, in the beautiful suburban area just outside Philadelphia. The cognomen for these highly aristocratic, ultra-conservative members of society has been in use since early in this century—but the distinction is fading, as elsewhere.

to kick against the pricks

To use vain efforts; be recalcitrant; knock one's head against a wall; suffer from one's own misdeeds; kick against thorns or spurs to one's own hurt. Saul, later called Paul, on his way to Damascus from Jerusalem, where he had received letters authorizing him to arrest any Christians and take them to Jerusalem for trial, was stopped on the road by a messenger from God, as related in Acts ix, "and suddenly there shined round him a light from heaven: And he fell to the earth, and heard a voice saying unto him, Saul, Saul, why persecuteth thou me? And he said, Who art thou, Lord? And the Lord said, I am Jesus whom thou persecuteth: it is hard for thee to kick against the pricks."

to turn a new leaf

To amend one's conduct; begin a new life; go straight; reform. The leaf that one turns is not that of a tree, but that of a book, a book of lessons or of precepts, the book on which our sins of omission and commission are recorded. And we have been doing that, or at least using that expression for something over four hundred years. Though not the earliest example, we find the expression in Raphael Holinshed's *Chronicles of England, Scotlande, and Irelande* (1577), "He must turne the leafe, and take out a new lesson, by changing his former trade of liuing into better."

to gird (up) one's loins

Another Biblical phrase that has been taken in its early figurative sense directly into the language. He who "girds up his loins" prepares for action, usually physical and strenuous, but it may also be mental. In the physical sense the allusion was to the workman who, in preparation for work, tucked the long skirt of his garment into his girdle or belt. The reference is to Proverbs xxxi, 17, which in the Coverdale translation (1535) reads: "She gyrdeth hir loynes with strength."

on the carpet

In the days when "carpet" retained its original sense, "a thick fabric used to cover tables," to have something "on the carpet" had the same meaning that we now give to "on the table"; that is, to have something up for discussion, for consideration. Such was the

usage in the early eighteenth century and is still common usage in England, and is, as well, the intent of the French *sur le tapis,* and the German *aufs Tapet.* But dainty ladies found, even in the fifteenth century, that these thick fabrics also made ideal floor coverings and began to use them, first, in their bedchambers, and then in other private or formal rooms of a house. But they were for the use of the gentry. The occasions when a servant might "walk the carpet," as the expression went, was when he or she was called before the mistress or master of the house for a reprimand. Though this latter expression, coined in the early nineteenth century, is still in use, it has been largely replaced, especially in America, by transferring its meaning to "on the carpet."

on the level (on the square)

In all sincerity, honesty, or truth; on the up-and-up; the real McCoy. Both of these expressions were taken from the ritual of Freemasonry and both are of legendary antiquity. In the rites of the lodges, however, the level, an instrument used by builders to determine a common plane, is actually a symbol of equality. The square, an instrument of equally great precision for determining accurately an angle of ninety degrees, the fourth part of a circle, is a symbol of morality, truth, and honesty. *The Encyclopedia of*

Freemasonry (1916 edition) relates: "In the year 1830, the architect, in rebuilding a very ancient bridge called Baal Bridge, near Limerick, in Ireland, found under the foundation-stone an old brass square, much eaten away, containing on its two surfaces the following inscription [dated 1517]:

> I. WILL. STRIUE. TO. LIUE.—
> WITH. LOUE. & CARE.—
> UPON. THE. LEUL.—
> BY. THE. SQUARE.

a lick and a promise

This is the act that Johnny—or Billy, or Jeff, or Chip—generally does with a washcloth. Just a hasty dab—enough, he hopes, to pass grandma's not too critical eye before sliding into his place at the table. The "lick," that is, has nothing to do with a thrashing, but pertains rather to the rapid lapping of the tongue such as that of a cat drinking milk. It's a small quantity or small amount, about the amount we mean when we say that so-and-so hasn't "a lick of sense." The "promise," of course, is in Johnny's indefinite future, something that may be long deferred. And both "lick" and "promise" may apply to any chore. Nor is the action limited to young males. It may apply to a chore performed incompletely or inadequately by anyone. The expression dates back at least to 1850.

nip and tuck

Of course every American knows that this means neck and neck, or just about as close a finish in any sort of competition as two or more contestants could get—a photo finish, in modern terminology. But why "nip," and why "tuck"? There have been variations of the expression in the hundred and twenty-odd years of recorded usage. James K. Paulding in *Westward Ho!* (1832), gives it, "There we were at rip and tuck, up one tree and down another." William T. Porter, a dozen years or so later, wrote it both "nip and tack" and "nip and chuck." But "nip and tuck" has been common usage through the years since. The dictionaries, playing safe, refuse even to guess at the source, but I'll stick my neck out to suggest that perhaps Paulding was right. A rip, of course, is the result of what mother does to a piece of cloth in reducing it to smaller portions; the tuck the fold she makes in one such portion to sew it to another, as in making a patchwork quilt. By successive rips and tucks the patchwork comes out even. Pretty thin? Well, even some dictionary derivations with all steps known look superficially thinner.

to play fast and loose

"Fast and loose" was the name of an old cheating game, known in the middle of the sixteenth century at least. The game was thus explained by James O. Halliwell in his *Dictionary of Archaic and Provincial Words, Obsolete Phrases, Proverbs and Ancient Customs, from the Fourteenth Century* (1847): "A cheating game played with a stick and a belt or string, so arranged that a spectator would think he could make the latter fast by placing a stick through its intricate folds, whereas the operator could detach it at once." In fact, the game must have been known at a considerably earlier period, for the present phrase in a metaphorical sense—to say one thing and do another; to be slippery as an eel; to have loose morals —appeared in one of the epigrams in *Tottel's Miscellany* (1547): "Of a new married student that plaied fast or loose"—i.e., was unfaithful.

according to one's lights

When I was young, this always struck me as a silly expression. The "lights" were the last things—bright red and closely adhering —that my mother removed in cleaning a fowl, the "liver and lights" always in combination. It was not until some years later that I learned that "lights" is an old, a very old, term for "lungs." In fact, it dates back to the twelfth century. Our present phrase has nothing to do with that usage. Here it is the light of knowledge that is meant; one's opinions, information, abilities, capacities, or the like.

plain as the nose on one's face

Ridiculously obvious; as conspicuous or evident as anything could possibly be. The comparison must have been known to Shakespeare, who used it ironically in *Two Gentlemen of Verona* (1591). The Lady Sylvia had enjoined Valentine, who loves her,

"to write some lines to one she loves." She affects to be displeased
with the result, though Valentine's servant sees plainly that the one
she loves is his master. When Sylvia leaves, the servant says:

O jest unseen, inscrutable, invisible
As a nose on a man's face, or a weathercock on a steeple!
My master sues to her; and she hath taught her suitor,
He being her pupil, to become her tutor.
O excellent device! was there ever heard a better,
That my master, being scribe, to himself should write the letter?

meddlesome Matty

One who sticks his (or, more likely, her) nose into the affairs of
others; or, among the young, one who inordinately busies oneself
with or constantly fingers objects belonging to others. The term

derived from a poem of that title, written
by Ann Taylor, first appearing in *Original
Poems for Infant Minds,* published in
1804–05, and written chiefly by members
of the family of Isaac Taylor, English
engraver. Among them, incidentally, was
the well-known "Twinkle, twinkle, little
star, How I wonder what you are," written by Ann's younger sister, Jane. The
nine verses of "Meddlesome Matty," too
extensive to be quoted here, are recom-
mended reading for all, children or adults, who have been accused
of possessing such propensities:

Oh, how one ugly trick has ſpoil'd
   The ſweeteſt and the beſt!
Matilda, tho' a pleaſant child,
   One ugly trick poſſeſſ'd,
Which like a cloud before the ſkies,
Hid all her better qualities.

Sometimes ſhe'd lift the teapot lid,
   To peep at what was in it;
Or tilt the kettle, if you did
   But turn your back a minute.

In vain you told her not to touch,
Her trick of meddling grew ſo much.

But Matilda went too far eventually and got her comeuppance:

Her grandmamma went out one day,
And by miſtake ſhe laid
Her ſpectacles and ſnuff-box gay
Too near the little maid . . .

She donned the "glaſſes," and "looking round, as I ſuppoſe, The ſnuff box too ſhe ſpied." Nothing would do, of course, but open it.

So thumb and finger went to work
To move the stubborn lid;
And preſently, a mighty jirk,
The mighty miſchief did:
For all at once, ah! woeful caſe,
The ſnuff came puffing in her face!

. . . .

In vain ſhe ran about for eaſe,
She could do nothing elſe but ſneeze!

no skin off one's nose

Nothing of concern to one; not one's affair. In today's slang, nose is sometimes replaced by ear, elbow, or back, but the implication is equally evident: If one doesn't butt into, or stick one's nose into, an affair that is none of one's business, he is not likely to suffer abrasions upon any prominent portion of his anatomy by being thrown out upon his nose, elbow, back, shoulder, or the like. The allusion is American, at least fifty years old.

lares and penates

The familiar things, the cherished possessions, the appearance, the indescribable atmosphere which combine to make a house a home. Actually, this phrase combines two groups of Roman gods, though minor gods, to be sure. The *lares* (two syllables, please—lar'eez) were divinities presiding over the hearth and the whole house, representing the spirits, not of all the ancestral dead lords of the house, but only of good men. The *penates* (three syllables—

pe-nah'teez) were the protectors and promoters of happiness, peace, and concord in the family.

Tell it to the Marines

A fish story: an expression of disbelief or incredulity. Lord Byron, in *The Island* (1823), who appears to have been the first to record the expression, added the note: " 'That will do for the marines, but the sailors won't believe it,' is an old saying." A year later, in *Redgauntlet,* Sir Walter Scott repeats it thus: "Tell that to the marines—the sailors won't believe it." The inference is most powerful that the British Royal Marines of that period were such gullible landlubbers that they would swallow any yarn hook, line, and sinker.

a fish out of water

One out of one's element or the setting or environment to which one is accustomed. But unlike the aquatic animal yanked from stream, pool, or sea, the person who merely feels like a fish out

of water rarely suffers death from the sensation, no matter how protracted. The metaphor in English is found as far back as the *English Works* of John Wyclif (*c.* 1380): "And how thei weren out of ther cloistre as fishis withouten water." But Apperson carries it back to the Greek patriarch, St. Athanasius, of the fourth century, though citing no reference, and thinks it may have had an even earlier Greek form. He connects it, amusingly, to the Latin expression, *mus in matella,* a mouse in the pot: said of a person who finds himself in a pretty predicament.

Mardi gras

Mardi, Tuesday, and *gras,* fat; hence, "fat Tuesday," as is the literal meaning in France—"Shrove Tuesday," as we call the day before the beginning of Lent in English. No one knows when these days of carnival began, though probably they are a survival of the Roman festival of Lupercal held at the same season of the year. The name is derived from an immemorial custom in Paris, now little observed, of leading an especially fattened ox (*boeuf gras*) at the head of the carnival procession of merrymakers. But except in certain cities of Italy and in New Orleans in the United States, where the carnival procession and merrymaking essay annually to outdo all predecessors, the customs of former years have gradually been dropped.

to throw a monkey wrench in the machinery

To gum up the works; to place an obstacle or hindrance into a project or undertaking; to interfere, or cause confusion or disaster. Undoubtedly this literally described an act of sabotage when it was first used—possibly no more than fifty years ago, though it seems to me I have known it all my life. However, I may be mistaken, as the earliest literary use so far dug up, and the figurative use at that, was only twenty-five years ago. Garry Allighan, in his *The Romance of the Talkies* (1929), wrote: "The Talkies threw several kinds of monkey wrenches into the machinery of production." The expression is undoubtedly American, as the British say "spanner wrench" for the same type of wrench.

Furthermore, though the source of the name of the implement is not certain, there is good reason to think it American, as well as the implement itself. The tool was known in 1858, and Dr. M. M. Mathews, writing in *American Speech* (February, 1953), refers to an item that appeared in the Boston *Transcript* sometime in the winter of 1932–33, which credits the invention to a man named Monk, in 1856, employed by Bemis & Call of Springfield, Massachusetts. The item adds that the wrench was first called *Monk's wrench,* later jocularly turned into *monkey wrench.* But Dr. Mathews makes it clear that he has no confirmation of this tale.

as mad as hops

Confoundedly irate; mad enough to bite nails; roaring mad. Although "as thick as hops" has a literal background, referring either to the density of the hedges or thickets of hop vines as grown in southern England especially, or to the close growth of the cones on the vines, and although "as fast as hops" pertains to the rapid growth of the hop vine, this present expression has no such relationship. Some distinguished individual, probably American—wholly unknown now, but with a sly bit of punning humor in his make-up—coined it some seventy or seventy-five years ago by giving a slight twist to the well-known "hopping mad," so mad, irate, or angry that one fairly dances or hops around, sputtering with rage. The first occurrence in print was in a story by an unnamed writer in the October, 1884, issue of *Harper's New Monthly Magazine*. It's a story about a youngster called Gus who is annoyed with a pupil who is teasing the teacher.

Agnes looked at her for a minute. Then she tried to speak, but she broke down, and laughed instead. The tears rolled down her cheeks, but she laughed on, for all she was sobbing at the same time. Then she just jumped up and ran out of the room. Lil she turned round and grinned at me—such a grin! It made me mad as hops.

to put one's foot in it

If your wife kicks you under the table or otherwise makes it plain to you that it would be best not to go on with what you were about to say, you may, she hopes, understand that she's trying to

head you off from "putting your foot in it," from committing a social blunder or doing something that had best be left unsaid or undone. The figurative phrase was in current use in the latter part of the eighteenth century, but what the original allusion was is anyone's guess. Personally, because such a blunder fits so patly, I have always been taken by an old rancher's literal description of a hand he had recently hired: "I declare, he's such an ass that if there was just one cow-flop in a ten-acre field he'd be sure to put his foot in it."

Mother Carey's chicken

Both this name bestowed by sailors, two hundred or more years ago, and the regular name, the storm petrel, carry us to the New Testament. *Petrel,* French for "little Peter," was so named from its seeming to walk on the water like the disciple Peter, as related in Matthew xiv, 29. And *Mother Carey* (or *Cary*) was the British seaman's version of the title often used by Levantine sailors, *Mater cara,* "beloved Mother." The small bird, so the sailors believed, exhibited great activity at the approach of a storm.

easy as rolling off a log

Nothing could be easier; the simplest action possible. Early American colonists, probably, moving into a wilderness with a hundred things to be done at once by both husband and wife, sought desperately for a safe and dry place to "park" the baby

temporarily. Just as a modern couple would do on a camping expedition, undoubtedly they would place the infant on a log—"just for a minute." The little round bottom of the baby, however, was no more stable on the big round log than a marble would be on a child's balloon. At least, this could have been the way the metaphor started, for it goes back into colonial days.

not for money, marbles, nor chalk

Not for any consideration whatever; absolutely not; utterly incorruptible. Although "marbles," in this expression, could be taken to mean "slight value," with "chalk" indicating "no value," I think it more likely to be a slight mispronunciation of *meubles,* a term of French origin used both in France and England to mean "personal property." Thus the expression would literally mean, "not for real property, personal property, nor useless property."

high jinks

Mad frolic; pranks; jollity. At the end of the seventeenth century this was a term applied at drinking bouts for the ludicrous performance put on by some members of the party selected for the purpose by a throw of dice. It is best described in *Guy Mannering* (1815) by Sir Walter Scott: "On the present occasion, the revel had lasted since four o'clock, and, at length, under the direction of a venerable compotator . . . the frolicsome company had begun to practise the ancient and now forgotten pastime of *High Jinks.* The game was played in several different ways. Most frequently the dice were thrown by the company, and those upon whom the lot fell were obliged to assume and maintain for a time a certain fictitious character, or to repeat a certain number of fescennine verses in a particular order. If they departed from the character assigned, or if their memory proved treacherous in the repetition, they incurred forfeits, which were compounded for by swallowing an additional bumper, or by paying a small sum toward the reckoning."

to get a kick (or charge) out of (something)

To become thrilled, excited, or stimulated by something physical, mental, or emotional. The older American slang with "kick" is gradually being replaced by the later "charge," having the same interpretation, but "kick" has served well for some fifty years. Originally the "kick" was that induced by spirituous liquor, or perhaps by a sharp condiment, and the effect was physical, though considerably milder than if delivered by a horse or mule or even a high-powered gun. Our metaphorical expression has also been accepted by English writers, as, for instance, by a correspondent to the *Daily Express* in 1928: "I was told I should get a kick out of that journey —and I certainly did."

to put one through a course of sprouts

To give one a thorough and disciplined course of training. In my earlier book, *A Hog on Ice,* I offered no explanation of the source of this phrase. Mary Gilbert Smith of Wallingford, Vermont, author of the series of Grandpa White stories which appeared for some years in the Boston *Globe,* states in a letter to me that it stems from the days when plowing and heavy farm work in New England were done with oxen. "If a yoke of oxen," she wrote, "proved obstreperous, an easy cure was to drive them through a course of sprouts—i.e., young trees springing up where the forest had been cut over. My uncle told me a story of my great-uncle, John Quincy Adams, who taught a yoke that wouldn't hold back on a hill by driving them down so fast that they couldn't turn at the 'elbow,' as was their amiable custom, but plunged into the maple sprouts below the road—tough young sprouts that switched them thoroughly before they came to a stop. Thereafter no yoke was more docile."

No doubt "a course of sprouts" could refer to a row or line of young trees or brush; nevertheless I do not see how oxen or other animals could be lashed or switched by such a growth in dashing—or lumbering—through it, as Mrs. Smith recites, though their overzealousness would certainly be tempered.

dead man (or soldier)

Just a liquor bottle—or, perhaps nowadays, can—that is empty; hence, worthless, good for nothing, as a dead man or soldier on a battlefield would be. The term was recognized in *A New Dictionary of the Terms Ancient and Modern of the Canting Crew,* printed about 1700, and must certainly have been used many years earlier to have received a listing in that collection.

neat but not gaudy

A friend, just returned from a trip to Spain, said to me, "Know what I saw in Barcelona, Charles? The mansion from which we got the word *gaudy!* Put up by a grandee named Gaudi." I said, "Well, it must be pretty old, then." "No," said he, "just recently finished." He was quite taken aback to learn that the word had been in our language at least four hundred years. But the present expression is not that old. Probably Charles Lamb started it. In one of his letters, written in 1806, he mentioned "A little thin flowery border round, —neat, not gaudy."

Several years later, whether from Lamb's phrase or not, the more popular expression, still in use in one form or another, came into circulation. It first appeared in print in an article written for the staid *Magazine of Architecture,* November 1838, by the nineteen-year-old John Ruskin, later noted as an art critic. He wrote: "That admiration of the 'neat but not gaudy,' which is commonly reported to have influenced the devil when he painted his tail pea green."

My own usage, from first hearing some fifty years ago, has always been, "Neat but not gaudy, as the devil said when he painted his tail sky-blue." More decorous speakers substitute "monkey." And the tail may be painted in any color of the rainbow.

to pull a boner

To blunder; to make a stupid or ridiculous mistake; also, to be a bonehead. By deduction, I figure that this American phrase, of about fifty years' standing, came from "Bones" or "Mistah Bones"

of the old-style minstrel show. Originally there was but one of him, the end man in the show who played the "bones"—two pairs of ebony sticks (or, sometimes, pieces of seasoned and polished rib bones), about one inch wide and six inches long, clapped together in the performer's fingers. The other end man was "Tambo" or "Mistah Tambo," from the tambourine played by him. Both end men were later called "Bones," but in either case the "interlocutor," sitting in the middle of the line, directed such questions at the end men as would bring out jests or would evoke ridiculous answers or stupid blunders. He would, that is, "pull boners" from them.

to raise (or play) hob

To raise Cain; play the devil; make mischief. In English folklore, "Hob" was the familiar name of the sprite, Robin Goodfellow, the household spirit full of mischievous, sometimes malicious, acts—the being who, at least, received the blame. Shakespeare, in *A Midsummer Night's Dream,* gives him also his earliest English name, Puck, dating back at least to the eleventh century, and thus describes him in Act II, scene 1:

Fairy: Either I mistake your shape and making quite,
   Or else you áre that shrewd and knavish sprite
   Call'd Robin Goodfellow: are not you he
   That frights the maidens of the villagery;
   Skim milk, and sometimes labour in the quern,
   And bootless make the breathless housewife churn;
   And sometime make the drink to bear no barm,
   Mislead night-wanderers, laughing at their harm?
   Those that Hobgoblin call you, and sweet Puck,
   You do their work, and they shall have good luck:
   Are not you he?
Puck: Thou speak'st aright;
   I am that merry wanderer of the night.
   I jest to Oberon, and make him smile,
   When I a fat and bean-fed horse beguile,
   Neighing in likeness of a silly foal:
   And sometimes lurk I in a gossip's bowl,
   In very likeness of a roasted crab;
   And when she drinks, against her lips I bob
   And on her withered dewlap pour the ale.
   The wisest aunt, telling the saddest tale,
   Sometime for three-foot stool mistaketh me;
   Then slip I from her bum, down topples she,
   And "tailor" cries, and falls into a cough;
   And then the whole quire hold their hips and laugh;
   And waxen in their mirth, and neeze, and swear
   A merrier hour was never wasted there.

without rhyme or reason

Lacking in sense or justification. The French still say, *ni rime ni raison;* but we borrowed the saying from the French of the late Middle Ages, *na Ryme ne Raison,* as reported by W. W. Skeat some years ago in *Notes & Queries.* English usage dates from the early sixteenth century.

a hurrah's nest

A disorderly, untidy mess; a place of wild confusion. This "nest" has been variously attributed to a *hurrah,* a *hurra,* and a *hoorah,* but, I regret to say, no naturalist or folklorist has ever yet attempted to describe the imaginary creature responsible for the untidiness. My one-time associates, compilers of *The Standard Dictionary of Folklore* (1949–50), ignore it. In fact, because it first appeared in Samuel Longfellow's biography of his brother, Henry Wadsworth Longfellow, in 1829, and next in *Twenty Years Before the Mast* (1840), by Richard Henry Dana, who was a student at Harvard under H. W. Longfellow, it may well be that the "hurra's nest," as the biographer wrote it, was a family term that entered unconsciously into the ordinary conversation of members of the Longfellow family and was picked up by others who heard them use it. Our language does sometimes grow in that manner.

to quarrel with one's bread and butter

To complain about one's means of livelihood; to act against one's best interests. And many's the time you've seen a child do that—throw his buttered bread or his piece of cake or even the ice-cream cone he's been whimpering for on the ground in a fit of rage. The human race has been thus quarreling since the days of Noah, but our English phrase for expressing such lack of reason dates back not more than two centuries.

to the queen's taste

To a fare-you-well; lock, stock, and barrel; completely; utterly; totally. There was no individual queen to whom this phrase alluded, but because a queen is the highest lady in the land, all virtues are ascribed to her, including possession of all that is complete and thorough. Curiously enough, the expression is American. It first appeared in William Harben's *Abner Daniel* (1902): "You worked 'im to a queen's taste—as fine as spilt milk."

in a pretty pickle

Behind the 8-ball; the devil to pay and no pitch hot; in trouble; in a sorry plight. The Dutch, from whom we borrowed "pickle" and also the original phrase some four or five hundred years ago, said *in de pekel zitten,* literally to sit in the salt liquor used for preserving vegetables and meats. Such a bath, one can well imagine, would not long be comfortable. From time to time through the years our forebears have intensified the expression in such manners as "ill pickle," "sad pickle," "sweet pickle," and nowadays, "pretty pickle."

to walk the plank

To force out of office or position. This refers to a method used in a literal sense for getting rid of undesired persons on shipboard—a method used primarily by pirates or corsairs, especially in the seventeenth century on the Spanish Main, for disposing of unwanted captives in the cheapest, most effective, and least messy way. That is, a plank was laid over the side of the vessel, the captive, hands tied behind, was blindfolded and, by pricks of a dirk or cutlass, compelled to walk along that plank until he fell into the sea.

to play possum

To pretend; to deceive; especially, to feign sickness or death. Early American hunters speedily learned that the opossum is a past master in the art of simulating death. If threatened with capture it will lie with closed eyes and limp muscles, and no amount of handling or ordinary abuse will cause it to show signs of life. Only when thrown into water will it become promptly active. That ability to show every ordinary indication of death gave rise to our expression at least two centuries ago.

as proud as Satan (sin, or Lucifer)

This notion of evil being arrogant, supercilious, or contemptuous arose in the minds of people more than four hundred years ago. The first record in English is in *The Pilgrimage of Perfection* (1526) with "as proude as Nabugodonosor [Nebuchadnezzar]." Then came "as proud as Hell," by Dean Swift in 1711. Then "as proud as Lucifer," by Madame d'Arblay in 1782. And we have since substituted Satan, sin, the devil, Beelzebub, the Prince of Darkness, Old Scratch, Old Harry, or whatever synonym of evil may occur to us.

to take a powder

It is at least interesting to speculate on the origin of a slang phrase, even if there is no possible way of determining who started it nor his line of reasoning. Here we have something meaning to depart rapidly, to flee, to go over the hill, to take it on the lam, to beat it, to dust off or do a dust. It could be, of course, that "flee" suggested "flea," and that powder is used to rid oneself of this pest. But to my notion, "powder" was suggested by "dust" which, in turn, arises from "beating" a carpet, rug, or the like.

to break the ice

To dispel coolness or aloofness; to break through reserve or formality, establish friendly relations; also, to start an enterprise. Literally, of course, it is the ice on a river or lake that is broken for the passage of boats in early spring. Because that denoted the start of the season's activity, it was but natural to connect the expression with the start of an enterprise, and it was thus used almost four centuries ago. The current significance, that of establishing friendly relations, of dispelling reserve, came into general usage through Lord Byron. In *Don Juan* (1823) Canto XIII, referring to the British people, he has the noble don say:

> And your cold people are beyond all price,
> When once you've broken their confounded ice.

hoist with one's own petard

Ruined or destroyed by the device or plot one has set for another; caught in one's own trap. Had it not been for Shakespeare this expression would undoubtedly have died out long ago. It is found in *Hamlet*, one of the most popular of his plays. In Act IV, Polonius, hoping to catch Hamlet in some treasonable utterance in a private conversation with his mother, the queen, has hidden behind an arras in the queen's chamber, but is discovered and slain by Hamlet, who later says, "For tis the sport to haue the enginer Hoise with his owne petar." The "petar," more correctly "petard," was not unlike the modern hand grenade, originally of metal, bell-shaped, charged with powder, and fired by fuse; later, a wooden container. It was used for blowing open a door or making a breach in a wall, and, thanks to poor construction and general ignorance, not uncommonly also blew up the one operating it.

to pile (or heap) Pelion on Ossa

To heap difficulty upon difficulty; to attempt that which is all but impossible. Pelion is a mountain peak in Thessaly, about 5,300 feet high; Ossa, another peak in Thesssaly, about 6,500 feet high. The story is told in Homer's *Odyssey* (Book XI) as follows, according to the Butcher and Lang translation:

And after her I beheld Iphimedeia, . . . and she bare children twain, but short of life were they, godlike Otus and far-famed Ephialtes. Now these were the tallest men that earth, the grain giver, ever reared, and far the goodliest after the renowned Orion. At nine seasons old they were of breadth nine cubits, and nine fathoms in height. They it was who threatened to raise even against the immortals in Olympus the din of stormy war. They strove to pile Ossa on Olympus, and on Ossa Pelion . . . that there might be a pathway to the sky. Yea, and they would have accomplished it, had they reached the full measure of manhood. But the son of Zeus . . . destroyed the twain, ere the down had bloomed beneath their temples, and darkened their chins with the blossom of youth.

come off your perch

Come down a peg or two; don't be too conceited, haughty, or arrogant. The allusion is to the twig serving as a resting place for a bird; hence, a point of vantage from which one may take a superior view. The present expression is American of some fifty years' standing.

to take down a peg

To pull one off his high horse; to knock one off his perch; to humble one; to lower one in his own or another's estimation. This is found as far back as the sixteenth century, but the original allusion has been lost. Shakespeare, in *Love's Labor's Lost* (1592), Act V scene 2, has, "Master, let me take you a button-hole lower," by some interpreted to have the same meaning as our present phrase, but by others as meaning, "Master, let me speak confidentially." Yet "peg" appears at about the same date in the work of debated authorship, *Pappe with an Hatchet* (1589), in lines addressed "To Huffe, Ruffe, etc.," general terms for arrogant bullies: "Now haue at you all my gaffers of the rayling religion, tis I that must take you a peg lower."

It is my surmise that "peg" was originally connected with some game, possibly with one that preceded the introduction of draughts ("checkers" in America) in England, but I have no proof.

neither head nor tail of (a matter)

Neither one thing nor another; nothing definite nor positive: usually in such construction as, I can make neither head nor tail of this story. In the expression, which dates back to the seventeenth century, *head* means "beginning" and *tail* means "end"; hence, I can understand neither beginning nor end of this story.

to keep one's hair on

To restrain one's temper; to remain calm and serene, unruffled despite provocation. This was popular American slang of less than a century ago. In fact, the earliest literary example appears to have been in *Dr. Claudius,* one of the first pieces of fiction written by

Francis Marion Crawford. As with most slang, a positive source of the expression cannot be determined. However, it could have reflected the Indian raids upon isolated homesteaders that were still taking place in some of the western territories. Settlers and wagoners who could remain unexcited in the face of any such raid were the most likely to be able to fight off a threatening horde and thus to retain their scalps. This is, of course, conjecture. Neither Crawford nor other writers of that period, the early 1880's, left any clue that would suggest the source.

Paul Pry

The name is that of the chief character in the play, *Paul Pry,* written in 1825 by John Poole. He was such a perfect exemplar of those who go through life spying and eavesdropping into the affairs of others that the name was speedily adopted into the language. *Brewer's Handbook* (edition of 1898) thus defines the character: "an idle, inquisitive, meddlesome fellow, who has no occupation of his own, and is for ever poking his nose into other people's affairs. He always comes in with the apology, 'I hope I don't intrude.'"

to dislike (or like) the cut of one's jib

To dislike, or be chary of, the appearance of a person, or his character; to have a feeling of distrust. (Only occasionally do we use the opposite, "like.") The saying arose from nautical terminology of the seventeenth century, when the jib—the large triangular sail stretching forward from top and bottom of the foremast to the outer end of the boom, or to the bowsprit—was introduced on sailing vessels. Certain characteristic shapes of this jib served, among sailors, to identify the nationality of a vessel, and, therefore, whether the vessel might be friendly or hostile. But it was not, however, until the early nineteenth century that Southey, Walter Scott, Marryat, and others began to give the phrase its modern meaning.

in the lap (or on the knees) of the gods

According to the will of the gods; in the hands of fate or Providence; beyond one's control. The origin is Greek; the earliest occurrence is found in Homer's *Iliad*, Book XVII, line 514. The speaker was Automedon, and the occasion was the fight over the body of the slain Patroclos, friend and companion of Achilles. The Trojans, led by Hector, had already stripped the body of its armor, armor lent by Achilles to Patroclos, and, to disgrace the Acheans further, sought to drag the corpse away, intending to cut off the head, carry it in triumph into the city, and throw the body to the dogs. It was at this juncture that Automedon, watching the ebb and flow of battle, said, "All is in the lap of the gods," or, as some translate it, "on the knees of the gods." But the threat of disgrace did serve, however, to bring about a reconciliation between the powerful Achilles and Agamemnon, leader of the Acheans, and to induce Achilles to re-enter the war, eventually to rout the Trojans and slay his arch-enemy, Hector.

to get one's monkey up

To get one's dander up; to become angry. Apparently, along about a hundred years ago, people first began to compare their sudden fits of anger with the unreasoning bursts of rage so often seen among members of the simian family. The expression is of British origin and, though sometimes heard on the western side of the Atlantic, is generally confined to the place of its origin.

ish kabibble

That, at least, is the usual way the expression appears. Some, however, write it as a solid word, *ishkabibble,* and others make it three words, *ish ka bibble.* Actually you may spell it as you wish, for, like the Missouri mule, it has no pride of ancestry and no hope of posterity. Its source, that is, is unknown. It sprang into popularity roughly about 1915, and was long thought to be a Yiddish phrase equivalent to "I should worry"—meaning "it is of no concern to me"—which came into vogue at about the same time. But the Jews disclaim the saying. In fact, the usual Yiddish expression is, *Es is mein daige,* "It is my worry."

drunk as a fiddler

Highly intoxicated; three sheets in the wind; squiffy; spifflicated; tanked. It would be quite an achievement to be able to prove that the "fiddler" in the case was Nero, who, somewhat shellacked himself at the time presumably, fiddled while Rome burned, during his

reign back in the first century, but alas, this is just one of a variety of men of trades or position who, proverbially, or in fact, have been guzzlers. Others through the centuries have been, drunk as a beggar, as a lord, a piper, tinker, emperor, and fool, and there have also been "rattes," back in the sixteenth century, and a wheelbarrow in the eighteenth, as well as a fish, a "mous," "swyn," ape, and owl. The "fiddler" has prevailed, and with the best of reasons. The fiddler, always presumed to be well pleased with a chance to play, has had to be content with meager pay. In times past it was proverbial that "fiddler's pay" was nothing more than thanks and all the wine he could drink, and even when the thanks did include a few pence, the wine was supposed to make up for its scantness. What could he do but get drunk?

biggest frog (toad) in the puddle

The person of most importance in any community or group. The group or community is always a small one, otherwise the person would be a personage and "the biggest fish in the sea." Daddy is,

usually, the biggest frog in a domestic puddle, especially if he wears the pants of the family, but in a small community the relatively important individual—and rarely does that importance spread beyond the community—may be the banker, the police chief, the preacher, or the boss politician. He is, at any rate, the one to whom everyone kowtows. He's the one making the loudest "kerchunk." We've had this Americanism for at least seventy-five years.

dark horse

Originally this was a racing term for a horse about which nothing was known; its abilities had been kept "in the dark"—secret, that is—until it appeared on the track. Benjamin Disraeli is credited with the first literary usage in that sense in *The Young Duke* (1831): "A dark horse, which had never been thought of . . . rushed past the grand stand in sweeping triumph." Though a recent anonymous newspaper columnist attributes the origin to a "dark colored horse named 'Dusty Pete' " owned by a Tennessean, "Sam Flynn," who "used to ride from town to town" entering the horse, which appeared to be lame, in local races and snapping up the money, the story is another instance of folk etymology. Disraeli, both before and after entering the British political arena, was a popular writer, accepted in America as in England. Accordingly, when, to break the deadlock in the Democratic convention of 1844 among the adherents of Van Buren, Lewis Cass, and James Buchanan, the name of James K. Polk was introduced on the ninth ballot, he was the "dark horse" that had not been thought of—and this was the actual introduction of the term into political usage.

to add insult to injury

To heap scorn upon one already injured. Apperson, in *English Proverbs and Proverbial Phrases* (1929), reports that this familiar expression first appeared in Latin—*iniuriae qui addideris contumeliam*, "injury which is added to insult"—in the fifth book of the fables written by the Roman writer of the first century, A.D., Phaedrùs. But we probably owe our acquaintance with it from its use by Dickens in *Pickwick Papers*: ' To offer me a sandwich, when I am looking for a supper, is to add insult to injury."

to stick (or stand) to one's guns

To persevere in one's course despite obstacles; to hold out for, or insist on, a desired course; to maintain one's position. Obviously, the origin is military, pertaining to any commander who is determined to maintain a present position in the face of heavy attack by an enemy. As such, it could have been said of any determined leader since the invention of the gun. Curiously, however, our figurative usage traces back little more than a century, the earliest being found in Samuel Warren's popular farcical novel, *Ten Thousand a Year* (1839), in which the timorous character, Mr. Titmouse, in an argument, "though greatly alarmed," is said to have "stood to his gun pretty steadily."

to go up in the air

This is said not only of balloons and aviators, but of ordinary persons, American fathers especially, who become vociferously enraged, who sputter furiously in resemblance to a skyrocket with an ignited fuse, from which the expression originated some fifty or sixty years ago. Its British equivalent is "to get one's monkey up," which arose from the readiness with which the short-lived ire of monkeys is aroused.

on the water cart (or wagon)

The watering or sprinkling cart was a much more familiar vehicle on our dusty American streets a few decades ago than it is today. In fact, nowadays one sees only a motorized version of it cooling hot paved city streets in midsummer. But from the use of this former vehicle in slaking the dust of the roads, those of our forebears, troubled with dusty throats but seeking to avoid strong drink, spoke of climbing aboard the water cart. The expression arose during the heyday of the Prohibition movement, in the 1890's. The earliest record cited in *The Dictionary of Americanisms* is that appearing in Alice Caldwell Rice's *Mrs. Wiggs of the Cabbage Patch* (1901). Mrs. Wiggs, speaking of Mr. Dick, who is "consumpted," said: "He coughs all the time, jes' like Mr. Wiggs done. Other day he had a orful spell while I was there. I wanted to git him some whisky, but he shuck his head, 'I'm on the water-cart,' sez he."

to bite the dust (or ground or sand)

In America it is always dust that the hated villain or redskin bites when slain in mortal combat; in England, ground or sand. However, it is merely a matter of translation, for the original picturesque phrase is to be found in Homer's *Iliad*, Book II, lines 417–18. This, in the almost literal translation of William Cowper (1838), Vol. I, page 49, reads: ". . . his friends, around him, prone in dust, shall bite the ground." Whereas the American poet, William Cullen Bryant (1870), Vol. I, Book II, lines 514–15, gives it: ". . . his fellow warriors, many a one, Fall round him to the earth and bite the dust." But earlier than Bryant to use the favorite American idiom was the British explorer in South Africa, Carl J. Andersson. In his *Lake Ngami* (1856), page 363, he tells of a hunter who "had made numerous lions bite the dust." Regrettably the expression, from overuse, is losing its punch. Modern slang has now so greatly reduced its force that it implies little more than to suffer disaster of moderate degree. A horseman "bites the dust" if he falls or is thrown; a boxer, if he is knocked down or knocked out; a businessman, if he fails.

beside the mark

This is very old. In fact, it is so old that, in the original **Greek**, it had passed from a proverbial phrase into a single word which expressed its figurative sense. That is, in the old Athenian contests, an archer who failed to hit the mark was said to be out of the lists or course; hence, beside the mark. The same thing, though in English, was said of the English bowman—sometimes by variation, "far from the mark," "wide of the mark," "short of the mark," "to miss the mark." The Greek single word, which may be represented by roman type as *exagonion,* had the figurative meaning, "irrelevant; not pertinent," precisely the meaning we give to the English phrase.

hocus-pocus

Flimflam; deception; deceit; nonsense; charlatanism; jugglery: sometimes corrupted to "hokey-pokey." Probably this was originally a form of reduplication—like hodgepodge, odd-bods, shilly-shally, and many others—and was based on Latin. One explanation is given in 1656 by Thomas Ady in *A Candle in the Dark; or, A Treatise Concerning the Nature of Witches and Witchcraft*: "I will speake of one man . . that went about in King James his time . . who called himself, The Kings Majesties most excellent Hocus Pocus, and so was called, because that at the playing of every Trick, he used to say, *Hocus pocus, tontus talontus, vade celeriter jubeo,* a dark composure of words, to blinde the eyes of the beholders, to make his Trick pass the more currantly without discovery." Whether from that conjurer or not is not certain, but early in that century—just as one magician or one boxer today adopts the name of a successful predecessor—the name Hocus Pocus, Hocas Pocas, Hokos Pokos, or the like was bestowed upon any juggler or conjuror.

to make one's hair stand on end

To frighten or terrify; to cause one to become rigid with fear; to scare the pants off one. This might almost pass as a literal condition, because when one is suddenly terrified the hair on one's head tends to rise, or feels as if it does, like the fur of a cat or the mane of a dog. Even a baldheaded man feels a prickling of the scalp from a sudden terror or fright. Undoubtedly the condition was recognized in early days, but the earliest English record is not found before 1530. Occurring in John Palsgrave's *Lesclarcissement de la Langue Françoyse* it may be, in fact, a translation of the French, *faire dresser les cheveux,* "to make the hair stand erect." But Palsgrave's line is: "When I passed by the churche yarde my heares stode upright for feare." Thereafter many writers took the metaphor to their bosom.

to be well heeled

In these days one is well heeled who has plenty of money, is well fixed or well-to-do, just the opposite of one who is down at the heels. Since the latter—down at the heels—alludes directly to the usual run-down condition of the shoeheels of one who is hard-pressed for money, it might be supposed that well heeled originally alluded to the reverse condition. But that is not the case. Originally, back in the eighteenth century, it was a game cock that was well heeled; that is, provided with a good "heel" or artificial spur before it faced an opponent in the pit. From that, in the United States, men began to "heel" themselves, to arm themselves with gun or pistol, before entering a zone in which trouble might be expected. If well armed, they were "well heeled," from the troubled days in the West, and in the South following the War between the States. Hence, perhaps because most troubles can be alleviated by money, the expression soon took on its present financial aspect.

to make a mountain (out) of a molehill

To make a great to-do over a trifle; to give something far greater importance than is justified. This is by no means a new idea. In fact, as dug up by Apperson, you will find that the witty Greek writer, Lucian (A.D. 125?–210?), used it in his "Ode to a Fly": "to make an elephant of a fly." This has passed into a French proverb of identical meaning, *faire d'une mouche un éléphant,* as well as into the German *aus einer Mucke einen Elefanten machen.* Just why the Greek saying did not pass by direct translation into English is something to be guessed at, but instead, about four hundred years ago the elephant became a mountain, and the fly, gnat, or flyspeck became a molehile. It is first found in *Foxe's Book of Martyrs* (1570): "To much amplifying things y^t be but small, makyng mountaines of Molehils."

handwriting on the wall

A forecast of some ominous event; a warning of probable danger. The allusion is to the account told in the fifth chapter of Daniel in the Old Testament. Belshazzar, to celebrate his access to the throne of Babylonia upon the death of his father, Nebuchadnezzar, declared a great feast, and, to signify the complete subjugation of the Jews, had the golden vessels that were taken out of the temple at Jerusalem brought out, "and the king, and his princes, his wives, and his concubines drank in them." At this sacrilege, "came forth fingers of a man's hand, and wrote over against the candlestick upon the plaster of the wall." The words written were, *"Mene, mene, tekel, upharsin."* The king demanded of Daniel, the Jewish prophet, an interpretation, and was told: "This is the interpretation of the thing: *Mene*; God hath numbered thy kingdom, and finished it. *Tekel*; Thou art weighed in the balances, and art found wanting. *Peres*; Thy kingdom is divided, and given to the Medes and Persians." The chapter closes: "In that night was Belshazzar the king of the Chaldeans slain. And Darius the Median took the kingdom."

in one ear and out the other

Through the mind, but leaving no impression; as though a sound traveled through a tube passing through the skull leaving no evidence of its passing. The notion is by no means new; probably

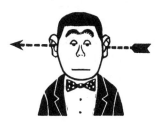

Adam gave utterance to something similar after giving some instruction to Cain and Abel. But the earliest English record concerned a sermon "upon Deuteronomie" by John Calvin which, according to his English translator, Arthur Golding in 1583, "goes in at the one eare and out at the other." There is little doubt but that many another sermon has shared the same reaction in the four centuries since.

like Hogan's goat

Poor old Hogan is merely an innocent bystander in this modern Americanism. Just as with "Hogan's brickyard," a slang designation of a baseball diamond, the goat could be the property of Jones, Smith, or Rockefeller, or VanTassel. That is, the name of the owner has no bearing whatever on the meaning of the expression. When one says that a given TV show, movie, book, or whatever is "like Hogan's goat," he is just with reasonable politeness saying that "it stinks terrifically."

playing to the grandstand (or gallery)

A contributor (David Shulman) to *American Speech* dug up a neat early description of the first expression, which he found in Thomas W. Lawton's *The Krank: His Language and What It Means* (1888): "Playing to the Grand-Stand. To accomplish this it is only necessary to smile, strike an attitude—and strike out." That is too often true, not only in baseball, as Lawton gives it, but in any sport or stage endeavor or whatever in which the performer strives or appears to strive to win the plaudits of the spectators, to show off his self-acclaimed marvelous skill or ability, especially to those he wishes to impress in the near-by high-priced grandstand seats. But one who attempts a grandstand-play, as we call it, must be very sure that he can carry it through, otherwise he may fall flat on his face and meet with hoots of derision. The earlier saying, "playing to the gallery," is still very much in use. Originally it had reference to those actors, especially in an English theater, who, going over the heads of the near-by, and frequently inattentive, occupants of orchestra seats or stalls, deliberately overacted their roles in seeking to gain the approval of the larger populace in the gallery. One had to shout and strike exaggerated attitudes and employ exaggerated gestures, just as the street orator, senator, or M.P. does today who is addressing his remarks primarily to the "dear peepul."

mad as a hatter

This doesn't mean irate, a sense one sometimes hears; it means crazy, utterly demented. There have been various theories advanced for this peculiar metaphor, and some of the theories are themselves peculiar. One is that "hatter" was introduced merely to add an intensive force, that the individual spoken of was just more "mad" than would be ordinarily expected under the circumstances. Another is that the original comparison was "mad as an adder," under the assumption, I suppose, that adders are always insane. But an explanation that I like was that given in an issue (Vol. 155, No. 3) of *The Journal of the American Medical Association*: "It seems that mercury is used in the making of felt hats. Often the unfortunate hatter who would work for years with the mercury would be afflicted with a violent and uncontrollable twitching of his muscles as a result of its poisoning effects. His friends, not understanding the cause of his strange gyrations, concluded that he was mad." Lewis Carroll's character, "The Mad Hatter," in *Alice in Wonderland* (1865) was derived from the expression, but it was in use by Thomas Haliburton in 1837 in *The Clockmaker,* and because mercury was used in hat-making much earlier than that, it may have already been in the argot of hatters long previously.

putting on the dog

Making pretensions of grandeur; assuming airs. This was American college slang of the 1860's. Whether or not it originated at Yale, it was so credited by Lyman H. Bagg who, in his *Four Years at Yale* (1871), wrote: "*Dog,* style, splurge. To put on dog is to make a flashy display, to cut a swell"—and the latter expression in the definition could be defined, "to appear important." The source of college slang even of today can be little more than guesswork, and to go back eighty-five years is necessarily conjectural. But it was then that the Blenheim and the King Charles spaniels were at the height of aristocratic popularity. Nothing could appear snootier, more high-toned than those dogs. Perhaps we owe this doggy phrase to them.

to pay the piper

To pay the fiddler; to settle the score; hence, to suffer the consequences; to take one's punishment, face the music, or take the rap. This had the same allusion as "to pay the fiddler"; that is, to pay the musician who led a dance, and the piper was one of the earliest to supply such music. Incidentally, until well into the nineteenth century, all such musicians, like the itinerant minstrels of earlier days, were considered to be scarcely a step above domestic menials. Hence, any pay they were given, beyond food and all the wine they could drink, was through the bounty of the master of the house.

a gone goose (or **beaver, chick,** etc.)

In *A Hog on Ice,* page 92, I repeated a couple of amusing but legendary yarns that might account for the expression "a gone coon," but I have been reminded that the coon is but one of various specimens of animal life which, in American speech, have and are similarly "gone" or hopelessly done for. "*A gone goose*" dates from 1830; "*a gone chick*" from 1834; "*a gone beaver*" from 1848; "*a gone horse*" from 1840; "*a gone gander*" from 1848, and James K. Paulding, in *Westward Ho!* (1832), even gave us "*gone suckers.*" But there are no legends to account for the hopeless state in which these creatures found themselves.

a Roland for an Oliver

Tit for tat; a blow for a blow; an eye for an eye. There was an actual Roland, a knight who fought under Charlemagne and who was killed in a rear-guard action in the Pyrenees in A.D. 778. From his heroic action grew the famous medieval *Chanson de Roland* (*Ballad of Roland*) and other legends that spread into all parts of Europe.

In one popular form the story was of a most romantic friendship between Roland and one of his companions, Oliver, who was the equal of Roland in every respect. They remind one of the Bobbsey twins! Whatever one could do, the other could do with precisely the same ability. Eventually the two engaged in a combat which, though fought for five days, ended in a tie. In some accounts, both were killed in the action in the Pyrenees, Roland by an accidental blow by his friend Oliver, who had himself received a fatal wound. Thus the two remained equal in death. Because of the various monumental deeds accredited to the two heroes, the saying is also sometimes employed to mean one tall tale to match another.

gosh all hemlock!

This is just one of various minced oaths or ejaculations by which a man who thinks he is nonprofane actually says "God Almighty!" *Gosh* has served as a substitute for "God"—usually in "By gosh"—for more than two hundred years. Some other similar substitutes that have appeared on the American literary scene are, gosh-a-mighty, gosh awful, gosh burned, and even, back in 1857, gosh all Potomac.

to have the goods on one

To catch one with the goods, or, that is to say, to have evidence or proof of one's guilt; to catch one red-handed. "Goods" in such usage refers to merchandise of any sort, whatever article a thief may purloin. The American expression dates from about the turn of the present century.

to warm the cockles of one's heart

To evoke a glow of pleasure in one; to produce a feeling of friendliness, affection, sympathy, or the like in one. Considering the fact that the study of anatomy—most other studies too, for that matter—was stagnant throughout the Dark Ages, or roughly from the time of Galen in the second century to that of Vesalius in the sixteenth, it is astonishing that anatomists of the seventeenth century were already likening the human heart to the shape and valves of the mollusk, common on European shores, and the cockle. That is to say, they saw sufficient resemblance between the two valves of the mollusk and the two ventricles of the heart to refer to the latter as the cockles. Thus, because the heart was long supposed to be the seat of the affections, men spoke of delighting, of rejoicing, of pleasing, and, more recently, of warming the cockles of one's heart.

to be a piker

To be a cheap-skate, tin-horn gambler, four-flusher, etc.; to be a poor sport or small better. Although this American term is less than a hundred years old, its origin is shrouded in uncertainty. It could have been derived from a regiment, commanded by Colonel Zebulon M. Pike in the War of 1812, so poorly armed that many of the men drilled with pikes instead of bayonets. Or it could have derived from the denizens of Pike County, Missouri (also named from Z. M. Pike), who, among the Forty-Niners of California, were called Pikes, Pikies, or pikers, any of which designated worthless, lazy, good-for-nothing persons. Or, in my own opinion it may have derived from a vagrant or tramp who, lacking means for other transportation, traveled on shank's mare—afoot, that is— down the pike; a foot traveler on the pike.

Barmecide feast (or banquet)

This comes from the "Story of the Barber's Sixth Brother" in *Arabian Nights*. A poor beggar, Schacabac, without food for several days, asked for bread at the door of the rich Persian noble, Barmecide. To his amazement he was invited to the table. Servants brought

golden platter after golden platter, and his host urged him to help himself freely But there was not a thing upon any of the platters. Nevertheless the beggar entered into the spirit of the jest, pretended to pile his plate full and to eat bountifully, and when, at the end of the repast, an empty jug of wine was brought, Schacabac pretended to fill and refill his goblet frequently and, eventually, to become quite drunk. In this feigned state he boxed his host heartily on the ears. This and the good nature of the beggar so delighted Barmecide that he then had a real banquet brought to the table. Thus, nowadays, a *Barmecide* is one who offers an unreal or disappointing benefit, and a *Barmecide feast* or *banquet* is a meal that, however inviting to the eye, fails to live up to expectations.

Shangri-la

A place of mystery; utopia. The place was fictional, some mysterious region in Tibet conceived by the late English-born novelist, James Hilton, in *Lost Horizon* (1933), where people lived for hundreds of years and attempted to preserve the best achievements in art and ideals of the outside world despite its tensions. The concept gained widespread appeal. Thus when, in World War II, President F. D. Roosevelt smilingly told reporters that the flyers under General James Doolittle in the bombing of Tokyo had taken off from Shangri-la, it was immediately understood that the point of departure was not to be made public, was to remain as undisclosed as Hilton's place of mystery.

Sam Hill

After long and diligent search for some American of sufficient prominence in a bygone generation to justify the continued use of his name, even to the present time, in such sayings as "to run like Sam Hill," "What the Sam Hill," "Who the Sam Hill," and so on, I have come to the reluctant conclusion that the editors of *The Dictionary of Americanisms* were right in calling the term "a euphemism for *hell.*" It may be, as Edwin V. Mitchell says in his *Encyclopedia of American Politics* (1946), that there was a Colonel Samuel Hill of Guilford, Connecticut, who continuously ran for and was elected to public office in both town and state, but this colonel, though perhaps locally prominent, does not turn up in any of the numerous biographical records I have consulted. Nor does Mr. Mitchell supply any dates. The expression itself had sufficiently widespread usage to extend into Schuyler County, New York, by 1839.

right as a trivet

Absolutely right; right as rain; all hunkydory; all to the mustard. Inasmuch as a trivet, a stand for supporting vessels in a fireplace, was always three-legged in former times, the housewife could set it anywhere upon her hearth, certain that a pot thereon would rest securely. The expression began to appear in literature early in the nineteenth century.

to go to rack (or wrack) and ruin

To go to destruction; go to pot; go haywire; go to the dogs. In the sixteenth century, and later, men spelled by ear, rather than through knowledge of the historical background of words. In fact, many of our present-day spellings are still affected by that custom. *Rack*, in this phrase, is one of them. It should have been, and should now be, *wrack,* which in turn was another spelling of *wreck* and with the same meaning. But we have had "rack and ruin" almost four hundred years and in the works of the best writers, even to the present day, and a change would be a slow process.

on the rocks

As used in American slang this respected and well-established phrase has taken on a variety of interpretations. They all relate to some form or another of dilapidation or ruin, however. Thus a person "on the rocks" may be ruined financially or "busted"; or he may be suffering a physical or mental collapse or "off his hinges," "minus some buttons," "gone haywire." A marriage "on the rocks" is one that is about to be, or has been, broken up. A business or other venture "on the rocks" has failed or, at least, is in a desperate plight. Figurative use in the sense of being destitute dates back some two hundred years, and was derived from the literal nautical sense of the condition of a vessel shipwrecked on a rocky coast.

to scare the daylights out of (a person)

To frighten extremely; to alarm intensely; to make one's hair stand on end; to scare stiff. The daylights here differ from those in the common saying, "to let daylight into a person." In that, the meaning is "light"—to make a hole in a person big enough for light to enter. But here, daylight means wits; hence, to scare a person witless. In my own span of life someone—at first, one or another of my brothers—has tried to scare the daylights out of me from the time I was two, and I'm sure the expression is just as well known and has been as long used in many another American family. Some people amplify it to "the living daylights," but it adds up to the same thing. However, the recorders of the language have heretofore missed this expression.

sacred cow

Any personal possessions cherished by its owner, or a person held in such high esteem or of such high office as to be above criticism or attack, someone on a pedestal. This twentieth-century term could have been derived from the cow, held to be sacred in India even at the present time, from the legendary hero, Prithu who assumed the form of a cow in order to encourage his subjects to raise edible vegetables. Or it could have been taken from Greek legend, the story of Io who was transformed into a heifer because Zeus had become too amorous. Or it could have had reference to the Egyptian Hathor, goddess of love, who, in the form of a cow, was served by princesses. Perhaps, even, it is somehow connected with the ejaculation "Holy cow!" made familiar in the 1940's to thousands of American radio listeners as the pet oath of "Oogie," boy friend of Corliss Archer. Most probably, however, the connection is with the sacred cow of India.

Indian sign

Evidently Frederick Webb Hodge, editor of the *Handbook of American Indians* (1907), issued by the Smithsonian Institution and still regarded as the leading authority on Indian life and customs, did not foresee that movies, radio, and television would perpetuate—at least, among children—an interest in those first inhabitants of the continent. On the meaning of this term he says merely: "A Western colloquialism of the earlier settlement days for a trace of the recent presence of Indians." It is no longer a colloquialism, nor is it confined to the West, nor to early settlement days. But Hodge missed an expression familiarly used in my boyhood—"to put (or hang) the Injun sign on someone." By that we meant, to mark a person for injury or for defeat in a contest; to put a jinx on one; to wish him ill luck.

taken to the cleaners

Defrauded; despoiled; mulcted; flimflammed; stung; played for a sucker; also punished or severely defeated. This is merely a modernized form of the slang term "cleaned out," used by some of our great-grandfathers in the early nineteenth century. The *New and*

Comprehensive Vocabulary of the Flash Language, written in 1812 by James H. Vaux, defined the older phrase: "Said of a gambler who lost his last stake at play; also, of a flat [dupe] who has been stript of all his money." The modern form, however, introduces a subtle play on words in the secondary meanings of punished or defeated in the suggestion that he who has been cleaned has been sent through a washing machine or has been subjected to the machinations of a dry-cleaning establishment.

to knock on wood

Why do even those among us who loudly proclaim utter freedom from superstition feel just a bit reluctant to state that such-and-such calamity has never happened without immediately feeling an urge to tap on some solid piece of wood? As everyone knows, the act is supposed to avert evil or misfortune which otherwise might attend vainglorious speech.

No one knows how the superstition arose, but George Stimpson, in *A Book about a Thousand Things* (1946), which the publishers, Harper & Brothers, permit me to quote, presents some of the numerous theories that have been offered. He says:

. . . Some attribute it to the old game known as "touching wood" or "wood tag," in which a player who succeeds in touching wood is safe from capture. Others hold that this game and "knocking on wood" had a common origin in primitive tree worship, when trees were believed to harbor protective spirits. To rap on a tree—the dwelling place of a friendly spirit—was to call up the spirit of the tree to protect one against impending misfortune. Later, people would place the hand on a wooden statue of a deity for the same purpose. It is said that among certain European peasants it is still common to knock loudly on wood to keep away evil spirits. Still others believe the superstition is of Christian origin and that it is in some way associated with the wooden cross upon which Jesus was crucified. Perhaps, they think, it is a survival of the religious rite of touching a crucifix when taking an oath or the beads of the rosary when praying.

a drop in the bucket (or sea, or ocean)

Any quantity far too small; a smithereen. The metaphor first appeared in the English translation of the Bible by John Wyclif

(1382) in Isaiah ix, 15: "Lo! Jentiles as a drope of a boket, and as moment of a balaunce ben holden." In the King James version the passage reads: "Behold, the nations are as a drop of a bucket, and are counted as the small dust of the balance." Charles Dickens gave impetus to the further alteration or expansion in *A Christmas Carol* (1844). In the first conversation between Scrooge and the ghost of his deceased partner, Marley, the ghost says: "The dealings of my trade were but a drop of water in the comprehensive ocean of my business." And nowadays the "drop" may be of any liquid into any proportionately great body.

to be in a hole

To be in debt; hence, in difficulty or trouble; in a predicament; on the spot; with one's back to the wall. The "hole" here is not the same one as that, in a poker game, in which one may have an ace in the hole, though this too is said to have had its origin at the poker table. That is, so says John P. Quinn in *Fools of Fortune* (1892), the proprietors of a gambling joint take a certain percentage out of the pot on each hand called as the amount due the house; "a pair of aces and another pair, and you must 'go to the hole' with a check. The 'hole' is a slot cut in the middle of the poker table, leading to a locked drawer underneath, and all checks deposited therein are the property of the keeper of the place."

to trip the light fantastic

To dance. In full, the expression is "to trip the light fantastic toe." It comes from John Milton's "L'Allegro" (1632), from the early lines beginning:

> Haste thee Nymph and bring with thee
> Jest and youthful Jollity,

and going on to—

> Sport that wrinkled Care derides,
> And Laughter holding both his sides.
> Come, and trip it as ye go
> On the light fantastick toe.

to be in the same boat

Obviously, two or more people or things occupying one boat must share equal risks, and the phrase has thus acquired such figurative meaning; to share risks equally, to have identical obligations or involvements, to be in or live under similar conditions. Literary usage of the phrase goes back only about a hundred years, but it may have had its origin in an older expression, by three centuries, "to have an oar in another's boat," that is, to interfere in or meddle with the affairs of another.

to take one's Bible oath

To be absolutely certain; to have no shadow of doubt. Alluding to the oath that one takes as a witness in a court, in which, under certain circumstances, one places his right hand upon the Bible or holds it, or the New Testament, in his right hand and swears "to tell the truth, the whole truth, and nothing but the truth; so help me God." Accordingly, an expression of willingness "to take one's Bible oath" is a statement that one is willing to enter such a court and to swear such an oath. Alas, unfortunately the statement is often, if not usually, that of a scoundrel, to whom the sanctity of the Bible or of such an oath is meaningless. The expression is criminal slang, and usage seems to have started in the past half century.

to hem and haw

To express hesitancy or uncertainty; sometimes to express a qualified disapproval. Actually we have made a compound verb out of two vocal sounds by which we ordinarily express such hesitance. That is, we "hem" when we clear the throat with a slight vocal effort, as if about to speak; we "haw," originally "hawk," when we clear the throat with greater effort. Back in 1580, in Gervase Babington's *A Profitable Exposition of the Lord's Prayer,* we find, "Wee gape and we yawne, we hem and we hawke." A

604

century earlier, however, in one of the *Paston Letters* written in 1469, we find: "He wold have gotyn it aweye by humys [hums] and by hays [ha's or haws], but I wold not so be answeryd." Shakespeare, as did some other writers of the seventeenth century, used "hum and ha."

touch and go

An uncertain, risky, or precarious state of things, a narrow escape; also, an immediate or rapid action. The expression arose in the early years of the past century, and both interpretations were in vogue from the beginning, probably because any narrow escape is averted through immediate or rapid action. For the origin, probably Admiral William H. Smyth was right in his definition of the term in *The Sailor's Word-book* (1865): "Said of anything within an ace of ruin; as in rounding a ship very narrowly to escape rocks, &c, or when, under sail, she rubs against the ground with her keel, without much diminution of her velocity."

Tom-and-Jerry

Nowadays this is a drink, one composed of brandy, rum, beaten egg, sugar, nutmeg, and hot milk or water. These components may vary somewhat, but those are the usual current ingredients in the United States. The name is derived from two characters in Pierce Egan's *Life in London; or, Days and Nights of Jerry Hawthorne and his Elegant Friend Corinthian Tom* (1821). This book, describing the sporting activities of that day, illustrated by George Cruikshank, was immensely popular. Hence, through the earlier "Jerry shop," a term for a low beer hall, the two names, *Tom* and *Jerry*, in this reversed order, began to be associated with drinking and carousing within a few years after the appearance of the book. A standard recipe for the drink, however—by one under the nom de plume, Jerry Thomas—did not appear until 1862.

on tick

On credit. Years ago, when this commercial term first came into use, it indicated a written document, a form of IOU. That is, it was just a contraction of "on ticket," and the "ticket" was some form of note of hand, or acknowledgment of indebtedness. The contracted form came into use in the fore part of the seventeenth century. *The Oxford English Dictionary* cites a usage of 1642: "They would haue . . run on tick with Piggin for inke and songs, rather than haue lost the show of your presence."

Tom, Dick, and Harry

This group of names signifying any indiscriminate collection of masculine representatives of *hoi polloi* was a more or less haphazard choice. It probably started with names common in the sixteenth century. Thus Sir David Lyndesay, in *Ane Dialog betwix Experience and ane Courteour* (*c.* 1555), has, "Wherefore to colliers, carters and cokes to Iack [Jack] and Tom my rime shall be directed." And Shakespeare, in *Love's Labour's Lost* (1588), gives us in the closing song, "And Dicke the Shepheard blowes his nails; and Tom beares Logges into the hall." And "Dick, Tom, and Jack" served through the seventeenth century. But our present group was apparently an American selection. It appeared (according to George L. Kittredge's *The Old Farmer and His Almanac,* 1904) in *The Farmer's Almanack* for 1815: "So he hired Tom, Dick and Harry, and at it they went."

with the tail between the legs

That's Fido for you. Put him up against a toy terrier half his size and his tail promptly turns down under his belly. Maybe he'll even turn on his back, all four legs limp. Brave dog! The attitude of a cowardly or scared dog is so typical that we have long said of a thoroughly cowed, utterly abased, or dejected person that he stands or runs "with his tail between his legs."

to take (something) lying down

Usually the "something" is an insult or act of scorn, contempt, derision, or the like that we do *not* take, or intend to take, with the submission implied by recumbency—passively, that is. In fact, he who does "take it lying down" is likely to be regarded as spineless, or perhaps as a bootlicker, stooge, apple-polisher, or toady. It is an American expression, perhaps twenty-five or thirty years old.

to play ball with one

To coöperate with one; to accept as a fellow; also, sometimes to accept as a friend or a confidant. In its literal sense the expression first alluded to the necessity for each member of a ball team—baseball or football—to coöperate with all other members in all possible ways during any game in order to play most effectively. From an admonition by the coaches of successful teams, the expression extended into social and commercial usage in the 1920's.

on Easy Street

Having an easy living; in comfortable circumstances; prosperous; riding on the gravy train. American slang from the close of the nineteenth century. The earliest record of this imaginary street in the *Dictionary of American English* takes it to George V. Hobart's *It's Up to You* (1902), in which the author tells of a young man "who could walk up and down Easy Street."

to swear like a trooper

To swear tremendous oaths; to use extreme profanity. Some anonymous newspaper columnist, recently, though using *trouper* instead of *trooper*, said, "This expression started and was used in church meetings as late as the 1900's. The troupers referred to are stage actors and the saying was used to denote the low esteem show people were regarded by many people." Sorry, but, except possibly for the lack of esteem in which actors were held by some unfortunate people, the statement is altogether untrue. The expression is at least a hundred and fifty years old, and the reference is to the habit of strong profanity among British cavalrymen at that period.

to cut a (big) swath

This was slang, back in the 1840's. It alluded to the wide sweep of grass mown by a scythe; hence, to the flourish made by a pompous person swaggering down the walk. In fact, the first literary use of this American slang was precisely that. It was in *High Life in New York* (1843), by Ann Stephens: "Gracious me! how he was strutting up the side-walk—didn't he cut a swath!" The popular creator of the fictional character, Sam Slick, undoubtedly helped perpetuate the phrase. In *Nature and Human Nature* (1855), that is, Thomas C. Haliburton had the lines, "The Miss A——s cut a tall swathe, I tell you, for they say they are descended from a governor of Nova Scotia, and that their relatiōns in England are some punkins too."

to make hay while the sun shines

Since hay is the resultant of mown grass dried for fodder, and the sun is the cheapest and most available drying agency, the literal sense of this aphorism is most obvious. Its figurative intent is equivalent to "Strike while the iron is hot," and in fact such are both the German and French phrases: *Das Eisen schmieden solange es noch heiss ist,* and *Battre le fer pendant qu'il est chaud.* That is, the English phrase means, if an explanation is needed, to seize opportunity by the forelock; to take advantage of a good thing before it slips past. John Heywood in his *All the Prouerbes in the Englishe Tongue* (1546) gave it: "Whan the sunne shinth make hay."

to splice the mainbrace

Either literally or figuratively this required the full crew of a sailing vessel. The mainbrace is the rope by which the mainsail is trimmed. To splice this rope requires the services of the entire crew, and at the conclusion of this arduous task it became the custom in the British Navy, in days of sail, to serve rum to all hands. From that custom, "to splice the mainbrace" became the accepted naval term in the early nineteenth century as a call to serve grog, a call speedily adopted among landlubbers and still in use by them, though long dropped in nautical lingo.

to knock the spots off one

Just what these spots were, which when knocked off gave one a victory, is a matter of guess. Apparently they were New England spots, and possibly localized still further in Vermont. At least the first printed reference leads to the latter inference. It was in an article on the breeding of Morgan horses in the publication, *Porter's Spirit of the Times*, November 22, 1856: "Addison County leads the van (or 'knocks the spots off,' as we say here) in Vermont and is celebrated over the world for its fine horses." I have a hunch that the "spots" were the prominent members of the countenance of one's adversary, the eyes, the nose, at which one would be most likely to aim one's fists.

to sing another (or a different) tune, or, to change one's tune

To speak or act in a different manner; to assume a different attitude; to change the subject, or, especially, to humble oneself. The school bully sings a different tune after brave Johnny, finally stirred to anger, gives him a thorough licking. And such has been the case, similarly expressed, for some six hundred years. Thus John Gower wrote in his *Confessio Amantis* (1390), "O thou, which hast desesed [disseised] The Court of France be thi wrong, Now schalt thou singe an other song." Because the saying is so old we can assume that it arose from frequent use among wandering minstrels of the Middle Ages who, traveling from court to court, found it discreet to change the wording of the songs they sang to meet the boasts of each successive baron.

Indian giver

The most blameworthy charge that one child can level at another, for he (or she) so charged is two-faced, without honor, faithless. To be brief, the present that Billy-B may bring to Robbie's birthday party is one that Robbie may look at while the party is in progress,

but Billy will demand its return when the party is over. That is to say, even back in colonial days an *Indian gift* referred "to the alleged custom among Indians," according to the *Handbook of American Indians* (1907) issued by the Smithsonian Institution, "of expecting an equivalent for a gift or otherwise its return." The same authority defines *Indian giver*—"A repentant giver." In my own youth, incidentally, although "Indian" was expected in formal speech, the normal everyday speech of all boys and many adults was "Injun."

stool-pigeon

An informer or telltale; a decoy used by the police to trap a wrongdoer. The term is neither new nor recent. In the literal sense of a decoy pigeon it was in use by American hunters early in the nineteenth century. And fowlers also used the term "stool-crow," a similar decoy for crows. It is fairly certain that *stool* as used here was formerly written *stale*, which also meant a living bird used to attract others of its kind. Thus, for example, we have in Shakespeare's *The Tempest* (1611), IV, 1, "The trumpery in my house, goe bring it hither For *stale* to catch these theeues." And this in turn was a variation in the same period of *stall,* as in lines from the so-called Chester Whitsun Plays (*c.* 1500), "Send forth women of thie countrye, namely those that beautifull be, and to thie Enemyes lett them draw nye, as *stalles* to stand them before."

to pull up stakes

To move from a place; change one's location. This takes us back to colonial days in New England, to the time when a settler, dissatisfied for any cause with the parcel of land allotted to him, took up the boundary stakes and either returned to England or moved to another location of his own choosing. The earliest citation is to an English lawyer, Thomas Lechford, who, after a stay of two years in Boston, 1638 to 1640, wrote to a friend in England, "I am loth to hear of a stay [in New England], but am plucking up stakes, with as much speed as I may, if so be I may be so happy as to arrive in Ireland. . . ."

old (familiar) stamping ground

A place to which one is accustomed. Back in the Revolutionary period, and probably long earlier, a *stamping ground* was a place known to our American forebears where horses or other animals gathered in numbers. The step was short in a transference of the term to a place to which a man, woman, or child was accustomed. First to use it in a published work was H. R. Howard, compiler of

The History of Virgil A. Stewart (1836): "I made my way from Milledgeville to Williamson County, the old stamping-ground."

shiver my timbers

It is not at all likely that any self-respecting sailor would have ever thought of using or even dared to use such an ejaculation or oath as this, but, in 1834, the sailor and novelist, Frederick Marryat, finding the necessity for an oath, in *Jacob Faithful,* chapter XI, that would not offend the ears of the most puritanical reader invented this most innocuous expression: "I won't thrash you, Tom. Shiver my timbers if I do." John B. Opdyke, in *Mark My Words* (1949), page 584, says "the expression 'shiver my timbers' belongs to cricket, referring to scattering or strewing wickets for which *timbers* is a slang substitute." The statement is partly true, and would have been entirely true if he had said "was adopted by cricket," in which game it is now used.

to have (a person) **where the hair is short; to get** (a person) **by the short hairs**

Both expressions are in equal use and have identical meaning: to have or get a person at one's mercy; to have or get complete mastery over; or, more moderately, to have or get a decided advantage over. The metaphor appears to be of American origin; at least the earliest instance of literary use of these short hairs that has been found occurs in *Memoirs of the United States Secret Service* (1872), by George P. Burnham. Nowadays, thanks to modern hairdressing, the general assumption is that the reference is to the hair at the back of the head, just above the nape of the neck, now usually trimmed rather short among English-speaking people with whom the saying is familiar.

The saying undoubtedly antedates the time of its earliest literary use, however, and if one looks at portraits of, say, our presidents or other important figures of the Civil War period, men likely to be tonsorially correct, it is immediately evident that hair was not then cropped short. Accordingly, I think we should look elsewhere for the short hairs on which a grip would give one complete mastery over an antagonist. The pubic hairs could be considered, but, if such was the original allusion, the conflict that could have given rise to such a painful hold would necessarily have been one in which at least one of the contestants, such as an Indian, had a minimum of clothing. But it is also quite possible that the beard was intended, as in a fight between two white men. Our own Washington Irving, in *Knickerbocker's History of New York* (1809), wrote, "A gigantic question . . . which I must needs take by the beard and utterly subdue." It would certainly be a far easier hold to seize a man by the relatively short hairs of the beard than by the pubic hairs or the short hairs of the modern haircutter's art.

to put one's shoulder to the wheel

To assist with might and main; to labor vigorously in behalf of a cause, project, etc. In the physical sense one put one's shoulder to the wheel to aid his horse in pulling a cart or other vehicle out of the mud or over an obstacle. And when a horse required such aid, it was certain that vigorous effort was needed. No halfway measures are implied by the expression. Figurative usage dates back to the seventeenth century, but I have no doubt that the captive Israelites under the Pharaohs of ancient Egypt were often obliged to perform the task literally in the building of the pyramids.

to lose one's shirt

It means to lose everything one has, and, though this expression is fairly new, the concept of one's shirt being the last thing one possesses, next to his skin, is not exactly new. Chaucer conveyed that thought when, in "The Wyf of Bathes Tale," he wrote, "Who that holt [hold] him payd of his povert [poverty], I holde him riche, al [though] had he nought [not] a schert." It is the same idea which, for several centuries also, others have had in speaking of one who has "not a shirt to his back," or who had "given away the shirt off his back"—the last of his possessions, that is.

in seventh heaven

In a state of ineffable bliss or delight; having great pleasure. This, especially in Islamic beliefs, is the heaven of heavens, in its literal sense, the abode of God and the highest angels. A similar concept prevailed among the Jews in pre-Christian times, probably acquired from Babylonian beliefs. The concept calls for seven heavens, one lying above another, graded according to the degree of merit one has acquired on earth, or, in some beliefs, according to the successive steps taken by the soul after death.

to give short shrift to

To cut short; to make quick work of. The literal sense appears in Shakespeare's *The Tragedy of King Richard* III, Act IV, scene 4. Lord Hastings has just been sentenced to execution by the Duke of Gloucester, shortly to be declared Richard III, and is interrupted in his reveries by Ratcliff, ordered to oversee the execution, who says: "Dispatch, my lord; the duke would be at dinner: Make a short shrift; he longs to see your head." That is, though a condemned criminal was permitted time for confession or shrift, urgency might require that he be allowed no more than a few minutes for his shriving. Hence, thanks to the long list of crimes punishable by execution, this urgency was so common in the seventeenth century that "short shrift" became a synonym with "least possible delay."

spit-and-polish

Finical smartness or ornamentation; furbishment; trimness. But whereas in the early nineteenth century, and many years before, the British officer, naval and military, demanded such finicky smartness—as if by the application of much spittle and elbow grease with a polishing agent—by the latter half of that century many naval officers, at least, regarded it as a wasteful affectation, having no bearing on efficiency. The first to voice that disapproval—and, incidentally, to record the term—was Admiral Lord Charles Beresford. In his *Memoirs* (1914), telling of his first independent command in 1873, he said that though at the outset he had a large working party holystone the decks until they were "as clean as a hound's tooth," from that day onward "I set myself steadily against bright-work and spit-and-polish." And he added, "Under the spit-and-polish system no doubt the men take a pride in keeping the ship bright, but such a process involves perpetual extra bother and worry, which are quite unnecessary."

no great shakes

Nothing out of the ordinary in proficiency or achievement; no particular bargain; nothing of importance or consequence; nothing to write home about; no prize. Maybe, as suggested by the great *Oxford English Dictionary*, the ultimate source alluded to the shaking of dice, in which the turn is so often nothing more than mediocre. But the expression was such common slang in the beginning of the nineteenth century that Lord Broughton, writing of an incident that occurred in 1816 (in his *Recollections of a Long Life*, 1865), recalled that, to quote him, "W. said that a piece of sculpture there was '*nullae magnae quassationes*,' and the others laughed heartily." That is to say, the others present not only knew their Latin, but immediately recognized that, translated literally, it meant "no great shakes."

to hold the bag

To be left in the lurch, or in an awkward or ludicrous position not of one's own devising; to be made the scapegoat for faults committed by others; to be the victim of a mean trick. As stated in *A Hog on Ice* this American expression was in use, and apparently

well understood, back in the time of George Washington, having been used in a comedy produced in 1787. But it did not occur to me, until reminded by several correspondents, that the expression undoubtedly arose from the "snipe hunt" known to (and probably participated in by) my father some ninety years ago, often gleefully described to me, nor, in fact, that the boyhood hoax of central Ohio of his generation could have been brought from earlier settlements. How old the prank may be and when or where it may have originated, perhaps under another name, cannot be determined.

For the benefit of those unfamiliar with the game, this is the procedure: A group of boys, initiating a new boy in a community, invite him to join them some night on a "snipe hunt"—generally where snipe have never been seen. They take him far into the woods, wholly unfamiliar to him, armed with lanterns (or, now-adays, flashlights) and burlap bags. At a "likely" spot the new boy is handed one of the lanterns, is given a bag, and is instructed to keep the bag open, with the lantern above it, while the rest of the crowd go off into the brush to scare up the birds. The birds, he is told, seeing the light, will make for it and be caught in the bag. Of course, the rest of the crowd actually reassemble at some appointed spot and return hilariously to town and their own warm beds, leaving the neophyte, shivering and alone in a strange place, "holding the bag" for birds that will never appear.

Incidentally, among the Pennsylvania Dutch the hoax is known as *elbedritsch,* and there may be other names for it in other parts of the country.

to start from scratch

To begin any enterprise, investigation, search, or other activity from the very beginning, often with no precedent as a guide; to begin at the beginning; to take the first step. Actually the expression is derived from the sporting world, from a race in which *scratch* designates the line or mark that is to be the starting point. Hence, he who starts from scratch starts from nothing; he has no preliminary impetus beyond his own ability, genius, or determination to carry him through the race.

to go scotfree

To be free of penalty, or exempt from punishment or injury. Little Pete goes scotfree if mother thinks the costly new glass candlestick was knocked on the floor by the cat. But the expression and its extended meaning are very old. Back in the twelfth century a *scot* was a tax or forced contribution payable by the subjects of a municipality, later including the payment for one's share for entertainment in a tavern. Thus, as originally intended, a person who went scotfree was merely one who was free from the burden of paying a fine or tax, or, in a tavern, was under no obligation to pay a share of the score. As John de Trevisa wrote in *Bartholomeus* (1398): "After souper that is freely yeue [given] it is not honest to compell a man to pay his scot."

between wind and water

We go back to naval craft of the sixteenth century for this, and thence onward through the history of wooden vessels in warfare to recent times. The allusion is to that portion of the side of a ship which, especially in rough seas, is alternately above and below water, exposed both to wind and to water. A shot from a hostile gun striking such an area would be peculiarly hazardous. The historian George Bancroft made use of the expression in his account of the action between the United States and Tripoli in his *History of the United States* (1876). The frigate *Congress* was, as he described the action, "hulled twelve times, and hit seven times between wind and water." But the phrase has also been applied metaphorically to man for some three centuries, usually designating unexpected attack. The usage is illustrated in the sentence from Thomas Fuller's *The Church-History of England* (1655): "The good old man was shot between Wind and Water, and his consent was assaulted in a dangerous joincture of time to give any deniall."

not to care a straw

To be completely and utterly indifferent, or to regard as of no value whatever; not to care a tinker's dam. Stone floors were cold, back in the days when carpets or rugs had not yet come into general use, or when, as among the peasantry, none could afford or were permitted to own such luxuries. Hence, in the halls of the gentry, it was the custom in winter to spread straw rather thickly over the stone floors or, in the hovels of the common people, over the dirt floors. Accounts of the Lord High Treasurer of Scotland, in 1501, show a sum paid to one James Dog "to buy straw for the kingis chamer in Invernes." In summer, green rushes were used. Naturally, as Maria Leach points out in *The Soup Stone* (1954), such straw soon became trampled, broken, and filthy dirty. More straw scattered over the top might improve appearances briefly, but not for long. Scraps of food, bones tossed to the dogs, did nothing to improve sanitary conditions either. Obviously, straw placed to such use soon lost what little value it had ever had, becoming wholly worthless, as indicated by our common saying. But the trifling value of straw after the grain has been separated from it had also been recognized from earliest times.

gone where the woodbine twineth

When we were boys and either of us inquired as to the whereabouts of some article or person, mysteriously disappeared or vanished into thin air, my brother or I might answer, "Gone where the woodbine twineth and the whangdoodle mourneth for his first-born." That is, somehow we picked up the saying in southern Ohio in the 1880's—both parts of the saying. Consequently, though I cannot produce proof, and though there is proof that the notorious stock manipulator, James Fisk, Jr., used the first clause in a statement quoted by New York newspapers in 1870 (when asked to account for a missing $50,000,000), and though the second clause appeared in an Illinois paper in 1858, I am confident that the whole expression was one of the highfalutin, boastful heroics of the rip-roaring breed of frontiersmen who salted their speech with all sorts of braggadocio in the early 1800's which we got in hand-me-down speech many years later. Jim Fisk, son of a peddler, could readily have picked it up in his youth, or later during his own peddling career.

to nourish a viper (or snake) in one's bosom

The saying takes us again to our old Greek friend, Aesop. The available translation tells this story under the title, "The Farmer and the Snake": "A Farmer found in the winter a Snake stiff and frozen with cold. He had compassion on it, and taking it up placed it in his bosom. The Snake on being thawed by the warmth quickly revived, when, resuming his natural instincts, he bit his benefactor, inflicting on him a mortal wound. The Farmer said with his latest breath, 'I am rightly served for pitying a scoundrel.' Moral: The greatest benefits will not bind the ungrateful."

as clean as a whistle

Robert Burns, in his poem, "Earnest Cry," used *toom* ("empty") rather than "clean"—"Paint Scotland greetan owre her thrissle; Her mutchkin stoup as toom's a whissle"—and other writers have had the whistle clear, dry, pure, or other adjective. The basic intent, however, is to indicate that, for a sweet, pure sound from a whistle or reed, the tube must be clean and dry.

to go west

Although it has never been determined who, during World War I, was the first to speak of a fallen British soldier—and thereafter any member of the Allied military force who died in service—as having "gone west," the choice of the expression does not impress me as having been out of the ordinary. Any classical scholar could have expressed it thus. The association of death with the west goes back at least to Roman times. In fact our word *Occident*, by which we mean "west," the opposite of *Orient*, was derived from the Latin *occidere,* meaning "to kill" or "to die." That is, to the ancients, the sun "died" at the close of each day; the place where it died was *occidens.*

to say (or cry) "uncle"

To eat crow; throw in the towel or the sponge; cry quits; yield; submit. When I was a boy, one "hollered 'cavy' " when he was licked, but we would have been the most astonished boys in the world had anyone told us we were talking Latin. That is, "cavy," as I learned much later, is a corrupted contraction of *peccavi,* meaning, I have sinned, or, I am at fault, and this acknowledgment of guilt or fault was English usage from the sixteenth century onward. How it came into southern Ohio, I don't know. And our present American expression, though arising only in this century, may also have had Latin birth. At least, when the Roman lad was in trouble, he cried, *Patrue mi patruissime,* "Uncle, my best of uncles!"

on velvet

Although the *Wardrobe Accounts of Edward II* state that that British sovereign (1307–27) had "1 couerchief de veluett" (kerchief of velvet), this material was still so rare and costly through the next two or three hundred years, so generally unfamiliar, as not to acquire any figurative application. Thus it was only about two centuries ago

618

that our present common expression began to indicate prosperity, a condition of ease or comfort. It was sufficiently well known, that is, to justify its use by Edmund Burke when, as Premier, in 1769, he stated in his notable *Observations on a Pamphlet on the Present State of the Nation* that not like the author of that pamphlet "who is always on velvet, he is aware of some difficulties."

tune the old cow died of

Any tune with which one has become thoroughly fed up, or the instrument upon which a tune is played ad nauseam, or the tedious or tiresome manner in which a tune is played. Some of the theme compositions of modern radio and television I would class as "tunes  the old cow died of." And the bagpipe and certain other so-called musical instruments could be consigned to the same category—in my humble opinion. In fact, concerning the bagpipe, I thought for a while I had the real reason for the death of the old cow. I figured that, in ancient times at least, the udder of the cow might have been used as the bag of the pipe and the various appendages might have been utilized for air intake, pipes, and drone respectively. The theory was good, but, alas, no history of bagpipe construction bears it out. All I can do, therefore, is to play follow the leader and report the childish yarn of the anonymous "old ballad" which would cause the death of any cow, old or young:

> There was an old man, and he had an old cow,
>   But he had no fodder to give her,
> So he took up his fiddle, and played her a tune;
>   "Consider, good cow, consider,
> This isn't the time for the grass to grow,
>   Consider, good cow, consider."

to wash one's dirty linen in public

All we did, about a century ago, was to reverse the French proverb, *il faut laver son linge sale en famille,* "one should wash one's dirty linen in private." The French idea, that is, is that family quarrels or matters that concern members of the family should be kept within the four walls of the home. Anthony Trollope seems to have heard the French saying, or was at least the first to give us the English equivalent. This was in *The Last Chronicle of Barset* (1867): "I do not like to trouble you with my private affairs;—there is nothing, I think, so bad as washing one's dirty linen in public."

to go to the wall

Though now it is usually a business house that, under insurmountable financial difficulties, "goes to the wall," it was—back in the sixteenth century—the adversary in a conflict that, forced to yield ground, went to the wall. The allusion is to the desperate straits of a wayfarer when set upon by ruffians in an unlighted street of former years. By giving ground and getting his back to the wall he was better able to defend himself by poniard or sword. From the same situation, by no means uncommon in the Middle Ages and later, came our expression, "to be driven (or pushed) to the wall," which we now use in a similar sense, to be forced to one's last resource.

to throw cold water

It's all a matter of habitual practice or personal taste. That is, if one is not accustomed to a cold shower, a sudden dash of cold water on one's naked body may be quite a shock. The very notion, a hundred and fifty years ago, gave one the jitters, or at least "dampened" one's ardor. Thus the deliberate throwing of cold water was taken to be an unfriendly act. And, in figurative usage, the thrower then became one who discouraged a plan or project or who was cool toward it.

to meet one's Waterloo

To get one's come-uppance; to meet defeat. Any reader of the life of Napoleon will recognize the source and the significance of the phrase. After the defeat of the "little Corsican" by the Allies in 1814 and his brief imprisonment on Elba, from which he escaped in February of 1815, Napoleon again took the field against his enemies

620

in June. Nominally he had an army of 500,000 men, but he actually mustered only 198,000. Opposed to him were the English, Dutch, Belgian, Prussian, and Austrian forces, numbering about 215,000 men—121,000 under Blucher and about 94,000 under Wellington. The two adversaries met near the little village of Waterloo, Belgium, some twelve miles south of Brussels. Despite a more advantageous position at the beginning of the battle on the morning of June 18, the French army was overwhelmingly defeated, its retreat ending in a rout. Napoleon was again forced to abdicate and was then imprisoned on the island of St. Helena until his death in 1821.

to beat (or belt) the living daylights out of one

To beat severely; flog unmercifully; lick the stuffing or tar out of one, or many other synonyms for thrash, punish, chastise. All these indicate severe punishment that is to be administered to a foe or even to a son, but none is so drastic as the original and less verbose threat. That is, back in the late eighteenth century or, most probably earlier, one threatened "to let daylight into" someone, usually a foe. This was, or was to be, accomplished by means of an opening made into his system by a dagger or sword or other sharp-pointed instrument or, in later times, by a bullet. But such actual punishment bore attendant risk of reprisal by law, so the threats became more moderate. One was less likely to swing for merely thrashing a person, and, certainly, "living daylights" could not be interpreted as a threat of death. The suspicion is that the modified phrase is of American origin, dating back perhaps seventy-five years.

like a bump on a log

Like a Stoughton bottle; stolid; unemotional; stupidly dumb. Usually any such dumb bunny is said to sit or stand like a bump on a log, meaning just to sit or stand in vacuous silence. The metaphor is American and may have referred originally to the stolid protuberance found on almost any log, or it may have been suggested as a comparison of the discomfort from sitting on a bumpy log with the discomfort of association with a superbly dumb companion. Undoubtedly the description was used long before her time, but it seems to have appeared first in Kate Douglas Wiggins' *The Bird's*

Christmas Carol (1899): "Ye ain't goin' to set there like a bump on a log 'thout sayin' a word to pay for yer vittles, air ye?"

double-cross

Betrayal; treachery; deception by double-dealing; or, as a verb, to bamboozle; to take one to the cleaners. Like any other slang expression this may have been current for many years before it received recognition on the printed page. Its formation, however, was a natural one: the adjective *double* in the sense, "characterized by duplicity; false," and the noun *cross* in its slang sense, "dishonesty; fraudulence." The first record we have is in the 1874 edition of John Hotten's *Dictionary of Modern Slang, Cant, and Vulgar Words,* with the definition—still in vogue in prize fights and some other sports—"A cross in which a man who has engaged to lose breaks his engagement, and 'goes straight' at the last moment."

to get one's come-uppance

To receive the fate one has merited; to get what is coming to one in the way of chastisement or rebuke. Though "come-uppance," in the sense here used, is said to be dialectal English, I think it is American, perhaps a modification of English usage, however. Our cousins spoke of one's "come-uppings," rather than "come-uppance," and the latter has been our usage since the Civil War at least. The phrase was in use long before his time, but William Dean Howells gave it the stamp of literary approval when, in *Silas Lapham* (1884), he wrote: "Rogers is a rascal . . . But I guess he'll find he's got his come-uppance."

trade last (or T. L.)

A quoted compliment offered by one who heard it in exchange for a compliment; reciprocal praise; adulatory tit-for-tat. Although a contributor to *American Speech* (October–December, 1948) tells of a friend of seventy-odd who "has known *trade last* in Kansas as far back as she can remember," the expression was sheer Greek to me when, coming from Ohio, I first heard it on Staten Island, New York, in the very early 1890's. In either case, however, that would indicate that it was used as early as the 1880's. But where it originated and under what circumstance cannot be guessed. "Last," in the expression, means that the speaker will not submit his tidbit of praise until the prospective recipient has first come across with a compliment, but why the adjective follows the noun is another mystery. The abbreviation to *T. L.* was introduced some forty years ago, probably a collegiate coinage which speedily became so popular that many young people are unfamiliar with the words so abbreviated.

to blow one's own horn

To advertise oneself; boast of one's own abilities; brag. In England, the same self-advertising is done by "blowing one's own trumpet," and there is every reason to assume that this saying, or

variants thereof, was the source of the American phrase. Fleming, in *A Panoplie of Epistles* (1576), "sounded" the trumpet of his own "merites," and writers of the eighteenth century "blew" their trumpets. The earliest American usage, according to Bartlett's *Dictionary of Americanisms* (1877), was "blowin' his bazoo," which was defined, "gasconade; braggadocio"—terms meaning boastful talk. At some time since that date—and on a guess I'd say about seventy-five years ago—the slang term "bazoo" began to drop out of favor and "horn" became the accepted substitute.

to make the air blue

Just why a vigorous and plentiful use of cuss words is supposed by us figuratively to affect the color of the atmosphere, especially to give it a blue tone, is a matter of guesswork. The history of our language does not show how the concept arose. The association of "blue" with evil is not altogether recent, however. Back in 1742 Edward Young in *Night Thoughts on Life, Death and Immortality*, wrote, "Riot, pride, perfidy, blue vapours breathe," in which he referred to "blue" as the color of plagues. And baleful demons were described as "blue devils" more than a hundred years earlier when, in 1616, these lines appeared in *The Times' Whistle*:

> Alston, whose life hath been accounted evill,
> And therefore calde by many the blew devill.

Joseph P. Roppolo, of the Department of English, Tulane University, discussing the use of "blue" in the sense, indecent, obscene, suggests the possibility of the following explanation, in *American Speech,* Vol. XXVIII, No. 1:

Early in its history, *blue* acquired symbolic meanings which are diametrically opposed. As the color of the clear sky and of the sea (both good), it came to be the symbol of purity, of fidelity, of staunchness, and of faith, and, by symbolic extension, it was chosen as one of the colors of the Virgin. Perhaps simultaneously (since both extremes involve morality and seem to be connected with the Christian religion), a flame which burned blue came to be associated with the flames of burning brimstone and therefore of hell; such a flame, quite logically, was regarded by the superstitious as an omen of death or other evil or was believed to indicate the presence of ghosts or evil spirits or of the devil himself. From these beliefs, it seems probable, developed *blue-blazes,* meaning hell, and such statements as "he talked blue" and "he made the air blue," meaning, respectively, "He talked obscenely" and "He cursed and swore": cursing or sinful talk would evoke evil spirits or the devil, whose sulphurous presence would cause flames to burn blue. Such talk, again logically, although this is admittedly conjecture, would become *blue talk*, and an oath or a curse a *blue word*.

cash on the barrelhead

Immediate payment; spot cash; payment on the nail. There is no doubt in my mind that the original scene here was the makeshift bar of the American frontier a century or more ago. The barrel itself, under improvised conditions, served as both container and counter, or, when empty, as counter only. But the wise bartender trusted none of his customers and extended no credit. Nor did he dare turn to serve another lest the first vamoose, and he unable to give chase. The expression dates back many years, but, regrettably, none but recent uses have been found. Its modern equivalent is the weak "cash on the counter."

to talk a blue streak

To talk rapidly and, usually, interminably. We seem to have made this up from two or more other American expressions, all referring to lightning. As long ago as 1830, for instance, mail coaches, though drawn by horses, moved with such rapidity as to leave a "blue streak" behind them. And if one "made a streak for home," or any other designation, he was in such a hurry to get there that, figuratively, he ran like lightning. Or it could be that we have partly taken a German expression, *das Blaue vom Himmel schwatzen,* to chatter the blue from the skies. The British equivalent is "to talk off a donkey's hind legs," which with us is "to talk one's arm off," in modern slang.

the real McCoy

In *A Hog on Ice* I attributed this expression to a prize fighter of the late nineties who traveled under the ring-name of "Kid McCoy." Another fighter of lesser skill, my story went, somewhat the worse for drink and unaware that McCoy was within hearing distance, declared in a barroom that he could lick any of the McCoys, any time and any place. When he picked himself up from the sawdust, after "The Kid" had delivered a haymaker, he amended his remarks by saying that he had meant any of the fighters who had adopted the popular name, "any but the real McCoy."

Although that version has earmarks of veracity, or at least of near veracity, other widely different explanations of the origin of the phrase have been made. Thus, in 1946 a writer in the New Orleans *Picayune,* as quoted in *A Dictionary of Americanisms* (1951), says, "The term originally was applied to heroin brought in from the island of Macao off the coast of China. . . . It was not cut. Dope addicts found out the stuff from Macao was the real Macao." The editor of that dictionary, however, Mitford M. Mathews, does not now accept that explanation, nor do I. Instead, according to his statement in *American Speech,* May, 1953, he regards with favor the solution proposed by Eric Partridge in *From Sanskrit to Brazil,* (1952). The corresponding British phrase, *the real Mackay,* Partridge says, dates from the 1880's and was originally Scottish, applied first to men of excellent quality and then to first-rate things, especially whiskey. The latter, namely the product of A. & M. MacKay of Glasgow, was exported to America where, Partridge believes, Scottish settlers in Canada and the United States were plentiful enough to "keep both the whisky and the phrase very much alive," though the phrase was later "transformed to *the real McCoy*, first under the impact of the hero worship that, in the late 1890's accrued to boxer Kid McCoy and then under that which, in the early 1920's, accrued, at least in New York State, to bootlegger Bill McCoy." I quote this theory for what it is worth, though it seems far-fetched to me. It is a fact, nevertheless, that the term *McCoy*, in slang usage, did refer to whisky of good quality back in 1908, a date earlier than any literary evidence of the usage of the entire phrase.

all my eye (and Betty Martin)

All humbug; sham; stuff and nonsense; apparent but not real; imaginary. The age, even of the first part of this expression, is unknown. Grose, in *A Classical Dictionary of the Vulgar Tongue* (1785), was the first to give it mention, but it is likely that "all in my eye"—that is, all imaginary—was an earlier phrase for the same thing. The second part, "and Betty Martin," has been the subject of much speculation. In commenting on the expression in *The Doctor* (1837), Robert Southey says, "Who was Betty Martin, and wherefore should she be so often mentioned in connection with my precious eye or yours?"

But Grose did not make proper nouns of the words. His listing of the phrase reads: "That's my eye betty martin." That gave some grounds for the explanation that appeared in some of the later editions of the apocryphal book, *Joe Miller's Jests*. Therein it was said that a sailor, attracted by the music, wandered into a Catholic church. The Latin words puzzled him. But finally a phrase caught his ear, *Ah mihi, beate Martin*, (Ah! grant me, blessed St. Martin), but to a comrade he later confessed that this he had understood to be, "All my eye and Betty Martin." This explanation might pass muster, except for the fact, alas, that no such Latin prayer is to be found in the formulary of the Catholic Church.

off one's base

This has a literal meaning in baseball, referring to a position taken by a runner away from the bag or base he has occupied, but in the slang sense it has nothing to do with baseball. Here *base* pertains to that which supports a person, and the expression thus means mentally unbalanced; crazy; off one's rocker or bean; screwy. One of the earliest to use the expression in print was George W. Peck, author of *Sunshine* (1882) and *Peck's Bad Boy and His Pa* (1883). In Chapter II of the latter: ". . . the boy has been for the three weeks trying to think of some innocent joke to play on his father. The old man is getting a little near sighted, and his teeth are not as good as they used to be, but the old man will not admit it . . . and he would bet a hundred dollars that he could see as far as ever. The boy knew the failing, and made up his mind to demonstrate to the old man that he was rapidly getting off his base." The means taken, incidentally, was that the bad boy cut up some small rubber hose and, with the connivance of the "hired girl," mixed it into his pa's serving of macaroni. The mischief was eventually discovered—and the boy had another session in the woodshed.

with a high hand

Overbearing in manner; arrogantly. In the Bible—Numbers xxxiii, 3—the chronicler used the expression in the sense of "triumphantly," in the description of the departure of the Israelites from Egyptian bondage: "And they departed from Rameses in the first month, on the fifteenth day of the first month; on the morrow after the passover the children of Israel went out with an high hand in the sight of all the Egyptians." In fact, it was through Wyclif's translation of the Bible in 1382 that we have the metaphor—"Therfor thei goon forth . . . in an high hoond."

627

to turn the heat on

Of course we "turn the heat on," in this modern age, when we adjust the thermostat to a higher thermometer reading, and thus start up the oil-burning or gas-fired furnace or the electric heater. But in current slang, the "heat" is of a different nature. At first, it would seem, it was that of the electric chair, called in criminal jargon the "hot seat." But then, approximately the time of the First World War, it became a slang substitute for the accepted colloquialism of three centuries standing, "to make it hot for," that is, to make one extremely uncomfortable, as by the grilling of a district attorney. More recently, the "heat" has been extended to include search for a person suspected of crime, and it may be even a master criminal who "turns on the heat" when grilling a subordinate.

to keep one's pecker up

To maintain one's courage or resolution; not to get down in the mouth; to keep a stiff upper lip. In fact, we might say that "lip" and "pecker" are two terms for the same thing, as the lip corresponds with the beak or pecker of a bird. The expression dates to about the middle of the nineteenth century.

to harp on one string

To repeat one thing endlessly; to dwell upon one theme at great length; to bore one to extinction with one bit of advice or caution or the like; to tell the same tale over and over again. The allusion is, of course, obvious. If a harpist were to play her instrument upon one note, the monotony would probably drive her nuts, if some unwilling listener had not already killed her. Although the harp was known in Biblical times, the English saying is first recorded in the early sixteenth century.

to split hairs

To quibble; to make fine distinctions; to cavil or become captious over trifles. Thanks to the great degree of refinement in modern equipment, a hair may be split or divided lengthwise into numerous fine filaments. In fact, not long since, we were told of a drill so fine that a series of minute holes could be bored transversely across a hair. But in the seventeenth, the eighteenth, and even the nineteenth century it was still considered no more possible to split a hair than for a camel to pass through the eye of a needle. Hence, anyone arguing over trifles or quibbling about inconsequential matters was likened to anyone who would attempt to split a hair.

in hot water

In trouble; in a pretty kettle of fish; in a pretty how-de-do; behind the 8-ball; on the spot; up Salt Creek; domestically, in the dog house. When one considers that, during the Dark Ages especially, one of the favorite tests of guilt or innocence of a crime called for the dipping of the hand or arm in boiling water and picking up a stone or ring, it might be reasonable to suppose that our present expression owes its origin to that ordeal. But, no. Though the phrase undoubtedly arose from the extreme discomfort produced by scalding water, the colloquial sense so familiar to all began merely as eighteenth-century slang.

by the great horn spoon

A mild oath, about as innocuous as "by the beard of the prophet," not as strong as "great jumping Jehoshaphat." Delvers into our language have been trying to figure out just what a "great horn spoon" was. So far, the search has been unsuccessful. Apparently it first occurred in a song printed in 1842 in which these lines occur: "He vow'd by the great horn spoon. . . . He'd give them a licking, and that pretty soon." I have tried to find a copy of that song in order to determine the allusions, but have not yet discovered one.

Of course, horn spoons—spoons shaped from the curved horns of cattle—were in common use for many centuries before the comparatively recent introduction of cheap, durable metals. But why a horn spoon should suddenly become "great" is still conjectural.

A correspondent, Francis W. Palmer, to the October–December, 1949, issue of *American Speech,* tries to connect the great horn with the American "bighorn," the Rocky Mountain sheep, which were called *gros cornes,* "great horns," by early French explorers. And he finds that Francis Parkman, in *The California and Oregon Trail* (1849), says the Indians made "ladles with long handles, capable of holding more than a quart, cut from such horns." But to me it does not seem likely that the writer of the song mentioned above could have known that fact in 1842.

to keep one's eye on the ball

To be closely attentive; to be alert, alive and kicking, on one's toes; to sit up and take notice. This has been popular American speech in a figurative sense for at least fifty years. In source, although applicable to any sport in which a ball is kept in motion—tennis, golf, billiards, bowls, polo—it was probably the game of football from which it was derived, from the urgent instructions of college coaches.

call off the dogs

Cease some objectionable line of conduct, procedure, conversation, inquiry, or the like; break off an unprofitable or disagreeable course. The analogy is that of the chase, in which dogs following a wrong scent are called off.

to hoe one's own row

To make one's own way; to be independent, beholden to no one; to paddle one's own canoe, peddle one's own papers, blow one's own nose. This was farm lingo, and is still applicable in a literal sense on any farm on which most labor is performed without benefit of machinery. Figurative application apparently dates to a time shortly after the death of William Henry Harrison (April 4, 1841), a month after inauguration, when John Tyler succeeded him as president. Tyler, a former Democrat, had broken with his party and was elected with Harrison on the belief that he had fully adopted Whig principles. But within a few months it became evident that such was not the case. With the exception of Daniel Webster, Secretary of State, the entire cabinet resigned (September, 1841). This led a writer in *The Knickerbocker*, a New York monthly, to say, "Our American pretender must, to adopt an agricultural phrase, 'hoe his own row,' . . . without the aid of protectors or dependents."

a sop to Cerberus

Cerberus, in classical mythology, was the three-headed dog that  guarded the entrance to Hades, permitting the dead to enter, but preventing their shades from leaving. Sometimes those who entered were greeted in friendly manner by the several heads, but others might be met by fierce and angry snarls. Accordingly, friends placed in the hands of those who died honey cakes to be fed to Cerberus, thus to permit them a friendly entrance, as described in Bishop Gavin Douglas's translation of the *Aeneid* (1513), VI, vi, 69:

. . . Cerberus, the hiduus hund, that regioun
Fordynnys, barkand with thre mowthis ſowm,
Onmeſurabill in his cave quher he lay
Richt our for gane thame in the hie way:
Quhom till the prophete, behaldand quhou in hy
Hys nekkis wolx of eddyrris all gryſly
A ſop, ſtepyt intill hunny als faſt,
And of enchant it cornys maid, gan caſt.

Hence, figuratively, "a sop to Cerberus" is any gift or compliment or the like that may placate an opponent, allay suspicion, or distract vigilance.

a long (or hard) row to hoe

A difficult or tedious task to perform; a dreary prospect to face. An American expression of obvious source, and there are few tasks more dispiriting to face than to start hoeing weeds from a long, long row of beans, say, or to hill a row of corn that seems to stretch ahead interminably. First to use the figurative sense in print was David Crockett, in his book with the lengthy title, *An Account of Col. Crockett's Tour to the North and Down East, in the Year of the Lord One Thousand Eight Hundred and Thirty-four* (1835): "I never opposed Andrew Jackson for the sake of popularity. I knew it was a hard row to hoe, but I stood up to the rack."

mad as a wet hen

Very, very vexed. Though, unlike a duck, a hen does not deliberately seek water in a pond and is not disposed to leave a dry shelter in search of food in the rain, this metaphor has never made good sense to me. My sons and daughters have, at various times, sought small fortunes from chickens (with much of the care devolving upon me), but I have never seen a hen becoming particularly perturbed from getting wet. If she has a brood of chicks, she will cluck them under the shelter of her wings during a shower, but she certainly doesn't stamp her feet and rave noisily, no matter how wet she herself becomes. Yet many a man, woman, and child, with far lesser cause, is said to become "mad as a wet hen." Be that as it may, whether sensible or not, the expression has been good American since at least 1823, as determined by a correspondent in *American Speech,* Vol. XXI: "Every body that was not ax'd was mad as a wet hen."

as scarce as (or scarcer than) hen's teeth

No one has ever yet found teeth in a hen, nor is likely to; so this is just another example (American) of exaggerated statement not intended to be taken literally, to impress the listener with the fact that the item under discussion, whatever it may be, does not exist, rarely occurs, or is rarely to be found. Thus one might say, "Elephants in Greenland are scarcer than hen's teeth," meaning that elephants are not to be found in Greenland. Just when this hyperbole first appeared has not yet been determined. *The Dictionary of Americanisms* reports its use by "Edmund Kirke," pen name of James R. Gilmore, in *My Southern Friends* (1862). But because this metaphor is thoroughly familiar in all parts of the country, there's good reason to believe that it may actually have had word-of-mouth use from colonial days.

from hell to breakfast

I have little doubt that the original expression was "hell-bent for breakfast," cowboy slang of the past thirty or forty years, typifying the rush from bunkhouse to cookshack at the clang of the breakfast gong—automobile-tire rim or triangle. In fact, some writers still have their characters say, "hell for breakfast," though the heading I have used is, I think, more common. But whereas "hell for breakfast" signifies in a hell of a hurry, "from hell to breakfast," though sometimes used with the same sense, usually connotes nothing more than "from Dan to Beersheba"; that is, a lot of territory.

cross one's heart

The most binding oath of childhood; solemn assurance of truthfulness, usually accompanied by motions of the right hand forming a cross over the general vicinity of the testator's heart. Probably the gesture and its binding nature were originally based upon the familiar Catholic sign of the cross. In my own Protestant childhood in Ohio, and my wife says the same was the case in Massachusetts, the oath was often accompanied by the irreverent doggerel: "Cross my heart and hope to die, And hope the cat'll spit in your eye."

old hat

Old stuff; information, experience, condition, or the like that is familiar. A gutter interpretation of the origin, based on the pun, "frequently felt," does not strike me as remotely plausible. In my opinion the familiarity that is implied is rather that of long usage, something to which one is as accustomed as he is to a hat so long worn as to fit the head snugly. The metaphor is comparatively recent, and is rarely heard in the United States.

duck soup

Extremely easy; easy as rolling off a log; hence, a cinch. American slang of some twenty-five years' standing. Probably derived from "a sitting duck," namely one resting on the water, thus easily shot by a hunter; hence, figuratively, an easy mark, any person who lays himself wide open to ridicule or any form of attack. Thus, to some persons, the solution of a cross-word puzzle or the putting together of a jigsaw puzzle is duck soup.

to ride the gravy train

To acquire wealth; become prosperous; live on Easy Street; have a profitable business or an easy or well-paid position. Probably the expression actually arose in railroading lingo, in which a *gravy run* or a *gravy train* meant an easy run with good pay for the train crew, for *gravy* in popular speech, has long meant money easily earned or obtained. Though the earliest quotation in which *gravy train* appears is in Benjamin A. Botkin's *Lay My Burden Down* (1945)—"They is on the gravy train and don't know it, but they is headed straight for 'struction and perdition"—even the full phrase, "to ride the gravy train," was undoubtedly in use ten or twenty years earlier than that date, because it appears in all the above senses in *The American Thesaurus of Slang* which was published in 1942 and was under compilation during the preceding ten years or so.

in the doghouse

In a predicament; in a pickle; in a pretty how-de-do; in disgrace. This American slang of the early twentieth century came into being through analogy. Anyone who was considered, usually by a man's wife, to be "going to the dogs" was, in theory at least, thought to  be fit to associate only with the family dog, especially for slumber; hence, figuratively, consigned to the dog kennel. The notion became enlarged. In due course the husband began to realize that any time he was going to have domestic difficulty, especially in explaining an action, he would again be out of favor and again be relegated to the doghouse.

getting down to grass-roots

This is something that politicians or office-seekers repeatedly do, or do in their speechifying preceding an election. Grass-roots, apparently, are rediscovered perennially at those times. Actually, this homely American phrase means nothing more than getting down to the underlying principles or basic facts of a matter, and may be appropriately used at any time. Popularity preceding an election indicates that it is then that politicians strive to convince their hearers that they know all basic facts troubling the nation.

Mencken, in *Supplement One: The American Language* (1945) says in a footnote: "The late Dr. Frank H. Vizetelly told me in 1935 that he had been informed that *grass-roots,* in the verb-phrase, *to get down to grass-roots,* was in use in Ohio *c.* 1885, but he could never track down the printed record of it, and neither could I." Well, I guess I'm the culprit. The phrase has been familiar to me, through my father's use of it, ever since I was still wearing skirts in my Ohio infancy, and it is probable that, questioned by my then boss, "Dr. Viz," I said that it had been used in Ohio for at least fifty years—and I still think I was right.

to ring a bell

To start a train of recollection; to strike a familiar chord; also, to appeal to one, to strike one's fancy. Partridge, in *A Dictionary of Slang,* says that this is from "the bell that rings when, at a shooting-gallery, a marksman hits the bull's-eye." I don't agree with that. In my opinion, this expression, with its indefinite article, is of nostalgic birth, relating rather to memories or responses evoked by the church bell or the school bell. Had he specified the American expression, "to ring the bell," always with the definite article, I could agree. That expression indicates success in one form or another; as, in a commercial transaction, to make a sale or obtain an order for goods; in law, to win a case; in games, to make a high score; in sports, to win; on the turf, to finish first; in gambling, to win a bet; in one's studies, to pass an examination. These all spring from target shooting.

come (or in spite of) hell or high water

Let the consequences be whatever they may, however ill. I'd say that this is considerably older than the date—1915—shown for it in *A Dictionary of Americanisms.* In fact, I heard it commonly employed in Colorado and Wyoming some years earlier, and it is the sort of expression that one would expect to find studded through Bret Harte's Western stories. And, though the dictionaries describe "high water" as either being about the same thing as ordinary highest tide or ordinary highest flow of a stream, I'd translate the "high water" of this saying as referring specifically to the flash floods of water that roll down a canyon after a heavy storm above, sweeping everything before it. Certainly that's the kind of destructive force worthy of comparison with "hell."

sound (or **all right**) on the goose

Back in 1854 Congress, admitting Kansas and Nebraska as territories, weakly made the slave question a matter of local option. But abolitionists among the new settlers were at first in the minority. "How are you on the goose?" became a customary question put to any newcomer in a community, especially in Kansas. It was never clear just how the term "goose" became involved in the question of slavery, but if the answer was "All sound (or all right) on the goose," the newcomer was recognized to be in favor of slavery and was usually welcomed to the community. But if the answer was "I'm a free-stater," one who wanted Kansas to become a free state, he was likely to be looked upon with disfavor or threatened or told to move on. Though Kansas eventually entered the Union as a free state, this particular "goose" brought about not only the John Brown rebellion, but also the birth of the Republican Party, replacing the Whig Party, and ultimately led to the disastrous War between the States.

to fish or cut bait

To make a choice; specifically, to be obliged to take a definite stand, as upon a political issue. Just how this personal decision, admitting of no argument, wandered from matters piscatorial to matters political is one of the many questions which contribute interest to the life of a lexicographer, questions that often remain unanswered forever.

Cutting bait is one of the essential duties on board a deep-sea fishing vessel. Live fish, carried for the purpose, are cut into chunks which are then dropped overboard in quantity to attract the quarry when the vessel has reached a favorable location. The duty is onerous, but is assigned summarily to a member of the crew who, in the opinion of the captain, has merited it.

Though this American expression had undoubtedly long been part of the common argot of fisher folk, it suddenly appeared with

636

political significance in the halls of Congress back in 1876, and from the mouth of a representative, not of a salt-water state, but of the inland state of Illinois, Joseph Gurney Cannon, then known as "the Hayseed Member from Illinois"—years later affectionately termed "Uncle Joe." On August 5th of that year in a discussion of a monetary bill, Cannon pointed out that the bill was open to amendment, and then declared: "I will offer what is known as the Kelley silver bill as an additional section to the bill." Then according to the *Congressional Record,* he added:

Now I want you gentlemen on the other side of the House to "fish or cut bait." This is the chance and the only chance you will have under the rules this session by which a bill can be passed by a majority vote, making the silver dollar a legal tender for all debts, public and private. Gentlemen of the other side [the Democratic side], do something positive for once during this session . . .

ivory tower

When Charles-Augustin Sainte-Beuve, French literary critic of the early nineteenth century, coined this term he thought of it as applicable to the aerie of a poet, a place where he could retire from the world, a retreat. The term occurs in his own poem, *Pensées d'Août* (*Thoughts of August*), written in October, 1837, and dedicated to François Villemain. The third stanza, in which Victor Hugo and Alfred de Vigny, both poets, are mentioned, runs in part—

Hugo, dur partisan
. . . combattit sous l'armure,
Et tint haut sa bannière ou milieu du murmure:
Il la maintient encore; et Vigny, plus secret,
Comme en sa tour d'ivoire, avant midi, rentrait.

[Hugo, strong partisan
. . . fought in armor,
And held high his banner in the midst of the tumult;
He still holds it; and Vigny, more discreet,
As if in his tower of ivory, retired before noon.]

Nevertheless, although Saint-Beuve may be credited as the originator of the thought, its intent is more pertinently expressed by Jules de Gaultier in *La Guerre et les Destinées de l'Art,* as given also in the Christopher Morley edition of *Bartlett's Familiar Quotations* (1948):

> The poet, retired in his Tower of Ivory, isolated, according to his desire, from the world of man, resembles, whether he wishes or not, another solitary figure, the watcher enclosed for months at a time in a lighthouse at the head of a cliff.

Though long held by the poets, the "ivory tower" has been invaded by others in recent years. It is still aloof from the common run and is still a sanctum, but, whether secluded or not, it is now a remote observation post that is open to philosophers, college professors, various writers, an occasional editor, and others who may, as from a place of vantage, watch the world go by.

a whipping boy

One upon whom is inflicted punishment for the faults or wrongs of another; a scapegoat. Under the belief that the body of a young royal prince was as sacred as that of the king, his father, and that, accordingly, no governess nor tutor should chastise him, a custom was introduced into England in the early seventeenth century to transfer any punishment merited by a princeling to the body of another. The first to benefit was the son of James I, the young prince who later became Charles I. The lad William Murray was appointed to be his playmate and fellow pupil, and to receive all punishment deserved by either of the two lads, to be the "whipping boy" of the prince and be flogged for all the faults of either. The custom died out as the royal household became more democratic, but the allusion has remained.

to suck the hind teat

In my youth, it was "tit" rather than "teat," of course, but there was then long established American usage for that. The allusion was to the supposition long existing among the breeders of domestic animals that the rearmost nipple of an udder supplied less nourishment to a calf, colt, piglet, or lamb than any of the others; hence, that any of a litter forced by its brothers and sisters to draw from that poor source of supply was bound to be a weakling. Accordingly, the expression as I have always known it has meant to lose out, to get the short end of the stick, to have the worst of a deal. However, in the Ozarks, according to E. H. Criswell, in *American Speech,* December, 1953, a meaning given to the phrase in that region is "to be always late or behind," though he offers no conjectural explanation. Typical American prudery affords no example of literary use.

over a barrel

When you have one "over a barrel" or put him over one you have him at your mercy, on the spot; you have him under your

thumb—hook, line, and sinker. I surmise that the literal expression was an act of mercy, arising from the use of a barrel, until better means of resuscitation were developed, in the attempt to bring a drowned person back to life. In that method the person taken from the water was placed face down over the curving surface of a barrel, which was then gently rolled. Needless to add, the one so placed was at the mercy of the attendant.

to throw in the sponge (or **towel**)

To say uncle; to holler quits; to admit defeat; to surrender, submit, or yield. In today's pugilistic encounters one is more likely to hear that the manager of one contestant throws in a towel, rather than a sponge, but the original occasion for the expression, which still stands in a non-physical sense, is explained in *The Slang Dictionary.* Though first published in 1860, the 1874 edition in my possession reads: " 'To throw up the sponge,' to submit, to give over the struggle—from the practice of throwing up the sponge used to cleanse a combatant's face at a prize-fight, as a signal that the side on which that particular sponge has been used has had enough— that the sponge is no longer required."

to crack the whip

To be in control; to have absolute dominance; to have under one's thumb; to rule the roost. The Florida "cracker," nowadays, tries to persuade himself and others that this nickname originated, not, as was actually the case, because his antecedents were notorious braggarts—i.e., cracked tall tales—but, as was not the case, because they were drovers, who cracked the whip over cattle or teams of oxen or mules.

Our present expression, however, did originate from the skill of drovers or teamsters in handling the vicious bullwhacker whip of, especially, the nineteenth century. Before the days of the railroad, or to areas unreached by them, large wheeled wagons drawn by two, four, six or more pairs of horses, mules, or oxen carted freight over mountains and plains to ever-extending Western frontiers. The whip or bullwhacker of the driver, though short-handled, carried a long heavy thong which, properly wielded, could be snapped through the air to sound like a shot from a gun. Some drivers became so expert as, reputedly, to be able to kill a horsefly from the flanks of the leading horse without disturbing a hair of the animal, or to flick a piece of the hide from a lagging "critter." All these were the ones who, originally, "cracked the whip."

to jump Jim Crow

To dance with a peculiar limping step. Although, according to the *Negro Year Book* for 1925–26, the name "Jim Crow" was that of a Negro born in Richmond about 1800, later emancipated and, in England, acquiring "quite a fortune," it is not probable that his name was in any way responsible for the application of that title to Negro discriminatory laws introduced, first, in Tennessee in 1875. The title came, rather, from a popular song, copyrighted in 1828 by Thomas D. Rice, which became part of a skit, *The Rifle,* written by Solon Robinson. The song and its accompanying dance, it is said, were based on the chance observance of an old Negro in Louisville, Kentucky, who shuffled as he sang, "Weel about, turn about, do jist so." In the skit, produced in Washington in 1835 and taken to London in 1836, where it became equally popular, Rice, in black-face, sang, as he danced:

First on de heel tap, den on de toe,
Ebery time I wheel about I jump Jim Crow.
Wheel about and turn about and do jis so,
And ebery time I wheel about I jump Jim Crow.

fatten (or sweeten) the kitty

No, in modern usage at least, this "kitty" is not a member of the cat family. The expression is a gambling term, chiefly poker nowadays, and today means to increase the stakes, to add chips to an unopened jack pot. According to Hoyle, however, "kitty" is "the percentage taken out of the stakes in a game for expenses of any kind." In this connection it refers to the "take" of the house, whether the gambling be cards, pool, racing, or other sport. The source is by no means positive, but I suspect that someone with a fine sense of irony derived this "kitty" as the natural offspring of the "blind tiger" of faro fame. (See *A Hog on Ice,* page 82.)

to pull one's leg

To coax, wheedle, blarney; bamboozle, delude, pull the wool over one's eyes; befool, make fun of one. Our cousins over the seas, among whom the expression originated, use it in the latter senses; the first is an American addition, carrying the tomfoolery into downright cheating and chiseling. The Scots were apparently the first with the idea, using "draw" rather than "pull," as in the following quotation from a rhyme written in 1867:

He preached an' at last drew the auld body's leg,
Sae the kirk got the gatherins [the money] o' our Aunty Meg.

Just why one's leg was something to be either drawn or pulled for the success of a delusion is most uncertain. Perhaps it had something to do with tripping a person; i.e., to catch him in an error, or to bring him into a state of confusion.

to hide one's light under a bushel

To conceal one's talents or abilities; keep in the background; be unduly modest. This has reference to the fifth chapter of St. Matthew, in which, following the Beatitudes, Jesus called upon his disciples to be "the light of the world," adding, in the fourteenth and fifteenth verses, "A city that is set on a hill cannot be hid. Neither do men light a candle and put it under a bushel, but on a candlestick." ("Bushel," here, is the vessel used as a bushel measure.) But the preachers were already using this simile from earlier translations than the King James Version. It was used in 1557, and, not in the present sense of humility, in a sermon by Bishop Robert Sanderson in 1627, in which he said: "The light of God's word, hid from them under two bushels for sureness: under the bushel of a tyrannous clergy . . . and under the bushel of an unknown tongue."

to take a leaf out of one's book

If you do it figuratively, it's all right. The person whose leaf is thus taken is likely to feel flattered, if he learns of it, because the implied meaning is to imitate, to copy, to ape another person, as in deportment, manner, or method, etc. But if you do it literally and are caught at it, you run a good chance of running afoul of the law against plagarism. Nowadays you may not take another man's book, copy a leaf from it, or even a paragraph from that leaf, and publish it as your own. You may not even print it without due credit or his (or his publisher's) written permission. The penalty can be costly.

a nigger in the woodpile (or fence)

Some fact of considerable importance that is not disclosed; something suspicious or wrong; something rotten in Denmark. The sayings with "fence" and "woodpile" developed about the same time and about at the period, 1840–50, when the "Underground Railroad" was flourishing successfully. Evidence is slight, but because early uses of the expressions occurred in Northern states, it is presumable that they derived from actual instances of the surreptitious concealment of fugitive Negroes in their flight north through Ohio or Pennsylvania to Canada under piles of firewood or within hiding places in stone fences.

to toe the mark

To conform with the rules or to standards of discipline; to fulfil one's obligations; to come up to scratch. Literally, this used to be a term in footracing, now replaced by the command "Take your marks." An order, that is, to all entrants in a race to place the forward foot on the designated starting line. The expression does not appear to be more than about a hundred and fifty years old and could have been of American origin. At least the earliest use thus far found is in James K. Paulding's *The Diverting History of John Bull and Brother Jonathan* (New York, 1813).

cutting off one's nose to spite one's face

Injuring oneself in taking revenge upon another; damaging oneself through pique. Apperson has traced this back to a French saying that was current in the seventeenth century. Among the *Historiettes* of Gédéon Tallemant des Réaux, written about 1658,

he finds: *"Henri iv conçut fort bien que détruire Paris, c'étoit, comme on dit, se couper le nez pour faire dépit à son visage"* (Henry IV well knew that to destroy Paris would be, as they say, to cut off his own nose in taking spite on his own face). Very likely there was some popular animal story similar to the account of *Reynard the Fox,* circulated by the troubadours of the Middle Ages, which told of a foolish creature that did, inadvertently, commit such an act, but the story has not come down to us, if it existed. But the French saying crossed the channel to England before the end of the eighteenth century and was recorded in Grose's *A Classical Dictionary of the Vulgar Tongue* (1796): "He cut off his nose to be revenged of his face. Said of one who, to be revenged on his neighbor, has materially injured himself."

to hit the nail on the head

To say or do the right thing; to express in words the exact idea; to speak to the point; to hit the bull's-eye. Our old Romans may have given us the grounds for this expression in the common saying, *acu rem tangere,* literally, "to touch a matter on the point," but which is ordinarily rendered, "to hit the nail on the head." For that matter, though the French say *mettre le doigt dessus,* "to hit on the finger," that too is ordinarily translated into our English saying. But our own expression goes back at least four and a half centuries. Apperson reports finding it in the *Vulgaria* (*c.* 1520) of John Stanbridge: "Thou hyttest the nayle on the head."

to stick one's neck out

To expose oneself to criticism; to take a chance, especially an extremely risky one; to monkey with the buzz saw. Although this American slang is of considerably later vintage, probably little more than thirty years old, it is my opinion that it arose also from the nineteenth-century slang, "to get it in the neck," or "to get it where the chicken got the ax." That is, as anyone who has beheaded chickens has learned, when the creature's head is placed upon the block the animal will usually stretch out its neck, thus making the butcher's aim more certain. Just some physiological reaction, I suppose. Of course, the expression could have originated from the victim of a lynching bee, but I do not think so.

to turn the tables

In my explanation of this expression in *A Hog on Ice* the assumption was made that it originated about three centuries ago from some unknown game of cards. The game from which the expression arose was backgammon, not cards. This is a game of considerable antiquity, thought to have been invented in the tenth century, but probably related to the game *Ludud duodecim scriptorum,* "twelve-line game," played in ancient Rome. In Chaucer's time and until the seventeenth century the game was invariably known as "tables" in England, and even in modern play the board is customarily divided into two (or four) "tables." The play is too involved to describe here, but there are often dramatic reversals of fortune due, not to reversing the position of the board, but to a rule which allows a player to double the stakes under certain circumstances—literally, to turn the tables. Sir St. Vincent Troubridge, to whom I am indebted for this correction, informs me that backgammon has again become popular in London social clubs and that stakes are sometimes very high.

snake in the grass

We owe this proverbial saying to the Roman poet Vergil (70–19 B.C.). In the third *Eclogue* is the line *Latet anguis in herba,* "A snake lurks in the grass." Apperson reports the appearance of this Latin proverb also in a political song in England round the year 1290: *Cum totum fecisse putas, latet anguis in herba,* "Though all appears clean, a snake lurks in the grass." The saying was used frequently thereafter. The earliest English translation was Edward Hall's *Chronicles* (1548): *The Union of the Two Noble and Illustre Famelies of Lancestre and Yorke:* "But the serpent lurked vnder the grasse, and vnder sugered speache was hide pestiferous poyson." The French put the snake under a rock, *quelque anguille sous roche.*

to bring (or put) under the hammer

It is the auctioneer's hammer that is meant, the small mallet used by him when tapping "once," to indicate that the item on sale is about to be "going" to the latest bidder; "twice," to give reluctant bidders another chance; "three times," as notice that the item has been "sold" or has "gone" to that latest bidder. The expression in present form goes back about a century and a half. For about an equal period before that the common expression was "to pass under, or sell at, the spear." This was translated from the Latin, *sub hasta vendere,* referring to the Roman custom of thrusting a spear into the ground at public auctions, the spear being a token of booty gained in battle and coming into the possession of the state.

to strain at a gnat and swallow a camel

To make a fuss over trifles but accept great faults without complaint. This, as are many others, is a Biblical expression. It is found in Matthew xxiii, 24–26: "Ye blind guides, which strain at a gnat and swallow a camel. Woe unto you, scribes and Pharisees, hypocrites! for ye make clean the outside of the cup and of the platter, but within they are full of extortion and excess. Thou blind Pharisee, cleanse first that which is within the cup and platter, that the outside of them may be clean also." But the translators of the King James

Bible of 1611 were already familiar with this figure of speech. It had appeared in *Lectures upon Jonas* by Bishop John King, first printed in 1594, reprinted in 1599, in which the bishop himself said, "They have verified the olde proverbe in strayning at gnats and swallowing downe camells."

to win one's spurs

To prove one's ability; to perform some deed by which one first gains honor among one's fellows. And there are a thousand ways by which it may be accomplished—a salesman by making his first sale, or his first important sale; a clergyman in delivering his first sermon; a doctor in attending his first patient; an author by the publication of his first story or book; an athlete by winning his first contest; or even, I suppose, by a yegg cracking his first safe. The allusion is to the young squire or princeling who, "when knighthood was in flower" in medieval days, had performed his first meritorious act or deed of valor by which he gained knighthood, by which his lord "dubbed" him a knight, tapping him with a sword lightly on the shoulder. After which accolade this lord or another presented the new member of the order with a pair of gilded spurs. Though early practices remain under discussion, this procedure, however, was apparently not adopted before the late fourteenth century. Thus we read in John Lydgate's *The Assembly of Gods* (c. 1425), "These xiiii knyghtes made Vyce that day; To wynne theyr spores they seyde they wold asay."

with tongue in cheek

This is something I'd like to see, or hear. Just how one can accomplish such a gymnastic lingual feat of lodging the tip or other portion of the tongue against the cheek and then uttering any distinguishable word is beyond my imagination. I can't do it. The English humorist, Richard Barham, seems to have dreamed up the feat. In *The Ingoldsby Legends* (1845), in the story of the "Black Mousquetaire," he has a Frenchman saying, " '*Superbe!—Magnifique!*' (With his tongue in his cheek.)" Perhaps that explains why I could never work up an interest in *The Ingoldsby Legends*. Other writers, however, have taken up the expression. Thus we have so eminent a writer as Matthew Arnold, in *Culture and Anarchy* (1869), saying, "He unquestionably knows that he is talking claptrap, and, so to say, puts his tongue in his cheek." From this we infer that the one so performing engages in irony or insincerity.

to eat salt with (a person); **to eat** (a person's) **salt**

To be on terms of amity. From time immemorial the sharing of salt with another has been a sign of hospitality and, therefore, a token of friendship. Among the ancient Greeks, the oath taken "with salt and over the table" was held as an expression of sacred hospitality. The Arabs say, "there is salt between us." And, in the Revised Standard Version of the Bible, we read in Ezra, Chapter iv, how the enemies of the Hebrews went to the king and, in token of friendship, said to him, "Now because we eat the salt of the palace and it is not fitting for us to witness the king's dishonor . . . We make known to the king that, if this city [Jerusalem] is rebuilt and its walls finished, you will then have no possession in the province Beyond the River"—because it was certain that the Jews would rebel and pay no tribute.

keeping up with the Joneses

Though I have been regretfully obliged to abridge, I'll let Arthur R. ("Pop") Momand, the creator of this expression, now adopted into the American language, tell in his own words, from a personal letter to me, how it originated:

Here is how it happened: At the age of 23 I was making $125 a week (good money in those days, with no income tax). I married and moved to Cedarhurst, L.I., joined a country club, rode horseback daily, and bought a fifty-dollar bull-pup; also we kept a colored maid who, as I recall, had the glamorous name of Beatrice Montgomery. And we entertained in the grand manner, or as grand as we could on $125 a week. Well, it was not long until the butcher, the baker et al were knocking gently but firmly on the old front door. In the end we pulled up stakes, headed for New York and moved into a cheap apartment.

Our Cedarhurst experience was a rude awakening, but I saw the humorous side of it. We had been living far beyond our means in our endeavor to keep up with the well-to-do class which then lived in Cedarhurst. I also noted that most of our friends were doing the same; the $10,000-a-year chap was trying to keep up with the $20,000-a-year man.

I decided it would make good comic-strip material, so sat down and drew up six strips. At first I thought of calling it *Keeping up with the Smiths,* but finally decided on *Keeping up with the Joneses* as being more euphonious.

Taking the strips to The Associated Newspapers at 170 Broadway, I saw the manager, H. H. McClure. He appeared interested and asked me to give him a week to decide. In three days he phoned, saying they would sign a one-year contract for the strip. *Keeping up with the Joneses* was launched—and little did I realize it was to run for 28 years and take us across the Atlantic 42 times.

The feature was released in February of 1913 and appeared first in the New York *Globe,* Chicago *Daily News,* Boston *Globe,* Philadelphia *Bulletin* and ten minor papers. At that time I signed it POP, a nickname I had acquired at school. Later I signed the drawings POP MOMAND. In 1915 I had it copyrighted in my name. The strip gained in popularity each year; it appeared in 2-reel comedies, was put on as a musical comedy, and Cupples and Leon each year published a book of *Keeping up with the Joneses* cartoons. I have made the drawings in London, Paris, Berlin, Madrid, Vienna, Amsterdam, Los Angeles, and South America, mailing them to the Syndicate from wherever I chanced to be.

After 28 years on the old treadmill I tired of it. Today I paint portraits, landscapes, and marines—and, yes, I hate to admit it, we are still trying to keep up with the Joneses.

to cry wolf

There are, I suppose, as many versions of *Aesop's Fables* as there are publishers who have reprinted them with added tales from other sources. The version from which I took this story of "The Shepherd-boy and the Wolf" runs as follows:

A shepherd-boy who kept his flock a little way from a village for some time amused himself with this sport: he would call loudly on the villagers to come to his help, crying, "Wolf! wolf! the wolves are among my lambs!" Twice, three times the villagers were startled, and hurried out, and went back laughed at, when finally the wolves really did come. And as the wolves made way with the flock, and he ran crying for help, they supposed him only at his old joke, and paid no attention. And so he lost all his flock.

648

It only shows that people who tell lies get this for their pains, that nobody believes them when they speak the truth.

to shake a stick at

Although this does have a literal meaning, to threaten with a stick, we in the United States give it much more fanciful interpretations. If we say, "There are more filling stations in town than one can shake a stick at," we mean nothing more than that the town contains an abundance of places at which one may purchase gasoline for one's motorcar. That American usage dates from early in the nineteenth century. One may speculate that it arose from the play at warfare by small boys—George Washington Jones flourishing a triumphant wooden sword over the considerable number of British soldiers who surrendered at Yorktown, more, in fact, than he could wave his "stick" at. Then, too, we use the expression to indicate a comparative that may express derogation, and have done so for well over a hundred years. David Crockett, in his *Tour to the North and Down East* (1835), wrote of one place at which he stayed, "This was a temperance house, and there was nothing to treat a friend to that was worth shaking a stick at."

to sit above (or below) the salt

He who sits "above" is among the elect, honored, or socially acceptable; he who sits "below" is just an also-ran, an ordinary person, perhaps even inferior in social standing. The allusion is to the dining customs in the houses of the nobility and gentry in medieval days. The saltcellar (properly "saler")—a large container—was placed about the center of the table and all guests of distinction were ranged in order of merit at the upper or master's end of the table "above" the salt, or saltcellar. The dependents, tenants, or persons of low degree sat "below" the salt, or at the lower end of the table. The prolific writer, Bishop Joseph Hall, in Book II of his *Satires* (1597), tells us:

> A gentle Squire would gladly entertaine
> Into his House some trencher-chapelaine,
> Some willing man that might instruct his Sons,
> And that could stand to good Conditions:
> First that He lie vpon the Truckle-bed,

Whiles his yong maister lieth ore his hed;
Second that he do, on no default,
Euer presume to sit aboue the salt. . . .

like a bear with a sore head

Very disgruntled; peevish; ill-tempered; soreheaded. Professor Hans Sperber of Ohio State University, in his studies of words and phrases in American politics, argues that the American term "sorehead," meaning a disgruntled person, is derived from the metaphor,  "like a bear with a sore head" (*American Speech,* Vol. XXVII). To add point to the argument he cites some uses of a century and more ago: Cincinnati *Gazette,* October 26, 1824, "The engineer, Dawson, a pussy fatwitted Irishman, was raving round the forecastle like a bear with a sore head, ever and anon vociferating corruption," and W. G. Simms, *The Partisan* (1835), "Art thou, now, not a sorry bear with a sore head, that kindness cannot coax, and crossing only can keep civil!" Then he goes on through the years with other quotations which lend support to his contention that the "bear with a sore head" became the source of the political term, "sorehead," used first in the campaign of 1848, "when the opponents of the newly founded Free Soil party characterized it as a motley crowd recruited from the refuse of other parties," demonstrated by a quotation from the Albany *Weekly Argus,* August 12th of that year: "As no other selection could be supposed so well to represent such a conventicel [sic] of 'sore heads,' it is perhaps quite as well it sho'd take direction as any other."

Although Professor Sperber modestly admits that he has indulged in a certain amount of guesswork in his etymology, his circumstantial evidence is nevertheless convincing. Regrettably, the origins of slang and colloquial expressions are rarely recorded at birth; consequently, later researchers are often obliged to resort to conjecture.

But Professor Sperber assumes in his discussion that the expression, "a bear with a sore head," grew out of the experience of hunt-

650

ers who learned that shooting a bear in the head was likely to lead to nothing more than to make the animal truculent, highly irascible and fighting mad. I doubt that explanation, though it stands to reason that any animal, bear or other, so injured by a non-fatal shot would not be exactly jovial. I suggest, therefore, though I have no record to prove it, that the metaphor arose belatedly either from bear-baiting, in which dogs were set upon a bear chained to a stake, or from the ancient tales of *Reynard the Fox*. You will recall that one of these tales relates how Reynard greatly discomfited Bruin by leading him to a succulent repast of honey, which, however, was stored in a cleft of a tree. When Bruin inserted his head to gorge upon the honey, the fox slyly removed the wedge left by the woodsman, and then led the farmer to the scene. Bruin made his escape only at the expense of losing most of the skin from his head, and was indeed "a bear with a sore head" when he returned to court.

hair and hide (horns and tallow)

The whole works; every part; the entirety. The first part, hair and hide, has long been used in the same sense. In fact, five hundred years ago, in the metrical *Life of St. Cuthbert,* we find: "pai were destroyed, bath hare and hyde." The second part, horns and tallow, is, I suspect, a fairly recent American additive probably of the wild-woolly-West school of literature to impress youthful readers. When the earlier part is reversed and used negatively, as in "I have seen neither hide nor hair of the cat since yesterday," the sense is that the speaker hasn't seen any part of the animal, and this usage dates back apparently little more than a century.

hold your horses

Don't be in too great a hurry; take it easy; watch your step; keep your shirt on; be patient; control your temper. This homely admonition traces back to the American county fair of old, to the races which, among the menfolk especially, were the main features of the day. The harness races were especially difficult to get started, for the horses, sensing the tautness of inexperienced eager drivers, were constantly breaking from the line and had to be called back. Figurative transfer to human restiveness and its restraint was but a step.

As early as 1844 we find in the old *New Orleans Picayune,* "Oh, hold your hosses, Squire. There's no use gettin' riled, no how."

itching palm

A wistful desire for money; a hankering for gain; avariciousness; readiness to receive a bribe. Other bodily parts were metaphorically said to itch, even before Shakespeare's time—such as an "itching tongue," a craving to repeat gossip; an "itching ear," a craving to hear something new; an "itching foot," a craving for travel. But Shakespeare gave us the "itching palm." It is to be found in *Julius Caesar* (1601), Act IV, scene 3. Cassius has come to the tent of Brutus to voice certain complaints, especially to criticize Brutus for condemning a friend of Cassius for taking bribes. In reply Brutus says: "Let me tell you, Cassius, you your selfe Are much condemn'd to haue an itching Palme."

to stick (or put) in one's oar (in another's boat)

To enter without invitation into the affairs of another; to interfere or meddle; to butt into a conversation or the like; to add one's two-cents' worth. There's no telling where this originated. Its first appearance in English is in the *Apophthegmes, That is to Saie, Prompte Saiynges* (1542), translated by Nicolas Udall from the collection, in Latin, of adages garnered by Erasmus, published in 1500. In Udall's translation it is thus given:

> Whatsoeuer came in his foolyshe brain,
> Out it should, wer it neuer so vain.
> In eche mans bote would he haue an ore,
> But no woorde, to good purpose, lesse or more.

Along in the eighteenth century the "boat" phrase was occasionally dropped, and we in America now use "stick" more frequently than either "put" or "have."

to get it in the neck

To get it where the chicken got the ax; to be defeated or punished; to be on the carpet; also, to be deceived. The first definition, in its literal sense, adequately explains the origin of this American slang, and the first definition used figuratively is fully synonymous with each of the other meanings. The expression is at least seventy years old, first reported in the Louisville (Kentucky) *Courier*, issue of January 20, 1887. The report dealt with the play, *The James Boys,* at the New Buckingham Theatre the previous Saturday evening. The galleries were filled with bootblacks, newsboys, and small boys generally. As half a dozen dark-visaged and heavily armed rogues crept on the darkened stage and gathered around a barrel marked in large white letters "Powder," one small urchin in a most excited stage whisper said, according to the reporter, "Dem dubs is goin' to get it in de neck in a minit."

casting pearls before swine

"Give not that which is holy unto the dogs, neither cast ye your pearls before swine, lest they trample them under their feet, and turn again and rend you." That is the sixth verse of the seventh chapter of Matthew. Of the passage John Wyclif wrote in 1380: "Þus [Thus] comaundeth crist þat men schullen not yeve [give] holy þingis to hondis [hounds] & putten precious perles to hoggis." That is, grandmother, don't bequeath the most revered among your treasured antiques to a daughter or daughter-in-law who cares only for modernistic décor, and, granddad, no matter how generous your instincts, you are merely casting pearls before swine in giving your six-year-old grandson a set of ivory chessmen at Christmas, rather than lead Indians.

to keep the pot boiling

To provide for one's living; to keep at gainful employment that will produce income; also, to keep interest from flagging; to keep the ball rolling. In former times when gentlemen and ladies were not supposed to work, to sell their time and effort for wages, some still found it necessary to produce some sort of salable commodity in order to continue to eat. It was genteel, not vulgar labor, to write or to paint, and many a man in the early nineteenth century especially (and from then to the present time) kept food in his domestic pot and a fire under it, through the judicious exercise of these talents and the generosity of a benefactor. Thus we find

William Combe, himself a "potboiler" through long practice, in *The Tour of Doctor Syntax in Search of the Picturesque* (1812), saying in his customary doggerel: "No fav'ring patrons have I got, But just enough to boil the pot."

something rotten in Denmark

Something of a highly suspicious nature; a nigger in the woodpile; something likely to be corrupt. We have it from Shakespeare's *Hamlet,* Act I, scene 4. Hamlet has been summoned by the ghost of his father, the murdered king of Denmark, into a conversation apart from his friends Horatio and Marcellus. His friends urge him not to go alone, for fear of injury, but Hamlet insists and will not be denied, saying, "Unhand me, gentlemen, By heaven, I'll make a ghost of him that lets me," and departs with the ghost. Marcellus then says, "Let's follow; 'tis not fit thus to obey him." Horatio replies, "Have after. To what issue will this come?" To which Marcellus responds, "Something is rotten in the state of Denmark."

to crash the gate

If Willy Smith, in fitting attire, enters the portals of Madame Astorbilt's house or grounds, to which he has not been invited, in order to mingle with her party guests, he has "crashed the gate" to do so. Or if little red-haired Sammy Jones finds a way to sneak past a ticket-taker at the Polo Grounds or Madison Square Garden, he too "crashes the gate." Neither one has literally crashed anything—other than social or legal convention—but such an entrance, uninvited or non-paid, has been popular American designation since, approximately, the end of World War I. No one knows and there is no clue to the person who became the first *gate-crasher.*

to get in one's hair

To have someone or something persistently annoy one; to become greatly irked. I doubt that this American expression was of Western origin, though its first reported appearance was in the *Oregon Statesman* in 1851: "I shall depend on your honor . . . that you won't tell on me, cause if you did, I should have Hetty Gawkins in my hair in no time." But there had been towns and villages in that territory for almost forty years by that time, so it is of course possible that the expression signified some annoying Oregonian factor that actually did get in one's hair. What that annoyance may have been, we are not told. Nevertheless since body lice were then regarded as a more or less necessary evil, it is certainly within the realms of probability that these were the pests of the early reference, literally irritating the scalp.

to cry for the moon

"Breathes there a man with soul so dead" that he has never done this! Any such would be utterly lacking in either desire or ambition, one who goes through life just a-settin' like a Stoughton bottle. That is, we all, at some time, strive for the impossible or the unattainable—and, perhaps, the disappointment over our inability to answer the siren's call or to catch up with the will-o'-the-wisp inclines us to follow the lover in Lord Tennyson's *The Princess* (1847): "I babbled for you, as babies for the moon." It was Charles Dickens, however, who, in *Bleak House* (1852), was the first to put on record the present saying, even though, undoubtedly, the babies of Adam and Eve and all babies since must have reached out their plump little hands and demanded, in no uncertain tones, that the pretty yellow ball in the sky be placed therein. Dickens, describing in Chapter VI the actions of Mr. Skimpole, had him say of himself, "Give him the papers, conversation, music, mutton, coffee, landscape, fruit in the season, a few sheets of Bristol-board, and a little claret, and he asked no more. He was a mere child in the world, but he didn't cry for the moon."

to skate over (or on) thin ice

To approach or treat a delicate subject without causing offense; to risk imprudence or indelicacy in language. The author, in fact, has skated over thin ice several times in this book in his attempt to explain one or another irreligious or indecent expression tactfully, without giving occasion to any reader to drop the book in the fire. The allusion is to the sport indulged in by daredevil boys and venturesome young men, in winter, in skating rapidly over newly formed ice on lakes or streams, ice so thin that it would not bear his weight if the skater stopped or slowed down; hence, the risk of being plunged into icy water. In my own youth, as in that of my sons in New England, the sport was called "tickledy-bendo," partly from the bending ice as the skater skimmed its surface. The expression also is used to mean to undertake a venturesome enterprise, especially one relying upon consummate skill or great luck.

to ride the goat

To be initiated or inducted into an organization, especially into a secret society. In all probability, although no facts are ever likely to be disclosed, this expression actually did arise from the practice in some college Greek-letter fraternity of introducing a goat into the hazing of prospective candidates for membership. But the earliest record of the phrase occurs in *Peck's Bad Boy and His Pa* (1883), by George Wilbur Peck. In Chapter XIX, "His Pa Is 'Nishiated," the bad boy and his chum train a goat to butt a bock-beer sign, borrowed from a neighboring saloon, and ask "Pa" if he would like to be " 'nishiated" into their lodge and take "the bumper degree." When "Pa" agrees, he is told to "come up pretty soon and give three distinct raps, and when we asked him who come there must say 'A pilgrim who wants to join your ancient order and ride the goat.' " The goat, as the bad boy says, is "loaded for bear," and when "Pa" repeats the order, "Bring forth the Royal Bumper and let him Bump," the goat, seeing the bock-beer sign pinned to "Pa's" back side, lets him have it with the best "bump" of which he is capable.

to lead one up (or down) the garden (or garden path)

This expression, in frequent use by English writers, has not yet gained much currency in the United States. It is relatively new, dating probably no further back than around the end of World War I. When I wrote to Sir St. Vincent Troubridge, whom I have quoted variously elsewhere, to inquire whether he could suggest a possible origin, I advanced the theory that seduction might have been the aim in the "leading." He did not agree with that view, though he was not able to offer anything more plausible. Nevertheless, to quote the *Supplement* (1933) to *The Oxford English Dic-*

tionary, the saying means "to lead on, entice, mislead," and the earliest printed quotation that is cited is from Ethel Mannin's *Sounding Brass* (1926): "They're cheats, that's wot women are! Lead you up the garden and then go snivellin' around 'cos wot's natcheral 'as 'appened to 'em." If that doesn't imply seduction, then what does it imply? Be that as it may, current usage rarely, if ever, carries other meaning than to bamboozle, to hoax, to blarney, to pull one's leg, to deceive.

other fish to fry

The French idea is *il a bien d'autres chiens à fouetter,* literally, "he has many other dogs to whip." The Germans, with no frills, give the actual meaning—*andere Dinge zu tun haben,* "to have other things to do," as do the Italians with *altro pel capo.* The Spaniards are equally direct though your translated version of *Don Quixote* may give you a different idea. Thus, in the Motteux translation (1712), part II, chapter XXXV, Merlin tells the noble Don that the only way by which "the peerless Dulcinea del Toboso" may be disenchanted is that Sancho—

> ". . . thy good Squire,
> On his bare brawny buttocks should bestow
> Three thousand Lashes, and eke three hundred more,
> Each to afflict, and sting, and gall him sore."

But Sancho, quite naturally, objects to being the recipient of such indignity; the disenchantment of the fair Duchess is of no immediate concern to him; hence, " 'I say, as I have said before,' quoth Sancho; 'as for the flogging, I pronounce it flat and plain.' 'Renounce, you mean,' said the Duke. 'Good your Lordship,' quoth Sancho, 'this is no Time for me to mind Niceties, and spelling of Letters: I have other Fish to fry. . . .' "

Cervantes actually wrote, *otras cosas en que pensar,* "other things on which to think," but Motteux, anxious to show off his acquaintance with English idiom, adopted the phrase already well known. Just how old the "fish" version may be is not known. The first appearance in print that has yet been found is in the *Memoirs* (1660) of the prolific writer John Evelyn. Undoubtedly, however, it had long been familiar to his readers.

657

unable to see the wood for the trees

Too beset by petty things to appreciate greatness or grandeur; too wrapped up in details to gain a view of the whole. In America we are likely to use the plural, "woods," or possibly to substitute "forest," but "wood" is the old form and is preferable. Yes, the saying is at least five hundred years old, and probably a century or two could be added to that, for it must have long been in use to have been recorded in 1546 in John Heywood's *A Dialogue Conteynyng the Nomber in Effect of all the Prouerbes in the Englishe Tongue.* He wrote: "Plentie is no deinte, ye see not your owne ease. I see, ye can not see the wood for trees." And a few years later, in 1583, Brian Melbancke, in *Philotimus: the Warre Betwixt Nature and Fortune,* wrote: "Thou canst not or wilt not see wood for trees." The saying has cropped up repeatedly from then to the present, becoming, in fact, more frequent with the passing years.

son of a gun

Nowadays this is likely to be a respectable or nice-Nelly substitute for an epithet of the when-you-call-me-that-Smile variety, a male offspring of the female of the canine family. But it is also used as a term of affectionate regard, as between pals. In general, however, it is the opposite extreme, accompanied usually by a derogatory adjective and used as a term of contempt. It has been in the language for at least two and a half centuries, and if one is willing to accept the story of its origin given by Admiral William Henry Smyth of the British navy in *The Sailor's Word-Book,* written about 1865, here it is: "An epithet conveying contempt in a slight degree, and originally applied to boys born afloat, when women were permitted to accompany their husbands to sea; one admiral declared he literally was thus cradled, under the breast of a gun-carriage."

hot dog

It would have been my guess that this term for the popular American comestible came into circulation, along with the item itself, during the great Columbian Exposition in Chicago in 1893. But the New York *Herald Tribune,* in an editorial, "The Hot-Dog

Mystery," June 2, 1931, was not able to carry the date earlier than 1900. It hardly seems necessary to explain that the name itself is applied to a frankfurter, a highly seasoned sausage of mixed meats, usually grilled and placed in a split roll, the name being suggested by the one-time notion that the sausage was made of dog meat. The *Herald Tribune* credited the invention of the concoction to one, Harry M. Stevens, caterer at the New York Polo Grounds, who at that time heated not only the frankfurter but also the roll. However, Stevens, as reported by the *Herald Tribune* in his obituary, May 4, 1934, credited the name to the late T. A. Dorgan (known as "Tad," from his initials), a sports cartoonist, though unable to recall the date. In more recent days "hot dog" has become an ejaculation expressive of surprise or approval.

to give one the gate

This might appear to be a descendant of a saying of the fifteenth century, "to grant one the gate," as in *The Knightly Tale of Golagros and Gawane*: "The king grantit the gait to schir Gawane, And prayt to the grete Dod to grant him his grace." That is to say, the king granted Sir Gawane permission to leave, to pass through the gate and to take to the road. But that expression died many years ago. Ours is of twentieth-century birth and is reasonably literal in that it means to show one the door; hence, to give one his walking papers, or, that is, to dismiss a person, give him a walkout powder, give him the air, or, in baseball terminology, to send a player to the showers, retire him from the game.

by hook or by crook

By fair means or foul; in one way or another. As stated in *A Hog on Ice*, this expression is so old, dating back at least to the fourteenth century, that, though many derivations have been advanced, no certainty of origin has been obtained. This statement brought a letter from Admiral Gerald J. FitzGerald of Chicago, which I am privileged to quote, and to which was attached a clipping: "Admiral Gerald J. FitzGerald—of the Knight of Glin branch, of the Lord (Earl) of Desmond branch, of the House of Geraldine—can trace his pedigree back to Adam and Eve."

In regard to "by hook or by crook," Admiral FitzGerald wrote: "The origin has an affinity with my family . . . When my ancestors, the FitzGerald barons, were invading Ireland around A.D. 1169–1170, it was decided to establish a beachhead at Waterford because of its excellent harbor. As the invading squadrons were cruising across the broad expanse of water, they saw on the Emerald Isle's left shore a lofty tower, and on the right a magnificent church. A spy was asked what these places were and he responded, 'On the left, the Tower of Hook, and on the right, the Church of Crook.' 'Then,' said the head lord and marshal, 'we'll invade and take this great Kingdom of Ireland by Hook or Crook.' "

This account has at least the novelty of differing from all the others that I have seen, and history does record the fact that Gerald, ancestor of the FitzGerald family, was among the Anglo-Norman leaders authorized by Henry II of England to invade Ireland.

a leap in the dark

Any undertaking the outcome of which cannot be foreseen; a venture of uncertain consequence. At least, such are the modern interpretations, and we apply the metaphor to just about anything we have under contemplation of which the consequences cannot be determined. But the earliest usage of which we have record gives the phrase a more sinister interpretation. That is, in Sir John Vanbrugh's *The Provok'd Wife* (1697), we find (Act V, scene 6), the words of one dying, "So, now, I am in for Hobbes voyage, a great leap in the dark." The allusion being that the English philosopher, Thomas Hobbes, 1588–1679, on his deathbed was alleged to have said, "Now I am about to take my last voyage, a great leap in the dark."

paying (or working) for a dead horse

Performing work for which payment has already been made; ergo, doing something which is no longer profitable. I have no doubt that the Greeks had a phrase for this, and the Egyptians before them, and so on back to the first time that man worked for hire— or at least to the first one who got paid in advance. Nothing is quite so irksome. The allusion, of course, is to that unfortunate man who at some remote period bought a horse to work his field only to have the animal die before the field was sown—and the animal still to be paid for. A modern parallel is to buy a car on time, only to wreck it before the second payment has been made. Literary record of the English phrase has been traced back to the seventeenth century.

to do (put on, pull, or play) the baby act

To act in a manner typical of a baby; that is, to whine, coax, wheedle, shed tears, yell, howl, scream, kick, or otherwise adopt a babylike action in order to evoke sympathy, gain attention, or get one's way; as, "He weakened when she pulled the baby act, for he

couldn't stand tears." The expression in any of its forms is modern, but the act itself undoubtedly traces back to Eve, who was the first female determined to have her own way. But the small boy also puts on the baby act when he thinks he may gain something thereby, and perhaps occasionally his older brother, for the act is not altogether confined to the female of the species.

This expression should not be confused with the phrase, "to plead the baby act." Here the defense may be (a) that a contract is legally void because it was entered into by one still a minor, or (b) that the person committing a stupid act was so ignorant or inexperienced as to warrant excuse. Thus, for example, a person who entered a Communist cell while in college may later "plead the baby act" on the grounds that, because of the inexperience of youth, he was not then legally responsible.

to flog a dead horse

To try to revive a feeling of interest that has died; to engage in a fruitless undertaking. The French express it more literally— *chercher à ressusciter un mort*, to seek to resuscitate a corpse. But whatever the language, the sense is clear: it is as useless to try to stir up interest in an issue that is dead as it would be to try to get a dead horse to pull a load by flogging it.

to wait for dead men's shoes

Though "deadman" may have a variety of meanings—a corpse; a log, concrete block, or other heavy mass buried in the ground to serve as an anchor; an empty liquor bottle, "dead soldier"; a timber, in logging, to which the hawser of a boom is attached—we are concerned with something more literal here. These shoes belong to a man still living which the one who is waiting is anxious to try on for size if only the "old geezer" would pass along to his final reward. Sometimes the "shoes" mean the job to which one hopes to succeed, or they may mean the possessions or title that will descend to one. The saying is old. It was recorded in John Heywood's *A Dialogue Conteynyng the Nomber in Effect of All the Prouerbes in the Englishe Tongue* (1546)—"Who waiteth for dead men shoen, shall go long barefoote"—and, therefore, is undoubtedly much older.

the daughter of the horseleech

"The horseleech hath two daughters, crying, Give, give." You will find that in Proverbs, xxx, 15. Of course, the horseleech is an aquatic sucking worm, of large size and great sucking facilities which veterinary surgeons of old employed to remedy common diseases of the horse; hence, the name. But the name, as far back as the sixteenth century, was therefore also applied to any veterinary surgeon and, because of the natural propensities of the worm itself, to any rapacious insatiable person, to any bloodsucker, clinging to another and robbing him of money, ideas, or other resources. His daughters, presumably, are even more grasping; hence, any "daughter of a horseleech" is anyone, especially any female, who is constantly crying, "Give, give."

to ride for a fall

To lose intentionally; also, to fail in an enterprise. Obviously the saying stems from horse racing, especially in a steeplechase, in which a rider, though on a favorite mount, deliberately rides in such manner as to disqualify himself by, apparently, being thrown from his horse. The expression—recent American—has been transferred to other contests and games in which one of the contestants or contesting sides deliberately, but very slyly, loses the contest. How-

662

ever, the expression has also been employed in a sense not at all sinister. Any person who embarks upon an undertaking—commercial, amorous, or whatever—that seems doomed to fail, is also said to be riding for a fall.

to throw the book at one

Many a man who has had "the book" thrown at him would infinitely prefer that it had been a literal book, no matter how large or hefty. But no, it is a figurative book, or, rather, the contents of a literal book. Originally, and usually, "the book" is the maximum sentence that a judge can legally impose upon one convicted of a crime, and is often interpreted to mean life imprisonment. However, the metaphor has now been taken into non-criminal slang and is variously interpreted. In military circles, for instance, it usually implies a severe sentence resulting from a court martial, but it also may mean nothing more serious than a stiff reprimand from a superior officer. In family circles, father may "throw the book at" an erring son or daughter by depriving him or her of certain privileges. The expression appears to be of American origin, but, as with most criminal argot, its history is dubious.

fly-by-night

Quite properly, anyone who is a "fly-by-night" is one who decamps secretly or who departs hurriedly or clandestinely, usually at night, from a scene of recent activity, as from solicitous creditors or from anxious purchasers of worthless mining stocks or the like. In any case, he is a four-flusher, a swindler, and his activities are fraudulent. But the term originally had a literal meaning, or at least a meaning that its users thought to be literal. Even so recently as a century and a half ago it meant a witch, one who, as popularly supposed, actually mounted her broom or besom at midnight and went off on her round of appointments, whatever they may have been, or to meet secretly the Old Boy himself.

to put the finger on someone

This American slang has a far different connotation than the older "to put (or lay) one's finger upon something." The latter, though in general use the past hundred years, has the specific meaning, to point out, to indicate precisely; especially to show meaning or cause. But the newer expression is gutter slang for "to mark a person for murder," or "to accuse one of being a stool-pigeon," or, somewhat with the older meaning, "to inform on a person."

Davy Jones's locker

Maybe there was once an Englishman whose name was really Davy Jones. Perhaps he was the barman of the sixteenth-century ballad, "Jones Ale Is Newe," and the locker, dreaded by seamen, may have been where he stored his ale. That is speculation, however. Actually the source of the name and the reason for bestowing it upon the bottom of the sea, especially as the grave of those who have perished in the sea—"gone to Davy Jones's locker"—cannot be fathomed. The first mention of Davy Jones—his locker came later—is to be found in *The Adventures of Peregrine Pickle,* written by Tobias Smollett in 1751. It occurs in the episode (Chapter XIII) describing the attempt by Peregrine and his two associates to frighten Commodore Trunnion by a dread apparition they have prepared, succeeding so well that the commodore exclaims:

"By the Lord! Jack, you may say what you wool; but I'll be damned if it was not Davy Jones himself. I know him by his saucer eyes, his three rows of teeth, and tail, and the blue smoke that came out of his nostrils. What does the black-guard hell's baby want with me? . . ."

This same Davy Jones [Smollet adds], according to the mythology of sailors, is the fiend that presides over all the evil spirits of the deep, and is often seen in various shapes, perching among the rigging on the eve of hurricanes, ship-wrecks, and other disasters to which sea-faring life is exposed, warning the devoted wretch of death and woe.

to get one's dander up

To get angry; to become riled or ruffled. Dad gets his dander up when neighbor Simpson implies that his new Chevvy runs better than dad's new Ford, but he also gets his dander up, good and plenty, when son Pete smashes a fender of that same Ford backing into a tree. *Dander* still means "anger" in the dialectal speech of several English counties, but the full phrase appears to be entirely

American. In the dialectal use we find it in Seba Smith's *The Life and Writings of Major Jack Downing, of Downingville* (1830–33), a book dedicated to General Andrew Jackson. In "Letter LXV," dated July 20, 1833, the Major tells about a quarrel between him and Mr. Van Buren at Concord, in which Van Buren belittles the major's qualifications for the presidency. "At this," says the Major, "my dander began to rise . . ."

Through the popularity of these humorous yarns and letters, Smith began to have several imitators. The most pretentious was Charles A. Davis, who, in 1834, brought out *Letters of J. Downing, Major, Downingville Militia, Second Brigade*. In the third "letter," after describing a dance, in which "Gineral" Jackson participated, the fictitious Downing goes on to say that several of the men, including Van Buren, then tried on Jackson's coat, after he had retired: "Then cum my turn; but I see how the cat jump'd, 'so,' says I, 'I'll jest step out and rig in another room:' and I went strait to the Gineral, and woke him up, and tell'd him all about it—he was wrathy as thunder—and when he gets his dander up, it's no joke, I tell you."

Hence, to Davis, rather than to Smith, goes the credit, for what it may amount to, for being the first to record this expression. Probably, however, it was a popular phrase of the period, as shortly thereafter it appeared in the works of other writers, among them, Colonel David Crockett in his *Life* (1835) and upon the lips of "Sam Slick" in Thomas Haliburton's *The Clockmaker* (1837–40).

weasel words

Slaps on the wrist; words that weaken or detract from the effectiveness or force of another word or expression. The expression is often erroneously accredited to Theodore Roosevelt. He did use it and define it, however, in a speech at St. Louis, May 31, 1916. Roosevelt, along with many others, thought that action, rather than chidings, should be taken by the Wilson administration for the depredations by the German navy on American shipping. He said the notes from the Department of State were filled with "weasel words," adding, "When a weasel sucks eggs the meat is sucked out of the egg. If you use a 'weasel word' after another there is nothing left of the other." But the expression first appeared in an article, "The Stained-Glass Political Platform," by Stewart Chaplin, in the June, 1900, issue of *Century Magazine*. In the course of the dialogue in which the article is written, one St. John, reading the "platform" aloud, quoted, " 'the public should be protected—' 'Duly protected' said Gamage. 'That's always a good weasel word.' "

to burn one's boats (or bridges)

To make retreat impossible; hence, figuratively, to make a categorical statement or to take a positive stand from which none but an ignominious withdrawal is possible. I have read that this expression with the "boat" terminus was an ancient Greek idiom, but if that is true I have not been able to find it. However, the literal burning of his boats after crossing rivers or seas with his armies into alien lands was a practice of Caesar's to make his leaders and men realize most definitely that a victorious campaign would offer the only chance of a safe return to Rome. In much later periods the generals of invading armies had bridges burned behind them with the same object, as well as to add difficulties to pursuers.

willing to give one's ears

Willing to make a marked sacrifice. The allusion is to a punishment for certain crimes in the England of the twelfth century and later—and in America, too—by which one or both ears of him or her adjudged to be guilty were cut off. But though the punishable crimes run on back through the centuries, our present expression itself is not much more than a hundred years old. Hence, it must be left to the imagination which of those various crimes—forgery, quackery, treason, adultery, and others—could have been so desirable as to make one willing to suffer such an undesirable penalty.

to throw (or cast) dust in one's eyes

The ancient Romans expressed this same thought by saying, "*verba dare alicui*," which, translated, is "to give empty words," and that is what we do when we throw dust in anyone's eyes. We say a lot of empty words or perform some action which will confuse or mislead that person, blinding him, as it were, to actual facts.

666

Probably the generals of ancient armies took advantage of nature's own dust storms, whenever possible, to conceal the movements of their forces. But the earliest instance of an English phrase similar to present-day usage is to be found in the translation by George Pettie (1581) of Guazzo's *Ciuilie Conuersation* (*Civil Conversation*): "They doe nothing else but raise a dust to doe out their owne eies." However, one form of the modern phrase appears in Thomas Birch's *The Court and Times of James the First,* published before 1766: "He [Salisbury, lord treasurer] found so little good at the Bath, that he made all the haste that he could out of that suffocating, sulphurous air, as he called it, though others think he hastened the faster homeward to countermine his underminers, and, as he termed it, to cast dust in their eyes."

hitting below the belt

Using unfair methods or actions. As anyone knows who has attended a prize fight or watched one on television, or who has witnessed any other pugilistic engagement, to strike one's opponent below the line of his belt is a foul blow and, if done deliberately or repeatedly, may cause the decision to be rendered against the offender. Both literal and figurative uses of the expression arose from the adoption in 1867 of the Marquis of Queensberry rules covering prize fighting.

tarred and feathered

Subjected to indignity and infamy. Not so long ago, and perhaps in some localities even yet, this was literal, a punishment or condemnation meted out upon someone adjudged to have merited such treatment. In its severest form the victim was stripped, sometimes shaved, and melted or even hot tar was poured or smeared over his head and body and he was then rolled in chicken feathers. The victim might then be ridden out of town on a rail or driven out by dogs. The punishment was first inflicted in England in 1189 by Richard I for one guilty of theft in the navy, but had been practiced in Europe in earlier years. In America a royal officer of the customs was tarred and feathered in Boston in 1774, and other Royalists, according to report, received similar treatment by hot-headed rebellious mobs in that period. The Ku Klux Klan and various American mobs repeatedly resorted to such measures in more recent years in attempts to rid a community of persons deemed by them to be undesirable.

to save (or lose) face

To maintain (or lose) one's dignity, prestige, or at least a semblance of such dignity or prestige or esteem before others; to avoid humiliation or disgrace. The Chinese use only *tiu lien,* which means "to lose face," though they have another expression, "for the sake of his face." It was the English residing in China who coined "to save face," and it is that expression, along with "to save one's face," that is in more common use among Occidentals than the translation of the phrase used by the Chinese themselves.

to draw (or pull) chestnuts from the fire

To be made a cat's-paw, to be used for the advantage of another. The story dates back at least to Pope Julius II (1503–1513) who, some say, owned the monkey of the tale. As related by Drexelius (in Latin, translated for me by Miss Phyllis L. Bolton), it reads:

I am told by an excellent and reliable man that there once was a monkey who, because he was a favored pet, ran free about his master's house. One day a soldier stood outside hungrily gazing into the kitchen. The cook pretended not to see him and failed to make the customary offering. Seeing his hopes frustrated, the soldier slipped into the kitchen and, the moment the cook disappeared, stepped to the hearth. As it happened, there were chestnuts roasting on the hearth and their fragrance, which had attracted the hungry watcher, was equally alluring to the monkey. He, too, was drawn to the fireplace where he beheld the cause of the enticing aroma and endeavored to pull them out of the coals. Failing sadly, unable to stand the heat, the monkey snatched back his singed fingers. At a loss what to do then, he sat scratching his head. Suddenly his eye fell upon the cat lying in wait for mice. In an instant he pounced upon her and forced her, struggling and spitting, to serve as his deputy. Seizing the cat's paw in his, he used it to draw one chestnut after another from the fire. The cat did not, naturally, take such servitude kindly, and back arched, fur on end, she howled piteously until her wails brought the cook to the rescue.

to get (or **be given**) **the bounce**

To be summarily ejected, as Polly Prim might say; to be ejected forcibly, as by a "bouncer," one employed to get troublesome characters—drunks, noisy persons, or the like—out of a saloon, bar, hotel, etc.; also, to be dismissed from employment, to be expelled  from membership in an organization or from attendance in some institution, or to be rejected as a suitor, etc.; in short, to be shown that one is not wanted. Apparently we Americans borrowed the expression, in translation, from the Dutch in some manner. At least, the Dutch have the phrase, *de bons geven,* "to give the bounce," which is employed to mean to jilt, dismiss, give the sack. We've had "bouncers" who performed the above-mentioned duties, since the days of the Civil War, but "bounce"—usually exaggerated to "grand bounce"—is recent American slang. Perhaps orally the expression itself, in one form or other, dates back to that period also, but literary usage carries it back only to O. Henry's story, "The Friendly Call," first published in *Monthly Magazine Section,* July, 1910. The story is about two friends who are always on tap to rescue one another from predicaments: Bell, who tells the story, went to the rescue of George from the attentions of a widow, asking Bell "to get her off his tail." Bell asks, "Had you ever thought of repressing your fatal fascinations in her presence; of squeezing a hard note in the melody of your siren voice, of veiling your beauty—in other words, of giving her the bounce yourself?"

to get one's Dutch up

To get one's dander up; to arouse one's temper. The reference is, of course, to the Pennsylvania Dutch, to the people of Germanic origin who, in the early seventeenth century, fled from continued religious persecutions in the Palatinate, chiefly, and brought their brands of Protestant faith into the sanctuary provided by William Penn in eastern Pennsylvania. They were a peaceful people, these paternal ancestors of mine. And they practiced their religion. Accordingly, they were slow to anger, keeping their tempers under subjugation. Nevertheless, so the historian Bancroft tells us, although representing only one-twelfth of the population at the time, the Pennsylvania Dutch composed one-eighth of the army in the Revolutionary War. And, from personal experience, I can vouch for the fact that some of their descendants, at least, had flaring tempers—although they might not let "the sun descend upon their wrath."

to go in at (or off) the deep end

This is variously interpreted. In England, where presumably it originated during or just before the First World War, it seems to have no other application than to get terrifically excited, especially without much cause. The notion, one judges, was that if one inadvertently stepped into a swimming pool at its deepest part one would momentarily become quite agitated until discovery was made that the water was no more than shoulder deep. But though we sometimes apply the same meaning to the expression in America, we also use it for other deeds. Chiefly, I think, we mean by it the great agitation of high dudgeon or roaring temper. When Johnny with his air rifle pings a neat hole in the windshield of the new car, granddaddy is likely to go off the deep end and whale the tar out of Johnny. And we use it in much weaker senses. Of one who is reckless, of one who has got into hot water, of one who has married, or of one who is dotty, we say that he has gone in at (or off) the deep end.

I'm from Missouri; you've got to show me

Colonel William D. Vandiver, representative in Congress from Missouri from 1897 to 1905, is often said to have originated this expression, though he never claimed that distinction, nor does the evidence bear it out. However, he did use it in the course of a jocular informal speech before The Five O'clock Club of Philadelphia in 1899. The preceding speaker, Congressman John A. T. Hull, of Iowa, had twitted Vandiver for being the only guest not in evening clothes. The fact was that neither guest, being on a naval inspection trip, had brought dress clothes, but Hull had somehow managed to obtain them. In Vandiver's reply, according to his own statement, as reported in Mencken's *Supplement Two: The American Language,* he said:

He tells you that the tailors, finding he was here without dress suit, made one for him in fifteen minutes. I have a different explanation: you heard him say he came here without one, and you see him now with one that doesn't fit him. The explanation is that he stole mine, and that's why you see him with one on and me without any. This story from Iowa doesn't go with me. I'm from Missouri, and you'll have to show me.

But Paul I. Wellman, in an article that first appeared in the Kansas City *Times* (reprinted July 11, 1941, in the St. Louis *Post-Dispatch*), reported other and earlier claims. One was that made by General Emmett Newton, who said that he had coined it when, as a boy, he had accompanied his father to a Knights Templar convention in Denver in 1892. Boylike he made a collection of badges. Another collecter said, "I'll bet I have a better collection." To which the young Newton replied, "I'm from Missouri; you'll have to show me."

Another report, made originally by W. M. Ledbetter in the St. Louis *Star* and quoted in *The Literary Digest,* January 28, 1922, was that the reporter had first heard the phrase in Denver in 1897 or 1898, and upon further investigation found that it—

had originated in the mining town of Leadville, Colorado, where a strike had been in progress for a long time, and a number of miners from the zinc and lead district of Southwest Missouri had been imported. . . . These Joplin miners were unfamiliar with [mining practice in Leadville]. . . . In fact, the pit bosses were constantly using the expression, "That man is from Missouri, you'll have to show him."

This report was later confirmed in a letter to the St. Louis *Post-Dispatch,* July 14, 1941, by Joseph P. Gazzam, who had been a mine superintendent in Leadville during that strike in 1896, and who had personally used the expression at the time.

But Wellman also reports a much earlier claim, made by Dr. Walter B. Stevens, author of *A Colonial History of Missouri* (1921):

. . . an officer of a Northern army [during the Civil War] fell upon a body of Confederate troops commanded by a Missourian. The Northerner demanded a surrender, saying he had so many thousand men in his command. The Confederate commander, game to the core, said he didn't believe the Northerner's boast of numerical superiority, and appended the now famous expression, "I'm from Missouri; you'll have to show me."

hell on wheels

Very tough, vicious, wild, or, especially of towns of the "wild and woolly West," lawless. During the construction of the Union Pacific Railroad back in the 1860's, as also on later western railroads, every temporary town successively at the end of the line—largely occupied by construction gangs living in boxcars, by liquor dealers, gamblers, and other "camp followers"—received the apt, though transient, name "Hell-on-wheels." As a result, any person or animal having vicious tendencies, especially a mule, or any vice-ridden, lawless town is said to be "hell on wheels." The expression is also applied derisively to men who pretend undeserved superiority.

to double in brass

To work in two jobs in order to increase one's income; to earn money from two sources; originally, and still, to play in the band as well as to perform. The expression is used primarily by theatrical people, especially by old-timers, when referring to an actor who, for economic reasons, appears as two different characters in a play. Undoubtedly, however, it originated in the circus, the American circus as developed by Phineas Taylor Barnum. And probably it was altogether literal in the early days of "The Greatest Show on Earth"—back, say, in the 1880's. Literal also in the one-ring circuses which hit the small towns today. The equestrian, the aerial trapeze artist, the clown who can also play a cornet, trombone, or clarinet in the street parade and when not engaged in his act has a better chance of employment than the straight musician or the straight performer. The expression, literal or figurative, seems to be unknown in England; at least it does not appear in the latest collections of British "unconventional English."

elbow grease

Just plain exercise for the elbows, or, rather, for the arms and elbows, such as scrubbing for the females of the species or polishing the car for the males. Elbow grease is the best kind of polish, it used to be said, to get furniture smooth and lustrous. The term was well known back in the seventeenth century, and was defined by a dictionary of slang at the end of that century—*A Dictionary of the Terms of the Canting Crew*—as, "A derisory Term for Sweat."

to be skinned out of one's eyeteeth

To be right royally hornswoggled, bamboozled or flimflammed, that is, cheated or deceived—and there are twenty or more less polite ways to express the unfair methods employed in such skulduggery. Whereas the expression "to cut one's eyeteeth" indicates that one has reached (presumably) years of discretion, "to have one's eyeteeth drawn"—or the American version, "to be skinned out of one's eyeteeth"—conveys the reverse impression, to be duped, to be made a fool. It is the hayseed taken over by city slickers or, conversely, the man or his wife coming from a big city to a country village who is most likely to be skinned out of his eyeteeth.

to tie the can to one

To give one the air; to fire, bounce, dismiss from employment; to expel. Although cans were in use a thousand years ago, this American slang could have had no meaning then, nor, for that matter, would we have recognized as cans the articles that then bore the name. Cans in those days, and for many centuries thereafter, were made of wood, or stone, or pottery. It was not until about the mid-eighteenth century that metal was introduced in the making. Today, though we still "can" things in glass or stoneware, we think of a can as always made of metal, usually tin. And it was the tin can that gave rise to our current expression. Before the S.P.C.A. became a great deterrent to such practices, it was considered a rare rowdy sport to win by blandishment the confidence of some stray dog, then, with a piece of string, to tie a tin can to its tail, with perhaps a small stone or two in the can. The released dog, at the first friendly wag of its tail, would be startled by the resulting rattle and go tearing down the street yelping in fright at the noise from the bounding can from which it could not escape. One to whom the can is tied is, thus, one whose presence is no longer desired. And "to can" a person is to dismiss him.

castle in the air (or in Spain)

Un château en Espagne has been the French expression since the fourteenth century, and as the Greeks and the Romans and the ancient Egyptians could build such marvelous yarns around the arrangement of stars in the constellations—Orion's belt, Cassiopeia's chair, the Great Bear (Ursa Major), and so on, and so on—it must be that they, too, had some equivalent for a castle in Spain or in the air. Sometimes the early Gallic dream site was *en Asie,* or sometime *en Albanie,* but always in some land or region where one could not conceivably acquire space for so impossible an edifice as a castle. We first adopted the translation, "a castle in Spain," which appears in *The Romaunt of the Rose* (*c.* 1400): "Thou shalt make castels thanne in Spayne, And dreme of Ioye [joy], alle but in vayne." Some dream architects of the sixteenth century began to design their structures for the skies or for the air, as we do today, and with a third site in Spain.

as queer (or tight) as Dick's hatband

Absurdly queer, or, as the case may be, inordinately tight. The "Dick" alluded to in this metaphor was Richard Cromwell, "Lord Protector" of England for a few months, September 1658 to May 1659. He had been nominated by his father, the powerful Oliver Cromwell, to succeed him in this high office, and was actually so proclaimed. But whereas the father had served, at least from the death of Charles I in 1649, as quasi-king of England, king in fact if not in name, Richard would gladly have accepted both title and crown, had not the army been hostile to such action and, indeed, to Richard, who was shortly dismissed from office. The crown was the "hatband" in the saying, which was deemed a "queer" adornment for the head of one so briefly in highest office, and too "tight" for him to have worn in safety. (Let me add, however, this account is not accepted by the *Oxford English Dictionary,* though no better substitute is offered.)

at daggers drawn

Ready for a fight or at the point of fighting; in a state of open hostilities. The dagger became a generally accepted part of the gentlemanly costume in the middle of the sixteenth century, and, naturally, with the means of reprisal so conveniently at hand, any insult, suggestion of an insult, or gesture or remark from which an insult might possibly be inferred became an occasion for the drawing of a weapon on the spot or for the more formal challenge to duel. The original expression was "at daggers drawing," implying readiness to draw one's weapon in defense or in maintaining one's honor. It is found in the translation (1540) by Jehan Palsgrave, *The Comedye of Acolastus,* a German story of the Prodigal Son: "We neuer mete togyther, but we be at daggers drawynge."

an also-ran

A loser in a contest; hence, an unsuccessful or insignificant person; a failure. The term originated on the American turf, applied to any horse failing to take a place among the winners or to a jockey riding such a horse. In political circles the term is applied to any unsuccessful candidate for office. The earliest literary example of the political use appears to have been in a headline in the Cincinnati *Enquirer* of February 6, 1904, which read: "George B. Cox— He Heads the List of Also Rans." Now, George B. Cox, saloon-keeper, was long the notorious political boss of Cincinnati; he determined who should be candidates for office, but never ran for any office himself. And there were no candidates for any office in February of 1904. So I wrote to the *Enquirer* for an explanation. Here is the answer to my query, printed in the issue of April 8, 1954:

On the above date under a heading: "Hoodoo Of the Race Horse" "Having A Horse Named After You Is Bad Luck." The Enquirer reprinted a New York *Sun* story about a horse that had been named "George B. Cox" after the famous boss of Cincinnati, evidently without his knowledge or consent.

Early in its career the horse had won a number of races and had captured the fancy of horse-players, especially Cincinnatians, and every time the horse went to post the home folks bet heavily on him. But they over-raced the old plater and he couldn't win a race.

Finally the notoriety that resulted from the continual losses of the horse became so derisive [as] to arouse the newspapers opposed to Boss Cox, and they seized on every loss during an election period to manufacture opprobrious slogans calling attention each time to such loss in page one headlines; while covering the election of Cox's candidates under a small head somewhere in the middle of the paper.

At what should have been the peak of its career, however, the horse disappeared from the tracks, but writers of the period reported a ringer as having been seen on several tracks in Ohio. Boss Cox had tried to get the owner of the horse to change its name. Whether he had succeeded or not was mere conjecture.

to cut capers

The sense, to anyone whose knowledge of Latin enables him to recognize that the zodiacal sign Capricorn is a he-goat, is to perform like a goat, especially a kid or young goat; that is, to frolic about in a grotesque manner. Although the expression and its meaning were still new in his day, Shakespeare introduces it in *Twelfth Night* (1601) in a dialog between the two cronies, Sir Toby Belch and Sir Andrew Aguecheek, Act I, scene 3:

Sir Andrew: I am a fellow o' the strangest mind i' the world; I delight in masques and revel sometimes altogether.
Sir Toby: Art thou good at these kickshaws, knight?
Sir Andrew: As any man in Illyria, whatsoever he be, under the degree of my betters; and yet I will not compare with an old man.
Sir Toby: What is thy excellence in a galliard [a lively French dance], knight?
Sir Andrew: Faith, I can cut a caper.
Sir Toby: And I can cut the mutton to it.

lead-pipe cinch

We borrowed "cinch" from the Spanish *cincha,* a saddle-girth, used by the early settlers of our present West and Southwest. And because the former girths of braided horsehair were so strong and could be drawn so tight that a rider could have no fear of a slipping saddle, "a cinch" became a synonym for a sure-fire certainty, something so assured that it could be considered easy. But why "lead pipe" was introduced into the phrase some fifty or sixty years ago has me mystified. An anonymous paragraph picked up a few years back says that a mythical cowboy, troubled by a bucking bronco that often snapped its cinch, throwing both saddle and rider, gave him the notion to make his cinch out of lead pipe. But as one who has had experience, not only with horses but also with lead pipe, I can imagine few materials more productive of uncertainty than the latter. Lead is far down the scale in tensile strength, and a cinch devised of lead pipe would be little more sturdy than cotton string.

ace in the hole

Something of especial effectiveness held in reserve or undisclosed; something kept up one's sleeve. The expression derives from the game of stud poker. In this game the first round of cards in each deal is dealt face down, and each such card remains undisclosed to all but its holder until the end of the hand. The next round is dealt face up, and that player with an exposed card of highest value may open the betting (or he may throw down his cards and pass the betting to the holder of the next best card). Bets may be called or raised, or a player may pass out, but when the bets are even among the remaining players the dealer deals the third round, also face up. Betting is resumed as before, the player with exposed cards of highest value having the privilege of opening. When betting is again even, the fourth round is dealt, again face up, and betting is again resumed as before. Upon the fifth and final round, also face up, each player then knows the full value of his own hand —his "hole card," the one undisclosed, plus the cards that have been exposed. After final bets are completed each player exposes his card "in the hole" and the best hand wins. Since aces are cards of highest value, that player with one, two, or three exposed aces and "an ace in the hole" has a card of especial effectiveness.

to get (or have) cold feet

This was discussed as an American expression in *A Hog on Ice,* and also so considered by the editors of *A Dictionary of Americanisms* (1951). But Kenneth McKenzie, professor emeritus of Italian at Princeton, has found a much older instance of its use.

In a letter to me after the publication of my earlier book he said: "This expression can hardly have originated in the 1890's, as you state, for it is found in Ben Jonson's *Volpone* (1605), where he refers to it as a 'Lombard Proverb.' Some years ago I published a short article on the subject, 'Ben Jonson's Lombard Proverb,' in *Modern Language Notes,* Vol XXVII (1912), p. 263. There seems to be no doubt that Jonson heard it used by some Italian friend."

The pertinent part of this article reads: "In the second act of the play, Volpone, disguised as a 'mountebank doctor,' explains to the crowd why he has fixed his bank in an obscure nook of the Piazza of St. Mark's instead of a more prominent place:

Let me tell you: I am not, as your Lombard proverb saith, cold on my feet; or content to part with my commodities at a cheaper rate than I am accustomed: look not for it.

In other words, he is not so 'hard up' as to be obliged to sell his wares at a sacrifice."

Professor McKenzie's article goes on to relate that the proverb— *Avegh minga frecc i pee,* to have cold feet—is still used in Lombardy, with the figurative meaning, "to be without money." "And if a card player, as a pretext for quitting the game in which he has lost money, says that his feet are cold, the expression might come to mean in general 'to recede from a difficult position,' or more specifically, 'to have cold feet.' "

playing horse with a billy goat

Of course, "playing horse" is a childhood pastime—playing as if riding upon a horse. And "playing horse with (a person)" is indulging in horseplay—taking advantage of, or picking on, or joshing a person. But neither of these expresses the sense of the phrase used by my father and which my children and grandchildren understand, even when abbreviated into "pee-ing h. with a b. g." Others of my father's generation in central Ohio also knew its meaning, though I have not heard it elsewhere. As used by the cognoscente it conveys "engaging in something of uncertain outcome; or, making something or doing something which, for the present at least, is secret." Probably the billy goat was dragged into the picture just because it used to be fashionable among families of the less wealthy, who could not afford pony carts drawn by real ponies for their children, to have the carts but to substitute a billy goat or two for the ponies and thus more or less keep up with the Joneses.

codfish aristocracy

He didn't coin the term, but Wallace Irwin neatly expressed its meaning in the first stanza of "Codfish Aristocracy," which he has given me permission to quote:

> Of all the fish that swim or swish
> In ocean's deep autocracy,
> There's none possess such haughtiness
> As the codfish aristocracy.

In fact, the name was coined thirty years or more before Irwin was born in 1876. It originated in Massachusetts to denote a class of *nouveau riche* who had acquired wealth from the codfishing industry. George Stimpson in *A Book about a Thousand Things* (1946) reminds us that John Rowe, a Boston merchant, made a motion in the legislature on March 17, 1784, that "leave be given to hang up the representation of a Codfish in the room where the House sits, as a memorial of the importance of the Cod-Fishery to the welfare of the Commonwealth," a motion that was carried, thus accounting for the painted wooden codfish still hanging in the chamber of the House of Representatives in Massachusetts.

Mrs. Grundy

Do you picture her as a hoity-toity person, nose in air, prim, precise, lips pursed as if always saying "prunes" and "prisms"? Well, actually you may paint your own picture, for the dear lady never existed. She was an imaginary person in a play, a character frequently referred to but never appearing. The play was Thomas Morton's *Speed the Plough* (1798). Dame Ashby, one of the characters, is constantly on edge, fearing that some occasion may arise that will provoke the scorn of her neighbor, Mrs. Grundy, apparently the supreme exemplar of perfect propriety. "What will

Mrs. Grundy say?" is so often on the lips of the good dame that, thanks to the popularity of the comedy on both sides of the Atlantic, it became proverbial. Thus, in the second act speaking of her daughter, she says to her husband, "If shame should come to the poor child—I say, Tummus, what would Mrs. Grundy say then?" "Dom Mrs. Grundy," replies Farmer Ashby; "what wou'd my poor wold Heart zay?"

The line inspired the poet Frederick Locker-Lampson, in "The Jester," 1857, to write:

> It is an ugly world. Offend
>   Good people, how they wrangle,
> The manner that they never mend,
>   The characters they mangle.
> They eat, and drink, and scheme, and plod,
>   And go to church on Sunday—
> And many are afraid of God—
>   And more of Mrs. Grundy.

to put (or have) one's nose out of joint

To supplant one in the affection or esteem of another; hence, to humiliate; also, to upset one's plans. Usually it is the arrival of a baby in the family nowadays that puts the nose of a slightly older brother or sister, hitherto greatly favored, out of joint. But it can be, and formerly generally was, an older person. A parson or priest can have his nose put quite out of joint in his congregation by a substitute acting in his absence. And so can a doctor when a younger practictioner hangs up his shingle. And on up or down the line. In earliest usage the intent of the phrase was that of upsetting one's plans, and that was what was meant by Barnaby Rich in *His Farewell to Militarie Profession* (1581): "It could bee no other then his owne manne, that has thrust his nose so farre out of ioynte." The present prevailing interpretation, however, had been reached by 1662 when the diarist Samuel Pepys had apparently become addicted to the use of the expression. At least it occurs twice in his diary, each time, curiously, referring to the mistress of Charles II. The first entry, May 31st of that year reads:

. . . all people say of her [the king's recent bride, Catherine of Braganza] to be a very fine and handsome lady, and very discreet; and that the king is pleased enough with her; which, I fear, will put Madam Castlemaine's nose out of joynt.

The second, July 22nd, 1663, is:

He [Lord Sandwich] believes that, as soon as the King can get a husband for Mrs. Stewart, however, my Lady Castlemaine's nose will be out of joynt; for that she comes to be in great esteem, and is more handsome than she.

to keep one's shirt on

Perhaps because the shirts of a hundred years ago were not Sanforized and, therefore, the American male was likely to be hampered in the free movement of his arms, it was his custom, whenever a fight seemed imminent in settling an argument, to remove his  shirt first, and thus be ready to wade in with both fists flailing. The opponent, however, might see that there were two sides to the matter under debate; therefore, that it would not be necessary to resort to fisticuffs. Accordingly, his admonition would be, "Now, just keep your shirt on." At least, such is still the meaning—avoid becoming excited or angry; keep calm, cool, and collected—and was when George W. Harris in *The Spirit of the Times* (1854) wrote, "I say, you durned ash cats, just keep yer shirts on, will ye?"

a tin-horn gambler (or sport)

We have to go back to the times of the Gold Rush of the Far West for the original specimen, and the people who used the term then thought they were giving a literal name to the person or persons who were thus described. In other words, the name was applied to those gamblers who could not take the chances of the more aristocratic and costly game of faro, and were obliged to content themselves with the less pretentious game of chuck-a-luck. This is a game played with three dice, the gamblers betting the house that (a) all three will turn up with the same number, or (b) that the sum of the three will equal a certain number, or (c) that at least one of the three will appear with a specified number on its face. To relieve the monotony of shaking the dice all evening long the operators employed "a small churn-like affair" which, popularly, was called a tin horn. The game was a cheap one and, in consequence, the would-be sports who played it became tin-horn gamblers or sports, a term nowadays applied to anyone making a flashy appearance on a cheap scale.

to hang by a thread

To be subject to imminent danger; to be in a hazardous position or precarious condition. The allusion is to one Damocles, a courtier in the reign of Dionysius of Syracuse in the fifth century B.C. All we know of this courtier is from the tale told both by Cicero and by Horace. He was given to extreme flattery of his ruler, and, one day, having praised extravagantly the power of Dionysius was invited to see for himself just how much happiness that power brought. Accordingly he was given a magnificent feast, and was surrounded by luxury and entertainment beyond description. In the midst of this, however, he happened to glance above him and saw, suspended by a single hair, a naked sword pointed directly over his head. The intent, of course, was to show that a king, perhaps even more than his subjects, could never enjoy unalloyed happiness. We also refer to the *sword of Damocles* as a symbol of impending doom or threat of danger.

badger game

A form of blackmail, employed upon a man of position or wealth who is enticed into a compromising situation by a woman and is then "discovered" by one professing to be her husband. To avoid disgrace under threat of legal procedure or newspaper publicity the victim is under the thumb of the conniving operators. To badger, in criminal slang, is to blackmail. This meaning arose from the cruel sport of badger baiting, practiced from time immemorial until comparatively recent years, in which a live badger was placed in an artificial hole, such as a barrel, and dogs were set upon it. Thus "to badger" came to mean "to worry, tease, pester," or, leading to

682

the sense above, "to subject a person in one's power to persecution; hence, to blackmail." This form of blackmail is probably as old as the hills, but association with the term "badger" and the present name of the practice are American innovations of the past hundred years.

ambulance chaser

Derogatory term for a lawyer who, after an accident, immediately seeks the person injured and, for a contingent fee, offers his professional services in a suit for damages. This profession of dubious ethics, or at least the descriptive term, apparently originated in New York City in the 1890's, during the period when the notorious partnership of criminal lawyers, Howe & Hummel, was entering the height of its career.

alpha and omega

The first and the last; the beginning and the end. Both the expression itself—the first and the last letters of the Greek alphabet—and its definition are from the Bible, The Revelation of St. John the Divine. The phrase is repeated four times—in the eighth and eleventh verses of the first chapter, in the sixth verse of the twenty-first chapter, and in the thirteenth verse of the twenty-second chapter.

hammer and tongs

With all the vigor at one's command; forcefully; with might and main. Usually one goes after another hammer and tongs; that is, with no holds barred; with every intent to take him apart literally or figuratively. But on the domestic scene, a wife may go after the spouse, or the reverse, hammer and tongs, orally flaying him or her, or perhaps even hurling crockery or other solid articles. The allusion is to the old-time blacksmith who, with his tongs, long-handled pincers, took a piece of red-hot metal from the forge, laid it upon his anvil and beat it into shape with his hammer. Nowadays the blacksmith with his forge, his hammer, and his tongs has just about disappeared from the scene; his art is being replaced by insensate machinery, but the language of his trade will long remain.

sailing under false colors

Assuming to be what one is not; being a pretender or hypocrite. This arose from the days of piracy on the high seas, when a pirate vessel, sighting a possible prey, hoisted the flag of a friendly nation to its halyards to allay suspicion while it drew within striking distance, thus catching the unsuspecting victim unprepared for defense. But "under false colors" was in earlier use in a similar sense, denoting a man, sect, or even an army appearing in the garb or under the badge or insignia of a house or party of which he was not a member. From this were derived such phrases as "to come out in one's true colors" and "to show one's colors"; that is, to reveal one's true nature or standing.

to cry over spilt milk

To grieve over that which is irretrievably lost or beyond recovery; to regret that which has been said or done. Though the actual occurrence, with high milk prices, is something over which housewives probably have wept—or over a torn fig leaf—since the time of Eve, they never think of the ones benefiting from the accident—the dog, the cat, or the milkman—just their own selfish loss. The first to give voice to this cold comfort in this manner, in print at least, was that prime humorist of the past century, Thomas C. Haliburton. In his first series of *The Clockmaker; or the Sayings and Doings of Samuel Slick of Slickville* (1836), a friend says, "What's done, Sam, can't be helped, there is no use in cryin over spilt milk."

to get one's goat

To bewilder, confuse, or baffle; to irritate, annoy, or vex; to fuss one; to make one nervous; to get under one's skin (as said of the chigger); to give one a pain in the neck. Efforts have been made to trace this American expression back to a Greek source, but without conspicuous success. The French, however, do have an expression, *prendre la chèvre*, which, though defined, "to take offense," has the literal meaning, "to take, or to snatch, the goat." Their expression is said to have appeared as early as the sixteenth century, and does appear in seventeenth century as well as current dictionaries. Nevertheless it is most probable that American usage, traceable only to the early twentieth century, was of independent origin: first, because the French phrase does not have the same literal meaning, and, second, even if it did, the borrowing and literal translation would have been much earlier. One account weakly explains our phrase as derived from the racing stable where, sometimes, a goat browses among the horses on the theory that it has a calming effect upon high-strung racers. Deliberate borrowing of the goat from such a stable might thus be considered an unfriendly act, according to that explanation. Be that as it may, the earliest literary quotation thus far exhumed appears in Jack London's *Smoke Bellew* (1912), Chapter VII, "The Little Man," in which the usage has nothing to do with horse-racing. Here "Smoke" and "the little man" face the danger of crossing a rotting snow-bridge over a crevasse. "The little man" crosses first and waits for "Smoke." " 'Your turn,' he called across. 'But just keep a-coming and don't look down. That's what got my goat. Just keep a-coming, that's all. And get a move on. It's almighty rotten.' "

six of one and half a dozen of the other

No choice; one and the same; even steven. There seems to have been no specific allusion involved in this expression, nothing beyond the fact that half a dozen is six. It first appeared in Marryat's *The Pirate and the Three Cutters* (1836). Several of the sailors, repairing the ravages of a storm, have fallen to talking about some of the passengers, especially about the black nurse of white twins on board. Jack says to Bill, "You've been sweet on that . . . girl for these last three weeks." "Any port in a storm," Bill replies, "but she won't do for harbor duty—it's the babies I likes." At which Jack jeers, "I knows the women, but I never knows the children. It's just six of one and half-a-dozen of the other, ain't it, Bill?"

(big) butter-and-egg man

Derisive term for one of the *nouveau riche,* for one ostentatiously displaying new wealth. The expression came into popularity about 1925, during the Coolidge regime of almost hectic national prosperity, when office workers and mill hands alike were sporting silk shirts. Everyone was playing the stock market and reaping enormous paper profits. A large army of short-lived millionaires was the result, many of whom, not to the manner born, threw their new-found money around in wild splurges, especially on chorus girls. Unlike the older and more respected "captains of industry," these men sought control of no big business, such as railroads, or mines, or motorcars. Lacking a specific appellation for such a spender, New York columnists dubbed him a "butter-and-egg man," taking the term from the title of a play by George Kaufman produced in 1925.

deus ex machina (a god from a machine)

This Latin phrase really refers to a stage effect in Greek plays. That is to say, Greek tragic playwrights frequently introduced one

or another of the gods for the purpose of explaining some situation or solving some difficulty. Representing gods, the characters who played the parts could not walk out upon the stage as did other players, but were let down upon the stage from above by the aid of a mechanical device constructed for the purpose. Such was a god from a machine, *deus ex machina,* one who appeared suddenly and unexpectedly, ready to solve any difficulty.

to pay the fiddler (or piper)

To bear the consequences; suffer the penalties; defray the costs. The first is the American version and "to pay the piper" is the English. Fiddles furnished the music for stately English ballrooms, but flutes or pipes were the conventional music for English rustic dances, whereas the country dances of America relied on fiddles. In its figurative sense the English phrase dates back to Thomas Flatman's *Heraclitus ridens* (1681): "After all this Dance he has led the Nation, he must at least come to pay the Piper himself." The American phrase is very probably much older than the first citation shown in *The Dictionary of Americanisms* which quotes John Edwards' *Shelby and His Men* (1867): "Those who dance must pay the fiddler, says an adage." The incongruity is that the proverbial "fiddler's pay," even in England, was nothing more than thanks and all the wine he could drink, hence the metaphor, "drunk as a fiddler."

to shoot the bull (bull session)

Back in my college days a "bull session" was a gathering of young men—always men and always young—congregated informally in some dormitory room over late coffee or beer or other refreshments, with conversation ranging over any topic or topics that might be argued or discussed. The topics might be religion, giving rise to a diversity of views or half-formed ideas, or sex, or music, art, literature, or anything discussable, but none of the participants in such a session certainly ever considered these sessions—sometimes, though rarely, including a college prof or instructor—to consist of "foolish talk, stuff, claptrap," in the words of a recent dictionary. The discussants took them seriously, no matter what others may have thought—though, of course, frivolity did enter now and then. But along about that time "bull" degenerated into another sense, euphemistically often called "bushwa," what one might describe as the end product of the domestic bull, used chiefly as fertilizer; its slang sense was idle talk, stuff, nonsense, claptrap. The "bull session" of earlier days then descended into any confabulation, male or female, devoted to such chatter, and "to shoot the bull" did then become hyperbole for "to talk nonsense" or, sometimes, "to brag," or "to cheat or defraud."

Anthony (or Antony) over

The great collector of Americanisms, Schele De Vere, calls this an American game and defines it (1872): "A game of ball played by two parties of boys, on opposite sides of a schoolhouse, over which the ball is thrown." He localizes it in Pennsylvania, but it was also played in southern Ohio in my boyhood, and, if I recall correctly, also in my later youth in the suburbs of New York City. But why the game carries the name Anthony (or Antony) is a mystery. Possibly the reference was to St. Anthony who, upon appeal, is credited with aid in finding lost objects, as it was always

687

an object by either of the "two parties of boys" to so throw the ball as to go far over the heads of the opposing party, perhaps to be lost in high grass or weeds.

as dead as the dodo

Utterly extinct; obsolete; completely washed up. The reference is to a peculiar flightless bird of which only two species were known, those found respectively on the islands of Mauritius and Réunion, lying east of Madagascar. The birds, as described by voyagers to  the islands in the sixteenth and seventeenth centuries, were larger than the swan and with much heavier bodies. Being slow of motion and unable, with their small wings, to fly, they were easily killed by voyagers and early settlers, who found them highly edible, and especially by the pigs introduced to the islands by colonists. Before the end of the seventeenth century the species on Mauritius had all been exterminated; a few still remained on Réunion into the early eighteenth century before complete extermination. As Will Cuppy said in *How to Become Extinct* (1941), "The Dodo never had a chance. He seems to have been invented for the sole purpose of becoming extinct and that was all he was good for."

to take a back seat

To take a seat or occupy a position among those of little importance; to practice humility or become humble; to go 'way back and sit down. There's little doubt that this expression was an outcome of the natural characteristics of Americans. The aggressive, those determined to be heard on any subject up for discussion, inevitably plant themselves toward the front of any assembly, so that they may rise and be seen readily by those whom they wish to persuade. The humble, those who instinctively avoid the limelight, as well as those who hide their lights under a bushel, willingly keep in the background. A back-seat driver, however, is a horse of another color. He—or usually she—knows not the meaning of the word

688

"humility." On the contrary, she is the aggressive one, dictating from the rear seat what the actual driver in the front seat, usually her husband, should do, what road he should take, how slow he should drive, what he should do in any emergency, and so on.

to cut the mustard

To accomplish, be able to, or succeed with; to meet expectations; to play, as music, expertly. To get at the origin of this altogether American expression we have to go back to the beginning of the century when "to be the proper mustard" was a slang phrase meaning to be the genuine article, possibly because some so-called "mustard" of that period would not pass today's pure food requirements. From that, immediately, came "all to the mustard," that is, all one could ask for, fine and dandy, "copesetic," as the late Bill Robinson would say. Then hotly, as early as 1907, came our present phrase. O. Henry used it in *Heart of the West* in that year: "I looked around and found a proposition that exactly cut the mustard." It's just a slang expression, bearing no connection to the use of the verb "cut" in the sense of to reduce the strength of.

to bury the hatchet

To settle differences and take up friendly relations. In *A Hog on Ice* I made the statement that, although we are accustomed to connect this expression with practices of the American Indian, I had not been able to find that there was any such ritual or saying among the tribes of North America. Accordingly I considered it a variation of the fourteenth-century English saying, "to hang up the hatchet," of similar meaning.

Mitford M. Mathews, in an article in *American Speech* (May, 1953), indicates unmistakably that I did not delve as deeply as I should have into the customs of the American Indian. He quotes, as the earliest record, this statement, dated 1680, from the writings of Samuel Sewall: "Meeting with the Sachem they came to an agreement and buried two Axes in the ground; . . . which ceremony to them is more significant and binding than all Articles of Peace the Hatchet being a principal weapon." *The Dictionary of Americanisms* (1951), edited by Dr. Mathews, carries further evidence confuting my statement. Thus, under *tomahawk*, is a quotation from Robert Beverley's *The History and Present State of Virginia* (1705): "They use . . . very ceremonious ways in concluding of Peace . . . such as burying a Tomahawk." Other quotations from those dates onward, under both *hatchet* and *tomahawk*, demonstrate that the custom was well established, as was also the custom of "taking up the hatchet" when warlike activities began.

raining cats and dogs

Dean Jonathan Swift has been given credit for originating this extravagant way of indicating excessive or torrential rain, but I doubt that he did. To be sure its first literary appearance in this

form is in his *Polite Conversation* (1783), but it must not be forgotten that these so-called "dialogues" are markedly satirical, and when he has Lord Sparkish say, "I know Sir John will go, though he was sure it would rain cats and dogs; but pray stay, Sir John," he is using what he regards as a hackneyed phrase, as he does deliberately throughout these dialogues. The hyperbole was probably more than a hundred years old by that time. As evidence, go back to Richard Brome's play *The City Witt* (*c.* 1652). In Act IV, scene 1, we find Sarpego—the pedant who, affecting a great knowledge of Latin, translates it entirely by ear— speaking: "From henceforth *Erit fluvius Deucalionis*/The world shall flow with dunces; *Regna bitque*/and it shall rain; *Dogmata Polla Sophon*/ Dogs and Polecats, and so forth."

to eat one's hat

To eat crow; to eat humble pie; to assert one's readiness to consume such an unsavory mess if a certain event should not turn out as one predicts. The present form of the saying is first found in

Charles Dickens' *Pickwick Papers* (1837): " 'If I knew as little of life as that, I'd eat my hat and swallow the buckle whole.' " Dickens could have coined the phrase, but it is more likely that it was merely his own adaptation of the older, "I'll eat old Rowley's hat," of the same general significance. Here "old Rowley" referred to Charles II, a nickname given to him, it is said, from his favorite race horse, but cherished by his adherents from the long struggle against Oliver Cromwell, through punning connection with the familiar saying, "a Rowley [Roland] for an Oliver."

to row (someone) up Salt river

To defeat, overcome, vanquish an adversary; especially, politically, to defeat an opposing candidate in an election. For many years the expression was used only in the latter sense, based on an alleged incident. The story, gravely cited by the recent *Dictionary of American History* on the authority of various earlier accounts, takes it back to the presidential campaign of 1832, when the Whig candidate, Henry Clay, was running against Andrew Jackson. Clay on a Western speaking trip, it was said, hired a boatman to take him up the Ohio river to Louisville, but the boatman, a Jackson supporter, took him up Salt river instead, causing Clay to miss his engagement by several hours. Clay's defeat was assumed to have hinged on that episode; hence, the political application of the phrase.

That story was accepted as the origin of the expression for more than a hundred years. Apparently it did not occur to anyone to doubt that Henry Clay, who had lived in Lexington, Kentucky, from the time he was twenty, could have been bamboozled into an acceptance of the comparatively narrow Salt river for the broad expanse of the Ohio, or that Louisville had suddenly been moved some thirty miles downstream. It was not until recently that doubt was thrown upon the accepted version.

The skeptics were Professor Hans Sperber of Ohio State University and Professor James N. Tidwell of San Diego State College. As they report in *American Speech* (December, 1951), the expression antedated the Clay-Jackson campaign by at least several years. Salt river was already notorious as the seat of Western tall talk among rivermen; it was the home of the "ring-tailed roarer or screamer of the half-horse, half-alligator breed," of backwoods braggarts or rowdies who would make life miserable for a stranger. Their conclusion: "*To row up Salt River* and *to row somebody up Salt River* as used in actual or fictional backwoods slang mean, respectively, to be engaged in a difficult or probably unsuccessful journey and to make somebody undergo hardships or, more particularly, to give him a beating. The corresponding political phrases are nothing but natural applications of these meanings to political conditions."

On my own, I surmise that the original speakers intended to "roar" a person up Salt river by their outrageously exaggerated tall talk; in their speech "roar" became "ro'," which the listener interpreted to be "row."

to draw the line

To reach one's limit; especially, to fix a definite limit of procedure beyond which one refuses to go. Although now figurative, the line that was drawn was originally actual. It was the cut of a plowshare across the field to indicate the limit of one's holding, back in the sixteenth century.

try it on the dog

To experiment on (someone or something); to try out the effects of something upon someone. In all probability, though proof is lacking, this was a literal test originally—experimentation, probably with meat, possibly tainted, or with some other doubtful food upon the household dog to determine alimental effect upon the human system. The idea, at least, traces back to the official taster in days when royalty was always fearful of being poisoned by a cook secretly employed by an envious brother or cousin. However, our present expression came into theatrical usage around the latter quarter of the nineteenth century, when, first in England, the producers of a new play sometimes decided to "try it out on the dog," meaning to test the reaction of some provincial or matinee audience and thus be able to correct any faults before introducing the play in London. In America, a play is "tried out on the dog" by being first played in Hartford, New Haven, Philadelphia, or perhaps Boston, before it appears on Broadway. But the expression is applied now quite generally; almost any new product is first tested upon a limited number of "dogs" before it is placed on general sale.

up Salt Creek (without a paddle)

In a pretty kettle of fish; behind the 8-ball; on the spot; in a predicament. Salt Creek is not the same body of water as Salt river (q.v.), up which a political party or candidate is sometimes rowed, or at least its political allusion is different. In fact, since one who is up this creek is often also said to be "without a paddle," the inference is that it was originally an actual salt-water indentation from the sea, a passageway through marshland, from which egress would be extremely difficult without proper means of locomotion. The American expression is at least seventy years old, having been used in a campaign song of 1884 called "Blaine up Salt Creek."

poor as a church mouse

Mighty poor; about as deprived of the necessities of life as the "fly on the wall" of which my wife used to recite lugubriously to the children:

> Poor little fly on the wall,
> Ain't got no shimmy-shirt,
> Ain't got no pettiskirt,
> Ain't got no nothing at all!
> Poor little fly on the wall.

But our church mouse is not found only in English-speaking countries. The Germans have the same saying, *arm wie eine Kirchenmaus;* in French it's *gueux comme un rat d'église,* and it is found also in other languages. The English saying goes back to the seventeenth century, but was probably taken over from French. It is likely that it arose from some folk tale relating the sad experience of a mouse trying to find food for itself and its starving little ones in a church. No pantry, no meal bag, no grain bin made the struggle for existence most difficult.

to set one's cap at (or for) a person

To strive to gain the affection of a person: always said of a woman or maiden who, perhaps modestly or perhaps ostentatiously, puts her best foot forward in her efforts to gain the attention and win the admiration of the male she favors as a lifelong companion in matrimony. The expression was once more literal than figurative. Back in the days when women considered a light muslin cap a necessary part of ordinary indoor attire, it was but natural for a maiden, a spinster, or a widow to don her most becoming or fanciest cap when an eligible swain came to call. Of course young brother or nephew Diccon would spot the dress-up headgear, and the family would adopt his remark that Molly or Aunty Prue was "setting her cap at" the young squire or the parson. The common expression may go back to the seventeenth century, but was certainly known to Oliver Goldsmith in the eighteenth. The younger generation of today probably does not know it.

a pain in the neck

Not an actual physical pain, nor is it located so much in the neck as in the head. That is, the pain is mental, rather than physical. One who is the cause, who is the pain or gives the pain, is just *persona non grata* to the recipient. Others may consider him or her a pleasant and entertaining person, even well informed, but to the sufferer he or she is an unmitigated bore. The cause of the pain may also be inanimate; that is, a house or a picture or a newspaper, or anything which one regards as contemptible or lacking in merit. The expression is American slang of the past fifty years, a polite variation of a pain previously associated with another part of the anatomy.

not to know B from a battledore (or broomstick, or from a bull's foot, or buffalo's foot)

To know not one letter from another; not to know beans; to be wholly illiterate, or extremely ignorant. This accusation of complete illiteracy dates at least to the late Middle English period, according to *The Rolls Series* (the chronicles and memorials of Great Britain

694

during the Middle Ages). The earlier expression, perhaps originating in an agricultural section, seems to have been that comparing B to the foot of a bull, but by the time of John Foxe's *Actes and Monuments of these Latter and Perilous Dayes* (1563) the more courtly battledore was the fashionable term: "He knew not a B from a battledore nor even a letter of the book." Broomstick and the American buffalo's foot were later variations, the latter first appearing in James K. Paulding's *Westward Ho!* (1832). Mere alliteration, not real or fancied resemblance, seems to have been the only motive back of any of the comparisons, just as in the antonym, "to know a hawk from a handsaw," indicative of intelligence.

iron curtain

This expression, in its allusion to the line across Europe beyond which are the countries under Soviet influence or control, was credited, in *A Hog on Ice,* to Winston Churchill, to its use in a speech delivered by him on March 5, 1946, at Westminster College, Fulton, Missouri. But the same metaphor may have been in other minds also and was certainly used by others before that date. Had the idea of an impenetrable curtain occurred to an American, it is likely that he would have called it "an asbestos curtain," having in mind the curtains used in American theaters to stop a backstage fire from spreading to the audience. But in Europe such fireproof curtains have long been made of iron.

Thus, some five months before Churchill's speech, there was an article in the *Sunday Empire News* (London), October 21, 1945, with the heading, "An Iron Curtain across Europe," describing the difficulties attending military government in Germany. It was written by a former staff officer in the G_5 Division of SHAEF, Sir St. Vincent Troubridge, who is also familiar with theatrical terms and expressions. In a letter to me he stated that the expression immediately caught the fancy of the London newspaper world and within a month or two appeared in leading articles and that it was used at least once in the House of Commons before Churchill gave it world-wide circulation.

However, though without doubt unknown to either Troubridge or Churchill, the same metaphorical application had been given to the expression eight months earlier by no less a person than Joseph Goebbels, German Propaganda Chief. As reported by John A. Lukacs in *The Great Powers & Eastern Europe,* 1953, Goebbels wrote in his editorial of February 23, 1945, in *Das Reich*:

If the German people should lay down their arms, the agreement between Roosevelt, Churchill and Stalin would allow the Soviets to occupy all Eastern and South-Eastern Europe, together with the major part of the Reich. An iron curtain [*eiserner Vorhang*] would at once descend on this territory, which, including the Soviet Union, would be of tremendous dimension. . . .

Goebbels was a good prophet.

To forestall the critics, let me add that other metaphorical applications of *iron curtain,* though not to the Soviets, may be found in the story, "The Food of the Gods," by H. G. Wells (1904), with reference to a person held incommunicado by the police; in a book, *A Mechanistic View of War and Peace* (1915), by George Crile, and in *England, Their England* (1933), by A. G. MacDonnell, each of the latter two with reference to a curtain of artillery fire in a military engagement.

to bite the thumb at

"I will bite my thumb at them; which is a disgrace to them, if they bear it," said Sampson of the house of Capulet to his fellow servant, Gregory, in Act I, scene 1, of *Romeo and Juliet*. But a moment later, when it appeared that the servants of the house of Montague were not going to "bear it," he amended the remark: "No, sir, I do not bite my thumb at you, sir, but I bite my thumb, sir."

That is, to bite one's thumb was, and still is, an ordinary act, as ordinary and inoffensive as to bite one's fingernail. But "to bite one's thumb at" a person was an insult of Shakespeare's time not to be taken lightly, a sure cause for quarrel. The gesture itself, as defined by Cotgrave (1611), meant, "to threaten or defie by putting the thumbe naile into the mouth, and with a ierke [from the upper teeth] make it to knack [click, snap]." But the commentators of Shakespeare and others have not been able to determine the significance of the gesture, what it was intended to represent. The conjecture is that it was equivalent to the indecent gesture of contempt, the thumb thrust between the fingers to represent a fig (see under "not worth a fig" in *A Hog on Ice,* p. 125), but it is difficult to see what relationship there could have been between the two.

tied to one's mother's (or wife's) apron strings

Apparently this whole idea of domination by one's mother—more rarely, wife nowadays—arose from a law going back at least three hundred years under which a man might have a tenure of property only by virtue of his wife, sometimes only through her  lifetime. That tenure was known as an "apron-string hold." The wife, obviously, controlled the finances of the family and, undoubtedly, frequently wore the pants. At least it was easy to extend the sense of the figure and to have the husband tied to his wife's apron strings, as Thomas Macaulay put it in his *History of England* (1849). But by that time also that which worked so successfully with papa was carried on by mama to such others of her family as might be benefited. Little Bud, who had looked to mama to wipe his nose as a child, continued to look to her through adolescence and even into adulthood. Perhaps the only blessing from a war is that it enables many young men to become untied from mother's apron strings.

to put the bite on one

To mooch, cadge, shake down, or, more plainly, to beg. This American slang seems to have developed from the entirely innocent token of fondness, "to bite one's ear." In *Romeo and Juliet,* Mercutio makes reply to a quip from Romeo, his dearest friend, "I will bite thee by the eare for that iest." The expression, though perhaps not the action, originated from the French, *mordre l'oreille,* a soft caress and whispered endearment accompanied by a gentle nip of the ear. Now, in making a request for a loan or in begging, one does not shout from the housetops, but if possible one whispers his wants in the ear of the intended victim. He is "putting the bite on," though from appearances he is but "biting a friend by the ear."

busman's holiday

Spare time spent in doing the same thing one does in one's regular occupation. The story is that the regular driver of a London bus actually did that—spent one of his days off riding as a passenger alongside the driver who was taking his place. But if that episode ever occurred, no report of it has yet been found. The age of the expression cannot be determined, but it had become proverbial many years before the first reported appearance in print—1921. A carpenter who, on a holiday repairs his own porch—a schoolteacher who uses his weekends as a Boy Scout master—a newspaper reporter who, at night, writes fiction; each may be said to take a busman's holiday.

drawing a longbow

One who numbers golfers or fishermen among his acquaintances should quickly recognize the nature of this expression. Any tale which in the telling makes use of unusual distance or unusual size that cannot be subjected to verification is very likely to be stretched in the telling. Thus it was even in the days of Robin Hood. For two hundred years—roughly between 1300 and 1500—the might of England rested on its archers. The kings, from Edward II to Henry VIII, in all ways encouraged an increase in this skill; in fact, successively they commanded the general practice of archery on holidays and Sundays, to the exclusion of all other pastimes. The weapon was the longbow (now often written "long bow"), a bow distinguished from the common bow in being not less than five feet in length, and sometimes specified as being one foot taller than the archer. Both skill and strength were required to draw such bows, but prodigious feats of skill and strength were shown by the bowmen—if one were credulous enough to accept the tales of the mighty archer or his friends. Outdoing the exploits of William Tell, an old English ballad recites the deed of an archer who, shooting

698

before the king, split a thin wand in two at a distance of a quarter of a mile (!), then in further proof of skill he sent his arrow through an apple placed on the head of his young son at a distance of 120 yards. And Robin Hood and the valiant Little John, 'twas said, could place an arrow a measured mile. 'Tis plain why our expression has long meant stretching the truth; exaggerating; telling a tall tale.

Cadmean victory

A victory in which the victor has suffered such great loss as hardly to be distinguished from the vanquished. The term derives from the mythological founding of Thebes. Cadmus, prince of Phenicia, searching for his lost sister, was advised by an oracle to abandon the search and to follow a cow and establish a city where she should lie down. The cow led him into Bœotia where, before Cadmus could carry out the charge to found a city, his companions were all devoured by a dragon. Cadmus thereupon slew the dragon and, at the command of the goddess Athene, scattered its teeth over the field. Immediately armed men sprang from the teeth and fiercely turned upon the hero. To divert the threat, however, Cadmus induced them to turn upon each other. When all but five were thus slain, Cadmus stopped the strange duel and persuaded the five to assist him in the founding of the city. Hence also the expression, *to sow dragon's teeth,* meaning, to sow seeds of strife and discord.

to take the bark off

To tan; give one a hiding; to lambaste, or, in simpler speech, to flog, chastise. Possibly the original idea, likening the bark of a tree to the skin of a man, was to castigate, to flog as with a cat-o'-nine-tails, or, that is, to whip so severely as literally to flay the skin from one's back.

As easily imagined, "to take the bark off one" gives greater pain than "to talk the bark off a tree," though both are severe. The first is entirely physical, both literally and figuratively. The second is entirely figurative. The implication is that the one who does the talking gives such a tongue-lashing, or uses such cutting remarks as to resemble in effectiveness the strippers used in removing bark from a tree. Both expressions are homely American, probably dating back to the days of peeled logs for frontier cabins and strict disciplinary parents. Literary records as far as traced, however, do not show great antiquity—the first to 1845, and the second only to 1891.

to kill the fatted calf

To prepare for a season of rejoicing; to prepare a warm welcome. The allusion is to the parable of the prodigal son, Luke xv, verses 11 to 32, the younger son who took his portion of his patrimony and journeyed "into a far country, and there wasted his substance with riotous living. And when he had spent all, there arose a mighty famine in that land; and he began to be in want." Then, employed as a swineherd, "he would fain have filled his belly with the husks that the swine did eat." Finally, coming to his senses, he decided to return home, knowing that his father would at least give him better employment. "But when he was yet a great way off, his father saw him, and had compassion, and . . . said to his servants, Bring forth the best robe, and put it on him; and put a ring on his hand, and shoes on his feet: And bring hither the fatted calf, and kill it; and let us eat, and be merry: For this my son was dead, and is alive again; he was lost, and is found. And they began to be merry."

in cahoots with (one)

In close coöperation with; in league with; in partnership with. It is highly probable that our American term came from the French *cahute,* a small hut or cabin, or the related Dutch *kajuit* of the same meaning. The connecting link has not yet been found—the use, that is, of a French or Dutch expression which our great-grandparents adopted—but the kind of partnership or league-ship indicated by "in cahoots with" is obviously that which would be expected of the fellow inhabitants of a small cabin, of men closely engaged in a joint undertaking. The expression dates at least from the early nineteenth century, if not back to the Revolution.

700

to go to the dogs

Sometimes things are thrown to the dogs or sent to the dogs, but nowadays, at least, it is usually the country or the younger generation that is going to the dogs. In any case, "to the dogs" means utter ruin, straight to hell, the demnition bow-wows. The dog, you see, was not always the house pet that it has now largely become. It was kept for its utility, chiefly in hunting. Such food as it received from its master might be no more than the bones tossed over his shoulder into the straw litter that covered the floor. Our first record of the figurative usage is in Thomas Cooper's *Dictionary* (1563), rightly named *Thesaurus Linguae Romanae et Britannicae,* in the Latin phrase: *addicere aliquem canibus,* to bequeath him to dogs.

to lock the barn (or stable) door after the horse is stolen

To take out automobile insurance after your car has been stolen, or after you've had an accident; to take belated precautions, especially on one's property. Apperson reports that the Romans had the same idea: as quoted from Plautus's *Asinaria,* he gives: *Ne post tempus prædæ præsidium parem* (After the time of plunder one provides protection). But the English aphorism is also very old. We find it in John Gower's *Confessio amantis* (1390): "For whan the grete Stiede Is stole, thanne he [Negligence] taketh hiede, and maketh the stable dore fast." And the saying has come down through the years. We in America are more likely to say "barn door" rather than "stable door," though we recognize either term.

not to know if one is afoot or on horseback

To be so completely confused, thoroughly upset, or beside one-self as to be unable to determine whether one is walking or riding; to be utterly befuddled. This degree of pixilation, or this way of expressing it, is apparently known only in America; at least the saying originated here. In literary usage it has been traced only as far back as 1895, in the *Century Magazine* of that year—"Sam he had a keg hat on, all shiny silk, and a red necktie thet Car' Jane hed made him git, and he didn't know whether he was afoot or a-hoss-back." But undoubtedly the saying was in fairly common use in some sections of the country many, many years before that. Both of my parents, born in the early 1850's in central Ohio, used it so familiarly as to indicate early acquaintance with it, as if from their own parents or grandparents.

talking through one's hat

To talk nonsense; to indulge in fanciful dreams. Just how this expression came into everyday American speech is now a mystery. From the printed evidence it's not very old, as expressions go; probably no more than seventy years. But what event or circumstance brought it into the language? Because of the date of the earliest record, and the medium in which it appeared—*The World,* New York, May 13, 1888—the notion persisted in my mind for several years that it had a political significance. It was at about that time that Benjamin Harrison's friends were advocating that he be the Republican nominee for the presidency at the forthcoming convention. One of Harrison's foibles was the beautiful tall beaver hat that he affected. It became his natural dignity, but later cartoonists, especially those on opposition papers, such as *The World,* made much of it, showing the president as almost overwhelmed by a prodigious beaver hat. But, alas, it was no cartoonist who coined the expression, and it was not Benjamin Harrison who was first said to be "talking through his hat." The phrase that appeared in *The World* was in an unsigned article entitled "How About White Shirts?" which dealt with a prosaic discussion of the fact that drivers and conductors of street cars in New York wore white shirts, although those in Chicago did not. The phrase was merely part of the conversation of a New York driver with the reporter. He was quoted as saying, in part, "Dis is only a bluff dey're makin' —see! Dey're talkin' tru deir hats." And since the driver did not have to explain his meaning to the reporter, nor the reporter to the readers of *The World,* it is certain that "talking through one's hat" was a familiar expression in 1888, at least in New York.

all wool and a yard wide

Of top quality, character, or the like; absolutely genuine; the real McCoy; fine in every respect; as, Knute Rockne was regarded by all who knew him as all wool and a yard wide. Fraudulence and deceit in the manufacture and sale of woolen cloth were practiced in England certainly as long ago as the reign of Edward IV, according to an act of 1464 against such practices. Further acts of 1483 and 1515 and even to the time of George III, however, indicate that, after a brief flurry, the laws were quietly disregarded until dishonesty again became too flagrant. An act in the short reign of Edward VI is specific, asserting that some clothiers "do daylie more and more studdye rather to make monye then to make good cloths . . . and doe daylie . . . practyse sleight and slender makinge, some by myngelinge of yernes of diverse spynnynges in one clothe, some by myngelinge Fell Wool and Lambes Wooll with Fleese. . . . some by overstretchinge them upon the tenter . . . fynallye by usinge so manye subtill sleights and untruithes as when the clothes soe made be put in the water to trye them, they ryse out of the same neither in lengthe nor bredeth as they ought to doe."

In America, as long as wool was spun and woven in the home for home consumption, it was honestly made, but when itinerant merchants began to travel around the countryside selling cloth from New England mills, their products were not always as represented. To bolster sales they began to adopt the slogan, "all wool and a yard wide," thus proclaiming, with tongue in cheek perhaps, that the cloth contained no shoddy or other adulterant and that it was full width. By the 1880's this slogan had passed into the language in its current meaning. The first it appeared in print was in *Peck's Sunshine* (1882), by George W. Peck, the author of *Peck's Bad Boy,* a favorite possession of my youth.

Ivy League

This Ivy label, in words of Leo Riordan in *The Saturday Evening Post,* November 7, 1953, "was an apt designation coined by a sports-writer to characterize old-line institutions." It refers specifically to the football teams of the colleges, Yale, Harvard, Princeton, Dartmouth, Brown, Cornell, Columbia, and University of Pennsylvania. The sportswriter to whom Riordan referred was Caswell Adams, now of the New York *Journal American.* In a letter to me, which I am privileged to quote, Adams thus described the episode:

It is true that, rather unconsciously, I did coin the phrase back in the mid-thirties. If I remember correctly, it was when Fordham's football team was riding high and playing big-name teams from all over the country. One afternoon mention in the office was made of Columbia and Princeton and the like and I, with complete humorous disparagement in mind, said, "Oh they're just Ivy League." Stanley Woodward, then sports editor of the New York *Herald Tribune* [with which Adams was then connected] picked up the phrase the next day and credited me with it.

But Mr. Adams does not mention the fact that, like "Main Line," the phrase is now sometimes used, also with humorous or even slightly sardonic disparagement, to designate institutions or, especially, literary groups which consider themselves somewhat superior to the rest of us.

like a bat out of hell

Moving or speaking, etc., with extreme speed; like greased lightning; hell-bent for election. Though this might have become a part

of British aviation slang in the First World War, as Partridge says in his *Dictionary of Slang and Unconventional English* (1953 edition), it was certainly in use in the United States at least by the turn of the century—and, I suspect, ten or twenty years earlier than that. It was familiar to my ears in my college days in Colorado, back in 1903–04. A possible explanation of source of origin is that because bats shun the light, they would be in great haste to escape from the incandescent flames of the lower regions.

Back Bay

A fashionable residential district of Boston, Massachusetts. Formerly this was a basin of the Charles River, an inner harbor of Boston. From 1856 it was gradually drained and filled in and laid out in fine wide streets, including Commonwealth Avenue, one of the finest boulevards in America. Hence, used attributively, representative of the culture, thought, accent, etc., of Boston.

flat on one's back

Helpless; without further recourse; at the end of one's rope. Although usually employed in a figurative sense, the original meaning was literal. One who is actually flat on his back is so completely disabled through sickness or injury as to be helpless, unable to fend for himself. Figuratively, the meaning may indicate helplessness through lack of power or through lack of financial means.

to back water

Literally, this was said of a ship, boat, canoe, or the like, to which the paddle wheel was reversed, or the oars or paddles were moved backward. Hence, figuratively, one is said to back water when obliged to retract a statement or reverse a position or withdraw from a situation. The expression dates from the early days of the steamboat, the early nineteenth century.

fifth columnist

This expression was wrongly attributed in *A Hog on Ice* to the Spanish general, Emilio Mola. It should have been credited to Lieutenant General Queipo de Llano, famous as the "broadcasting general" during the Spanish Civil War. In 1936, in the early days of the war, broadcasting to the Loyalist forces in Madrid he threatened, "We have four columns on the battlefield against you and a fifth column inside your ranks." This was the first recognition in modern warfare of organized forces behind the battle lines ready to sabotage the defense of a position.

brain trust

A group of experts; especially, a group organized to aid in the shaping of policies, etc.; hence, derisively, any group of advisers. The term was first coined by James M. Kieran, a reporter for *The New York Times*. It had been announced at Hyde Park that Franklin D. Roosevelt, the Democratic candidate for the presidency in 1932, was preparing a series of campaign speeches and that the services of three Columbia University professors—Rexford G. Tugwell, Raymond Moley, and Adolf A. Berle, Jr.—had been engaged to assist, as experts in economics and political science. Kieran tried unsuccessfully to label this group the "Brains Trust," in his articles for *The Times,* but it was not until after Roosevelt took office and other reporters had adopted the term for the augmented group of non-political advisers which the president retained that it became generally used, now reduced to "brain trust." The first printed use was apparently in *Newsweek,* September 2, 1933: "The President's Brain Trust, a little band of intellectuals, sat at the center of action as similar bands have done in revolutions of the past."

African dominoes (or golf)

Popular names for the game of craps, a gambling game played with a pair of dice. The game is especially favored among American Negroes, hence, "African"; the term "dominoes" alludes to the combined number of pips on the two dice, identical with those on the face of dominoes. "Golf" is in ironical reference to the usual financial status of the players and to the great disparity in the comparative cost of equipment.

asleep at the switch

Unprepared; lacking alertness; inattentive. Undoubtedly this American expression was originally railway terminology and was almost literal in meaning. It dates from the time when railroad switches or turnouts were thrown or turned by levers operated by hand, either by switch-tenders or brakemen. In a freight yard especially, where it was the duty of the switch-tender to shunt cars to the proper tracks, alertness was an essential. Lack of attention gave rise to the charge that he was "asleep at the switch."

right down (or up) one's alley

Peculiarly adapted to one's ability or talent, or particularly attractive to one: "By virtue of his knowledge of Greek and Latin, work on a dictionary was right down Phil's alley"; "That ad for a young man to drive a car to Mexico was right up my alley." It has been suggested, learnedly, that these expressions may have originated from baseball, from the fact that "down the alley" means a ball so hit as to go between the fielders, usually good for a home run. But I am inclined to think that "alley," in these phrases, is merely a substitute for "street," or the locality on which one lives, that "right down (or up) my alley" is merely a figurative way of saying "right in the locality (or specialty) in which I am most at home, or most familiar."

to have hold of the wrong end of the stick

To have the wrong slant; to have another guess coming; to be misinformed, or to misinterpret a story. The *stick* was originally a *staff,* and he who had "the worse end of the staff," as was the saying in the sixteenth century, was on the receiving end of a bout  with quarter-staves, those six- to eight-foot rods made familiar to us through the tales of Robin Hood and his merry band. Obviously, the one on the receiving end was getting the punishment, which accounts for the former and still occasional meaning of the phrase, to be at a disadvantage. And also obviously, the one being worsted in such a combat must confess that he is in the wrong, which accounts for the meaning of our present saying. Curiously, however, no instance of this current saying has been found earlier than the late nineteenth century.

alley cat

Any homeless or stray cat, especially one frequenting alleys in search of food in garbage cans, etc. By extension, a prostitute or a street-walker furtively seeking customers.

to get the drop on (a person)

To have a marked advantage; literally, to have a person covered with a gun before that person is able to draw his own weapon.

According to Mary A. Jackson's *Memoirs of Stonewall Jackson* (1895), this phrase originated during the War between the States. At least, she wrote: "They had seventy-three pieces of artillery, one battery being siege guns or thirty pounder Parrotts, but the elevated position of McLaws and Walker gave them decidedly the drop, not only on the big guns but on the whole Federal line." Nevertheless, long before her *Memoirs* were written, back in 1869 in fact, the traveler, Alexander K. McClure, wrote in his *Three Thousand Miles through the Rocky Mountains:* "So expert is he with his faithful pistol, that the most scientific of rogues have repeatedly attempted in vain to get 'the drop' on him." And, for that matter, I think it most likely that the literal phrase was in use during the famous days of the Forty-Niners, or possibly much earlier.

a Donnybrook fair

Strife and contention; a melee; Bedlam broke loose; hell's a-popping. Why? Because Donnybrook, now a part of Dublin, was a place where, every year for six centuries beginning in 1204, a riotous fair was held each August. Originally the fair lasted for two weeks, but eventually that became too taxing for even the most fun-loving of the natives of the town and the exhibitions and festivities were cut down in later years to one week. Needless to say, huge quantities of usquebaugh were consumed even in that one week, and a quick-tempered Irishman found ample occasion to crack a crown with his stout shillelah. Probably to the regret of none, the fair was discontinued in 1885.

Philadelphia lawyer

An astute person; sometimes one whose cleverness leads him into shady practices. In my explanation of this phrase in *A Hog on Ice* the account of its origin as given by the historian John Fiske was accidentally omitted, as I was reminded by a correspondent.

According to Fiske, the expression stems from the noted trial of John Peter Zenger in 1735. Zenger, a New York printer, began to publish a newspaper, the New York *Weekly Journal* in 1733, which became the organ of the popular party in that colony. Attacks upon the administration of the governor of the colony, William Cosby, brought about the arrest of Zenger on a charge of libel, and he was held in jail, awaiting trial, for about eight months. Friends busied themselves in his behalf and eventually secured the services of Andrew Hamilton, former Attorney General of Philadelphia. At the trial Hamilton admitted the publication of the statements charged by the prosecution, but maintained that inasmuch as the statements were true no libel had been committed. The jury supported that contention and gave a verdict of not guilty, thus establishing the principle of freedom of the press in America. Thus Fiske reports, people then proclaimed, "It took a Philadelphia lawyer to get Zenger out."

Fiske's statement may be true, but, regrettably, no proof has yet been discovered that people in New York or elsewhere had actually made such a remark. Nevertheless the expression was certainly in use before 1788. In that year, as found by Allen Walker Read, the *Columbian Magazine* of Philadelphia printed a "Letter from a Citizen of America," "written in London," to his "Correspondent in Philadelphia," a portion of which reads, "They have a proverb here [London], which I do not know how to account for;—in speaking of a difficult point, they say, it would puzzle a Philadelphia lawyer."

But there are other accounts. One credits it to an unnamed attorney in colonial days who rescued two British sailors from some unnamed difficulty they experienced in the City of Brotherly Love. Again, it is reported that there was a saying in New England that any three Philadelphia lawyers were a match for the devil, though I have found no proof of that report—nor substantiation of the statement.

to know where the shoe pinches

Though the Romans of old said *calceus urit,* they meant it physically—the shoe or sandal frets or pinches. However, the figurative sense—where hardship occurs or difficulty lies or trouble may be experienced—has been in English usage for at least six centuries. Chaucer had it in *Canterbury Tales* (*c.* 1386) when, in "The Merchant's Tale," he has the merchant's brother say:

". . . Myn neighebours aboute
Sayn that I have the moste stedefast wyf,
And eek the meekest oon that berith lyf;
But I woot best [know best], wher wryngith [pinches] me my scho."

The French phrase, a direct transalation, is *c'est là que le soulier me pince,* though *c'est là que le bât me blesse,* literally, "that's where the saddle galls me," is heard more frequently. Germans say, *wissen wo einen der Schuh druckt,* "to know where the shoe pinches one." Spaniards say, *Cada uno sabe donde le aprieta el zapato,* "Each one knows where the shoe pinches him."

absent treatment

In the United States this expression is used with two differing meanings. Originally, and properly, it is a term in Christian Science for a treatment by a healer given at the request of and for the benefit of an absent person. But the term has also acquired a slang sense: treatment such as that shown to a person or an animal not present. One gives a child, a dog, another person the absent treatment by speaking of him or it as if he were non-existent or not within hearing distance, though actually the speaker knows him to be present and able to hear what is said.

the devil to pay

Serious difficulty; great trouble or misfortune; perplexity; confusion; mishap. "There'll be the devil to pay if I don't get home in time for dinner." There are two schools of thought about the original meaning of this. One is that it related to witchcraft, to the selling of one's soul to the devil and the payment exacted for its release. This would seem to be the sense in the earliest quotation that we have, occurring under date of approximately 1400 in the poem, "Titivillus," in the collection of ancient manuscripts, *Reliquiæ Antiquæ*—"Beit wer be at tome for ay, Than her to serve the devil to pay."

But "devil" is also a nautical term for the seam nearest the keel of a vessel, and "pay" means to calk. Hence, among sailors "the devil to pay" could mean to calk the seam nearest the keel. This could be done, in former days, only when the vessel had been careened, tipped on its side. Such an operation, between tides, would be difficult, especially so if the expanded form of the expression is considered—"the devil to pay and no pitch hot," as we find it in Sir Walter Scott's *The Pirate* (1821): "If they hurt but one hair of Cleveland's head, there will be the devil to pay, and no pitch hot." Proof is lacking that the nautical was the original sense, but this is the logical source of the phrase.

tooth and nail

Yes, it means exactly what cute little Mary Ann means when she goes after her pestiferous older small brother who is torturing her

dolly. She bites and digs in with her nails. And she and her ancestors before her, both sides of the family, have been using those natural weapons of offense and defense since Noah was a pup. Thus *with tooth and nail* long ago became an English phrase signifying "with all the powers at one's command." The old Latin equivalent was *toto corpore atque omnibus ungulis,* "with all the body and every nail." In France, it's *bec et ongles,* closely approaching our English phrase, but with the literal meaning, "beak and talons."

to the bitter end

To the last extremity; to death or utter defeat. This expression has a double meaning, but it is hardly likely that the poetic resemblance between the two meanings is anything more than chance. That is, in the words of the famous Captain John Smith in his *A Sea Grammar* (1627): "A Bitter is but the turne of a Cable about the Bits, and veare it out [let it out] by little and little. And the Bitters end is that part of the Cable doth stay within boord." Or, as a later seaman put it, "When a chain or rope is paid out to the bitter-end, no more remains to be let go"—when the end of the chain or rope reaches the bitts, obviously no more can be paid out. But death, the end of life, has long been thought to be bitter, and it is no more than natural that, poetically, we should say that when one has come to the end of life, the "end of one's rope," that he has come "to the bitter end." (It has been contended that nautical usage is, properly, "to the better end," the end of the rope or chain which, being inboard, is little used. But the language of the sea does not substantiate this argument.)

loaded for bear

To be fully prepared for any contingency; to be well prepared; hence, ready to fly into a rage. Originally this had a hunting significance; the bear, being the largest of dangerous American wild animals and likely to be encountered in any region of wild game, a hunter did not regard himself as prepared unless his gun carried a charge heavy enough to kill a bear. Undoubtedly, use of the expression—often written and spoken, "loaded for b'ar"—goes back to the days when the West was wild and woolly, but evidence of this has not yet been turned up in our literature. Modern slang has introduced a new meaning into the phrase—to be well loaded; spifflicated; drunk as a boiled owl.

blowing one's top

Possibly the "top" in this expression alluded originally to the top of a volcano, which would be shot into a thousand pieces with a tremendous noise during a violent explosion and scattered over the neighborhood with a devastating effect. "Blow," at least, has been used in the sense of "to erupt; to go to pieces by explosion" for several centuries. Much the same effect occurs when, in modern slang, a person "blows his top." He lets off steam in a violent explosion of temper; he shouts; he cares not a whit where or upon whom the pieces may fall. In short, he gets furious with rage. The expression is also used in a far milder sense: a crazy person, that is, or a person who is befuddled by drink and acts brainless is now sometimes said to have blown his top.

to bleed one white

Literally, this is to cause one to lose so much blood that he becomes pale, but for the past three hundred years men have been said to "bleed" when they have unwillingly or through fraud parted with an undue sum of money, as through blackmail or the like. When the victim has been "bled white," in modern parlance, he has paid through the nose to such an extent that the extortionist sees that his racket has come to an end.

not worth a rap

Having no intrinsic value; not worth a straw, nor a tinker's dam, nor beans. We don't know just how *rap* got its name, but it was a very small coin which, though not legal tender, was passed for a halfpence in Ireland during the early eighteenth century. It was because of the lack of legal small currency and in protest against a lopsided patent issued to one William Wood by George I for the coinage of copper halfpence in Ireland that Dean Jonathan Swift wrote the celebrated *Drapier Letters* in 1724. Concerning the *rap,* he wrote in one of the letters, "Copper halfpence or farthings . . . have been for some time very scarce, and many counterfeits passed about under the name of raps."

And when we say, "I don't care a rap," it is the same worthless coin to which we refer.

fourth estate

The newspaper press as a distinct power in the state, from the license it exercises, the liberties it enjoys, or the power it wields. (The first three estates, as ultimately represented in the British Parliament, are the Lords Spiritual, the Lords Temporal, and the Commons.)

Thomas Carlyle, in *Heroes and Hero Worship* (1841), credited the expression in this sense to the statesman, Edmund Burke— "Burke said there were three Estates in Parliament, but, in the Reporters' gallery yonder, there sat a Fourth Estate more important far than they all"—but the statement is not recorded anywhere in Burke's published works. Moreover, in the *Edinburgh Review* in 1826, Thomas Macaulay used the phrase in an essay on Henry Hallam's *Constitutional History,* in the eighth paragraph from the end: "The gallery in which the reporters sit has become a *fourth estate* of the realm." As Carlyle himself was a Scottish reviewer and wrote for the *Edinburgh Review,* it is probable that he attributed the thought to the wrong author.

In strict justice, however, the novelist, Henry Fielding, should receive some of the credit. Seventy-six years earlier, writing for the *Covent-Garden Journal,* he said: "None of our political writers . . . take notice of any more than three estates, namely, Kings, Lords, and Commons . . . passing by in silence that very large and powerful body which form the *fourth estate* in this community . . . The Mob." And, though erroneously, Lord Lucius Cary Falkland has been similarly credited. While Richard Cromwell was Lord Protector of England, according to Charles Knight's *Popular History of England,* Lord Falkland, in the course of a speech in 1660 in Parliament, said: "You have been a long time talking of the three estates; there is a *fourth* which, if not well looked to, will turn us all out of doors"—referring to the army. The army did ultimately turn Cromwell out, but Falkland made no such speech —he died sixteen years before Cromwell's short-lived tenure of the office his brilliant father, Oliver, had created.

to go by the board

"Board," in nautical language, is the side of a ship. Thus "overboard," for example, means over the side of a ship; hence, out of the ship, into the sea, and "by the board" has the same meaning— i.e., down the ship's side, overboard. Accordingly, "to go by the board," in its literal sense, is to go down the ship's side, to fall overboard and to be carried away; hence, to be lost for good. These several literal meanings date back at least three centuries, and some are older. But the figurative sense of our present phrase—meaning, to be utterly lost, as if carried away by the sea—is scarcely more than a hundred years old. The earliest literary usage thus reported occurs in *The Autobiography of a Beggar Boy* (1855) by James D. Burn: "Every instinct and feeling of humanity goes by the board."

to leave no stone unturned

To use every expedient at one's command. Some say that this was the reply given by the Delphic oracle when Polycrates, the

Theban general, asked for aid in discovering the treasures said to have been buried by the slain leader of the defeated Persian army, Mardonius, before the battle of Plataea, 479 B.C. Actually, according to the historian Herodotus, the answer of the oracle is usually translated, "to leave no stone unturned," by which was meant, "to move all things." The English saying arose sometime in the first half of the sixteenth century and could have been common before that to indicate any exhaustive search, as for some valued object lost in the destruction of a baronial hall or the like. The earliest mention in print is in *A Manifest Detection of the Most Vyle and Detestable Use of Dice-play* (c. 1550): "He wil refuse no labor nor leaue no stone vnturned, to pick vp a penny." Probably this was at first a variation of the older "to leave no straw unturned," which, with the straw-littered and dust-covered floors of the Middle Ages, meant an even more exhaustive search than among stones.

talking to one like a Dutch uncle

In *A Hog on Ice* I expressed the opinion that the concept of a severe reprimand from an uncle of Dutch ancestry appeared to be American. Though I have nothing to offer to contradict that opinion, I have run across literary instances which indicate that the original of such an uncle was Roman. The poet Horace, that is, living in the first century B.C., twice referred to the tongue-lashings of an uncle. In the *Satires,* II, 3, is the line, *Ne sis patruus mihi,* which may be translated, "Do not play the uncle over me," and in the later *Odes,* III, 12, is the more positive, *Metuentes patruæ verbera linguæ,* "Fearing the tongue-lashings of an uncle."

baby-kisser

An aspirant for public office who attempts to win the favor of parents by a show of affection toward their children. Probably the Greeks and Romans had a word for this also, for the politicians of ancient days certainly practiced all the other arts known to modern office-seekers. Especially in Rome in the time of the republic. Here the *ambitor,* literally he who went around (seeking votes), resorted to every known expedient of that day to influence voters in his favor, even in the face of stringent laws against bribery and corruption, so if the kissing of babies and the patting of small boys on the head would ingratiate him, he could not have missed such a chance. The first application of the American term appears to have been in the presidential campaign of 1884 when General Benjamin F. Butler, disaffected with the Democratic nomination of Grover Cleveland, ran on an independent Greenback-Labor ticket. In the election, however, against Cleveland, Democrat, and Blaine, Republican, Butler was an also-ran. As the Cincinnati *Times-Star* put it, "As a baby-kisser, Ben Butler is not a success."

all quiet on the Potomac

Peaceful; undisturbed; a time of ease or quiet enjoyment: from the frequent repetition of the phrase in bulletins issued during the War between the States, 1861–1865. The original expression has been ascribed to General George B. McClellan (1826–85), who was in command of the Army of the Potomac in 1861 and 1862, but who received much criticism in Washington because of alleged dilatory policies and lack of aggressiveness. The phrase sometimes appears as "all quiet *along* the Potomac," from the poem, "The Picket Guard" (1861), by Ethel Lynn Beers, the sixth stanza of which is—

> All quiet along the Potomac tonight,
>   No sound save the rush of the river,
> While soft falls the dew on the face of the dead—
>   The picket's off duty forever.

to get ahead, to be ahead (of the game), to come out ahead

We, in America, use the first expression in two differing ways. Thus when we say, "Jeff is getting ahead in the store he has recently opened," we mean that Jeff is prospering, is on the way toward a successful venture. But when we say, "Maggie Jones has thought up a new scheme to get ahead of conceited Mary Smith," we mean that Maggie is contriving to surpass, or outdo, or outwit Madam Smith.

"To be ahead" and "to come out ahead" also carry the thought of financial gain, of having more than one started with, the converse of "to be behind." Such is the meaning in "He was ahead on the deal with Aaron, but he got behind when he began to trade with Simon." This idiom is often expanded into "to be ahead of the game," because business transactions so often present the aspects of gambling; as, "When I sold the business I was twenty thousand dollars ahead of the game." And when we say, "The women came out ahead on the church bazaar," we mean that they did well, or at least that the financial gain was greater than the cost.

to give the air to (a person)

To tie the can to; to fire; to dismiss; to discharge from employment; literally, to put out of doors. A British counterpart of this modern American slang is "to give one the sack" (see *A Hog on Ice*). The expression also has a negative meaning in the language of love. When Joan gives the air to John, she terminates a courtship by giving John to understand definitely and unmistakably that his attentions are unwanted, or she breaks off an acquaintance before John can begin to get romantic notions.

eager beaver

A person who is always "rarin' to go," eager to start at whatever is to be done. Undoubtedly the term developed naturally from one who "works like a beaver," one who works rapidly and assiduously. It bears no relation to the "beaver" or full beard worn by some men. This latter term was transferred from ancient helmets, from the movable part of the helmet covering the chin, called "beaver" from Old French *bavière,* a bib. Let me add, before I'm accused of missing a point, that the modern "eager beaver" is usually so overly zealous as to attempt duties that do not concern him, and thus he becomes an obnoxious character, one thoroughly disliked by his associates.

HORSEFEATHERS

and Other Curious Words

To B. M. F. and A. G. F.

FOREWORD

No, this book does not pertain to slang terminology, though, undoubtedly, some of the words discussed herein did originate as  slang. The title arose from a bit of information I stumbled upon some ten years ago when the old Vermont farmhouse we occupy during the summer months was about to undergo a face-lifting operation. The clapboards, after many, many years of unpainted exposure to sun, rain, hail, sleet, snow, and wind, were adhering to the structure apparently only through force of habit. An aged master carpenter to whom I appealed for advice said, "Well, seems if 'bout the only thing ye kin do is to rip off all them clabbuds. If they wa'n't so old an' curled up, ye moight put horsefeathers over 'em, and then cover yer hoose with asphalt shingles, but it's too late for that."

"Horsefeathers," I learned from him and other old-timers of New England and New York in the building trade, refers to rows of clapboards laid with the butt edges against the butt edges of shingles or clapboards so as to provide a flat surface over which asphalt or other shingles or siding may be laid. Subsequently I sought verification from the National Board of Fire Underwriters. This is the answer, in part, from its Chief Engineer, Mr. J. A. Neale:

723

We cannot document the following but some of our men who have been interested in building construction and building codes over the years remember its past use.

It refers, as indicated in your letter, to the tapered boards laid on wood shingle roofs to provide a flat surface for asphalt shingles to be laid on in re-roofing. The term "feathering strips," meaning the same thing, is found in some roofing manuals.

The term "horsefeathers" is used colloquially in New England and New York. Its use other than in the slang sense is disappearing and it is only the old-timers who now understand it.

Regrettably, neither the age of this legitimate, though trade, usage nor that of the slang usage can be determined. No printed record of the trade usage has been found, but the old-timers with whom I have talked, men in their seventies at least, say they knew its use forty or fifty years ago. And it may be older. Printed record of the slang usage—in senses equivalent to "bosh," "stuff and nonsense," "hogwash," "tommyrot," "applesauce," or, in ejaculation, "Heavens to Betsy!"—is also undated as to birth, but, to the best of my recollection, did not occur before 1925 or thereabouts. It is my belief, therefore, that some bright chap heard the term used by an upstate builder, cleverly told the tale in a New York speakeasy of the period, and that "Horsefeathers!" was then picked up by doubting Thomases and used thereafter to greet any incredible statement.

Why apply the term to ordinary feathering strips? That can't be determined. Perhaps the successive layers of new wood reminded one at a distance of the feathers on the wings of a chicken, except as to size. Relatively, then, they were feathers fit for a horse.

The parentage of the great bulk of all the words that we use in our speech or see upon the printed page is, in general, adequately explained in any dictionary that carries word derivations. One need know no more about the word "include," for instance, than that its source was the Latin preposition *in* and verb *claudere*, "to close," hence "to nclose," or about "liberty" than that it derives from Latin *liber*, "free," or about "speak" than that it comes from an Old English (Anglo-Saxon) word, *specan*. Such brief explanations, giving the Greek, Latin, French, Germanic, or like sources,

724

suffice for thousands of words. It would be, to use a sesquipedalian erudite term of my youth, a work of supererogation, a superfluous act, to carry those explanations further.

The words discussed in this book are, accordingly, mainly those that piqued my own curiosity in younger days, terms usually left unexplained or but partly explained even in unabridged dictionaries. Why, for example, is a common tall roadside weed known in some parts of the country as a joe-pye weed? Why is butterscotch so named? Or belladonna? How did the nuthatch get its name? Or that insect, the earwig? Why is a certain Southern comestible called hush-puppy? How did it happen that, in a fireplace, the log supports became known as andirons or, sometimes, firedogs? There are hundreds of such peculiar terms, terms that appear to be compounds, though they are not always so.

And there are also other hundreds of words for which, for lack of space, the usual dictionary of household size can supply no more than the skeleton of the story accounting for them. We are told, for instance, that our word *arctic* is from a Greek word meaning "a bear," but the connection with the north polar region may be left to the imagination. We see by the morning's paper that So-and-so "has entered the arena of politics." The dictionary tells us that Latin *arena* meant "sand." How did the sense become transformed? *Grotesque,* we may learn, came from the same Italian source as "grotto," a cave or cavern. How did it then acquire so diverse a meaning as "incongruous, ridiculous, fantastic, monstrous"?

The serious purpose of this book is, then, to supplement the dictionary, to fill gaps where filling seems to be warranted and to supply explanations for many of the curious words the significance of which is not evident from the parts that compose them. But as I do not think that a reference work need be a dry-as-dust compilation; it has been my aim to provide a little fillip of entertainment here and there, to indulge in fancy—which I hope is always plainly labeled as such—when there is no clue to the original source of a word or term.

I am indebted, of course, to all recent dictionaries, abridged and unabridged; especially to the *Oxford English Dictionary* and its *Supplement,* to Wyld's *Universal Dictionary* for its excellent etymological treatment, and to Mathews' *Dictionary of Americanisms*. The works consulted in the preparation of material, however, are legion, embracing about every book on my shelves and including books of special nature, such as those on common plant names, borrowed from university libraries. Despite precaution, however, I have little doubt that I have gone astray from time to time in statement or in surmise. I shall welcome correction.

ADDENDUM TO FOREWORD

After having lived a full and, on the whole, happy life, my father died suddenly, as he would have wished, on April 16, 1957. He had just passed his seventy-sixth birthday less than two weeks previously.

At the time of his death, he had been working on the manuscript of this, his final work on the study of the origins and histories of English words and phrases, for upwards of a year, and had completed approximately 70 per cent of the task he had set himself. *Task,* though, is not the word to use, for he loved the study of words and took keen pleasure in successfully tracing an obscure use or etymology to its ultimate source. He also immensely enjoyed passing on to others the knowledge of those things that his research turned up. I can distinctly recall his surprise when he found that I, a chemical librarian, knew what horsefeathers were, without having to consult any reference, for my knowing the term took the edge off the story he was about to relate and which he has told here in his foreword. (The reason for my foreknowledge of this lies in the fact that I am among the legion of do-it-yourselfers. I had just recently re-roofed my house by laying asphalt shingles over the original wooden shingles and, on consulting *my* expert before the job was started, had been told that the practice of using horsefeathers, once common, had been pretty well abandoned in my locality. An explanation of what constituted horsefeathers had, of course, followed.)

(Incidentally, lest it occur to some reader that the original name for these feathering strips might have been *house*feathers, later corrupted through mispronunciation to *horse*feathers, let me point out to him in advance that this possibility has been explored. No substantiation for such a theory has been found.)

The interest that my father's stories aroused, as demonstrated by the success of his earlier books, led me to undertake to complete the present work along the lines he had begun. He had prepared a list of the words he planned to choose from in compiling the present group of tales, and I have generally based my selections on this list, as he had done. For the record, that part of the book covering the alphabet through *P* is, for the most part, my father's work. My contribution to this first part consists only of minor editing of his rough draft plus the addition of a few entries on which his research had been incomplete at the time of his death (*cuspidor, kangaroo court, Paris green*). That part of the book covering the alphabet from *Q* on is, for the most part, my work based on his list. My father had not conducted his search strictly in alphabetical order, though, and a few of the entries in the latter part of the alphabet are his (*starboard, sub rosa, tadpole, thank-ye-ma'am, thimblerig, thoroughfare*).

Like him, I have leaned heavily on the *Oxford English Dictionary* and on the *Dictionary of Americanisms* as primary reference tools, but to enumerate and acknowledge separately all of the works consulted would, in effect, constitute a catalogue of both his and my own libraries, and even so would be incomplete. Blanket acknowledgment is hereby tendered to all my sources of information, with grateful thanks.

HORSEFEATHERS

and Other Curious Words

stirrup cup

The Anglo-Saxon word which has become *stirrup* was *stigrap,* and if this were to be literally translated into modern English, it would become *"sty-rope"* or "climbing-rope." The Anglo-Saxon word is composed of the root *stig-,* from *stigan,* "to climb" (see under **steward** for *sty,* "to climb"), plus *rap,* "rope." This leads us to the conclusion that the first stirrups were merely short lengths of ropes thrown over the back of the steed, and having loops tied in either end. But the *stirrup cup* had nothing to do, either then or later, with any resemblance of these loops to cups. Instead, it could be translated today as "one for the road," for it was the cup of wine or other refreshment offered to the traveler who, having mounted, was in the stirrups and ready to take off upon a journey.

hoity-toity

Nowadays one rarely hears this except as an expression of surprise coupled with annoyance or indignation, usually uttered by a precise elderly person in condemnation of the behavior of a niece or granddaughter. And that reflects its source, for *hoity* at one time—some three centuries ago—described a person who indulged in *hoiting,* an obsolete word, but meaning "acting like a *hoyden.*" The *toity* was added just for rhyme, as *scurry* to rhyme with *hurry* in *hurry-scurry.* The variant exclamation *highty-tighty* arose through mispronunciation, from the same change in vowel sound that, in the seventeenth century, caused *oil* to be pronounced "ile"; *boil,* "bile"; *join,* "jine," etc.

cucking stool

Often confused with the later and much less immodest *ducking stool*. The earlier device dates back, in England, at least to the eleventh century and was sometimes disguised under the Latin *cathedra stercoris* of the same meaning. When used, as it generally was, for the punishment of viragoes, and perhaps then modified in form, it was often merely called a *scolding stool*. Actually the *cucking stool* was a crudely constructed commode, upon which the culprit was securely fastened and exposed to the jeers of the towns-people for such length of time as the magistrate might determine. The punishment might be meted out also to dishonest bakers or other tradesmen. (See also **ducking stool.**)

mushroom

Another beautiful example of what will happen to an English-man's attempt to pronounce a foreign word. Nothing whatsoever of *mush* in it, nor of *room*. It was, in the fifteenth century, a poor English rendition of the Old French *moisseron,* modern *mousseron.* Some then spelled it, and probably pronounced it, *muscheron,* and in following years at least a score of other forms appeared. But before the French name was introduced, the fungus had the far more descriptive name, *toad's hat.* If only that name were still in use we might now use that for the edible fungus and *toadstool* for the inedible.

steward

Authorities are in general agreement that *steward* is a descendant of the Anglo-Saxon *stigweard,* a combination of *stig,* "sty," and *weard,* "ward, keeper." However, they are quick to point out that it should not be inferred that this proves that the exalted position of steward, as major-domo, arose from such humble beginnings as the keeper of the pigsty. *Sty* is an old, old word, and its relatives are to be found in many, if not all, of the Teutonic family of languages, with a number of meanings, quite dissimilar. Even in English there have been such different meanings as "a path," "a ladder, or stair," and a verb sense, "to climb," as well as the common meaning today, "a pigpen." Skeat, in his *Etymological Dictionary of the English Language,* seems to have resolved the matter very prettily in saying, for steward, "The original sense was one who looked after the domestic animals, and gave them their food; hence, one who provides for his master's table, and generally, one who superintends household affairs for another." The key phrase is "one who provides for his master's table." This, far from being a menial task, has assuredly always been an important one, and it would be only natural that such a trusted servant would be given the greater responsibility of looking after the household in all other respects, too.

proud flesh

It is *proud* only by virtue of being swollen, as if by pride. In the same sense, we speak of grain which, by luxurious growth, is unseasonably *proud,* swollen beyond the normal stage of advancement.

stevedore

The Spanish, at one time the rulers of the seas, have left their contributions to seafaring terms, and one of these is *stevedore.* It is derived from the Spanish noun of agency *estivador,* "one who stows cargo," of which the corresponding verb form is *estivar,* "to stow cargo." From the same source is the English verb, now little used, *to steeve,* "to pack tightly." A further derivation takes us to the Latin *stipare*, "to press closely together."

cubbyhole

One might suppose that this had developed from the hole or den in which the young of the bear or fox may be found, but no. In rural parts of England one may still find places where *cub* means the shed or pen or stall for cattle, or the coop for chickens, or the hutch for rabbits, or even a monk's cell. It is a term, that is, for any small shelter. The diminutive, used chiefly by children referring to any small retreat of their own, is *cubby,* frequently extended to *cubbyhole.*

Amazon

To speak of a woman as an Amazon is to imply that she is physically well proportioned, but large—above average in height  and figure. The term was first applied by the ancient Greeks to a tribe of warlike women who dwelt along the shores of the Black Sea and in the Caucasus mountains. Men were barred from the state, the ladies devoting themselves to fighting the Greeks, according to anecdotes related by professional storytellers of old. They also said that the name meant "without a breast," from a belief that each Amazon had had her right breast removed that it might not interfere with the use of javelin and bow. That derivation is regarded as doubtful nowadays. The Amazon river in South America was so named by the early Spanish explorer Orellana, who, in descending the river in 1541, battled with a tribe of Tapuya Indians whose women fought alongside the men.

hornswoggle

Nothing much can be said about this peculiarly American substitute for bamboozle, cheat, defraud, hoax, swindle. It was, apparently, a Kentucky coinage of the early nineteenth century, a period in which frontiersmen, especially, attempted to outvie one another in the creation of extravagant, highfalutin speech. Not much of it survived, so it is to the credit of the unknown hero who coined *hornswoggle*, based on heaven knows what, that it not only lived, but ultimately found its way into our dictionaries.

stereoscope

Over the space of many years, inventors and would-be inventors have been trying various means of making pictures more and more true to life. One avenue has been in portraying action, another has been in portraying solidity, that is, the reproduction or viewing of pictures in such a way that the pictures seem to be three-dimensional. The first to achieve some measure of success in this latter undertaking was Sir Charles Wheatstone, a nineteenth-century English physicist. Although it remained for a later scientist to perfect the device, yet it was Sir Charles himself who coined its name in 1838. *Stereoscope* is a compound from two Greek roots, the first, *stereos,* meaning "solid," the second, *scopein,* meaning "to look at." Adding these together, we get "solid to look at," or, more truthfully, "when looked at, seems to be solid."

crowbar

As said of various other words, some of our remote ancestors must have possessed wonderful gifts of imagination. Someone, about six hundred years ago, discovered that if the end of the ordinary iron prize or prise were sharpened to a point or beak, its use as a lever would be more effective. Someone then likened that beak to the neb or beak of a crow—and *crow* then became the name of such a tool, especially of one curved or bent toward its wedge-shaped end. The addition of the *bar* was notice to steel-makers, several centuries later, that the desired *crow* must be a straight rod.

tyro

To the Romans, an ordinary soldier was *miles* (pronounced *mee-less*), from *mille,* which literally means "a thousand" but in the figurative sense means "a great many, a horde." The new recruit, to distinguish him from the seasoned campaigner, was a *tiro* (plural, *tirones*). In Medieval Latin, the words were often spelled *tyro, tyrones,* and it is with this spelling that the word is most often used in English, although the spelling *tiro,* which may be preferable on an etymological basis, is sometimes used. The English plural, incidentally, is *tyros* or *tiros,* and the word has come to have the extended meaning of "a novice in any field, a greenhorn."

grubstreet

It refers nowadays to a literary hack who, for needed money, will turn out an article or even a speech on whatever subject he may have a call. But the designation actually alludes to a street in London formerly bearing that name, since 1830 called "Milton Street," which from the early seventeenth century was, as Dr. Johnson said, "much inhabited by writers of small histories, dictionaries, and temporary poems." The description might apply to Johnson himself, forced into literary drudgery for many years after reaching London merely to obtain "grub."

stenography

By no means the invention of John Robert Gregg, nor even of his predecessor, Sir Isaac Pitman, stenography was an art known many centuries before either of these men walked the earth. As an English word, *stenography* has been recorded as early as 1602. It is derived from two Greek words, *stenos,* "narrow," and *graphein,* "to write," thus, literally, it is "narrow writing" as opposed to the "broad writing" that is the more ordinary script. Even *shorthand* is only slightly younger as a synonym for stenography—it has been in use since at least 1636 as a substitute for the now obsolete older word *short-writing* of the same meaning. This latter is an Anglicization of the still older word *brachygraphy,* the first part of which is from the Greek *brachus,* "short." *Brachygraphy* has been found in English as early as 1590 and is not yet wholly obsolete, although, I'm sure to the satisfaction of today's secretaries, it is only rarely encountered. Actually, of course, stenography, call it what you will, is of much greater age than even these word histories would indicate. It is known to have been practiced in the Roman Senate and there is some evidence that it was practiced by the ancient Greeks before the time of Christ. However, it is known that modern shorthand systems originated in England about the close of the sixteenth century.

aroint

"Aroynt thee, Witch, the rumpe-fed Ronyon cryes," is the way Shakespeare wrote it in *Macbeth* (Act I, Scene iii), and here, as well as in *King Lear* (Act III, Scene iv), his obvious meaning was "Begone! Get out! Scram!" but the source of his term may never

736

be known. No earlier instance of use has been turned up. Nor do we know positively what he meant by a *ronyon,* which, in *Merry Wives of Windsor* (Act IV, Scene ii), he spelled *runnion.* Dr. Samuel Johnson, in his dictionary of 1755, defined the latter spelling as "a mangy creature," but defined *ronion* as "a fat bulky woman." You may take your pick. *Rump,* of course, pertains to the posterior of an animal.

pot-walloper

A term gradually falling from repute. In its original form, *pot-waller,* in the early eighteenth century, it designated an Englishman who, by virtue of having his own pot to boil (to *wall,* in the speech still current then), was entitled to vote in a parliamentary election. An early alteration of *potwaller* was *pot-walloper.* For a hundred years it carried the same meaning. But then one who boiled a pot was thought, by some, to be in a demeaning occupation and, accordingly *pot-walloper* became a term of contempt, indicating one with the mind or ability of a scullion.

crosspatch

Back in the fifteenth century the jester or fool attached to the retinue of prominent persons was sometimes referred to as a *patch,* probably because his costume was often "a thing of shreds and patches." And whether or not this term was applied to him only when he was ill tempered is not now known, but such was the case by the end of the sixteenth century, and so it remained for another hundred years, though other than court fools were included. It was then, for additional force, that some genius made assurance doubly sure and labeled a person of ill-nature a *cross-patch.*

hopscotch

Back in the seventeenth century this children's game was called *scotch-hoppers,* which appears to be the earliest English name, although one writer says that the game itself probably "dates back to the beginning of the Christian era." But the "scotch" part of the name is in nowise related to the country of Scotland nor to its people. A giveaway to its real meaning is that in some English shires the game is called *hop-score,* for the lines marking the squares to be hopped are scored or *scotched* in the ground. Compare **butterscotch.**

Annie Oakley

She was born in Ohio in 1860; her full name, Phoebe Anne Oakley Mozee. At the age of sixteen she married Frank Butler, a vaudeville actor, and became a superb marksman; her skill, it was said, was such that by 1,000 shots with a rifle on one occasion she broke 942 glass balls tossed in the air. Touring with Buffalo Bill's Wild West Show in the 1880's and 1890's, she would demonstrate her marksmanship by successively centering shots through the pips of a playing card, usually the five of hearts. Through this feat her name became synonymous with a complimentary pass to a show, which, formerly, was a ticket punched by the manager when issued, not unlike the card perforated by Annie's shots. She died in 1926.

quagmire

He who ventures into a new undertaking, seemingly sound, only to find himself inextricably entangled in a hopeless mess, has become quagmired, bogged down, on shaky ground. The last term here is a nearly literal equivalent of the first, as *quag* seems certainly to be a variant of *quake,* "to shake," and *mire* is "muddy or swampy ground." Thus a quagmire is a piece of ground that looks firm, but shakes when walked upon, only to engulf the traveler. An obsolete form is *quickmire,* and the relation to *quicksand,* which has much the same treacherous properties, immediately comes to mind.

ducking stool

More modest than the *cucking stool* (which see), though still an unpleasant device for the punishment of scolds, prostitutes, or women judged guilty of witchcraft. It replaced the older device during the sixteenth century, though the older term was then sometimes used for it, and was still in use until the early nineteenth century. The device consisted of a chair, in which the culprit was secured, mounted at one end of a seesaw at the edge of a pond or stream. Those operating the other end of this seesaw could determine the number of times the culprit was ducked or dipped and the length of each immersion. The victim sometimes died, either from shock or drowning. In a similar device, a *ducking tumbrel,* the chair could be rolled into the water.

steadfast

"Guarding the town." Not exactly what most of us think of today in connection with *steadfast,* but etymologically speaking, this comes close to the original meaning. For *stead,* from the Anglo-Saxon *stede,* is closely related to the Dutch *stad,* "town," and *stede,* "place"; and to the German *Stadt,* "town," and *Statt,* "place." Words with similar spelling and meaning exist in most languages of Teutonic origin, and all stem back to a common ancestor, the Sanskrit *sthiti,* "standing, position." The Greek *stasis,* "standing, stoppage," and the Latin *statio,* "station," are from the same origin. *Fast,* in the meaning of "firm," comes from the Anglo-Saxon *fæst,* and it, too, has close relatives in many languages of Teutonic origin such as the German *fest,* "firm." The common origin of these seems to be the Old Teutonic root *fastu-,* "to keep, guard, observe." The Anglo-Saxon combination of these, *stedefæst,* "fixed in position," dates to the tenth century, and is the direct precursor of our modern *steadfast,* "steady, unchanging."

tympany

Used, today, as a collective noun to designate the aggregation of kettledrums in an orchestra, this word is actually the Anglicized form of the Latin *tympanum,* "a drum," from the Greek *tympanon,* "a drum," from *typtein,* "to strike, beat." The Latin word has also been taken directly into English with the original spelling preserved, in the same meaning, and there also exists a much older Anglicized form, *tympan,* which may have come through the Old French *tympan* rather than directly from the Latin. It seems probable that the modern use of *tympany* may have arisen from the mistaken belief that this spelling, or at least the pronunciation thereof, represented the plural of *tympanum* (i.e, as though the Latin plural were *tympani*), whereas its true plural is *tympana.*

Prince Albert

The prince himself was English, eldest son of Queen Victoria, ultimately reigning as King Edward VII. As prince, he traveled extensively, first visiting the United States in 1860. Social leaders were then greatly impressed by the long double-breasted frock coat worn by the prince at afternoon occasions and promptly adopted it, calling it a *Prince Albert* or *Prince Albert coat.*

arena

Thanks to the fact that the citizens of ancient Rome liked to see gory contests—gladiators fighting one another to the death,

 starved wild animals turned loose upon human victims—the ground of the amphitheaters was always liberally covered with sand to soak up spilled blood. And the Latin word for sand is *arena.* Nowadays an "arena" may never know blood, it may never see sand; it merely denotes a scene of contest—physical, mental, or even figurative.

starling

The Latin word for starling, and still the scientific name for the genus of which starlings are members, was *Sturnus.* This word, with the usual changes in spelling and pronunciation, became

740

adopted into one after another of most of the European languages, finally reaching the Anglo-Saxon as *stær,* from which it became, in Middle English, *stare.* This name for the starling, although rare for many years, has still been in limited use as late as the early part of this century. However, it was over nine hundred years ago that someone applied to the stare the affectionate diminutive suffix that has become, in modern form, *-ling,* the original combination having had the form *stærlinc.* And it was this combination that has become our familiar *starling.*

hogwash

This is not slang, nor is it a recent coinage. Five hundred years ago it was the common term for the swill fed to swine. And, curiously enough, the earliest instance of its use traced by the *Oxford English Dictionary,* dated about 1440, reads "They in the kechyn, for iape, pouryd on here hefd hoggyswasch" (They in the kitchen, for jest, poured hogwash on her head). Some joke! In figurative contemptuous usage the term dates to the early eighteenth century.

star-chamber

Somewhat over five hundred years ago, the royal palace at Westminster contained an apartment which, it is presumed, was decorated with gilt stars upon the ceiling. By virtue of its decoration, the room became known as the *Starred* or *Star Chamber.* It was the practice of the reigning monarchs to hold special high courts of jurisdiction in this room—courts on which the king's council sat as judges, and from which there was no appeal. It is good politics, of course, for the king's counselors to play along with the wishes of their sovereign, and the natural result was that this special court came to be used by the king for the exercise of tyranny. The flagrant misuse of the power of the court became so great during the rule of James I and that of Charles I that, in 1641, the court was abolished by Act of Parliament. But the notoriety of the court had become such that the phrase *star-chamber court,* or just *star-chamber,* was applied to any trial proceedings in which the defendant could expect nothing better than arbitrary and oppressive treatment, and in this sense the term continues to live today.

hoosegow

We changed the spelling most decidedly, but that was done only to preserve the American idea of a phonetic pronunciation— spelled as sounded to an American ear. That is, the Mexican term is *juzgao,* derived from Spanish *juzgado,* a tribunal. But to the ordinary Mexican the term means a jail, and that is the meaning given also to the American term. Literary use did not appear, or has not been traced, before 1920, but I am certain it was in collcquial Western speech a dozen or more years earlier.

dragonfly

So called because if a Walt Disney were to magnify this insect to airplane size it would be as fearsome a creature as any dragon slain by St. George: huge eyes; long, slender, glittering body of variegated hues; two pairs of large wings; and extremely strong jaws. And there's little doubt but that to the insect world upon which it feeds voraciously it is as dread as any dragon that walked the earth or flew above it. Another common name for this insect is *devil's-darning-needle* (which see). The scientific name of the genus is *Libellula,* "little book," fancifully conceived because the wings at rest remain partly open, resembling the leaves of a booklet.

twilight

The prefix *twi-* almost invariably has the meaning of *two,* in the sense of twice, or double, the nature of the suffix. This is certainly not the meaning here, yet it is a little difficult to trace the reason for the origin of the use of the prefix in this combination. One possibility is that the *two* meaning is that of *in two,* that is, half, rather than double. A second is that *twilight* may be a corruption of *'tweenlight,* in the sense of "between light and dark." This last may have occurred not in English, but first in German, for there was a Middle High German word *zwischenliecht,* from *zwischen,* "be-

742

tween," and *liecht,* "light," whereas modern German has *Zwielicht.* *Zwie,* here, could be a contraction of *zwischen,* and, since it usually has the value of *two* in a compound term, could have been translated literally into English as *twilight* rather than as *'tweenlight,* which would have been more accurate.

starboard

It has no reference to stars at all, but probably few sailors, even, know why this designates the right side of a vessel. Its origin takes us back to the early ships of the Norse and other Teutonic people. Though, with favoring winds, those vessels were driven by sails, they were steered, not by rudders from the rear, but by a paddle (*bord,* "board, paddle") over the right side. It was the "steering paddle, or board." In Old English, *steorbord;* whence, "starboard."

crawfish, crayfish

Either way you say it, American with *w* or British with *y,* the name is derived from Old French *crevice* or *crevisse,* meaning "crab," a term that then covered almost any of the larger crustaceans. And because of the propensity of the critter to navigate rearward, we have made a verb of the term, using it figuratively to indicate an attempt, usually conspicuous, to withdraw oneself from a stand or a commitment that has become undesirable.

oyez

Although pronounced "oh yes," it has no further tie with those two words. It was an Old French addition to the law courts of England after the Norman conquest. In the French of the period it was written *oiez,* from the verb *oir,* "to hear." Used by the court crier at the opening of the court, or by an officer calling for attention to a proclamation, it meant, "Hear ye! Hear! Hear!"

preface

"*Peter Rice eats fish and catches eels,*" was the favorite acrostic carefully lettered above PREFACE in all schoolbooks in my gen-

743

eration. This, of course, had then to be reversed by some bright spirit and, on the lower edge, we read, "*Eels catch alligators; fish eat raw potatoes.*" But the term itself is merely from the Latin *praefatio,* "a saying beforehand."

Argyll socks (sox)

Perhaps originally, ten or fifteen years ago, the American woman who first knitted a pair of these socks for husband, son,

or sweetheart did follow the traditional plaid pattern of the clan of Campbell of Argyll—light green crossed with dark green, and narrow independent cross lines of white. If so, though the name was retained by followers who adopted the idea, the plaid speedily lost all resemblance to that claimed by the Scottish clan. The Argyll sock of today's American, whether home knitted or machine produced, has become a variegated plaid affair of bright colors.

standpatter

The voluminous and authoritative *Oxford English Dictionary* offers 104 meanings of the verb *to stand,* alone and in combinations. Of these, the thirteenth reads:

Card-playing. To be willing, or announce one's willingness, to play with one's hand as dealt. Opposed to *pass.*

The same source gives three meanings of the adverb-adjective *pat.* The third, in part:

Exactly suitable or to the purpose.

Combination of these led to the verbal phrase *to stand pat,* which, incidentally, is the fourteenth meaning given for *to stand.* The phrase was coined by a poker player, and it meant, "to *stand* (that is, to play without drawing) with a hand that is *pat* (one not apt to be improved by drawing)." But then followed the almost inevitable extension of meaning into a nonspecialized sense, and

744

to stand pat came to be used, especially in politics, to denote the inactivity of a man who accepted the existing situation, not trying to improve it but at the same time doing nothing that would worsen it. Such a person, eventually, came to be known as a *standpatter,* a conservative.

hoodlum

The country is indebted to some unknown and unheralded genius in San Francisco for this underworld character. Time: about 1870. Attempts to trace the source of the word have persisted almost ever since, but without success. The first theory, advanced by Bartlett in 1877 on the strength of hearsay evidence, described it as an accidental coinage of a reporter assisted by his paper's compositor. A gang of ruffians, the story was, was under the leadership of one Muldoon. Fearing reprisals, the reporter spelled the name backward—*Noodlum.* Poor writing led the compositor to mistake the initial *N* for *H;* hence, *Hoodlum.* This account is still often circulated, though there is nothing factual to back it. Barère and Leland, in their *Dictionary of Slang* (1889), though admitting uncertainty, thought the word may have been derived from Pidgin English *hood lahnt,* "very lazy mandarin," because of the many Chinese in San Francisco, but they exited gracefully from that poor guess through the preface that the word was "probably of Spanish origin." The latest theory, and the most tenable in my opinion, was advanced by Dr. J. T. Krumpelmann in 1935 in *Modern Language Notes.* On the basis of the large percentage of Germans, many of them Bavarians, in San Francisco in the sixties and seventies, he thought it probable that *hoodlum* was nothing more than a slight mispronunciation of the dialectal Bavarian *hodalump* of identical meaning.

turtledove

The Romans listened to them coo, then named them in imitation of the sound they made, *turtur.* And this is the name that was taken directly into Anglo-Saxon before the time of the Norman Conquest. But in Old High German, the final *r*-sound was converted to an *l*-sound, giving *turtulo* for the male, *turtula* for the female, and these forms were separately adopted into Anglo-Saxon as *turtla* and *turtle*, respectively. The two were later combined into *turtle*, regardless of sex, and this name eventually superseded the former *turtur* entirely. It was several hundred years later that the second element of the name was added, and the addition was really redundant, for a *turtle* was a dove and nothing else. Several hundred years more passed by (bringing us to the mid-seventeenth century) before the word *turtle* was applied, from an entirely different derivation, to the marine tortoise.

grotesque

Paintings discovered on the walls of the Baths of Titus, excavated by archaeologists in the sixteenth century, gave us our word "antic" through the Italian *antica,* "antique." But, though the learned world thus attributed the paintings to the ancients, the general public was more impressed by the finding of them in the excavated chambers, or *grotte,* of ancient buildings, and, therefore, called them *grotesca.* Any kind of comic distortion or unnatural exaggeration at all akin to the figures in these old Roman murals then became *grotesca,* a term that, through French influence, evolved into English *grotesque.*

stalemate

Originally, the term was just *stale*—the *mate* part was added, possibly originally in jest, because a stalemate, like a checkmate, serves to end the game. Unlike *checkmate,* and *chess* itself, both of which come from Arabic, *stale* seems to have originated in the French *estaler* (*étaler*), one of the meanings of which is "to fix," in the sense of "to set in place." The latter is related to the German *stellen,* "to place," which, in turn, has been traced to the Teutonic *stal,* "a fixed place."

craps

The book *Sucker's Progress* (1938), by Herbert Asbury, tells the entire story in half a dozen pages or so, but in brief the original

746

game was a simplified form of the old game of hazard. In that game, *crabs* was the lowest throw. When hazard moved into France its name became *crabs* or *craps,* and it was the latter name by which the game became known in New Orleans, where it was introduced about 1840. Needless to add, the game did not remain confined to New Orleans. Within fifty years it became highly popular and has remained so, especially among Negroes, among whom it is often called "African golf" or "African dominoes."

potter's field

The original was a piece of ground outside Jerusalem bought by the chief priests with the thirty pieces of silver which, according to Matthew 27: 7, had been given to Judas for the betrayal of Jesus and which he later returned. The field was then set aside for the burial of strangers and the poor. The supposition is that the clay used by potters had formerly been obtained in this field.

attic

Yes, odd as it may appear, that portion of our homes that lies between the roof and the ceiling of the uppermost rooms which

we call "the attic" is derived from *Attica,* the country of ancient Greece of which Athens was the chief city. The architecture of the country was outstanding, the name, thus, being applied to various characteristic structural types. One such, conspicuous chiefly in structures of large design, included a low story above the main cornice, originally set off, on the façade, by short pilasters above the main pillars. Though the decorative effect was later omitted, the name *attic* was still applied to the low space, eventually also to any garret.

artesian

Centuries ago—some authorities place the date definitely as the year 1126, and others merely vaguely as recent as "about

1750"—an unknown genius bored a well in the region of France now known as Artois. By accident or design he hit upon a geological formation where a tilted porous stratum lay between two tilted impervious strata, and, in consequence, water was forced by natural pressure above the surface of the boring. But anything or anyone native to the province of Artois is, from its ancient name, *Artesien,* in French; transformed in English to *artesian.*

cockroach

Captain John Smith described this unattractive insect in 1624: "A certaine India Bug, called by the Spaniards a Cacarootch, the which creeping into Chests they eat and defile with their ill-sented dung." The Spanish name, however, is *cucaracha,* which the English, with usual disregard for foreign languages, converted to *cockroach.*

German measles

Though the existing amenities between nations may cause a German to name something unpleasant as *französisch,* a Frenchman to name the same thing as *anglais,* and an Englishman to call it *German,* the name of this ailment honors, rather than derogates, its specification. The disease was identified, that is, by the German physician Friedrich Hoffmann in 1740. Hence called, by some, *German measles.* Another name, sometimes used for the same disease, is *French measles.* This, it has been said, is in commemoration of the French physician De Bergen, who has been credited with making additional discoveries concerning the disease in 1752, but I have not been able to verify this, nor even to discover De Bergen's full name.

slowpoke

Of the many different meanings for the word *poke,* one, an Americanism dating to about 1860, is "a lazy person, a dawdler." The origin of this meaning is easily traced to the British use of the verb *to poke,* "to potter." But there is no indication of the reason for Jane Austen's use of the verb with this sense, for it was she, in *Sense and Sensibility,* who is the earliest on record with this meaning. But it must have been an American who first became discouraged with the extreme laziness of some poke of his acquaintance, and who coined the term to describe one who was the epitome of dawdlers—a *slowpoke.*

tomahawk

First rendered by Captain John Smith as *tomahack,* this word first came into English through him from the Renape Indian dialect of Virginia, whose word for this all-purpose ax was *tämähak,* a shortened form of *tämähakan,* "cutting tool," related to *tämäham,* "he cuts." Closely similar words are found in a number of other Indian dialects, for example in Pamptico (of the Carolinas), *tommahick;* in Mohegan, *tummahegan;* in Delaware, *tamoihecan;* in Abenaki, *tamahigan;* in Micmac, *tumeegun;* in Passamaquoddy, *tumhigen.* Captain Smith also reported the existence of a tool used as a pick-ax, which he named a *tockahack,* but there is no evidence that this was taken into English in general use.

dog Latin

Properly, this is just very bad Latin, a mongrel Latin—whence the name—composed of a mixture of Latin and English. But in my own childhood (in Ohio), what we called *dog Latin* was a gibberish of decapitated English words, the initial letters transposed to the rear, plus "ay"; as, "Ohnny-jay ust-may o-gay ome-hay." In other areas this form of lopped English was called "hog Latin," or "pig Latin," possibly because the sound resembled the grunting of hogs.

pipe dream

A dream full of illusions such as results from the smoking of an opium pipe, which was the source of the term. As American slang heard just about at the beginning of the present century, and apparently first appeared in print in Wallace Irwin's *Love Sonnets of a Hoodlum* (1901):

> *To just one girl I've tuned my sad bazoo,*
> *Stringing my pipe-dream off as it occurred.*

cockhorse

This plaything first attained notice early in the sixteenth century, but it is not certain why it was so named. The best guess is that the make-believe horse was one upon which its young rider was "a-cock," that is, was jauntily set upon the wooden horse or Father's knee.

auburn

The modern auburn-haired beauty has tresses of golden or reddish brown, but that was far from the color the Normans had  in mind when, after the Conquest of 1066, they invaded England. They used it to describe the prevailing hue of the Saxon hair—flaxen or yellowish white, that which we now ascribe to a towhead. Careless speech and faulty writing of the sixteenth and seventeenth centuries contributed to the shifted meaning. Old French *auborne* often appeared as *abrun* and *abroun* and even *abrown*, from which, by inference, "a brownish tint" was the natural conclusion.

blindman's buff

Probably Will Shakespeare played this when he was boy. At least he could have; the children of his day did play it, and were, perhaps, no more gentle in the sport than are some of today. One youngster would consent to be blindfolded and attempt, then, to grab one of the other players, each of whom would push or jostle him or, especially, give him a buffet, a slap upon the rump with open hand. And that, in the language of the period, was a *buff;* whence the name of the sport.

flophouse

Although labeled slang in some dictionaries, this early-twentieth-century substitute is certainly convenient and expressive. It will undoubtedly gain prestige and, as long as need exists, remain in our language. We in America are barely acquainted with the Englishman's equivalent, *doss house,* and don't particularly like it; it sounds Chinese, though actually derived from Latin *dorsum,* "the back." But here in America we "flop" down on a bed, when tired, and a *flophouse* is a house or lodging for the weary who need a bed at a very, very low rate and must be content with other inmates, whether human or vermin.

slogan

It is very unlikely that advertising copywriters, who must spend many sleepless nights trying to devise catchy phrases to describe their wares, realize that the resulting *slogans* are direct descendants of ancient Gaelic battle cries. But the original was just that, for the origin of *slogan* is *sluagh-ghairm,* literally, "the cry of the host," from the Gaelic words *sluagh,* "host," and *gairm,* "a cry or shout." For the most part, these battle cries consisted chiefly or solely of the name of the clan or of the leader of the host, repeated over and over by the body of soldiers, in unison, as they moved into battle. This part of the technique, at least, is retained by today's slogan writers, who try, if it all possible, to work the name of their product into their phrases.

toilet

This word has had a rather curious development in the little more than four hundred years it has been in the language. Its origin was the French *toilette,* the diminutive of *toile,* "cloth." Its first use in English was as the name for the fragment of cloth used for wrapping clothes. Then it was applied to the cloth cover for a dressing table, such a cloth often being of rich fabric and workmanship. From here it was used for the collection of articles found on or associated with the dressing table, and then for the table itself. Next the term was transferred to the process of dressing, and some time later to the manner or style of dress as well as to the dressing room. It is almost exclusively in the United States that the use of the word has been extended to apply to the bathroom and particularly to the water closet, these being sometime adjuncts to the dressing room itself.

cobweb

Though this was, in fact, a web made by a cop, I don't mean a trap set by a policeman. No, six hundred years ago an ordinary spider, though more commonly called a spider, was also known as a *cop,* and when that term was combined with *web* its pronunciation was softened to *cob.*

doggone

Popular notion nowadays is that this is an affected or prim American version of "God damned." The fact is, however, that British writers, long before any record of American usage is found, were using "dog on it," as a form of mild oath, much as earlier writers had been using "a pox on it." I think it most likely, therefore, that *doggone* is nothing more than a misspelling of *dog on.*

claptrap

This definition which appeared in Nathan Bailey's dictionary of 1720 tells the full story: "*A Clap Trap,* a name given to the rant and rhimes that dramatick poets, to please the actors, let them go off with: as much as to say, a trap to catch a clap, by way of applause from the spectators at a play."

flapdoodle

Here's another coinage of the same nature as "flabbergast," but of later vintage. Its anonymous creator left no blueprint, but probably drew it from the seventeenth-century slang *fadoodle*, which was used in like sense. The first use in print of the surviving term was apparently in Frederick Marryat's *Peter Simple*, published in 1834, and of course this writer may have been the one who modernized the older term. Its meaning? Twaddle; sheer nonsense.

ballyhoo

Several suggestions have appeared as the source of this term for the glib patter of the showman: (a) the village of *Ballyhooly*,  Ireland; (b) a circus blend of *ballet* and *whoop;* (c) the cry of dervishes, *b'allah hoo,* "Through God it is," at the 1893 World's Fair in Chicago. Dr. Atcheson L. Hench (*American Speech,* Oct., 1945) suggests that it may have come from the seaman's term, the *ballahou,* for a fast-sailing, two-masted vessel, with foremast raked forward, mainmast aft, rigged with high fore-and-aft sails, much used in the West Indies. The contemptuous term *ballyhoo of blazes,* used in 1847 by Melville in *Omar,* in derision of a slovenly vessel, may have been picked up by landlubbers, he thinks.

tocsin

Back in the days before systems of mass communication had been developed to anything like the extent they are today, it was necessary that some means be used to call the inhabitants of a community together in case of a general alarm or for the dissemination of important news. This was frequently done by means of an alarm bell, which was struck only on such special occasions. And a *tocsin* is literally "a striking of the bell." The word was taken into English directly from the French, where it had slowly developed in form from the Old French *toquassen,* and to which, in turn, it had come from the Provençal *tocasenh,* "strike the bell." This is made up of *tocar* (from which came the French

753

toucher), "to touch, to strike," together with *senh,* "sign, bell," the latter part from the Latin *signum,* "sign," which, in Late Latin, also had the meaning of "bell."

skin game

It was as early as 1812 when the verb *to skin,* meaning "to strip a person of his money," was first entered into an English dictionary of slang, so the meaning undoubtedly existed in speech long before that. But it was not until 1862 that the first recorded use of the compound word *skin game* made its appearance. The meaning was, at first, a game, such as a card game, in which the player had no chance to win, the house "skinning" him of his purse. Later the sense was expanded to its present status, when any person subjected to a set of circumstances wherein he has no choice but to emerge the worse for the experience is said to have been the object of a *skin game.*

germane

If you will cross-check the entry **cousin-german** it will be seen that *german* means "having the same parentage; closely related." And *germane* may be substituted, and frequently is. Nowadays, however, there's a growing tendency to apply the latter term to matters that may bear close relationship, that may be relevant or pertinent, rather than to persons having close relationship.

skiagraph

(Also spelled *skiograph, sciagraph.*) Long, long ago—reputedly in ancient Corinth—the art of making shadow pictures was born. That is, the practice of casting a shadow of the person or object upon a wall or other surface, then filling in the shadow with pencil or charcoal. Today we know such a picture as a *silhouette,* but they were earlier known by the name of *skiagraph,* from the two Greek words, *skia,* "shadow," and *graphon,* "picture." Later, when the art of taking pictures of people and objects by means of Roentgen rays was developed, it was realized that these pictures, too, were really a sort of shadow picture. By that time the word *skiagraph* had been pretty well superseded by *silhouette* for the original meaning, so it was adopted by Roentgenologists to describe what many of us know better as an X-ray picture.

pin money

I suppose that the very earliest notion of *pin money* was literal —just enough money with which a wife could buy pins. This would have been an exceedingly small sum, indicated by the expression "not worth a pin," one of the earliest in our language. But in the early sixteenth century and onward the amount was considerably larger. "Money to buy her pins" was enough, not only for the purchase of pins, but for all other personal expenses. It was usually a fixed annual allowance in the olden days, and, in England, is still often provided for by the annual rentals of certain properties settled upon the wife.

highfalutin

It has been in the written language of America since 1839, so it was undoubtedly in wide use in much earlier common speech. But, regrettably, not until we reach a lexicographer's idea of heaven can the source of the term or the name of its coiner be ascertained. Bartlett (*Dictionary of Americanisms,* 1877) quotes a speech delivered in 1848 by Leslie Coombs, thus:

"I was at the Barnburner's convention in Utica, and the first person I heard was a good-looking, fat, rosy-looking man, who got up and ground out what we term at the West a regular built fourth-of-July— star-spangled-banner—times-that-tried-men's-souls—Jefferson speech, making gestures to suit the *highfalutens.*"

Black Maria

A police van for the conveyance of prisoners. Tradition says that the original, in Boston, Massachusetts, in the early 1800's, was named after a huge Negress, Maria Lee, but known as "Black Maria," who ran a lodging house for sailors, but who co-operated with the police in the arrest of any lodger who became unruly or violated the law. It is not known when the first van acquired the name, but a Boston paper of 1847 tells of "a new Black Maria" being put into service.

flibbertigibbet

Strangely enough, this does not appear ever to have been considered as slang. As evidence thereof the first printed appearance of which we have record was in a sermon, and at that, a sermon before His Majesty the King—King Edward the Sixth in the year 1549, sermon by Bishop Hugh Latimer. The word he used, however, was *flibbergib,* which he spelled *flybbergybe.* His meaning was that of today, a garrulous or flighty person. But Shakespeare, who wrote *flibbertigibbet* in *King Lear,* used it as other writers had done, as the name of a devil. And Scott, in *Kenilworth,* had it mean an impish youngster.

bandy-legged

Bowlegged; having the legs shaped for greater comfort in riding a horse, parenthesis-fashion. The term probably arose, back in the seventeenth century, through a comparison of legs so shaped with the curved stick, then called a "bandy," in the game of hockey as then played.

clapboard

Our English forebears just partly anglicized a German term back in the sixteenth century. The word that came to them was *klappholt,* in which *holt* (modern *Holz*) meant "wood, board," and *klapp* apparently referred to the clacking sound from boards smacking together. This *klappholt* and the early *clapboard* was used by coopers in making casks and was later used for wainscots. The American pilgrim, however, took the term and applied it to lengths of wood that he split much thinner. These later evolved into boards

756

thinner at one edge, so they would underlie the board above, affording greater protection against inclement weather.

skewbald

A *skewbald* horse (or other animal) is one that is basically white, but whose coat also has patches of some other color. It is thus similar to *piebald* (which see, especially for the derivation of *-bald*), and is sometimes used synonymously therewith, but when a distinction is made, *piebald* is used when the patches are black, *skewbald* when they are other than black. As a compound word, *skewbald* dates to the seventeenth century, but its predecessor, *skewed,* of the same meaning, is some two hundred years older. The derivation seems to be from the Anglo-Saxon *scuwa,* "shadow," which may be related to the Latin *obscurus,* "dark, shadowed," in the sense that the animal's otherwise white coat is shadowed by the other color.

guttersnipe

He, or quite often she, frequently a child or street Arab, gathers a living from the gutter, or less literally, from discarded rags, trash, or other refuse, including food. His mode of living, that is, resembles that of the snipe which pokes its bill into the mud lining a body of water for its food. The term, originating as slang, is not quite a hundred years old.

shenanigan

Many sources have been suggested for this Americanism, which seems to have been originated in California during or soon after the Gold Rush. The first recorded use was in that state in 1855. As the word has the sense of "trickery, deceit," most possible sources suggested have had similar meanings, such as the Spanish *chanada,* "a trick," and the Irish *sionnachuighim,* "I play tricks." However, despite the fact that, as Mencken remarks, the word has "an Irish smack," a very strong case is made by Spitzer (*American Speech,* Vol. 23, 1948 p. 210) for a derivation from the German *schinnagel,* "the nail holding the rim to the wheel," through the cant word *schinageln,* "to work," and *Schenigelei,* "a trick."

hubbub

The best I can do is to say "probably." That is, this term for a confused din, an uproar of sound from a multitude of voices, was probably taken from an ancient Irish war cry. The cry itself appears to have been *abu! abu!,* repeated over and over from the throats of yelling hordes. Edmund Spenser, in *The Present State of Ireland* (1596), describes it: "They come running with a terrible yell and *hubbabowe,* as yf heaven and earth would have gone together, which is the very image of the Irish *hubbabowe,* which theyr kerne [foot soldiers] use at theyr first encounter."

madcap

In its earliest sense, as in Shakespeare's day, this meant simply one who was crazy, a maniac. *Cap,* just because it covered the head, was sometimes used for "head," and *mad,* used literally, meant "crazy." Of course it was also used, and still is, somewhat playfully, in describing one who acted impulsively or recklessly, in much the same manner as we now say, "He's got bees in his bonnet."

billingsgate

Just why the gate, once an entrance to the old city of London, was known as *Billings,* even back in the thirteenth century, cannot be determined. Presumably that was the name of its builder, but Newcourt's map of the city in 1658 says the gate was "Founded by Belen ye 23th Brittishe Kinge." At any rate, a fish market became established near it in the sixteenth century which soon acquired an unenviable reputation for the coarse vituperative language of the fishwives. Hence, to this day *billingsgate* denotes vulgar and violent abuse, though the market itself passed out of existence long ago. (P.S. The theory seems not to have been advanced before, but it seems to me quite probable that "Belen's gate," with careless pronunciation, could easily have been corrupted to "Billin's gate" and then to "Billingsgate."—C.E.F., Jr.).

highbinder

One's immediate interpretation of the sense of this word is largely sectional. In eastern America it is associated with a ruffian, a gangster, and that was its earliest application—a member of a gang of rowdies in New York City who, in 1806, called themselves *Highbinders.* But, especially in California and later in New York City, the term was applied, in the 1870's, to any member of a Chinese secret society organized for blackmail or assassination.

banjo

In Thomas Jefferson's *Notes on Virginia* (1788) he says that this instrument is "proper to the blacks, which they brought

hither from Africa, and which is the original of the guitar, the chords being precisely the four lower chords of the guitar." But your dictionaries tell that *banjo* is probably a Negro corruption of the far older *bandore,* known ˇto the ancient Greeks as *pandoura,* a musical instrument of three strings. It seems not to have occurred to anyone that both may be right. The Greeks had contact with Ethiopia, as well as Egypt, from the days of Homer, and might well have introduced the *pandoura* into such regions of Africa.

flittermouse

It isn't a mouse, for it has wings, and mice don't. But it does fly rather swiftly and dartingly, so it can be said to flitter, and being a mammal with a body not unlike that of a mouse in size, and sometimes in color, it is not surprising that this creature was known to our ancestors as a *flittermouse,* after the German *Fledermaus* or the Dutch *vledermuis.* But the older and better-known English name was *back,* a name now lost in English dialects, though remaining

759

as *bawkie-bird* in Scotland. Today we know this flying mammal as a *bat*.

skedaddle

There has been a great deal of controversy, which has still not been resolved, over the origin of this word, and even some difference of opinion as to whether it was born in England or in America. The earliest recorded use for the American *skedaddle*, "to flee precipitously," that has been found is 1861—that for the English, "to spill (as milk)," is 1862, but since spilt milk has, in effect, fled abruptly, this sense may actually derive from the former. Bartlett, in his *Dictionary of Americanisms* (4th ed., 1877), reviewed the controversy thoroughly as of that date, and little new has been turned up since. Thus various writers claim to have traced it to the Greek *skedannumi,* "rout"; the Welsh *ysgudaw,* "to scud about"; and the Irish *sgedadol,* "scattered." Others have claimed Swedish and Danish origins, but no one really knows, for sure.

high-muck-a-muck

We take into our speech words from all manners of strange sources. Thus when Canadian and American reached the Chinook tribes dwelling north of the Columbia River in the far West, they adopted many terms known to all the tribes, combining them sometimes with French and English words. Among the Indian phrases, according to Charles J. Lovell (*American Speech,* April, 1947), was *hiu muckamuck,* meaning "plenty to eat." It was catchy, and it is Lovell's conjecture that, as we do with numerous slang expressions, the traders began to use it without regard to its original meaning, but in the sense "big bug; chief man." And, naturally, because they "could not frame to pronounce" *hiu* aright, they made it *high.*

pink-stern

Pinkeye designates an inflamed eye, but *pink-stern* has nothing to do with color. It names a type of small boat, one with its stern shaped like that of a sailing vessel known as a *pink* or *pinky*. Both names are corrupted from the Middle Dutch *pincke,* first applied to a flat-bottom sailing vessel which was subsequently built with a narrow stern, the so-called *pink-stern.*

tintinnabulation

Chiefly known to us because of its use by Edgar Allan Poe in "The Bells," this word is based on the Latin *tintinnabulum,* "a bell," from *tintinnare,* "to ring." It seems probable that *tintinnare* and its relatives were coined in imitation of the sound of bells, quite as our *ding-dong, ting-a-ling,* etc., were coined for the same purpose.

chucklehead

Has the same meaning as *chowderhead,* but the first element is from the dialectal word *chuck,* meaning "a chunk," such as "a chunk of coal; a chunk of bread," any lump, that is, which is of irregular size.

runabout

My son, now in his teens, drives a convertible. When I was in my teens, I drove a roadster. In my father's youth, the automobile body style of equivalent popularity to these was the *runabout,* but in his father's youth, the *runabout* was a light, horse-drawn vehicle. All of these are, or were, handy means of transportation for the driver with, perhaps, one or two passengers. But here, again, we have an example of changing meaning for a long-established word, for ever since the fourteenth century a *runabout* has also meant a footloose wanderer, a vagabond, or tramp, having been used in *Piers Plowman* in this sense.

arrowroot

A tropical American plant now cultivated commercially for the nutritious starch obtained from the root. The name, however, according to Sir Hans Sloane, a British naturalist who wrote of this plant in 1696 in his catalogue of Jamaican plants, arose from its use by Indians to counteract the effect of poisoned arrows. "But," says the *New International Encyclopedia,* "it is not improbable that the name is really another form of *ara,* an Indian word." No one now living can be certain. I'd love to be able to assert confidently that the Indians used the root to tip their arrows with poison, thus opposing Sir Hans.

barrel house

Now it's a form of music, crude jazz, or a type of blues performed originally in low-class night clubs. The name itself came from any

rough or low booze joint in which drinks were drawn from the barrels in which the liquor was delivered or where such barrels were prominently displayed. It is at least seventy-five years old. *Peck's Bad Boy* (1883) has the "Boy" tell that his "Pa . . . thought he had a snap with me in the drug store . . . ; but after I had put a few things in his brandy he concluded it was cheaper to buy it, and he is now patronizing a barrel house down by the river."

flimflam

"She maketh earnest matter of euery flymflam," was listed as one of the *Prouerbes in the Englishe tongue,* compiled by John Heywood in 1546. So the word must be considerably older than that date, the earliest in recorded print. It had no known source, except that it seems to have been a reduplication, for added effect, on *flam,* "a whim," "a falsehood," or just "nonsense."

shyster

This Americanism was probably coined early in the nineteenth century, since its first recorded use, as cited in the *Dictionary of American English,* was in 1846. Partridge, in his *Dictionary of Slang and Unconventional English,* suggests that *shyster* is a variant of *shicer*, "a person or thing of no account, worthless," although the latter may actually be the newer word. In any event, there is some reason to believe that both are derived from the German (possibly through Yiddish) *Scheisse*, "excrement."

doch-an-doris

Any Scot can tell you that this has the same meaning as "stirrup cup," and is literally "a drink at the door," that is, a parting drink. Sometimes it is written *doch-an-dorach*, but in any case it represents the Gaelic *deoch*, "drink," *an*, "the," and *doruis*, "door."

gazebo

If the eighteenth-century inventor of this term had known, he might have had many a chuckle over the labors he invoked upon later scholars. From what source did he obtain it? Some think it from some unknown Oriental source, but the general consensus now is that he just made it up. As he wanted a term for a structural lookout, he may have taken the ordinary word *gaze* and, under the pretense that it was from a hypothetical Latin verb of the second conjugation, *gazeo*, produced the future form, *gazebo*, "I shall see." Incidentally, the term is wholly unrelated to the American slang *gazabo*, which is also sometimes spelled and pronounced *gazebo*, but which is from Spanish *gazapo*, "one who is shrewd."

Stygian

Derived from the Latin adjective *Stygius*, from the Greek *Stygios*, all are related to the River *Styx*, that river in Greek mythology which separated the land of the living from Hades, the land of the dead. The name of the river is closely related to the Greek adjective *stygnos*, "hateful, gloomy," and this, too, is the meaning most often associated with our adjectival use of the river's name.

horse chestnut

Our English name is nothing more than a translation of the sixteenth-century Latin botanical name, *Castanea equina*. The name, according to a late-sixteenth-century writer, was "for that the people of the East countries do with the fruit thereof cure their horses of the cough." It is much more probable, however, that *horse* merely indicated "large," as is the case with a number of other materials—the horse bean, horse mackerel, horse-radish, for example.

choler

The ancient Greek physicians believed that there were four *humors,* or primary fluids, which governed the body—the blood, or *sanguis;* the yellow bile, or *chole;* the black bile, or *melas chole* (giving our word *melancholy*); and the phlegm, or *phlegma*. A superabundance of *chole* in one's system was supposed to cause that individual to become hot tempered, highly irascible, ready to fly off the handle; *choleric,* in fact.

shinplaster

In early colonial days there were both poverty and hard work, the work being of such a nature that cuts, bruises, and blows could well have been the daily fare of our forebears. When the injury was to the shin, it was usual to apply a poultice of sorts, and, among the poorer classes, this often took the form of a small square of paper previously soaked in vinegar, tobacco juice, or some other decoction of soothing, if not medicinal, value. These, of course, were *shinplasters*. With the advent of paper currency of dubious value, the size thereof being reminiscent of the makeshift poultice and the value often also of the same magnitude, the term was transferred to the scrip, and even yet paper scrip of low real or imagined value is known by the same term.

pinafore

That's what it was; "pinned afore," pinned at the front (of a dress). The item pinned was some sort of wash material which served as an apron or bib to protect the front of a child's dress— a dress then worn by either girl or boy child. That was back in the latter part of the eighteenth century. Many years ago, however, though the name was retained, the garment underwent a face-lifting. As now worn, by women or girls, it requires no pins and covers most of the dress.

blunderbuss

Though it's a loud blusterer to whom we give the name now, it was formerly, from the mid-seventeenth century, a short gun of  large bore and short range which scattered many slugs or balls. The Dutch, who invented it, called it, accurately enough, *dunderbus,* "thunder tube," because of its noisy firing. The English in adopting it, quick to see how blindly the shots were carried, just substituted *blunder* for *dunder.*

knickerbockers

We are so accustomed to this term that we can scarcely realize it is barely a hundred years old. It seems that it must date back to the days of Peter Stuyvesant, when the Dutchmen on Manhattan Island all wore flaring breeches now called *knickerbockers.* But, though the name of this garment is often credited to Washington Irving, and some credit is certainly due him, we really owe it to the British caricaturist George Cruikshank, who, in the 1850's, illustrated an English edition of the satire *A History of New York,* written by Irving in 1809 under the pseudonym "Diedrich Knickerbocker." The garments of the alleged author, in these illustrations, and of his fellow Dutch burghers led to the adoption of *knickerbockers* for knee breeches of any kind.

hurly-burly

We're all familiar with Shakespeare's "When the Hurley-burley's done, When the Battaile's lost, and wonne." But the earlier form was *hurling and burling*—or, as written in 1530, *hurlynge*

765

and burlynge. Hurling had long then meant "strife" or "commotion"; *hurling-time* referred specifically to the Wat Tyler rebellion in the reign of Richard II. But, despite the fact that *burl, burling,* and *burly* have each been long in the language, none has been used in a sense that would normally associate it with *hurling* or its contracted form, *hurly.* We are forced to conclude that *burling* and *burly* were added merely to duplicate an effect by sound.

piebald

Thank fortune, one may be *bald* without being *piebald.* The element *pie,* in this case, relates to the *magpie,* a bird with feathers splotched with two colors, a bird called *pica* by the Romans, whence the English *pie.* Originally one of the two colors was, as with the bird, always a white spot, having thus the appearance of a *bald* spot. Actually, therefore, *piebald* originally related to the white-spotted *pie.* (See also **skewbald.**)

three-tailed bashaw

In Turkey the title of *bashaw* or *pasha* is applied to military officers and civil servants of high rank, being comparable to general, admiral, or governor. There are three grades of bashaw, and it was formerly the practice, especially during military maneuvers, to designate the grade by tying an appropriate number of horse tails to the standard of the officer, that with three tails denoting the highest rank. Thus a *three-tailed bashaw* was in fact a commanding general or admiral. The term came into English slang to describe a man of great importance, or, more often, a man who disported himself in such a way as to imply that he thought himself of great importance.

shilly-shally

When first recorded (1674), the air of indecision expressed by this term was rendered in much more recognizable form. The picture we have is of some Caspar Milquetoast of the day standing irresolutely and murmuring, *"Shall I? Shall I?"* In the course of

766

literary evolution, the question became reduced to *shally-shally,* but was accompanied by a parallel change of vowel, retaining the form of the question, to *"Shill I? Shall I?"* Ultimately both paths of alteration converged, yielding the present *shilly-shally.*

chop suey

The *chop* is English, in the sense of "chipped" or "cut," but the *suey* is Chinese *sui,* "bits." Like the term itself, the concoction or comestible is of mixed origin. As explained to me, forty years ago, it was first devised by a Chinese operating a restaurant in Brooklyn, who composed it of bits of fried or stewed chicken or pork, rice, noodles, and sesame seeds or oil, and served the steamy mess in its own juice. But I'll accept as more authentic the statement by Herbert Asbury in *Gangs of New York* (1928) that it was the invention of a dishwasher in San Francisco about 1860. Yes, you're right; I've never asked for it a second time.

shindig

Although one authority cites a purported Southern United States meaning of "A sharp blow on the shins," this may only be a transferred meaning, from the appearance of the word, to an accidental kick received during a spirited dance or party. It seems much more likely that a *shindig* is a U.S. alteration of the much older British word *shindy,* which is preceded by *shinty* and *shinny.* This last is a ball game of considerable antiquity (seventeenth century or older) somewhat resembling field hockey. Its name may have been derived from a call used in the game, *"Shin ye! Shin you!"* or from the Gaelic *sinteag,* "a skip, jump."

dingbat

Mr. Bartlett, in the fourth edition (1877) of his *Dictionary of Americanisms,* decided that this owed its origin to a *bat,* or piece of wood or metal, that could be *dinged,* or thrown. Well, maybe so. That's probably as good as any explanation, though the source of any bit of slang is, usually, highly dubious. At any rate, we Americans use it, as we do its derivative, *dingus,* as a momentary name of anything of which the proper name is out of mind or unknown. (See also **thingum.**)

unkempt

The verb of which *kempt* is the past participle is *kemb,* "to comb," and it derives from the Anglo-Saxon *cembam* and ultimately from the Old Teutonic *kembjan.* The only  modern survivor of the verb is this form as it appears in the combinations *unkempt* and *well-kempt,* but the meanings most often implied in modern usage are, respectively, "ill-groomed, slovenly" and "well-groomed, neat," rather than the literal meanings of "uncombed" and "neatly combed." In all other uses, *kemb* has been replaced by its descendant, *comb.*

(Apologies to H. Hoffman)

bluenose

Nowadays it is (a) a person of puritanic habits, such as, allegedly, those of the Back Bay area of Boston, or (b) a Nova Scotian to whom this term is applied. But in the first quarter of the nineteenth century it was applied generally to one from northern New England or adjacent provinces of Canada. The indicated color of the nose was not due to overindulgence in strong drink, one may assume, but to long-continued exposure to cold and inclement weather, such as experienced by lumberjacks, mariners, and fishermen. The term is also given to a variety of blue potato grown in Nova Scotia.

garrote

They did it first with cords twisted tighter and tighter by a stick, a method copied from carriers who thus secured loads upon their mules. The stick itself was the *garrote.* "They" were the Spanish Inquisitors of the fourteenth century and later, who sought and employed all sorts of methods of torture to extract confessions. In this, the muleteer's cord, passed around a stake, was tied about the arms, legs, and thighs of the victim and slowly tightened by the *garrote,* even perhaps cutting its way to the bone. At a later time the term was applied to an instrument of capital punishment in Spain and Portugal whereby death was accomplished by strangulation.

shilling

Shilling is a purely Teutonic word, found in all languages of the Germanic group with appropriate spelling in each. In English, it dates back to the Anglo-Saxon *scilling*—from there to the Gothic *skilligs.* It has been adopted into most of the Romance languages, again with appropriate changes in spelling. The root is uncertain, but seems probably to be *skel-,* "to divide." It seems always to have been a unit of currency, and a subdivision of the major piece of currency of the country, e.g., in England, of the pound. As for the *pound* itself, it was originally so-called because, in fact, it was a pound (Troy) of silver, though this has not now been true for many years. But despite the purely Teutonic background of the *shilling,* but not of the pound, the abbreviations of both come from their Latin equivalents. Thus the £, denoting the pound of money and the *lb.* indicating the pound of weight are both from the Latin *libra,* "pound," while the *s.* for shilling is the abbreviation for the Latin *solidus,* a monetary unit equal to 25 *denarii* (from which comes the *d.* for pence). The English abbreviation for shilling is *sh.* rather than *s.* In former times the abbreviation actually used for shilling was the long *s* (ſ). Written quickly, this soon degenerated into nothing more than a slant line (/), and it is from this degeneration that the slant line has received the name, *solidus,* that it is now known by.

bigwig

Although humorously employed nowadays to designate a person of real or self-fancied importance, the start of the allusion was in fact indicated by the size of the wig a man wore. That was back in the times of Queen Anne of England and Louis XIV of France. Wigs had been courtly fashion for a half century or more, but by the beginning of the eighteenth century they attained exaggerated proportions, some covering the back and shoulders and floating down the chest. The status of a man was marked by the style of wig he wore, and the more important in state or occupation, the more imposing his wig. Eventually the fashion passed, though the wig or peruke is still retained in British courts of law.

pickaback

If we count only three generations to a century, our ancestors were carrying their children or others *pick-a-back* twelve generations ago and calling the manner by that name, or one very like it. That is, in the original dialect the term may have been *pick pack,* which may have referred to a *pack picked* (pitched) on one's shoulders. In the past hundred and fifty years the term has often been corrupted to *piggy-back* or the like, but great honored men have, on occasion, been carried *pickaback;* none has yet been carried *piggy-back.*

thoroughfare

Strange that New York thought it had to create a new word for its cross-state toll road—the Throughway. Beyond the temporary distinction of application to that one highway, there is nothing in the word that does not already exist in the long-established—six hundred years—word *thoroughfare. Thorough* is the ancient spelling of *through; fare,* now used chiefly for "passage money," formerly meant "passage, way." And *thoroughfare* has long indicated a "through way between places."

love apple

Just the ordinary common tomato, but my mother was averse to eating it. In rural Ohio, the home of her girlhood, it was known only as *love apple* and, believed to possess aphrodisiac properties, was therefore feared by virtuous maidens. The reason for the name, with the properties suggested by it, was entirely due to a mistake in translation. From South America, where the plant was discovered, it was introduced into Spain in the sixteenth century and from there into Morocco. Italian traders then brought it to Italy, where it was called *pomo dei Moro,* "apple of the Moors." From Italy it went to France, and there is where the mistake was made. Whoever the grower, his knowledge of Italian was faulty. Guided by the sound, he obviously thought *pomo dei Moro* meant, in French, *pomme d'amour,* "apple of love." And it was by the latter name or its English translation that the tomato was introduced into England in the early seventeenth century and thence to North America. And in Germany the common name is still *Liebesapfel,* "love apple," although *Tomate* is gaining ascendency. Needless to add, perhaps, any notion that the tomato arouses sexual desire or is even faintly poisonous has now completely died out.

daisy

One wonders whether coming generations will think that we, in this day of countless new inventions, have shown like imagination

and poetry in the coining of names as that given to our early forebears. It does not so appear. Certainly not in such words as telephone, automobile, airplane, radio, television, electric refrigerator. But consider the common field plant, the *daisy.* Even a thousand years ago it was observed that the white rays of its flower opened with the rising sun, exposing its golden disk through the day, and folded again in the evening. They called it *daeges eage,* "day's eye."

gantry

You may spell this *gauntry* if you like, or even *gauntree,* but the present preference is *gantry.* Nowadays the chief application of the name is to a traveling crane, a wonderfully ingenious device mounted on overhead rails in machine shops or the like by which the operator is able to hoist and transport heavy pieces to any portion of the shop. Our word, greatly altered through transition in French, came from Latin *cantherius,* "trellis" or "framework," probably of the nature of the "horse" used by modern carpenters.

Big Ben

This is the great deep-toned bell which strikes the hours of the clock in the clock tower of the Houses of Parliament, London. The tower carries five bells in all, the other four striking the quarter hours in the famed Westminster chimes. The great bell, weighing thirteen and a half tons, was cast in 1858, and was named Big Ben after Sir Benjamin Hall, who was First Commissioner of Works at the time when the clock was erected.

flea-bitten

Maybe the dog or horse with coat of the color that we call *flea-bitten* has been at some time infested with fleas, but, whether so or not, that is unessential. The color term originated back in the latter half of the sixteenth century. Some discerning groom or dog fancier saw that the reddish flecks on the coat of his lighter-colored animal were very similar in appearance to the reddish marks left on his own hairy arms by the bites of fleas. So what more natural than to describe the coat of his animal as *flea-bitten?* It saved time searching for a more definite color; easier to think of than, say, mottled gray or speckled sorrel.

sherry

The Romans of Caesar's day are remembered for, among other things, their fondness for good wines, so it may be fitting that Caesar's title has been perpetuated, even though indirectly, in this common table wine. For the name *Caesaris* was given to a town in Spain in his honor, but the name soon became modified to the more native-sounding *Xeres,* and still later to *Jerez.* And it was in this town that the wine was made, and from which it found its way to England. Unable to cope with Spanish pronunciation, the English gave the wine the name of *sherris* as a close approximation, and later, since this sounded like a plural, the name was changed to the synthetic singular, *sherry*.

gangplank

In England it's a *gangboard,* though both here and there the same thing is also called a *gangway*. In any case, whether plank, board, or way, it's a means of "going" aboard or off a ship. And that, in Old English, is what a *gang* was—a "going." In later times *gang* began to mean also a set or group of things that "go" together, thus giving us the sense of a band of persons who go or act co-operatively.

sub rosa

Under the rose; i.e., confidentially, in secrecy. Legend attributes the origin to a rose handed by Eros to Harpocrates, god of silence, accompanied with an injunction not to reveal the love affairs of Venus. Accordingly, in the customs of ancient councils, said to date back to the fifth century B.C., a rose hanging from the ceiling enjoined all present to observe secrecy on matters discussed. In later times, and until quite recently, the ceilings of dining rooms, decorated with roses or rosettes, were indication that private conversation would be confidential. Because the German *unter der Rose* is also of great antiquity and has identical significance, the custom of a rose on the ceiling was probably a Teutonic observance.

dillydally

Who first used it, or when, is not known; probably some harassed mother back in the sixteenth century, annoyed with the dalliance of a loitering son—or husband—made *dally* more emphatic by duplicating it with *dilly*. At least, the *dilly* prefix has no separate meaning of its own, any more than *shilly* has in the analogous term, *shilly-shally*.

loophole

The kind of *loop* now attached to this *hole* is seldom used or heard of any more. In the late Middle Ages, however, a *loop* was a narrow window, in a castle or other fortification, through which an archer could direct his missiles, but so narrow as to be a baffling target for an opposing bowman. The masonry of the window widened inwardly to permit a wider range for the defending archer. Possibly to avoid confusion between *loop,* "window," and *loop,* "a fold," the first became identified as *loophole.*

daystar

It is usually Venus, though it may at times be Jupiter, Mars, Saturn, or Mercury. At any rate it is the planet that appears in the eastern sky shortly before the sun rises, accordingly also called the morning star.

dormouse

This creature is certainly not a *dor,* or beetle, nor related to anything that flies, nor is it exactly a *mouse,* though small and a  member of the rodent family. In fact, the source of its name has long been a matter of speculation and is still obscure, though in use for some five hundred years. But because the animal is noted for sleepiness, the consensus is that the first element, *dor,* is from the same source as *dormant,* or, that is, from the Latin *dormire* "to sleep," to which *mouse* was then added because of general appearance.

highball

There's no doubt that this term has long been used by American railwaymen as that of a signal to the locomotive engineer to proceed. The signal itself was a ball large enough to be plainly visible which, when hoisted to the top of a mast at the approach to a small station, indicated that a train could proceed without stopping, that neither passenger, freight, nor express was awaiting it. Presumably this sense was somehow transferred to an iced alcoholic beverage about sixty years ago, but if so, the connection has not yet been determined. Possibly some passenger who had over-indulged in the beverage vaguely saw a resemblance between the floating ice at the top of the glass to the ball of the signal, and the tall glass to the mast.

chopfallen

"To lick one's chops," usually interpreted as indicating supreme pleasure, such as that from lapping the last taste of gravy or the last crumb of cake from one's jaws, not only shows us the meaning of *chop* in this term, but also pictures the exact opposite, the antonym, of the whole term. One who is *chopfallen* has been made supremely unhappy; he has had the ground knocked out from beneath him; he is crestfallen; he has a hangdog appearance, or, in brief, he has been so taken aback, so discomfited, that his chop, or jaw, has fallen open.

sheet anchor

The derivation is somewhat obscure, although some authorities believe that the name for this emergency anchor comes from *shot-anchor,* or *shoot-anchor,* since, if an emergency actually came about, it would have been "shot" (dropped quickly) from its supports. To bolster this theory, attention is called to the derivation of *shoot,* which came into the language through the Anglo-Saxon *sceotan.* which then passed through the Middle English form, *scheten.* It may also be worth noting that Scottish dialect *sheet* for "shoot" may have had something to do with our present form, as many capable British shipmasters were drawn from Scotland. Be that as it may, the modern meaning, "something which may be relied upon," is a direct descent from the emergency nature of the *sheet anchor.*

belladonna

"Beautiful lady," but why this name for the deadly nightshade? Two highly contradictory accounts have been given. The English

775

naturalist John Ray (1627–1705) said that a cosmetic made from the juice of this plant was used by, especially, Venetian ladies to enhance their beauty. This is probably the true origin of the name. But a botanist of the mid-nineteenth century asserts that its name arose from the use of the deadly juice by an Italian criminal, one Leucota, who poisoned beautiful women with it.

hurry-scurry

Oddly enough, in the earliest use of *hurry*, in the last years of the sixteenth century, it was nothing more than a variant of *hurly*, meaning "disturbance, tumult." That is the sense in Shakespeare's *Coriolanus* (Act IV, Scene vi): "His remedies are tame, the present peace, And quietnesse of the people, which before Were in wilde hurry." And, in fact, through the next century or two we had *hurry-burry*, *hurry-durry*, and *hurry-curry*, all imitating *hurly-burly*, before finally settling upon *hurry-scurry* in the middle of the eighteenth century. But not only was *hurry* coined in this manner; so was *scurry*, though it did not find separate place in the language until another hundred years had passed.

pettifogger

One could be pardoned for thinking this was a person who "fogged" an issue by quibbling over petty matters, which is exactly what he does. Such was not the origin of the word, however, as *fog* was not used in such a sense in the mid-sixteenth century when *pettifogger* made its appearance. Nevertheless the true source is uncertain. Some think that *fogger* came from the name of a prominent family of German merchants, *Fugger*, of that period, and indicated a trickish lawyer. Others connect it with *pettifactor*, an agent or factor who handles small matters. The safest course is to throw up one's hands and say, "I don't know."

thingum, thingumajig, thingumbob, thingummy

All of these are meaningless extensions of the word *thing* in its special use as a term to denote an object or person which the speaker cannot or will not name specifically. *Thingum* was first recorded in the late seventeenth century, the other forms followed (not in order) in the eighteenth and nineteenth centuries.

chestnut

An old joke or oft-repeated story. The reason for this designation has never been proved, but George Stimpson, in *A Book about a Thousand Things* (1946), says: "The generally accepted story is that [it] originated in a play entitled 'The Broken Sword,' in which the chief characters are Captain Zavier, a Baron Munchausen type of storyteller, and Pablo, a comic person. This play contains the following colloquy:

CAPTAIN ZAVIER: I entered the woods of Collaway, when suddenly from the thick boughs of a cork tree—
PABLO: A chestnut, Captain, a chestnut.
CAPTAIN ZAVIER: Bah, I tell you it was a cork tree.
PABLO: A chestnut; I guess I ought to know, for haven't I heard you tell this story twenty-seven times?"

Mr. Stimpson attributes the perpetuation of *chestnut* in this sense to the English-born American actor William Warren, who had played the part of Pablo, at a stage dinner where he repeated Pablo's concluding line after hearing an old joke. But as this William Warren died in 1832, whereas *chestnut* only came into popular use about fifty years later, it is more likely to have been his son, William Warren, Jr., also a player of comedies, who died in 1888, who repeated Pablo's line.

arras

In English this is the name of a kind of tapestry richly woven with scenes and figures, and also of the hangings of this material which, in olden days, were hung around the walls of large rooms, often so spaced as to furnish concealment for an eavesdropper, a lover, or a knave The French call such material *tapisserie;* the English name is that of a town, Arras, in Artois, France, which was famed for the excellence of tapestry of this nature produced there. (See also **tapestry.**)

earwig

As none of these insects has any interest whatever in wigs, why this curious name? The clue, nevertheless, lies in that second part.

For many, many centuries, popular superstition had it that the insect's chief aim in life was to enter the ear of any warm-blooded animal, chiefly man, and then by the aid of the pincerlike appendage at the end of its abdomen, bore its way into the brain—to *wiggle*, that is, through the inner ear into the brain. It doesn't do any such thing, of course, yet if we called it an "ear wiggler" the old popular notion would be self-explanatory. The scientific name is *Forficula auricularia*, Latin for "ear forceps" or "ear pincers."

upholstery

To uphold means, among other things, "to maintain, to preserve intact," and it was but a slight extension of this to arrive at "to keep in repair." It was in this latter sense that the word *upholder* was coined, to apply to one who dealt in the sale, manufacture, or repair of clothing and furniture. Such a person was also called an *upholdster* (which has the equal meaning of "one who upholds"), and, by elision of the hardly pronounceable *d,* this became an *upholster.* Hence the materials with which an upholster dealt were named *upholstery,* but by now with complete loss of any reference to clothing except occasionally in a figurative sense. Also, in the course of time, the noun *upholster* became obsolete, to be replaced by the longer *upholsterer.*

shambles

Suppose your wife (or mother) came home after two weeks of vacation in which you were left to shift for yourself, took one look at the house, threw up her hands and exclaimed in dismay, "This place! It's a shambles!" Would you interpret her remark to mean: (1) "I don't know how, but you've turned everything into a footstool"; (2) "I see you've opened up a butchershop"; (3) "Have the stockyards expanded? How come our home is now a slaughterhouse?"; or (4) "You're a rotten housekeeper—the whole place is a mess!" Today, of course, meaning (4) would be the one she intended, but, strangely enough, at different times in history, any of the other interpretations would have been accurate, for this is the curious path that the word *shamble* (now usually in the plural form but with singular case) has taken. It all started with the Latin *scamellum*, "a footstool," the dimunitive form of *scamnum*, "a bench." Going through the Teutonic *scamel* and the Scandinavian *skamel*, it became the Anglo-Saxon *sceamel* (remember that the Scandinavian *sk* and the Anglo-Saxon *sc* had the value of *sh* in modern English), while retaining the meaning of "a low bench, footstool." This happened over a thousand years ago. Even before the Norman Conquest, the meaning began to change, having, by then, the sense of "a merchant's display counter," and by the fourteenth century it was specifically "a counter or shop for the sale of meat." Various spellings were used during this period, of course, and the *b* had been introduced probably during the fifteenth century. Before 1600 the meaning had been expanded to include "a slaughterhouse," or, figuratively, "a place of carnage," and the modern spelling had been evolved. The modern, milder meaning, of "a place in general disorder," is so recent that none but, perhaps, the most up-to-date dictionaries will be found to give this sense, although some fairly recent ones do give the sense just preceding this, i.e., "a place laid waste as by bombing."

petcock

None of the various word tracers has attempted to explain why the small shut-off valve was so named. Though a *cock*, it is distinctly no one's *pet*. Until someone turns up with a better explanation, I suggest that *pet* was merely a contraction of *petty* or *petit*, meaning "small, minor, inferior." An objection to this theory is that we have no record that the valve was ever known as a "petty cock"; it was *petcock* (or *pet-cock*) from the earliest printed use, around the mid-nineteenth century.

galosh

Seldom encountered but in the plural, *galoshes*. Nowadays it is rarely other than a rubber or rubberized-fabric overshoe, but in former days, extending back to ancient Greek times—yes, it's a very old term, though its antique form was then *kalopous*—it may have been of wood, like the French *sabot,* or a sandal with a wooden sole and leather upper, or even like the Mexican *huarache,* all of leather. Whatever the material, with us it's *galosh;* in France, *galoche;* in Spain and Portugal, *galocha;* and in Italy, *galoscia.*

shako

This time our modern word shows evidence of Hungarian influence, even though the ultimate derivation seems to be from the Germans. Starting with the German *Zacke,* "a peak," the trail leads next to the Hungarian *csákós suveg,* "a peaked cap." This became abbreviated to *csákó,* which was then taken into French as *schako,* and back into German as *Tschako,* still with the meaning of "a pointed cap." From the French, we took our word, dropping the *c,* but retaining the meaning. This was applied to a form of military headgear, which did, then, come to a point. Proving to be rather impractical as an item of battle dress, the point was flattened off, until now the military *shako* is a flat-topped hat best described as a truncated cone. The one-time peak is retained only symbolically by affixing a pompon or a plume at the front of the hat.

beachcomber

Lives there a man who hasn't at some time envied the *beachcomber,* that wastrel who, without a care in the world, strolled some beneficent Pacific isle, taking shelter from sun or storm under a broad tree, and deriving sustenance from plentiful vegetation and marine life, free for the taking? Such, at least, was the *beachcomber* of a century back; literally, one who combed the beach in carefree manner. More recently the term has taken on a sinister bent and denotes, perhaps, a person of low character who, on alien shores, makes his living through disreputable means.

fanfare

Nothing at all to do either with a fan or a fare, but, as still happens when we try to take a foreign word into our language, a

syllable or two got lopped off the original word, some three centuries ago, and the meaning was altered. That is, the original was the Spanish word *fanfarria,* meaning "bluster, presumption, haughtiness." And, because persons of that sort demand that notice be taken of them, their approach had to be announced by the blast of a trumpet or the like. So, in the progress of the Spanish term through French and into English, it came to mean the flourish of a trumpet or the call of a bugle or a noisy demonstration.

ultramontane

As the Church of Rome grew stronger, it acquired converts in many of the lands both near to and distant from Italy, including those in Europe to the north. And, of course, to retain these converts, it was necessary to appoint representatives in these countries who would represent the Church to the natives. Now, the north of Italy is bounded by mountains (the Alps), and it became the practice to refer to one of these representatives as *ultramontanus,* "one who is beyond the mountains," which is made up of the Latin *ultra,* "beyond," plus *mont-,* the combining form of *mons,* "mountain," together with a masculine personal suffix. The word (with suitable variations appropriate to the language) was taken into French as early as the fourteenth century, and also into Spanish, Portuguese, Italian, German, and Dutch. It entered English in the late sixteenth century, since which time there have been a number of minor variations in meaning. That now most commonly in use is "one who supports papal policy."

pernickety

We have not much to say about this; no one knows its ancestry. It is alleged to have been born in Scotland, chiefly, I'd say, because the earliest appearance in print so far noted was in the works of Scottish writers. But the date of such appearance was 1808, and that would scarcely account for the use of the term—or its variant, *persnickety,* as we used it in Ohio seventy years ago—in all parts of the United States. If of Scottish origin it must have been early enough to have been carried to America by emigrants in the first half of the eighteenth century.

xerography

A word of very recent coinage, dating only to about 1940, this, like most words in English having the initial *x,* is based on Greek roots. It is made up of the combining forms of *xeros,* "dry," and *graphein,* "to write," hence has the literal meaning of "dry writing." Although on an etymological basis it could be applied, therefore, to writing with a pencil rather than with ink, actually it is used exclusively in connection with a photographic process in which the latent image is formed as an electrostatic charge and is developed through the adhesion of a dry powder to the charged areas. This is in contrast to other photographic processes where the latent image is developed by processing with solutions of chemicals.

cheesecake

Though originally—fifteenth century and later—this denoted a cake or pie of light pastry containing cheese, the custardlike preparation used as filling by today's good cooks may or may not include cheese in the composition. But the modern product is delicious. And because it also delights the eye, users of American slang have applied the term, in recent years, to photographs featuring attractive feminine legs.

flabbergast

Someone whose identity will never be known dreamed this up about the year 1770. At least it was reported as a new word in 1772—"Now we are *flabbergasted* and *bored* [another new word] from morning to night." Possibly the inventor coined it by joining forcibly the two words *flabby* and *aghast*, but he left no notes to furnish a definite clue.

Jolly Roger

The earliest of pirates' flags was, when displayed, no more, likely, than a plain black sheet. Later some of the pirates began to embellish them with designs in white of grinning skull and crossbones, and by the mid-nineteenth century such was the general ensign. To the English, about the middle of the eighteenth century, the black flag of pirates became known as a *Roger* or, eventually, a *Jolly Roger*. No writer of the period gives a reason for such designation, so a guess may be in order. *Roger*, perhaps then pronounced with a hard *g*, among members of the underworld —the "canting crew," as they were called—had long been a term applied to a beggar or "rogue." *Jolly*, of course, meant "carefree." It would follow, therefore, that the *Jolly Roger* would represent the flag of carefree rogues. Please, however, this surmise has nothing to do with the reply "Roger!" used in radio communication to signify "Right! Received!" That is an arbitrary term for the letter *r*, derived from military signaling.

cuspidor

The "spit-box" and the "spittoon" were known early in the past century, the former usually containing sand or sawdust and more or less immovable, and the latter of earthenware or metal, small enough to be cleaned from time to time. They were reasonably necessary adjuncts to a saloon or club frequented by men who chewed tobacco. The euphemistic *cuspidor* (variantly spelled *cuspidore, cuspadore*) has had a vague and largely unrecorded history. The mighty *Oxford English Dictionary* has been able to trace its use to 1779, but the manner in which it was then used implies that it was already a well-known term. No further printed use has been recorded until 1871, when one Eugene A. Heath patented an "Improvement in Cuspadores (Cuspidores)" in both the United States and England. No dictionary printed in the interim includes the word, but Bartlett's *Dictionary of Americanisms,* 4th ed., published in 1877, does so. Since six years is usually much too short a time for a term not already in common use to become entered in a dictionary, there is a strong implication that it existed in the intervening century in the spoken, if not in the written, language. The derivation is commonly ascribed to the Portuguese *cuspir,* "to spit" (*cuspidor,* "one who spits"), from the Latin *conspuere,* "to spit into," but Mencken also notes a Dutch word, *kwispedoor,* or *kwispeldoor,* "a cuspidor," which he suggests may be the source of our English form. Only in Spanish do we find a close cognate which is probably also of the same common origin, *escupidera.*

stopgap

One of the many meanings of *to stop* is "to dam, to plug up," as in "to stop a leak," or "to stop a drain." And a *stopgap,* even in its modern sense of some temporary measure to fill a need, is, both literally and figuratively, something to "stop" a "gap."

shakedown

Shake, which comes ultimately from the Teutonic *skakan,* at one time during its life in our language had the meaning "move away from, travel, wander." From this sense it acquired the meaning of "take away without permission, steal." This, in turn, led to the coining of *shakedown* in the sense of extracting unwilling tribute, as may be practiced by those who exact "protection" payments from their inferiors. A *shakedown* cruise of a new ship, on the other hand, comes from the more modern sense of *shake,* "tremble, quiver." When grain, for instance, is measured out, rather than weighed, full measure is not obtained until the grain is literally *shaken down* in the container, in order that all the voids are filled as tightly as possible. In the case of the ship, the agitation due to the voyage fills the analogous function of bringing any faults to light.

hidebound

The literal sense related first to cattle which, under conditions of extreme emaciation resulting from disease, lost the fatty tissue normally lying under the skin. After death, then, the hide of any such animal cannot be loosened from the ribs or backbone. The condition, using this term, was first described in 1559. The figurative sense, however, is actually derived from the costive condition sometimes affecting some of us mortals, during which the skin seems to be rigidly constricted. From this condition those persons whose minds are firmly fixed, inelastic, cramped, of set and rigid opinion, are said to be *hidebound*.

Ferris wheel

It was first seen at the Columbian Exposition held in Chicago in 1893, the "World's Fair," and was the greatest attraction of all the

amusements then offered. No doubt larger ones have since been built, but this first one, rotating between two pyramids, was a framework of steel, 250 feet in diameter, and carried 36 cars, each capable of holding 40 passengers. It was designed by and named for George Washington Gale Ferris (1859–96), an engineer of Galesburg, Illinois.

battledore

This was originally a paddle-shaped wooden bat used by women as a mangle, or "beetle," for linens, back in the fifteenth century. There is no certainty as to the origin of the name, but it might then have been a play upon words—*battle* instead of *beetle,* and because *beetle* was also the name for a hard-sheathed insect for which another name was *dor* or *dore,* the two might have been combined humorously into *battledore.* Our ancestors enjoyed their jokes, too. The name also denoted a paddle for removing loaves from an oven or for propelling a canoe. And, when the game of rackets, subsequently called "battledore and shuttlecock," reached England in the sixteenth century, the name was applied to the racket, because of its shape.

flagstone

Among the four or five words spelled f-l-a-g recorded in your dictionary may be: (1) a banner; (2) a plant; (3) a wing feather of a bird; (4) a coin; (5) a flat slab of stone. And, though there are some differences of opinion, your dictionary may indicate that these *flags* are independent of one another, separate words from separate sources. It is the fifth that gives us *flagstone*. But this *flag*, possibly left by Norse invaders, originally referred to a slice of turf, a piece of sod. It is only through resemblance to such a slice of turf that a pavement stone is a *flagstone*.

hiccup

We say, somewhat fatuously, that this name is an echo of the sound, yet, strangely, the French idea of the same sound, written *hoquet*, is pronounced "aw'keh," and the Spanish idea, written *hipo*, is pronounced "ee'po." We also spell our term *hiccough*, though without affecting the pronunciation. Prior to the seventeenth century our English ancestors said *hicket*, more nearly representative of the actual sound, to my ears. And it is close to the Dutch *hikke*, Danish *hicke*, and Swedish *hicka*.

thimblerig

The trick may have been practiced in the time of the Pharaohs; if not, probably some variant of it was. Certainly someone then knew that the hand is quicker than the eye. In England it was known as "the thimble trick" two and a half centuries ago, and then, as now, the trickster at horserace or fair would exhibit a pea and three thimbles or small cups, then, at first with modest wager, challenge a bystander to guess under which thimble he had hidden the pea. A hundred years later, when *rig* became a slang term for "to cheat or trick," our present word came into use, and it was, of course, a simple step to transfer the application to any form of trickery or jugglery.

786

sesquipedalian

It was the Roman poet Horace who coined this very long adjective that is used to define a word that is very long. It appears in line 97 of one of the last of his works, published shortly before his death in 8 B.C., the *Epistle to the Pisos,* better known as *Ars Poetica* (The Poetic Art):

> *Et tragicus plerumque dolex sermone pedestri*
> *Telephus et Peleus, cum pauper et excul, uterque*
> *Projicit ampullas, et sesquipedalia verba,*
> *Si curat cor spectantis tetigisse querela*

I am indebted to Miss Dorothy Gardner for assistance with the translation, of which the following is a free rendition into verse:

> *By use of ponderous speech to tell each tragic part*
> *Did Telephus, the pauper, and Peleus, outcast,*
> *Attempt to touch with grief the watcher's kindred heart,*
> *Emitting yard-long words and spouting forth bombast.*

Literally, *sesquipedalian* means "a-foot-and-a-half long," from *sesqui-,* "one-and-one-half," and *pedalis,* "foot-long," from *pes,* "a foot." Figuratively, and it is in this sense that Horace coined it, the word is entirely equivalent to our *yard-long, block-long, mile-long,* etc., which we use to express an indeterminate length that is substantially more than is necessary, or than is expected. Miss Gardner also points out to me that the Greeks anticipated us here, too, with terms such as *amaxiaia remata,* "words large enough for a wagon."

pennyroyal

Somewhere along the line someone with a cleft palate or a mouthful of mush must have been responsible for this word. Its Latin name, in the thirteenth century was *pulegium,* corrupted along with French usage to *puliol.* To distinguish it from wild thyme, *rial,* "royal," was added. But then, along in the sixteenth century, Mr. Mushmouth came along, and through means that have not yet been figured out, managed to induce people to alter *puliol* to *penny,* thus educing *pennyroyal,* as the alteration of *rial* to *royal* followed natural steps. In France it's still *pouliot.*

thespian

Some two and a half millenniums ago—specifically, in the sixth century B.C.—there lived a Greek playwright whose name was Thespis. None of his plays or poems have lived to the present, and his name is remembered almost entirely because of the generally accepted view that it was he who invented the Greek tragedy. From his name the adjective *thespian* was coined to describe, first, a tragic play, then, a tragic actor. By now the word is used as a name for any actor, tragic or otherwise.

fiddler crab

It is also known just by the simpler name, *fiddler.* The reason? Merely because it brandishes its outsize larger claw in a manner suggestive of the action of a violinist handling his bow.

Argus-eyed

Extraordinarily vigilant. This, too, comes from Greek mythology. The goddess Hera, wife of the supreme god Zeus, jealous of his affection for the nymph Io, turned her into a cow and then appointed Argus, possessed of a hundred eyes and able to see in all directions, as guardian and caretaker. Notwithstanding this precaution, Zeus had his messenger, Hermes, kill the hundred-eyed Argus, whose eyes were thereupon transferred to the tail of the peacock.

fizgig

Chaucer and other early writers called a frivolous or giddy girl a *gig,* and such was indeed slang usage even to the eighteenth century. So, presumably because she seemed to fizz or sputter as she ran gadding about, such a girl or woman became a *fysgygge,* as it appeared in sixteenth-century spelling. Since then varied meanings have been applied, all associated in one way or another with *fizz.*

barnstormer

He did not take barns by storm, as a soldier might; he merely did his storming in barns—his furious dramatic declamations. He was an actor, that is, or one who would be. He was one of the large number of second-rate itinerant players who roamed the countryside in bands, giving a play wherever they could attract an audience. Dickens describes such a troupe in *Nicholas Nickleby.* Whenever a proper theater was not available, they made shift in a barn. It was not until about the mid-nineteenth century, however, that *barnstormer* was applied to such an actor. Late in the century the term was also applied to any American political speaker making a rapid campaign tour to arouse the electorate in his behalf.

jolly boat

Chances are that the members of the crew handling one of these rarely were, if ever, rollicking or gayhearted. It is, or was, a workboat, one used formerly around sailing vessels, chiefly in harbors, in carrying out errands in small duties about the ship. It was, in fact, a yawl of small size, the source of the name being the Danish *jolle,* "yawl." Another of the numerous instances of English mispronunciation of alien words.

dewclaw, dewlap

Though the names of different parts of animal anatomy, the terms may have, in part, a common explanation. That is, the *dewclaw* is that rudimentary inner claw, sometimes present in dogs, which hangs loosely in the skin above the other toes and which brushes, not the soil, but only against the "dew" on the grass. Similarly, the *dewlap* of cattle, dogs, or turkeys is the *lap* or fold of skin hanging loosely under the throat, and which, some say,

789

brushes against the "dew" on the grass. In this latter term, however, others think that the element *dew* is a corruption of some word that can no longer be traced.

serendipity

Perhaps the best definition that I've heard for this is that "Serendipity is the art of finding what you're not looking for." This agrees pretty well with the explanation of Horace Walpole, who coined the word in 1754 after reading the old fairytale *The Three Princes of Serendip*. Walpole wrote that these princes "were always making discoveries, by accidents and sagacity, of things they were not in quest of." Even though Walpole, in coining the word, made quite clear the meaning he intended it to have, Bernard E. Schaar has conducted research into the matter that convinces him the princes were being maligned (New York *World Telegram & Sun,* Sept. 10, 1957). He is convinced, after close study of the fairytale, that the princes of Serendip (now known as Ceylon) were highly educated, and that their seemingly fortuitous discoveries were no more accidental than are the wondrous results achieved by today's highly trained scientific investigators, whose very training leads them to recognize the worth of an experimental result even when the experiment does not proceed according to plan.

wormwood

Nothing to do either with worms or with wood, the word is an alteration, adopted beginning in the fifteenth century, of the earlier *wermod,* which is found in eighth-century Anglo-Saxon. It is known that the Teutonic *wer,* in other applications, means "man," and that *mod* is an ancestor of *mood* with the meaning of "courage." On this basis, it has been suggested that the herb was named "man's courage" in reference to its medicinal or aphrodisiac qualities. The word, incidentally, has been traced to the Old High German *wermota,* which has come down to modern German as *Wermut* (pronounced *vehr-moot*) and which, in turn, became the French *vermouth.*

banister (baluster)

"Over the banister leans a face," sang the poet, little knowing perhaps, the true poetry of his song. *Banister,* you see, is a careless mispronunciation of *baluster,* introduced about three hundred years ago. And *baluster,* the proper word, was formed from Greek *balaustion,* which was originally the term for a specific flower. Our poet thus sang, in effect, "Over the flower of the wild pomegranate leans a face, Tenderly soft and beguiling." Greek architects used the outlines of these flowers—doubly curved, slender above and bulging below—for series of short pillars supporting handrails or copings, thus giving us the modern sense.

figurehead

It was ornamental only, usually carved (from wood) into the figure or bust of a person, sometimes quite imposing, and it was

 placed beneath the bowsprit at the very bow of a ship, directly above the cutwater. Thus, most grandly, it led the vessel. Whatever the country, wherever the port, it was in the fore. But it had no function. However beautiful the carving, however emblematic the design, the vessel could have been handled just as well without it. And so it is with him or her who accepts an appointment or position that carries neither duties nor responsibilities. The imposing name of such a figurative *figurehead* lends prestige to the enterprise or organization.

johnnycake

I wish it were possible to tell with certainty why this New England corn pone is so named, but all accounts are tinged with speculation. The present name was in use early in the eighteenth century, and, though some folks did speak of the same rather durable ration as *journey-cake,* it is much more probable that *johnny* preceded *journey* than the reverse. However, some fifty or sixty years earlier than our first record of *johnnycake,* New England housewives were serving what was then called *Jonakin* or *Jonikin* to their households. Susan F. Cooper, many years later, described these as "thin, wafer-like sheets, toasted on a board . . . eaten at breakfast, with butter." Dr. M. M. Mathews, in *Dictionary of Americanisms,* suggests the possibility of a relationship between *Jonakin* and *johnnycake.*

chowderheaded

Here's a curious bit of slang traceable back more than four hundred years, though, like much current slang, the earliest term cannot be explained. *Chowder* here does not denote a stew; it's just a mispronunciation of *cholter,* for *cholter-headed* was the form that began to appear in the early nineteenth century. But that, which made no sense either, was a corruption of *jolter-headed,* used through the previous century, and, in turn, it was derived from the earliest form, *jolthead.* Heaven knows the source of that, but it, too, meant a blockhead, a stupid or clumsy person.

seneschal

The final syllable rhymes with the second syllable of *marshal.* *Seneschal* has had an odd history. It comes into English in its present form from the French word of the same spelling, but it originated with the Old Teutonic *seniscalc,* "senior servant," from the roots *seni-,* "old," and *skalk,* "servant" (the pronunciation of the *sk* in *skalk* was probably similar to that of the *sk* in the modern Scandinavian languages, or roughly similar to *sh* in modern English). The word was taken into the Romance languages generally, with suitable modifications of spelling, and was even Latinized (*siniscalcus*), being finally adopted back into modern German in the form *Seneschall.* The functions of a seneschal are quite similar to those of the major-domo—both are in charge of the retinue of house servants. *Marshal* has had a very closely similar history. The second part of the word has the same derivation as the above, and the first part is from the Teutonic *marah,* "mare." The antecedent of a mare was, originally, any horse, or even, specifically, a stallion, our word having been derived from the feminine form of the original. So a *marshal,* at least by the origin of the word, was literally a horse servant, a groom, or stable boy.

joe-pye weed

Legend hath it that this common tall weed of New England, blossoming with purple flowers in late summer, was so named "from an Indian of that name, who cured typhus fever with it, by copious perspiration," in the phrasing of the botanist Constantine S. Rafinesque in 1828. Though that legend has been repeated over and over again by subsequent botanists, its veracity has been questioned in recent years by hard-headed fact finders. Since typhus has been known by that name only since 1785, when and where was this cure effected? To what New England tribe did this Indian of curious name belong?

Probably the entire story will now never be uncovered, but, writing in *The Scientific American* (vol. 61, 1945), "On the Fable of Joe Pye," anthropologist F. G. Speck and librarian Ernest S. Dodge tell of learning through old diaries of the existence of a Joseph Pye, alias Shauqueathquat, in 1787, and, from other evidence, advance the possibility that he was a descendent of the original Joe Pye, a medicine man probably living near Salem, Massachusetts, in colonial times.

wishbone

The little innocent game was probably known to Shakespeare— that where two people break the fork-shaped breastbone of a fowl while making a wish. And, of course, it was the act of *wishing* upon a *bone* that resulted in this name for, in technical language, the bone known as the *furcula.* But the name *wishbone* seems to be an Americanism, and it dates only about to the middle of the nineteenth century. The much older British name is *merrythought,* undoubtedly because of the merry thoughts that take place during the wishing game, especially if the two people playing are of opposite sexes. Incidentally, the technical name, *furcula,* is the diminitive of the Latin *furca,* "a two-pronged fork."

John Barleycorn

This legendary gentleman, sometimes styled Sir John Barleycorn, was apparently conceived about the year 1620. That we gather from the use of the name as a title to "A pleasant new ballad . . . of the bloody murther of Sir John Barleycorn," of that period. And the gentleman, if so he was, was even then a personification of malt liquor, or the grain of which it was made. But it is not likely that his name would still be known were it not for Robert Burns. "Inspiring bold John Barleycorn," he wrote in "Tam o' Shanter," "What dangers thou canst make us scorn!" See also his poem "John Barleycorn."

barefaced

Bottom, in *Midsummer Night's Dream,* has suggested that he play the part of Pyramus in a "French-crowne colour'd beard, your perfect yellow," and Quince replies, "Some of your French Crownes haue no haire at all, and then you will play bare-fac'd." The meaning is thus clear, "having no hair upon the face, beardless." Because it is the stripling or boy who is beardless, and because the stripling or boy is usually bold, impudent, shameless, or audacious, the latter is now the usual use. For example, Dickens has the beadle, Mr. Bumble, say to Oliver Twist, who pleads not to be apprenticed into the "chimbley-sweepin' bisness," "Well, of all the artful and designing orphans that ever I see, Oliver, you are one of the most bare-facedest."

sedan

This is a curious example of a word for which the true etymology is not known with certainty, yet for which many authorities have proposed almost as many possible derivations. The only item upon which there is relative unanimity is that the sedan, an enclosed chair seating one person and carried by bearers, was introduced into England in 1634 by Sir Sanders Duncombe, it having been brought from Italy. Dr. Samuel Johnson began the guessing by suggesting that the name was taken from the town of Sedan in northern France, but modern authorities find nothing to support this, even though the 1864 edition of Webster's dictionary cites this as an alleged derivation. The *Oxford English Dictionary* hazards the guess that the word may be derived from the Latin *sedes,* "seat," through the Italian *sedere,* "to sit," but admits the etymology is obscure. The 1941 printing of *Webster's New International Dictionary,* 2nd. ed., offers the observation that the word comes from the Latin *sella,* "chair, saddle," through the Spanish *sillón,* "armchair, side-saddle." The 1946 revision of the *New Standard Dictionary* takes an entirely different slant, proposing that the word is a play upon the first five letters of Sir Sanders' given name, with transposition of the *de,* reversed, ahead of the *an.* About equally plausible would be the suggestion which, so far as I know, has not been advanced before: that Sir Sanders was one of those given to spelling names backward, did so with his name (*srednas*), and, to get a pronounceable word, eliminated the *r* and reversed the *na,* finally dropping the last *s* to avoid the appearance of a plural.

forecastle

Now it is merely the forward and, usually, raised part of a ship; the part, below the deck, where the sailors live. That still explains

fore, but the *castle* section has become so completely obsolete that, indeed, anyone pronouncing the entire word other than "fo'ksl" labels himself immediately as a landlubber. But in the fourteenth and later centuries that forward part of a vessel used in naval warfare served as a floating fortress or *castle.* By its eminence the captain could command the decks of an enemy, and through embrasures in its parapet, shot could be directed.

hellgrammite

This must have started as an Indian name, though if so no one as yet has succeeded in figuring it out. Undoubtedly the name was in wide use long before his time, but present records indicate its first appearance in print in a July, 1866, issue of the publication *Wilkes' Spirit of the Times*, by the American explorer Admiral Charles Wilkes, who wrote thus: "There is another bait for bass called *kill devil*—a sort of indescribable Barnum-what-is-it thing, about three inches in length. An old friend of mine denominated them hell gramites." Other names are *dobson* and *grampus*. They are the larvae of the large four-winged insect, the dobson fly or *Corydalis cornutis*.

tête-à-tête

This adverbial phrase, implying an intimate conversation, is a direct lift from the French, and has the literal meaning "head-to-head." The phrase has been given both adjectival and noun uses in English as applied to chairs so designed as to permit the exchange of confidences, meals served for two persons, and the like. It is interesting to note that the French *tête*, "head," has no relation whatever to the Latin *caput*, "head," as would be expected, but instead is derived (through the Old French *teste*) from the Latin *testa*, "a pot," a slang term for "head."

devil's-darning-needle

The common name in the United States of the dragonfly (which see). We abridge it sometimes to *darning-needle*, and, a hundred years ago, Thoreau and others spoke of the insect as *devil's-needle*. The name is fairly obvious: large staring eyes which remind one of Satan himself, and an extremely slender and long body, not unlike a needle.

windjammer

The earliest use of this term in English is reported to have been in the 1870's, with the meaning of "a horn player." It seems probable that the nickname was coined from the German word for *wind*, which has the same spelling, and from the German verb *jammer* (pronounced *yahmmer*, and from which we get the English *yammer*), which means "to moan, cry, wail." Hence the horn player, who might seem to an unappreciative hearer to be making moaning or wailing sounds with his wind, was given the slang name of *windjammer*. The next oldest use in English is the meaning "a talkative person, blowhard, windbag," and since such a one, too, is making noises with his wind, this meaning seems to be a logical extension of the first. But the most common meaning in English today, which dates from the very last of the nineteenth century, is "a sailing vessel or one of its crew." Here we can only suppose that, in the great rivalry between steam and sail, the men of the sailing ships bragged so loudly of the merits of sail that the supporters of steamships tacked onto them this term, from where it was transferred to the ships as well.

bandoline

Could be that under another name this hair dressing is in use today. It was a sticky aromatic ointment used by dandies of a century back for keeping hair smooth and mustache waxed and pointed and it was made from the boiled pips of the quince. Later it was also used in the making of jellies and soups. The name was probably coined from the French *bandeau,* "band" or "fillet," and Latin *linere,* "to anoint."

subtle

Light as a feather—or better, thin as gossamer. Either of these expressions describes fairly accurately the gentleness which is characteristic of true subtlety, but "gossamer" is a close translation of the Latin word from which *subtle* originates. *Subtle* was brought into English from the Old French *soutil* (alternately spelled *sotil* or *sutil*) with the meaning of "thin (rarefied), fine, delicate." But the French word came from the Latin *subtilis,* a contraction of *subtexilis,* "finely woven" (literally, "underwoven"), from *sub,* "under," and *texare,* "to weave." For many years an alternate spelling of the English word, *subtile,* existed in parallel with the presently accepted spelling, this being based directly on the Latin ancestor.

jimjams

Maybe you think *jimjams* is a new word. Well, in the plural form, it is—relatively so, though it dates back about sixty years. But as a singular it goes back four hundred years. A rhymester of that period wrote:

> *These be as knappishe knackes [knick-knacks]*
> *As ever man made,*
> *For iavells [rascals] and for iackes [jacks],*
> *A iymiam for a iade [jimjam for a jade].*

But from some fantastic trifle, as the slang term then meant, when resurrected sixty years ago it was in the sense of fantastic manners, peculiarities of behavior. And, pray tell, what manner of behavior is more peculiar than that of one overcome by continued overindulgence in spirituous liquor? So *jimjams* became synonymous with delirium tremens. Always seeking novelty of expression, generally ephemeral, we Americans often substitute such variations as *jimwillies,* or just *jimmies,* or even *willies.*

dead horse

Undoubtedly there was once a pathetic story about a poor man who, painfully, saved enough money to make a down payment on a horse that he greatly desired to help him till his land; the sad part being that the horse died long before the buyer had made enough to pay the remainder of his debt, demanded by the seller. Hence the expression, known for two hundred years, "paying for a dead horse." But alas, the story is now entirely hypothetical. No one knows what the original tale may have been.

scalawag

The word, which seems to be a true Americanism, has had several other spellings, the most common of which is *scallywag,* but *scalawag* seems to be the original and, today, is the one most favored. It was first recorded by John Russell Bartlett in the first edition (1848) of his *Dictionary of Americanisms,* in which he defined it as "a favorite epithet in western New York for a mean fellow; a scape-grace." In his fourth edition (1877) he says, "A *scalawag* has been defined to be, 'like many other wags, a compound of loafer, blackguard, and scamp.'" Although many authorities have speculated on the probable origin of this term, with little agreement, I find what seems to be a significant entry in Elwyn's *Glossary of Supposed Americanisms* (1859), wherein he says, "*Scaly,* for a shabby, mean person, is our New England word." Thus, considering the contributions of Bartlett and Elwyn together, and bearing in mind the close proximity of New England and New York, there seems to be an excellent chance that a *scalawag* was. at first, a *scaly wag,* or, in modern parlance, a "crumb bum."

Frankenstein

In 1818, Mary Wollstonecraft Shelley, wife of the poet, Percy Bysshe Shelley, published her first novel. It dealt with the super-

natural, though bearing the noncommittal title *Frankenstein, or the Modern Prometheus.* It was a story telling about a young Swiss student, Victor Frankenstein, who found a way to create life artificially and who, eventually, constructed a body in human form and endowed it with life. But he had no way to imbue it with a soul. Without that controlling element the monster was abhorrent to all whom he would make his mate, and when Frankenstein, his creator, refused to create a mate, he took revenge by murdering, first, Frankenstein's friend, and then his brother, his bride, and finally Frankenstein himself. The book became very popular, but, unfortunately, Mrs. Shelley had not thought to give the creature a name. Hence, readers and others who wished to refer to it acquired the habit of using the title of the book instead. The consequence is that *Frankenstein* has been often applied to any agency of whatever nature that brings about harm or ruin to its proponent or its creator.

penny-a-liner

Always used contemptuously of writers who write to fill space, who use many words but say little. It was applied originally to journalists of the early nineteenth century who, paid at space rates, padded their copy with all the bombast it would bear. With all due respect to the lovers of Dickens there are many, many pages in some of his novels which lead one to suspect that he was, at times, an accomplished *penny-a-liner.*

terrier

Hunting dogs are used for different purposes, according to their several natures, and the peculiar property that distinguishes the class of *terriers* is their ability to dig out burrowing animals from their lairs. It is this earth-moving attribute that has given the class its name. An old name was *terrier dog,* which is a half-translation of the French *chien terrier.* If fully translated, we would have had *burrow dog,* for the French word *terrier* has the meaning "a burrow, a hole in the ground." It comes from their *terre,* "earth," which is from the Latin *terra,* "earth."

argosy

A merchant vessel, especially one richly laden. The term dates to the sixteenth century, to a period when such vessels plied a brisk trade with England from a certain port in Italy. That port was Ragusa (now in Yugoslavia and called Dubrovnik). A ship hailing therefrom was, of course, "a Ragusa," a term rapidly degenerating in dockside language into "a Ragusy," and hence to *argosy.* In *The Merchant of Venice* Shakespeare has:

> *There where your Argosies with portly saile*
> *Like Signiors and rich Burgers on the flood*
> *Or as it were the Pageants of the sea,*
> *Do ouer-peere the pettie Traffiquers*
> *That curtsie to them, do them reuerence*
> *As they flye by them with their wouen wings.*

bandog

Dictionaries for the collegiate trade, slavishly following one another, continue to carry this term, though, except in the works of Sir Walter Scott, a student might never run across it. It simply means a dog, usually a large one such as a mastiff, that is kept tied—*band* here being used in the sense of that which binds, a strap, chain or the like. The word used to be spelled, more properly, *band-dog*. Scott contracted it to *bandog* and so it remains.

saturnine

The planet Saturn was named after the Roman god of the same name, but any symbolic similarity ends there. For Saturn, the god, was feasted with unrestrained merrymaking, and we still recall these riotous feasts in our term *Saturnalia*. On the other hand, Saturn, the planet, was the seventh and most remote planet known to ancient astronomers, and this remoteness was presumed to confer a cold and gloomy attitude upon those under its influence. In sharp contrast to the gay Saturnalia, then, we have the adjective *saturnine,* "gloomy, dull."

haversack

Just think, as far as original meaning is concerned, this soldier's carryall might just as properly have been called a "gunny sack." That is, the original German term was *haber sack,* literally "sack for oats," and it referred especially to the bag, usually of canvas, in which a cavalryman carried oats for his mount. French and English cavalry adopted both bag and name, with slight alteration, and, naturally, found the bags convenient for holding personal items in moving from place to place. And so did other travelers, the flexible *haversack,* with strap over the shoulder, being easier to carry than is the modern suitcase, though perhaps less commodious.

charwoman

In the United States she would be called a Martha-by-the-day; a general houseworker; cleaning woman; mother's helper; or, perhaps, housemaid or maid. We're not familiar, that is, with *char* or *chare* as a synonym for *chore,* "a piece of work, an odd job," applied especially to any of the multitudinous small tasks involved in household labor. But such feminine laborers have been *charwomen* in England for some four hundred years.

galligaskin

Although Noah Webster tried hard to determine the sources of words included in his dictionary of the English language, a hundred-odd years ago, he went far astray at times. And this term, rarely used in America but formerly common in England, was an instance. It is the name of the wide, very loose breeches worn in the sixteenth and seventeenth centuries. The intrepid Webster said that the name came about because "these trowsers were first worn by the *Gallic Gascons,* i.e., the inhabitants of Gascony." But it is really a greatly perverted form of Old French *garguesque,* which meant, "after the fashion of the Greeks," referring to a style of Greek nether garment.

tenterhooks

When cloth is fabricated, it is necessary or desirable to stretch the piece in order to even out the threads and to make the material straight. Before the development of modern machine methods, whereby this is accomplished in the mill as a part of the routine of manufacture, it was the practice to stretch the fabric on frames, usually out of doors, which frames were known as *tenters.* The frames were fitted with pins or hooks to hold the cloth, and these were, of course, *tenterhooks.* The precise derivation of *tenter* is not well established, but it is fairly certain that it comes, eventually, from the Latin *tendere,* "to stretch," through the French. *To be on tenterhooks* is, literally, "to be stretched torturously, to be on the rack," hence, figuratively, "to be subjected to agony approaching that of torture."

heirloom

Sad might you be if told that, as heir to your grandfather's estate, the only things you would receive after all taxes were paid would be "all my various *looms,*" but it might be far better than you think. The old gentleman may have been testing your knowledge of Scottish or northern English dialect and used an old, old meaning that survives only in those areas. A *loom,* that is, might just possibly include the mechanical device used for weaving, but in its earliest meaning a thousand years ago it included all implements, tools, and household items of any kind, everything other than real estate. Such were the original *heirlooms,* but that sense has long since been lost and the term has degenerated into a coverall for any item of whatever nature that has been in a family for two or more generations.

quacksalver

Known in our language for some four hundred years, the term nevertheless was soon felt to be unmanageably long and was reduced to *quack,* with which we are more familiar today. The *quacksalver* was originally an unscrupulous or false physician, one who *quacked* (hawked, or bragged of) his *salves* (ointments). Today, the quack is any charlatan, though still often a make-believe or unethical medical doctor. The word is supposed to have come to us from the Dutch, but the ultimate origin is in considerable doubt, as the same term, with suitable modifications in spelling, is known widely throughout the Germanic languages.

lollipop, lollypop

Travelers in England must have, at least, known of this confection, for it has been familiar to English children, and perhaps their parents, for more than a hundred and fifty years. But to the best of my knowledge and belief it remained unknown to American children until the early twentieth century, perhaps about 1910. Be that as it may, however, the sad fact remains that the origin of the name is a deep dark mystery, though it may somehow have been related to the dialectal word *lolly,* sometimes used in northern England to mean "tongue."

satire

Not too long ago, an inept actor or group of actors might have been driven off the stage by being pelted with an assortment of fruits and vegetables thrown by the disgruntled audience. If the play were a satirical one, the object of the satire would, figuratively, also have been the recipient of the barrage, for *satire* is indirectly derived from the Latin *lanx satura,* "a full dish"—that is, a dish composed of several sorts of food, a potpourri. Dropping the dish (*lanx*), *satura* came to have the meaning of a medley, or more specifically, a short play with a great variety of subject material. Along the way, the spelling became *satira,* and the play developed into a critical commentary. Finally, with the same meaning, the word was adopted into English with its present spelling.

dauphin

As this is French for "dolphin," one may be excused for the thought that its use (from 1349–1830) as the title of the eldest son of the King of France was in playful jest. That was not so. It was originally the title of the lords of the province of Dauphiné, the last of whom, dying childless, bequeathed his possessions to Philip of Valois, with the proviso that his title should pass continuously to the heir to the throne.

hedgehog

This is one of the European members of the porcupine family. Or rather, it is the English name of that member, as its French name is *hérisson,* which might be translated "bristler," and its German name is *Igel.* But despite the *hog* part of the name, neither it nor the porcupine is remotely related to the porcine or swine species of the animal kingdom; *hog* refers merely to the swinelike appearance of the snout. And in England it makes its home chiefly among the hedgerows bordering the roadsides; hence the name. As for the *porcupine*, its name seems to be a highly corrupted form of the Latin *porcus spinosus*, "thorny pig."

gargoyle

Architects and masons of the thirteenth century certainly had an odd sense of humor. Obviously it was their duty to provide  means whereby rainwater should be diverted away from the walls immediately below the roof of cathedral or other imposing edifice. So expert workers in stone were set to carve spouts for this purpose. And these sculptors undoubtedly vied with one another to think up and effect fanciful concepts, thoroughly practical, but also agreeably ornamental, and, often, highly amusing. Many of these were grotesque animals in form; another might be in the shape of a demon; others, perhaps, angels; and another a monk or prelate. But whatever might be represented in stone, all spewed forth streams of water from throat and mouth during a fall of rain. French for "throat" at that period was *gargouille,* giving rise to our English *gargoyle,* by which we know these monstrous carvings.

unmentionables

Prudery is always with us, only the subjects about which we are prudish vary. Often it is difficult—even impossible—for a later generation to understand the reason for some particular prudery of its ancestors. Toward the end of the eighteenth century, for example, it became impolite to mention the words *trousers* or *breeches.* Since it was obviously necessary to refer at times to these ubiquitous garments, various euphemistic terms were coined for the purpose, and *trousers* became *inexpressibles, inexplicables, ineffables,* or *unmentionables.* Later, when *trousers* regained its standing in polite society, it became imprudent to talk about undergarments, especially women's undergarments, and these became *unmentionables.* Modern advertising practice has, by now, pretty well removed all traces of prudery, at least with respect to items of clothing, leaving *unmentionables* without definite standing at present.

sucker

Literally, "one who or that which sucks." In this sense, one application is to the not-yet-weaned young of any animal, and it is this application that has led to the figurative meaning of "dupe, simpleton." For the greenhorns, those "not yet dry behind the ears," are by this term endowed with the ingenuousness and naïveté that are presumably characteristic of a babe too young to be removed from his mother's breast.

Charterhouse

This is the name of one of the great public schools of London. But whether or not the institution has a charter, the fact has no bearing on its name. Its site was originally that of a Carthusian monastery, an order which derives its name from that of the French village where it first arose. That village was La Grande Chartreuse. Its early English spelling was *Chartrous*. Combined with the fact that the monastery then bore the French name, *maison Chartreuse,* "Carthusian house," the Londoners quite naturally amplified *Chartrouse* into *Charterhouse*.

fifty-fifty

In equal amounts: an Americanism which, since early in the twentieth century, has had the contracted meaning of 50 per cent for you (or one person) and 50 per cent for me (or another person).

Charles's Wain

The wain—four-wheeled wagon—of Charles the Great, and this is the name applied by some, even back around the year 1000, to the constellation, the Great Bear, *Ursa Major,* the Big Dipper.

To some eyes, that is, the bowl of the Dipper had the appearance of the huge wagons of old, the stars in the handle being the long shaft. And, of course, no greater man ever lived worthy of such a wain than Charlemagne, Charles the Great. Tennyson, in "New Year's Eve," has the line, "Till Charles's Wain came out above the tall white chimney-tops."

sarcastic

True sarcasm wounds the one against whom it is directed as deeply as though it were the flesh rather than the spirit receiving the attack. The Greeks recognized this, and invented an appropriate metaphor. From the word *sarx*, "flesh," they had already coined *sarkazein*, "to tear the flesh in the manner of a dog." And from this they invented *sarkastikos*, "bitterly cutting, caustic," or, exactly, *sarcastic*.

willy-nilly

Many years ago there existed, in Old English, a verb that was the negative of *will*, "to desire, to be in an acceptable or purposeful frame of mind." This verb of negation was *nill*, "to be unwilling, not to will." It is known to have existed as early as the ninth century in Anglo-Saxon, and its use continued in good standing until about the first of the seventeenth century. Since then it has become obsolete or archaic except as it has been used specifically in conjunction with *will* in one of several expressions signifying known futility. These expressions have included such combinations as *willing . . . nilling; will I, nill I; will ye, nill ye; will he, nill he* (sometimes in the reverse order), all of which imply that "such a thing will be, or will happen, regardless of the desires of the person affected." All these forms have now been contracted into the single expression of futility which is our *willy-nilly*.

bandbox

This box had nothing to do with a company of musicians, as I thought when a very young child. But, back in the seventeenth century, it was a box of thin wood—chip, it was called—in which lords and ladies kept the very wide collars or "bands" of lace or plain linen that were then in vogue. When starched to stand up, they were simply "bands," but when extending flat across the shoulders and down the chest, they were called "falling bands." Our Puritan forebears are depicted with small plain falling bands, and the clerical collar of today owes its origin to that band.

gremlin

He was born during the early stages of World War II, sired by British aviators, but otherwise of uncertain parentage, though  possibly from the womb of the Irish term *gruaimin,* "an ill-natured runt." He was very small, though wholly invisible. And it was his delight to ride in anyone's airplane and perform mischievous tricks upon engine, wings, gun, propeller, flaps, or other part, unaccountable but most annoying or disastrous to the flyer. He was just some sort of goblin who resented man's use of the air for the waging of warfare.

strait-laced

Often, because of the similar pronunciation, misspelled "straight-laced." The first element was *streit* in Middle English, having been introduced in about the fourteenth century. It came from the Old French *estreit,* "tight, close, narrow," and similar words (Spanish *estrecho,* Portuguese *estreito,* Italian *stretto*) are to be found in the other Romance languages. All are derived from the Latin *strictus,* the past participle of *stringere,* "to tighten, bind tightly." *Lace* came in to the languge at about the same time, also from the French (*lacier*) from the Latin *laciare,* "to ensnare." Here, too, there are closely related words in the other Romance languages. The two words have been found together as early as 1430 in their literal significance of "tightly laced," but the compound term is not found until the sixteenth century. It was about at the same time that the figurative use of the term became established, for the

808

strictures laid upon the body through the tight lacing of the bodice were quickly seen to be closely similar to those laid upon one's conduct through what seemed to be excessive prudishness.

cutpurse

The pocket as an ordinary adjunct of man's outer attire is not very old, dating back only a few centuries. Before that time anything that a man carried with him had to be in his hands or hung about his person. And money was just as necessary an evil then as it is now. And, being gold or silver, it was heavy and difficult to conceal. Such coins were customarily carried in leather pouches or purses hanging from one's girdle. What could be simpler than for three or four ruffians to jostle the wearer while one of the number cut the purse and released the coins, or for a deft hand to cut the cord by which it hung? The penalty for detection, however, was severe. Thereafter a *cutpurse* was marked by the absence of one or both ears.

harlot

An old dictionary in my possession, Thomas Blount's *Glossographia* (1656), has this to say of the origin of this word: "Metonymically"—a word used as a substitute for another—"from *Arlotta* and *Harlotha,* Concubine to *Robert* Duke of Normandy, on whom he begat *William* the Bastard, Conqueror, and King of *England;* in spight to whom, and disgrace to his Mother, the English called all Whores Harlots." But, though an interesting story, it was taken by Blount from a piece of vague guesswork made by another writer a hundred years earlier, William Lambarde. The word is actually a modification of Old French *harlot,* used in such a manner as we use "fellow."

tenderfoot

First appeared in the literal sense of "having tender feet," as applied to horses, and recorded in this sense in the late seventeenth century, in England, as the adjective *tenderfooted.* The use of the word as applied to a person is conceded to be an Americanism, and probably arose also in the literal sense, referring to one who, unused to traveling, became footsore. However, the earliest recorded use of the word is not in this literal meaning, but in the figurative one of "a greenhorn, a novice." This meaning has been dated to as early as 1849, and was popularized by the emigrants to California in the gold rush of that time. A slightly earlier use (1842) of the adjective in the sense of "timid" has also been found in American usage, but this sense has not survived.

pell-mell

Authorities disagree here. Some have it that, of Old French origin, this was a combination of *pesle,* a "shovel," and *mesle,* "to mix." Hence, "mixed as with a shovel." But others, though agreeing with the source of the second element, take it that *pell* was never more than a reduplication. The French coiners, back in the twelfth century, are not telling. It was widely borrowed by English writers of the sixteenth century, used by Shakespeare in *Henry IV,* Part I (Act V, Scene i): "Nor moody Beggars, staruing for a time Of pell-mell hauocke, and confusion."

jew's-harp

As far as has yet been ascertained, no Jew had anything to do with the introduction of this so-called musical instrument into England, with its naming, or with its previous invention, or with the slightly earlier name, *jew's-trump.* Both names date from the sixteenth century, and both are peculiar to the English language, the latter still used in Scotland. The French name, formerly *trompe,* is now generally replaced by *guimbarde.* All sorts of theories have been advanced to account for the name, but none stands up in the cold light of day.

logrolling

Now political slang expressing exchange of support upon favored legislation, this found its birth in an honorable custom among neighboring American frontiersmen establishing a new settlement. A house of some sort was, of necessity, the first consideration. It might be temporary and of rude construction. But as soon as opportunity permitted, a site was selected for a permanent home. For warmth, as well as protection against marauding Indians, such homes were erected from the trunks of trees cleared from land to be used in later planting—log cabins or log houses. And for mutual assistance, neighbor would assist neighbor in bringing logs to the site and erecting the walls. This mutual assistance constituted *logrolling*.

wigwam

The 1864 edition of Webster's *Dictionary of the English Language* (G. & C. Merriam) offers the following etymology, and most other authorities are in general agreement:

From Algonquin or Massachusetts *wēk*, "his house," or "dwelling place"; with possessive and locative affixes, *wēkou-om-ut*, "in his (or their) house"; contracted by the English to *weekwam*, and *wigwam*.

char-à-banc

Even if you know your French, but have never actually seen this vehicle, the name, "car with bench," will not give you much of a picture of it. Actually this "benched carriage" strongly resembled the motor bus that has replaced it. It was long and narrow, and the transverse "benches" or seats faced forward.

telltale

Tell and *tale* are closely related in an etymological sense, one being the verb form and the other the noun form of the same word. The original sense was in the concept of counting, and related parallel terms are found in the Anglo-Saxon *tellan, talu;* Dutch *tellen, taal;* German *zählen, Zahl* (number); Old Norse *telja, tala*. *Tell*, in the sense of "to count," exists today as *teller*, "one who counts money or votes"; *tale* in the counting sense has pretty well vanished (*tally,* which would seem to be related, is of different origin). So it would seem likely that a *telltale* might have been a scorekeeper or reckoner, but there is no evidence that the word was ever applied in this sense. Instead, a *telltale* is simply a bearer of tales, a tattler.

G string, gee string

Let me say at the outset that the reason one or the other of these terms was given to the type of breechclout worn by some

 American Indians has never been definitely determined. The early plainsmen who, apparently, were first to use it did not leave explanatory notes. But I shall offer a conjecture: That which the American Indian used for a cord was, of course, a length of sinew or a strand of gut, and, naturally, such a strand tied around one's waist to carry the single strip of cloth or flexible hide running between the limbs from front to back was of such thickness as not to cut the flesh. Now, among any group of plainsmen in frontier days there was likely to be one, at least one, who toted and played a fiddle. Necessarily having to replace its string from time to time, it would occur to him that the cord of the Indian breechclout might serve as the heaviest of its strings. That would be the *G string.*

roundabout

One of the earlier descriptive names of that form of a hoop-skirted dress known as a *farthingale* (which see), *roundabout* was obviously coined with particular reference to the encircling lower part of that garment. Later, in extension of the same sense, it became applied to garments which encircled the body completely, such as a greatcoat, as well as a woman's dressing gown. Finally, early in the nineteenth century (and the use has persisted into the twentieth), American clothiers effected a major shift of emphasis

812

with respect to the area surrounded by adopting the same word, *roundabout*, as the name of a short jacket reaching no lower than the waist, such as is worn by small boys.

harebell

Dictionaries hazard merely the guess that these wild hyacinths, so common in England and Scotland, were "perhaps" so named because they grow in places frequented by hares, but I prefer to think the ancient Saxons had a more poetic notion. "Yes," they may have said, "they are plentiful where hares abide, and the hares love to tinkle them as they pass, so we shall call them the *harebell*."

telegraph

An old pun has it that there are three ways to spread news rapidly: telegraph, telephone, or tell a woman. But the French inventor Chappe had no pun in mind when he gave this name to the instrument which he had devised in 1793, for transmitting messages by means of a sort of semaphore. It comes from two Greek words, *tele*, "far off," and *graphein*, "to write." There have, since Chappe's day, been other devices known as telegraphs, but the word has now become restricted almost entirely to the electromagnetic instrument invented by Morse in the 1830's. *Telephone*, too, was coined much earlier than the invention of the instrument with which it is now associated. The first element is the same as above—the second is the Greek *phone*, "sound, voice."

banana oil

Actually an aromatic liquid having the odor of a ripe banana, chiefly employed as a solvent for lacquers. Chemically it is isoamyl acetate, if you know what that is. But when your young son says, "Aw, that's just banana oil," in terms of derision or of praise, his slang usage is that he regards the "that" as either nonsense or as flattery.

daredevil

One so reckless as to be willing to dare the devil himself. Curiously enough, though we've had all sorts of foolhardy, devil-may-care, harebrained madcaps throughout history, it was less than two hundred years ago that the term *daredevil* was pinned upon such an individual. And, as is so disheartening to the researcher, there is now no clue as to the identity of the person so described. The earliest literary usage is insipid: "I deemed myself a dare-devil in rhime," said John Wolcott in *Odes to Mr. Paine* (1794).

roughrider

It may surprise many of the younger generation—those who grew up in this age of mechanization—to learn that the term *roughrider* was not coined specifically as a name for Teddy Roosevelt's cavalry regiment of the Spanish-American War. Instead, the word originally was used to describe a man who specialized in breaking horses to harness, that is, a bronco buster. The word has been known in print at least since the early eighteenth century, and probably existed in speech long before that time. As for the Rough Riders of Roosevelt, a major reason for their acquiring the sobriquet was that many of the members of the regiment were just that—bronco busters and cowboys recruited from the "Wild West" by Roosevelt himself.

lodestar, lodestone

Obviously, *lodestar* indicates the star or other force or attraction that points the "lode." But if that isn't clear, perhaps it should be explained that, early in our language, *lode* carried the meaning "way" or "course." Similarly, a *lodestone*, now more frequently spelled *loadstone*, was originally a piece of stone containing strongly magnetized iron which was used by mariners to point out the way, to direct them on their course.

Sanhedrin

Historically, this is the correct spelling for this ancient Jewish council, but the spelling *Sanhedrim* is often seen. The word comes from the Greek *synhedrion,* "council," which is made up of *syn,* "together," and *hedra,* "seat," hence, literally, "seat together."

halibut

For the past six or seven hundred years, the common name in England for any of the flatfish—skate, flounder, plaice, turbot, or

whatever—has been *butt.* The most highly prized of all, the one formerly reserved for eating upon holy days, was the largest of the flatfish, so large that some run up to three or four hundred pounds and to seven or eight feet in length. These, some five centuries ago, were termed *haly* (holy) *butts,* whence cometh our present spelling. But the eating of this "holy flounder" is no longer confined to feast days of the church.

chapbook

This item still circulated when I was small, though it was begun in the early nineteenth century. It and its kind were, in a way, the forerunners of the modern "comic" books, though the reading matter in any that came my way, at least, could never be called lurid. The contents—short stories, poems, tales by explorers—of those presented to me at Christmas were highly moral, as I recall, and the illustrations most demure. But the name of these board-covered cheap volumes was in no wise connected with the young "chaps" who read them; originally they were "chapmen's books," some of the various items sold by retailers or peddlers—*chapmen* —especially in England.

bamboozle

My third edition (1737) of Nathan Bailey's *Universal Etymological English Dictionary,* first published in 1721, contains "A Collection of the Canting Words . . . used by Beggars, Gypsies, Cheats, House-Breakers, Shop-Lifters, Foot-Pads, Highway-men, etc.," and carries this entry: "A BAM, a Sham or Cheat; a knavish Contrivance to amuse or deceive." *Bamboozle,* a verb of like sense, is not shown but is the same age, late seventeenth century, and is among the terms listed by Jonathan Swift in 1710 as among the slang terms of "Continual Corruption of our English Tongue." Others were *banter, put, sham, mob, bubble, bully.* The word is not related to *bamboo.* In fact, clues to its origin are lacking.

linsey-woolsey

One rarely knows through what influence a word has been created. Possibly some little Ælfrida of the fifteenth century at her mother's knee could not rightly say "linen," and the mother and father, thereafter humoring the child, also said *linsey.* No one knows. But, if we add to the fanciful story, we may then also assume that the father, weaving a textile of flax and wool, went a step further in childish speech and called his weave *linsey-woolsey.*

teetotum

This ancient gambling game was played by spinning a toplike device having four sides or segments which were marked, respectively, with the letters A, T, N, D. The players spun the device one after another, and their fate was established by that face of the toy that lay upward at the end of the spin. Each letter was the initial of a Latin word having, in the game, some special significance, as follows: T, *totum,* player wins the pot; A, *aufer,* player takes one stake from the pot; D, *depone,* player puts one stake into the pot; N, *nihil,* player takes or puts nothing. Later the letters were changed to correspond to English words, but it is from the winning face of the older form that the device and the game took their name—T for totum, shortened to *teetotum.*

Argonaut

An adventurer, especially one who sails the seas in search of fortune or adventure. This present-day interpretation arose from those so called who, in 1849, lured by reports of vast gold fields in

California, endured great hardship to reach that land of promise, especially those who went by sea first to Central America, thence by land through jungle and mountain to the Pacific, and by ship again to San Francisco. The name actually derives from the Greek legend of the search by Jason, in the ship *Argo*, for the golden fleece. He and his fifty companions were *Argonautes*, from *Argo*, the ship, and *nautes*, "sailor."

lich gate

Our remote forebears went all out at a burial, and this is just one of the reminders. The *lich* (rhymes with *rich*) was the corpse, borne from house to churchyard. It was carried over a *lich way* or path to the solemn sound of a *lich bell,* and at the *lich gate,* or roofed entrance to the churchyard, the coffin was placed upon a *lich stone* to await the arrival of the clergyman, and was then finally carried to the *lich rest* or grave. Previous to death, perhaps, a *lich owl* may have shrieked its ominous prophecy.

whippersnapper

The word itself is merely a balanced extension of *whip-snapper,* "one who cracks a whip." Its use is most often in the sense of "one who cracks a whip loudly to make a fearsome noise because he himself would have no attention paid to him otherwise." In other words, "an insignificant, impudent nobody."

chaparajos

We picked this up from our Mexican neighbors and have abbreviated it to *chaps*. Rightly, we should say *chaparreras,* a term used by Mexicans for a kind of leather breeches worn over the trousers to protect the legs when riding through *chaparral,* a dense tangle of dwarf oak and thorny shrub common in the Southwest.

jerrybuilt

Jerry, whoever he was, was a bad egg, or at least one held in contempt. He first appeared on the literary scene in the early eighteenth century as *jerrymumble* or *jerrycummumble* in some such sense as a tumbler or one who is knocked about. Scott, gruesomely, has a *jerry-come-tumble* dancing at the end of a hangman's rope. And we had a *Jerry-Sneak,* an unkind appellation for a browbeaten husband. Latest to appear was the *jerrybuilt* cottage of about a hundred years ago, certainly too unsubstantial to be still standing, but being replaced daily through the efforts of modern *jerrybuilders.* No record exists of the identity of the first Jerry deserving such continued reproach.

hangdog

There's no evidence that I have found of the actual hanging of any dog nor of the actual appearance of any person who had committed such an act. So the only inference that can be drawn is that someone gifted with high imaginative powers, about three centuries ago, figured that a dog, if hung, would have a cringing abject demeanor, or that the person capable of hanging it would have a contemptible sneaky aspect, and thus applied the term to one of such character or appearance.

leghorn

Whether it be straw hat or chicken is all the same. The original of either was produced at Legorno, Italy, or, as the English had previously misnamed it, *Leghorn.* Even yet, though the Italians have renamed it Livorno, it remains *Leghorn* on British and American maps.

roulette

See entry under **roué.** As shown there, the French word *roue* (no accent) means "a wheel." A *roulette,* of course, is "a little wheel." And all those who have played the game of chance of the same name are well aware that it is a little wheel that governs the destinies of the players.

818

bambino

Italian for "infant, baby," and applied specifically to images of the infant Jesus in swaddling clothes now exhibited generally at Christmas. The term has the same root as Greek *bambaino*, "to stutter," and was probably suggested by the prattle of an infant.

sanguine, sanguinary

So similar in appearance, so similar in etymology (both are derived from the Latin *sanguis*, "blood"), these words are quite different in meaning, and care must be exercised not to use one when the occasion requires the use of the other. *Sanguine*, literally "bloody," has been used to describe something that was actually bloody or was blood-colored (and is still correctly, though rarely, used in this sense). From this, it was used to describe a person of ruddy complexion, that is, one of good blood, healthy. Then it was but a slight change of meaning to apply it, in its present sense, to one who is of hopeful disposition, or confident of success, for these are attributes supposedly borne by one who is healthy. *Sanguinary*, also with the literal meaning of "bloody," is used more with respect to bloodshed, and is properly applied to a person who is bloodthirsty, delighting in carnage, of cruel disposition.

Darby and Joan

Typification of marital contentment. Names and allusion are assumed to be from a set of verses appearing in *The Gentleman's Magazine* in 1735 under the title, "The Joys of Love Never Forgot: a song." The author was presumably Henry Woodfall, though that is not certain. The third stanza reads:

> *Old Darby, with Joan by his side,*
> *You've often regarded with wonder:*
> *He's dropsical, she is sore-eyed,*
> *Yet they're never happy asunder.*

soft sawder

To treat a man with soft sawder is to flatter him—to "butter him up." But why? Well, *sawder* is an obsolete spelling of *solder*, and is still a phonetic spelling of a dialectal pronunciation of the word. And *solder,* a low-melting alloy used for uniting certain metals, is derived from the Latin *solidus,* "solid." The transition from *solidus* to *solder* took place through a now obsolete verb form, *sold* (approximate pronunciation is *sawd*), meaning "to unite by soldering or welding." Now, one of the objects of flattery is to get the flatterer "in solid" with the person being flattered. And soft solder is easier to apply than is the hard variety, even though it may be less durable. The final link in this particular chain of evidence is obvious.

hillbilly

Probably the best and, according to the *Dictionary of Americanisms,* the first printed description appeared in the New York

Journal, April 23, 1900: "A Hill-Billie is a free and untrammelled white citizen of Alabama, who lives in the hills, has no means to speak of, dresses as he can, talks as he pleases, drinks whiskey when he gets it, and fires off his revolver as the fancy takes him." In more recent years the territory has been vastly increased and the habits enlarged to include addiction to stringed musical instruments, often as accompaniments to group or individual nasal singing of so-called "hillbilly songs." *Billy,* tracing back through some four centuries of usage, just means "fellow."

teetotal

There are various accounts of the origin of this word, all more or less well documented, and the evidence indicates that it probably came into being both in America and in England, independently, within the space of a few years, early in the nineteenth century. The earliest use, though, seems to have been American, in the form *tetotally,* the extra *e* being added later. In any event, the word was coined in connection with the temperance movement to signify absolute abstinence from alcohol by emphasizing, through repetition, the initial sound of *total—T-total.*

820

chanticleer

In the old, old tales of the exploits of *Reynard the Fox,* fragments of which have been traced to the tenth century, this was the proper name of the cock—"So sawe they comen doun the hylle to hem chauntecler the cock," in the first printed edition by William Caxton in 1481. The name, taken from some old French version, was in recognition of the far-reaching early-morning summons of the cock, "the clear singer," from *chanter,* "to sing," and *cler,* "clear."

jerkwater

Strongly divergent views appeared in 1945 in relating the origin of this. James L. Marshall in *Santa Fe, the Railroad That Built an Empire* says that that railroad was so named because the crews "jerked water" by bucket from wayside streams to fill the locomotive tender. But the *Engineman's Magazine* in September of the same year gives the laurels to the New York Central, which, in June, 1870, made the first installation, at Montrose, New York, of water pans between the tracks whereby locomotives could scoop up water.

Both of these explanations strike me as lame and inadequate, however. Marshall may have been partly right, though certainly not in applying "Jerkwater Line" to the whole Sante Fe Railroad. A branch line, yes—one feeding one or more towns too small and insignificant to have regular main-line service. Train crews on such lines had plenty of time to fill tenders by bucket brigades, and, naturally enough, the one-horse towns on such branch lines were scornfully "jerkwater towns."

Arctic

It relates, of course, to the region around the North Pole, but the ancient Greek astrologers and mariners called it by this name from the constellation that circumscribes the area of the heavens above it, the Bear, which in Greek is *arktos.* That about the South

Pole then became *antarktos,* from *anti,* "opposite," and *arktos,* "Bear"; hence, "opposite the north." Through Latin adaptation, the names have been further modified to *arctic* and *antarctic.*

mumble-peg

It was *mumbly-peg* in my boyhood, probably contracted from *mumblety-peg* from an earlier *mumble-the-peg.* But the game seems to have disappeared from the American scene entirely. I don't know why, unless it may be that mothers are more fearful lest their young roughnecks cut themselves with a sharp knife. The name derives from the manner in which the game was played in England from the early seventeenth century and as brought by boys thence to America. From various positions, toe, knee, elbow, fingers, each player in turn flipped his opened knife with sufficient force to stick in the ground. If unsuccessful, the other players had the privilege of driving a peg into the ground with an agreed number of blows struck with the handles of their knives, a peg which the loser was then supposed to withdraw with his teeth. My memory may be faulty, Mummy, but I doubt that after one game of *mumbly-peg* any knife was then sharp enough to produce serious injury.

fifth wheel

Nowadays used contemptuously or at least disrespectfully of a person or thing as useless or needless as an extra wheel for the support of a vehicle ordinarily running on four. But in original use the term was applied to a metal wheel or circular plate (sometimes a segment of one) having an important service and never touching the ground. It lay horizontally beneath the forward part of the body of a wagon or carriage and was attached to the upper side of the front axle, thus supporting the body while the vehicle turned a corner or the like.

wardrobe

There are a few words native to the Teutonic languages which, in these, are spelled with *w,* but which, on having been adopted

822

into the Romance group, were spelled with a *g,* or, perhaps, with *gu.* One of the latter is represented by our word *guard.* This started in Old Teutonic as *warda* and was taken into most Romance languages as *guarda,* but became modified, in Old French, to *guarde* or *garde.* It seems to have been in France that a room, generally adjoining a bedchamber, was set aside in which to keep clothing, and this room was named *garderobe*—or it may have been in Italy that it began, where the room was called *guarda-robba.* But in northeastern France, where the language was under the influence of the neighboring Teutonic tongues, the first element underwent a reversion to the Teutonic form, and the word became *warderobe,* in which form it was taken into English, elision of the first *e* following later.

hobbyhorse

The term itself is merely repetition, as, six centuries ago, a *hobby* was a horse, a small horse, probably a nickname for *Robin.* But

hobbyhorse comes to us from the sixteenth-century morris dance, commonly held throughout England at Whitsuntide —mid-May. Although the characters in these festivals chiefly represented Robin Hood and others of his company—Friar Tuck and Maid Marian invariably—there was also always a horseman ostensibly astride a small horse, dancing fantastically among the group. In reality the horse was a gaily caparisoned framework of wicker or the like, surmounted by an imitation of a horse's head, all carried by the rider. The morris dance has long since departed; the *hobbyhorse,* considerably modified for the sport of young children, is the sole survivor.

chameleon

Ancient Greeks had some of the most peculiar and original notions. Heaven knows wherein anything in the nocturnal skies to warrant the names they gave to many of the constellations, and here again they seem to have let imagination run riot. This small lizardlike reptile, for reasons one can't even guess, rejoices in the Greek name *chamai*, "dwarfed," *leon*, "lion"—"the dwarfed lion." And the ancients also thought these creatures could go for interminable periods living only on air.

sang-froid (sahn·frwah)

We are all impressed by those, like the "private eyes" of television and whodunits, who remain calm, cool, and collected amid the greatest stress. This time it was the French who had a word for it—actually, two words telescoped by frequent use into one. *Sang-froid* is a direct lift into English from the French, dating back at least to the eighteenth century, and possibly introduced about the time of the Norman Conquest. The literal meaning is "cold blood," and the derivation is from the Latin *sanguis*, "blood," plus *frigidus*, "cold." We would say that a man who exhibits *sang-froid* is "cool as a cucumber."

hardtack

If this term were not already available it is possible that today's mariner would invent a term of similar import, such as "hard grub," as all that was intended by *tack*, a hundred years ago, was food of any sort. *Hard tack* was literally hard food, or, that is, biscuit of more than ordinary hardness to have on hand in rough weather. The modern slang equivalent is *dog biscuit*.

tattletale

This word is an American colloquialism, but its antecedents are well established in English. The first part, *tattle*, dates back to 1481 with the publication of Caxton's translation of *Reynard the Fox* from the Flemish. As then used, the word had the meaning "to speak hesitatingly, to stammer," being Caxton's rendering of *tatelen* ("tattling"), a variant of *tateren*. Low German has a related *tateln*, "to gabble, cackle." But *tattle* acquired other meanings, such as "to chat," "to gossip," and eventually, "to tell tales." It is presumably to indicate precisely which meaning was intended that our Americanism was invented, for a *tattletale* is specifically a tale bearer.

April fool

Since April is the first month of spring, when all things are green, it stands to reason that people are green then too, and, no more than half awake after a long winter hibernation, in prime condition to be easily hoaxed. The custom was apparently brought across the channel from France to England about the beginning of the eighteenth century, as Jonathan Swift, in his *Journal to Stella,* enters under March 31, 1713, that he and others had been contriving "a lie for tomorrow."

chafing dish

We are so accustomed to the use of *chafe* in the sense of "to abrade; to fret," as to overlook that its earliest meaning (derived from Latin *calefacio*) was "to make warm." And the *chafing dish,* or *chafer,* as first called, was designed for that purpose. They were used and so named five hundred years ago. In a will of the following century a man bequeathed to his sister "a chaffyndyche."

hotspur

This title, or designation of extreme impetuosity, was first bestowed upon Sir Henry Percy, eldest son of the first Earl of Northumberland, born in 1364. He was only a lad of fourteen when he saw active service, but it was not until six years later that gained the title "Hotspur"—a name by which he was known the rest of his life—in another of the continuing conflicts against the bordering Scots. In later years, dissatisfied with the treatment he received from Henry IV, by whom he had previously been greatly honored, Hotspur took up arms against the king, but was killed in battle, July, 1403.

mugwump

According to the King James Version of the Bible, Genesis 36:15 reads: "These were dukes of the sons of Esau . . ." But when John Eliot, in 1663, translated the Bible into the tongue of the native Indians of Massachusetts, he used *mugquomp,* meaning "chieftain," as the equivalent of "duke." As *Mug-Wump,* the word appeared in 1832 in the ironical sense of one who would like to be considered a chieftain or vastly important great man. But fifty years later, or, to be exact, in the presidential campaign of 1884, though at first applied in derision to members of the Republican party who, it was said, thought themselves too virtuous or too important to support the Republican nominee, James G. Blaine, it was taken over by those men themselves as a term for an independent Republican. Since then anyone, even in England, who fails to vote in accordance with the policies of his party is considered a *mugwump,* or, as waggishly said of one such independent, "His mug is where his wump should be."

hoodwink

To get the original significance we must go back to the old, old meaning of *wink*—to have one's eyes closed. Thus, in the sixteenth

century, when fashion decreed head coverings of cowls or hoods, often attached to the cloak, one became *hoodwinked* or blinded when the hood fell or was drawn over the eyes. Thieves and purse snatchers took advantage of the fashion to *hoodwink* victims. But the term and practice were also employed in the game of blindman's buff. Hawks and falcons were also *hoodwinked* when being carried.

fife rail

A mariner's term, now indicating a rail round the mainmast of a sailing vessel with holes into which belaying pins may be inserted. Originally, however, according to Admiral W. H. Smyth's *The*

Sailor's Word-Book (1867), it formed "the upper fence of the bulwarks on each side of the quarter-deck and poop in men-of-war." By repute, the fifer had his seat on this "upper fence" while the anchor was being hoisted.

dandelion

They used to call it *lion's-tooth* in England before the sixteenth century, but someone then got fancy notions and began to use the French name of this common European weed, *dent de lion,* though it has the same meaning. Of course, it didn't make sense to the average Englishman to spell something *dent de* and pronounce it *dan de,* so he soon changed the whole thing into *dandelion.* The name, incidentally, refers to the shape of the deeply indented leaf, not to that of the flower.

saltpeter

An alternative spelling, preferred in England, is *saltpetre.* Chemically, saltpeter is potassium nitrate, a compound essential to the making of gunpowder and also of important value as a fertilizer. The name comes from the Latin *sal petrae,* "salt of the rock," so-called because it is sometimes found in nature as an efflorescence on rocks or soil. However, saltpeter is definitely not to be confused with *rock salt,* even though it has a saline taste. Rock salt is merely sodium chloride (table salt) which has been induced to form large, rather than small, crystals.

viscount

In Latin, the word *vice* (two syllables) meant "alternate, in place of," and, although it had the standing of a noun, there arose the practice in later Latin, and particularly in medieval Latin, of using it chiefly as one element of a compound noun. A number of these compounds were taken into the various other Romance languages, and they are found in French chiefly with the spelling *vis-* or *vi-*. So the Old French word for that member of the lower nobility who was an alternate count became *visconte* or *viconte* (modern French, *vicomte*), from the medieval Latin *vicecomes.* On being taken into

English, the spelling of the first part retained the French form, whereas the spelling of the second part was altered to the English form, to give us the half-French, half-English term *viscount.*

peanut

So called only because the nut somewhat resembles a pea in size. In the early days of American colonization it was known as the *ground-nut* or *ground-pea,* because it developed under the surface of the ground, and those names still occur, especially in England. Another name is *earth-nut.* Discovered first in South America by Spaniards, it was introduced by them into equatorial Africa, from whence Negro slaves brought the name *nguba* with them to the plantations of the Southern United States, where it speedily became *goober.* The English, slow to accept the shelled and roasted nuts for human consumption, long knew peanuts as *monkey-nuts,* because the simians in the zoo avidly consumed all that were tossed to them.

St. Swithin's Day

Many of the saints' names have become associated in folklore with vagaries of the weather, some with actual occurrences (cf. **St. Martin's summer**) and some with respect to weather to be anticipated. Swithin (sometimes *Swithun*) was Bishop of Winchester in the ninth century A.D., and upon his death was buried in the churchyard. According to some reports, during the century after his death it was recalled that he had performed many miraculous cures, and it was decided that he should be canonized and his remains re-interred in the cathedral. The date selected was July 15, 971. On this date, rain fell so hard as to require postponing the ritual, and continued for forty days thereafter. Hence the saying that, "If it rains on St. Swithin's day [July 15], it will rain for forty days," which dates to at least the sixteenth century.

fiddle-faddle

There was no definite source; the word *fiddle* was in the language and, four hundred years ago, it had taken on the meaning "to act aimlessly," so, just like such duplications as flip-flop, jim-jams, helter-skelter, and the like, someone turned it into *fiddle-faddle*. Thus since the sixteenth century this nonsense word has implied aimless or idle action or conversation, or any thing or occupation that is of little consequence: "Pete's sudden interest in postage stamps is just so much fiddle-faddle."

larboard

The first element, *lar,* is often assumed to have been a corruption of *lade,* thus making *larboard* the side of a vessel for loading, the side opposite the "steering side" or *starboard*. The assumption is logical, but the sad fact is that it cannot be traced—as a lawyer would say, "not proven."

hushpuppy

Which of the Southern states is your preference? The invention of this comestible, or at least the name for it, has been claimed by  most of those south of the Potomac, though never even approximately dated by any, so you may make your own choice. The account of the origin of the name, however, is always strikingly similar, the difference being chiefly in the personnel of the group assembled for the meal and the one distributing the largesse. The account now circulated by the Tallahassee (Florida) Chamber of Commerce is the most colorful of those I have seen, so, without prejudice, I shall follow it. It is taken from *The Southern Cook Book* (1939), compiled and edited by Lillie S. Lustig, S. Claire Sondheim and Sarah Rensel, and published by Culinary Arts Press, Reading, Pennsylvania. With the permission of the publishers to quote, this account, slightly abridged, reads:

"Years ago the Negroes of Tallahassee . . . would congregate on warm fall evenings for [sugar] cane grinding. . . . After their work was completed, they would gather around an open fire, over which was suspended an iron pot in which fish and corn pones were cooked in fat.

"The Negroes were said to have a certain way of making these corn pones which were unusually delicious and appetizing. While the food was sizzling in the pot, they would spell-bind each other with 'tall' stories of panther and bear hunts. On the outer edge of the circle of light reflected by the fire would sit their hounds, their noses raised to catch a whiff of the savory odor of the frying fish and pones. If the talking ceased for a moment, a low whine of hunger from the dogs would attract the attention of the men, and subconsciously a hand would reach for some of the corn pone which had been placed on a slab of bark to cool. The donor would break off a piece of the pone and toss it to a hungry dog, with the abstract murmur, 'Hush, puppy.'

"The effect of this gesture on the hounds was always instantaneous and the Negroes attributed the result to the remarkable flavor of what eventually became known as 'The Tallahassee Hush Puppy.' "

I take no responsibility for the accuracy of this account. In fact, a more recent cookbook says that the fried dainty and its naming were inventions of colonial days. And another, also recent, attributes the naming to Northern soldiers accompanying General Sherman on his famous march through Georgia. The "puppies" similarly "hushed," according to this account, were hungry dogs which followed the Northern army.

roué

Back in the days when criminals, real or fancied, were punished by being put to torture, the French word *roue* (no accent mark), meaning "wheel," and derived from the Latin *rota,* came to have the special meaning "torture wheel." From this, in turn, was coined the verb *rouer,* "to torture (break) on the wheel." Now the Duke of Orleans, about 250 years ago, was rather a disreputable rake-hell, and surrounded himself with companions of the same ilk. Of these, it was said that they were *roués* (note accent mark), "men deserving to be broken on the wheel." And the term is still applied to one who is a dissolute wastrel.

830

causeway

Although now a dialectal word, *causey* is the basis for this, and no pun is intended. That is, a *causey* is a raised footway or embankment over marshy ground made firm by stamping or pounding. Probably it is derived from Latin *calx,* "heel." Such an original footway might later be widened for the accommodation of carriages. If so, it then was known as a *causey-way,* or, eventually, *causeway.*

sumpter horse

This story goes all the way back to the ancient Sanskrit, in which language was the word *sakta,* "attached," the past participle of *sanj,* "to adhere." This led to the Greek *sattein,* "to fasten," which later became, "to pack, to put a burden on a horse," from which was derived *sagma,* "a pack saddle." The latter was taken directly into Latin, where it was eventually corrupted to *salma* with the meaning of "a pack, a burden." The next path on the journey was Old French, into which the Latin word was adopted with the spelling *somme,* and the French modified their word to *sommetier* to describe the pack-horse driver. And this is the word that was taken into English, early in the fourteenth century, with the spelling *sumpter,* "a pack-horse driver." It was the horse he drove, of course, that was called the *sumpter horse,* this term having been recorded in the fifteenth century. In the following century, the name of the horse became shortened to *sumpter,* and these two terms have continued to exist to the present time as synonymous expressions describing a pack horse.

mud puppy

One wonders sometimes what sort of beverage our forebears may have been consuming when they bestowed names upon some of the odd-looking critters they found in America. These salamanders, either the hellbender or the Necturus, no more resemble a puppy than they do a cat. They have four legs, and the resemblance stops about there. They look more like undersized alligators than like anything canine. Undoubtedly the name was bestowed by an early traveler or settler, but it did not break into print much before seventy-five years ago. Another, and more fitting, name for the hellbender was *mud devil.*

padlock

The lock of this name dates from the fifteenth century, but the name poses a riddle. Our language contains *pads* of varying kinds and descriptions, but there was only one, totally obsolete now, which was in use before that date. The toad. So it may have been that the removable lock of five centuries ago had somewhat of a likeness to the shape of a toad, and was thus so called.

daffodil

It's a long way 'round, but the name of this plant and its flower were originally and properly still should be *asphodel,* though the later name denotes a kind of narcissus rather than a true asphodel. In the fifteenth century, perhaps at first in imitation of some king or prince who lisped, folks began to change *asphodel* to *affodill.* Then in the sixteenth century, perhaps to give the word a Frenchified aspect (such as in altering *Albert* to *D'Albert*), the name suddenly gained a new initial, and *daffodil* was born. The names *daffodilly* and *daffodowndilly* are merely poetic substitutions, used as early as the sixteenth century, even by so renowned a poet as Edmund Spenser.

vinegar

In times past, the only source of vinegar generally known was wine that, on turning, became sharp and acrid to the taste. And it is precisely this that is shown by the name, for it comes from the Old French *vyn egre* (which led to the modern French *vinaigre*). *Vyn,* or *vin,* comes from the Latin *vinum,* "wine," and *egre,* or *aigre,* is from the Latin *acer,* "sharp, pungent."

St. Martin's summer

The phenomenon of a spell of warm, bright, pleasant weather occurring well after the official start of autumn is known to people in many parts of the world, and the event, known to North Americans as *Indian summer,* is known by many names. Thus, St. Martin's Day is November 11, and when the summerlike weather occurs near that date, it is *St. Martin's summer* to the British (*été de la Saint-Martin* to the French). Similarly, St. Luke's Day is October 18, and All Saints' Day is November 1, and thus we may have, if the weather co-operates, *St. Luke's summer* or *All Saints'* (or *All Hallows'*) *summer* at an earlier time of year. Incidentally, the reason for the name *Indian summer* has never been explained with full satisfaction to all concerned. It has been known and used at least since the late eighteenth century.

jackanapes

Now, any man or boy who apes his betters or pretends to be more than he is. Apparently, however, this was originally an ex-

tended meaning of the earliest application, perhaps when memory of the first use had faded. That is, the first historical use was derisive, applied to William, Duke of Suffolk, when that knight was baselessly arrested for treason against Henry VI in 1450 and ultimately beheaded. The satirical appellation arose from his heraldic emblem, a clog and chain such as were then characteristic of the fastening attached to a tame ape. But within a hundred years the significance of the satire was gone, and, though the name remained, it referred just to any ape, whether tame or not, or to a man or boy behaving as one.

tatterdemalion (-demallion)

It is generally conceded that the first part of this word (which dates to the early seventeenth century) is nothing more than *tatter,* or, more probably, *tattered,* "ragged." With respect to the second element, it has been suggested that it may have come from the French *maillot,* from Old French *maillon,* "swaddling clothes,"

833

also, "an acrobat's tights." However, most authorities agree that the second part of the word was coined from pure fancy, just as was the second part of *ragamuffin,* with which *tatterdemalion* is synonymous.

applejack

Sorry, but there was no Jack who had a hand in naming the American brandy derived from cider, nor any John either, unless it may have been John Barleycorn. Perhaps the tippler who first discovered that cider would ferment just happened to use the John-apple, so named because it ripened on or about St. John's Day, June 24. New Jersey, back in the early nineteenth century, was the great producer of applejack. Hence, because of its prompt action, the brandy was also known as "Jersey lightning." New England was slow to adopt either name, preferring to call the juice by the more sedate name, "apple-john."

knapsack

As an essential of a soldier's field equipment, both knapsack and haversack are now obsolete. Whereas the latter carried his field rations, the *knapsack* was for personal items, such as changes of clothing. However, such were not in accord with the original German military usage. The *haversack,* as stated elsewhere, carried grain for a cavalryman's horse; the *knapsack,* as its name implies —German *knappen,* "to eat"—was a sack or wallet of considerably lesser size which held the rations of the soldier.

daddy longlegs

A frequent name in America for this insect is *granddaddy long-legs,* as any reader of Mark Twain knows. In England it is sometimes called *father-long-legs* or *Harry-long-legs,* the latter possibly in allusion to a fancied resemblance to his Satanic majesty, the Lord Harry. But the paternal or patriarchal name, applied without any regard whatever to the sex of this member of the spider family, is due only to the fact that its slender legs are excessively long, perhaps because some men appear to have legs reaching from the neck down. The crane fly, a fly with very long slender legs, is also sometimes called *daddy longlegs.*

St. Elmo's fire

St. Elmo, even though described in some reference works as the patron of navigators, seems likely to be a figment of the imagination, although it has been suggested that his name may be a corruption of St. *Anselm,* St. *Erasmus* (the patron of Neapolitan sailors), or of *Helena,* the sister of Castor and Pollux. In *An Etymological Dictionary of Modern English,* Weekley agrees that the saint, whether Elmo or Helen, is probably apocryphal, and suggests, with much merit, that the phrase goes back to the Greek *elene,* "a torch." Certain it is that this play of electric luminosity about the mast tips of a ship would strongly resemble a torch of magnificent, though eerie, proportions.

handsome

The meaning has changed a bit. Five hundred years ago the idea behind it was "somewhat handy; easy to deal with," but that original sense has now disappeared. Or, rather, it has given place to a more miserly notion that that which is most handy, most easy to deal with, is that which is also most pleasing. And thus, for more than three hundred years, men have spoken of a *handsome* sum of money, a *handsome* cargo from Spain, *handsome* praise from Sir John, and, most commonly nowadays, a *handsome* man, implying one of admirable face or figure, one pleasing to the eye.

ant lion

Hundreds upon hundreds of these have their diminutive pitfalls amid orange groves of Florida or wherever ants are numerous and the soil is composed of dry and very fine sand. Properly the name should be confined to the larvae, known also as doodlebugs, rather than to the adult insect, which resembles a dragonfly. The louse-like larva buries itself in the sand and, by throwing descending sand away from the edge by violent motions of its head, digs a funnel-shaped pit with smooth sides that may be an inch to two inches in depth, so smooth and steep than an incautious ant may slip to the bottom, where it is immediately seized by the formidable projecting mandibles of the "lion" awaiting it. Rainfall must be most discouraging; all trace of the laborious construction is wiped out by the first few drops, and the infant must wait until the sand is again bone dry before it may begin to set the table for the next meal. (See also **doodlebug.**)

tapestry

The art of decorative weaving seems to have been well developed in many of the Oriental countries long before it was learned in Europe, and Persia, especially, has long been known for the craft of its weavers in turning out fine fabrics. Thus it is probably from the Persian that this word stems, though it has been traced with certainty only back to the Greek *tapes*, "cloth wrought with figures in various colors." The diminutive is *tapetion*, and this was taken into Latin as *tappetium* or *tapetium* from which it spread into the Romance languages as *tapiz*, finally settling in French as *tapis*. One who wove such figured cloth was then called, in French, a *tapissier*, and his products were known, collectively, as *tapisserie*. This is the form that was taken into English as the ancestor of our present word, with the spelling *tapissery*, which spelling was very soon corrupted to that still used.

recipe, receipt

Whether your wife cooks from a *receipt* or from a *recipe* makes no difference, for today the terms are equivalent in meaning. Both are derived from the Latin, *recipere*, "to receive," the former from the participial form, *recepta*, the latter from the imperative form, *recipe*, "take!" The *receipt* was originally any set of directions for making up a formulation, whether in cookery or medicine, but in the course of time has pretty well lost its medicinal meaning. *Recipe* was used in its literal sense by physicians as the first word in a set of directions for compounding a medicinal preparation (in this sense, now abbreviated ℞), but, because of similarity to the older term, also came to be used as the name for the set of directions, and thence also to a set of directions in cookery.

John Bull

The long-drawn-out War of the Spanish Succession, 1701–1714, in which the allied armies of England, Austria, the Netherlands, and Prussia were finally victorious over the combined forces of France and Spain, was not altogether popular in England. It cost many lives; it disrupted commerce, and the expense was enormous. All this was seen by the eminent physician and witty author Dr. John Arbuthnot. To get others to share his views he resolved, in 1712, to satirize the struggle for power. The first of his satires bore the title, *"Law is a Bottomless Pit. Exemplified in the case of the Lord Strutt, John Bull, Nicholas Frog, and Lewis Baboon, who spent all they had in a lawsuit."* These characters were intended to represent, respectively, Spain, England, Holland, and France—especially, as of the first and fourth, their rulers, Charles II of Spain and Louis XIV of France. The satires were later expanded into five parts, published under the title, *History of John Bull.* From Arbuthnot's generalized characterization of the English people in this series England has subsequently been personified as *John Bull.*

cat-o'-nine-tails

In this day it seems amazing that this instrument of punishment was actually authorized in the British Navy until as recently as 1881. It came into use in the late seventeenth century, and was probably greatly modified from time to time according to the nature of the person commanding the punishment and its duration, but at best the bare back of its victim might be literally flayed. A description in 1788 says it "consists of a handle or stem, made of rope three inches and a half in circumference, and about eighteen inches in length, at one end of which are fastened nine branches, or tails, composed of log line, with three or more knots upon each branch."

feverfew

French is not the only language to suffer mutilation when lifted bodily into English. Latin has also suffered. In Roman times a plant, the centaury, was known to possess properties which could soothe a feverish person. For that reason the plant was also known as *febrifugia,* from *febris,* "fever," and *fugare,* "to drive away." Passing through French, the people of England took this at first to be *feferfuge,* later corrupted in common speech to *feather-few, fetter-foe,* and, eventually, *feverfew.*

jayhawker

Though natives and residents of Kansas now proudly proclaim themselves to be *Jayhawkers,* such publicity a hundred years ago was likely to be followed by a fight and bloodshed. Among the settlers of the territory they were abolitionists, men chiefly from nonslaveholding states who fought against pro-slavery settlers to keep Kansas free. Who coined the term and when are not now likely ever to be known. We know only that it was prior to 1858. Some folks maintain that there was once, and perhaps may yet be, an actual *jayhawk,* a bird which robbed the nests of other birds. The bird has never been seen, so, in order to supply a deficiency, Mr. Kirke Mechem, of the Kansas State Historical Society, gaily provided a description in 1944 in a brochure, "The Mystical *Jayhawk.*" His account was from the writings, "now unfortunately apochryphal," of "a famous Spanish ornithologist" with Coronado's expedition. And the mythical bird described by this mythical Spaniard somewhat resembled a huge parrot, curved beak, iridescent blue and red feathers, and wings and talons so powerful as to enable the bird to fly off with a buffalo in each claw. Well, far be it from me to be unable to invent something less staggering. I think it at least possible that some early spinner of yarns, inspired by authentic, though incredible, tales of the curious habits of the pack or trade rat, would not be outdone and came up with a bird having the keen vision of a hawk and the garrulity of a jay. Or, if that doesn't suit, we could suppose that the original *jayhawker* was given the title by fellow plainsmen in complimentary recognition of his keenness of sight coupled with humorous recognition of his constant flow of chatter.

caterwaul

This is just the *waul* or alluring musical call (or howl)—musical, presumably, to the female, that is—of a courting tomcat. Chaucer has the Wife of Bath say, in the Prologue:

> *"Thow saist thus that I was lik a cat;*
> *For who so wolde senge the cattes skyn,*
> *Than wold the catte duellen in his in;*
> *And if the cattes skyn be slyk and gay,*
> *Sche wol not duelle in house half a day;*
> *But forth sche wil, er eny day be dawet,*
> *To schewe hir skyn, and goon a caterwrawet."*

And the cat with fine clothes, male or female, does the same to this day.

tantamount

Our present adjectival use, which dates to the mid-seventeenth century, was preceded by a noun use, of slightly greater age, and a verb use some 350 years older, both now obsolete. It is to the verb use that originated in the tongue known as Anglo-French that we must look for the beginning of the word, which was then rendered as *tant amunte*, "to amount to as much," made up of the French *tant*, "as much," plus the Anglicized French *amunter*, "to amount to." From these beginnings it was only a matter of time until first the noun, "that which amounts to as much," and then the adjective, "that amounts to as much, equivalent," senses were developed.

St. Anthony's fire

St. Anthony, "The Great" (A.D. 251?–356?), was an Egyptian ascetic, and one of the pillars of the early Christian Church. During his life he was reportedly tempted sorely by the devil, who took many forms, including that of a pig. It was through this temptation that St. Anthony became the patron of pigs, which, in turn, has given his name to *St. Anthony's nut* and *St. Anthony's turnip*, both of which are foods favored by swine. His bones, discovered in 561, were finally enshrined at Vienne, France, where they are said to have performed miracles of healing during an epidemic of erysipelas in the eleventh century. For this reason, erysipelas, a feverish disease accompanied by reddening and itching of the skin, has since been popularly named *St. Anthony's fire*.

rasher

In the United States, we refer to "a slice of bacon"; our British cousins more commonly would order "a rasher of bacon," and expect to receive the same portion implied by our term—a single thin slice. Some have suggested that the *rasher* is so-called because, being thin, it may be cooked *rashly* ("quickly"). Others prefer to believe that the word is derived from the long-obsolete verb, *to rash*, "to cut, slash." I find more plausible than either the suggestion made by Dr. James Mitchell in his book, *Significant Etymology*, where he offers the theory that *rasher* is a misspelling of *rasure*, "a thin slice, a shaving," from the Latin verb *rado, rasi, rasum, radere*, "to scrape, shave, scratch."

handkerchief

An incongruous word, when you come to analyze it. The *chief* is an early misspelling of Old French *chef*, "head," and *ker* is a corrupt contraction of Old French *covrir*, "cover." Thus *kerchief*, back in Chaucer's time, was a square of cloth used as a head covering, though, approaching the Norman French, he wrote it *coverchief*. But of course the idea of a *kerchief* being only a head covering was quickly lost, and in no time at all both men and women began to appear wearing a "brest-kerchief," a "shuldur-kerchief," or a "nekke-kerchief," furnishing protection of a sort for breast, shoulder, or neck. But it was not until the early sixteenth century, apparently, that our English ancestors adopted the refinement of wiping the nose with a square of cloth, though the "napkin" for wiping the mouth or face after a meal had been introduced in the previous century. So, as *kerchief* had long since lost any distinctive application, this new soft square, equally useful as a napkin or for wiping the nose, and, in the fashion of the day, carried negligently in the hand, became a *handkerchief,* a *kerchief* to be carried in the *hand.* Later still, when garments were designed with pockets, we had *pocket handkerchiefs,* literally (now follow this closely), coverings for the head to be held in the hand inserted in one's pocket. A literal accomplishment is somewhat more difficult as one recalls that the *pocket handkerchief* is now usually an adjunct of feminine attire and that it commonly reposes, not in a pocket, but in a handbag.

juke box

According to Lorenzo D. Turner, in the dialect of the Negroes living on the islands lying off the coast of South Carolina, Georgia,

 and Florida—a dialect called Gullah—*juke* is associated with anything connected with a place of ill repute; a *juke house* (sometimes just a *juke*) is a disorderly house. From his researches he found evidence also that the term was derived from dialects in Senegal, French West Africa, whence came the ancestors of most of these Negroes. Thus we may ascribe to African tribes the common name of our electrically operated, nickel-in-the-slot music box.

rarebit

It may have been a deliberate attempt to "glamourize" the dish; it may have been suggested in humorous vein; or it may have been a failure to understand the country humor in the original name, but whatever the reason, the word *rarebit* is used only to designate the cheese dish, *Welsh rabbit,* normally also in combination, as *Welsh rarebit.* Similar terms originating in popular humor are *Adam's ale* (water), *Scotch coffee* (hot water flavored with burnt biscuit), *Missouri meerschaum* (corncob pipe), *Cape Cod turkey* (codfish), and so on.

annus mirabilis

A wonderful year. It now means any year which the speaker regards as especially outstanding, notable. But, in England particularly, the term refers to the year 1666, the year that marked two notable events: a victory over the Dutch fleet and, in September, the great London fire in which a large part of the city was destroyed. Both events were commemorated in a poem by John Dryden having the title "Annus Mirabilis."

paddywhack

In England, perhaps because all Irishmen (each known as "Paddy") have no love for the English, a *paddywhack* generally denotes a towering rage or, sometimes, the kind of thrashing that is most likely to accompany such a rage—a real, genuine, downright whacking. But in America, where "Pat" or "Paddy" may be less given to fits of temper, the *paddywhack* has become considerably gentler. It is still a punishment for a misdemeanor, usually one committed by a child, but it is rarely more than a spanking, often not very drastic.

Oh yes, for unfathomed reasons the ruddy duck is locally called *paddywhack,* often abridged to *paddy.*

catchpole

The original of this, back in the twelfth century, was the surname of mixed language, *cassa pullum,* "the fowl catcher," denoting a legitimate occupation, such as "cowboy" does today. But the fowls so caught were seized for the payment of taxes. Hence, in time the *catchpole* or *catchpoll* became a minor court officer, a bailiff.

exclamation point (or mark)

It is the American practice to add *point* or *mark;* the British are content with *"exclamation,"* or occasionally with the older terms, *ecphonesis* or *epiphonema.* The mark itself(*!*), however, came into English use about three hundred and fifty years ago, borrowed from earlier Italian usage.

dachshund

True, Harold, *Dach* does mean "roof" *auf Deutsch,* but what, then, will you do with *shund?* It's meaningless. No, the first element is not *Dach,* but *Dachs,* and the meaning of that is "badger." This low-built hound (*Hund*), in other words, was especially used in Germany for hunting badgers, during the years long gone by when the baiting of badgers was a popular sport. This breed of dogs is thought to be very old, as its counterpart appears in ancient Egyptian paintings.

hand-in-glove

Originally, about three hundred years ago, those using this metaphor worded it *hand and glove*—that is, being on terms of intimate relationship comparable to that of one's hand and the glove for it. But whether through elision—*hand 'n' glove*—or through deliberate intent to indicate even closer intimacy, a snuggling intimacy as it were, seventeenth-century *hand and glove* became nineteenth-century *hand-in-glove.*

sadism

It is too often true that men of infamy tend to live in history longer than do men of good will, and so it is with Comte Donatien Alphonse François de Sade, usually called the Marquis de Sade. The Comte was a French soldier who lived from 1740 to 1814, but he is better known as a sexual pervert and an author of obscene writings. Most of his adult life was spent either in prison or in asylums for the insane. A form of perversion described by him consists in the obtaining of gratification by practicing cruelty upon the loved one, and it is to this practice that his name has been given. By extension, *sadism* is now applied to a love of cruelty, and a *sadist* is one who receives pleasure through the practice of cruelty.

kangaroo court

In *A Hog on Ice,* my father stated that, "The source of the name [kangaroo court] is mysterious, for it is American, not Aus-tralian." That he was not wholly convinced of this is indicated by his having entered into correspondence, shortly before his death, with Mrs. H. E. L. Patton, of Kew, Victoria, enlisting her assistance in trying to establish whether, in fact, the term may not have originated in Australia. Mrs. Patton's efforts were, at first, wholly fruitless, seeming to substantiate the belief expressed earlier. Ultimately, however, the query was published in the Melbourne *Age* (April 22, 1957), where it elicited the following letter to the editor from Mr. J. D. Seymour of Longwarry North, Victoria, published April 26:

"Many years ago when I was working on Hamilton Downs station, about 200 miles south of the present site of Alice Springs, I put the same question to an old hand. I had seen many 'sundowners' calling at homesteads and huts for a handout and wondered why the irresponsibles didn't take a chance and steal a horse for their long walkabouts.

"The oldtimer answered: 'If they did, maybe they'd soon find themselves in hoppers' court.' Asked what he meant, he said: 'That's what we call it.'

"The manager was more explicit. 'It comes,' he said, 'from the kangaroos in the back country where they seldom, or never, see a white man, and the only lethal weapon they know is a blackfellow's spear. They feed in small bunches. When they sight a man out of spear range they sit up and stare, sometimes for five minutes, and then turn and leap for the horizon. It is from that dumb sense of inter-communication common to all animals and the resemblance of the staring bunch to an inquiring council and quick decision that we got the term Kangaroo Court.'

"No doubt Australian 'forty-niners' took the term to California as the Americans brought their idioms to this country less than a decade later."

tam-o'-shanter

Robert Burns, the national poet of Scotland, wrote of the wild ride of Tam o'Shanter (Tom of Shanter), when Tam rode through a furious storm "whiles holding fast his gude blue bonnet." Tam's bonnet, presumably, was the wide floppy hat favored by the Scottish Lowlanders and faintly resembling a beret. Just why is not clear, but some time after Burns' poem was published, the name of its hero became applied to this type of headgear, and the association remains down to the present, although now often abbreviated to "tam," or at times "tammy."

huggermugger

Perhaps this term should be passed over in silence, for its source is certainly as concealed and secret as is meant by *huggermugger* itself. Undoubtedly the rhyming term in one or another of its several variations—*hoker-moker, hocker-mocker, hucker-mucker,* or even *hudder-mudder*—had long been in colloquial use before the sixteenth century, but it first appeared in print in Sir Thomas More's *Dyaloge on the Worshyp of Ymagys* (1529): "He wolde haue hys faythe dyuulged [divulged] and spredde abrode openly, not alwaye whyspered in *hukermoker.*" And on another page of the same work he wrote, ". . . these heretyques [heretics] teche in *hucker mucker.*"

andiron

The only excuse for the present formation of this word is that the object itself is usually, though not always, composed of iron. The name of this device for supporting wood in an open fireplace came into the language from Norman French and, properly, we should still be calling it *andier* or the equivalent Saxon word, *aundyre.* The latter, through misinterpretation, produced our present word. The ending *yre,* you see, was also an independent spelling of *yren* or *yron,* five hundred years ago, and consequently was thought also to mean "iron."

king's evil

The "evil," scrofula, was not possessed by a king, but, because the kings of France and those of England were all anointed with consecrated oil, it was formerly a popular belief that, merely by a touch—"the king's touch"—a person afflicted with scrofula would be cured. In France, the power of so healing *le mal de roi* was first ascribed to Clovis in the fifth century; in England, the claim was that Edward the Confessor of the eleventh century was the first ruler to possess such divine power. Actually, however, the practice of "touching" an afflicted subject for the *king's evil* can be traced only to Louis IX in France and Edward III in England, of the thirteenth and fourteenth centuries respectively. It was abolished in both countries during the nineteenth century.

Javelle water

Correctly, we should always spell it *Javel water,* and even more properly call it *eau de Javel,* as the encyclopedias generally record it and as it appears in French. The chlorinated bleaching agent known by the name was first produced by the Javel works near Paris in 1792.

ambergris

As any Frenchman knows, this is a misspelling of *ambre gris,* meaning "gray amber," and is used to distinguish the soft, animal secretion of the sperm whale, gray in color, from the hard, fossilized resin, *ambre jaune,* "yellow amber." But at one time, because both of these were found along coasts of the sea, the yellow amber, that which we now call "amber," was thought to be hardened ambergris of different color. Amber itself was known in ancient Greece, but was called *elektron.* Through this name and the properties exhibited by the material when rubbed were derived our terms "electric," "electricity," etc.

846

fetlock

Sorry, but maybe it would be best to slide over this. It is the tuft or *lock* of hair that grows at the back of the pastern joint of the leg of a horse, or the part of the leg where this lock grows, but the word experts of our language have been able to do little more than make a wild stab at any early meaning of *fet*. Some think that it may have been a dialectical form of "foot," but others do not agree with this notion.

catchpenny

Descriptive of any novelty, whether true or flimflam, that might literally "catch a penny." Its first use, two hundred years back, was of any printed matter that might conceivably inveigle a purchaser to the investment of a penny.

katydid

The name of this American insect is customarily said to be due to the repetitious sound produced by it—as if, over and over again,

it were saying *Katie did!* It does my heart good to be able to record that others also have not detected this flat statement in the creature's stridulous tones. To the naturalist John Bartram in 1751 the sound was *Catedidist*. To Meriwether Lewis, of the Lewis and Clark expedition in 1804, it was *Chittediddle*. To a writer in *Western Monthly Review* in 1827 it was *Cataded*. And I have the notion that many would agree in saying that the sound is *Kaykihet*.

pea jacket

Frederick Marryat, in *Poor Jack* (1840), thought the spelling should be *P-jacket:* "A short P-jacket (so called from the abbreviation of *pilot's jacket*)," he wrote, "reached down to just above his knees." But Marryat was wrong. The original first element was *pee,* back in the fifteenth century, taken from Dutch *pij,* and that was the name of a kind of coat made of a coarse cloth and worn by men. Coat and name died out in England, but were revived in America in the early eighteenth century, first as *pee-jacket* and later in the present form, both apparently from Dutch *pij-jakker* of the same meaning—a short, double-breasted coat of thick woolen material, worn by sailors in severe weather.

tambourine

Etymologically speaking, there seems to be little doubt that *tambourine,* which comes to us from the French, is the diminutive of *tambour,* "a drum." The actual instrument, as we know it, though, is that which was known in France as *tambour de Basque,* because of its popularity in Biscay. *Tambour* is apparently a variant spelling of *tabor,* which is a much older name for a drum, and seems to have come from either of two Persian words, both of which mean "drum," *tabirah* or *taburak.* Both *tabor* and *tambour* have, in English, become practically obsolete since the introduction of the word "drum" into the language in the mid-sixteenth century, except in some specialized uses.

hamstring

We are so accustomed to the thought of a *ham* as consisting of that part of the upper leg which includes thigh and buttock as to forget entirely that this is, literally, an extended meaning. Originally the *ham* of a man or beast was only that part of the leg directly back of the knee. The *ham strings* were (and still are, though now united into *hamstrings*) the tendons at the back of the knee, or in an animal, the great tendon at the back of the hock. To be *hamstrung* is to be disabled or crippled through the severing of a *hamstring.*

balm of Gilead

Jeremiah, in the King James Version of the Bible, says: "Is there no balm in Gilead; is there no physician there?" But, so

848

says the *Oxford English Dictionary,* "The term 'balm of Gilead' is modern, and . . . originated in the assumption that this is the substance mentioned in the Bible as found in Gilead." The Hebrew term, it adds, was *tsori,* "resin," which Miles Coverdale (1488–1569) mistakenly rendered "balm" in his translation of the Bible. However, the term is now applied to several Oriental trees and to various other aromatic plants, as well as to the resinous exudations which they yield.

mortarboard

Inasmuch as, nowadays, even American kindergartners appear in "cap and gown" upon the eve of stepping into the first grade, to say nothing of youngsters about to take the great step of entering high school, it may be well to know what the *mortarboard* they wear as a cap originally indicated and why it was so named. In its early form, back in the sixteenth century, the crown of this cap, though square, was unstiffened and was little more than a rim extending about the upper part of the cap proper, topped with a round knob. It was then worn only by high dignitaries of the church. Though continued as a churchly vestment, the squared crown was gradually extended in the seventeenth century and eventually required a stiff support to keep it in shape. And in the eighteenth century the crown was frankly a cloth-covered board, surmounted by a round knob and held to the head of the wearer by a skullcap. By this time the cap was worn not only by high officers of the church, but also by deans and rectors of universities. By the early nineteenth century a cap of the same style, but with a tassel replacing the round knob, both cap and tassel of black, was a required head covering of university students. With a black robe, also required, no distinction of rank was then in evidence.

Thanks to the squared shape, these flat caps reminded some wag in the mid-nineteenth century of the square boards used by masons for holding the mortar used by them. He then dubbed them *mortarboards.* As usual, no one knows who this wit may have been, but, though at first classed as college slang, the name is now definite. Alas, however, in America neither cap nor gown is limited to academic wear, nor is its color limited to black. Nor is it a required garb upon a college campus. In fact, it is more frequently seen as the vestment of a choir, the cap worn only by the feminine members. And, though black remains the customary color for male students in a college or university, female students sometimes appear in white. In lesser halls of learning, fabrics in any hue of the rainbow may appear.

By curious coincidence, the cap worn by certain French judges has also the name *mortier,* "mortar." The object from which this name is derived, however, is the vessel used with accompanying pestle by pharmacists or cooks, and in which ingredients are pounded or ground.

fer-de-lance

The name of this extremely poisonous snake, whose bite is most likely to be fatal, actually indicates the shape of the head—*fer,* "head" or "iron," *de lance,* "of the lance"; i.e., lance head. But it might also indicate the speed with which the serpent strikes or the fact that it springs at its victim like a charge with a lance. This lance-headed or yellow viper is found chiefly in tropical America, infesting especially the sugar plantations of the West Indies.

catboat

Entered merely not to skip a curious word, though little can be said about it. Two hundred years ago the name was applied to vessels of four to six hundred tons, built according to Norwegian design and used in the British coal trade, but no reason has been found for the designation and none for the transfer of the name to the small single-masted sailboat, with mast stepped well forward, used for pleasure.

vinaigrette

Taken directly from the French *vinaigrette,* "vinegar sauce," a condiment prepared with vinegar, from *vinaigre,* "vinegar." The name, though, became transferred to the container rather than to the sauce, and to similar containers, finally being settled on a container of smelling salts.

ladyfinger

The poet Keats, who knew these delicate pastries back in 1820,  called them *lady's-fingers*. Both of these were fanciful names, however, merely indicative of size. As applied to the modern bakery-made American product the name is distinctly inappropriate. The name *finger biscuit,* also in early use, would be more fitting: the finger could be that of a heavyweight prizefighter.

ember days

Three days (Wednesday, Friday, and Saturday) of fasting observed quarterly in the Roman Catholic and Anglican churches. Though the first is but a week after Ash Wednesday, the term *ember* has no relationship to the ashes of a fire. It is, in fact, only a corruption of the Old English word *ymbrene,* meaning "quarterly," or "seasonal," for the periods of fasting celebrate the four seasons—spring, summer, autumn, and winter.

talisman

Completely unrelated to **talesman** (which see), despite all similarities of spelling, this word comes to us through the Romance languages from the Arabic *tilsam,* "a magic charm." The earlier derivation is from the Greek *telesma* of the same meaning, but having had the former meaning of "a religious rite," and coming from *telein,* to "fulfill," from *telos,* "end."

sadiron

In its original sense in English, *sad* had the meaning "fully satisfied, sated." From this sense it underwent alteration, as so many

English words do, and came to have the meaning of "solid, heavy, dense." It is in this sense that it is used in the *sadiron,* which is a heavy, solid flatiron used for pressing and smoothing clothes. Regardless of how sorrowful the housewife may be that she is compelled to use this weighty tool, her sadness has no part in its name.

villain

Originally, apparently, one of the retinue attached to an estate, for the word stems from the Latin *villanus,* from *villa,* "a country house," and this meaning was largely retained in an alternate spelling of the English word, *villein.* But, progressing from the general sense of "a peasant," in which sense the word dates back to the early fourteenth century, the use of the term was broadened to include anyone of low birth, then to one of ignoble instincts, and finally to its present sense where it applies to a scoundrel or criminal. Related terms are known in most of the Romance languages, and the immediate source of the English form was the Anglo-French of the same or slightly different spelling.

catawampus

No one now knows the source. It showed up in print shortly after 1840 and, most likely, had already been American slang for ten or fifteen years before that. With humorous reference to General Zachary Taylor at the Battle of Buena Vista in the Mexican War, the New York *Herald* carried the squib (June 17, 1846):

> *On Taylor came and met the foe*
> *All marshall'd forth so pompously,*
> *And there he's slain two thousand men,*
> *All chaw'd up catawampously.*

That is, to translate the meaning, as if they had been met by a fierce or savage bogy.

umpire

Although this word has been in the language since the late fourteenth or early fifteenth century, it is a variant of a still older word, *noumpere,* which entered the language in the mid-fourteenth century but lasted less than a hundred years. For *a noumpere* became altered to *an oumpere,* which then underwent many changes of spelling until the one we know was adopted in the seventeenth century. The original English form was adopted from the Old French *nonper, nomper,* "not equal," from *non,* "not," plus *per,* "peer." It has reference to the third man who was called in to settle a dispute when the two arbitrators first appointed could not agree, that man thus making the total number of referees unequal so that there would necessarily be a majority opinion.

fearnought

You may run across this in your reading of tales of the sea especially. That is, it is the name of a heavy woolen cloth, or the outer clothing made from it, that is specially adapted for use by sailors aboard ship in inclement weather. Those wearing it "fear nought" from the elements. Sometimes the cloth is known as *fearnought* and the garments made from it are *dreadnoughts,* but the terms are often used interchangeably.

peacock

Six hundred, even four hundred years ago, this bird was just called a *po,* though by the latter time *pokok* and *pocock* had begun to come into favor. (The female was the *pohenne* or *pohen.*) But the *o,* sounded as in "cost," gave rise also to the spelling *paa.* Carelessness turned this into the sound *pay,* which, by the pronunciation of the English alphabet of that period, caused it in turn to be spelled *pe* and thence to *pea,* for "ea" then represented the sound we still have in "break," "great," "steak." Change to the present pronunciation began in the eighteenth century. (See also **Argus-eyed.**)

rambunctious (rambustious)

This Americanism (possibly brought to us by Irish immigrants) seems to be a variant of the British term of equivalent meaning, *rambustious.* The latter, it is suggested, may have been coined from *ram* plus *bust*. To *ram*, of course, is "to butt, strike," and generally to behave in the manner of a frolicsome male sheep. And *bust?* The earliest recorded use of the verb, which has been traced to the early thirteenth century, is in the sense, "to beat, thrash." (This sense still exists, as in the colloquial, "I'll bust him in the nose!") So if we have a man, or especially a small boy, in boisterous mood, *ramming* around and *busting* people, he may certainly best be described as *rambustious!*

leapfrog

It is the boy beneath who is the *frog,* his bent back, chin on chest, somewhat resembling a ranine attitude. The sport is not recent. Shakespeare speaks of it when, writing *Henry V,* in 1599, he has the king say to Katherine of France that he would marry, "If I could winne a Lady at Leape-frogge, or by vawlting into my Saddle, with my Armour on my backe."

eggnog

There is nothing particularly tricky about this term; it, like the concoction it designates, is a combination of *egg,* the product of the hen, and *nog,* "strong ale," the product of the brewer. Originally, that is, strong ale was the spirituous ingredient, but it is often replaced by wine, rum, cider, or other spirits. Incidentally, the beverage is of American origin, known by this name in Revolutionary times.

amateur

Though this was derived from Latin *amator,* "a lover," the French gave it a slight alteration in sense, which we have adopted, "a lover or devotee of an art, pastime, sport, or the like." And, nowadays, we have even extended the sense to include one who is a dabbler or tyro, one without training in an art, sport, or skill, but who enjoys its activity.

854

catamount

In North America, a name applied to the cougar or the lynx. Although the *Hazlitt Diary,* describing the appearance of one on Cape Cod, says: "It was said to be five feet long; besides, the tail was as much more; and it could mount trees, whence its name," the name is actually formed by contraction from "cat of the mountain," because the critters are usually to be found in hilly country —or, at least, the critters of the cat family known to the English by this name, the leopard or the panther, frequent such regions.

kingfish, kingpin, etc.

Long years before radio gave Amos and Andy, and their pal, the Kingfish, to the American audience *kingfish* was a name bestowed upon any of several fish notable for size or importance. It is for similar cause that *king* became the first element in such terms as *kingbolt, kingpin, kingpost, king snake, kingwood,* etc.

landlubber

Though we might honestly say that a *landlubber* is one who "lubs de land," we would rightly be called a punster, rather than a tracer of origins. The fact is that a *lubber,* even six hundred years ago, was a clumsy lout, one who didn't know B from a bull's foot. And so he was to sailors who, through later centuries, had to put up with him on shipboard. First it was new green seamen who, in contempt, were called *lubbers,* then, as *landlubbers,* it was applied with equal contempt to passengers or others who knew not one rope from another.

talesman

It was formerly the practice (and may still be in some places) to make up a trial jury in whole or in part of men selected from among the bystanders in the court. Men of law, like doctors, like to express things in Latin when possible, and people drawn on to fill a jury in this manner were called *tales de circumstantibus,* "such persons as those standing around." This was soon shortened to *tales,* which is the plural of *talis,* "of such a kind." So it follows that a *talesman* was one of such persons impaneled to complete a jury, from which it has become, simply, any juror.

jalousie

In our own Southern states this is now a misnomer. In Spain, back in the sixteenth century, spelled *gelosia,* and later in France as *jalousie,* both indicating "jealousy," the term denoted a kind of slatted blind somewhat similar to the modern Venetian blind. It was then made of wood, however, and the immovable slats excluded not only rain and sun, but also the prying eyes of possible suitors of señoritas within. But, less than a score of years ago, Florida genius found that rain could still be excluded and sunshine admitted by replacing the wooden slats with slats of glass, and that the admission of air could be controlled by having these slats movable. They are still called *jalousies,* but no longer safeguard a jealous husband or father.

litterbug

A term coined by an unknown person, probably about 1945, and now designating one who strews litter wherever he goes. The term

was descried in 1950 on the back of a truck by Mrs. Henry W. Land, a member of the Mount Dora, Florida, Lakes and Hills Garden Club, and it was suggested that *litterbug* be adopted by the club in connection with a roadside clean-up campaign planned by that organization. Announcement of the plan, in the June 22, 1950, issue of the weekly *Mount Dora Topic,* closed with the statement, "The cleanup campaign . . . will carry the theme: 'Don't be a litter-bug!' " The slogan and litter campaign were subsequently adopted, in order, by the Florida Federation of Garden Clubs, Inc., The South Atlantic Region, and the National Council of Garden Clubs.

catacomb

The name was, originally, merely applied to a low-lying plot—Greek *kata,* "down," *kumbe,* "hollow"—on the outskirts of Rome along the Appian Way. The church of San Sebastiano was erected on this plot, and, by tradition, the bodies of St. Peter and St. Paul were briefly interred beneath it. In consequence, however, the ground here was considered peculiarly blessed among early Christians and, in time, thousands, after death, were interred in niches carved along innumerable galleries leading in all directions in the soft tufa beneath the church. Other similar subterranean cemeteries, some in tiers of galleries, were developed in other parts of Rome, all known as *catacombs,* but all were closed and forgotten in the ninth century until chance rediscovery in 1578.

talbotype

One of the words describing a process or product that was named after the inventor (like *daguerreotype* and *pasteurize*), the *talbotype* is named after W. H. F. Talbot, an English inventor, who, in 1841, patented his discovery of making photographic images directly upon sensitized paper. Talbot himself called his process *calotype* (from the Greek *kalos,* "beautiful," plus *typos,* "type"), but his friends renamed it after the discoverer.

castanet

Identical in sound though it may be with the words "cast a net," this comes through Spanish *castañeta* from Latin *castanea,* "a chestnut," probably from resemblance in form, faint though it may be. The instrument, used as an accompaniment to dancing, was introduced to Spain by the Moors, but is actually a variation of the *crotalum* used by Roman dancers and the corresponding *krotalon* of the Greeks.

eavesdropper

The eighteenth-century jurist, Sir William Blackstone, really told the whole story: *"Eaves-droppers,* or such as listen under walls or windows or the eaves of a house to hearken after discourse, and thereupon to frame slanderous and mischievous tales, are a common nuisance, and presentable," he adds, "at the court leet." Regrettably, however, the old "court leet" having jurisdiction over such offenses has gone out of existence; eavesdroppers frame their "slanderous and mischievous tales" with impunity nowadays.

jackstone

The name of this children's game comes from its similarity to the older name, *chackstone,* which in its turn came from *chuckstone,* in Scotland called *chuckiestone.* Nowadays, in America at least, the game is played with five or six six-pointed (or knobbed) small iron pieces which are tossed or *chucked* into the air by the player and caught in the hand. Formerly, however, the pieces so chucked were pebbles or small *stones.* In still earlier times, dating back to ancient Rome and Greece, the objects so tossed and caught were the ankle bones of sheep, the *tali* and *astragaloi.*

Paris green

This term, which dates at least to the 1870's, seems to be of American origin, but has spread to Europe by this time. Today, it refers to the compound copper aceto-arsenite, which has had extensive use both as an insecticide and as a pigment, and which is better known in Europe as *Schweinfurt green.* When the name *Paris green* was first coined, it was more often used to designate the related compound, copper arsenite, of similar use and color, more commonly known as *Scheele's green. Paris green* has also been used as a name for the color obtained on using these pigments. The origin of the term is obscure—it may have indicated that the material was manufactured in or exported from Paris, but it seems equally plausible to suggest that the name was coined by some shrewd Yankee merchant who reasoned that "Paris green" would be a much more attractive shade of paint or wallpaper to the American housewife than would one of "Schweinfurt green" or "Scheele's green."

taffeta

Although this name has been applied and misapplied to many different fabrics during the span of the nearly six centuries during which it has been in the language, its original sense, "a plainly woven, glossy silk," reflects its origin closely. The word has been through just about all the Romance languages on its way toward English (Old French *taffetas* or *taphetas,* Medieval Latin *taffata,* Italian *taffeta,* Portuguese *tafeta,* Spanish *tafetan*), but it came originally from the Persian *taftah,* "silken cloth," a substituted use of the past particle of *taftan,* "to shine."

lotus-eater

According to ancient Greek myth, the people dwelling in a certain region in northern Africa derived particular enjoyment from

 the fruit of a tree which the Greeks called *lotos.* The fruit itself was pleasant to the palate, but a wine made from it was especially enjoyable. Those who partook of it forgot all cares and worries. Thus, to the Greeks, these people, and also any others who allowed themselves to become similarly lulled into a state of indifference or a sense of luxurious ease, were *lotophagi,* "lotus-eaters." It was said by Homer that the companions of Odysseus lost all desire to return to their native land when, in their wanderings, their vessel reached these shores and they tasted the fruit and wine of this tree. Botanists have identified the tree with the jujube; today's lozenge so named is flavored with the juice of its fruit or an imitation thereof.

jackknife

Certainty is lacking of the source of this American name, known since the early eighteenth century. Obviously *jack* was not employed in the sense of smallness, for the true jackknife is always large. This has given rise to the surmise that the American name is a corruption and contraction of the Scottish (later also English) clasp knife, the *jockteleg*. If so, there is a possibility that the Scottish historian, Lord David Hailes, gave the true source of both names in 1776 by attributing the latter to a corruption of the French name *Jacques de Liége,* the original maker of the knife. However, though admitting the plausibility of this account, Sir James A. H. Murray, editor of the *Oxford English Dictionary* and a Scot himself, was unable to find confirmation of the statement.

moonstruck

"The sun shall not smite thee by day, nor the moon by night," said the Hebrew psalmist. And from early Greek and Roman times, Selene of the Greeks and Luna of the Romans, goddesses of the moon, were also believed to be capable of affecting the brains of mortals. Those, especially, who slept with head exposed to the light of the moon would become *selenobletos* or *lunatikos,* maddened by Selene or, in Rome, by Luna. No one knows the age of the superstition; it was held also by the ancient Egyptians.

fata morgana

Nothing to do with "fate"; the expression is Italian for "the fairy Morgana," and you'll see it in French as *Morgan le Fay.* By English legend she was the fairy who reported to King Arthur, her brother, the love affair between his wife, Guinevere and the knight Lancelot. But the fairy appears in many medieval romances, especially Italian. And, because she was anciently supposed to have been the cause, her name, *fata morgana,* has long been applied to the kind of mirage most frequently seen in the Strait of Messina, in which the spectator may see images of men, houses, ships, sometimes in the water, sometimes in the air, or doubled, with one image inverted above the other.

ball peen

This is recorded merely for the benefit of those who don't know one kind of hammer from another. But this one is used chiefly by metalworkers. It is one in which the side opposite the face or flat surface of the hammer or sledge is rounded or ball-shaped. *Peen,* that is—also sometimes spelled *pane, pean,* or *pein*—designates that end of the head of a hammer, and it may be pointed, sharp, thin, or ball-shaped.

yardarm

There is some uncertainty about the origin of *yard*. It is known to be descended from the Anglo-Saxon *gierd* of which there are related forms in the Teutonic languages generally, and it has been suggested that the ultimate origin may be either the Latin *hasta,* "spear," or the Russian *zherd',* "a thin pole." Either, though, is relatively long and slender and could as easily have led to the nautical *yard,* the relatively long and slender spar that is hung upon and crosswise to the mast of a ship to support a square sail. As is so for other such crossed configurations, either part of the cross-member is one of its *arms*—hence, *yardarm,* "one of the arms of a yard."

viking

The word is found in Anglo-Saxon, with the spelling *wicing,* as early as the eighth century, but, curiously, it is not found in modern English until the early nineteenth century, having been introduced then from the Norwegian *vikingr.* However, the evidence indicates that it was the Anglo-Saxon term that was the earliest ancestor, having been formed from *wic,* "camp." The name was apparently formed because of the practice of the vikings to set up temporary encampments while carrying out a raiding expedition. The word was adopted into the various Scandinavian languages and, in Old Norse and Icelandic, acquired the meaning of "the practice of piracy."

gagman

Apparently on the theory, "If an audience will swallow this joke or yarn it won't *gag* on anything," *gag* developed, some hundred and fifty years ago, as an improbable story, some tale or yarn taxing the credulity of the listener, or, eventually, a joke that would bring forth hearty laughs from the hearers. In the theatrical world the *gag* was likely to be a line or so of his own inserted into his part, usually to evoke a laugh. He was the original *gagman*. But, especially when radio began to make heavy demands upon the wit of professional humorists, the capacities of others were needed in the promotion of laugh-producing mirth. Then the writers of humorous lines, rather than the speakers, became the *gagmen*.

Queen Anne's lace

I am indebted to Dr. Nellie Payne for this tale of the origin of the common name of the wild carrot, *Daucus carota*. She recalls having read it in a child's primer published perhaps some fifty years ago. It seems that a ward of the Queen, learning to tat, had chosen the delicate flower of this weed to use as a pattern. Having been found innocent of a suspected childish prank, the little girl came to the attention of the Queen, who observed and praised the child's handiwork, and gave her her royal permission to name the pattern for Her Majesty. It soon followed that the name of the pattern was transferred to the flower itself, and to the plant. As for the Queen, Dr. Payne believes it was Anne of Bohemia, who married Richard II of England in 1382.

ultimatum

Diplomatic negotiations between countries are traditionally carried on with the utmost of politeness and in courteous language. When, however, an impasse is reached, the "mailed fist in a velvet glove" is extended, by one side or the other, in the form of an *ultimatum*. The word itself is the neuter singular of the past participle of the Late Latin verb *ultimare*, "to be at the end," from *ultimus*, "last, final." Although *ultimatum* is Latin in form, it is probable that it came into English through the French, which is, historically, the language of diplomacy. The word is known in the same form in many of the European languages, both Romance and Teutonic.

862

monkey wrench

Though this useful device is little more than a hundred years old we can't even be sure whether it was of English or American origin,  let alone how it came by its name. Stimpson, in *A Book about a Thousand Things* (1946), believed that it was devised by a London blacksmith named Charles Moncke, and that *monkey wrench* was a corruption of *Moncke wrench*. But Mencken, in *The American Language* (1936), points to the fact that our cousins-across-the-sea call this wrench a "spanner wrench." In an effort to establish a case for an American origin, Dr. M. M. Mathews, in *American Speech,* February, 1953, reporting on a number of newspaper clippings about words that had been collected over a period of years by Dr. John W. Cummins of Boston, largely undated, had this to say about *monkey wrench:* "There is in the Cummins material a digest that appeared in the Boston *Transcript* sometime during the winter of 1932–33. According to this note, about 1856 a Yankee named Monk employed by Bemis & Call of Springfield, Mass., invented a movable jaw for a wrench. It was given a special name there in the shop, but it soon came to be called *Monk's wrench* and then *monkey-wrench*. This explanation is suspiciously easy and 'pat,' but it is somewhat odd that the date given, 1856, tallies pretty well with that of the first occurrence of the term in the *Oxford English Dictionary* [a listing of the name in Simmonds 1858 *Dictionary of Trade Products*]. I am hoping that Mr. Monk may stand up under investigation, but he may have been disposed of long ago in some article not seen by me."

hamlet

Yes, it does mean "a little ham," but the *ham* therein has nothing to do with any member of the *Sus,* or hog, family. It had originally, that is, to do with members of *Homo sapiens,* those who, in the times of Alfred the Great, lived in a small collection of cottages, a small village, then called a *ham*. The term survives in such place names as Shoreham, East Ham, Oakham, and others.

farthingale

Heaven grant that this garment doesn't come into style again, but it may, of course, though it can have nothing to recommend it. It was a kind of hooped skirt, extending from hips to feet, and as nearly a perfect cylinder as skill could make it, the top covered by flounces. It was the height of fashion in England just three hundred years ago. But the name had to do with neither farthings nor gales; it was a curious corruption, through French, of Spanish *verdugo,* meaning "rod," for the garment owed its shape to a framework of rods.

alyssum

The Greeks had the notion that if one were bitten by a rabid dog, hydrophobia or madness could be averted by promptly chewing the leaves of this plant. Accordingly they gave it the name *alyssos,* from the negative prefix *a* and *lyssa,* "madness," hence, "preventive of madness." The meaning was preserved in the Roman alteration, *alyssum*. None of our modern physicians, however, recommends it as a cure for hydrophobia.

carpetbagger

Shortly after the War Between the States—in the North, the Civil War—hordes of gentry, mostly poor whites, piled their paltry belongings into the traveling bag of the period, its sides made of carpet, and moved South. Their intent was to pick up what they could, financially, socially, and politically, with the aid of the newly enfranchised Negro, from the impoverished former slave owners. The selfish "carpetbagger," operating through unworthy motives, became "a hissing and a byword" among Southerners and a disgrace to the North.

jack-in-the-pulpit

This American wildflower, growing only in marshy woodlands, is unknown in some parts of the country. To anyone who has seen it in springtime, the cause of the name is obvious. The upright sturdy spadix or flower spike stands under a protecting canopy or spathe, vividly resembling a priest at his pulpit with sounding board curved above him. The plant is also called *Indian turnip,* but woe betide the unfortunate lad whose mates beguile him into being misled by the name! The tuber, edible when properly cooked, is burningly pungent when eaten raw, the effect lingering for hours.

moonshine

Perhaps a good covering definition would be an operation or a product achieved in the light of the moon. In England, the operation is that of smuggling spirits into the country without the payment of excise. In America, the end objective is the same and the product is also spirits, but the spirits are produced within the country by stealth and in violation of law. Neither usage is old. That of England dates back barely more than a century and a half, and that of America has perhaps half that age.

carboy

It's the genius of any language, I suppose, to alter an adoption from another language into familiar syllables. It was the famous grapes of Shiraz in Iran—or rather, the wine from those grapes— to which we owe this word. The wine was put up in large bottles of green or blue glass, which, for protection, were encased in basket-work. The native name for such a globular bottle was, by transliteration, *qaraba,* a term difficult to English tongues. But merchants and traders speedily surmounted that difficulty by resolving it into the convenient syllables, *carboy.*

rakish

Many years ago some enterprising naval architect, perhaps tired of the squared-off look of the vessels of his day, or perhaps to increase the deck area of his ship, designed a craft with bow and stern at sharp angles fore and aft of the keel—literally *reaching* out over the water. To our forefathers, a craft so designed was described as *rakish,* and the slope of the bow or stern as the *rake* thereof. The word is said by some authorities to have been derived from the Anglo-Saxon *ræcan* or *reccan,* "to reach, stretch," and probably to be cognate to the German *ragen,* of similar meaning. Regardless of origin, our word has been extended in use so that it now applies to various things, including ships, that "reach out" from their bases at a sharp angle.

Mother Hubbard

Greatly remembered, not so much by what she lovingly tried to do, but by what she wore while trying. She was unable, you remember, "to get her poor dog a bone," because the cupboard was bare. But she was not. At least, according to the crude illustrations adorning the pages of *Mother Goose's Melodies* of the early nineteenth century, she was robed in a cloaklike coverall, unconfined from shoulder to hem. And it was upon that shapeless garment her name was imposed.

allspice

This aromatic spice was not known in Europe before the discovery of the West Indies. The Spanish name was *pimienta,* "pepper," and because of that and the place of origin the dried seeds of the berry were known to English traders as "Jamaica pepper." However, because the housewives of England thought the seeds conveyed the combined flavor of cinnamon, cloves, and nutmeg, they began, in the seventeenth century, to demand *all spice* of their tradesmen. Nowadays, incidentally, the name is also given to other aromatic shrubs of North America and Japan.

tadpole

If this name of the early stage of frog or toad had gone along with other changes in our language through the centuries, no explanation of its source would be needed. *Tad* is merely a survival of the way *toad* was spelled and pronounced four hundred years ago, and *pole* was a seventeenth-century substitution for *poll,* "head." The name *toadhead* for the larva in the stage when it consists of little more than a round head with a tail is simple.

panhandle

Undoubtedly, in the sense of "to beg," this originated among the hoboes or vagrant tramps of the United States in the late nineteenth century. The significance is by no means evident, but I see no likelihood that it had any direct reference to any of the geographical regions known as "Panhandles," such as northern Texas, western Oklahoma, or northern West Virginia. But possibly, taking the idea of "to pan out," meaning to yield good returns, from the placer-miner's lexicon, some hobo evolved a *panhandler* as one who handles the pan hopeful of good returns.

ventriloquist

The first record of a related word is found in a book, *The discouerie of witchcraft,* by Reginald Scot, printed in 1584, where the author speaks of a *ventriloqua* (feminine of *ventriloquus,* "a ventriloquist"), and of her "practising hir diabolicall witchcraft and ventriloquie." It is not surprising that men of that time thought of witchcraft in this connection, for a *ventriloquist* is, both literally and in the original meaning of the word, "one who speaks in his belly," from the Latin *ventri-, venter,* "belly," plus *loqui,* "to speak." It was only later that the practitioner's art improved to the point that he could seem to cast his voice to distant places, and the word was transferred to mean "a voice-caster."

hamfatter

Theatrical slang, of course, now often abridged to *ham* or altered to *ham actor.* Whatever you wish to use, it is applied somewhat contemptuously to an actor or actress who may wish ardently to succeed on the stage, but who just can't act. A writer in *Century Magazine* in 1882 said the term came from an old Negro song, "The Hamfat Man," but H. L. Mencken, in *Supplement II* of his *The American Language,* says that among theatrical people the preferred belief is that the term first denoted those actors who, probably from the cost of cold cream, used ham fat instead to remove grease paint.

balderdash

A dash more bald than others of its kind? No, the fact is that no one knows for a certainty how this word originated. When, in the late sixteenth century, it first appeared in print it referred apparently to a light frothy or bubbly liquid—"barber's balderdash" was the term used. Not long after, in 1637, John Taylor, the "Water Poet," said that beer mixed with wine was called *balderdash*. Beer and buttermilk, said Ben Jonson, is "balderdash." Thus anything frothy, bubbly, or impossibly mixed, whether liquid or language, became so termed. As to origin, it may have been formed from the slang *balductum,* a hundred years the elder but itself of unknown ancestry, which also met Jonson's definition.

neat's-foot oil

When I was very young and my dad, of a Sunday morning, would apply this dressing to my rather scuffed shoes, by natural logic the inference was that the oil gave one a neat foot, hence the name. But not so. Though now so rare as to be called obsolete, *neat* was formerly a general term for cattle, more especially for oxen. *Neat's-foot oil,* accordingly, was and still is an oil extracted from the hoofs, now also the shin bones, of oxen or cattle. Now used as a lubricant and for dressing leather, it was at one time also used medicinally.

taciturn

It has nothing to do with any other kind of a turn, but comes to us almost unchanged from the Latin *taciturnus,* "silent," through *tacitus,* the past participle of *tacere,* "to be silent." Although *taciturn,* today, rarely implies the absolute silence suggested by its ancestor (meaning, rather, "disinclined to conversation, uncommunicative"), the expression of this quality has been retained in *tacit,* which is also derived from *tacitus, tacere.*

nightmare

A relic of ancient superstition dating in England at least from the eighth century, but, under the name *incubus,* known to the

Romans of Caesar's time. People thought this kind of *mare,* said to appear only at night, to be a female monster, spirit, or goblin. She sat upon the bosom of a sleeper, causing a feeling of suffocation, from which, in later times, the sleeper sought to free himself. The male counterpart was termed a *succubus.* We moderns attribute our nightmares to overindulgence in food or drink.

cantilever

In college speech this becomes, "Can't I leave her?" Though most certainly this interpretation has no bearing whatsoever on this type of "flying-lever bridge," no satisfactory source of the *canti-* element has been determined. As a term in architecture, the name appeared in the seventeenth century, pertaining to a masonry bracket of much greater length than depth. Two such brackets united at the tips became a *cantilever bridge* early in the nineteenth century.

ultima Thule

Thule (pronounced *thew'-lee* or *thoo'-lee,* with *th* as in *thank*) is the ancient Greek and Latin name for the most northerly habitable place in the world, said to be six days' sail north of Britain. Although it was presumably named for a real place, there is considerable uncertainty as to just what place was that designated

869

as Thule, and guesses range from Norway to Iceland. The Thule in Greenland at which the United States has recently established an Air Force base is named in remembrance of this unknown land of the ancients and is pronounced *too'-lee*. But *Thule* has also acquired a figurative meaning, which is "the extreme limit of travel," and this has led to the phrase *ultima Thule* ("farthest Thule"), with the meaning of "the utmost attainable, the limit, 'the most.'"

backgammon

A game of considerable antiquity, believed to have been invented in the tenth century, but possibly related to the game *Ludus duodecim scriptorum,* "twelve-line game," played in ancient Rome. In England the game was always called *tables* prior to the seventeenth century, when the new name was introduced. Apparently the name was made up of *back* and *gammon,* a variant form of *gamen,* "game," because the rules provide that a player's pieces must be taken up, under certain circumstances, and go back to the starting point.

sundowner

Sundown itself is presumed to be a contraction of "sun-go-down" or perhaps the archaic "sun-gate-down," and a *sundowner* is either a person who times a certain action relative to sundown, or a deed performed at sundown. There are at least three quite distinct applications of the term. The oldest is an Australian usage found as early as 1875, and applies to a nomad who times his arrival at a dwelling with sundown, so that he will be invited to spend the night. The second is an Americanism, found near the turn of the century, denoting a person now known as a "moonlighter"—a hustler who holds down a secondary job, usually in the evening, in addition to his regular employment. The third, dating to the 1920's, is a South African term applied to a drink of conviviality taken at sundown.

870

zodiac

The Greeks reckoned their calendar from the twelve principal constellations as they took their turns in the sky overhead, but the calendar was represented graphically by a circle in which figures representing the constellations were entered. This representation was called *zodiakos kyklos,* "the circle of the figures," from *zodion,* "a figurine" (diminutive of *zoön,* "animal"), and *kyklos,* "a circle" (which led to our *cycle*). The term became abbreviated to *zodiakos,* which was taken into Latin as *zodiacus* and hence through the Romance languages and into English with appropriate spelling changes along the way.

fantan

Neither portion of this is an English word; the whole merely approximates the Chinese name of a simple game of chance. In the native form a small heap of coins is covered by a bowl and the players then place bets, not on the number of coins so concealed, but on the remainder—one, two, or three—when the total is divided by four. The Chinese name means "remainder." Variations have, of course, been introduced.

hackamore

Easterners and Englishmen may rarely hear this word, but it is common among horsemen and cattlemen of the West. No one ever accused the forty-niners in early contact with California Mexicans of a close ear for the Spanish words they adopted, but it is now generally accepted that *hackamore* was intended to represent the sound of the Spanish *jáquima,* a term in that language for the part of the harness of a horse that we call "halter" or, more exactly, "headstall."

hallmark

Whatever the present application, the original term has designated the official stamp or mark of the Goldsmith's Company of

London or other assay office applied to gold and silver articles to indicate their purity. Such stamping was introduced by order of Edward I in the year 1300, and there have been but few changes in the designs so employed since that date.

nuthatch

This small bird, of several varieties, got its name from certain of its feeding habits. Although it eats a profusion of insects, it is  especially notable as an eater of acorns and the nuts found in pine cones, the shells of which it breaks with its sharp beak. Our ancient forebears therefore gave it a descriptive name, combining *nut* with *hatch,* a term borrowed from French *hacher,* "to chop, hack"; hence, a bird that hacks nuts for its food. Our words *hatchet,* "that which chops," and *hash,* "that which is chopped," came from the same French source.

alewife

Although the early settlers on our New England shores knew this plentiful fish by this name (*New Plymouth Laws,* 1633), so many other pronunciations were also used in the early years that to this day there is no certainty of its source. Some think that an Indian name was adopted which sounded something like "alewife." Nevertheless, the traveler John Josselyn in his *An Account of Two Voyages to New England,* 1674, wrote: "The alewife is like a herrin, but has a bigger bellie, therefore called an alewife."

nightingale

Bits of our language have been picked up from almost every people with whom our English forebears came in contact. Thus, in remote times, when Norse vikings made settlements along the coasts of England, the Norse *gala,* "to sing," entered the native speech. Thus *nahtigala,* the early name of the bird, merely meant "night singer." At some time down through the years, as spelling altered, an *n* was inserted without rhyme or reason. In fact, by all rules and precepts, our name for the bird should be *nightgale.*

pallbearer

In England, to this day, a *pallbearer* is one who does about what the name indicates—one who, at a funeral, is assigned the duty of holding up the corners or edges of the pall draping the coffin. But in America, unless serving in an honorary capacity only, he is one of those delegated to the bearing of the coffin itself.

sackbut

This musical instrument, a precursor of the trombone in that it contained a hairpin-shaped bent tube which was slid in and out to vary the tone, may have derived its name from the Old Norman French *saqueboute,* a lance with a curved hook at the end, which was used to pull riders from their horses. The further etymology of *sackbut* may remind my contemporaries of the *pushmi-pullyu,* that mythical animal found in Hugh Lofting's tales of Doctor Dolittle which had a head at either end, for it is based on the fusion of *saquier,* "to pull," and *bouter,* "to push."

akimbo

One can't be certain about this, but the prevailing opinion among the word-delvers is that this arose from a corrupted pronunciation of the medieval phrase *in kene bowe,* meaning "in a sharp bend," just as is the shape of one's arm when the hand rests on the hip, the present usual sense of the word. But there was an Old Norse word, *kengboginn,* "bent double; crooked," which may have been the source of our word. Our language has undergone some mighty strange transformations, yet I mention this only because it has been given serious consideration.

fakir

Through the fact that some of the practices of certain religious devotees, especially of India, appear to be quite fictitious, clever trickery, the word *fakir* is sometimes considered to be merely another spelling of *faker*. It isn't; it's an Arabic term and, strictly speaking, it should be applied only to those followers of Mohammed who, with him, can truly say, "Poverty is my pride," *el fakr fakhri*. However in India the Hindu *fakir* is likely to be an expert juggler, adept in sleight of hand, in hypnotism, in ventriloquism, and in producing illusions.

bachelor's button

Almost any kind of small round flower the petals of which present a jagged appearance goes by this name. Why? Because garments anciently worn were held by buttons of cloth which, in the case of helpless bachelors, became frayed around the edges.

sabotage

The etymology of *sabotage* is clear—it is derived from the French *sabot,* "a wooden shoe," which, in turn, has been traced to the Spanish *zapato,* "a shoe," probably from the Biscayan *zapatu,* "to tread." The origin of the present-day meaning of *sabotage,* though, is less clear. It has been suggested that it may have been derived from the clatter of children in their noisy sabots, driving their parents or teachers to distraction; or that it may have arisen as an allusion to shoddiness, as by the comparison of crude wooden shoes with those of leather; or that it may have been applied to the practice attributed to French millworkers who, averse to the introduction of mechanization, cast their sabots into the looms; or, because it is also applied to the cutting of shoes or sockets used in attaching the rails of a railroad to the ties, that this sense of the word became warped to the deliberate destruction of these same rail attachments with the concomitant disabling of the railroad. In any event, *sabotage,* as an instrument of industrial warfare, had become firmly established by the French General Confederation of Labor in 1887, and was adopted into English by 1910, being accepted as a labor weapon by the I.W.W., though Weekley, writing in 1911 (*The Romance of Words*), said that it was not even then known to the great French dictionaries in that sense.

874

O.K.

Although these initials are now known and used around the world and have been in common American usage for a hundred  years, the source was a matter of great disputation through most of that period. Some attributed it to illiteracy displayed by Andrew Jackson, who, they said, wrote *O.K.* as the initials of *"Oll Korrect."* Others thought the source was a misreading of the initials *O.R.,* "Order Recorded," indicating official approval of a document. And some believed that the initials were an erroneous rendering of the Choctaw *okeh,* "it is so." All dispute ceased in 1941. In that year, in the July 19 issue of the *Saturday Review of Literature,* in an eight-page article, "The Evidence on *O.K.,*" Allen Walker Read laid the ghost for all time. By dint of much research he traced the initials back to 1840, finding the first appearance in print in the New York *New Era* of March 23. The reference was to a political organization supporting the candidacy of Martin Van Buren for a second term in the White House. The members called themselves the Democratic *O.K.* Club, taking the initials from *Old Kinderhook,* a title bestowed upon Van Buren from the name of the village, *Kinderhook,* in the valley of the Hudson where he was born. The mystifying initials, as a sort of rallying cry, caught the fancy of other supporters immediately, and were used, according to the New York *Herald* of March 28, by these supporters in a raid upon a meeting of the Whigs the previous evening. "About 500 stout, strapping men," the paper reported, "marched three and three, noiselessly and orderly. The word *O.K.* was passed from mouth to mouth, a cheer was given, and they rushed into the hall upstairs, like a torrent."

kickshaw

And of all the ways in which we who speak English have altered words of other languages this is literally something. Yes, that is what it meant—"something." It began as the French plural, *quelque choses,* which, especially when used in cookery, and,

875

generally, with a shrug of the shoulders, indicated, "just something dainty; mere trifles." By the elite, the pronunciation was *que'que choses,* which became in English speech, of the seventeenth century, *keck shaws.* Our forebears then turned this back into a singular and the permanent pronunciation, *kickshaw.*

numskull

If the first syllable were spelled *numb,* as it once was, the sense and source would be clearly recognized. *Numb* in the *skull,* with the brain benumbed, dulled. Actually, however, if we were to follow *numb* back through the centuries we would find that it should be spelled *num* after all. Anciently, our language had a verb *nim,* meaning "to deprive, to take away." A past participle was *num,* "deprived, taken away." But *nim* has been *num* from our speech these five centuries.

humbug

My, but how the learned scholars of the 1750's did rave and rant against this neologism. After its coinage—out of whole cloth, presumably—it must have sprung into immediate popular favor. But here is what was said of it by one writer, probably Thomas Warton, in *The Student:* "I will venture to affirm that this *Humbug* is neither an English word, nor a derivative from any other language. It is indeed a blackguard sound, made use of by most people of distinction! It is a fine make-weight in conversation, and some great men deceive themselves so egregiously as to think they mean something by it." Nevertheless, despite all railings, *humbug* assumed a place of utmost respectability in the language as a synonym for "Nonsense!"

quarter-

The casual student of etymology may well be intrigued by various compound words starting in *quarter-,* as there seems a good likelihood that certain of these may have odd and unusual beginnings. But *quarterback,* for instance, is found to be, in football, the back whose position is one-quarter of the way between the line and the fullback; *quarterdeck* is, on a ship, a deck for the use of officers which covers approximately one-quarter of the area over the main deck; and *quartermaster* was originally a petty officer who was responsible for the troops' living quarters, but whose duties have now been enlarged to include responsibility for supplies in general as well as for quarters.

falderal, folderol

It had no basic meaning; originally used just as a refrain in songs, probably first in Scotland about three hundred years ago. But just because it was so often employed as a meaningless termination to silly little songs it did eventually come to be employed for a flimsy trifle, an empty bit of nothingness.

hunky-dory

Some of the dictionaries say, "Source unknown." I'll agree with that as to the *dory* element, but, considering that the common meaning of the American term is "Quite satisfactory; all safe and secure," the *hunky* element is logically explainable. Though not recorded until a hundred years ago, to be "all hunk" was probably as familiar to New York City schoolchildren from the time of Peter Stuyvesant as to be "O.K." is today, and had a similar meaning—to reach goal; to be home. It was from the Dutch *honk*, "goal." Change from *hunk*, "home," to *hunky*, "safe at home; hence, safe," was as natural as the modern change in slang *corn* to slang *corny*. Printed use goes back to 1861.

The full *hunky-dory* seems to have arisen during or soon after the Civil War. Definite record occurs in 1868. Credit for its introduction is thus stated by Carl Wittke, in *Tambo and Bones* (1930): " 'Josiphus Orange Blossom,' a popular song with many disconnected and futile stanzas, in a reference to Civil War days, contained the phrase, a 'red hot hunky dory contraband.' The Christy's [well-known blackface minstrels of that period] made the song so popular, that the American public adopted 'hunky-dory' as part of their vocabulary."

877

vampire

Neither of the living nor yet of the dead, a vampire is a reactivated corpse doomed, not to peaceful rest in its tomb, but to spend each night in search of a living victim of whose blood to drink. Belief in vampires is virtually world-wide, but the Slavic countries and their neighbors are the center of this belief. Thus, although the word comes to us from the French of the same form, its origin is the Hungarian *vampir,* in which form it is also known, together with variations, in Russian, Polish, Bulgarian, and other languages of the area. It has been suggested that the ultimate source may have been the North Turkish *uber,* "witch."

cantankerous

We must thank Oliver Goldsmith for developing this word from an older source. In *She Stoops to Conquer,* he proclaims, "There's not a more bitter cantanckerous road in all christendom," meaning that the road would try one's soul, is perverse, contrary, ill natured. Apparently Goldsmith dug up a word of similar meaning, long since obsolete or surviving only in country speech, *contecker,* a person who "contecks," quarrels, disputes, is contentious. But whatever his source, he gave us a mighty useful word.

pantywaist

This American appellation for an effeminate young man is not much more than thirty years old. The idea, however, takes us  back to about 1890. Small American children, then, and some perhaps not so small, were encased in a sleeveless undervest, bedecked with buttons at the waistline, to which their panties were severally attached. The garments were for children and, especially, for girls; ergo, feminine and nonheroic.

Fahrenheit

He was only fifty when he died, in 1736, and only twenty-eight when he introduced the mercury-filled thermometer and devised the scale for measuring temperature still called by his name, Gabriel Daniel *Fahrenheit,* a German citizen, born in Danzig. His father was a merchant, and the son had been trained to follow that pursuit, but, interested more in the science of physics than in commerce, he removed to Holland.

ladybug

The usual American name; *ladybird,* the usual name in England. So named, not, as childish fancy may have assumed, because these beneficial insects are all female, but in honor of "Our Lady," the Virgin Mary.

table d'hôte

Lifted directly from the French over three hundred years ago, this literally means "the host's table." The original sense was that of a common table set for the guests at a hotel or other eating place, but from this has come the more usual meaning today, which is the complete meal served at a hotel or restaurant.

camelopard

No, no one ever thought this beast was a cross between the camel and the leopard, but the Greeks of old gave it the name—*kamelopardalis*—simply because its body somewhat resembled that of the camel and its spots were like those of the *pard* or leopard. We call the animal by the shorter name, *giraffe.*

strawberry

Although derived from the Anglo-Saxon *streawberige,* this word is curious in that its parallel is not found in other Teutonic languages. A synonymous Anglo-Saxon word was *eorthberge* (earthberry), which failed to live in English, but is related to the German *Erdbeere* of the same meaning. Both *straw* and *berry*, though, have living relatives in the other Teutonic languages. *Strawberry* is of great age in its English ancestry, the early forms having been found to date from about the tenth century. The age of the word leaves us in considerable doubt as to the reason for its origin, but the best accepted derivation is that the small seed-like growths on the berry (called "achenes") were taken to resemble bits of straw, giving the fruit its name.

nincompoop

Sorry, but there's not much we can do with this word. It was coined sometime in the last half of the seventeenth century, though variously spelled *nicompoop, nickumpoop, nincumpoop,* but no source has been established. Dr. Samuel Johnson, in his dictionary of 1755, believed it to have been a corruption of the Latin phrase, *non compos,* "without ability," but the earliest forms of the word do not support that theory. It looks to me as though someone had merely elaborated upon the older *ninny* of almost identical meaning.

yesterday

Related forms of the word are to be found throughout the entire group of the Teutonic languages, and, indeed, more distant relatives are known in many of the languages of the large Indo-European family of which the Teutonic and Romance are two important branches. In English, the word goes back to the Anglo-Saxon *geostrandæg* or *gestordæg* (sometimes as two words, *geostran dæg*). It is uniquely in English, though, that the two elements always go together (some writers have experimentally written *yester* or *yestern* alone, but the practice has never won wide acceptance). In German, for example, "yesterday" is expressed by the simple word *gestern*. Interestingly, in some languages the related term has also had the sense of "tomorrow," so it is presumed that the original sense was "a day either before or after today."

haberdasher

The term is so old and so beguiling in appearance that there really should be a good story behind it. We have record of its continuous use through more than six hundred years, back to the early fourteenth century. John Minsheu, a dictionary compiler of around 1617, derives it from the German, *Hab' Ihr das?* "Have you that?" as a shopkeeper might say in showing his wares to a customer. But, though our word probably crept into English usage as a corrupt version of some alien term, the most likely being the Old French *hapertas,* "a dealer in furs," there is no clear account of its source. However, the original *haberdasher* sold hats and caps, as well as the notions he now deals in.

petticoat

In the fifteenth and sixteenth centuries this garment was actually, as the name indicates, a "little coat." At first it was a

man's coat, worn under his armor as a protection against chafing. Later he wore it as an undergarment beneath his doublet, as a waistcoat or sort of vest. And it was thus, then, that women first wore it, as a sort of chemise. But in the seventeenth century women began to extend the name to the underskirt appended from the chemise, or, as at present, to any underskirt.

jack-in-the-box

Nowadays the name is usually applied to a toy, a box from which a frightening figure, such as a dragon, serpent, clown, or the like, springs out when the fastening of the lid is released. The toy, however, is a very modest proxy for the original box of the sixteenth century, which was also designed to delude or deceive the person who opened it. That is, it was a box, empty or containing worthless trash (the *jack*), which a clever cheat or sharper substituted for the box or small chest of money that a tradesman expected to receive for his merchandise. Hence, the sharper himself became a *jack-in-the-box*. One of the *Satirical Poems of the Time of the Reformation*, in 1570, has the lines, in modern spelling:

> *Jack in the box,*
> *For all thy mocks*
> *A vengeance might [on] thee fall!*
> *Thy subtlety*
> *And palliardy [knavery]*
> *Our freedom brings in thrall.*

gaffer, gammer

The terms did not break into print before the latter end of the sixteenth century, but both must have been in common dialectal speech many long years earlier. And, of course, dispute reigns as to what were the original words. As now used, almost wholly only in rural England, they are usually terms of address, respectively, to an elderly man and an elderly woman. The present consensus is that they have gradually evolved as contractions of *godfather* and *godmother,* but there is also a strong belief that the original forms were *grandfather* and *grandmother.*

humdrum

Hum, yes, because that which is *humdrum* has the monotony of the humming of a bee or other insect. But *drum*—well, did this added syllable, back in the sixteenth century, also convey the monotone of a drumbeat? It is doubtful, though such could have been the case. But it is more likely that *drum* was added merely because it rhymed with *hum* and just happened to be a word itself.

stripling

The etymology of this word is uncertain. Most authorities suggest that it is derived from the noun *strip,* "a narrow piece of substantially even width," plus the suffix -*ling,* "one having some specified attribute." This derivation is based on the use of *stripling* as "a youth, not yet having filled out in manhood, hence, one slender as a strip." However, the best authorities then immediately point out that *strip,* as a noun, was not recorded in the language until more than a half-century after the first recorded use of *stripling.* The verb to *strip,* to divest someone of something, though, is much older, and it seems remotely possible that *stripling* may have originated with the sense of beardless, i.e., one *stripped* of his beard. This is not too likely, since presumably such a person never had had a beard of which to have been stripped.

ait

If it were not for the needs of crossword puzzlers, this rarely used word might peacefully fade away from American dictionaries. In England, where it is still applied occasionally as a term of ancient lineage for a small island, especially in the Thames river, the spelling may be *ait, eyot,* or *eyet,* according to one's whim, each having the same pronunciation as "eight."

rabble

Every generation has them—people who lose their tempers quickly, people who make more noise than they do sense—and the Romans had a name for them. (The Greeks did, too, but right now it's the Romans who concern us.) The Latin term meaning "to rave, to rage" is *rabo,* and the petty advocate who pleaded his cause with more temper than temperateness was a *rabula.* Although the derivation is not clear, it seems probable that this term became applied to any noisy person and finally to a noisy collection of people—a mob—which is the sense of our modern word, *rabble.*

callithump

Back in 1856, B. H. Hall, in *College Words and Customs,* attributed this name to a noisemaking band composed of Yale College students. Maybe he was right, but if so, the *callithumpians,* as members of any similar band were known, had also spread out by 1830 from New Haven to New York. At least the term sounds as if it had a college source—made up from Greek *kalos,* "beautiful," and *thump;* "a beautiful thump." What did these beautiful thumpers do? Strummed on pans, kettles, coal buckets, and any other discordant noisemaker to make the night hideous. The name, sometimes degenerated to "cowthump," was also applied to the "shivaree" or *charivari.*

tabernacle

This word first entered our language in the mid-thirteenth century as applied to the curtained tent that, in the Old Testament, contained the Ark of the Covenant and other sacred items. Its use in the broader sense of "a portable, temporary dwelling, such as a tent" began about a century later, as so used in the Wyclif translation of the Old Testament, although there exist some records of its use in differing senses in the interim. The word comes to us through the French (of the same spelling) from the Latin *tabernaculum,* "a tent, booth, shed," this being the diminutive of *taberna,* "a hut, booth" (from which we also get *tavern*).

polecat

A *cat,* sometimes called "pussy," that is fond of *poles*—not, however, the kind stuck in the ground. This *pole,* back in the four-

teenth century, was a French word which, in modern French, is spelled *poule.* It means a chicken. For the *polecat* is a chicken thief, just as is its American cousin, the skunk. Incidentally, the European polecat does not have the broad stripe down the back, so characteristic of the American skunk.

oakum

You might not think it to be so, but in its original form *oakum* was "off-combing." It referred to the hard, coarse strands of retted flax which were combed out before spinning, the tow. The Old English word was *acumba,* considerably modified in spelling down through the years. This tow, or "hards" as also called, was found to be useful in the calking of boats, and later the name was transferred to the strands of old rope, untwisted into its fibers and used for the same purpose.

keelhauling

By comparison, this, in the modern navy, constitutes a mild punishment. It actually amounts to nothing more castigating than a severe tongue-lashing. Not so in former days. The literal procedure was so severe a punishment that many a sailor failed to survive. It is said that the device was first copied by the Dutch in the sixteenth century from earlier practices among Mediterranean pirates, and it was then speedily adopted by the British. The malefactor to be punished was dropped from the end of a yard and hauled under the vessel from side to side, a weight being attached to his feet to keep him clear of the ship's bottom. Or if his misdeed were adjudged worthy of more severe treatment, he was hauled lengthwise under the vessel, from stem to stern. This latter, called *keelraking,* was more likely to be fatal.

gadabout

One *gads* who merely roams here and there idly or as if in meditation, but without special destination. But the *gadabout,* though he may have no special objective, does have a definite purpose in mind, and his roaming is rarely meditative. He seeks news. And the news he wants is that which will satisfy curiosity or some choice bit of gossip about a neighbor. Perhaps the pronouns should be changed from "he" and "his" to "she" and "hers," for the typical *gadabout* is more likely to be feminine than masculine. The term is little more than a hundred years old; a short-lived predecessor was *gad-abroad.*

Babbitt

No relation whatsoever to the chief character in Sinclair Lewis's satire of that title. This is the name of a soft, whitish alloy used to reduce friction in machine bearings and was that of its American inventor, Isaac Babbitt (1799–1862), who first produced it at Taunton, Massachusetts, in 1834. The invention contributed so greatly to the development of the "Machine Age" that Babbitt later received a Congressional award of $20,000.

mooncalf

In Shakespeare's youth this was a figment of the imagination, a monster of some horrendous sort conjured up by moonlight in the eye of a frightened person too scared to see straight. But by the time Shakespeare wrote *The Tempest* (1613), he or others took it to be an actual being, a congenital monstrosity such as a malformed calf. The term was then applied to a person who was a congenital idiot or, as though moonstruck, acted as if deranged.

eaglestone

Actually these small, hollow, globular, stony balls, varying in size from a golf ball to a man's head, were so named by the Greeks —*aetites,* which, translated, is "eaglestone." According to Pliny, that is, this early name arose from a belief that unless the eagle were able to transport one of these stones into its nest the eggs would not hatch. How that belief came about is, of course, unknown, but as the nests are just about inaccessible, it is possible that an ancient climber, finding such a stone near a nest, embellished the tale of his daring ascent with the story, and the stone itself as proof of his discovery. The Greeks had their "tall stories" too.

stereotype

One of the greatest advances in the art of printing was the invention of movable type, for this permitted the printer to be free of the time-consuming process of having his plates individually engraved by hand. Yet movable type, too, had disadvantages, for it had to be carefully adjusted for even depth of impression and, once set up, had to be firmly locked in place to avoid becoming "pied" (i.e., scrambled). Then there came another great advance, said to be the invention of Firmin Didot, a French printer, in about 1798. This was *stereotype,* from the Greek *stereos,* "solid," plus *typos,* "type" (from *typtos,* "to strike"); hence, "solid type." In this process, movable type is set, as before, but it is then used to form a mold which, in turn, is used to cast a solid plate of type, releasing the original type for reuse and avoiding pieing. But one of the greatest advantages to the printer was that the invention of stereotype permitted the running of much larger editions, at lower cost, than had theretofore been possible, and each copy assuredly being exactly like all its mates. This absolute duplication of copies led to the figurative use of the word to describe people who behave in uniform patterns, also to characterize hackneyed phrases or those who use them, hence any formalized or uniform pattern of behavior.

Milquetoast

This fictitious character—in full, *Caspar Milquetoast*—was created by the cartoonist H. T. Webster. The series, continued at intervals through the 1930's and 1940's, depicted episodes in the life of "The Timid Soul," episodes of harrowing nature to a nonassertive, timorous man.

ragtime

As all cool cats know, this precursor of jazz is heavily syncopated, but with a strong beat. To its listeners in the late nineteenth century, the timing was most certainly ragged, compared to the tunes with which they were more familiar. What more logical than that this music of "ragged time" should become popularly known as *ragtime?*

leatherneck

Doughboy, gob, and *leatherneck,* as familiar designations of members of the Army, Navy, and Marine corps, respectively, of the

887

United States, have long been subject to speculation—and still are. No one knows; the origins remain inscrutable. As to *leatherneck,* H. L. Mencken said at one time, "It obviously refers to the sunburn suffered by marines in the tropics," overlooking the fact that sailors, with their low-cut collars, were even more exposed to sunburn. Among the theories advanced is the Navy version as it appears in George Stimpson's *Book about a Thousand Things* (1946): "Many sailors maintain that *leatherneck* originally referred to the dark and leathery appearance of a dirty and long-unwashed neck. It may be a myth, but according to Navy tradition marines in the early days were dirty of person. In sailor slang, washing without removing the undershirt and jumper is called a 'leatherneck' or 'marine wash.' When a sailor washes, according to the sailors, he usually strips to the waist and washes his face, neck and arms; but when a marine washes he does so after the fashion of civilians, that is, he merely takes off his coat and rolls up the sleeves of his shirt to the elbows and washes his hands to the wrist and his face to the neck. That, at any rate, was the version formerly given by sailors."

ignis fatuus (jack-o'-lantern, will-o'-the-wisp)

All names apply to the same natural phenomenon, which was apparently of quite frequent occurrence at one time, but is now infrequent. From printed records it would seem that the Latin term, appearing in the sixteenth century, was the earliest in English use, but it is more likely that *ignis fatuus,* "foolish fire," was some unknown scholar's translation into Latin of the French *feu follet,* of the same meaning, accepted by other writers as more learned, more highbrow, than the colloquial *jack-o'-lantern* and *will-o'-the-wisp*—sprites or hobgoblins locally termed Jack or Will and supposedly misleading unwary foot-travelers with lighted lantern or blazing wisp of hay into treacherous bogs. German *das Irrlicht* and Spanish *fuego fatuo* are respective translations of the Latin.

blue-sky law

Any law enacted for the protection of suckers who, without some such safeguard, might part with cash for the purchase of hot air, scenery, or even the blue sky from unscrupulous promoters. The first of the laws that acquired the term was enacted in Kansas in 1912. Our "blue sky" in such connection is the equivalent of the German *blauer Dunst,* literally "blue haze," but in colloquial speech, "humbug."

Airedale

Literally, "valley, or dale, of the Aire," a river in the southern part of Yorkshire, England, joining the Ouse and emptying into the Humber. The name is applied specifically to a breed of terrier originating in this valley, wire-haired, with crown, back, and sides black, and face, throat, and limbs tan. The dog, usually 40 to 50 pounds in weight, is noted for speed, sagacity, and scenting ability; hence, an excellent hunter. The Airedale is also said to be a pleasant companion and a good watchdog, though, never having owned one, I can't vouch for that.

dragoman

Even a woman may be a *dragoman,* for the terminal syllable is not an English word, even though we do, through long custom, make its plural *-men,* rather than *-mans,* as we should. We borrowed the term from the French, who had borrowed in turn from Spain, and there it had come, through the Moors, as a transliteration of Arabic *targuman.* When you hear some traveler use it, or meet it in the works of some author, be lenient; he wants to air his knowledge. He'd rather say *dragoman* than the English equivalent, "interpreter."

hocus-pocus

It is often stated as positive fact that this conjuror's formula, this indication of sham or trickery, owed its origin to a mocking corruption of the first three Latin words of the Consecration in the Catholic Mass, *Hoc est corpus meum* (This is my body). There is no proof of that. The conjecture was first advanced in 1694 in a sermon by the Protestant Archbishop, John Tillotson, seventy years after the term first appeared in print, though then in the form *Hocas Pocas.* Even at the early appearance there is repeated evidence that the term had been taken by various conjurors in imitation of an earlier and more famous one. At least Thomas Ady (c. 1656), though writing of witches and witchcraft, tells of a conjuror in the time of James I who called himself "Hocus Pocus, and so was called, because that at the playing of every Trick, he used to say, *Hocus pocus, tontus talontus, vade celeriter jubeo*," which, as Ady goes on to say, was "a dark composure of words, to blinde the eyes of the beholders."

Frankly, that is to say, I do not know the source of *hocus-pocus,* and neither does anyone else. It may have had some such blasphemous Latin origin, and so may have had the Norwegian equivalent, *hokuspokus filiokus,* and the American expression current in my childhood, *hocus-pocus dominocus,* possibly corrupt Latin, respectively, for "This is the body of the Son," and "This is the body of the Lord."

But there is abundant evidence that "Hoky-poky," the cry of street vendors of ice cream in my childhood who so named the commodity they cried, was derived from the old juggler's term, and it is also probable, though not a certainty, that *hoax,* the art of the conjuror, is a shortened form of *hocus.*

firecracker

England knows this jubilant explosive as merely a *cracker,* though if part of a pyrotechnic display, such as a set piece, it is there, as here, a *firework.* Both terms have been in use from the sixteenth century. But with us, especially with a child, a *cracker* is first of all something to be eaten, harmlessly known as *biscuit* in England. Consequently the paper tube containing gunpowder which explodes with a bang when fire is applied became, naturally enough, a *firecracker* to American childhood from at least the early nineteenth century.

banshee

The Gaelic is *bean sidhe,* "female fairy," which, believe it or not, is transcribed phonetically as *banshee* in English. The *Standard*

Dictionary of Folklore (1949) describes her as, usually, a beautiful woman, though sometimes a hag, whose appearance, according to Irish folklore, foretells the death of someone close to one's family.

ramshackle

The Icelandic language has contributed relatively little to English, which has drawn so heavily on the various languages of the

world for its present make-up, but there seems good reason to believe that *ramshackle,* in its present sense of "tumbledown," or "on the verge of falling to pieces," is derived from the Icelandic *ramskakkr*. (Remember that in the Scandinavian languages, of which Icelandic is one, *sk* has a value very close to *sh* in English.) *Ramskakkr* is made up of the words *ramr*, "very," and *skakkr*, "wry, twisted"; hence is *very twisted,* and this is very close to what we mean when we call Sonny's old jalopy a "ramshackle automobile."

marchpane

Included merely to show that it wasn't overlooked, but there is little of a positive nature to explain its origin, despite much discussion. Similar forms appear in various of the languages of Europe, apparently all derived from Italian *marzipani*. Some say that that was derived from the name of a Venetian coin, the *matapanus,* and was transferred to the confection purchasable by that coin. Others say its source was the Latin *Martius panis,* "bread of Mars." The latter certainly bears greater plausibility.

sweepstakes

Used more or less interchangeably with the singular form. It is generally conceded that the original sense was "winner take all," that is, that the person winning the race or game "swept" all the "stakes" into his own pocket. Later the winnings did not accrue entirely to a single winner, but were divided in some set manner among the first several winners, and still later the term became applied to the event occasioning the wagering (for example, the famous Irish *Sweepstakes*) rather than to the disposition of the spoils. Curiously, though, *Sweepstake* (also spelled *Swepestake*) is recorded as used as a ship's name at least a hundred years earlier than its first recorded use in the gambling sense, but without any sound clue as to the reason for its choice as a nautical term.

martingale

Whether part of a harness, part of the rigging of a ship, or a gambling term, the name is supposed to be connected, in some peculiar manner, with a type of stinginess characteristic of the inhabitants of the town of Martigues in Provence, France. At least such is the deduction that one draws from the sixteenth-century writer Rabelais. *Chausses à la martingale,* according to him, were hose or breeches fastened at the back in the custom of Martigues. I should add, perhaps, that some authorities prefer to say, "Source uncertain."

aftermath

Consequences; especially, in current general use, ill consequences. Also, which indicates the origin of the term, a second crop of hay after one crop has already been cut. *Math,* a term no longer in use, meant "a mowing" in olden days, or the produce of a mowing; hay, that is. Thus an *aftermath* was a later or "after" mowing. Used figuratively it meant later results or effects; consequences.

periwig

False hair, called *phenake* by the Greeks and *galerus* in Rome, was worn by the ancients. But, though imitated in the Middle Ages, especially in the early sixteenth century, attendants at the courts of Louis XIV of France and of Charles II of England brought the wearing of false hair into fashion. Men went so far as to have their own natural hair cut off and converted into wigs. But they were not then called "wigs." That word had not yet been coined. The term was the French word *perruque*—a word which, of course, few Englishmen could correctly pronounce, though which was eventually turned into the pronounceable *peruke*. But *perruque* was first corrupted to *perwyke,* to *perewig,* and ultimately to *periwig.* We still have both *peruke* and *periwig* in the language, but the latter, perhaps because there was long such diversity of its forms, became abbreviated to the much more convenient *wig* before 1675, while Charles II still reigned over England.

synagogue

Literally, a congregation or assembly, it has also come to mean the place of assembly, specifically the meeting place for Jewish worship. The word comes to us through the Late Latin *synagoga* from the Greek *synagoge,* "assembly," from *synagein,* "to bring together," a compound of *syn,* "together," with *agein,* "to lead, bring." The Greek, in turn, is a direct translation of the Hebrew *keneseth,* "assembly," from *kanas,* "to collect, assemble."

draggletail

Just what it appears to be—a tail, especially a skirt tail, that drags, and particularly the person thus dragging her skirt in wet and mud. And inasmuch as one so careless of appearance is likely to be careless in morals as well, the term has frequently denoted a woman of loose character. Not always, though, and not always applied to women. A group of woebegone soldiers, for instance, defeated in battle, anxious for nothing but to save their skins, too tired to maintain any semblance of order, just dragging themselves along, may also be *draggletails.*

aide-de-camp

Without by-your-leave or even the courtesy of an attempt to observe the original pronunciation, we "borrowed" this from the French. Literally it means "an assistant of the field"; hence, one upon whom a general officer relies, on the field of battle, to receive and transmit orders. However, the duties of such a confidential assistant nowadays are not limited to attendance upon a field officer.

roorback

Political campaigns have rarely been entirely free of invective and diatribe regarding the candidates for office, and the presidential  campaign of 1844 was no exception. Widespread publicity was given by those opposing the election of James Polk to a purported book by a mythical Baron von Roorback (sometimes Roorbach), in which certain unsavory practices involving Polk were said to have been described. The falsity of these allegations was soon exposed, and a lie, particularly a lie told for political advantage, is still sometimes referred to as a *roorback*.

milksop

Perhaps it's too obvious; just an infant, or one of infantlike caliber, who sops up milk; hence, one unfit by temperament for conflict. But of interest is the fact that this term for one lacking in spirit is very old in our language. It was used, not only by Chaucer, but a hundred years before his time.

tycoon

Commodore Perry's expedition of 1852–54, which played so great a part in bringing Japan into the fellowship of the world's nations, brought back with it the Japanese word *taikun*, "great prince," the descriptive title of the army's commander-in-chief, whose military title was *shogun*. Upon being taken into American English, the word was respelled phonetically, becoming *tycoon*, and wholly losing all resemblance to its actual Chinese origin. For much of the Japanese language is borrowed from the Chinese, and *taikun* is made up of the Chinese *ta*, "great," plus *kiun*, "prince." Once in English, of course, the word quickly lost its strict meaning, and became applied to anyone who displayed real or imagined power, particularly in the business world.

stucco

Taken into English directly from the Italian, without change of spelling or meaning, this word seems originally to have come from a Teutonic rather than a Romance background. Specifically, the Italians apparently adopted the Old High German *stucchi* or *stukki,* one of the meanings of which was "crust," although the more common meaning was "piece, fragment." *Stucco* has been taken back into modern German with the spelling changed to *Stuck,* whereas the original German *stucchi* has also lived with the spelling modified to *Stück,* but with the meaning "piece" retained.

Jack

As a familiar form of *John,* one of the most common of English masculine names, *Jack* was early applied to any male representative of the common people, especially to a serving man, a laborer, sailor, odd-jobs man, etc. Thus came such names as *steeplejack, jack-tar,* etc. Through association of the name with common labor it became attached also to mechanisms or devices that might be substituted for common labor. Hence such terms as *jackscrew* (now usually contracted to *jack* and operated often by means other than a screw), *bootjack, jackhammer,* etc. Or again, the name was applied to animals, birds, and plants, either because of their common occurrence, their usefulness, or their smallness. Hence such names as *jackass, jackrabbit, jackdaw, jack oak, jack pine, jack plane,* and so on. The list of applications is by no means exhausted though most of them fall within the categories mentioned.

surly

Although, today, *sir* is commonly used as a title of respect for any man, when it first entered the language in the late thirteenth century (as a shortened form of *sire,* which preceded it by a scant hundred years) it was employed solely as the title of a knight or baronet. With the growth of the language, it followed shortly that a man, not necessarily knighted but who comported himself in knightly fashion, came to be described as *sirly*—that is, he was "like a sir." But, as has been remarked so many times, spelling in those days was much more of an art than a science, and individual authors followed their own whims. Thus *sir* was sometimes spelled *sur,* and *sirly* became *surly,* the latter becoming fixed. And the meaning changed from "knightly" to "haughty" to "arrogant" to "rude," which is its present sense.

firedog

No fireplace has less than two, one on either side for supporting logs or grate. But today, possibly because the name sounds more highfalutin, we speak of them as andirons. Formerly, however, the dogs, as they were then called, were of utilitarian iron, serving as supports, and the andirons, in households that afforded them, were state affairs of highly polished brass. Why *dog?* Because they were low, serviceable, and stood (usually) on four legs.

agate

A gem or semiprecious stone of quartz, waxy in texture and marked by bands of color. The name was formerly and should still be *achate* (pronounced *ak'ate*), after the Sicilian river Achates, near which, according to Pliny, the stone was first found.

hellbender

This peculiarly repulsive amphibian looks not unlike an uncouth young crocodile, and I can well imagine that the first white men to run across it in the valley of the Allegheny thought it a salamander direct from hell. Why the *bender* part of the name is not certain, but it may be that the man who named it thought it to be "bent for hell," rather than to have come direct from hell. Another common name for the hideous, though harmless, creature is *mud puppy,* for, though it is able to live several hours out of water, its natural habitat is in the muddy bottom of a stream.

rubberneck

As Mencken has so amply documented, Americans are well known for their adroitness in coining a catchy and appropriate  phrase, yet they seem to have been a little slow in connecting the elasticity of caoutchouc with the craning of the over-curious. *Rubber,* as a contraction of *India rubber,* first appeared in print at least as early as 1788, but it was over a century later, in 1896, before *rubberneck* did so. To be sure, it was probably known in the spoken language a little sooner, but Americans also have the practice of pub-lishing their catchy phrases soon after they are coined, so very little additional age can be assigned this colorful term for a snooper.

finnan haddie

Either of two fishing villages in Scotland is credited with the first source and naming of this delicacy, but no report has been circulated that either has claimed first honors. The delicacy, if your taste runs that way, is merely smoked haddock—*haddie* to the Scots—haddock usually smoked with green wood. Sir Walter Scott attributed the source and name to *Findhorn,* a village on Moray Firth, but a few years earlier, Walter Thoms, in his *History of Aberdeen* (1811), gave the credit to the village of *Findon,* to the south of Aberdeen.

coxcomb

The spelling, though common from Shakespeare's time, conceals the source. The original was *cock's comb,* the comb or crest of a cock, and, back in the time of Queen Elizabeth I and later, it de-noted the cap worn by the professional fool or jester, having the cut and color of such a crest, sometimes with small bells sewn to the tips. The jester himself became the *coxcomb,* and, because of his foolish pretensions and conceits, it was not long before any man of like characteristics, any pretender, became a *coxcomb* in the eyes of his fellows.

kaleyard, kailyard

It is likely that few of the so-styled literati who speak with authority are aware of the fact that a *kaleyard* (also spelled *kailyard*) is nothing more nor less than a cabbage patch or kitchen garden. The Scottish authors—Barrie, "Ian Maclaren" (John Watson), S. R. Crockett, and others—who wrote, a half century ago, of common Scottish life in ordinary Scottish villages were said in sarcasm by their critics to have introduced their readers to a "kaleyard school of writing." Despite these sneers, nevertheless, the books of these authors became immensely popular—another proof of Lincoln's "God must love the common people; He made so many of them."

isinglass

One seeing this for the first time could not be blamed if he thought it to be "is in glass." Nor did I, as a boy, comprehend that the thin, transparent, noncombustible material through which fire could be seen in the pot-bellied parlor stove, and which we called *isinglass,* was not *isinglass* at all, but sheets of mica. Our English name is again the result of mispronunciation and perhaps faulty hearing. Merchants who introduced the product from Holland in the early sixteenth century did not correctly give it the Dutch name, *huysenblas.* They dropped initial *h* and substituted *g* for *b.* The name meant "sturgeon's bladder," and the product was then used in cookery in the making of jellies, or for other purposes in which gelatin is now employed. When this gelatinous substance dried out into thin sheets, such as one can now observe with, say, glue allowed to harden on a pane of glass, the resemblance to mica was striking, thus giving rise to the erroneous substitution—carried from the mid-eighteenth century to the present—of the name *isinglass* for *mica.*

streetwalker

Literally, of course, a *streetwalker* is merely a pedestrian—anyone who is out for a walk either in or along a street. Even though this sense of the word is known and has been used for many years, a still older use is the one applied to a woman of easy virtue, and again the origin has been lost in the mists of antiquity. This sense dates to the sixteenth century, and was probably known to Shakespeare. It seems probable that the term was coined as being descriptive of the practice of prostitutes in pursuing their trade openly on the streets rather than awaiting a customer's chancing to seek them out at home.

quarterstaff

Those who have read *Robin Hood* and other adventure tales of the same period will certainly recall this ubiquitous weapon of the period. One theory is that it got its name from its having been constructed by quartering the bole of a young tree lengthwise, yielding a *quartered staff*. It seems more generally accepted, though, that it is named from the manner in which it is held in combat—one hand at the center, the other at the quarter point, midway between the center and the untipped end (the striking end was tipped with metal). The staff itself was between six and eight feet long.

merry-andrew

If there ever was an Andrew whose jokes and antics were so remarkable that all other men of like disposition would subsequently be known by his name, it's a doggone shame that the history books overlooked him. An attempt was made by Thomas Hearne in 1735 to tie the first *Merry Andrew* down, but it was quickly proved that Hearne had insufficient knowledge of the man he designated. In his work, *Benedictus Abbas Petroburgensis,* he pointed to Dr. Andrew Boorde, a man who, two centuries earlier, had been physician to Henry VIII of England. Some color was given to the statement, because Boorde did have the reputation for attending country fairs and for enjoying salacious jokes. But he was not a buffoon nor a mountebank, however, nor, as sometimes said, the author of a joke book. The fact is that *Andrew,* in the seventeenth century, was a name carelessly bestowed upon any manservant, just as today we call a Pullman porter George.

899

whortleberry

A general name for the fruit (or the plant) of a number of the members of the genus *Vaccinium,* in particular *V. myrtillus.* An earlier name for the fruit was *hurtleberry,* from which the present form was derived, and the shortened forms *whort* and *hurt* are also known. There have been several suggestions attempting to explain the formation of the first part of the word, one of the more interesting of which is that, since the berry has some resemblance to a small black-and-blue mark as might be obtained by a smart blow upon the person, it was named a *hurt,* even as the mark has been so called. The other forms are then presumed to have followed as extensions of this, although in fact the first recorded form is the longer *hurtleberry* (as *hurtilberyes*). The American word *huckleberry* is presumably derived from one of these.

sack coat

A *sack coat* is not (or at least, is hardly ever) made of sack-cloth, but, because it is a loosely fitting garment, hanging straight from the shoulders, is so-called simply because it gives the impression of having been fashioned from a sack. *Sackcloth* is just that—a coarsely woven cloth from which sacks are made.

two-by-four

Although *two-by-threes* and even *two-by-twos* are known and employed for certain purposes, the *two-by-four* is the smallest size of standard dimension lumber used today in the construction of frame buildings. The name refers to the nominal size, in inches, of the thickness and width, respectively, of the piece, although the actual size of the standard, dressed two-by-four is, at the present time, one and five-eighths by three and five-eighths inches for a net cross-sectional area of just under six square inches rather than the eight square inches the name would imply. The smallness of the size has led to the figurative use of the term as a derogatory appellation for anything of small or insignificant area, such as, "He lives on that little two-by-four farm on the edge of town," or, "His shop is that two-by-four hole-in-the-wall in the middle of the block."

syllabus

A word created by a printer's error, but which is now firmly fixed in the language. Cicero had written, in his *Epistles to the Atticans,* "indices . . . quos vos Graeci . . . *sittubas* appellatis" (indexes, which were called *sittubas* by the Greeks). The key word was misprinted *syllabos* in a fifteenth-century edition of Cicero, and the misprint was adopted as a learned synonym for "index" (with our present spelling). From its use as "index" or "table of contents," the meaning has spread to its modern sense —"the subjects of a series of lectures."

quahog, quahaug

Early settlers in New England found that the Indians prized this bivalve for a twofold reason. First, the succulent meat provided many a welcome feast; finally, the dark spot on the inside of the shell was cut out and used for money—black wampum. Our word is a contraction of the Narraganset *poquauhock,* or the Pequot *p'quaughhaug,* meaning "hard clam." The ever-romantic biologists, however, seized upon the monetary use of the clam in assigning it its Latin name, *Venus mercenaria. Quogue,* another variant spelling, is also the name of a small community on Long Island, New York.

Adam's apple

"In Adam's fall We sinned all," ran the first stanza of the seventeenth-century *New England Primer.* His "fall" has since been marked on all mortals, by superstitious belief, by a projection on the fore part of the neck representing, 'tis said, a piece of the forbidden fruit of the Garden of Eden that stuck in Adam's throat as he ate it. Eve did the tempting and ate first, but the projection is much larger in men than in women, often quite con-

spicuous in the adolescent male. Physicians call it *pomum Adami,*
just to say "Adam's apple" in Latin.

hodgepodge

Although originally a corruption of *hotch-potch,* taking over
most of the sense of the older term, this became the more common
form from the seventeenth century onward, probably because
hotch was assumed to be an altered form of the proper name
Hodge, nickname for Roger. But *hotch-potch* was itself a rhyming corruption of a still earlier (thirteenth century) *hotch-pot,*
from French *hoche,* "a shaking," and *pot;* hence, "a shaking together in a pot." At that early period it was a law term, relating
to the commixture of property in order to secure an even distribution, and it is still so used. But probably suggested by *pot,* the
hotch-pot became a culinary potpourri, especially a stew of mutton broth and vegetables. By the late sixteenth century, *hotch-potch*
had become the usual term in cookery and is still so used in England. Figurative usage, indicating a jumbled assembly of miscellany, persons or things, dates from the fifteenth century, and is
the sense most familiar to us in America in the term *hodgepodge.*

firedamp

Damp in this word has nothing to do with moisture, as we
ordinarily associate it, but rather with deadening, or choking, or
stifling. In fact the earliest meaning of *damp* when it mysteriously
appeared in the language in 1480 was as a kind of noxious gas
exhaled by a goat. "After this dragon," wrote Caxton in *The
Cronicals of Englond,* "shal come a goot and ther shal come oute
of his nostrel a *domp* that shal betoken honger and grete deth of
peple." So *firedamp,* then, is in itself a choking gas, often encountered in coal mines, that may become violently explosive
upon contact with a flame.

lazy Susan

One is tempted to parody Shakespeare: "Who was Susan?
what was she?" All that I have learned is that this "Susan"

appeared on the American scene perhaps seventy-five years ago and probably in New England. She, or rather it, was the successor of the dining-room article which, in both England and America, had been called a "dumb waiter." This device, known since the mid-eighteenth century, usually stood alongside the host, its three shelves, laden with wine, rotating about a common spindle. Presumably—the presumption being entirely mine—in some American family this silent servitor replaced a living, energetic, and anything-but-dumb waitress. In ironic honor of her activity, let us say, they called it *lazy Susan*. We can readily assume that the name would remain when, as a matter of further convenience, the shelves were reduced to one and the shortened device was lifted to the center of the dining table.

madstone

The New Orleans *Times-Picayune Magazine* of June 19, 1949, as quoted by *Dictionary of Americanisms,* reported a statement to the effect that there had been an estimated "4000 actual cases in which the application of the Mad Stone brought about instant relief and final cure of snake bites, black widow spider stings, bee stings, and mad dog bites," etc. Obviously we should know what this miraculous stone is, especially as no less a person than Abraham Lincoln believed in its efficacy when he took his son Robert, bitten by a dog, to Terre Haute to have a madstone applied to the wound. Actually, various substances of stonelike nature have been given the name. Generally, however, it is a hard substance that may occur somewhere in the digestive system of an animal, such as a calculus within the gall bladder or a mass of hair or calciferously coated pebble within the stomach of, say, a deer. Where and how the popular belief arose in America is not known. Literary reference goes back only to the early nineteenth century, but it was undoubtedly much earlier.

hogshead

For six hundred years, at least, this measure of liquid capacity has been in our language (and taken into other Teutonic languages, with *hog* sometimes changed to *bull* or *ox*), but as yet the mystery of its source or a plausible reason for the name remains unsolved. One guess, quoted by the learned W. W. Skeat, is that the earliest cooper of these casks of two-barrel size branded his product with the outlines of the head of a hog or of an ox. But Skeat also says that most of the conjectural sources are "silly." And I have nothing to add to that.

Sam Browne belt

General Sir Samuel James Browne was a British army officer of the nineteenth century who was born, and later served, in

India. It may be presumed that some time during his career he became annoyed at the drag of his sword on his belt, which most certainly caused the belt to go askew, marring his smart military appearance. If the general had smallish hips, the weight of the sword may even have tended to pull his belt down over his posterior. In any event, it was General Browne who attached an auxiliary strap to his belt, passing it over his right shoulder (the sword being hung on the left side), thus supporting the sword and permitting the general to maintain his poise. The military belt with strap over the shoulder is still known by the name of its inventor, Sam Browne.

green soap

Anyone who has ever had occasion to use it, in the treatment of impetigo or other skin affection, knows that its color is brown, not green. Nevertheless the name is a reminder that the color was formerly green. Possibly to make the appearance less repulsive, indigo was added to the soft soap, imparting a green hue.

turncoat

In medieval times, the retainers and servants of any given nobleman were clothed in livery of distinctive color and design for easy recognition. If, as might happen under the stress of war or of sharp political differences, it became expedient that a man not be recognized as associated with another, it was a simple matter for him to slip his coat inside out, thus disguising his allegiance. One who so *turned* his *coat* was, literally, a *turncoat,* and the designation soon came to be applied in the figurative sense as well. Legend has it that one astute landholder, whose estate lay on the border between two warring factions, had a coat fashioned with the colors of one army on one side and those of the other on the reverse. According to the tides of battle, he wore first one side out, then the other.

pot cheese

Now we call it "cottage cheese," probably because the old-fashioned names, *pot cheese, bonnyclabber,* and *smearcase* (which comes to us from the German *Schmierkäse,* "spreading cheese"), are no longer sufficiently elite for the modern dining room. But in grandmother's time the curds were separated from the water by heating the coagulated milk in a pot. Hence the name, *pot cheese.*

cranberry

Most of the dictionaries agree that we Americans got this name from the Low German *kraanbere,* "crane berry," from the fact that the plant flourishes in marshy lands frequented by cranes. But Dr. Mathews, in *Dictionary of Americanisms,* questions this assumption. The name, he points out, was used by John Eliot in *Day-breaking,* written in 1647. He doubts that the Low German word would have penetrated to eastern Massachusetts at that early date, and thinks it more likely that our word was already in dialectal English use.

squash

Roger Williams (he who settled Rhode Island) called them "vine apples," and described them as being about the size of apples, and as quite tasty. From this it can be inferred that the gourds which the Narragansett Indians called *asquutasquash* were a sort of melon, especially since the Indian word, literally translated, means "that which is eaten raw." But it is the abbreviation of that same Indian word that gives us *squash,* which, as we know it, is rarely eaten raw. An earlier, now obsolete form was *squantersquash.*

groundhog

We should properly call this largest member of the squirrel family a marmot, or even a woodchuck, for there is definitely nothing hoggish about him. (Or her, as the case may be. It is a "her" who rears her young annually under the pantry of my summer home.) Because there is American usage, a theory has been advanced that the name is a translation of the Dutch *aardvark,* earth pig or hog, an animal of South Africa which, though somewhat larger, has similar burrowing propensities. Dutch colonists in America may have supposed the two to be members of the same family. (See also **woodchuck.**)

sans-culotte

In the latter part of the eighteenth century, it was still fashionable for men to wear knee breeches, this fashion prevailing both in this country and in Europe. The labor-

ing class of France, largely responsible for the first French revolution of 1789, sought for some symbol of dress which would distinguish them from the aristocracy against whom they were pitted, and decided to abandon knee breeches in favor of trousers. Their aristocratic adversaries thereupon bestowed upon them the epithet *sans-culotte,* literally, "without breeches" (*sans,* "without," plus *culotte,* "breeches," from *cul,* "posterior"). Having been applied to the "rabble" of France, the word has now been transferred to apply to any ragamuffin.

quadroon

The descendants of mixed racial unions have been known by many names, most of them sufficiently distinctive to identify immediately the races of the parents. Many of these names can be traced to the Spanish, who were the great adventurers and explorers of the sixteenth and seventeenth centuries. We owe to them the terms *mestizo* and *mulatto,* the former the child of a European and an American Indian, the latter the child of a European and a Negro. The Spanish word *cuarteron* (from *cuarto,* "one fourth") identifies the child of a European and either a mestizo or a mulatto, and from this word we have our *quadroon* as a corruption of the French spelling, *quarteron.* In more recent times it has acquired the unequivocal meaning indicating an ancestry three-fourths white and one-fourth Negro.

cracker

A name now used with pride by native whites of Florida as a distinction from the influx of residents from other states, but also applied in other Southern states to ignorant, shiftless white people, commonly called "poor whites." Among various explanations, one often recurring is that the term originated from the "cracker" or snapping of long whips in the hands of expert freighters over early Southern roads. In fact, however, back even in 1509 a *cracker* was one given to boastful braggadocio, tall stories, or, to speak plainly, lying. In a letter written in 1766 to the Earl of Dartmouth, those known by the name in America were said to be "a lawless set of rascalls on the frontiers of Virginia, Maryland, the Carolinas, and Georgia, who often change their places of abode."

honeymoon

The definition in an old dictionary, Blount's *Glossographia* (1656), on my shelves delights me: *"Hony-moon,* applied to those married persons that love well at first, and decline in affections afterwards; it is hony now, but will change as the moon." Thomas Blount, however, merely paraphrased the definition in

Richard Huloet's *Abecedarium,* printed a hundred years earlier, reading: *"Hony moon,* a terme prouerbially applied to such as be newe maried, whiche wyll not fall out at the fyrste, but thone [the one] loueth the other at the beginnynge excedyngly, the likelyhode of theyr excedynge loue appearing to aswage, ye which time the vulgar people cal the hony mone, *Aphrodisia."*

turkey

It was apparently just about four hundred years ago that the bird, native to Africa, that we know today as guinea fowl was imported into England by way of Turkey, even though the bird itself had been known for its delectable qualities for long previously (it had been mentioned by Aristotle and Pliny). Because of coming from Turkey, and ignoring its African origin, the birds were named *Turkey-cocks* and *Turkey-hens*—later just *turkeys.* A few years later some of the same variety of bird were imported directly from Guinea in West Africa. Not, at first, being recognized as the same species, the latter were called *Guinea-fowl,* and, for a while, the two terms were used interchangeably. Then, with the exploration of America, the large, native game birds found there were at first thought to be the same, and they, too, were called *turkeys.* When it was realized that the two were distinct species, the American bird was given the older name of *turkey* and the African bird retained the name of *guinea fowl.* Unfortunately, though, the distinction was not recognized in time to avoid confusion in their scientific names, the genus of the former and the species of the latter both having been given the name *Meleagris,* which is the ancient name by which Aristotle and Pliny knew the African bird.

dovetail

In the mid-sixteenth century, when this term used in joinery and carpentry first appeared in print, the joint was also known as "swallowe tayle," to follow the spelling of the period. You can see an example of the joint on well-made bureau or desk drawers. It is composed of a series of wedge-shaped tenons and mortises which fit snugly into a corresponding series of mortises and tenons.

The name arises from the shape, that of the V-like or wedgelike shape of the tail of dove or swallow.

portmanteau

In France, back in the sixteenth century and earlier, a *porte-manteau* was an officer in the king's service who carried the mantle (*manteau*) of the king when traveling—the royal mantle bearer, we might call him. The mantle or cloak was precious, of course, and was accordingly carried in a case of soft leather. Eventually, in England, the case itself became the *portmanteau* and was used as a traveling bag for carrying articles of various nature. Lewis Carroll (Charles L. Dodgson) adopted the term, coining *portmanteau-word,* to designate his blendings of two words into one suggesting the meanings of each, a device that he employed in *Through the Looking Glass,* such as *chortle,* from *chuckle* and *snort; mimsy,* from *miserable* and *flimsy.*

coxswain

The spelling *cockswain,* sometimes used, better indicates the source. Five hundred years ago a *cock* was a small rowboat, often called a *cockboat.* Such a boat was usually carried on a larger vessel for the use of the captain, to take him ashore or the like. And the *swain* in charge of that small boat, assigned to row the captain where he listed, was the *cockswain.* With passing years the boat under his charge increased in size and, whether manned by many oarsmen or moved by sail, his prime duty was that of helmsman. The corrupted spelling, *coxswain,* has been general since the seventeenth century.

greenroom

That's what is was, originally—a room near the stage in a theater, the walls and, sometimes, the furniture of which were painted or covered with green cloth. Some say that color was selected for the relief of the eyes of the actors, who rested in that room between appearances on stage, from the glare of the footlights. But it is more likely that the first assemblyroom for artists when dressed just chanced to be painted green. Such is also the opinion of Sir St. Vincent Troubridge, for whom the theater has long been of special interest and study, and to whom I am indebted for the further statements. That first assembly room was in the Dorset Garden theater, mentioned in Thomas Shadwell's *A True Widow,* produced in that theater in 1678. Four years later, 1682, from economic causes, the Dorset Garden and Drury Lane companies were amalgamated at the latter theater. Then at some time within the next eighteen years a room similar to that at Dorset Garden and now called a *greenroom* made its appearance at Drury Lane. Definite reason for the choice of name is not known, but Sir St. Vincent surmises that "one half of the amalgamated company said so often and naggingly 'I wish we had a retiring-room here like the greenroom at Dorset Garden,' that the management had to provide one at Drury Lane, and it was in consequence called the *greenroom* generically for the first time."

But, as Sir St. Vincent adds, any notion that the actors were affected by eyestrain from footlights at that period can be dismissed. It was the spectators, especially those in the galleries, who suffered from the overhead chandeliers above both stage and auditorium. The diarist Samuel Pepys records in 1669, "the trouble of my eyes with the light of the candles did almost kill me." Not until the next century, about 1758, were footlights introduced.

sputnik

This word which, as I write, has so recently leaped into the headlines of just about every newspaper in the world is not, as may have been felt, a pet name coined by the Russians to describe their man-made moon, but is actually the Russian word for "satellite." In the nonastronomical sense, it means "a companion or associate." *Sputnik* is derived from the root *sput-,* implying entanglement or admixture, plus the suffix *-nik,* which is closely equivalent to the English suffix *-er,* that is, one who or that which is involved in the action of the verb root. *Sput-* is probably a compound of the preposition *s,* "with," plus *put,* "road." Thus a literal translation of *sputnik* would be "a traveling companion."

scaramouch

Like our stock companies today, traveling groups of actors in the Middle Ages had a limited repertory, which then was often but one play. Such a group of strolling  players, from Italy, visited London in the latter part of the seventeenth century, bringing with them a pantomime in which one of the chief characters was *Scaramuccia,* a representation of a Spanish don who was a coward and a braggart. His part in the play involved a series of *skirmishes* with the hero, and his name is, appropriately, the Italian word for "skirmish." This character made a great hit with the London audiences, and they took his name, later modified by the French spelling, *Scaramouche,* into the language, applying it to a person having the characteristics of the boastful coward who was the original *Scaramuccia.*

butterscotch

This candy—toffee, in England—does not concern Scotland nor the Scottish people, nor does it contain any of the liquid known as "Scotch." No, the chief ingredients are just butter and sugar. Where does the *scotch* come in? Well, all directions for the preparation of this candy after it is properly cooked close with some such statement as: Pour upon oiled paper or well-buttered pan and when slightly cool *score* with a knife into squares. And "to *scotch"* is merely an old-fashioned word for "to score, notch, mark with shallow cuts."

trousers

The more recent etymology is fairly certain; the earlier is somewhat cloudy. The turning point comes with the medieval Irish and Scottish Gaelic *triubhas,* pronounced *triwas.* This was taken into English in the sixteenth century, and became *trouse.* Although the term describes the entire garment, the word has the appearance of a singular and the garment that of a plural, so that the word was given the plural form *trouses* which, perhaps in analogy with such words as *tweezers, scissors* (plural forms describing singular objects), became altered to *trousers* soon afterward. Meanwhile, in a parallel development, *trouse* was adopted into Scottish English as *trews,* as the name of a particular form of trousers still worn by certain Lowland regiments. As for the earlier development, it may be that the Gaelic *triubhas* is derived from the French *trebus,* a sort of leg covering, from Latin *tubracos.* This, it has been suggested, is a word coined as a play on the words *tibia,* "shin," and *braca (bracca),* "buttocks," that is, "they are called *tubracos* because they reach from *tibia* to *bracas* (accusative plural of *braca*)." But "buttocks" is only a derived meaning of the term *braca,* the primary meaning of which (usually as the plural *bracae*) is "breeches." And *braca* has been identified as coming from the Old Celtic *bracca,* "covering for the legs." Which brings us around nearly full circle, for Old Celtic is one of the ancestors of Irish Gaelic, and *bracca* has, with fair certainty, been identified as the ancestor of the Irish *brog,* "a shoe," from which we get our English *brogue,* "a shoe." And just to make the whole thing slightly more confusing, an obsolete meaning of *brogue* is, you guessed it, "trousers."

cowslip

Sorry, but the name of the plant has nothing to do with the lip of the cow. The English wildflower, the primrose or *Primula veris,* to which the American plant is allied, commonly grows in cow pastures, and the name pertains to the *slip,* anciently *slyppe,* "dung," among which the plant flourishes.

doughboy

In her book, *Tenting on the Plains* (1887), Elizabeth Custer, wife of the General, says, "A *doughboy* is a small, round doughnut served to sailors on shipboard, generally with hash. Early in the Civil War the term was applied to the large globular brass buttons on the infantry uniform, from which it passed, by natural transition, to the infantrymen themselves." That is a reasonably logical explanation. It might be acceptable if it were not for the fact that twenty years earlier, just two years after the close of the Civil War, a writer in *Beadle's Monthly* said, "To us *doughboys* (the origin of the name is one of the inscrutable mysteries of slang) who wore light blue shoulder-straps and chevrons, and were our own pack-horses, . . . the constant . . . skirmishing into positions, only to abandon them, . . . became a wearisome iteration." Regretfully, then, we must continue to say, "Origin uncertain."

sponging house

A sponge is characterized as "readily absorbing fluids and yielding them on pressure." It is the latter part of this that led to one of the slang senses of sponge—the noun, "an object of extortion," and the verb, "to deprive one of something." It is this meaning of extortion that resulted in the coining of *sponging house,* sometime in the sixteenth or seventeenth cenury, as a slang name for the house (usually the bailiff's home) in which men arrested for debt were held overnight prior to being led off to debtors' prison. The reason is that the bailiffs made a good thing of this. They charged exorbitant prices for food and items of comfort given their prisoners, pocketing the profits, and also took advantage of their wards' temporary quarters to try to pry from the prisoners' friends either payment of the debt or further tribute intended to ensure the comfort of the "sponge."

holystone

This term for the soft sandstone formerly used by sailors for scouring the wooden deck of a vessel has led to all sorts of speculation. Why *holy?* One opinion was that *holy* was just a humorous corruption of *holey,* the stone being full of holes like a sponge. Admiral Smythe, in *The Sailor's Word Book* (1867), allowed us other choices: "So called," he said, "from being originally used for Sunday cleaning, or obtained by plundering church-yards of their tomb-stones, or because the seamen have to go on their knees to use it." In *Naval Customs* (1939), by Lt. Comdr. Leland P. Lovette, U.S. Navy (now Vice Admiral, ret.), is the statement that the name came from fragments of gravestones "from Saint Nicholas church, Great Yarmouth, England," first used by English sailors. One hesitates to doubt so positive a statement, but, unable to find other mention of a specific churchyard, I sent a letter of inquiry to Admiral Lovette. His reply, which I am privileged to quote, was, "I don't think we will ever get the full story. One British authority, Rear Admiral Gerard Wells, R.N., definitely states: 'So called because when using them an attitude of prayer is taken.' You know the larger ones in the British Navy were called 'hand bibles,' the smaller ones 'prayer books.' I think the fact that all were of tombstone material and many from old tombstones got the word launched."

porterhouse

Originally, about the beginning of the nineteenth century, a house at which *porter* was served. This *porter* was a kind of dark brown beer or ale favored by porters and ordinary laborers, often called *porter's beer* or *porter's ale*. The *porterhouse steak* is supposed to have been introduced about 1814, according to the *Dictionary of Americanisms,* in the porterhouse conducted by Martin Morrison in New York City.

trombone, trumpet, tuba

The common grandfather of all these seems to have been the straight bronze war trumpet of the ancient Romans, which they called a *tuba*. The word is undoubtedly related to the Latin *tubus,* "a tube." It has been suggested that, in passing into the modern Romance languages, there took place a threefold change in this word—insertion of an *r*, change of vowel, and insertion of an *m* —resulting in the Italian *tromba*, Provençal *trompa*, French *trompe*, "a trumpet." This came into English as the now archaic or poetic *trump*. But there came to be different sizes of the instrument, and in Italian, the larger was given the augmented form of *tromba*, which is *trombone*, whereas in French the smaller was given the diminished form of *trompe,* namely *trompette,* this then coming into English as *trumpet.* Finally, with the development of the extra-large size, the original name of *tuba* was revived and applied to it.

shuttlecock

Although this name has only been in the language since the sixteenth century, it is composed of two words, *shuttle* and *cock,* that are found in the earliest forms of the

language. *Shuttle* is the modern spelling of the Anglo-Saxon *scytel,* "an arrow, missile," and is related to our verb *to shoot.* The name became applied to the weaver's shuttle, probably because it seemed to shoot back and forth across the web, but this has resulted in having the back-and-forth concept become more closely tied to the shuttle than the shooting concept (as a *shuttle train*). When, then, a cork was fitted with a crown of feathers, thus gaining some resemblance to a bird, or cock, and was batted back and forth, as in badminton or its predecessor, battledore and shuttlecock, the *shuttlecock* itself (shuttled cock) was born.

avoirdupois

The *Oxford English Dictionary* calls this "a recent corrupt spelling," and adds: "The best modern spelling is the 17th century *averdepois;* in any case *de* ought to be restored for *du,* introduced by some ignorant 'improver' *c* 1640–1650." The term was borrowed from France about the year 1300. Though its literal meaning was "goods of weight," the sense of its early use was merchandise sold by weight. "Avoirdupois weight" became legalized in England in 1303, but we have long discarded the longer name.

cousin-german

This matter of cousinship is sometimes made more complicated than it should be. *German* is now rarely used in such relationship, replaced by the more readily understood *first* or *full*, coming from Latin *germanus,* denoting such relationship. My brother's son is my son's *cousin german,* or first or full cousin. My brother's grandson is my son's first cousin once removed, and is my grandson's second cousin. If you wish to carry it further, my brother's great-grandson is my son's first cousin twice removed, my grandson's second cousin once removed, and my great-grandson's third cousin. But, even in the South, this degree of relationship scarcely constitutes a "kissing cousin," unless the third cousin is female and very pretty.

greenhorn

Yes, it did at first apply to horns that were green—green, that is, in the sense of young and tender, such as those of a young ox. Then the term was next applied in a more figurative sense to raw, untrained, and inexperienced soldiers, those who might be characterized as not yet dry behind the ears. And from that, still in the seventeenth century, the final extension was easy, and the *greenhorn* became what he is today—one who is a novice or an ignoramus in any given trade, line, or profession.

spindrift

Years ago, the verb *spoon* had a now obsolete meaning, "to run before the wind, to scud." The origin of this sense is not known, but the similarity in sound to *spume* (from the Latin *spuma,* "foam") led to an alternate spelling, *spoom*. Then, through some confused process of reasoning quite difficult to reconstruct, the two meanings, "foam" and "scud," were connected in *spoondrift,* the sea foam generated by high winds. As though this weren't sufficiently complicated, there now came the problem of dialectal pronunciation. In parts of England, *spoon* was pronounced *speen;* in other parts, *spin*. From the latter, *spoondrift* became *spindrift,* and this, some seventy-five years ago, became stabilized as the accepted spelling and pronunciation.

Dutch treat

We of Pennsylvania Dutch extraction have always been of an independent spirit, unwilling to be "beholden" to anyone—and, by the same token, taking it for granted that a neighbor or companion is of the same spirit. In consequence, though far from any justifiable accusation of ungenerosity, we expect that anyone fully able to pay his own way will do so. Thus, when, by design or chance, one of us is accompanied by an acquaintance into a place of entertainment or refreshment, we think it but natural that each pay his own scot. And that is Dutch treat—or Dutch lunch, Dutch supper, or Dutch party.

trespass

The original sense was "to pass beyond or across," and the word comes to us from the Old French *trespasser* from the Medieval Latin *transpassare,* "to pass beyond." This is made up of *trans,* "beyond" (which became *tres* in French), and *passare,* "to pass." Modern French has developed a derivative meaning, "to pass away, to die," which also existed briefly in English in the fifteenth and sixteenth centuries, but did not survive. The sense of passing beyond some limit became applied to passing beyond the limit of some law or regulation, which led to the meaning of "transgression, sin." This is the sense implied by the use of the word in the Lord's Prayer, as first appears in Wyclif's translation of 1382.

quatchgrass

A variant form, of minor importance, of the common name for various grasses, especially *Agropyron repens.* This is only one of several onomatopoetic names for the same thing. Others include *couchgrass, quitchgrass, quackgrass,* and *twitchgrass,* or just *couch* or *quitch.* This last is the oldest known form, and it seems to be related to older forms of *quick.* From this, we assume that the name was given to show that this weed grows and spreads *quickly* unless the farmer is on his toes and roots it out promptly.

stockade

One of those curious words which have entered English with both Romance and Teutonic backgrounds, *stockade* comes to us through the French *estacade* from the Spanish *estacada,* "a fortification consisting of a row of stakes." But *estacada* is from *estaca,* "a stake," which is derived from the Teutonic root *stak-,* a variant of the verb root *stek-,* "to pierce." In more normal fashion, this same Teutonic root has given us our own *stake* through the Anglo-Saxon *staca,* "a post stuck in the ground." *Palisade,* which is a quite similar fortification, is purely of Romance origin, coming from the French *palissade,* from *palis,* "a fence"; *pal,* "a stake"; and ultimately from the Latin *palus,* "a stake, especially one used for punishment of criminals."

sitz bath

This term, describing both the process of taking a bath while in the sitting position, with the legs and feet outside, as well as the  tub in which this uncomfortable process may be accomplished, is taken directly from the German word for the same. The curious feature of the term is that it is half the original, half the English translation. The German is *Sitzbad,* literally "a sitting bath," but the first element has been left in German, possibly to introduce an aura of mystery to the process and render attractive, psychologically, a process that most certainly has nothing to commend it from the standpoint of comfort.

buckwheat

This reminds one of the noted comment on *oats* in Johnson's *Dictionary of the English Language* (1755): "A grain which in England is commonly fed to horses, but in Scotland supports the people." Buckwheat in Europe has been grown for many centuries as a grain for cattle, horses, and poultry, but in the United States a meal is ground from it for making the breakfast delicacy, buckwheat cakes. Because the grain appears similar to the seed of the beech, the Dutch called it *boekweit,* "beech wheat," from which came the English *buckwheat.*

spindleshanks

A quick review of *The Legend of Sleepy Hollow* reveals that Irving seems not to have used the term, but it would most certainly have well described Ichabod Crane. "He was tall, but exceedingly lank, . . . long arms and legs, hands that dangled a mile out of his sleeves, . . . and his whole frame most loosely hung together." For this is the picture one gets of a person so unfortunate to be hailed as "*Spindleshanks.*" *Spindle,* from *spin,* is the slender, tapered rod upon which fiber is twisted into thread, and *shank* is from the Anglo-Saxon *sceanca,* "leg." Specifically, then, a *spindleshank* is a long, thin leg, but in the plural it commonly refers to the possessor of such legs. German and Dutch, respectively, have *Spindlebein* and *spillebeen,* "spindle-leg," while French has *doigts fuselés,* "spindly fingers."

dornick

Had anyone, in my youth, told me that a *dornick* was a kind of fabric, I would certainly have thought either that he was trying to spoof me or he was an ignoramus. In Ohio, and later in Brooklyn, it was a brickbat or cobblestone that could be, and was, hurled by hoodlums through store windows. But this, I learned later, is an American usage, the name probably derived from Irish *dornog,* "a small stone." The fabric *dornick,* known since the fifteenth century, was so named from the Flemish town where first made, the town known to the French as Tournai.

graham bread, crackers, flour

We take our food fads very seriously in this country, and some continue for many years. Along about 1830, a young Presbyterian minister, Sylvester Graham (1794–1851), an ardent temperance advocate, got the notion that if one lived wholly on a vegetable diet he would have no interest in any alcoholic beverage. *Graham boardinghouses* sprang up in many of the larger cities. Then within a year or two he extended his dietetic reform into encouraging the substitution of unbolted flour for all wheaten products. The latter advocacy still meets with much medical favor and it is due to the efforts of this preacher that we continue to have *graham flour, graham bread,* and *graham crackers.*

buckram

Despite the appearance of a compound word, this is wholly unrelated to either *buck* or *ram.* In fact, though it has counterparts in other European languages, its ultimate source is unknown. The fabric itself was originally of fine linen or cotton, costly and delicate. Such was its nature through the Middle Ages. But in the fifteenth century the name was transferred to linen of coarser weave and stiffened with paste, henceforth serving as a stiffener for clothing, as a backbone in bookbinding, and similar purposes.

span-new

This concept of absolute, perfect newness is very old in itself, dating back past medieval English to the Old Norse, in which its form was *span-nyr,* from *spann,* "a chip," plus *nyr,* "new." The allusion is to the newness of a chip freshly cut by the woodsman's ax. Variants such as *spang-new, spanking new,* etc., are merely inventive expansions giving additional emphasis, as is the longer term *spick-and-span-new.* In this last, *spick* is identical to *spike,* and the allusion is to a spike just off the blacksmith's forge. The later extension of *spick-and-span* to imply neatness or cleanliness, of course, is with reference to the appearance of newness. *Brand-new* (*bran-new*) refers to the newness of something, such as pottery, perhaps, fresh from the fire (*brands*), and this has led to the sometimes-heard *bran-span-new.*

hockshop

The term is included here simply because someone may look for it, but I can't retail much information. *Hock,* in the sense of "pawn," has been in American usage at least seventy-five years; hence, a *hockshop* is a pawnshop, but no one knows why. It is my supposition that our *hock* is related to the first element of the English *hock-day, hocktide, hock Monday* or *Tuesday,* which referred to an ancient custom: on the second Monday after Easter the women of a parish seized and bound men, holding them for redemption by a payment of money; on the second Tuesday, men had their turn. Men and women were thus, in effect, held in pawn. In modified form the custom persisted in some parts of England through the nineteenth century.

country-dance

Attempts have been made to give this a French background, insisting that it was first the *contre-danse* of French, Italian, or Spanish origin. Such is not so. It was the other way round. Those dances were eighteenth-century adaptations from the English country-dances. It is not known when nor in what part of England these folk dances originated, but they were certainly much older than the earliest printed record of late sixteenth century.

slipshod

A *slipshoe* was, at one time, the name used for a shoe or slipper that fitted loosely and was worn for comfort, within the home,  rather than for street wear. However, it happened that even back in the sixteenth century, when the term was in vogue, there were certain of the citizenry who valued comfort more than propriety, and who allowed themselves to be seen in public wearing slipshoes, hence, were *slipshod.* Proper people looked down their noses at such goings-on, of course, and thus it came to be that anyone careless of dress in general came to be described as "slipshod." From this it was an easy step to apply the adjective to any thing or action kept or performed in careless, slovenly fashion.

hobnob

We don't use it as Shakespeare did. With us it is a verb—to hold intimate conversation with (another); to be convivial with. But Shakespeare used it (*Twelfth Night,* III, iv) as an adverb: "He is [a] knight . . . ; but he is a diuell in a priuate brall; . . . and his incensement at this moment is so implacable, that satisfaction can be none, but by pangs of death and sepulcher. Hob, nob, is his word: giu't or take't." And the sense then was that of the earlier *hab nab,* "have it, have it not"; hence, "give or take," "hit or miss." The supposition is that our present sense developed from social drinking among two or more with clinking of glasses, giving or taking wine with one another alternately. So, at least, was the occurrence of the expression onward from the eighteenth century.

curtail

The "curtal friar," Friar Tuck, of the Robin Hood ballads, was merely so called because the frock worn by the friar was short, *curtal* being derived from the Latin *curtus,* "short." Other things were also "curtal" four hundred years ago, especially a horse whose tail had been bobbed—a "bobtailed horse," we would say now. And just through this association of *curtal* and *tail,* pronunciation and spelling were altered and remained altered to *curtail.*

poppycock

Now and then difficulties are presented in stating the sources and original meanings of some of our words, especially, as here, of words which through use in a different sense have become completely respectable in our language. Thus, in America, *poppycock* is merely an equivalent of "stuff and nonsense; bosh," but among the Dutch ancestors of some of us or by a present-day Netherlander the original form, *pappekak,* would never be used in polite society. In euphemistic terms: soft ordure.

soupçon

Coming to us directly from the French, in which it has the same meaning, "a trifle," this has gone through several spellings as the

922

French language itself was evolved. It stems from the Late Latin *suspectio,* which comes, in turn, from the Latin *suspicio,* "a suspicion." A *soupçon,* therefore, is a quantity so small that it may exist only in the imagination.

furbelow

One could make a poor pun by asking, "Was it fur below?" But the source of this stylish flounce of bygone years did not derive from a mispronounced "far below" nor from the pelt of an animal. The flounce was much more likely to have been made of silk than of fur. No, we owe the term only to the carelessness of the dressmakers or their customers of the early eighteenth century. The true name, used also in other languages though from an unknown origin, was *falbala,* accented on the first syllable. Through ignorance, perhaps, this became *falbeloe* and, eventually, *furbelow.*

Pollyanna

The "glad" girl. She was created by Eleanor Hodgman Porter in a novel of that name published in 1913, with a sequel, *Pollyanna Grows Up,* in 1915. She was an orphan, turned over, after the death of her missionary father, to live with a stern puritanical aunt. But Pollyanna steadfastly practiced a game taught to her by her father of always finding something to be glad about, no matter how grim the immediate circumstances. Through her continued unquenchable optimism, always seeing a bright side in every catastrophe, the entire community became infected and developed an air of friendliness. Thus anyone who appears unduly optimistic or cheerful in the face of discouragement is now a *Pollyanna.*

atlas

Greek mythology tells us of a terrific struggle between the gods and the rebellious Titans, a race of giants, led by the powerful Atlas. When defeated, Atlas was compelled in punishment to bear the heavens upon his shoulders through all eternity. Ancient artists pictured him as supporting an enormous globe, and a copy of such a picture was used in the sixteenth century by the Flemish geographer Mercator as a frontispiece to his collection of maps. Through his and the subsequent use of some such picture, any volume of maps came to be known by the name of the mythical Greek hero.

treble

The usual sense, of course, is "threefold," and in this sense the word is fully equivalent to *triple*. Whereas *treble* came to us from the Old French, of the same spelling and meaning, which, in turn, was derived from the Popular Latin *tripulus, triple* came directly from the latter source. The original Latin form was *triplex,* from the Greek *triplous,* "threefold." The musical sense of *treble* seems to be from the soprano part having been the third part to be added to harmonized musical composition, in about the fifteenth century.

solfeggio

In the eleventh century, there lived an Italian monk and musician, one Guido d'Arezzo, who proposed the group of syllables that is

 now known as "Guido's scale," or the "Aretinian syllables." These were to be used, in lieu of words, in singing exercises, one for each note of the scale, now known to every school child as the familiar *do, re, mi, fa, sol,* etc. (Our *do* was *ut* to Guido, though.) These syllables were widely adopted, and the verb *to sol-fa* was coined to describe singing with them. The corresponding verb in Italian is *solfeggiare,* and the noun *solfeggio,* taken into English directly from the Italian, is a musical exercise sung with the Aretinian syllables.

asses' bridge

Sometimes called *pons asinorum,* which, perhaps more politely, says exactly the same thing in Latin. Germans translate the Latin into *Esels-brücke;* French use *pont aux ânes,* but they all refer to the fifth proposition of the first book of Euclid: If a triangle has

924

two of its sides equal, the angles opposite these sides are also equal. The proof of this simple bridge-shaped figure is so difficult for those beginning the study of geometry as to give rise to the name, whatever the native country of the student.

sophomore

An older spelling was *sophimore,* and it is believed that this resulted from *sophism* plus the suffix *-or,* "one who practiced sophism," which is the art of argumentation, especially on a fallacious premise. The present spelling stems from the theory that a second-year college student, having acquired some measure of erudition, tends to exploit this knowledge to a degree far beyond its actual worth. In so doing he is wise (Greek *sophos*) to the point of folly (Greek, *moros*), that is, he is a wise fool, *sophomoron,* or, in Anglicized form, a *sophomore.*

counterpane

Oddly enough, it started life as *counterpoint.* This was not the musical term of the same spelling derived from Latin *contra punctus* relating to combined harmonies, but a corruption of an Old French term which was itself corrupted from Latin *culcita puncta,* meaning "a quilt." As the early heavy quilt began to give way to a lighter and ornamental outer bedcover in the seventeenth century, the second element, *point,* was gradually replaced by *pane* (French *pan,* "cloth"), long previously in use for "coverlet."

funny bone

This name for that portion of the elbow over which the ulnar nerve is drawn has never seemed appropriate to me. To strike or be struck on that edge of bone distinctly gives rise to a tingling pain rather than to anything remotely amusing. The American synonym, *crazy bone,* is more fitting. But it has been *funny bone* since at least the early nineteenth century. Barham, in "Bloudie Jacke of Shrewsberrie," in *The Ingoldsby Legends* (1840), has these lines:

They have pull'd you down flat on your back,
And they smack, and they thwack,
Till your "funny bones" crack,
As if you were stretched on the rack,
At each thwack!
Good lack! what a savage attack!

soothsayer

As used today, a *soothsayer* is a person who can, or at least is alleged to be able to, forecast the future accurately. This is not a new meaning—it has been in use for about three hundred years —but it is not in agreement with the original sense. *Sooth* was, to start with, an exact synonym for *truth,* and a *soothsayer* was merely one who was truthful. But charlatan fortunetellers have been with us a long time, and they are most anxious that their gullible patrons should believe in the truth of their predictions. Hence it was quite to be expected that they should protest that they were *saying sooth,* i.e., "telling the truth." *Sooth,* today, lives only in this word and in *forsooth* ("in truth! certainly!"; chiefly ironically), except that it is sometimes used as a deliberate archaism.

doodlebug

The larva of the ant lion. But why this immature insect is held to ridicule by the contemptuous name *doodle,* "simpleton," is not easy to understand, for he's a wise little gazebo, well versed himself in the follies of ants, as you will see under the item **ant lion.** Because of the power, like that of a miniature rotary snow plow, with which he expels sand particles from his excavation, one would expect to connect *doodle* with *doodlesack,* the bagpipe, played by a current of air, but there is no such connection.

polliwog

If we called this immature amphibian a *polwygle* as our English forebears did five centuries ago, the source of the name might be more easily identified. That is, *poll,* "head," and *wygle,* which we now spell *wiggle*—a "wigglehead." *Tadpole* (which see) is the usual name in England; in America we use one or the other, whichever may first come to mind.

assassin

In today's underworld slang, he would be a gangster, a gunman, a gorilla, a trigger boy, or, from the murderous qualities ascribed to the tribe, an Apache. But the old term, dating to a band of Saracens in the eleventh and twelfth centuries, came from the practice by the members to dope themselves heavily with hashish, more powerful than marijuana, when ordered by the chieftain to commit a murder. A person thus doped to fanatical zeal was a *hashashin*, "eater of hashish." European Crusaders understood it to be *assassin*.

sombrero

Like the other head coverings *parasol* and *umbrella, sombrero* is named to describe its benefit when worn. Thus this wide-brimmed hat from sunny Spain is so-called

from the shade it affords its wearer, the Spanish for "shade" being *sombra. Umbrella* is similarly named, from the Latin *umbra,* "shade," with a diminutive ending, hence, "a little shade." *Parasol* is from the Italian *parasole,* from *para,* a form of the verb *parare,* "to ward off, parry," combined with *sole,* "sun," hence, "warding off the sun."

gooseberry

Sorry, but nothing has ever been found which would indicate that anyone anywhere ever thought geese were at all eager for these berries, or were even averse to them. They're just not interested. In fact, no reason for associating the bird with the plant or berry has been discovered.

sooner

In 1889 the Federal Government decided to throw open the Territory of Oklahoma for settlement, and those in charge took great pains to try to see that no potential settler received any unfair advantage over another with respect to the more choice land. The borders were closed, and policed to keep them closed until the starting gun was fired, whereafter the race was on, and the swiftest to reach a chosen site was the winner. But, despite all precautions, a few managed to cross the border *sooner* than the rest, and to nab some of the best spots. In so doing, they unwittingly caused the coining of a new noun, for not only were these cheats named "sooners," but the same appellation was applied to anyone thereafter who jumped a deadline. And, too, Oklahoma itself is now nicknamed "the Sooner State."

hobgoblin

Here again, as in *hobbyhorse,* we find *hob* as a nickname, this time as a variant form of *Rob,* the diminutive of *Robin.* And the allusion was to the tricksy sprite of ancient superstitious belief, Robin Goodfellow. But whereas *hob,* among our remote ancestors, was rarely more than mischievous, when they united his name with *goblin*—Robin the goblin, as it were—the mischief ascribed to him was usually ill humored, often malicious. And he himself was alleged to be a bogey, an ill-favored imp—to children, something bad "that'll git you, ef you don't watch out."

corn dodger

It's made of corn meal, all right, plus a little salt and water or milk, and then fried in a hot skillet, three or four at a time, and it's perfectly delicious, especially served hot at breakfast. Why it is virtually unknown north of the Mason-and-Dixon line is a mystery, as it is very filling and cheap. But what this comestible is or was supposed originally to "dodge" is beyond my comprehension, unless, possibly, its creator contrived it as a "dodge" to cover a shortage of another breadstuff. Earliest available record carries it only to the 1830's, but I have little doubt that Southern tables knew it long before that.

928

treadmill

The verb *to tread* is one of the oldest words known in the English language and its forebears, being found in that most ancient of Anglo-Saxon writings, *Beowulf,* which dates to the seventh century A.D. It, or rather, its close relatives, are also known in all the languages of the Teutonic group, with the general meaning of "to step upon, to walk on." The noun is less old, and that particular sense of the noun applying to the steps of a set of stairs is as recent as about the eighteenth century. Yet it is this sense that has entered into *treadmill,* for this machine, invented about 1820 as a means of employing prisoners, was a large cylinder, or wheel, arranged with a series of horizontal *treads* around its circumference. As the wheel was rotated by means of men "climbing" these steps, the resultant movement of the axle was used to operate a *mill,* thus giving us the compound term *treadmill.*

polka dot

Along about 1830 a lively dance originated in Bohemia which speedily took all of Europe and America by storm. It was named *Polka,* meaning a Polish woman, just as *Polak* means a Polish man. So popular did the dance become that tradesmen vied with one another to attach the name to jackets, hats, gauze, and even articles of food. About 1880 or a year or so later an American dress fabric was introduced, ornamented with round, evenly spaced dots of uniform size which, following the prevailing custom, the maker called *polka dots.* Actually, however, the textile bears no other connection whatsoever with the dance.

brimstone

Because this was formerly the common name for sulfur, one would suppose that it was so called because it could be stone taken from the brim, say, of a volcano. But, no; *brim* is just the surviving form, in this word, of a dozen ways in which *burn* was spelled four and five centuries ago. It was, that is, a "stone" which could "burn." "Brimstone and treacle" was a prime household remedy of Dickens' day, which, to the American grandmother, became "sulfur and molasses."

corduroy

The Draper's Dictionary (1882) blandly says, "The name is of French origin, where it was originally *corde du roi,* the king's cord." But, alas, no such name has ever been used in France. The French name for the material is *velours à côtes,* "ribbed velvet." First mention of the fabric was in the 1790's, but no hint accompanied that or later mention as to the reason for the name. It has the semblance of clever advertising. Material disguised as "the king's cord" would undoubtedly interest a prospective buyer.

sphinx

The name comes to us from the fabled monster of Thebes, which had a woman's head on the winged body of a lioness. This creature

would stop passers-by and propound to them the riddle, "What is it that in the morning travels on four feet, during the day on two feet, and in the evening on three feet?" All who could not give the answer were strangled and devoured. Finally, the Greek hero Œdipus gave the solution: "Man, who as a child creeps on all fours, in adulthood travels erect, and in old age needs the aid of a stick." Whereupon the monster destroyed herself. The tale was first recorded by the Greek poet Hesiod (circa eighth century B.C.), and the name itself is the Latin transliteration of the Greek *sphigx,* "the strangler," from the verb *sphiggein,* "to bind tightly, to strangle."

son of Belial

Belial is the Anglicized form of the Hebrew *b'li-ya'al,* from *b'li,* "not," and *ya'al,* "worth, profit." Thus the original sense of *belial* was merely "unprofitable." From this sense, though, the term came to have the meaning of "wickedness," and the many references in the Old Testament to a *"son of Belial," "daughter of Belial,"* etc., refer to someone who is very wicked. Later,

Belial, although never previously a proper name, became used as one of the names of the devil, the personification of all wickedness, so that now the phrase *"son of Belial"* is most often taken to be synonymous with "spawn of Satan."

dogwood

Sorry, there doesn't seem to be any valid explanation of the animal prefix. A botanist of the seventeenth century called the European plant the *dogberry* tree, because of its dark purple berries, but that throws no light on the "dog" element. One writer only gives this explanation: "It is called Dogwood, because a decoction of its leaves was used to wash dogs, to free them from vermin," but that was written in 1838 and no previous writer seems ever to have heard of such usage. In this I am inclined to agree with the statement in the *Century Dictionary:* "In this, as well as . . . in similar popular names of plants, it is not necessary to assume a definite intention in the use of the animal name."

somersault

Acrobats have been doing this for years, and the word has been in the language at least since the sixteenth century. It came to us from the Old French *sombresault,* which is from the Provençal *sobresaut.* An obsolete English spelling of equal age is *sobersault.* But to get back to the derivation. The Provençal word is equivalent to the Spanish *sobresalto,* and this, in turn, comes from the Latin word *supra,* "over," plus *saltus,* "jump." Thus *to somersault* is "to jump over," or, in practice, "to jump over oneself."

goldbrick

Of course the original *gold brick* was of the pure metal which, for convenience in handling, had been melted and molded into brick form. But skullduggery reared its ugly head among Western promoters of mining properties, and, especially after 1880, many of these gentlemen began to create bricks of identical form of lead, coated with gold. Gullible Easterners with money to invest were taken in by scores in mines from which these "gold bricks" were alleged to have been produced, until eventually the term became synonymous with a swindle, with faking. Later, first as military slang, to *goldbrick* became "to fake industrious toil, to shirk"; and *goldbricker,* "a shirker."

plus fours

Knickerbockers, such as we used to wear in the early years of the twentieth century, were gathered just below the knee. They were thus likely to be stretched pretty tight over the kneecap, especially on a growing boy or in certain sports, such as golfing. Some brave English tailor along about 1920 came to the rescue and, though still buckling the trousers just below the knee, he made the leg much fuller and added just four inches (*plus four*) to the length of the cloth. The garment was not becoming. Any man who wore it looked as if he had two bags suspended from the waist.

trainband

Nothing to do with any railroad, the *trainband* was a group of citizen soldiery organized to serve as reserves in depth for the regular militia. The term arose in the sixteenth century and lived in this sense as long as the practice of having such citizen reserves continued—that is, into the eighteenth century. It has continued to live in attributive senses with respect to especially trained groups of people or of animals. The word itself is merely a shortening of *trained band.*

bowie knife

The brothers Bowie—John J., Rezin P., and James—enjoyed better reputations after death than in life. The three, that is, were in the slave trade in Louisiana in the 1820's, smuggling Negroes into the country from Jean Lafitte's stronghold on Galveston Island. But James was among the defenders of the Alamo, butchered on his sickbed at its fall, and his name has henceforth been honored. The knife carrying the family name, though accredited to Colonel James Bowie, was actually the invention of his brother, Rezin P. It is a strong hunting knife, blade ten to fifteen inches in length, double-edged near the point, with hilt, cross-piece, and sheath.

stalking-horse

Hunters, almost since time immemorial, have made use of a variety of tricks and ruses devised to enable them to approach their quarry (or vice-versa) without being noticed. One of the oldest of these is the *stalking-horse*. At first, as the name indicates, it was an actual horse, behind or alongside of which the hunter walked in concealment. Later, the horse was draped with cloths or the like, and the hunter might be beneath rather than behind the covering. Either way, the game could see only the horse, and was duped into thinking there was no hazard. As time went on, the term became used as a general one to describe something used to conceal a secret project, usually a somewhat dishonorable one. In the political field, it has been employed to describe a third candidate deliberately entered into a race in order to draw votes from the more popular of the original entries with the hope that the less popular would become the winner.

touchstone

Ever since mankind began to practice chicanery upon his fellows, it has been found necessary to develop techniques for ascertaining the true value of those materials that are to be found in the marketplace—particularly gold and silver. Long ago it was discovered that if suspected gold were rubbed on the mineral known as basanite, and if the streak left on the stone was compared with the streaks deposited by gold of differing known purities, the quality of the unknown could be assayed with reasonably good accuracy. The Greeks called this stone *basanos,* which also

933

has the meaning of "inquiry, especially by torture." The Romans were less picturesque—the Latin term is *lapis Lydius,* "the stone of Lydia." But the French got right down to brass tacks and called it *touchepierre* (modern French, *pierre de touche*), literally, *touchstone,* with that sense of *touche* that means "assay."

hobbledehoy

The dictionaries try to satisfy consultants by saying, "Origin unknown," or something of similar import. It might be more honest to confess, "I don't know." A lot of speculation by brainy men has been given, but no one knows yet whether the term came into England from some other language, or whether it was an English coinage. In fact, no one can be certain how it should be spelled, as there were some thirty different spellings used in the years following its introduction. It was first recorded back in 1540, under the spelling *hobledehoye,* with the definition, "the yeres that one is neyther a man nor a boye." Thirty-three years later, Thomas Tusser, though recognizing the term to mean an adolescent stripling, assumed it to have a French source in the lines, from his *Fiue Hundreth Pointes of Husbandrie:*

> *The first seuen yeeres bring vp as a childe,*
> *The next to learning, for waxing too wilde,*
> *The next keepe vnder sir hobbard de hoy,*
> *The next a man, no longer a boy.*

four-in-hand

Today most of us think of this only as a necktie, to be tied in its own special loop. But the horsemen among us may have another notion. To them it means four horses harnessed to a single vehicle and driven by one person. And it is to these sportsmen of the nineteenth century we are indebted for the necktie and its name. They formed themselves into "Four-in-Hand Clubs," and vied with one another for distinctive garb, especially as to neck scarfs. Just as some unknown sportsman evolved the knot which, commemorating the racecourse, is still called an *ascot,* so another

934

anonymous individual along about 1890 produced for his fellow members, and the rest of us, the *four-in-hand*.

soliloquy

St. Augustine, one of the most renowned fathers of the Christian Church, was, in his youth, rather a dissolute profligate. After embracing Christianity in his early thirties, though, he became a most devout member of the faith, eventually being awarded a bishopric. He was always a prolific writer, and many of the books of his later life were strongly introspective and devoted to criticism of his wanton youth. One of his books was entitled *Liber Soliloquiorum* (freely translated, "Book in which I talk to myself"), whereby he coined a word compounded from *solus,* "alone," and *loqui,* "to speak." As Augustine was not the first, nor yet the last, to talk to himself, his new word was found to be quite useful, and it lives today in our *soliloquy,* "a talk to oneself."

dogwatch

A two-hour vigil on shipboard, so arranged as to alternate from day to day the regular four-hour watches of the divisions of a crew. That is, instead of dividing the twenty-four hours of the day into six periods of four hours each, they are divided into five such periods and two of two hours each, one from four to six and the other from six to eight. The name derives from the fact that each of such crew has only a short period of rest before being aroused into alertness, comparable to the alertness expected of a watchdog.

sojourner

The verb *sojourn* comes to us from the French *sojorner,* which, with the related Italian *soggiornare,* has been traced to the Popular Latin *subdiurnare,* compounded from *sub,* "under," and *diurnus,* "day-long" (from *dies,* "day"). Thus the original sense was applied to some event lasting for less than a day, especially a short visit. The sense has become expanded with time, until now *to sojourn* is to visit for any length of time, but not permanently, and a *so-journer* is one who is temporarily staying somewhere other than at home.

quicklime

Here, *quick* has its original sense of *living,* and our popular term for this substance is a direct translation of the Latin *calx viva,* "living lime," as taken through the French *chaux vive.* To the chemist, quicklime is calcium oxide, and it was called "living" by virtue of its intensely vigorous reaction when brought into contact with water, seeming to be possessed of a living spirit. *Lime,* in its older sense of *"mortar,"* or *"glue,"* is closely related to the German *Leim,* "glue," and both have been traced to the Latin *limus,* "mud." *Calx* has come down to modern English as *chalk,* the great chalk deposits in England being the principal sources of lime to that country.

touchhole, touch-powder, touchwood

Touch-, in each of these compound terms, has the special sense of "to set fire to" or "readily ignited"—a sense not found in other uses of "touch" either alone or in combination except those derived from the above. There are two distinct theories to explain the origin of this special meaning, but it is uncertain which is correct—possibly both have contributed in some degree. The first is based on a passage in *Piers Plowman,* a tale written in the late fourteenth century, where the following quotation is found:

Bote thou haue tache to take hit with tunder and broches, Al thy labour is lost. [Unless you have touchwood to take it (i.e., the spark) with tinder and tapers, all your labor is lost.]

Skeat, in his *Etymological Dictionary of the English Language,* suggests that *tache,* in the above, is derived from the Low German *takk,* one of the meanings of which is "twig," and that the subsequent development of the word *touchwood* represents a tautological development giving the equivalent of "stick-wood." Skeat also considers that this development represents a change in spelling from *tache* to *touch*. Militating against this theory is the absence of the use of *tache* in this sense by any other author, as well as the fact that *touchwood* is first found only two hundred years later (as *touchewoode*, but very soon afterward in its present spelling) with no intermediate forms representing what should have been expected in a change of this magnitude. The second theory is that presented in the *Oxford English Dictionary*, where it is suggested that *touch-* in the present sense is apparently from the Old French *tochier* (*le feu*), *touchier*, "to set fire." Thus *touch-powder*, which is found as early as 1497, probably represents a translation of an Old French *poudre-à-toucher* (*le feu*).

bonnyclabber

The Earl of Strafford, in the seventeenth century, wrote of this dish, "it is the bravest, freshest drink you ever tasted," a verdict with which I agree. But my sons agree with Ben Jonson, who, at about the same period, called it "balderdash." What is it? Just milk that has coagulated in souring. I always sprinkle it with a little sugar before eating. The name is anglicized from Irish *bainne*, "milk," and *clabair*, "thick."

stark-naked

Stark, in many of its senses in English, is closely—sometimes very closely—related in meaning to the German word of the same

spelling and with the meaning "strong." But this is not the case with *stark-naked,* for here *stark* is a corruption for the original term in the phrase, which was *start. Start-naked* dates to the thirteenth century, when *start* had the Anglo-Saxon form *steort,* with the meaning of "tail, rump," such as in *redstart.* Thus the meaning of *stark-naked* in its original form was not "strongly naked," but rather "naked even to the tail."

cofferdam

Though in my impious youth one was considered as very clever who could work this in as, "Let her cofferdam head off," it really has no connection with an oath. A coffer is merely a tight chest, as for the storing of valuables. By extension, it denotes a water-tight box or caisson. And a *cofferdam* is nothing more than a series of such caissons so constructed as to become a dam for holding out water.

go-devil

I think our American male ancestors of a hundred-odd years ago took keen delight in playing with the word *devil*. It sounded just short of a swear word—and probably annoyed their wives. At least it is certain that farmers especially took to calling various mechanical implements which, in early stages of development, acted erratically or mysteriously, *go-devils*. Or perhaps, through comparative speed, because they went "like the devil." How many of such were so called is now uncertain, but the name was early applied to corn cultivators, hay rakes, road scrapers, snow plows, logging sleds, and later in other fields to instruments for clearing pipes of obstructions, to explosive devices in oil-well drilling, to handcars, etc., etc.

torpedo

In the slang of the submarine arm of the navy, a *torpedo* is called a "fish," and in applying this nickname our sailors are more nearly correct than they are probably aware with respect to the origin of the name. For the object which was the first torpedo was indeed a fish — in particular, that fish that is also called the electric ray, because of its ability to emit electric discharges that benumb the person who may unsuspectingly come into contact with it. And it is that ability that gave the fish its name. *Torpedo* has the meaning of "stiffness, numbness" in Latin, from *torpere*, "to be stiff or numb," and it is exactly this quality that led the word to be applied to military mines of both land and sea. In the evolution of military parlance, the term is now used almost exclusively for

938

the self-propelled marine mines that so closely resemble the action of the fish from which they took their name.

glamour, gramarye

If those who seek to entice us into a movie theater with repetitions of the word *glamour* knew its source, perhaps they would use it less freely. Or more freely. Who knows? But originally it was just a Scottish mispronunciation of *grammar*. The reference was then to Latin grammar, the only grammar that anyone knew anything about before the seventeenth century. And, among the ignorant, anyone so learned as to be able to speak and write Latin was believed also to possess occult powers, to be able to work magic. In England he was said to have *gramarye;* the Scots, who had difficulty with the word, said he had *glamour*. Both meant that such a wonderfully knowing person must have the ability to effect charms. Perhaps today's ad man would have us believe he can read and speak Latin. Both *gramarye* and *glamour* are still associated with the sense of magic, ability to charm or allure, but *grammar* has not moved from its rut.

coconut

Though regarded as slang, it is fitting, nevertheless, to use this in reference to one's head, for it was from that that the nut had its name. Portuguese explorers of the fifteenth century, sailing around Africa, found this fruit growing upon islands of the Indian Ocean. Not only was the nut about the size and shape of a small head, but the addition of the three dark hollows at its base conveyed so strongly the resemblance to a grinning face as to impel the explorers to call it "a grinning face," which is what *coco* means in Portuguese.

bock bier (or beer)

One couldn't do better than quote from an item in an issue of the 1856 *Illinois State Register:* "There is a Bavarian lager beer which is called 'bock'—in English buck or goat—and is so called

939

because of its great strength making its consumers prance and tumble about like these animals." This beer, incidentally, requires about two months for brewing, being brewed usually in midwinter, and is usually drunk in early spring.

sofa

The most curious feature of this word is its ubiquity, for it is to be found in all the Romance languages—French, Italian, Spanish, Portuguese—and has even been adopted into German, with the same spelling and meaning. It is thus far from clear as to the immediate source of the word into English; it could as well have been from any of these sources. What is clear is its origin, which is the Arabic *soffah,* "a raised and richly carpeted bench or platform upon which to recline."

cocktail

H. L. Mencken, in *The American Language: Supplement One* (1945), relates that he had accumulated "numerous etymologies" purporting to account for the name of this American beverage, but only seven of them could be regarded as plausible. His list, with dates, highly condensed, is: (1) from French *coquetier,* "egg cup," New Orleans, about 1800; (2) from *coquetel,* a mixed drink, introduced from France "during the Revolution"; (3) from English *cock-ale,* a concoction from the seventeenth century; (4) from a later *cock-ale* fed to fighting cocks; (5) from *cock-tailed,* "having the tail cocked up"; (6) from *cock-tailings,* tailings from various liquors dumped together; (7) as a toast to the cock, after a fight, which had the most feathers left in its tail. But, reduced to the last analysis, all that is so far definitely known is that Washington Irving, in *Knickerbocker's History of New York* (1809), called it a Dutch invention, and that in *The Balance,* Hudson, New York, of May 13, 1806, occurs this description: *"Cock tail,* then, is a stimulating liquor, composed of *spirits* of any kind, *sugar, water,* and *bitters* . . . It is said, also, to be of great use to a democratic candidate: because, a person having swallowed a glass of it, is ready to swallow anything."

stiff-necked

The use of "a stiff neck" to denote obstinacy can be found in Deuteronomy 31:27, where Moses uses the term to describe the  Levites to whom he entrusted his book of laws. The adjective *stiff-necked* is used in the same sense in Acts 7:51, where Stephen is pleading his defense against blasphemy. The German *hartnäckig* and the Vulgate Latin *dura cervice* have the same significance, and both have the literal meaning "hard neck." All are derived from the Greek, from which much of the Bible has been translated, where the term is *sklerotrhachelos,* a compound from *skleros,* "hard," and *rhachis,* "spine," and the Greek is a direct translation of the Hebrew *keshay oref.*

ascot

This was a popular tie affected by us young males in the late 1890's, narrow around the neck and broad and slightly padded where it was loosely tied at the throat, the broad sections then crossing diagonally. Popularity and name sprang from sporting circles attending the fashionable races held annually at Ascot Heath in Berkshire, England.

tornado

It is from the Spanish, who were the principal explorers and masters of the Atlantic in the sixteenth century, that we get this word. It originated from *tronada,* "a thunderstorm," from *tronar,* "to thunder." Somehow, very likely through a spelling error, the word was taken into English as *ternado.* Later, when it became noted that these strong tropical storms were characterized by whirling winds, it was theorized that the spelling should more aptly reflect this trait, and it was revised to *tornado,* as if the derivation had been from the Spanish *tornar,* "to turn, return," of which the participle is *tornado,* "returned." With the change in spelling, there was an accompanying generally accepted change in use of the word away from thunderstorms and more particularly to those storms chiefly characterized by whirlwinds.

horehound, hoarhound

The name of this herb is really contained in the second element, which, though considerably altered through the centuries, seems to have been earliest in use. That is, in England of about a thousand years ago, the name of the plant seems to have been *hune,* and, to distinguish the one covered with white cottony hairs and small white flowers from others similar, but less attractive, it was described as the *hare hune,* from *har,* "hoary, white." Both elements underwent change, *hune* becoming *houne* in the fourteenth century, *hounde* in the fifteenth, and *hound* in the sixteenth—and there's no association whatsoever between the plant and any member of the canine family.

plum duff

This delicacy originated in the north of England, probably early in the last century. It was a kind of plum pudding, boiled in a bag, but the "plums" in the dough, raisins or currants, lacked the variety expected in a pudding. Why *duff?* Well, in the north of England, *dough* then rhymed with *rough* and *tough.* In fact, though still so pronounced, the pudding was sometimes spelled *plum dough.*

dog's letter

The surest proof that the letter R was not formerly sounded as "ah," the approximate current pronunciation in parts of England, New England, and some of our Southern states, lies in the fact that, as Ben Jonson put it (1636): "R is the dog's letter, and hurreth in the sound, the tongue striking the inner palate, with a trembling about the teeth." That is, as still heard in the speech of Scotland, Ireland, and our Midwestern states, it resembled the snarl of a dog.

gewgaw

Probably this term for a gaudy ornament of little value was originally nothing more than a contemptuous duplication of nonsensical sounds, such as *shilly-shally, fiddle-faddle,* and many others. No definite source has yet been found for the term, but it is very old. Though then spelled *giuegoue,* it appears in the text of *Ancren Riwle* (Rule of Anchoresses) written in the first quarter of the thirteenth century.

soda jerker

The average drugstore soda fountain clerk would be quite upset to be called a drunkard, but this is what was meant by a *jerker* some hundred and fifty years ago. A habitual drunkard, in time, loses his ability to move smoothly; his actions become quite jerky, and this led to the coining of the slang term to describe such a person, then to *beer jerker* for the sot who was principally a drinker of beer. By 1873, the term *beer jerker* had been transferred to the bartender who dispensed the beer. With the widespread growth and popularity of soft drinks early in the present century, the many resulting soda fountains required the services of clerks who dispensed these more innocuous beverages, and it was quite natural that they should be called by the trade name of their predecessors, becoming *soda jerkers.*

sulky (carriage)

A sulky person is one who, at least for the moment, wants nothing but to be let alone, and it is directly from this meaning

that the vehicle *sulky* gets its name. For this vehicle is designed to seat a single person, and one choosing to ride therein presumably feels that degree of aloofness best described by the adjective giving it its name. The same line of reasoning has led to the application of the same name to such things as a bathing machine designed for one, a horse-drawn plow having a seat for a single rider, etc.

hors d'oeuvres

Your French dictionary will define the expression, "in composition, art, or the like, that which is not an essential part of the work." Then it may go on to say, "In cuisine, something such as radishes, olives, etc., served before the main dish." From this you may see that the literal idea of the phrase is, "Aside from the work; not essential."

stool pigeon

Today, a *stool pigeon* is usually someone engaged in illegal or shady activities who, to save his own neck, voluntarily turns informer against his confederates. Earlier, he was someone deliberately planted by the authorities to serve as a decoy to gather evidence against those among whom he was sent to spy upon, or to influence them in some way, such as at the polls. The modern usage dates to about the first of this century, and the former has been found as early as 1830. Authorities are in substantially unanimous agreement that both senses are derived from a still earlier literal meaning of *stool pigeon*—a pigeon fastened to a stool or perch (some say with its eyes stitched closed), thereby serving as a live decoy to entice others into the snare set for them by the hunter. To the dismay of students of word origins, though, no recorded use of the term in this literal sense has been found earlier than 1836, and even this is only suggestive rather than being a certain instance. Their belief, however, is supported by the recorded use of *stool-crow* in the sense of "decoy" in 1811, and of the use of *stool* alone in the same sense in 1825, this latter being presumably a shortened form of the supposedly earlier but yet unfound *stool pigeon*. All these terms are generally accepted as being Americanisms.

forget-me-not

In Germany they call the flower *Vergissmeinnicht;* in France it's *ne m'oubliez pas;* in Sweden, *förgäta mig ej;* in Italy, *non ti scordar di me;* in Spain, *nomeolvides,* all meaning "forget me not," and in these, as in other countries, the flower is used as a token of friendship or, by lovers, in token of undying love. How old may be these sentiments attached to the flower is anyone's guess, but the widespread symbolism leads to the inference of considerable antiquity.

boatswain

He was, back in Old English days, merely the lad—*swain*—with the duty of attending to the small open boats of that period. His duty involved the care of the boat, of its oars and steering paddle, of its sails and rigging, if so equipped, and the summoning of its crew. In very early days it is probable that the latter duty was performed by whistling through his own lips, but, by the fifteenth century or earlier, we may read that he "blewe his whystell full shryll." Corruption of the pronunciation to *bosun* was in colloquial use before the middle of the seventeenth century.

swashbuckler

Quite a number of words that have existed in the English language (and in other languages, as well) were coined in imitation of some sound. One of these is  *swash*, little used now, but apparently originally created as descriptive of the sound of a blow. A *buckler*, back when knighthood was in flower, was a particular kind of small shield, chiefly used to catch the blows of an adversary. So a *swashbuckler* was one who, when fencing, put on a show by making a great noise, striking his opponent's buckler with his sword. From this, the term was broadened to describe any swaggering show-off.

plaster of Paris

Gypsum would be a much simpler name. But English artisans of the fourteenth and fifteenth century thought the best quality of gypsum for conversion into plaster and mortar came from the

945

large deposits in the region of Montmartre on the outskirts of Paris, and thus insisted upon *plaster of Paris*. The name remains, but has long been applied to any calcined gypsum, regardless of place of origin.

sobriquet, soubriquet

Depending upon the circumstances prevailing at the time, any act of familiarity may be interpreted in either of two ways. On the one hand, it may be an expression of friendly companionship— on the other, it may be a deliberate puncturing of pomposity. One such act of familiarity, very common today, is the bestowal of a nickname. Another, not so common today as at times in the past, is a chuck under the chin. In Old French, the latter was *sous bruchet* (modern French would have it *sous-brechet;* the synonymous term in Italian is *sottobecco*), "under the throat (beak)." This came to be applied also to the giving of a nickname, and the two-word phrase became telescoped to the single word *sobriquet,* in which form it was taken directly into English over three hundred years ago.

topsy-turvy

To have the world seem to turn upside-down is a feeling that must have been common to mankind for many years, and for at least almost that number of years people have needed to express this feeling. *Topsy-turvy* was coined for this purpose over four hundred years ago, and has the literal meaning of "top turned over." The first element is just *top,* to which the suffix *-sy* was apparently added for euphony. The second element is based on the now obsolete *tirve* (*terve*), "to turn," especially, "to turn over." Thus it is seen that *topsy-turvy* is, just as you probably thought all along, "top turned over."

sockdologer

It is characteristic of the American "man in the street" that he displays very little reverence for the purity or tradition of his language. If he can coin a new, catchy phrase, or twist an old one into a new meaning, he delights in so doing. Thus, early in the nineteenth century someone, just who is not known, observed that the singing of the doxology always meant that his church service was finished. Mental play with "doxology" revealed that reversal of the consonant sounds of the first and second syllables gave him "sock-dology." The similarity to *sock,* "a blow," was obvious, and forthwith was born the *sockdologer,* the mighty blow that was to the battle as the doxology was to the service, the finish.

tandem

The Latin word *tandem* means "at length (with respect to time)," that is, "for a long time." Back in the eighteenth century,

when the study of Latin was a normal part of English university curricula, some student noticed a carriage harnessed to two horses, one before the other, and, being somewhat of a wag, he coined a pun on the word by applying it, in the sense of "at length (with respect to distance)," to a team so harnessed. The pun caught popular fancy, so that it has lived long after most people realize that it is a pun, and the sense has become broadened to include any of many things or events which may be arranged in consecutive order, one after another.

cocksure

The great *Oxford English Dictionary* waxes facetious about this. It says, in effect, this should mean "as sure as a cock," that is, "as secure, safe, certain, trustworthy, reliable, etc.," as a cock. But what kind of cock? Certainly not a rooster. So, the dictionary suggests, possibly the reference, four and a half centuries ago, "may have been to the security or certainty of the action of a cock or tap in preventing the escape of liquor, or perhaps of a cock with a removable turning-key in leaving the contents of a tun secure from interference."

947

footpad

That brave hero Robin Hood was one—that is, a highwayman who, having no horse, *pads* along on *foot* to hold up and rob people in carriages or on horseback. Or, let us say, Robin might have been called one, had he lived in the seventeenth century, for it was then that the term came into use, during a long period of great destitution throughout Europe and when governmental authority was ineffective. (See also **slyboots.**)

thank-ye-ma'am

This, gratefully appreciated in rural American courtship in grandfather's day, is now rapidly disappearing, replaced by hum-

drum metal or concrete culverts on hilly roads everywhere. On early roads in such country, an earthen diagonal ridge served to carry rain water or melting snow from high side to low side, thus preventing excessive wash. But, passing over it in carriage or wagon, the passenger on the side first hitting this ridge would sway involuntarily toward the other. The rural swain, needless to say, chose roads accordingly. With the head of the fair one thus within kissing distance, the grateful murmur, "Thank ye, ma'am," was of course passed along to the humble cause.

tomato

The explorers who invaded Mexico in the sixteenth century found, in addition to treasure of silver and gold, a vegetable treasure in the form of a new fruit, unknown in Europe, which the Mexican Indians called *tomatl*. They thought sufficiently well of this fruit to take samples back to the Old World, and the name they took into the Spanish and Portuguese languages was *tomate* (three syllables). On moving north to France the spelling was retained, but the pronunciation was shortened to two syllables, and this was also the spelling and pronunciation first taken into

English. It wasn't until the mid-eighteenth century that the present spelling first appeared, apparently having been coined in the belief that the word was of Spanish origin, the *-o* ending being common in Spanish. At an early date, the tomato was believed to have aphrodisiac qualities, because of the one-time name of *love apple,* (which see) for the fruit.

cockshy

It is to the credit of humanity that the original practice of this eighteenth-century "sport" was suppressed, in England and America, before the close of the same century. As practiced, by men and boys, a broomstick was cast from a distance of twenty yards at a cock tied by a cord attached to its leg. A small fee for the privilege was demanded by the owner, and he who succeeded in killing the bird might carry it off. But if the bird were merely lamed, it was propped up so that the sport might continue. It is the opinion of Professor Hans Sperber of Ohio State University (*Language,* vol. 31, 1955) that the verb "to shy," in the sense "to throw," descended from this sport, for it was the custom of the owner of such a bird to teach it in advance to become wary of objects thrown at it. That is, to quote, "in order to make the throwing competition a lucrative venture, it is necessary to make the bird shy, or, as it certainly would be expressed—*to shy him.* Since this 'shying' was accomplished by throwing at him, *shy* became a restricted synonym of *throw.*"

snood

The oldest words in the language sometimes seem to be among the most difficult to trace to their origins, perchance because these origins have become lost in the mists of age. *Snood* is such a word. It has been found to have been in English, in much its present meaning ("a fillet or ribbon for binding the hair"), since the eighth century. For quite some time it was to be found particularly in Scotland, where this type of hair covering was reserved to maidens alone, as a sign of virginity, being replaced by other forms of head-dress after marriage. Skeat (*Etymological Dictionary of the English*

Language) suggests that the origin is to be found in the Teutonic root *snu-*, implying turning or twisting, from which come the Danish *snoe,* Swedish *sno,* "to twist, twine"; also the Swedish noun *sno,* "twine, string." The modern German *Schnur,* "string, cord, lace," is easily seen to be related. The etymological implication is that the first Anglo-Saxon snood may have been but a bit of string, or perhaps a fillet of string lace, about the hair, more likely to keep it from being blown into the wearer's eyes rather than for its decorative effect.

artichoke

Beyond the spelling, the name of this plant has no connection either with art or with choking, although the latter was at one time seriously suggested. Actually the name has been highly corrupted through various European versions of the original Arabic name, *al-kharshuf.* Italians eventually made that into *articiocco,* and through some four centuries of struggling with a score or more of various spellings we have, at least temporarily, settled upon *artichoke.*

trousseau

Taken into English directly from the French, in which it is the

diminutive of *trousse* (from which we get *truss*), "a bundle, a pack." If taken literally, then, it would seem that a bride's trousseau would be "a little bundle," presumably consisting only of a few of her most needed personal effects and household linens.

hitchhike

The date of coinage is not definite but was probably during the period of training of American boys in military camps in the First World War. Making their way home on a brief furlough, that is, the boys would *hike* until a car or truck approached going their way, then *hitch* a ride. The term shortly passed into the general language—and into a recognized form of travel.

foolscap

Now it is a size of paper, usually folded, and running in size from 12 to 12½ inches in width and 15 to 16 inches in length. Rarely, if at all, does the paper now carry as a watermark the design in outline of a fool's cap, but that is what gave it the name. A specimen of paper with such a design, dating to 1540, is said to have been found. But why any papermaker ever marked his product in this manner is no longer to be determined. An often repeated story is that the Long Parliament, finally dissolved by Cromwell in 1653, ordered that paper with this design should replace that carrying the royal crown, but, though interesting, the account lacks foundation.

ultramundane

With all the current interest in space travel, rocketry, and so on, this is a word that should become ever more important, although,  being polysyllabic, it may never become part of the argot of the "man in the street." For, with the literal meaning of "out of this world," it can well apply to the various aspects of the exploration of outer space. As the appearance of the word would indicate, it is of Latin origin, coming from the Late Latin *ultramundanus,* from *ultra,* "beyond," and *mundus,* "the world."

slyboots

Although slyboots has the meaning of "a crafty or cunning person," it is closely related to *footpad,* "a thief"; *gumshoe,* "a detective"; *pussyfoot,* "a prying, nosy person"; also to the German *Leisetreter* (light treader), "a sneak, spy"; and the French *pied plat* (flat foot), "a sneak, knave." All of these carry the common connotation of a person who moves with quiet or stealth, and always these movements are contrary to the well-being or comfort of the one applying the term (even the *gumshoe* is so-called only by the one who is attempting some clandestine act). The American *flatfoot,* of course, is quite different from the French, being a policeman—specifically, one who has walked on patrol for so long that his arches are presumed to have fallen and, in fact, he has acquired flat feet.

hijack

It came into American speech shortly after the First World War, during the "silk shirt" era of prosperity when the prohibition amendment was still in force and people with money to spend wanted to spend it on liquor. Some say it originated in the Middle West, in reference to the activities of hoboes who preyed upon harvesters, even to murder, but the general consensus is that it originally indicated a holdup, at night, especially of a load or cargo of illicit liquor. The holdup might be with or without murder, and might include the transference of the load or cargo to another truck or vessel. Though the source of the term cannot be definitely traced, I think it probable that it came from the friendly hail, "Hi, Jack!" intended to disarm the suspicions of a truck driver by another who was apparently in trouble by the side of the road.

German silver

It was named in honor of the country where discovered, for the original alloy was found in nature in ore found in Hildburghausen, Germany. Actually, it contains no silver at all, but is about one-half copper and one-quarter each nickel and zinc. Being silvery in appearance, the alloy has been used for inexpensive decorative effects, and it also has useful electrical properties. During the First World War, when any name suggestive of Germany was anathema, it was given such euphemistic titles as *silveroid* and *nickeline,* but these have not lived.

slubberdegullion

It is said, and I believe it to be true, that there are far more English words having insulting or derogatory meaning than there

952

are those carrying a complimentary connotation. Certainly *slubberdegullion* would rank among the most degrading of epithets short of foul speech. For *slubber* is an older form of *slobber,* "to befoul as with saliva, to slaver." The *de* may be a meaningless connective, or may be in imitation of the French *de,* "of." *Gullion* seems to be a variant of *cullion,* "a vile or despicable fellow," from the French *couillon* (*coion*), "a dastard, coward." Hence both the etymological and actual meanings of *slubberdegullion:* "a slobbering, worthless sloven."

velocipede

Early in the nineteenth century, a German, Baron von Drais, invented a machine that had a remarkable likeness to a modern bi-  cycle, except that it lacked pedals, chain, and sprockets. The rider sat upon a saddle and propelled himself by pushing with the feet, and is said to have been able to achieve a speed of up to five miles per hour. The device was introduced into England and manufactured by one Denis Johnson in 1818, by whom it was patented under the name of *velocipede.* Although this name is now applied chiefly to a tricycle fitted with pedals, it was used extensively throughout most of the nineteenth century for nearly all the descendants of the original machine, whether of two or more wheels, with or without pedals. The name seems to have come from the French of the same form, but is of Latin ancestry, being made up of the combining forms of *velox,* "swift," and *pes,* "foot"; hence, "swift-footed."

highroad, high seas, etc.

It was not that the road, sea, way, or the like was elevated above others of its kind that it was labeled *high,* tracing back to Old English times, but that it possessed some quality that made it outstanding, especially notable. The *highroad* and *highway* were main or principal roads; the *high seas* were oceans; *high Mass* was celebrated in full ceremonial. And in a later day, *high tea* was an evening meal at which meat was served.

woodchuck

"How much wood would a woodchuck chuck if a woodchuck could chuck wood?" "He'd chuck as much wood as a woodchuck

could, if a woodchuck could chuck wood!" Confirming this old tonguetwister, a woodchuck can't and doesn't chuck wood, nor does *wood* as such have anything to do with his having been so named. The name comes from a Cree Indian word that has been rendered as *wuchak* or *otchock* (Chippewa *otchig*). Early settlers gave the word various spellings reminiscent of familiar English words, such as *wejack, woodshock,* and *woodchuck* (also *-chuk*),

but all these names applied originally to the animal known as the fisher or pekan. Later, either through error or guile, the name of *woodchuck* was transferred by traders to the groundhog, and the two terms are now synonymous. (See also **groundhog.**)

INDEX

956

958

Caesaris, Spain, see under
   sherry, 772
cahoots, in, with (one), 700
Cain, to raise, 42, 579
cake, one's is dough, 533
cake, see under cheesecake,
   johnny-cake
cake, to take the, 130
calf, fatted, to kill the, 700
calf, see under mooncalf,
   886
Calicut, see under calico,
   268
Calker's Club, see under
   caucus, 279
call a spade a spade, to, 184
call off the dogs, 630
call the turn, 533–34
callithump, 883
calotype, see under
   talbotype, 857
Cambrai, see under batiste,
   29, cambric, 269
camel, to strain at a gnat and
   swallow a, 645–46
camelopard, 879
candid, see under candidate,
   273
candle, the game is not
   worth the, 86
candle, to burn the, at both
   ends, 163
candle, to hold a, to
   (someone), 86
candor, see under candidate,
   273
canoe, to paddle one's own,
   41, 630
cantankerous, 878
cantilever, 869
canvass, see under canvas,
   275
can, to tie the, to one, 673–
   74, 717
cap, to set one's, at (for) a
   person, 694
Cape Cod turkey, see under
   rarebit, 841
capers, to cut, 676
caprice, see under caper,
   275

capricious, see under caper,
   275
Caraffa, Cardinal, see under
   pasquinade, 433
carboy, 865
card, to speak by the, 533
Carew, Sir George, see under
   blarney, 250
Carey, Henry, see under
   namby-pamby, 414
carpet, on the, 568, 652
carpetbagger, 864
Carroll, Lewis, see under
   portmanteau, 909
carrot, see under Queen
   Anne's lace, 862
carry coals to Newcastle, to,
   45
carry the ball, 555
carry the torch for one, to,
   127
cart before the horse, to put
   (or set) the, 30
Carthage, see under vandal,
   504
cash in one's checks (chips),
   534
cash on the barrelhead, 624
cash on the counter, 624
Cassianus, Joannes, see
   under collation, 292
cast sheeps eyes at, to, 63
castanet, 857
casting pearls before swine,
   653
castle, see under forecastle,
   65
castle in the air (in Spain),
   674
Castor and Pollux, see under
   academy, 217
cat, alley, 707
cat, Cheshire, to grin like a,
   126
cat, room to swing a, 72
cat, see under polecat,
   884
cat, to bell the, 145
cat, to let the old, die, 93
cat, to let the, out of the bag,
   138

cat, to see which way the,
   jumps, 67
cat, to skin the, 112
cat and mouse, to play, with
   one, 527
catacomb, 857
catamount, 855
catawampus, 852
catboat, 850
catch a Tartar, to, 75
catch as catch can, 162
catchpenny, 847
catchpole, 112
catchup, see under ketchup,
   381
caterwaul, 839
Catherine wheel, 144
cat-o'-nine-tails, 837
cats and dogs, raining, 37,
   690
cats, Kilkenny, to fight like,
   149
cat's-paw, to be made a,
   668
catsup, see under ketchup,
   381
cattle, see under chattel, 282
caught flat-footed, to be,
   57, 544
caught with one's pants
   down, to be, 88
causeway, 831
causey, causey-way, see
   under causeway, 831
cavalier, see under chivalry,
   285
cavalry, see under chivalry,
   285
caviar to the general, 95
Cerberus, a sop to, 631
Cervantes, Miguel de, see
   under quixotic, 451
chackstone, see under
   jackstone, 858
chafe, chafer, see under
   chafing dish, 825
chafing dish, 825
chagrin, see under shagreen,
   469
chalk, not for money,
   marbles, nor, 576

960

962

eager beaver, 98, 717
eaglestone, 886
ear, cute as a bug's, 536–37
ear, in one, and out the
    other, 593
ear, itching, 652
earn one's salt, to, 128
ears, to set (persons) together
    by the, 557
ears, willing to give one's,
    666
earthberry, see under
    strawberry, 879
earth-nut, see under peanut,
    828
earwig, 778
easy as rolling off a log,
    576
East Street, on, 607, 633
eat crow, 157, 618, 690
eat humble pie, to, 47, 690
eat one's hat, 690–91
eat salt with, 647
eavesdropper, 857
ecphonesis, see under
    exclamation point, 843
Edward VII, King of
    England, see under
    Prince Albert, 740
eel, to be slippery as an, 570
eft, see under newt, 417
egg, a bad (or good), 97
egg, to lay an, 120
eggnog, 854
egregious, see under
    gregarious, 350
"Egyptian days," see under
    dismal, 314
eight, pieces of, 112
eight ball, behind the, 108,
    581, 629
elbow grease, 673
election, hell-bent for, 23,
    704
electric, electricity, see under
    ambergris, 846
elephant, white, 122
eleventh hour, at the, 527–28
Eliot, John, see under
    mugwump, 411
Ely, see under tawdry, 489

ember days, 851
encaustic, see under ink, 370
end, to the bitter, 711–12
English pale, see under pale,
    426
envy, see under vie, 505
Ephraimite, see under
    shibboleth, 470
Epicurus, see under epicure,
    324
Epimetheus, see under
    promethean, 446
epiphonema, see under
    exclamation point, 843
Erasmus, Saint, see under St.
    Elmo's fire, 835
Eric the Red, see under
    Greenland, 349
Erne, Ear of, see under
    boycott, 256
errant, see under arrant, 231
erysipelas, see under St.
    Anthony's fire, 840
essence, time is of the, 556–
    57
Essex, Earl of, see under
    derrick, 308
estate, fourth, 713–14
etcetera, see under
    ampersand, 227
Etheldreda, see under
    tawdry, 489
Euclid, see under trapezium,
    497
even steven, 548, 685
every dog has his day, 546
evil, see under king's evil,
    846
exchequer, see under check,
    284
exclamation point (mark),
    843
expedite, see under impede,
    367
eye, all my (and Betty
    Martin), 626
eye, to keep one's, on the
    ball, 630
eye for an eye, 596
eyelashes, to hang on by the,
    559

eyes, to keep one's, skinned
    (peeled), 545
eyes, to pull the wool over
    one's, 641
eyes, to throw (cast) dust in
    one's, 666–67
eyet, eyot, see under ait, 883
eyeteeth, to be skinned out
    of one's, 673
eyeteeth, to cut one's, 185,
    673
eyeteeth, to have one's,
    drawn, 673

fa, see under gamut, 341
fable, see under fib, 333
face, cutting off one's nose
    to spite one's, 643
face, plain as the nose on
    one's, 570–71
face, to have one's, made of
    a fiddle, 562
face, to save (lose), 668
face the music, to, 192
fadoodle, see under
    flapdoodle, 752
Fahrenheit, Gabriel Daniel,
    879
fair means or foul, 659
fakir, 873
falconet, see under musket,
    413
falderal, folderol, 877
fall, to ride for a, 662–63
fall between two stools, to
    27
false colors, sailing under,
    684
fanfare, 781
fantan, 871
fantastic, to trip the light,
    603
fare-you-well, to a, 581
farthingale, 864. See also
    roundabout fat, see
    under hamfatter, 867
fast and loose, to play, 85,
    570
fast as hops, 575
faster than greased lightning,
    96

give the bag, to, 56
glamour, 939
glove, see under hand-in-glove, 843
gnat, to strain at a, and swallow a camel, 645–46
go against the grain, to, 75
go off half-cocked, to, 63
go the whole hog, to, 152
go to Halifax, 192
goat, billy, playing horse with a, 678–79
goat, like Hogan's, 594
goat, to get one's, 684–85
goat, to ride the, 656
goblin, see under hobgoblin, 928
god from a machine, 686
go-devil, 938
godfather, godmother, see under gaffer, 882
gods, in the lap (on the knees) of the, 586
going to town, 131
goldbrick, 931
golf, African, 706
gone coon, 92
gone to Jericho, 78
gone to pot, 165
goober, see under peanut, 828
good egg, 97
goodness, I declare to, 550
goods, to have the, on one, 597
goose, a gone, 596
goose, sound (all right) on the, 636
goose, to cook one's, 142
goose, to get the, 49
goose chase, a wild, 70
goose hangs high, the, 137
goose summer, see under gossamer, 348
gooseberry, 927
goose-egg, 120
Gordian knot, to cut the, 139
Gordon, Wm., see under caucus, 279

gosh all hemlock, 597
graham bread, crackers, flour, 919
Graham, Sylvester, see under graham bread, 919
grain, to go against the, 75
gramarye, grammar, see under glamour, 939
grammar, see under glamour, 346
grampus, see under hellgrammite, 795
grandfather, grandmother, see under gaffer, 882
grandmother, to teach one's, to suck eggs, 136
grandstand, to play (playing) to the, 138, 594
grapes, sour, 154
grass, see under quatchgrass, 917
grass, snake in the, 645
grass widow, 180
grass-roots, getting down to, 634–35
gravy train, to ride the, 633–34
grease, elbow, 673
grease (a person's) palm, to, 81
greased lightning, faster than, 96
greased lightning, 566, 704
greasy luck, 66
Great Bear, see under Charles's Wain, 76
green, see under Paris green, 858
green soap, 904
greenhorn, 916
greenroom, 909
Gregory I, see under iconoclast, 365
Gregory XIII, see under January, 374
gremlin, 808
grenadier, see under grenade, 351
grin like a Cheshire cat, to, 126
groove, to be in the, 191

grotesque, 746. See under antic, 229
ground, to bite the, 590
ground, to run (something) into the, 83
groundhog, 906
ground-nut, ground-pea, see under peanut, 828
grubstreet, 735
Grundy, Mrs., 679–80
G string, 812
Guido of Arezzo, see under gamut, 341
Guido's scale, see under solfeggio, 194
Guillotin, Dr. Joseph I., see under guillotine, 352
guinea-fowl, see under turkey, 908
gullion, see under slubberdegullion, 952
gum up the works, 574
gumshoe, see under slyboots, 951
gun, son of a, 658
gun, to jump the, 129
gunpowder plot, see under guy, 353
guns, to spike one's, 190
guns, to stick (stand) to one's, 589
guttersnipe, 757
gymnasium, see under gymnast, 354
gypsum, see under plaster of Paris, 945

hab nab, see under hobnob, 922
haberdasher, 881
hackamore, 871
haddock, see under finnan haddie, 897
Hades, see under lethal, 386
hair, not to turn a, 156
hair, to get in one's, 654–55
hair, to have where the, is short, 611–12
hair, to keep one's, on, 585
hair, to make one's, stand on end, 591–92, 600

hair and hide (horns and
tallow), 651
hair of the dog that bit you,
78, 529
hairs, to split, 51, 628–29
Haiti, see under buccaneer,
258
halcyon days, 140
half-cocked, to go off, 63
half-seas over, 175
halibut, 815
Halifax, go to, 192
Hall, Sir Benjamin, see
under Big Ben, 772
hallmark, 871
ham actor, 549
hamfatter, 867
Hamilton, Duke of, see
under Whig, 506
hamlet, 863
hammer, to bring (put) under
the, 645
hammer and tongs, 683
hamstring, 848
hand, high, with a, 627
hand in glove, to be, 121,
843
hand in one's checks (chips),
534
hand over fist (or hand), 71
handkerchief, 840
handle, see under panhandle,
867
handle, to fly off the, 196
handsaw, not to know a
hawk from a, 695
handsome, 835
handwriting on the wall, 593
hang by a thread, 682
hang on by the eyelashes,
559
hangdog, 818
hanged, drawn, and
quartered, 556
Hannah More, not amount
to, 124
Hanno, see under gorilla,
347
Hansom, John A., see under
cab, 264
hansom, see under cab, 264

hardtack, 824
Hare, William, see under
burke, 262
harebell, 813
harlot, 809
harp, see under jew's-harp,
810
harp on one string, 628
hash, see under nuthatch,
872
hashish, see under assassin,
232
Hassan ben Sabbah, see
under assassin, 232
hat, old, 633
hat, talking through one's,
702
hat, to eat one's, 690–91
hat, to keep under one's, 90
hatband, as queer (tight) as
Dick's, 674–75
hatch, hatchet, see under
nuthatch, 872
hatchet, to bury the, 144,
689–90
hatter, mad as a, 594–95
haul, see under keelhauling,
885
haul over the coals, to, 48
Hausmann, Irving, see under
jeep, 375
hautbois, see under hobo,
360
haversack, 801
hawk, not to know a, from a
handsaw, 695
hawk, see under jayhawk,
838
hay, to make, while the sun
shines, 608
haywire, gone (go), 201,
562, 600
head, neither, nor tail, 585
head, sore, like a bear with
a, 650–51
head, to hit the nail on the,
643–44
head, to knock one's, against
a wall, 567
head or heels, not to know if
on, 538

heap coals of fire on one's
head, to, 97
heart, to cross one's, 633
heart, to warm the cockles of
one's, 597
heart in one's shoes, to have
one's, 60
heart on one's sleeve, to
wear one's, 29
heat, to turn the, on, 121,
628
heathen, see under pagan,
425
heaven, in seventh, 612–13
Heavens to Betsy, 515–17
Hecate, see under trivial,
500
hedgehog, 804
heeled, to be well, 592
heels, down at the, 592
heels, to cool one's, 25
heels, to kick up one's, 25
heirloom, 803
Helen, see under academy,
217, nepenthe, 416
Helena, see under St. Elmo's
fire, 835
Helios, see under phaeton,
439
hell, go to, 546
hell, like a bat out of, 566,
704
hell for leather, 85
hell on wheels, 672
hell or high water, come (in
spite of), 635–36
hell to breakfast, 632–33
hellbender, 896. See also
mud puppy
hell-bent for election, 23,
704
hellgrammite, 795
Helmont, J. B. van, see
under gas, 344
hem and haw, 538, 604–5
hemlock, gosh all, 597
hen, wet, mad as a, 632
Henderson, Robert W., see
under tennis, 491
Henry VIII, see under
sirloin, 475

hen's teeth, as scarce as
(scarcer than), 632
Heracles, see under
Promethean, 446
Hermes, see under hermetic,
359, stentorian, 481,
trivial, 500
Herrick, Robert, see under
cabbage, 265
herring, dead as a, 544–45
het up, to get, 551
hiccough, see under hiccup,
786
hiccup, 786
hide, hair and, 651
hide nor hair, neither, 99
hide one's light under a
bushel, 641–42
hidebound, 785
hiding, to give one a, 699
high horse, on one's, 26
high horse, to pull one off
his, 584
high horse, to ride the, 26
high jinks, 576–77
high Mass, see under
highroad, 953
high seas, high tea, see
under highroad, 953
highball, 774
highbinder, 759
higher than Gilderoy's kite,
160
highfalutin, 755
high-muck-a-muck, 760
highroad, 953
highty-tighty, see under
hoity-toity, 731
highway, see under
highroad, 953
hijack, 952
hike, see under hitchhike, 950
Hill, Sam, 599
hill, to go over the, 583
hill of beans, not worth a,
539
hillbilly, 820
hinges, off his, 600
hit the bull's-eye, 643
hit the nail on the head,
643–44

hitchhike, 950
Hitti, Philip K., see under
tennis, 491
hitting below the belt, 667
hitting on all six (or four),
188
hoarhound, see under
horehound, 942
hoax, see under hocus-
pocus, 889
hob, to raise (play), 579–80
Hobbard de Hoy, see under
hobbledehoy, 934
hobbledehoy, 934
hobbyhorse, 823. See under
hobby, 359
hobgoblin, 928
hobnob, 922
Hobson's choice, 31
hock-day, -tide, etc., see
under hockshop, 920
hocker-mocker, see under
huggermugger, 845
hockshop, 920
hocus-pocus, 591, 889
hodgepodge, 902
hoe, a long (hard) row to,
631
hoe one's own row, 630
Hoffmann, Friedrich, see
under German measles,
748
hog, root, or die, 564
hog, see under groundhog,
hedgehog
hog, whole, to go the, 152
hog Latin, see under dog
Latin, 749
hog on ice, independent as a,
7
hog wild, to go, 551
Hogan's goat, like, 594
hogshead, 903
hogwash, 741
hoiden, see under hoyden,
362
hoist with one's own petard,
583
hoiting, see under hoity-
toity, 731
hoity-toity, 731

hoker-moker, see under
huggermugger, 845
hold a candle to (someone),
to, 86
hold at bay, to, 188
hold one's horses, to, 83
hold the bag, to, 56
hold water, to, 38
hold your horses, 651–52
holding the bag (or sack),
116
hole, ace in the, 677
hole, to be in a, 603
holiday, busman's, 698
Holland, Philemon, see
under curmudgeon, 301
Holmes, Oliver Wendell, see
under pants, 431
holystone, 913
home, nothing to write,
about, 614
Homer, see under nepenthe,
416
honey-apple, see under
marmalade, 398
honeymoon, 907
hoodlum, 745
hoodwink, 826
hook, line, and sinker, to
swallow (a tale), 123
hook or by crook, 44, 659–
60
hoosegow, 742
hops, as mad (thick, fast), as,
574–75
hop-score, see under
hopscotch, 737
hopscotch, 737
Horace, see under
sesquipedalian, 787
horehound, hoarhound, 942
horn, to blow one's own,
623
horn, to come out at the little
end of the, 123
horn spoon, by the great,
629–30
horns, hair and hide, and
tallow, 651
horns, to draw (or pull) in
one's, 112

970

limb, out on a, 131
lime, see under quicklime, 936
line, to draw the, 692
linen, dirty, to wash one's, in public, 619–20
linen, see under linsey-woolsey, 816
linsey-woolsey, 816
lion, see under ant lion, 835
lion, to beard the, 106
lion's share, the, 49
lion's-tooth, see under dandelion, 827
lip, to keep a stiff upper, 551, 628
literate, see under stigma, 481
litterbug, 856
little end of the horn, to come out at the, 123
living the life of Riley, 170
Livorno, Italy, see under leghorn, 818
loaded dice, playing with, 556
loaded for bear, 712
loadstone, see under lodestar, 814
lock, see under fetlock, padlock
lock, stock, and barrel, 144, 581
lock the barn (stable) door after the horse is stolen, 701
Locke, James, see under tweed, 502
locker, Davy Jones's, 664
lodestar, lodestone, 814
lodestone, see under magnet, 396
log, easy as rolling off a, 576
log, like a bump on a, 539, 621–22
Logeman, Dr. Henri, see under Yankee, 507
loggerheads, at, 170
logrolling, 810
loins, to gird (up) one's, 567–68

lollipop, lollypop, 803
Lombardy, see under lumber, 390
London, Jack, see under hobo, 360
longbow, to draw the (drawing a), 43, 698–9
Longinus, see under lounge, 389
look a gift horse in the mouth, to, 155
lookout, to keep a sharp, 545
loophole, 774
loose, to play fast and, 510
lose one's shirt, 612
lotto, see under lottery, 388
lotus-eater, 859
Louis, Dr. Antoine, see under guillotine, 352
Louis XIV, see under martinet, 399
Louis XV, see under pompadour, 441, silhouette, 472
Louvain, F. M. le Tellier, see under martinet, 399
love me, love my dog, 554
lover apple, 40. See also tomato
lubber, see under landlubber, 855
Lucifer, proud as, 582
Lucullian feast (banquet), 561
Luke, Saint, see under St. Martin's summer, 832
Lupercalia, see under February, 331, valentine, 503
lurch, to be left in the, 187, 614–15
lute, a rift in the, 528
Luze, Albert de, see under tennis, 491
Lydgate, John, see under derring-do, 309
lying down, to take (something), 606
Lynch, Capt. William, see under lynch, 391

Lynch, Col. Charles, see under lynch, 391

Macassar, see under antimacassar, 230
Macaulay, Thomas, see under Machiavellian, 394
Maccabees, see under macabre, 392
machinery, to throw a monkey wrench in the, 574
Macintosh, Charles, see under mackintosh, 394
Macklin, Charles, see under panjandrum, 429
mad as a hatter, 594–95
mad as a wet hen, 632
mad as hops, 574–75
mad enough to bite nails, 574
madcap, 758
madstone, 903
Maenius, see under rostrum, 458
Magdalen, see under maudlin, 401
Maggie Lawder, see under blatherskite, 251
Magnesia, see under magnet, 396
magpie, see under piebald, 766
Mahound, see under termagant, 492
main, with might and, 683
Main Liner, 566–67
mainbrace, to splice the, 608
make no bones about, 536
make one's mouth water, to, 128
man of my kidney, 104
mandragora, see under mandrake, 397
manger, a dog in the, 41
manna from heaven, 84
marbles, not for money, nor chalk, 576
marchpane, 891

Marco Polo, see under khan, 382, post, 442
Mardi gras, 573–74
Marforio, see under pasquinade, 433
Marines, tell it to the, 573
mark, beside (far from, wide of, short of, miss) the, 591
mark, see under hallmark, 871
mark, to toe the, 642–43
marry over the broomstick (or besom), to, 174
marshal, see under seneschal, 792
Martigues, France, see under martingale, 892
Martin, Betty, all my eye and, 626
Martin, Saint, see under chapel, 281, gossamer, 348, St. Martin's summer, 832
martingale, 892
marzipani, see under marchpane, 891
matchlock, see under match, 400
matchwood, see under match, 400
Matty, meddlesome, 571–72
Maundy Thursday, 32
mausolus, see under mausoleum, 403
McAdam, John L., see under macadam, 393
McCarthy, Cormac, see under blarney, 250
McCoy, the real, 180, 568, 625–26, 702
measles, German, French, see under German measles, 748
meddlesome Matty, 571–72
Medusa, see under gorgon, 347
melancholic, see under humor, 363
melancholy, see under choler, 34

melon, to cut (split), 564–65
Mencken, H. L., see under caucus, 279, yankee, 507
Menderes, see under meander, 404
Mercer, John, see under mercerize, 406
Mercury, see under Wednesday, 506
merry-andrew, 899
merry-go-round, see under carousel, 277
merrythought, see under wishbone, 793
Mesmer, Friedrich A., see under mesmerism, 406
message to Garcia, to take a, 100
mi, see under gamut, 341
mica, see under isinglass, 898
might and main, with, 683
Milan, see under fife, 333, magenta, 395, milliner, 407
mile, see under furlong, 340
milk, spilt, to cry over, 684
milksop, 894
mill, see under treadmill, 929
Miller, Elizabeth S., see under bloomers, 252
Milquetoast, Caspar, 887
Milton, John, see under joke, 377, pandemonium, 428
mimsy, see under portmanteau, 909
mind one's P's and Q's, to, 199
Minerva, see under egis, 321
minimum, see under miniature, 407
Minotaur, see under clue, 288
Minsheu, John, see under tennis, 491
mint, see under money, 408
miracle play, see under maudlin, 401

mire, see under quagmire, 738
Mirmir, see under Wednesday, 506
Missouri, I'm from; you've got to show me, 670–72
Missouri Compromise, see under buncombe, 261
Missouri meerschaum, see under rarebit, 841
Mitchell, Dr. Samuel, see under knickerbocker, 384
mitten, to get (or give one) the, 102
Mjolnir, see under Thursday, 494
Mogul Empire, see under nabob, 414
molehill, to make a mountain (out) of a, 592–93
Moncke, Charles, see under monkey wrench, 863
Moneta, see under money, 408
monetary, see under money, 408
money, marbles, nor chalk, not for, 576
money, to spend, like a drunken sailor, 551
Monk (toolmaker), see under monkey wrench, 863
monkey, to get one's, up, 587, 589
monkey wrench, 863
monkey wrench, to throw a, in the machinery, 574
monkey-nut, see under peanut, 828
monkey's, see under reynard, 455
Montagu, Lady Mary, see under blue-stocking, 252
Montague, John, see under sandwich, 462
Montgolfier, see under balloon, 239
month of Sundays, 84
moon, blue, once in a, 61

not to know (one) from
  Adam, 35
not to turn a hair, 156
not worth a continental, 172
not worth a fig, 125
not worth a tinker's dam (or
  damn), 184
nothing to write home about,
  614
nothing, to make much ado
  about, 528
notice, to sit up and take, 630
nought, see under
  fearnought, 853
Numa, see under March,
  398, May, 404,
  terminus, 493
numb, see under numskull,
  876
numbskull, 876
nut, see under coconut,
  peanut
nut to crack, 530
nuthatch, 872

Oakley, Annie, see under
  Annie Oakley, 738
oakum, 884
oar, to stick (put) in one's
  (in another's boat), 652
Oates, Titus, see under tory,
  496
oath, Bible, to take one's, 604
oats, feeling one's, 560
oboe, see under hobo, 360
ocean, a drop in the, 602–3
Octavius Augustus, see
  under August, 234
Odin, see under Thursday,
  494, Wednesday, 506
Odysseus, see under siren,
  470
off ox, Adam's, 96
oil on troubled waters, to
  pour, 67
ointment, a fly in the, 198
O.K., 875
old hat, 633
"Old Man of the Moun-
  tains," see under
  assassin, 232

Oliver, a Roland for an,
  596–97
Omar, see under admiral,
  220, caliph, 268
omega, alpha and, 683
omnibus, see under bus, 263
on tenterhooks, 148
on the anxious seat (bench),
  37
on the bandwagon, 136
on the beam, to be, 170
on the bum, 162
on the nail (or nailhead), 189
on the nose, 186
once in a blue moon, 61
once, see under one, 421
one-horse town, 34
orange, see under apron, 230
Orellana, see under amazon,
  224
Ossa, to pile (heap) Pelion
  on, 584
Othman, see under ottoman,
  424
out of the frying pan into the
  fire, to jump, 56
out on a limb, 131
outside the pale, 181
over a barrel, 639
Ovid, see under morphine,
  409
oxhead, see under hogshead,
  903
oyez, 743

pad, see under footpad, 948
paddle, up Salt Creek
  without a, 693
paddle one's own canoe, to,
  41, 630
paddywhack, 842
padlock, 832
pain in the neck, 694
pain in the neck, to give one
  a, 684
paint the lily, 560
paint the town red, to, 73
Palatine Hill, see under
  palace, 425
pale, beyond (or outside) the,
  181

pallbearer, 873
palm, to grease (a person's),
  81
palm itching, 652
Pan, see under panic, 428
Pandarus, see under pander,
  428
Pandora, see under
  Promethean, 446
pane, see under counterpane,
  ball peen
panhandle, 867
pantaloons, see under pants,
  431
pants, to be caught with
  one's, down, 88
pants, to scare the, off one,
  591
pantywaist, 878
papers, to peddle one's own,
  630
parable, see under palaver,
  426
Paracelsus, see under
  bombast, 254, sylph,
  484
Paris, see under boulevard,
  255
Paris green, 858
Parnell, Charles S., see under
  boycott, 256
parson's nose, 165
pasha, see under three-tailed
  bashaw, 766
Pasquino, see under
  pasquinade, 433
pass in one's checks (chips),
  534
pass the buck, to, 117
paternoster, see under patter,
  434
path, garden, to lead one up
  (down) the, 656–57
Patroclus, see under hector,
  358
Paul Pry, 585–86
pay, the devil to, 538, 581,
  710–11
pay the fiddler (piper), 596,
  686–87
pay through the nose, to, 190

polish, spit-and-, 613
polka dot, 929
poll (head), see under
  polliwog, tadpole
pollice verso, 188
polliwog, 926
Pollyanna, 923
polwygle, see under
  polliwog, 926
pomegranate, see under
  grenade, 351
Pompadour, Madame de, see
  under silhouette, 472
poor as a church mouse,
  693
poor as Job's turkey, 175
Pope, Alexander, see under
  namby-pamby, 414,
  sylph, 484
pope's nose, 165
poppycock, 922
porcupine, see under
  hedgehog, 804
pork barrel, 548
Porter Eleanor Hodgman, see
  under Pollyanna, 923
porterhouse, 914
portmanteau, 909
possum, to play, 582
posthaste, see under post,
  442
pot, gone to, 165
pot, to go to, 600
pot, to keep the, boiling, 45,
  653-54
pot cheese, 905
Potomac, all quiet on the,
  716
potter's field, 747
potwaller, see under pot-
  waller, 737
pot-walloper, 737
pound, see under shilling,
  769
pound, see under soldier,
  478
pour oil on troubled waters,
  to, 67
powder, to take a, 582-83
praise from Sir Hubert,
  552

precipice, see under
  precipitate, 444
preface, 743
pricks, to kick against the,
  567
Priestly, Joseph, see under
  rubber, 458
Prince Albert, 740
Proclus, see under trapezium,
  497
Procopius, see under
  anecdote, 228
Procrustean bed, 146
procrustes, see under
  procrustean, 496
prodigy, see under monster,
  409
Prometheus, see under
  Promethean, 446
promise, a lick and a, 569
prophet, by the beard of the,
  629
proud as Punch, 65
proud as Satan (sin, Lucifer),
  582
proud flesh, 733
prunes, full of, 560-1
Prussia, see under spruce,
  479
Pry, Paul, 585-86
P's and Q's, to mind one's,
  199
Ptolemy II, see under
  Septuagint, 468
public, to wash one's dirty
  linen in, 619-20
puddle, biggest frog (toad) in
  the, 588
pull a brodie, to, 133
pull in one's horns, to, 112
pull the wool over one's
  eyes, to, 87
pull wires (or strings), to, 63
pulpit, see under jack-in-the-
  pulpit, 865
Punch, proud as (or pleased
  as), 65
puppy, see under hushpuppy,
  mud puppy
purse, see under cutpurse,
  809

pussyfoot, see under
  slyboots, 951
put a spoke in one's wheel,
  to, 89
put in one's best licks, to,
  118
put one through a course of
  sprouts, to, 94
put one's back up, to, 72
put (or set) the cart before
  the horse, to, 30
put the kibosh on, to, 22
put the screws on, to, 79
Pye, Joe (Joseph), see under
  joe-pye weed, 793
pyritegium, see under
  curfew, 300
Pyrrho, see under skeptic,
  476

quackgrass, see under
  quatchgrass, 917
quacksalver, 803
quadroon, 907
quagmire, 738
quahog, quahaug, 901
quake, see under quagmire,
  738
quarrel with one's bread and
  butter, 581
quarter-, 876
quarterback, quarterdeck,
  quartermaster, see under
  quarter-, 876
quartered, hanged, drawn,
  and, 556
quarterstaff, 899
quatchgrass, 917
Queen Anne's lace, 862
queen's taste, to the, 581
queer as Dick's hatband,
  674-75
quicklime, 936
quickmire, see under
  quagmire, 738
quiet, all, on the Potomac,
  716
quisle, see under quisling,
  449
quitchgrass, see under
  quatchgrass, 917

Quogue, New York, see under quahog, 901
quoin, see under coin, 291

R, see under dog's letter, 942
rabble, 883
Rabelais, Francois, see under gargantuan, 343
rack and ruin, to go to, 600
racket, see under tennis, 491
rag, to chew the, 132, 534
ragamuffin, see under tatterdemalion, 833
rag-tag and bobtail, 563
ragtime, 887
Ragusa, Italy, see under argosy, 800
raid, see under road, 456
rail, see under fife rail, 826
rain, right as, 599
rain cats and dogs, to, 37, 690
raise Cain, to, 42
raise oneself by his bootstraps, 517–18, 557–58
rake, see under rakish, 865
rake over the coals, to, 48
rakish, 865
Raleigh, Sir Walter, see under eldorado, 321, potato, 443
rambunctious (rambustious), 853
ramshakle, 891
rap, not worth a, 713
rap, to take the, 596
rapture, see under rapt, 452
rarebit, 841
rarin' to go, 560
rasher, 840
raspberry, to get the, 49
rasure, see under rasher, 840
re, see under gamut, 341
Read, Allen Walker, see under blizzard, 251
read the riot act, to, 141
reason, without rhyme or, 580
receipt, see under recipe, 836
recipe, receipt, 836

reckon without one's host, to, 105
red herring, to be neither fish nor flesh nor good, 93
red herring, to drag a, over the track (or trail), 91
redstart, see under stark-naked, 937
red-handed, to catch one, 597
red-letter day, 35
rehearse, see under hearse, 357
renard, see under reynard, 455
return to one's muttons, to, 113
revenon à nos moutons, 113
Rha, see under rhubarb, 455
Rhodes, see under colossal, 293
rhyme or reason, without, 580
rich as Croesus, 531
ride, to take for a, 137
ride for a fall, 662–63
ride shanks' mare (or pony), to, 191
ride the goat, 656
ride the gravy train, 607, 633–34
ride the high horse, to, 26
rift in the lute, 528
rig, see under thimblerig, 786
right as a trivet (rain), 186, 599
Riley, living the life of, 170
ring a bell, 635
ring the changes, to, 29
riot act, to read the, 141
river, sold down the, 100
road, see under highroad, 954
rob Peter to pay Paul, to, 90
Robert, Earl of Essex, see under derrick, 308
Robin Hood's barn, all around, 197
Robinson, Bill, see under copesetic, 297

Robinson, Capt. Andrew, see under schooner, 467
rock salt, see under saltpeter, 827
rocks, on the, 600
Roger, see under Jolly Roger, 783
Roland for an Oliver, 596–97
Rolf, see under bigot, 248
rolling, to keep the ball, 653
rolling off a log, easy as, 576
Rome, see under roam, 457
Romulus, see under inaugurate, 368
ronyon, see under aroint, 736
room to swing a cat, 72
roorback, 894
Roosevelt, Theodore, see under roughrider, 84
roost, to rule the, 77, 640
root, see under arrowroot, 761
root hog or die, 36, 564
rope, to come to the end of one's, 119
rope of sand, 127
ropes, to know the, 51
rose, under the, 158
rotten, something, in Denmark, 654
roue, 830
roughrider, 814
roulette, 818
round robin, 159
roundabout, 812
row, long (hard), to hoe, 631
row, to hoe one's own, 630
row (someone) up Salt river, 691–92
rubber, see under mackin-tosh, 394
rubberneck, 897
Rubicon, cross the, 552
rug, snug as a bug in a, 537
Ruggle, George, see under ignoramus, 366
ruin, to go to rack (wrack) and, 600

rule the roost, to, 77, 640
rump, see under aroint, 736
run amuck, to, 177
run (something) into the ground, to, 83
run the gantlet (or gauntlet), to, 178
runabout, 761
runnion, see under aroint, 736

sabotage, 874
sack, holding the, 116
sack, see under haversack, knapsack
sack, to get (or give one) the, 91, 717
sack coat, 900
sackbut, 873
sackcloth, see under sack coat, 900
sacred cow, 601
Sade, Marquis, de, see under sadism, 113
sadiron, 851
sadism, 843
sail between Scylla and Charybdis, to, 52
sailing under false colors, 684
sailor, drunken, to spend money like a, 551
St. Anthony's fire, 840
St. Anthony's nut, turnip, see under St. Anthony's fire, 840
St. Audrey, see under tawdry, 489
St. Augustine, see under soliloquy, 935
St. Elmo's fire, 835
St. George, see under dragon, 316
St. John's Day, see under bonfire, 255
St. Luke's summer, see under St. Martin's summer, 832
St. Martin's summer, 832. See under gossamer, 348

St. Swithin's Day, 98
St. Vitus's dance, see under tarantula, 487
saker, see under musket, 413
salt, to earn one's, 128
salt, to eat with, 647
salt, to sit above (below) the, 649–50
salt, with a grain of, 172
salt, worth one's, 128
Salt Creek, up (without a paddle), 629, 693
Salt river, to row (someone) up, 691–92
saltpeter, 827
salve, see under quacksalver, 803
Sam Browne belt, 904
Sam Hill, 599
sand, rope of, 127
sand, to bite the, 590
Sandwich, 4th Earl of, see under sandwich, 462
Sandwich Islands, see under sandwich, 462
sang-froid, 824
sanguine, sanguinary, 819. See under humor, 363
Sanhedrin, 814
sans-culotte, 906
sarcastic, 807
Sardinia, see under sardonic, 464
sardonyx, see under sardonic, 464
Satan, proud as, 582
Satan, see under daddy longlegs, 834. See also devil
satire, 804
Saturn, see under Saturday, 464
Saturnalia, see under saturnine, 801
saturnine, 801
save one's bacon, to, 183
sawder, see under soft sawder, 819
sawder, soft, 163, 819
scalawag, 798

scallywag, scaly, see under saclawag, 798
scaramouch, 911
scarce as (scarcer than) hen's teeth, 632
scare the daylights out of, 600
scare the pants off one, 591
sceptic, see under skeptic, 476
Scheele's green, see under Paris green, 858
Schlick, Count of, see under dollar, 315
schoenobat, see under acrobat, 219
Schroter, C. G., see under piano, 441
Schweinfurt green, see under Paris green, 858
sciagraph, see under skiagraph, 754
scolding stool, see under cucking stool, 732
scot free, to go, 40, 615
Scotch coffee, see under rarebit, 841
scotch-hoppers, see under hopscotch, 737
Scott, Sir Walter, see under glamour, 346
Scotus, John Duns, see under dunce, 318
scratch, to come up to, 642
scratch, to start from, 615
screws, to put the, on, 79
scrofula, see under king's evil, 846
scurry, see under hurry-scurry, 776
Scylla and Charybdis, to steer (or sail) between, 52
sea, a drop in the, 602–3
sea, between the devil and the deep blue, 50, 538
seas, the biggest fish in the, 588
second fiddle (or violin) to play, 60
sedan, 794

981

slipshod, 921
slobber, see under
    slubberdegullion, 952
slogan, 751
slowpoke, 748
slubberdegullion, 952
slyboots, 951
small fry, 31
smearcase, see under pot
    cheese, 905
snake in the grass, 645
snake, to nourish a, in one's
    bosom, 617
snap, see under whipper-
    snapper, 817
snipe, see under guttersnipe,
    757
snood, 949
snug as a bug in a rug, 537
soap, see under green soap,
    904
sobersault, see under
    somersault, 931
sobriquet, soubriquet, 946
sockdologer, 946
soda jerker, 943
sofa, 940
soft sawder, 819
soft soap (or sawder), 164
sojourner, 935
sol, see under gamut, 341
sold down the river, 100
solder, see under soft
    sawder, 819
solfeggio, 924
Soli, see under solecism,
    478
solidus, see under soldier,
    478
soliloquy, 935
sombrero, 927
somersault, 931
somnolent, see under
    morphine, 409
Somnus, see under
    morphine, 409
son of a gun, 658
son of Belial, 930
song and dance, 157
sooner, 928
soothsayer, 926

sop, see under milksop, 894
sop of Cerberus, 631
sophimore, sophism, see
    under sophomore, 925
sophomore, 925
sore head, like a bear with a,
    650–51
soupçon, 922
sour grapes, 154
sow dragon's teeth, 699
sow one's wild oats, to, 115
spade, to call a, a spade, 184
Spain, castle in, 674
spang-new, spanking new,
    see under span-new,
    920
Spanish, to walk, 39
span-new, 23, 920
speak, 724
speak by the card, 533
spear, to pass under (sell at)
    the, 645
specan, 724
spend money like a drunken
    sailor, 551
Spenser, Edmund, see under
    derring-do, 309
sphinx, 930
Sphinx, see under spinnaker,
    479
spice, see under allspice,
    866
spick and span, 23
spick-and-span-new, see
    under span-new, 920
spike one's guns, to, 190
spill the beans, to, 54
spilt milk, to cry over, 684
spin, spindle, see under
    spindleshanks, 919
spindleshanks, 919
spindrift, 916
spirits, in high, 560
spit an' image, the, 121
spit-and-polish, 613
spite one's face, cutting off
    one's nose to, 643
splice the mainbrace, 608
split hairs, to, 51, 628–29
spoke, to put a, in one's
    wheel, 89

sponge, to throw in the, 618,
    639
sponging house, 913
spoom, spoon, spoondrift,
    see under spindrift,
    916
spoon, horn, by the great,
    629–30
Spooner, Rev. Wm. A., see
    under spoonerism,
    479
sport, a tin-horn, 681–82
spot, on the, 603, 629
spots, to knock the, off one,
    608–9
spout, up the, 90
sprouts, to put one through
    a course of, 94, 577–
    78
spud, see under potato, 443
spur, see under hotspur,
    825
spurs, to win one's, 646
sputnik, 910
square, on the, 568–69
squantersquash, see under
    squash, 905
squash, 905
stab in the back, to, 129
stable door, to lock the,
    after the horse is stolen,
    701
staff, see under quarterstaff,
    899
stake, see under stockade,
    sweepstakes
stakes, to pull up, 610
stalemate, 746
stalking-horse, 933
stamping ground, old
    (familiar), 610–11
stand the gaff, to, 190
standpatter, 744
Stanton, Elizabeth Cady, see
    under bloomers, 252
star, see under daystar,
    lodestar
starboard, 743
star-chamber, 741
stark-naked, 937
starling, 740

tail, with the, between the legs, 606

take a message to Garcia, to, 100

take for a ride, to, 137

take French leave, to, 185

take the bull by the horns, to, 27

take the cake, to, 130

take time by the forelock, to, 157

take to the tall timber, to, 164

Talbot, W. H. Fox, see under photography, 440, talbotype, 857

talbotype, 857

tale, see under tattletale, telltale

talesman, 855

talisman, 851

talk a blue streak, 625

talk off a donkey's hind legs, 625

talk one's arm off, 625

talk straight from the shoulder, 536

talk the bark off a tree, 699– 700

talk turkey, to, 46

talking through one's hat, 702

talking to one like a Dutch uncle, 715

tall timber, to take to the, 164

tallow, hair and hide, horns and, 651

tambourine, 848

Tamerlane, see under nabob, 414

tam-o'-shanter, 845

tandem, 947

tant pour tant, 98

tantamount, 839

tapestry, 836. See also arras

tar, to lick the, out of one, 621

tar out of, to knock, or beat the, 22

tarantella, see under tarantula, 487

tarantism, see under tarantula, 487

Taranto, see under tarantula, 487

Tarentum, see under tarantula, 487

Tarifa, see under tariff, 488

tarred and feathered, 667– 68

tarred with the same brush, 107

Tartar, see under tartar, 489

Tartar, to catch a, 75

taste, to the queen's, 581

tatterdemalion, 833

tattered, see under tatterdemalion, 833

tattletale, 824. See also telltale

tavern, see under pavilion, 435, tabernacle, 884

taxi, see under cab, 264

teach one's grandmother to suck eggs, to, 136

teacup, a tempest in a, 528

teat, hind, to suck the, 638– 39

teeth, by the skin of one's, 107

teeth, dragon's, to sow, 699

teeth, hen's, as scarce as (scarcer than), 632

teeth, to lie ine one's, 162

teeth, to set one's, on edge, 163

teetotal, 820

teetotum, 816

tele, see under telegraph, 813

telegraph, 813

telein, telesma, see under talisman, 851

Telemachus, see under mentor, 405

telltale, 811. See also tattletale

tempest in a teacup, 528

tenderfoot, tenterhooks, 802

tenterhooks, on, 148

term, see under terminus, 493

ternado, see under tornado, 941

terrier, 800

terve, see under topsy-turvy, 946

tête-à-tête, 796

tether, to come to the end of one's, 119

tetotal, see under teetotal, 820

Thames, to set the, on fire, 41

thank-ye-ma'am, 948

that's the ticket, 173

Theseus, see under academy, 217, clue, 288, Procrustean, 445

thespian, 788

Thespis, see under thespian, 788

thick as hops, 574–75

thimblerig, 786

thin ice, to skate over (on), 655–56

thingum, thingumajig, thingumbob, thingummy, 776. See also dingbat

third degree, to give (get) the, 543

Thor, see under Thursday, 494

thoroughfare, 770

Thoth, see under hermetic, 359

thread, to hang by a, 682

three cheers and a tiger, 550

three sheets in the wind, 168, 587

three-tailed bashaw, 766

through thick and thin, 58

throughway, see under thoroughfare, 770

throw in the sponge (towel), 618, 639

throw the book at one, 663

Thule, see under ultima Thule, 869

thumb, to bite the, at, 696– 97

985